Helping Countries Develop
The Role of Fiscal Policy

Editors

Sanjeev Gupta, Benedict Clements, Gabriela Inchauste

INTERNATIONAL MONETARY FUND

Production: IMF Multimedia Services Division
Cover design: Martina Vortmeyer

Cataloging-in-Publication Data

Helping countries develop : the role of fiscal policy / editors, Sanjeev Gupta, Benedict Clements, and Gabriela Inchauste — [Washington, D.C. : International Monetary Fund, 2004]

    p. cm.
    Includes bibliographical references.
    ISBN 1-58906-318-X

    1. Fiscal policy — Developing countries. 2. Expenditures, Public. 3. Government spending policy. I. Gupta, Sanjeev. II. Clements, Benedict J. III. Inchauste, Gabriela.

HJ192.5.H34 2004

Price: $40.00

Address orders to:
External Relations Department, Publication Services
International Monetary Fund, Washington, D.C. 20431
Telephone: (202) 623-7430; Telefax: (202) 623-7201
E-mail: publications@imf.org
Internet: http://www.imf.org

Contents

II. Public Spending and the Millennium Development Goals

III. Revenues and Growth

IV. Fiscal Policy and Aid

V. Special Topics

Foreword

The role of fiscal policy in catalyzing economic development continues to attract the attention of policymakers and academics alike. The macroeconomic role of fiscal policy, as well as its impact on economic efficiency and the supply side of the economy, remain at the center of the debate. The increased focus of the international community on helping countries achieve the Millennium Development Goals (MDGs) has further sharpened interest in what governments should (and should not) do with fiscal instruments to foster economic development.

The role of fiscal policy in promoting development can be seen both through its effects on growth and, more broadly, through its impact on human development. There is widespread agreement in the economics profession that over the longer term, a prudent fiscal position, comprising low budget deficits and low levels of public debt, promotes economic growth, which is essential for reducing poverty and improving social outcomes. There is much less consensus, however, regarding the appropriate role of fiscal policy in the short run. Some economists have argued that—just as in industrial countries—fiscal policy can be an effective tool to stimulate aggregate demand and revive a stagnant economy. Others have argued that activist fiscal policy may not have its intended salutary effects in developing countries, given their high and often unsustainable levels of public debt.

The long-term effects of tax, expenditure, and financing policies are also of keen interest to policymakers as they design strategies to help achieve the MDGs. On the expenditure side, the question is whether increased spending on education, health, and infrastructure are effective in boosting long-term growth and improving human development outcomes, given the weaknesses in public administration that plague these countries. On the revenue side, a key issue is whether the existing structure of taxation and the underlying tax policies in developing countries are sufficient to yield the necessary revenue to finance poverty-reducing spending. Finally, on the financing side, there is an ongoing and lively debate over the benefits of foreign assistance (both loans and grants), and whether international aid is effective in reducing poverty and spurring economic growth. The question is not only how much aid should be delivered, but also how to improve the quality of aid.

These issues are important for the IMF, particularly after the transformation of the Enhanced Structural Adjustment Facility—a concessional financing window for low-income countries—into the Poverty Reduction and Growth Facility in November 1999. The new facility places the goal of poverty reduction at the center of policy formulation and requires countries to articulate their macroeconomic, structural, and social policies in a poverty reduction strategy paper (PRSP). With the implementation of the new approach, questions have been raised regarding how fiscal policy can be used to help achieve the policy goals countries describe in their PRSPs, and the precise channels through which fiscal policy affects economic activity and social outcomes. This volume seeks to answer some of these questions.

The Fiscal Affairs Department is playing an important role in taking forward the research agenda on macroeconomic and microeconomic aspects of fiscal policy. This is being done by (1) drawing lessons and best practices from its experiences in different countries, and (2) conducting research on different aspects of fiscal policy, including in developing countries. This volume compiles a significant amount of the research on developing countries undertaken in the past few years, with the hope that it will stimulate further research and wider discussion, both within and outside the IMF.

Horst Köhler
Managing Director
International Monetary Fund
March 1, 2004

Contributors

Emanuele Baldacci

Economist,
Fiscal Affairs Department, IMF

Rina Bhattacharya

Economist,
Fiscal Affairs Department, IMF

Aleš Bulíř

Senior Economist, Policy Development
and Review Department, IMF

Shamit Chakravarti

Programs Officer,
Asian Development Bank, New Delhi

Stanley Sang-Wook Cho

Former summer intern,
Fiscal Affairs Department, IMF

Benedict Clements

Deputy Division Chief,
Fiscal Affairs Department, IMF

Ousmane Doré

Senior Economist,
African Department, IMF

Kevin Fletcher

Economist,
Fiscal Affairs Department, IMF

Sanjeev Gupta

Assistant Director,
Fiscal Affairs Department, IMF

Peter S. Heller

Deputy Director,
Fiscal Affairs Department, IMF

Arye L. Hillman

William Gittes Professor of Economics
at Bar-Ilan University

Gabriela Inchauste

Economist, IMF Institute, IMF

Eva Jenkner

Economist, Western Hemisphere
Department, IMF

Michael Keen

Division Chief,
Fiscal Affairs Department, IMF

Naoko C. Kojo

Economist,
Fiscal Affairs Department, IMF

Timothy Lane	Assistant Director, Policy Development and Review Department, IMF
Ian Lienert	Senior Economist, Fiscal Affairs Department, IMF
Paul R. Masson	Former Senior Advisor, Research Department, IMF
Carlos Mulas-Granados	European Economy Group, Universidad Complutense de Madrid
Sonia Muñoz	Economist, Asia and Pacific Department, IMF
Toan Nguyen	Former summer intern, Fiscal Affairs Department, IMF
Alexander Pivovarsky	Economist, Fiscal Affairs Department, IMF
Alejandro Simone	Economist, Fiscal Affairs Department, IMF
Erwin R. Tiongson	Economist, World Bank
Marijn Verhoeven	Senior Economist, Asia and Pacific Department, IMF

Acknowledgments

This volume is the product of the collective effort of many individuals. In particular, we are grateful to the contributing authors for their papers. Most papers were originally issued as IMF Working Papers and the revised versions of many of these papers were published in journals. Thanks are due to Elsevier Science, Ltd.; John Wiley & Sons, Ltd.; Blackwell Publishing; and NTC Economic and Financial Publishing for allowing us to reprint these articles.

We are grateful to Teresa Ter-Minassian for supporting this effort, as well as to the staff of the Fiscal Affairs Department's Expenditure Policy Division, who provided valuable assistance. We are particularly grateful to Emanuele Baldacci, Erwin Tiongson, Larry Cui, and Chris Wu for their assistance and advice in compiling this volume. Special thanks are due to Meike Gretemann, Merceditas San Pedro-Pribram, and Viswanathan Krishnamoorthy, who managed the correspondence with publishers and prepared the volume for publication. Marina Primorac of the IMF's External Relations Department edited the manuscript and coordinated production of the book.

The views expressed are those of the authors and do not necessarily reflect those of the IMF.

Sanjeev Gupta
Benedict Clements
Gabriela Inchauste
Editors

1

Fiscal Policy for Economic Development: An Overview

BENEDICT CLEMENTS, SANJEEV GUPTA, AND GABRIELA INCHAUSTE

Fiscal policy can foster growth and human development through a number of different channels. These channels include the macroeconomic (for example, through the influence of the budget deficit on growth) as well as the microeconomic (through its influence on the efficiency of resource use). But how precisely do these channels work in developing countries? Do the insights gleaned from the vast body of research on these topics in industrial countries carry over to developing countries?[1]

From a macroeconomic perspective, one of the central insights from past research on developing countries is that prudent fiscal policy—that is, low budget deficits and low levels of public debt—is a key ingredient for economic growth, which in turn is essential for reducing poverty and improving social outcomes.[2] Small budget deficits also reduce the risk of economic crises caused by concerns about the government's ability to service its debt. They prevent interest bills from rising to levels that squeeze critical social spending and ensure that the stock of debt remains at levels consistent with a country's capacity to service

The authors are grateful to Emanuele Baldacci, Robert Gillingham, Naoko Kojo, and Antonio Spilimbergo for helpful comments on previous drafts.

[1]The methodology of the World Bank Atlas defines developing countries as those with per capita gross national income below US$9,075 in 2002 prices. Within this broader group, low-income countries are those with per capita national income of US$735 or less (based on 2002 prices).

[2]See Chen and Ravallion (1997), Rodrik (2000), Dollar and Kraay (2001), and Easterly, Rodriguez, and Schmidt-Hebbel (1994).

this debt. Indeed, the macroeconomic stability associated with the absence of such crises yields numerous benefits, including higher rates of investment, growth, and educational attainment.[3]

Economists have traditionally posited that, in the short term, fiscal policy should be used to mitigate fluctuations in output and employment, and most of the available empirical evidence supports this view.[4] Thus, countercyclical fiscal policy can be used to stimulate aggregate demand and revive a stagnant economy. However, there is growing recognition that, in some circumstances, activist fiscal policy may not have its intended salutary effects on economic activity. These circumstances include cases where the level of public debt is high and unsustainable. Even for countries that expect to receive significantly more foreign assistance, expansionary budgets may not be a viable option because of adverse macroeconomic consequences associated with high aid flows and the lack of capacity to absorb them in an efficient manner.

A growing body of research—primarily on industrialized countries—has concluded that when the level of public debt is high and unsustainable, reducing budget deficits can accelerate growth. This occurs because reduced government borrowing to finance deficit spending pushes down interest rates generally, thereby catalyzing higher private investment. Lower interest rates also raise asset values, and this wealth effect encourages private consumption. Furthermore, shrinking deficits lead the private sector to reduce its estimates of current and future tax liabilities, providing a further boost to investment and consumption. Finally, higher investment can also ease supply constraints on growth. As a result, fiscal contractions can be expansionary. The question is whether the same type of phenomenon holds true for developing countries, and under what circumstances.

In addition to the short-run impact of fiscal policy on macroeconomic imbalances, tax, expenditure, and financing policies also have important effects on growth. From a microeconomic perspective, taxes distort private agents' decisions to save and invest, which in turn could alter the growth rate of the economy.[5] The empirical evidence on the impact of taxes on growth, however, is inconclusive. Easterly and Rebelo (1993) note that the effects of taxation are difficult to isolate

---

[3] Gavin and Hausmann (1998) and Flug, Spilimbergo, and Wachtenheim (1998).

[4] Most empirical research supports the idea that fiscal policy can have real effects in the short run. That is, there is little support in favor of the "Ricardian equivalence" argument, whereby any increase in government spending is offset by higher individual savings in anticipation of future tax increases (see Barro, 1989). This is because the underlying assumptions for Ricardian equivalence to hold ignore short time horizons, less than perfect foresight, and imperfect capital markets. For recent discussion on this subject in developing countries, see Khalid (1996) and Giorgioni and Holden (2003).

[5] Milesi-Ferretti and Roubini (1998).

empirically. The lack of clear evidence on how tax policy affects growth could partly be accounted for by the expenditure policies simultaneously being pursued.

On the expenditure side, several categories of expenditure and expenditure policies influence long-run growth. For example, the burgeoning work on endogenous growth theory suggests that fiscal policy can either promote or retard economic growth through its impact on decisions regarding investment in physical and human capital.[6] In particular, increased spending on education, health, infrastructure, and research and development can boost long-term growth.[7] Higher growth, in turn, generates greater fiscal resources to finance spending on human capital, further bolstering the dynamism of the economy.

Beyond its effects on growth, public expenditure can also have a direct impact on human development outcomes. The recent literature on fiscal policy and human development has focused on the Millennium Development Goals (MDGs).[8] These goals grew out of the agreements and resolutions of world conferences organized by the United Nations in the past decade. They have been commonly accepted as a framework for measuring development progress, and indicators of achievement of these goals are being monitored by the international community. The goals are directed at reducing poverty in all its forms. They include halving global poverty, achieving universal primary education, reversing the spread of HIV/AIDS, reducing child and maternal mortality, and ensuring environmental sustainability. The issue is whether government expenditure policy has a role in attaining the MDGs, and in particular in fostering improved education and health outcomes. In this respect, empirical evidence on the impact of spending on health and education on social outcomes provides clear evidence that it is not just the level of spending that matters, but also the efficiency of these outlays and how well they are targeted to the poor.

On the financing side, there is an extensive literature on the relationship between external debt and economic activity. In general, the literature indicates that foreign borrowing has a positive impact on investment and growth up to a certain threshold level, beyond which its impact is adverse. There has also been considerable discussion on how high interest bills on debt, including that held by local residents, have constrained productive spending by countries.

---

[6] Barro (1990, 1991); and Barro and Sala-i-Martin (1995).

[7] Lucas (1988); Bloom, Canning, and Sevilla (2001); Barro (1990); and Romer (1990).

[8] See Besley and Burgess (2003); Collier and Dollar (2001); and the MDG website, http://www.developmentgoals.org/.

However, the empirical evidence on this matter is mixed. Some have questioned whether public spending financed from foreign assistance raises growth in developing countries. Burnside and Dollar (2000) found that aid raises growth in a good policy environment. However, recent research contends that this finding is not robust (Easterly, 2003). This debate has assumed special importance in the context of the MDGs, since one of the objectives is to increase aid flows to 0.7 percent of GNP of industrialized countries. The question is not only how much aid should be delivered, but also how to improve the quality of aid.

The IMF is keenly interested in fiscal issues, given its mandate to promote economic stability and foster international cooperation. There has been considerable research on fiscal aspects of macroeconomic policy in developing countries. In 1989, for example, IMF staff compiled a volume on fiscal policy, stabilization, and growth in developing countries.[9] Since then, there has been growing interest in understanding the relationship between fiscal policy, growth, and poverty in these countries, particularly in low-income ones. This book brings together some of this research. Most of the chapters were circulated for discussion within the IMF as working papers, and several have been published in academic journals. Drawing on both theory and country experience, the chapters attempt to provide, where possible, insights into how fiscal policy can be used to spur equitable growth.

The volume is organized around five broad topics. The chapters in Part I assess how fiscal policy affects growth in the aggregate, including the short run. The papers assess whether reductions in the budget deficit are good for growth, and under what conditions; what determines the persistence of fiscal adjustment efforts; and the channels through which changes in the fiscal stance affect growth. The section then discusses the conditions under which borrowing and the resulting debt buildup is conducive to growth, and the conditions that influence debt sustainability in a country. Parts II through IV address specific aspects of fiscal policy. Part II comprises chapters on expenditure policy and the MDGs, focusing on health and education spending. Taxation, revenue composition, and the impact on growth and the poor are the focus of Part III. Part IV examines the role of international aid and the potential difficulties for fiscal management in the presence of large donor inflows. Finally, the chapters in Part V touch on selected topics, including the fiscal consequences of armed conflict and terrorism, and public expenditure management systems in Africa.

---

[9] Blejer and Chu (1989).

Macroeconomic Policy in Developing Countries

Fiscal Adjustment and Growth

Some critics have argued that the IMF recommends that countries undertake fiscal adjustment in cases where fiscal problems are not the cause of macroeconomic imbalances, and without taking into account the adverse consequences of fiscal retrenchment.[10] Implicit in these arguments is that an easing of fiscal policy might be a better alternative for countries facing deep losses of output during crises. At issue here is the effect of changes in the fiscal stance on growth. As noted earlier, for countries with relatively high public debt levels and borrowing costs, fiscal consolidation can actually boost growth by raising market confidence, improving market access for private as well as public borrowers, and reducing interest rates. For countries that do not have access to markets, fiscal consolidation can also spur growth, especially if consolidation takes place through structural reforms that increase labor market flexibility and factor productivity.

The empirical research, primarily on industrial countries, has sought to understand the conditions under which fiscal consolidation leads to stable or increased output. Giavazzi and Pagano (1990), for example, show that consolidations tend to be expansionary when debt is high or growing rapidly. In this context, they argue that private spending responds positively to a credible commitment to debt reduction and a lowering of the risk premium. Furthermore, Alesina and Perotti (1995) and Alesina and Ardagna (1998) find that in addition to the size and persistence of the fiscal impulse, budget composition matters in explaining different private sector responses to fiscal policy (and, hence, the effect on growth). Fiscal adjustments that rely primarily on cuts in transfers and the wage bill tend to last longer and can be expansionary, while those that rely primarily on tax increases and cuts in public investment tend to be contractionary and unsustainable.[11]

What has yet to be explored in the literature is how relevant these concerns are for developing countries, and low-income countries in particular. Are smaller budget deficits good for growth? Should developing countries refrain from public spending, especially those that are likely to receive massive increases in aid inflows? There is limited evidence in the literature on the short-term effects of countercyclical fiscal policy in the context of developing countries. However, there are

---

[10] Stiglitz (2003).

[11] The idea is that cuts in transfers in the form of health and pension expenditures require legislation that would lead to permanent changes in the composition of government expenditure. See von Hagen and Strauch (2001).

institutional features specific to developing countries that will affect the impact of fiscal policy on economic activity differently than in an industrialized country setting. On the one hand, the availability and cost of financing is often a major constraint in countries that do not have access to international capital markets. Therefore, an increase in the fiscal deficit beyond a level that can be financed in acceptable terms will have strong crowding-out and inflationary effects, while raising the stock of debt to unsustainable levels. On the other hand, the relatively high marginal propensity to consume would tend to increase the size of the fiscal multiplier.[12] These issues have taken on greater prominence in recent years, as some have argued that fiscal policy in IMF-supported programs is too tight, causing developing countries to forgo economic growth in the name of fiscal austerity. Three main empirical questions arise from this debate:

- What is the impact of the fiscal stance, expenditure composition, and budget financing on economic growth in developing countries?
- How do these and other factors affect the persistence of fiscal adjustments?
- Through which channels does fiscal consolidation affect growth?

Chapter 2 of this volume contributes to this literature by analyzing the first of these questions. Gupta, Clements, Baldacci, and Mulas-Granados find that, as in the industrialized world, fiscal adjustment can bolster growth in low-income countries suffering from macroeconomic imbalances. Moreover, they find that allocating a higher share of public spending for public investment spurs economic growth. Cutting selected current expenditures triggers higher growth rates than do adjustments based on revenue increases and cuts in more productive spending, a result that is consistent with the findings for industrial countries. They also find that fiscal consolidations that trim domestic financing of the deficit are the most pro-growth. In contrast, in countries that have achieved macroeconomic stability in terms of low budget deficits and low inflation rates, an expansion of selected current expenditures is compatible with higher growth.

In some countries, fiscal adjustments take place, but do not last long enough to ensure a positive effect on growth. There is a consensus among researchers that fiscal consolidation needs to persist in order to maximize their effect on growth.[13] Therefore, a second relevant ques-

---

[12] For a recent survey of theoretical and empirical studies in industrialized and developing countries, see Hemming, Kell, and Mahfouz (2002).

[13] Alesina and Ardagna (1998); von Hagen, Hughes Hallett, and Strauch (2002); and Adam and Bevan (2003).

tion is what determines how long a fiscal adjustment program lasts. In Chapter 3, Baldacci, Clements, Gupta, and Mulas-Granados assess the factors determining the end of a fiscal consolidation episode and analyze whether improvements in the composition of public expenditure have positive repercussions for the duration of fiscal adjustment in low-income countries. They find that protecting capital expenditure during fiscal adjustment leads to a longer fiscal consolidation episode, as does an increase in the share of current spending on nonwage goods and services. Further, when fiscal consolidation is supported by a strengthening of the revenue effort, adjustment is likely to continue, while expenditure reductions play a minor role. This contrasts with findings in the literature on industrial countries, which have emphasized that expenditure reductions are the key ingredient for achieving persistent fiscal adjustment.

Finally, a third, related issue relates to the channels through which fiscal consolidation affects growth in developing countries, and whether they differ from those in industrialized countries. The principal channel for the increased growth in industrial countries is the higher private investment that follows reduced real interest rates and enhanced price and external stability.[14] In Chapter 4, Baldacci, Hillman, and Kojo review these channels for low-income countries and find that fiscal adjustment spurs growth principally through its effect on factor productivity. The investment channel is not as critical, owing to the low productivity of public spending in countries plagued by weak governance. Moreover, they find that changes in spending composition that increase the share of public-sector wages and salaries and reduce capital spending, tend to retard growth because they are associated with rent-seeking behavior. Finally, as in Gupta and others (Chapter 2), these authors find that fiscal contractions that reduce borrowing from domestic sources are the most conducive for growth.

Debt and Growth

There is widespread concern in the international community that the debt burden in developing countries has retarded growth, and that debt-service payments effectively crowd out public spending on health, education, and other poverty-reducing programs. In response to these concerns, the Heavily Indebted Poor Country (HIPC) Initiative was launched to provide debt relief to a group of countries confronted by high levels of debt. As a result, for the 27 countries for whom debt relief

---

[14]Giavazzi and Pagano (1990); and Bertola and Drazen (1993).

was approved by end-2003, debt service falling due between 1998 and 2004 will drop by more than half in relation to both exports and government revenue. In the context of this Initiative, three basic questions emerge. When does the debt burden begin to have a negative impact on growth? Has debt service squeezed spending on public investment? Will the HIPC Initiative help in this regard? In a study presented in Chapter 5 of this volume, Clements, Bhattacharya, and Nguyen analyze the relationship between debt, growth, and public investment for a sample of low-income countries. They find that the marginal impact of debt on growth becomes negative at about 20–25 percent of GDP when debt is measured in terms of net present value. Taking into account the average debt relief for countries under the Initiative, their results imply that per capita growth could be boosted by 0.8–1.1 percent a year. They further find that on average, every 1 percentage point increase in gross debt service reduces public investment by about 0.2 percentage point. Thus, reduced debt service—especially if a large share of the resulting savings is allocated for higher public investment—can help further boost growth.

Given that excessive debt burdens have an adverse impact on a country's growth prospects, it is important for policymakers to assess the sustainability of the fiscal position continuously and systematically. Such assessments are thus essential for evaluating whether fiscal adjustment is needed. In Chapter 6, Baldacci and Fletcher propose a framework for assessing debt sustainability in low-income countries that can be easily adapted to the specific circumstances of a country and can be used to assess the extent to which existing policies and financing are consistent with the country's broader development agenda. For example, countries may need higher public spending to achieve the MDGs. In these cases, debt sustainability analysis can be useful in highlighting the trade-offs while maintaining a sustainable debt position. In cases where investment in human and physical capital cannot be funded by cuts in less productive spending, analysts may need to carefully weigh the possible trade-offs between the growth-enhancing effects of such investment and the costs of the borrowing needed to finance them. An unsustainable debt position can also be addressed through higher foreign grants and/or through higher domestic revenue mobilization.

Fiscal Rules and Budgetary Convergence: The Case of WAEMU

Chapters 2–6 present evidence on how fiscal policy can promote growth in the short and long term. Toward this end, some countries have established fiscal rules to help promote fiscal consolidation and achieve fiscal sustainability. In Chapter 7, Doré and Masson study the issue of fiscal stability in the case of the West African Economic and Monetary Union (WAEMU). They find that cyclical variations and terms-of-trade fluctuations affected the WAEMU's experience with the convergence criteria (fiscal rules) applied since 1999. The setting of budgetary rules was predicated on the belief that fiscal consolidation would lead to sustainable growth by freeing up resources for the private sector. Despite considerable progress, the WAEMU's experience has produced mixed results since the 1994 devaluation. After an initial period of robust growth and fiscal consolidation, a marked deterioration of the fiscal balance was observed in most countries after 1997. Unfavorable developments in terms of trade undoubtedly had a negative impact on growth and budget deficits, but in several countries, a weakening of economic policies was the main cause of the fiscal slippages, which hindered the achievement of strong, sustained growth within the Union. The analysis also suggests that for governments to meet the fiscal convergence standards, they will have to pay more attention to reducing the share of public wages and monitoring other current operating expenditures. It further suggests that in light of the limited scope for reducing the aggregate level of expenditure while simultaneously attempting to combat poverty, it would be helpful to focus on the quality of fiscal adjustments and on strengthening the tax effort, in line with the results in Chapters 2 and 3. This would mean streamlining expenditures (for instance, better deployment of civil service staff) and engaging in sustained revenue-raising efforts.

Public Spending and the Millennium Development Goals

An improvement in the composition of expenditures is critical for low-income countries receiving debt relief. A larger number of countries are also articulating their plans for poverty reduction in poverty reduction strategy papers (PRSPs).[15] The additional resources freed by debt relief and those provided by donors are meant to be spent on poverty-reducing programs so that, over time, there is an improved performance on social indicators. However, a critical question is whether higher public spending in the past has actually led to improved outcomes. There is at least some evidence that budgeted resources are not

---

[15] IMF and World Bank–supported programs in low-income countries are framed around PRSPs, which are prepared by governments with the active participation of civil society and other development partners. PRSPs are then considered by the Executive Boards of the IMF and World Bank as the basis for concessional lending from each institution.

always used for their intended purposes.[16] Moreover, the empirical evidence on the relationship between actual levels of public spending on these activities and outcomes (e.g., educational attainment and health status) is mixed.[17] In some cases, the weak relationship between spending and outcomes owes to the fact that public spending crowds out private outlays on education and health care; in other cases, public resources may be used inefficiently and inequitably, and thus have little effect on the well-being of the poor.

Public Spending on Education and Health

This section analyzes three related questions: (1) What is the impact of public spending on health and education on outcomes? (2) If spending is reallocated within sectors, can outcomes be improved? (3) Do social indicators for the poor respond differently to public spending than those for the nonpoor?

In Chapter 8, Gupta, Verhoeven, and Tiongson assess whether increased public spending on education and health influences social indicators and whether improvements in the intrasectoral allocation can boost social outcomes. The results indicate that increases in overall education spending, as well as in spending on primary and secondary education as a share of total education spending, have a positive impact on educational attainment. Similarly, increased health care spending reduces child and infant mortality rates. For example, an increase of 1 percentage point of GDP in education spending increases gross secondary enrollment by more than 3 percentage points. A 5 percentage point increase in the share of outlays for primary and secondary education in total education spending increases gross secondary enrollment by over 1 percentage point. A 1 percentage point increase in health spending in relation to GDP decreases infant and child mortality rates by about 3 deaths of every 1,000 live births. These results suggest that policymakers need to pay attention not only to the level of social spending, but also to its allocations within sectors.[18]

Existing studies have typically relied on aggregate social indicators to study the impact of public spending. This is because data on the distribution of indicators by income classes are rarely available. As a result, studies based on aggregate indicators do not necessarily reveal the full

---

[16] Reinikka-Soininen and Svensson (2001).

[17] Psacharopoulos (1994); Glewwe (2002); Landau (1986); Filmer, Hammer, and Pritchett (1998); and Bidani and Ravallion (1997).

[18] Baldacci, Guin Siu, and de Mello (2003) found larger elasticities of spending on education using a latent variable approach.

impact of spending on the poor. In Chapter 9, Gupta, Verhoeven, and Tiongson assess the relationship between public spending on health care and the health status of the poor. They not only find that the poor have significantly worse health than the nonpoor, but also show that the poor are more strongly affected by public spending on health care. For example, a 1 percent increase in public spending on health reduces child mortality by twice as many deaths among the poor. Infant mortality rates follow a similar pattern. In addition, there is some evidence that returns to public spending on health are higher among the poor, regardless of the benefit incidence. The estimates of the elasticity of health status of the poor to health spending suggest that projected increases in health spending due to international initiatives such as debt relief may have led, on average, to a reduction in child mortality rates by 5 deaths out of 1,000 live births among the poor between 1999 and 2000/01. A similar reduction could be expected for infant mortality rates. To further strengthen the nexus between spending and outcomes for the poor, governments should aim to improve the incidence and targeting of public spending.

User Payments for Education

Ideally, all children should have access to free, publicly financed, quality schools. However, in some cases, there may be inadequate government resources to provide free education, or, even when these resources are available, the funds are not used for their intended purposes. In other cases, children may have access to education, but cultural factors or user charges prevent them from going to school. It has been proposed that user payments for basic education should not be permitted or, where present, should be abolished. In Chapter 10, Hillman and Jenkner assess the circumstances under which user payments have been introduced. They note that in cases where there are voluntary user payments, parents have taken responsibility for the education of their children in situations where they would otherwise not have access to schooling. In some cases, this reflects the lack of alternative financing or more general problems in public expenditure management. Compulsory user payments can also reflect administrative and governance impediments to replacing regressive taxation with broadly based taxation or insufficient donor funding as a means of financing schools. Therefore, the authors conclude that proposals to disallow or abolish user prices for basic education in poor countries should be made with caution, and with detailed reference to the case-by-case circumstances that explain why these user payments exist in a given country.

Efficiency of Government Spending

In discussions on making progress in achieving the MDGs, the focus has been on increasing public spending on sectors impacting on different dimensions of poverty. However, attention also needs to be paid to the need to improve the efficiency of spending of *existing* resources. In Chapter 11, Gupta and Verhoeven assess the efficiency of government spending on education and health in 37 countries in Africa, both in relation to each other and in comparison with countries in Asia and the Western Hemisphere. The results reveal that there is wide variation in the way government spending in the African countries affects measurable output indicators. On average, governments in Africa are less efficient in the provision of health and education services than in Asia and the Western Hemisphere, with those in Asia appearing most efficient. The results suggest that the inefficiencies observed in Africa are unrelated to the level of private spending, but may be due to relatively high government wages (in the case of education spending) and the intrasectoral allocation within the social sectors. The analysis suggests that improvements in educational attainment and health output indicators in Africa and the Western Hemisphere are feasible by correcting inefficiencies in government spending on education and health. Relatively low allocations for primary education, relatively high allocations for curative health care, and poorly targeted spending that primarily benefits upper-income groups are all symptomatic of expenditure inefficiencies. This suggests that some progress on the MDGs can be made by spending existing resources more wisely.

Tax Policy and Development

We turn now to the links between tax policy and development.[19] Developing countries face formidable challenges in implementing efficient tax systems owing to (1) large informal sectors; (2) lack of reliable data that allow for effective monitoring and analysis; (3) ineffective tax administrations; and (4) powerful high-income groups that preclude the introduction of more equitable taxes.

Given the complexity of the development process, a key question is how to improve the tax structure within existing constraints. In this context, Keen and Simone discuss the experience with tax policy in developing countries during the 1990s. Their findings show that revenue has at best been stagnant in the poorest countries and regions of the devel-

---

[19] For a survey of tax issues facing developing countries, see Tanzi and Zee (2000). For a historical survey of tax advice given to developing countries, see Goode (1993).

oping world; taking seignorage into account, it has generally fallen. Although sales tax revenues have increased markedly owing to the widespread introduction of the VAT (albeit less in the poorest countries and regions), it is not easy to show clear efficiency gains from the VAT. The primary task going forward will be to ensure proper functioning of the refund and credit mechanisms—a key part of the wider reform of conducting tax business. Second, trade tax revenues have fallen significantly, though least in the poorest countries. Developing countries, especially the poorest, have had difficulties in dealing with the revenue consequences of trade liberalization, which points to the need for greater attention to be paid to the sequencing of trade reform and the strengthening of the domestic tax system. Finally, Keen and Simone document the decline in corporate tax revenues in developing countries. While corporate tax reform among developed countries has been rate reducing and base broadening, in the developing world it has been rate reducing but also base reducing (or, at best, base neutral) at least partly owing to international tax competition. This is problematic, since developing countries have traditionally relied more heavily on corporate tax revenues, reflecting the relative administrative ease of collection, which is typically highly concentrated in a relatively small number of large firms. Like the decline of trade tax revenues, the erosion of the corporate tax may thus jeopardize a convenient tax handle—and so could raise the same difficult issue of developing alternative revenue sources.

Aside from the impact of tax policy on revenue collection, tax policy can also have important implications for income distribution. There have been increasing calls for the evaluation of distributional implications of reform programs in low-income countries. One of the key features of the IMF's Poverty Reduction and Growth Facility (PRGF), designed for low-income countries, is to undertake such an analysis of key policy reforms. In Chapter 13, Muñoz and Cho assess the distributive impact of the introduction of the VAT in Ethiopia, and compare it to the sales tax that it replaced. The results show that the VAT is progressive. However, it is not as progressive as the sales tax, and as such its introduction had an adverse impact on the poorest 40 percent of the population (reducing their consumption by about 1 percent). Moreover, Muñoz and Cho's estimates indicate that if the additional revenues from the VAT were allocated for higher spending on primary education and health, the poorest 40 percent of the population would be net beneficiaries.

Not only will the structure of taxation in developing countries need to improve to help meet the MDGs, but also the level of revenues reaped by the tax system. In this regard, a critical issue is how foreign assistance affects the revenue effort of aid-receiving countries. The debate on the effectiveness of foreign aid has revolved around the relative efficiency of loans versus grants. Since the early 1960s, an oft-repeated view has been that loans are used more efficiently than grants because they are expected to be repaid. This issue has reemerged with recent calls for a shift from loans to grants. Some observers consider that excessive lending has led to massive debt accumulation in many developing countries, while failing to help countries reach their intended human development objectives and worsening the debt sustainability outlook. These critics have therefore argued that grant financing is a better option. In Chapter 14, Gupta, Clements, Pivorarsky, and Tiongson empirically test whether the revenue effort in aid-receiving countries depends on the form of delivery of foreign aid—grants or loans. Their results indicate that concessional loans are generally associated with higher domestic revenue mobilization, while grants have the opposite effect. In countries plagued by high levels of corruption, the empirical results suggest that any increase in aid would be fully offset by a reduced revenue effort. Thus, grants to these countries cannot be expected to increase the aggregate amount of resources available to finance government expenditure. Loans, on the other hand, do not suffer from this drawback. A shift from loans to grants and the resulting fall in revenue-to-GDP ratios in recipient countries would, however, shift the burden of taxation to donor countries. The results also suggest that the aggregate amount of resources needed for achieving the MDGs would be larger than hitherto estimated.

International Aid and Fiscal Policy

It has been estimated that $40–$60 billion of additional resources annually would be required to achieve the MDGs.[20] This has resulted in repeated calls at the international forums to raise official development assistance (ODA) from its current level of 0.24 percent of GNP of industrial countries. During the 2002 Monterrey meeting, new commitments were made to increase ODA by $12 billion a year by 2006.

Macroeconomic Challenges in the Presence of Aid

Heller and Gupta (Chapter 15) consider the macroeconomic and microeconomic challenges that developing countries would face if industrial countries were to meet the international target for increased development assistance to 0.7 percent of GNP, about $175 billion, slightly more than three times the current level. First, they consider

---

[20]See Devarajan, Miller, and Swanson (2002).

what the appropriate criteria should be for allocating the aid across countries. If one were to distribute the full 0.7 percent of GNP in aid only to the world's *least* developed countries, then the scale of transfers would be massive relative to these economies' size. In particular, the average ratio of ODA to GDP in recipient countries would be 32 percent, almost two and a half times what it is now, and the resources available for government programs would almost triple. In fact, the ratio of ODA to GDP would amount to 90 percent in Ethiopia, 48 percent in Vietnam, 43 percent in Nicaragua, 57 percent in Guyana, and 74 percent in the Kyrgyz Republic. Moreover, applying such a distributional criterion would result in enormous differences in per capita transfers to the "absolute poor" of the world. On the other hand, if the increased ODA resources were distributed proportionally to the share of the world's absolute poor in a country, the bulk of aid would then go not to the poorest countries in the world, but to the larger countries such as China and India. Heller and Gupta ask whether developing countries would have the capacity to absorb these funds. They discuss the macroeconomic and microeconomic challenges countries would face, including (1) the ability of governments to keep their exchange rate competitive in the face of large foreign resource inflows; (2) the difficulties in ensuring sound fiscal management, particularly in the context of weak local government reporting systems; and (3) the potential aid dependence that could result from higher donor flows. They conclude that any significant expansion of ODA must be accompanied by a concerted effort by all partners in the development community to anticipate the challenges associated with utilizing external resources effectively.

In Chapter 16, Lane and Bulíř look at the related issue of the volatility and unpredictability of aid inflows and the implications of this volatility on fiscal policy management in aid-receiving countries. Although a number of recent papers have documented a pattern of aid volatility and aid procyclicality with respect to output and fiscal revenues,[21] the impact on output and growth has received relatively less attention. Lane and Bulíř find that aid is significantly more volatile than domestic fiscal revenue, and is procyclical vis-à-vis domestic fiscal revenue. Further, they find that rather than smoothing out cyclical shocks, aid tends to exacerbate them. As a result, recipient countries can either devise a flexible fiscal framework in which tax and spending plans can be adjusted in response to aid receipts, or they can try to smooth out fluctuations in aid disbursements by running down international reserves. Budgets can be designed to accommodate aid disbursements in excess of

---

[21] Gemmell and McGillivray (1998), and Pallage and Robe (2001).

a conservative fiscal baseline, provided that established budgetary proce-dures are made more flexible. However, the flexibility of fiscal frameworks to adjust to variations in aid receipts is limited. On the revenue side, vari-ations in tax rates to compensate for temporary fiscal shortfalls shift un-certainty onto taxpayers and, through their effects on expectations, may result in changes in behavior that vitiate these intended effects. On the expenditure side, it is generally disruptive to turn expenditures on and off at short notice, unless these expenditures are not serving an important purpose in the first place. Moreover, expenditures that are turned off for short-term reasons are often difficult to turn on again. For this reason, in-dustrial countries have relied increasingly on "built-in fiscal flexibility" stemming from the income sensitivity of tax and spending items, rather than hoping to fine-tune activist policies.

Food Aid

Lane and Bulíř's results are important, as the procyclicality of aid im-plies that aid flows cannot stabilize fluctuations in consumption. However, aid can take many different forms, including ODA, technical assistance, and food aid. In Chapter 17, Gupta, Clements, and Tiongson focus on food aid. They investigate whether it helps to stabi-lize food consumption in recipient countries, and whether food aid has been targeted to those countries most in need. They conclude that food aid is acyclical—that is, neither pro- nor countercyclical. This has two major implications for macroeconomic and fiscal management. First, to the extent that food aid is not disbursed in a countercyclical manner and recipient governments rely on counterpart funds generated from the sale of commodities provided through aid as a revenue source, the instability of budgetary revenues associated with declines in food pro-duction, and therefore in output, is not alleviated. Second, shortfalls in food supply increase demands on the government budget for programs to shield the consumption of the population. In the absence of coun-terpart funds from food aid, governments will have to rely on domestic resources for funding such programs. Therefore, falling revenues and rising demand for budgetary programs are likely to complicate macro-economic management for countries receiving food aid. In these cir-cumstances, food aid fails to act as an "automatic stabilizer."

Special Topics

The volume ends with a couple of special topics that are critical for fiscal policy and development. First, the fiscal consequences of armed

conflict and terrorism in low- and middle-income countries are analyzed. Then, a comparison of expenditure management systems in
Africa is presented.

Armed Conflict, Terrorism, and Development

Post-conflict countries such as Iraq, Afghanistan, and the Democratic
Republic of Congo face special challenges in formulating and implementing sound macroeconomic and fiscal policy. An institutional
framework, underpinned by a simple but realistic policy stance, must
be quickly put in place to reestablish macroeconomic stability and lay
the ground for a resumption of growth. In the fiscal area, conflict or
post-conflict countries typically confront a collapsed revenue base and
extraordinary expenditure needs. Although some studies have assessed
the economic consequences of armed conflict and terrorism, few have
focused on their fiscal implications. Several studies have analyzed the
economic costs of armed conflicts,[22] while others have found an inverse relationship between different measures of political instability
and violence and growth and investment.[23] For example, Arunatilake,
Jayasuriya, and Kelegama (2001) estimate that the conflict between
1983 and 1996 cost Sri Lanka about twice that country's 1996 GDP.
Prolonged terrorist activities, like armed conflict, have also been found
to reduce growth, both directly and indirectly.[24] For example,
Walkenhorst and Dihel (2002) estimate the global welfare losses due
to the tighter security precautions put in place following the attacks of
September 11, 2001, at about $75 billion. In Chapter 18, Gupta,
Clements, Bhattacharya, and Chakravarti find that there are sizable
economic gains in terms of economic growth, macroeconomic stability, and the generation of tax revenues to support poverty-reducing
spending for countries that end conflicts and tackle terrorism.
Moreover, the results suggest that conflict- and terrorism-affected
countries are likely to experience a pickup in government tax revenues
and a reduction in military spending (albeit with a lag) following the
cessation of violence, and that this would help in restoring macroeconomic stability. These results underscore the potential for the
"peace dividend" to contribute to economic development.

---

[22]See Richardson and Samarasinghe (1991); and Arunatilake, Jayasuriya, and
Kelegama (2001).

[23]See Barro (1991); Alesina and Perotti (1993, 1996); Alesina and others (1996); and
Rodrik (1999).

[24]Abadie and Gardeazabal (2001), Drakos and Kutan (2001); Enders and Sandler
(1991); Enders, Sandler, and Parise (1992); and Nitsch and Schumacher (2002).

Expenditure Management in Africa

Although previous chapters have focused on the role of fiscal policy in attaining the MDGs, it is clear that fiscal policy is ineffective if it is not accompanied by strong institutions. In particular, expenditure management systems are critical to ensuring that additional aid flows are spent efficiently on programs to reduce poverty and improve social indicators. In Chapter 19, Lienert analyzes the differences between the public expenditure management systems of anglophone and francophone Africa. The paper finds that although the francophone countries' budget execution and government accounting systems have a number of potential advantages, these have not produced better results. On the contrary, the desirable features of the francophone system have not been accompanied by better aggregate expenditure control. Since there are big variations within the francophone or anglophone groupings, the disappointing experience is due not to the public expenditure management systems themselves, but to the way they operate. Thus, even if budget legislation and implementation instructions are clarified, in the absence of changes in the behavior of all players in the budget process—in the executive, legislative, and judicial branches of government—it is unlikely that significant improvements will occur. In this regard, it will be critical to enhance budget discipline and improve the accountability of all those responsible for budget preparation, execution, and reporting. To bring about lasting improvements in public expenditure management, it will be necessary to enforce existing rules with rigor, and apply sanctions where necessary. This will require strong political will in both anglophone and francophone Africa. Although this is largely a domestic issue, the international community can contribute to durable solutions by understanding more fully the actual operation of public expenditure management systems, and by making foreign assistance conditional on efforts to improve the accountability of the public sector.

References

Abadie, Alberto, and Javier Gardeazabal, 2001, "The Economic Costs of Conflict: A Case-Control Study for the Basque Country," NBER Working Paper No. 8478 (Cambridge, Massachusetts: National Bureau of Economic Research).

Adam, Christopher, and David Bevan, 2003, "Staying the Course: Maintaining Fiscal Control in Developing Countries," paper prepared for the Brookings Institution Trade Forum Conference.

Alesina, Alberto, and Silvia Ardagna, 1998, "Tales of Fiscal Adjustment," *Economic Policy*, Vol. 27 (October), pp. 487–546.

Alesina, Alberto, and Roberto Perotti, 1993, "Income Distribution, Political Instability, and Investment," NBER Working Paper No. 4486 (Cambridge, Massachusetts: National Bureau of Economic Research).

———, 1995, "Fiscal Expansion and Fiscal Adjustments in OECD Countries," Economic Policy, Vol. 21, pp. 205–48.

———, 1996, "Fiscal Adjustments in OECD Countries: Composition and Macroeconomic Effects," IMF Working Paper 96/70 (Washington: International Monetary Fund).

———, and others, 1996, "Political Instability and Economic Growth," Journal of Economic Growth, Vol. 1 (June), pp. 189–212.

Arunatilake, Nisha, Sisira Jayasuriya, and Saman Kelegama, 2001, "The Economic Cost of the War in Sri Lanka," World Development, Vol. 29 (September), pp. 1483–1500.

Baldacci, Emanuele, Maria Teresa Guin Siu, and Luiz de Mello, 2003, "More on the Effectiveness of Public Spending on Health Care and Education: A Covariance Structure Model," Journal of International Development, Vol. 15 (August), pp. 709–25.

Barro, Robert J., 1989, "Ricardian Approach to Budget Deficits," Journal of Economic Perspectives, Vol. 3 (Spring), pp. 37–54.

———, 1990, "Government Spending in a Simple Model of Endogenous Growth," Journal of Political Economy, Vol. 98 (October), pp. S103–S125.

———, 1991, "Economic Growth in a Cross Section of Countries," Quarterly Journal of Economics, Vol. 106 (May), pp. 407–43.

———, and Xavier Sala-i-Martin, 1995, Economic Growth (New York: McGraw-Hill).

Bertola, Giuseppe, and Allan Drazen, 1993, "Trigger Points and Budget Cuts: Explaining the Effects of Fiscal Austerity," American Economic Review, Vol. 83, pp. 11–26.

Besley, Timothy, and Robin Burgess, 2003, "Halving Global Poverty," Journal of Economic Perspectives, Vol. 17 (Summer), pp. 3–22.

Bidani, Benu, and Martin Ravallion, 1997, "Decomposing Social Indicators Using Distributional Data," Journal of Econometrics, Vol. 77 (March), pp. 125–39.

Blejer, Mario, and Ke-young Chu, eds., 1989, Fiscal Policy, Stabilization and Growth in Developing Countries (Washington: International Monetary Fund).

Bloom, David E., David Canning, and Jaypee Sevilla, 2001, "The Effect of Health on Economic Growth: Theory and Evidence," NBER Working Paper No. 8587 (Cambridge, Massachusetts: National Bureau of Economic Research).

Burnside, Craig, and David Dollar, 2000, "Aid, Policies, and Growth," American Economic Review," Vol. 90 (September), pp. 847–68.

Chen, Shaohua, and Martin Ravallion, 1997, "What Can New Survey Data Tell Us About Recent Changes in Distribution and Poverty?" World Bank Economic Review, Vol. 11 (May), pp. 357–82.

Collier, Paul, and David Dollar, 2001, "Can the World Cut Poverty in Half? How Policy Reform and Effective Aid Can Meet International Development Goals," *World Development*, Vol. 29 (November), pp. 1787–802.

Devarajan, Shantayanan, Margaret J. Miller, and Eric V. Swanson, 2002, "Goals for Development: History, Prospects and Costs," World Bank Policy Research Working Paper No. 2819 (Washington: World Bank).

Dollar, David, and Aart Kraay, 2001, "Growth Is Good for the Poor," World Bank Policy Research Working Paper No. 2587 (Washington, World Bank).

Drakos, Konstantinos, and Ali M. Kutan, 2001, "Regional Effects of Terrorism on Tourism: Evidence from Three Mediterranean Countries," Center for European Integration Studies (ZEI) Working Paper No. B26 (Bonn: Universität Bonn).

Easterly, William, 2003, "Can Foreign Aid Buy Growth?" *Journal of Economic Perspectives*, Vol. 17 (Summer), pp. 23–48.

———, and Sergio Rebelo, 1993, "Fiscal Policy and Economic Growth: An Empirical Investigation," *Journal of Monetary Economics*, Vol. 32 (December), pp. 417–58.

———, Carlos A. Rodriguez, and Klaus Schmidt-Hebbel, 1994, *Public Sector Deficits and Macroeconomic Performance* (New York: Oxford University Press for the World Bank).

Enders, Walter, and Todd Sandler, 1991, "Causality Between Transnational Terrorism and Tourism: The Case of Spain," *Terrorism*, Vol. 14, pp. 49–58.

———, and Gerald F. Parise, 1992, "An Econometric Analysis of the Impact of Terrorism on Tourism," *Kyklos*, Vol. 45, No. 4, pp. 531–54.

Filmer, Deon, Jeffrey Hammer, and Lant Pritchett, 1998, "Health Policy in Poor Countries: Weak Links in the Chain," World Bank Policy Research Working Paper No. 1874 (Washington: World Bank).

Flug, Karnit, Antonio Spilimbergo, and Erik Wachtenheim, 1998, "Investment in Education: Do Economic Volatility and Credit Constraints Matter?" *Journal of Development Economics*, Vol. 55 (April), pp. 465–81.

Gavin, Michael, and Ricardo Hausmann, 1998, "Macroeconomic Volatility and Economic Development," IEA Conference Volume No. 119 (London: Macmillan), pp. 97–116.

Gemmell, Norman, and Mark McGillivray, 1998, "Aid and Tax Instability and the Government Budget Constraint in Developing Countries," CREDIT Research Paper No. 98/1 (Nottingham England: University of Nottingham, Centre for Research in Economic Development and International Trade).

Giavazzi, Francesco, and Marco Pagano, 1990, "Can Severe Fiscal Contractions Be Expansionary? Tales of Two Small European Countries," *NBER Macroeconomic Annual 1990*, pp. 75–110.

Giorgioni, Gianluigi, and Ken Holden, 2003, "Does the Ricardian Equivalence Proposition Hold in Less Developed Countries?" *International Review of Applied Economics*, Vol. 17 (April), pp. 209–21.

Glewwe, Paul, 2002, "Schools and Skills in Developing Countries: Education Policies and Socioeconomic Outcomes," *Journal of Economic Literature*, Vol. 40 (June), pp. 436–82.

Goode, Richard, 1993, "Tax Advice to Developing Countries: An Historical Survey," *World Development*, Vol. 21 (January), pp. 37–53.

Hemming, Richard, Michael Kell, and Selma Mahfouz, 2002, "The Effectiveness of Fiscal Policy in Stimulating Economic Activity: A Review of the Literature," IMF Working Paper 02/208 (Washington: International Monetary Fund).

Khalid, Ahmed M., 1996, "Ricardian Equivalence: Empirical Evidence from Developing Countries," *Journal of Development Economics*, Vol. 51 (December), pp. 413–32.

Landau, Daniel, 1986, "Government and Economic Growth in Less Developed Countries: An Empirical Study for 1960–1980," *Economic Development and Cultural Change*, Vol. 35 (October), pp. 35–75.

Lucas, Robert E. Jr., 1988, "On the Mechanics of Economic Development," *Journal of Monetary Economics*, Vol. 22 (July), pp. 3–42.

Milesi-Ferretti, Gian Maria, and Nouriel Roubini, 1998, "Growth Effects of Income and Consumption Taxes," *Journal of Money, Credit and Banking*, Vol. 30 (November), pp. 721–44.

Nitsch, Volker, and Dieter Schumacher, 2002, "Terrorism and Trade," paper presented at the German Institute for Economic Research (DIW) workshop on "The Economic Consequences of Global Terrorism," Berlin (June). Available via the Internet: http://www.diw.de/deutsch/service/veranstaltungen/ws_consequences/ws_programme.html.

Pallage, Stéphane, and Michel A. Robe, 2001, "Foreign Aid and the Business Cycle," *Review of International Economics*, Vol. 9 (November), pp. 641–72.

Psacharopoulos, George, 1994, "Returns to Investment in Education: A Global Update," *World Development*, Vol. 22 (September), pp. 1325–43.

Reinikka-Soininen, Ritva, and Jakob Svensson, 2001, "Explaining Leakage of Public Funds," World Bank Policy Research Working Paper No. 2709 (Washington: World Bank).

Richardson, John M., Jr., and S.W.R de A. Samarasinghe, 1991, "Measuring the Economic Dimensions of Sri Lanka's Ethnic Conflict," in *Economic Dimensions of Ethnic Conflict*, ed. by S.W.R. de A. Samarasinghe and Reed Coughlan (London: Pintner), pp. 194–223.

Rodrik, Dani, 1999, "Where Did All the Growth Go? External Shocks, Social Conflict, and Growth Collapses," *Journal of Economic Growth*, Vol. 4 (December), pp. 385–412.

———, 2000, "Growth Versus Poverty Reduction: A Hollow Debate," *Finance & Development*, Vol. 37 (December), pp. 8–9.

Romer, Paul M., 1990, "Endogenous Technological Change," *Journal of Political Economy*, Vol. 98 (October), pp. S71–S102.

Stiglitz, Joseph E., 2003, *The Roaring Nineties: A New History of the World's Most Prosperous Decade* (New York: Norton).

Tanzi, Vito, and Howell Zee, 2000, "Tax Policy for Emerging Markets: Developing Countries," *National Tax Journal*, Vol. 53 (June), pp. 299–322.

von Hagen, Jürgen, and Rolf Strauch, 2001, "Fiscal Consolidations: Quality, Economic Conditions, and Success," *Public Choice*, Vol. 109 (December), pp. 327–46.

von Hagen, Jürgen, Andrew Hughes Hallett, and Rolf Strauch, 2002, "Budgetary Consolidation in Europe: Quality, Economic Conditions, and Persistence," *Journal of the Japanese and International Economies*, Vol. 16 (December), pp. 512–35.

Walkenhorst, Peter, and Nora Dihel, 2002, "Trade Impacts of the Terrorist Attacks of 11 September 2001: A Quantitative Assessment," paper presented at the German Institute for Economic Research (DIW) workshop on The Economic Consequences of Global Terrorism, Berlin (June). Available via the Internet: http://www.diw.de/deutsch/Produkte/veranstaltungen/ws_consequences/docs/diw_ws_consequences200206_walkenhorst.pdf.

Xu, Bin, 1994, "Tax Policy Implications in Endogenous Growth Models," IMF Working Paper 94/38 (Washington: International Monetary Fund).

2

Fiscal Policy, Expenditure Composition, and Growth in Low-Income Countries

SANJEEV GUPTA, BENEDICT CLEMENTS, EMANUELE BALDACCI, AND CARLOS MULAS-GRANADOS

1. Introduction

A large body of empirical research supports the notion that healthy budgetary balances are, over the long run, good for growth (Easterly, Rodriguez, and Schmidt-Hebbel, 1994). The effect of fiscal consolidation on growth in the short run, however, remains open to question as a number of studies—largely for industrial countries—have drawn the conclusion that under some circumstances fiscal contractions can stimulate growth.[1] A central theme in these works is that the composition of fiscal adjustment plays a key role in determining whether fiscal contractions lead to higher growth and are also sustainable over time. These studies show that improving fiscal positions through the rationalization of the government wage bill and public transfers, rather than

This chapter is reprinted from the *Journal of International Money and Finance*, Vol. 23, Sanjeev Gupta, Benedict Clements, Emanuelle Baldacci, and Carlos Mulas-Granados, "Fiscal Policy, Expenditure Composition, and Growth in Low-Income Countries," ©2004, with permission from Elsevier. The authors wish to thank Shamit Chakravarti and Erwin Tiongson for their help in preparing this paper, and Guido Tabellini and an anonymous referee for their useful comments on an earlier version. Carlos Mulas-Granados was a consultant in the Fiscal Affairs Department in the fall of 2001.

[1] See, for example, McDermott and Wescott (1996); Alesina and Perotti (1996); Alesina, Perotti, and Tavares (1998); Alesina and Ardagna (1998); Buti and Sapir (1998); von Hagen, Hughes Hallett, and Strauch (2002); Alesina, Ardagna, Perotti, and Schiantarelli (2002).

increasing revenues and cutting public investment, can foster higher growth even in the short run.

The purpose of this paper is to assess whether fiscal consolidation and improvements in the composition of public expenditure have positive repercussions for growth in low-income countries. While some aspects of this issue have been assessed in other studies,[2] an in-depth econometric evaluation—drawing on a wide sample of low-income countries—has yet to be undertaken. For example, in the group of 36 different empirical studies that Kneller, Bleaney, and Gemmell (1998) identify as the core of the empirical research on the effects of fiscal policy on growth, only three studies (including Landau, 1986; and Easterly, Rodriguez, and Schmidt-Hebbel, 1994) were based on developing countries, and none were based on low-income countries alone.

A number of important related issues have not yet been fully examined in the literature. None of these studies, for example, have addressed whether deficits that are financed from abroad have a different impact on growth than those financed from domestic sources. In addition, the important issue of whether the macroeconomic effects of fiscal policy differ in low-deficit countries—as opposed to those that have yet to achieve a modicum of macroeconomic stability—has yet to be assessed for a wide sample of countries.[3]

This paper attempts to fill some of these gaps and aims to provide some empirical evidence of the effects of fiscal adjustment and expenditure composition on economic growth. More specifically, the paper addresses the following two questions:

- What is the impact of the fiscal stance, expenditure composition, and nature of budget financing on economic growth in low-income countries?
- Are these effects independent of initial fiscal conditions?

This paper does not restrict its analysis to episodes of fiscal adjustment as has been done in studies for industrial countries. Instead, it assesses the effects of both fiscal expansions and fiscal consolidations on growth in 39 low-income countries with IMF-supported programs in the 1990s.[4] These programs, on average, have targeted relatively small

---

[2] See Mackenzie, Orsmond, and Gerson (1997); Abed et al. (1998); and Kneller, Bleaney, and Gemmell (1999).

[3] See Adam and Bevan (2000) for a study based on 17 low-income countries.

[4] This includes countries that have obtained concessional loans from the IMF since 1999 under the Poverty Reduction and Growth Facility (PRGF), which replaced the Enhanced Structural Adjustment Facility (ESAF). One of the basic tenets of the PRGF is that a stable macroeconomic position is critical for promoting growth and reducing poverty. For further information on the characteristics of the PRGF, see http://www.imf.org/external/np/exr/facts/prgf.htm.

reductions in budget deficits.[5] Furthermore, the elimination of budget imbalances has not been the sole aim of these IMF-supported programs, which also sought, inter alia, to improve the composition of public expenditure and revenues. As such, an exclusive focus on episodes of fiscal adjustment—defined as periods of sharp deficit reduction—would be of only limited interest in examining the impact of fiscal policy on growth in low-income countries.

The results of this study confirm that there is a strong link between public expenditure reform and growth, as fiscal consolidations achieved through curtailing current expenditures are, in general, more conducive to growth. Fiscal consolidations tend to have the most positive effects on growth when they lead to a reduction in the domestic borrowing requirement of the government. When public investment is also protected, the positive effect of fiscal adjustment on growth is further accentuated. The fiscal consolidation–growth nexus is also influenced by a country's initial fiscal conditions—in particular, whether a country has reached a certain degree of macroeconomic stability or not.

The rest of the paper is structured as follows: Section 2 surveys the literature on the effects of fiscal policy and budget composition on economic growth; Section 3 describes the data used in the empirical sections; and Section 4 presents some baseline econometric results of the effects of fiscal policy and expenditure composition on economic growth. Particular attention is given to examining the robustness of the results, and whether results differ for low-deficit ("post-stabilization") countries. Finally, Section 5 concludes the paper and elaborates on some policy implications of the results.

2. Literature Review

The effects of fiscal policy on economic growth have been the subject of long debate. With respect to short-term effects, a large body of empirical research, primarily for industrial countries, has been devoted to understanding under which conditions fiscal multipliers can be small (and even negative) (Alesina and Perotti, 1996; Alesina and Ardagna, 1998; Perotti, 1999). Perotti (1999), for example, shows that consolidations tend to be expansionary when debt is high or growing rapidly, while Alesina and Perotti (1995) and Alesina and Ardagna (1998) find that, in addition to the size and persistence of the fiscal impulse, budget composition matters in explaining different private sector responses to fiscal policy (and, hence, the effect on growth). Fiscal adjustments

---

[5]For example, for ESAF-supported programs over the 1986–95 period, the deficit was targeted, on average, to decrease by about 1 percentage point of GDP relative to the pre-program year (Abed et al., 1998).

that rely primarily on cuts in transfers and the wage bill tend to last longer and can be expansionary, while those that rely primarily on tax increases and cuts in public investment tend to be contractionary and unsustainable (von Hagen, Hughes Hallett, and Strauch, 2002).

The potential effects of fiscal policy on long-term growth have also generated substantial attention (Tanzi and Zee, 1996). Most recently, the burgeoning work in the field of endogenous growth suggests that fiscal policy can either promote or retard economic growth as investment in physical and human capital—both of which can be affected by taxation and government expenditures—can affect steady-state growth rates (Barro, 1990, 1991; Barro and Sala-i-Martin, 1995; and Mendoza, Milesi-Ferretti, and Asea, 1997).

In both strands of the literature, the effect of fiscal policy on growth can be nonlinear. This may occur, for example, because the private sector's response to fiscal policy may be nonlinear, implying a complex relationship between the size and the composition of public spending and revenues and growth. Giavazzi, Jappelli, and Pagano (2000), for example, find that in industrial and developing countries the nonlinear effects of fiscal policy on national savings tend to be associated with large and persistent increases in the primary deficit.

There are good reasons to believe that for some (but not all) low-income countries fiscal contractions may also be expansionary. As in the industrial countries, expansionary contractions are more likely to be observed in countries that have not yet achieved a degree of macroeconomic stability.[6] For these countries, the overriding imperatives of reining in inflation and achieving low budget deficits are such that increases in public spending—even if potentially productive—may not have a salutary effect on growth. By contrast, countries in a "post-stabilization" phase can exercise more choice over expenditure priorities, including by allocating resources to important structural reforms, such as the decompression of the civil service payscale. In these countries, higher public spending—even if it results in higher deficits—could raise, rather than contract, economic activity. In sum, the relationship between the fiscal policy stance and growth will differ across countries depending on their initial fiscal conditions. This also has important implications for the econometric specifications used to link fiscal policy and growth (see below).

Another important issue to be considered in the analysis is the nexus between the composition of fiscal deficit financing and growth. Many

---

[6]For an empirical analysis of the impact of initial conditions on the effectiveness of fiscal policy during recessions in industrial and middle-income countries, see Baldacci et al. (2001).

studies found that fiscal consolidations can have an indirect impact on private investment (and thus growth) by affecting the level of aggregate demand and monetary variables. Deficits largely financed by domestic sources may also lead to inflationary pressures. High levels of inflation have been found to reduce growth and can lead to macroeconomic and financial instability (Fischer, 1983; Sarel, 1996).

In sum, the theoretical framework underlying the empirical analysis carried out in this paper assumes that fiscal policy can affect the steady-state and short-run growth rate through its effects on private sector behavior and on human and physical capital formation. It also acknowledges that initial and accompanying macroeconomic and fiscal conditions are important.

Statistical Data and Descriptive Analysis

Data

In this paper, three aspects of a country's fiscal policy are examined in relation to their impact on growth: the fiscal policy stance as measured by the level and changes in the general government budgetary balance; the financing of budgetary deficits; and expenditure composition. Data for these variables were constructed on the basis of the World Economic Outlook (WEO) database as well as a database for 39 ESAF- and PRGF-supported countries during the period 1990–2000.[7]

The fiscal policy stance is measured by the general government budget balance on a cash basis. This is defined as total revenues and grants minus total expenditures and net lending.[8] A positive change in the budget balance can be interpreted as a consolidation and a negative change as an expansion. As reported in Table 1, the average budget deficit for the sample is 6.3 percent of GDP. Deficits were generally reduced during the period with an average annual improvement of approximately ½ percentage point of GDP.

The deficit can be financed from either domestic or external sources. Domestic financing includes both bank and nonbank financing, with the latter measure including privatization receipts. For the countries

---

[7]The countries are Albania, Armenia, Benin, Bolivia, Burkina Faso, Cambodia, Cameroon, the Central African Republic, Chad, Djibouti, Ethiopia, The Gambia, Ghana, Georgia, Guinea, Guinea-Bissau, Guyana, Honduras, Kenya, the Kyrgyz Republic, Laos, Lesotho, Macedonia (FYR), Madagascar, Malawi, Mali, Mauritania, Moldova, Mozambique, Nicaragua, Niger, Rwanda, São Tomé and Príncipe, Senegal, Tajikistan, Tanzania, Vietnam, Yemen, and Zambia.

[8]The difference between revenues and expenditures can be different from the cash deficit for countries that measure expenditures on a commitment basis.

Table 1. Descriptive Statistics
(As percent of GDP, unless otherwise specified)

Variable	Observations	Mean	Standard Deviation
Budget balance	429	−6.30	7.9
Tax revenue	425	15.00	7.5
Nontax revenue	423	2.50	2.2
Grants	426	4.20	4.6
Current spending	425	19.70	9.5
Capital spending	425	9.00	7.2
Domestic financing	372	1.70	4.9
External financing	372	4.60	6.1
Per capita real GDP growth	429	−0.50	8.3
Change in:			
Budget balance	390	0.40	5.8
Tax revenue	386	0.02	3.2
Non-tax revenue	384	−0.06	1.2
Grants	386	0.03	2.6
Current spending	386	−0.50	4.8
Capital spending	386	0.05	3.4
Domestic financing	333	−0.20	4.8
External financing	333	−0.10	5.2
Per capita GDP growth	390	0.50	10.1

Source: Authors' calculations.
Note: Sample averages using data from 1990 until 2000.

included in the sample, external financing predominated while domestic financing averaged less than 2 percent of GDP.

Fiscal deficits are also used to identify "post-stabilization" countries. Post-stabilization countries are defined as those that had an average budget deficit (after grants) below 2.5 percent of GDP in the 1990–2000 period.[9] Based on this criterion, only seven countries can be considered post-stabilizers (Benin, The Gambia, Lesotho, Macedonia (FYR), Mauritania, Senegal, and Tanzania).

Macroeconomic indicators have also been extracted from the WEO database. Following earlier studies, growth is measured on a real per capita basis.[10] Other variables used in the regression analysis to control for initial and accompanying conditions include the labor force (as a percentage of total population); terms of trade; and private investment.

---

[9]This roughly corresponds to the low-deficit country group identified in the ESAF Review (Abed et al., 1998).

[10]Growth of per capita GDP is used most frequently in the empirical literature assessing the effects of fiscal policy on growth, as this controls for differences among countries in the population growth rate. See, for example, Aschauer (1989); Barro (1990, 1991); Easterly and Rebelo (1993); Devarajan, Swaroop, and Zou (1996); Easterly, Loayza, and Montiel (1997); and Kneller, Bleaney, and Gemmell (1999, 2000).

These variables are used to control the effects of private sector and external sector activity on growth. We also control for the levels of initial primary and secondary enrollment as indicators of human capital endowment in each country. Data are taken from the *World Development Indicators* of the World Bank.

Fiscal Policy and Growth: Bivariate Analysis

Simple correlations reported in Table 2 show a significant association between deficit reduction, expenditure composition, and growth consistent with previous findings in the literature on industrial countries. For example, stronger budget balances are positively associated with per capita growth. The composition of public expenditure also matters for growth; higher capital outlays are associated with more buoyant growth, while higher current expenditures and domestic financing of the deficit are associated with less favorable economic performance.

These results hold for the short-run correlations as well. Annual changes in the budget balance are positively correlated with changes in per capita growth. Correlation coefficients[11] are also significant for the various measures of public expenditure (including capital outlays) and for domestic financing.

These preliminary findings are consistent with the empirical results obtained by Easterly and Rebelo (1993) and Kneller, Bleaney, and Gemmell (1999, 2000), who found that balanced budgets and investment in transport and communications are consistently correlated with growth in a sample of low-income countries.

Econometric Analysis

The Econometric Models

The relationship between expenditure composition, fiscal adjustment, and growth can be estimated by regressing the annual rate of real per capita GDP growth on a set of regressors, including fiscal variables and other control variables. Three specifications of the relationship are used here. In Model A, fiscal variables are measured as a share of GDP without a variable included on the fiscal balance; this allows us to capture the effects of particular expenditure items (e.g., wages) not only on the composition of expenditure, but also on the deficit. In Model B, we measure fiscal variables in relation to total expenditures or total

---

[11]Correlation coefficients are calculated using the Spearman rank correlation formula to avoid the effect of outliers.

Table 2. Bivariate Correlations
(Variables expressed as percent of GDP, unless otherwise specified)

Variables	Per Capita Real GDP Growth	Number of Observations
Budget balance	0.23***	429
Tax revenue	−0.03	425
Nontax revenue	0.03	423
Grants	0.05	425
Current spending	−0.24***	425
Capital spending	0.16***	425
Domestic financing	−0.25***	372
External financing	−0.07	372
Change in:		
Budget balance	0.20***	390
Tax revenue	0.09**	386
Nontax revenue	0.08*	386
Grants	0.11**	384
Current spending	−0.16***	386
Capital spending	0.12***	386
Domestic financing	−0.16***	333
External financing	−0.01	333

Source: Authors' calculations.
Note: Bilateral correlations using annual data from 1990 through 2000.
*significant at 10 percent; **significant at 5 percent; ***significant at 1 percent.

revenues so as to assess directly the impact of expenditure or revenue composition on growth, while at the same time including a variable for the budget balance. In Model C, we address how the nature of the financing of the deficit affects growth by substituting the budget balance variable with variables for domestic and external financing of the deficit. Each of the three models is formulated as follows.

- Budget components (revenue and expenditure) measured as a share of GDP (Model A):

$$g_{i,t} = \alpha + \sum_{l=1}^{k} \beta_l Y_{ilt} + \sum_{h=1}^{q} \beta_h XGDP_{iht} + u_{it}, \tag{1}$$

where $g_{i,t}$ is the growth rate of real per capita GDP; Y_{ilt} is a vector of nonfiscal independent variables (initial level of GDP per capita, private investment ratio, terms of trade, labor force, and initial level of primary and secondary enrollment rates); and $XGDP_{iht}$ is a vector of independent fiscal variables aimed at capturing the effect of the composition of the budget. These variables are measured in percent of GDP and include public sector wages and salaries, expenditures on other goods and services, transfers and subsidies, interest payments on government debt, capital expenditures, tax revenues, nontax revenues, and grants. In order to avoid perfect collinearity among regressors, the budget balance is not included.[12, 13]

- Fiscal balance as share of GDP and expenditure composition by economic category (Model B):

$$g_{i,t} = \alpha + \sum_{l=1}^{k} \beta_l Y_{ilt} + \sum_{h=1}^{q} \beta_h XBALEXP_{iht} + u_{it}, \tag{2}$$

where $g_{i,t}$ and Y_{ilt} are defined as before and $XBALEXP_{iht}$ is a vector of independent fiscal variables aimed at capturing the effect of the budget balance and the composition of expenditures. The budget balance is measured as a percentage of GDP, while all expenditure items are measured as shares of total public expenditures. The expenditure categories include public wages and salaries, public transfers and subsidies, interest payments on government debt, public expenditures on other goods and services, and public capital expenditures.

- Sources of deficit financing expressed as a share of GDP and expenditure composition by economic category (Model C):

$$g_{i,t} = \alpha + \sum_{l=1}^{k} \beta_l Y_{ilt} + \sum_{h=1}^{q} \beta_h XFINEXP_{iht} + u_{it}, \tag{3}$$

where $g_{i,t}$ and Y_{ilt} are defined as before and $XFINEXP_{iht}$ is a vector of independent fiscal variables aimed at capturing the effect of the deficit financing (both domestic and external financing in percent of GDP), and the composition of expenditures as shares of total public expenditures. This specification is the same as the previous one, but it replaces the budget balance with its financing sources (expressed as ratios to GDP).

The baseline regressions use a fixed-effects estimator. The results are then tested for robustness by running a Generalized Method of Moments (GMM) estimator to address potential problems with endogeneity and

---

[12] Theoretical models have generally incorporated government budget constraint, which implies that a change in revenues or spending of a given magnitude has to be matched by offsetting changes elsewhere. This has not, however, been the approach taken in the empirical literature. In many cases, applied studies estimate the effect of selected expenditures and revenues on growth, which implicitly assumes that the effect of the excluded items on growth is neutral. We avoid this by including all budget items in the specification. In this respect, we follow Kneller, Bleaney, and Gemmell (1999), who emphasize the need to include all fiscal policy variables in the equations to avoid omitted variables bias.

[13] For example, adjustment based on selective increases in import tariff rates would most likely have a more adverse effect on growth than raising revenues from a broad-based VAT.

serial correlation arising from the dynamic specification of the models above. A pooled mean-group estimator (PMG) is also used to capture the effects of both short-run and long-run dynamics and relax the assumption of homogeneity of short-run coefficients. The relative merits of these methods are discussed in the respective sections.

Baseline Regressions

The models above are estimated in levels and in first differences (changes) in order to capture both long- and short-run effects of fiscal policy on growth. An alternative formulation of this model, involving a nested specification in which both short-run and long-run effects are estimated simultaneously, is found in Bassanini, Scarpetta, and Hemmings (2001). This model could not be fully estimated in the present context due to the relatively short length of our sample. The results from an abridged version of the Bassanini, Scarpetta, and Hemmings model are discussed in the section on sensitivity analysis.

An important problem that is encountered in panel data estimation is the presence of unobserved country-specific effects (Easterly, Loayza, and Montiel, 1997).[14] Excluding unobservable country-specific effects could lead to serious biases in the econometric estimates, notably when these effects are correlated with the other covariates. To address this, we used a least squares dummy variable (LSDV) estimator that allows the intercept in the regression to be country specific for the estimation of Models A, B, and C.[15, 16]

Results from the baseline regressions (Table 3) are consistent with the empirical literature and show that, on average, fiscal adjustments have not been harmful for growth, both in the long and in the short term. According to these results, a 1 percent improvement in the fiscal balance has a positive and significant impact in the long term on the rate of GDP growth, raising it by ½ percentage point (Model B). An even larger coefficient is estimated for the short-term effect of a change in the fiscal balance on growth. The composition of deficit financing also matters. Domestic financing of the budget tends to be more harmful for growth than external financing (Model C): in the long term, an

---

[14]Unobservable time-specific effects are less common. In fact, following Greene (2000), when such effects do exist, it would be more efficient to include an explicit linear or nonlinear time trend in the equation.

[15]Tests for serial correlation for the three models revealed no first-order autocorrelation of the residuals.

[16]The number of countries includes in the regression varies according to the specification. On average, about 28 countries are included.

Table 3. Budget Composition and Growth in Low-Income Countries: Fixed Effects

	Model A. Budget Composition (as percent of GDP)		Model B. Budget Balance and Composition of Expenditures		Model C. Budget Financing and Composition of Expenditures	
	Real per capita GDP growth	Change in real per capita GDP growth	Real per capita GDP growth	Change in real per capita GDP growth	Real per capita GDP growth	Change in real per capita GDP growth
Initial GDP per capita level[a]	0.205 (0.92)	0.203 (0.10)	−0.816 (−0.39)	0.475 (0.23)	−0.314 (−0.14)	0.332 (0.16)
Labor force	0.837*** (2.88)	2.894*** (5.24)	0.618** (2.21)	2.799*** (4.68)	0.687** (2.33)	2.329*** (3.85)
Terms of trade	−0.003 (−0.52)	0.001 (0.18)	−0.005 (−0.90)	−0.362 (−0.04)	−0.005 (−1.01)	−0.005 (−0.55)
Private investment	0.267* (1.77)	0.279 (1.44)	0.396*** (2.75)	0.582*** (2.81)	0.391** (2.28)	0.75*** (3.27)
Initial primary enrollment	−0.136 (−0.99)	−0.006 (−0.05)	−0.159 (−1.21)	−0.016 (−0.11)	−0.211 (−1.54)	−0.031 (−0.21)
Initial secondary enrollment	0.057 (0.51)	−0.048 (−.037)	0.162 (1.51)	−0.051 (−0.36)	0.150 (1.33)	−0.034 (−0.25)
Budget balance (as percent of GDP)			0.458*** (4.22)	0.551*** (3.39)		
Domestic financing (as percent of GDP)					−0.797*** (−5.08)	−1.336*** (−5.94)
External financing (as percent of GDP)					−0.383*** (−2.93)	−0.595*** (−3.22)
Wages and salaries (as percent of GDP)	−0.525* (−1.78)	−0.396 (−0.87)				
Wages and salaries (as percent of total expenditure)			−0.213** (−2.23)	−0.229 (−1.53)	−0.250** (−2.38)	−0.235 (−1.51)
Transfers and subsidies (as percent of GDP)	0.110 (0.42)	−0.424 (−1.08)				
Transfers and subsidies (as percent of total expenditure)			0.054 (0.49)	0.033 (0.19)	−0.047 (−0.37)	−0.008 (−0.05)

Table 3 *(concluded)*

	Model A. Budget Composition (as percent of GDP)		Model B. Budget Balance and Composition of Expenditures		Model C. Budget Financing and Composition of Expenditures	
	Real per capita GDP growth	Change in real per capita GDP growth	Real per capita GDP growth	Change in real per capita GDP growth	Real per capita GDP growth	Change in real per capita GDP growth
Interest payments (as percent of GDP)	-0.293 (-0.90)	-0.367 (-0.73)				
Interest payments (as percent of total expenditure)			-0.118 (-1.11)	-0.370*** (2.20)	-0.227* (-1.92)	-0.415** (-2.35)
Other goods and services (as percent of GDP)	0.420 (1.36)	1.722*** (3.96)				
Other goods and services (as percent of total expenditure)			0.015 (0.16)	0.068 (0.45)	0.043 (0.44)	0.175 (1.10)
Capital expenditure (as percent of GDP)	0.567*** (2.96)	0.874*** (3.52)				
Capital expenditure (as percent of total expenditure)			0.154* (1.96)	0.282** (2.25)	0.072 (0.82)	0.237* (1.81)
Tax revenue (as percent of GDP)	-0.056 (-0.29)	0.053 (0.17)				
Nontax revenue (as percent of GDP)	0.095 (0.81)	1.49*** (2.63)				
Grants (as percent of GDP)	0.079 (0.33)	0.209 (0.71)				
Number of observations	249	220	250	221	225	197
Adjusted R-squared	0.10	0.33	0.16	0.21	0.17	0.31
F test	1.77	3.86	2.41	2.62	2.30	3.50
Probability	0.00	0.00	0.00	0.00	0.00	0.00

Note: t statistics in parentheses. * significant at 10 percent; ** significant at 5 percent; and *** significant at 1 percent.
[a] Multiplied by 100.

increase in domestic financing by 1 percent reduces the per capita growth rate by ¾ percentage point. The estimated coefficient for the short-term relationship is even larger.

Expenditure composition is also critical for growth. In Model A, a 1 percentage point of GDP increase in spending on wages and salaries reduces growth by ½ percentage point, while a 1 percentage point increase in the ratio of capital outlays to GDP increases growth by more than ½ percentage point. Expenditures on other goods and services are also found to raise the growth rate, but only in the short term. Interest payments have a statistically insignificant impact on growth. Finally, in the models that assess the impact of expenditure composition directly (Models B and C), the coefficients for spending on wages are significant, but only in the long run. The share of capital expenditures in total outlays is positively related to growth under all model specifications, except for the long-run coefficient estimated in Model C. The results suggest that a 1 percent increase in the allocation of public spending to capital outlays can raise the growth rate by 0.1 percentage point in the long term and by almost ¼ percentage point in the short term. The share of public outlays devoted to the interest bill is also negatively correlated with growth. A 1 percent increase in the ratio of interest to total public spending tends to reduce growth by ¼ percentage point in the long run and by more than ⅓ percentage point in the short term.

Sensitivity Analysis

In order to assess the sensitivity of the econometric results presented above, this section reports the main results of the robustness analysis.

Reverse causality is not found to affect significantly the parameter estimates. A common issue in the literature on fiscal policy and growth is the likely presence of endogeneity or reverse causality. It could be the case that economic growth itself influences fiscal variables. For example, when economic growth slows down, the ratio of government spending to GDP is likely to increase if the nominal level of expenditure is fixed, or if the revenue effort is sensitive to cyclical developments. Moreover, some degree of reverse causality could also be present in the relationship between growth and investment.[17] If economic growth is a determinant

---

[17] A related issue is whether the model fully captures the effect of the budget balance on growth, as the inclusion of private investment (as an independent variable) de facto blocks the indirect effects of the budget deficit on growth via its effects on private investment. Estimates that omit private investment from the specification, however, do not lead to significantly different results, including for the fiscal balance. This assessment should be viewed as preliminary, however, given the need to assess the deficit-investment relationship in a model especially specified for that purpose.

of any of the right-hand-side variables in our model, estimation techniques that do not take into account this endogeneity will yield biased and inconsistent parameter estimates. To address this concern, we estimate the previous models using a GMM estimator,[18] instrumenting for the investment rate, fiscal balance ratio, and shares of government spending and revenues to GDP. We use as instruments the lagged values of these variables, the other exogenous variables in the model, and a set of instruments not included in the model.[19] Results are presented in Table 4 and broadly confirm the findings of the previous section. Accounting for the endogeneity of fiscal balances leads to the same positive effect of fiscal consolidations on growth as in the baseline regressions. However, a difference in the results is that the coefficient for the share of wages and salaries becomes insignificant in Model A, although it remains significant and negatively correlated with growth in the remaining specifications. The short-run effect of capital outlays on growth is not affected by the use of the GMM estimator; however, the long-run coefficient turns insignificant.

The specification used in the regression above does not allow for any dynamics between the dependent and the independent variables. However, growth relationships are dynamic in nature, as growth in a given period is not uncorrelated with past growth trends. If the true model is not static, parameter estimates based on a static fixed-effects estimator are biased and inconsistent, even when the error terms are not serially correlated. Thus, we estimated Models A, B, and C using unobserved country-specific effects and allowed for the lagged growth rate to be included among the determinants of economic growth. These models can be estimated using the GMM estimator proposed by Arellano and Bond (1991). The GMM estimate also controls for endogeneity by using the lagged values of the levels of the endogenous and the predetermined variables as instruments. Both the validity of the instruments and the presence of serial correlation in the residual, which would eliminate the consistency of the estimator, can be tested once the equation is estimated.

Introducing a dynamic specification does not lead to significantly different results from the baseline, while it improves the results compared to the static GMM estimator. GMM estimates of the dynamic model with country-specific effects are reported in Table 4. The results are, in general, consistent with the static fixed-effects estimates presented in the previous

---

[18] The GMM estimator used here deals with a heteroscedastic error process. This estimator is more efficient than the traditional instrumental variables estimator.

[19] The instruments include total revenue, current government spending and total government spending, all as a ratio to GDP. All instruments were found to be valid according to the Hansen-Sargan test.

Table 4. Fiscal Policy, Budget Composition, and Growth in Low-Income Countries: Controlling for Reverse Causality, 1990–2000

	Model A. Budget Composition (as percent of GDP)				Model B. Budget Balance and Composition of Expenditures				Model C. Budget Financing and Composition of Expenditures			
	Real per capita growth (GMM-IVREG)	Real per capita growth (GMM ABond)	Change growth (GMM-IVREG)	Change growth (GMM-ABond)	Real per capita growth (GMM-IVREG)	Real per capita growth (GMM ABond)	Change growth (GMM-IVREG)	Change growth (GMM-ABond)	Real per capita growth (GMM-IVREG)	Real per capita growth (GMM ABond)	Change growth (GMM-IVREG)	Change growth (GMM-ABond)
Per capita growth ($t-1$)		-0.109** (-2.05)		-0.329*** (-9.24)		-0.265*** (-21.78)		-0.371*** (16.38)		-0.229*** (-6.18)		-0.424*** (-16.21)
Initial GDP per capita level[a]	0.396* (1.96)		0.039 (0.31)		-0.041 (-0.22)		0.033 (0.34)		-0.061 (-0.32)		-0.006 (-0.06)	
Labor force	0.847* (1.74)	1.784*** (9.60)	2.89*** (3.12)	2.669*** (11.30)	0.75 (1.60)	0.936*** (4.32)	2.120** (2.03)	2.18*** (16.72)	0.802* (1.74)	1.149*** (5.38)	1.76* (2.05)	1.69*** (5.90)
Terms of trade	-0.003 (1.34)	0.003*** (3.66)	0.001 (0.42)	0.004 (1.47)	-0.005** (-2.94)	-0.002*** (-2.64)	-0.001 (-0.29)	0.003 (1.01)	-0.005*** (-3.18)	-0.004*** (-3.38)	-0.004 (-0.73)	-0.001 (-0.62)
Private investment	0.266* (1.69)	0.106 (1.49)	0.279* (1.69)	0.167 (1.30)	0.383** (2.84)	0.393*** (5.28)	0.466** (2.29)	0.642*** (5.97)	0.356** (2.36)	0.760*** (3.90)	0.602** (2.26)	0.533*** (3.14)
Initial primary enrollment	-0.797 (-1.80)		-0.068 (-0.89)		-0.546 (-1.27)		0.006 (0.09)		-0.519 (-1.24)		0.072 (0.67)	
Initial secondary enrollment	0.346 (1.45)		-0.021 (-0.23)		0.352 (1.58)		-0.052 (-0.77)		0.335 (1.51)		-0.072 (-0.87)	
Budget balance (as percent of GDP)					0.435*** (4.24)	0.536*** (9.59)	0.462** (2.21)	0.662*** (17.35)				
Domestic financing (as percent of GDP)									-0.606*** (-3.06)	-0.929*** (-6.80)	-0.977*** (2.73)	-0.991*** (-6.79)
External financing (as percent of GDP)									-0.415*** (-3.54)	-0.459*** (-7.07)	-0.511** (-2.57)	-0.605*** (-8.86)
Wages and salaries (as percent of GDP)		-0.385* (-1.89)			-0.214* (-1.85)	-0.350*** (-7.09)	-0.244* (-1.76)	-0.263*** (-6.26)	-0.220* (-1.65)	-0.280*** (-3.58)	-0.255* (1.83)	-0.344*** (-3.14)
Wages and salaries (as percent of total expenditure)	-0.521 (-0.86)		-0.396 (-0.58)	-0.511* (-1.92)								
Transfers and subsidies (as percent of GDP)	0.109 (0.46)	-0.059 (-0.50)			0.081 (0.92)	-0.004 (-0.09)	-0.001 (0.00)	-0.005 (-0.09)	0.039 (0.40)	-0.018 (-0.19)	-0.070 (-0.21)	0.230*** (3.00)
Transfers and subsidies (as percent of total expenditure)			-0.424 (-0.58)	-0.528***								

Table 4 *(concluded)*

	Model A. Budget Composition (as percent of GDP)				Model B. Budget Balance and Composition of Expenditures				Model C. Budget Financing and Composition of Expenditures			
	Real per capita growth (GMM-IVREG)	Real per capita growth (GMM ABond)	Change growth (GMM-IVREG)	Change growth (GMM-ABond)	Real per capita growth (GMM-IVREG)	Real per capita growth (GMM ABond)	Change growth (GMM-IVREG)	Change growth (GMM-ABond)	Real per capita growth (GMM-IVREG)	Real per capita growth (GMM ABond)	Change growth (GMM-IVREG)	Change growth (GMM-ABond)
Interest payments (as percent of GDP)	−0.298 (−0.74)	−0.188 (−1.63)	−0.367 (−0.87)	0.005 (0.03)								
Interest payments (as percent of total expenditure)					−0.139 (−1.09)	−0.248*** (−4.42)	−0.303 (−1.59)	−0.379*** (−6.17)	−0.218 (−1.47)	−0.194** (−2.08)	−0.314* (−1.67)	−0.412*** (−5.16)
Other goods and services (as percent of GDP)	0.400 (0.95)	1.417*** (6.26)	1.72*** (3.05)	0.932*** (4.12)								
Other goods and services (as percent of total expenditure)					−0.002 (−0.03)	0.129** (2.28)	0.048 (0.40)	0.035 (0.87)	0.003 (0.05)	0.149** (2.44)	0.109 (0.89)	0.064 (0.77)
Capital expenditure (as percent of GDP)	0.552 (1.57)	0.710*** (7.10)	0.874*** (2.41)	0.735*** (5.48)								
Capital expenditure (as percent of total expenditure)					0.116 (1.35)	0.185*** (5.03)	0.194 (1.38)	0.358*** (10.35)	0.071 (0.69)	0.180*** (3.69)	0.145 (1.00)	0.293*** (4.44)
Tax revenue (as percent of GDP)	−0.043 (−0.18)	0.067 (1.04)	0.053 (0.20)	0.059 (0.31)								
Nontax revenue (as percent of GDP)	0.104 (0.27)	1.518*** (5.01)	1.49** (2.35)	1.44*** (3.88)								
Grants (as percent of GDP)	0.090 (0.25)	0.185 (0.97)	0.209 (0.61)	0.328*** (5.10)								
Number of observations	249	201	220	172	250	201	221	172	225	179	197	151
Regression tests—Wald χ^2 (12)	...	3,644.13	...	18,158.87	...	26,400.36	...	18,255.63	...	7,060.64	...	108,082.74

Note: Absolute value of t and z statistics in parentheses. * significant at 10 percent; ** significant at 5 percent; and *** significant at 1 percent. Model A: Hansen-J Test: (GMM 0-levels = 0.01); (GMM 0-changes = 0.00); serial of over 2: (GMM-ABond-levels = 0.00); serial of over 2: (GMM-ABond-levels) = 0.41; (GMM-ABond-changes) = 0.25 Model B: Hansen-J Test: (GMM 0-levels = 0.62; (GMM 0-changes) = 1.32; serial of over 2: (GMM-ABond-levels) = 0.08; (GMM-ABond-changes) = 0.21. Model C: Hansen-J Test: (GMM 0-levels) = 1.04; (GMM 0-changes) = 2.32; serial of over 2: (GMM-ABond-levels) = 0.12; (GMM-ABond-changes) = 0.10

GMM = Generalized Method of Moments; IV = Instrumental variables; REG = regression; GMM ABond = GMM by Arellano and Bond (1991).
a Multiplied by 100.

section. The effect of fiscal consolidation on growth is larger and more significant than under the GMM and LSDV estimates of the static model. The contributions of capital outlays and government spending on wages are still correctly signed and statistically significant, and in most cases larger in size than in the baseline and GMM regressions. The negative effect on growth of an increase in domestic financing is larger, while the effect of external financing of the deficit is broadly unchanged. The coefficient of the lagged dependent variable is negative and significant, as expected,[20] for all models. Finally, both the Sargan test for the validity of instruments and the test for the serial correlation of residuals confirm that the dynamic GMM provides consistent estimates of the parameters.

A variety of other estimators were utilized to test the robustness of the results, including the Generalized Least Squares (GLS) estimate of the random effects model. The results confirm the main findings of the previous section.[21] Results are also consistent with these estimates when we use a robust technique to control for the possible presence of outliers in the data. The method is based on an iterative algorithm that first runs OLS estimates and calculates Cook's D statistics for the residuals, eliminating those observations for which $D > 1$.[22] The second step of the algorithm is to run a regression on the new dataset, and calculate case weights based on the inverse of the residual.[23] The results show that the effect of outliers in our data is not substantial.

A further robustness test was carried out by replicating a modified version of the model used by Bassanini, Scarpetta, and Hemmings (2001). This specification tries to capture the effect of the simultaneous inclusion of both short-run and long-run effects of fiscal variables in the growth equation using the PMG estimator. We were not able to fully replicate the nested specification used by Bassanini, Scarpetta, and Hemmings, given the short time dimension of our sample. Instead, we included the most important fiscal variables in first differences[24] in the

---

[20] A negative coefficient for the lagged growth rate can be interpreted as the tendency of the annual growth rate to converge toward an average long-run trend. Countries would still tend toward different, specific growth rates as a result of the error component structure in the equation.

[21] These and other results not reported in the paper are available from the authors upon request.

[22] Although most results are consistent with the baseline regression for models A and B, in the case of model C, the coefficient of the level of domestic financing is not statistically significant. For the majority of the short-run coefficients, the variables are significant and correctly signed.

[23] For a full description of this procedure, see Hamilton (1991).

[24] In Model A, we use the first difference of total government spending and total revenues as a share of GDP. In Models B and C, we use the fiscal balance and domestic and external deficit financing, respectively.

level specification of the three models, and allowed their coefficients to be country-specific to account for differentiated short-term responses of growth to fiscal policy. We estimated this model using a fixed-effects estimator. The results confirm the stability of the fiscal coefficients estimated in the baseline regressions (Table 5). The negative effect of fiscal deficits on growth is confirmed by these estimates. In Model B, the long-run coefficient of the fiscal balance is significant and positively signed, but smaller in size than the corresponding coefficient in the baseline regression. Similar significant and consistently signed coefficients are also found for the share of wages on total government spending and the ratio of capital to total public outlays. Results for Model A show a much larger and significant negative effect of the wage bill on growth. However, the ratio of capital spending to GDP becomes insignificant in this specification. Model C also confirms the main findings of the baseline model. However, in this model, while domestic financing is found to be detrimental for growth, external financing does not significantly affect growth.

Finally, results do not change much when the possible effects of the business cycle and time trends are removed from the data. The possible effects of the business cycle are partially eliminated by smoothing the data using a three-year moving average filter. Once again, the results are not sensitive to this transformation of the original data. The reason why business cycle effects may be weaker in low-income countries than in the industrial countries is the absence of automatic stabilizers. This feature makes it very unlikely that business cycles affect tax collection or public expenditures, and thus the overall budget balance. Moreover, in our sample, we do not find sufficient evidence that unobservable time effects are a serious problem, as evidenced by the results for regressions that include time dummies to control for nonlinear time trends in the data.

Nonlinear Effects of Fiscal Policy on Growth:
Pre- and Post-Stabilization Countries

The results in the previous sections suggest that fiscal consolidation is not harmful for growth in low-income countries. Quality fiscal adjustments based on the reallocation of public expenditure to more productive uses, and the reduction of the budget deficit, were found to be conducive to higher growth. Of interest is whether these results hold for all countries in the sample, in particular, for countries that have already achieved a modicum of macroeconomic stability (i.e., "post-stabilization" countries).

Table 5. Budget Composition and Growth in Low-Income Countries: Nested Models with Fixed Effects [a]

(Dependent variable: Real per capita GDP growth)

	Model A. Budget Composition (as percent of GDP)	Model B. Budget Balance and Composition of Expenditures	Model C: Budget Financing and Composition of Expenditures
Initial GDP per capita level [b]	0.003	−0.001	−0.001
	(1.07)	(−0.38)	(−0.43)
Labor force	0.510*	0.443	0.413
	(1.77)	(1.48)	(1.06)
Terms of trade	−0.006	−0.006	−0.007
	(−1.00)	(−0.93)	(−0.92)
Private investment	−0.026	0.343*	0.452*
	(−0.15)	(1.91)	(1.80)
Initial primary enrollment	−0.139	−0.130	−0.139
	(−0.36)	(−0.91)	(−0.67)
Initial secondary enrollment	0.020	0.133	0.135
	(0.10)	(1.19)	(0.94)
Budget balance (as percent of GDP)		0.348**	
		(2.54)	
Domestic financing (as percent of GDP)			−0.521*
			(−1.79)
External financing (as percent of GDP)			−0.378
			(−1.63)
Wages and salaries (as percent of GDP)	−0.833***		
	(−2.82)		
Wages and salaries (as percent of total expenditure)		−0.196*	−0.145
		(−1.79)	(−0.96)
Transfers and subsidies (as percent of GDP)	0.287		
	(0.76)		
Transfers and subsidies (as percent of total expenditure)		0.063	0.084
		(0.50)	(0.50)
Interest payments (as percent of GDP)	−0.023		
	(−0.07)		
Interest payments (as percent of total expenditure)		−0.159	−0.138
		(−1.33)	(−0.83)
Other goods and services (as percent of GDP)	0.424		
	(1.28)		
Other goods and services (as percent of total expenditure)		0.032	−0.016
		(0.27)	(−0.10)
Capital expenditure (as percent of GDP)	0.214		
	(1.05)		
Capital expenditure (as percent of total expenditure)		0.172*	0.213*
		(1.96)	(1.71)
Tax revenue (as percent of GDP)	−0.300		
	(−1.31)		
Nontax revenue (as percent of GDP)	−0.049		
	(−0.12)		
Grants (as percent of GDP)	0.041		
	(0.15)		
Number of observations	229	230	201
Adjusted R-squared	0.68	0.30	0.17
F test	3.07	2.53	1.47
Probability	0.00	0.00	0.02

Note: *t* statistics in parentheses. *significant at 10 percent; **significant at 5 percent; and ***significant at 1 percent.

[a] The regression includes the following variables, denoted in changes, and their interaction with country dummies: total expenditure and total revenue (Model A); deficit (Model B); and domestic and external financing (Model C).

[b] Multiplied by 100.

With the purpose of assessing the effect of initial fiscal conditions on the fiscal policy-growth nexus, we split the sample into post- and pre-stabilization countries. A post-stabilization country is defined as a country that maintained an average fiscal deficit (after grants) below 2.5 percent of GDP during the period 1990–2000.[25]

Results for post-stabilization countries point to the positive effects of capital outlays and selected current expenditures on growth. Econometric results for the two subgroups are reported in Table 6 using LSDV.[26] Interestingly, the results suggest that for countries with low budget deficits additional fiscal consolidation may not yield higher growth. Even more importantly, domestic financing is not harmful for growth in the short run and less harmful than external financing in the long run in these countries, unlike the case of countries that have not yet achieved stabilization. These results should be interpreted with caution, though, in light of the small sample size for post-stabilization countries and the poor performance of some of these models in terms of F-tests. Nevertheless, the results support the notion that the relationship between budget deficits and growth in these countries differs from that of the sample as a whole. Results for pre-stabilization countries are fully consistent with the "expansionary contractions" thesis.

Conclusions and Policy Implications

The empirical evidence provided in this study suggests that in low-income countries fiscal consolidations were not harmful for long- or short-term growth in the period 1990–2000. This paper sought to shed light on the relationship between fiscal adjustment, expenditure composition, and economic growth in low-income countries. Consistent with the previous findings in the literature on industrial countries, the results point to a significant relationship between fiscal adjustment and per capita growth. A reduction of 1 percentage point in the ratio of the fiscal deficit to GDP leads to an average increase in per capita growth of ½ percentage point both in the long and in the short term. This implies that a

---

[25] The criterion used to group the countries in the sample is similar to the one used in a study of ESAF-supported programs from 1986–95 (see Abed et al., 1998), where "low initial deficit" countries were defined as those with initial deficits (before grants) of 5 percent, with grants of approximately 2½ percent of GDP. Post-stabilization countries included in the regressions are The Gambia, Lesotho, Macedonia (FYR), Mauritania, Senegal, and Tanzania. Benin is the seventh post-stabilization country, but is excluded because data on the other control variables are unavailable.

[26] Results were also replicated using GLS and GMM estimators, which broadly confirmed these findings. These results are not included in the paper for the sake of brevity but are available from the authors upon request.

Table 6. Fiscal Policy, Budget Composition, and Growth in Low-Income Countries (Pre- and Post-Stabilization Countries), 1990–2000: Fixed Effects

	Model A. Budget Composition				Model B. Budget Balance and Composition of Expenditures				Model C. Budget Financing and Composition of Expenditures			
	Real Per Capita GDP Growth		Change Real Per Capita GDP Growth		Real Per Capita GDP Growth		Change Real Per Capita GDP Growth		Real Per Capita GDP Growth		Change Real Per Capita GDP Growth	
	Pre-stabilization countries	Post-stabilization countries	Pre-stabilization countries	Post-stabilization countries	Pre-stabilization countries	Post-stabilization countries	Pre-stabilization countries	Post-stabilization countries	Pre-stabilization countries	Post-stabilization countries	Pre-stabilization countries	Post-stabilization countries
Initial GDP per capita level [a]	1.466 (1.55)	-1.423 (-0.41)	-0.018 (-0.02)	-0.012 (-0.05)	1.010 (1.21)	-3.402 (-1.18)	0.290 (0.31)	-1.483 (-0.61)	0.013 (1.51)	-9.726 (-2.75)	0.422 (0.48)	-0.132 (-0.55)
Labor force	0.833** (2.62)	0.967 (0.63)	2.792*** (4.73)	0.218 (0.11)	0.571* (1.87)	1.68 (1.29)	2.56*** (4.03)	0.605 (0.29)	0.601* (1.91)	4.591*** (2.83)	2.10*** (3.32)	4.50 (1.52)
Terms of trade	-0.004 (-0.63)	-0.004 (-0.09)	0.002 (0.23)	0.045 (0.73)	-0.006 (-1.00)	0.033 (0.86)	-0.001 (-0.09)	0.30 (0.50)	-0.007 (-1.13)	0.030 (0.79)	-0.006 (-0.65)	0.043 (0.70)
Private investment	0.600*** (2.83)	-0.207* (-2.01)	0.518** (2.01)	-0.285** (-2.34)	0.650*** (3.29)	-0.192* (-1.91)	0.990*** (3.71)	-0.367*** (-2.91)	0.695*** (2.95)	-0.114 (-0.96)	1.22** (4.12)	-0.346** (-2.48)
Initial primary enrollment	0.052 (0.40)	-0.179 (-0.31)	-0.009 (-0.10)	-0.015 (-0.30)	-0.010 (-0.09)	-0.55 (-1.12)	0.0197 (0.21)	-0.031 (-0.59)	0.018 (0.15)	-1.638* (-2.73)	-0.003 (-0.04)	-0.055 (-1.03)
Initial secondary enrollment	-0.469 (-1.57)	1.463 (0.44)	-0.045 (-0.16)	0.050 (0.23)	-0.273 (-1.03)	3.21 (1.18)	-0.151 (-0.48)	0.157 (0.69)	-0.527 (-1.54)	9.154** (2.72)	-0.116 (-0.36)	0.153 (0.69)
Budget balance (as percent of GDP)					0.563*** (4.16)	0.118 (1.41)	0.804*** (4.11)	-0.043 (-0.36)				
Domestic financing (as percent of GDP)									-1.09*** (-5.36)	-0.206* (-1.98)	-1.57*** (-6.21)	0.141 (0.75)
External financing (as percent of GDP)									-0.44*** (-2.81)	-0.364*** (-3.02)	-0.723*** (-3.31)	-0.108 (-0.70)
Wages and salaries (as percent of GDP)	-0.305 (-0.86)	-0.768* (-1.91)	-0.896* (-1.74)	-6.01 (-0.82)								
Wages and salaries (as percent of total expenditure)					-0.233* (-1.97)	0.019 (0.25)	-0.300* (-1.68)	-0.064 (-0.52)	-0.246* (-1.98)	0.033 (0.28)	-0.283 (-1.58)	0.002 (0.02)
Transfers and subsidies (as percent of GDP)	-0.039 (-0.11)	0.411 (1.28)	-0.985** (-2.08)	0.862** (2.37)								

Table 6 *(concluded)*

	Model A. Budget Composition				Model B. Budget Balance and Composition of Expenditures				Model C. Budget Financing and Composition of Expenditures			
	Real Per Capita GDP Growth		Change Real Per Capita GDP Growth		Real Per Capita GDP Growth		Change Real Per Capita GDP Growth		Real Per Capita GDP Growth		Change Real Per Capita GDP Growth	
	Pre-stabilization countries	Post-stabilization countries	Pre-stabilization countries	Post-stabilization countries	Pre-stabilization countries	Post-stabilization countries	Pre-stabilization countries	Post-stabilization countries	Pre-stabilization countries	Post-stabilization countries	Pre-stabilization countries	Post-stabilization countries
Transfers and subsidies (as percent of total expenditure)	-0.538 (-1.44)	-0.756 (-1.02)	-0.526 (-0.97)	0.755 (0.74)	-0.010 (-0.08)	0.338*** (3.36)	-0.110 (-0.53)	0.306** (2.11)	-0.159 (-1.06)	0.527*** (4.45)	-0.188 (-0.84)	0.429** (2.76)
Interest payments (as percent of GDP)					-0.150 (-1.25)	0.290* (1.79)	-0.403** (-2.20)	0.444* (1.72)	-0.260** (-2.00)	0.277 (1.61)	-0.454** (-2.41)	0.313 (1.07)
Interest payments (as percent of total expenciture)	0.667 (1.63)	0.655** (2.33)	1.932*** (3.59)	0.711* (2.01)								
Other goods and services (as percent of GDP)					0.037 (0.31)	0.142* (1.80)	0.041 (0.22)	0.197* (1.87)	0.090 (0.73)	0.060 (0.67)	0.135 (0.72)	0.125 (1.06)
Other goods and services (as percent of tot. expenditure)	0.682*** (3.00)	-0.037 (-0.18)	1.327*** (4.32)	-0.032 (-0.18)								
Capital expenditure (as percent of GDP)					0.148 (1.56)	0.139* (1.98)	0.327** (2.21)	0.171* (1.86)	0.044 (0.44)	0.248*** (3.15)	0.221 (1.48)	0.260** (2.65)
Capital expenditure (as percent of total expend ture)	-0.057 (-0.21)	-0.099 (-0.48)	0.238 (0.60)	-0.312 (-1.45)								
Tax revenue (as percent of GDP)	-0.387 (-0.58)	0.524*** (2.08)	1.306* (1.85)	0.479 (1.16)								
Nontax revenue (as percent of GDP)	-0.100 (-0.35)	0.487 (0.85)	-0.099 (-0.31)	0.554 (0.94)								
Grants (as percent of GDP)												
Number of observations	200	49	177	43	201	49	178	43	184	41	161	36
Adjusted *R*-squared	0.13	0.16	0.39	0.14	0.20	0.33	0.28	0.13	0.22	0.51	0.38	0.30
F test	1.97	1.59	4.64	1.45	2.71	2.74	3.37	1.48	2.69	4.08	4.29	2.07
Probability	0.00	0.12	0.00	0.19	0.00	0.00	0.00	0.18	0.00	0.00	0.00	0.06

Note: *t* statistics in parentheses. *significant at 10 percent; **significant at 5 percent; and ***significant at 1 percent.
[a]Multiplied by 100.

reduction in the average deficit in low-income countries from about 4 percent of GDP to 2 percent of GDP could boost per capita growth by about 1–2 percentage points per annum.

Tilting the overall composition of public expenditure toward more productive uses is particularly important for boosting growth. Fiscal consolidations achieved through cutting selected current expenditures tend to trigger higher growth rates than adjustments based on revenue increases and cuts in more productive spending—a result consistent with the findings for industrial countries. According to the results of our analysis, protecting capital expenditures during a fiscal adjustment leads to higher growth. Reductions in the public sector wage bill are not harmful for growth for the sample as a whole.

The composition of deficit financing is also a key factor affecting growth in low-income countries. Fiscal consolidations, especially those leading to a sizeable reduction in domestic financing of the deficit, are likely to trigger higher growth rates. The empirical estimates indicate that adjustments based on reducing domestic financing have about 1½ times the effect on growth as adjustments based on reductions in both domestic and external financing.

The effects of fiscal policy on growth tend to be nonlinear. The results above hold for countries that have not yet achieved stable macroeconomic conditions. In post-stabilization countries, fiscal adjustments no longer have a salutary effect on growth. In this context, an expansion of selected current expenditures for these countries is compatible with higher growth. The design of fiscal frameworks in PRGF-supported programs is consistent with these results, as post-stabilization countries target relatively larger increases in public spending and in the fiscal deficit (IMF, 2002).

Additional research is needed to disentangle the channels through which fiscal policy affects growth. Given the reduced-form model tested here, the paper has not examined the demand- and supply-side channels through which fiscal policy affects growth, nor the role of accompanying policies (such as monetary and external sector policies), which have been underscored in previous work in this field (Baldacci et al., 2001; Thomas, 2001). Additional research is needed in this area.

References

Abed, G.T., Ebrill, L., Gupta, S., Clements, B., McMorran, R., Pellechio, A., Schiff, J., Verhoeven, M., 1998. Fiscal reforms in low-income countries: experience under IMF-supported programs. IMF Occasional Paper 160 (International Monetary Fund, Washington).

Adam, C.S., Bevan, D.L., 2000. Fiscal policy design in low-income countries. Paper prepared for UNU/WIDER research project on New Fiscal Policies for Poverty Reduction and Growth (unpublished, November).

Alesina, A., Ardagna, S., 1998. Tales of fiscal adjustment. Economic Policy: A European Forum, 27, 487–546.

Alesina, A., Ardagna, S., Perotti, R., Schiantarelli, F., 2002. Fiscal policy, profits, and investment. American Economic Review, 92, 571–589

Alesina, A., Perotti, R., 1995. Fiscal expansion and fiscal adjustments in OECD countries. Economic Policy, 21, 205–248.

————, 1996. Fiscal adjustments in OECD countries: composition and macroeconomic effects. IMF Working Paper 96/70.

————, Tavares, J., 1998. The political economy of fiscal adjustments. Brookings Papers on Economic Activity, 1, 197–248. Brookings Institution.

Arellano, M., Bond, S., 1991. Some tests of specific action for panel data: Monte Carlo evidence and an application to employment equations. Review of Economic Studies, 58, 277–297.

Aschauer, D.A., 1989. Is public expenditure productive? Journal of Monetary Economics, 23, 177–200.

Baldacci, E., Cangiano, M., Mahfouz, S., Schimmelpfennig, A., 2001. The effectiveness of fiscal policy in stimulating economic activity: an empirical investigation. Paper presented at the IMF Annual Research Conference, International Monetary Fund.

Barro, R.J., 1990. Government spending in a simple model of endogenous growth. Journal of Political Economy, 98 (1), 103–117.

————, 1991. Economic growth in a cross section of countries. Quarterly Journal of Economics, 106, 407–443.

————, Sala-i-Martin, X., 1995. Economic growth. McGraw-Hill, New York.

Bassanini, A., Scarpetta, S., Hemmings, P., 2001. Economic growth: the role of policies and institutions. Panel Data Evidence from OECD Countries. Economics Department Working Paper 283. Organization for Economic Cooperation and Development, Paris.

Buti, M., Sapir, A., 1998. Economic policy in EMU. Oxford University Press, Oxford.

Devarajan, S., Swaroop, V., Zou, H., 1996. The composition of public expenditure and economic growth. Journal of Monetary Economics, 37, 313–344

Easterly, W., Rebelo, S., 1993. Fiscal policy and economic growth: an empirical investigation. NBER Working Paper 4499. National Bureau of Economic Research, Cambridge, Massachusetts.

Easterly, W., Rodriguez, C.A., Schmidt-Hebbel, K., 1994. Public sector deficits and macroeconomic performance. World Bank, Washington.

Easterly, W., Loayza, N., Montiel, P., 1997. Has Latin America's post-reform growth been disappointing? Journal of International Economics, 43, 287–311.

Fischer, S., 1983. Inflation and growth. NBER Working Paper No. 1235. National Bureau of Economic Research, Cambridge, Massachusetts.

Giavazzi, F., Jappelli, T., Pagano, M., 2000. Searching for nonlinear effects of fiscal policy: evidence from industrial and developing countries. NBER Working Paper 7460. National Bureau of Economic Research, Cambridge, Massachusetts.

Greene, W., 2000. Econometric analysis. Prentice Hall, Upper Saddle River, N.J.

Hamilton, L.C., 1991. How robust is robust regression. Stata Technical Bulletin, 2, 21–26.

International Monetary Fund, 2002. Review of the key features of the Poverty Reduction and Growth Facility—staff analyses. Available via the Internet: http://www.imf.org/external/np/prgf/2002/031502.htm.

Kneller, R., Bleaney, M., Gemmell, N., 1998. Growth, public policy and the government budget constraint: Evidence from OECD countries. University of Nottingham, Department of Economics Discussion Paper 98/14.

———, 1999. Fiscal policy and growth: evidence from OECD countries. Journal of Public Economics, 74, 171–190.

———, 2000. Testing the endogenous growth model: public expenditure, taxation and growth over the long run. University of Nottingham, Department of Economics Discussion Paper 00/25.

Landau, D., 1986. Government and economic growth in the less developed countries: an empirical study for 1960–80. Economic Development and Cultural Change, 35, 35–75.

Mackenzie, G.A., Orsmond, D., Gerson, P., 1997. The composition of fiscal adjustment and growth: lessons from fiscal reforms in eight economies. IMF Occasional Paper 149.

Mendoza, E., Milesi-Ferretti, G.M., Asea, P., 1997. On the ineffectiveness of tax policy in altering long-run growth: Harberger's superneutrality conjecture. Journal of Public Economics, 66, 99–126.

McDermott, C.J., Wescott, R.F., 1996. An empirical analysis of fiscal adjustments. IMF Staff Papers, 43 (December), 725–753.

Perotti, R., 1999. Fiscal policy in good times and bad. Quarterly Journal of Economics, 114 (4), 1399–1436.

Sarel, M., 1996. Nonlinear effects of inflation on economic growth. IMF Staff Papers, 43 (March), 199–215.

Tanzi, V., Zee, H., 1996. Fiscal policy and long-run growth. IMF Working Paper No. 96/119.

Thomas, A., 2001. An exploration of the private sector response to changes in government saving across OECD countries. IMF Working Paper 01/69.

von Hagen, J., Hughes Hallett, A., Strauch, R., 2002. Budgetary consolidation in Europe: quality, economic conditions, and persistence. Journal of Japanese and International Economies, 16 (4), 512–535.

3

Persistence of Fiscal Adjustments and Expenditure Composition in Low-Income Countries

EMANUELE BALDACCI, BENEDICT CLEMENTS, SANJEEV GUPTA, AND CARLOS MULAS-GRANADOS

There is a consensus among researchers that fiscal consolidations need to persist if they are to have a positive effect on growth. In general, the persistence of high-quality fiscal adjustment can improve macroeconomic stability and reduce expectations that higher taxes and interest rates will be needed in the future to finance fiscal imbalances. Short-lived fiscal consolidations, on the other hand, can be harmful for growth, as they signal that the initial improvement in the fiscal budget cannot be maintained and could be reversed in the medium term. An understanding of what makes fiscal consolidations sustainable is therefore essential to unraveling how fiscal adjustment influences growth (von Hagen and Strauch, 2001).

This chapter assesses what are the factors determining the end of a fiscal consolidation episode and analyzes whether improvements in the composition of public expenditure help fiscal adjustments in low-income countries last longer. Many studies have analyzed episodes of fiscal adjustment in industrial countries (for example, Alesina and Perotti, 1995), but similar studies for developing countries—and in particular low-income countries—are lacking.

The authors wish to thank Shamit Chakravarti and Erwin Tiongson for their help in preparing this chapter. Carlos Mulas-Granados was a summer intern in the Fiscal Affairs Department in the summer of 2001.

The methodology traditionally used to assess the sustainability of fiscal adjustment episodes over time focused on large fiscal consolidation spells. Data on fiscal consolidation periods were used to analyze the features of successful fiscal adjustments, defined as those cases where fiscal control was maintained over an adequate period of time (Alesina and Ardagna, 1998). A number of recent papers (Maroto and Mulas-Granados, 2001; Gupta and others, 2002; von Hagen, Hughes Hallett, and Strauch, 2002; and Adam and Bevan, 2003) have chosen to treat the persistence of fiscal consolidations over time as endogenous, in contrast to previous studies. In this framework, survival analysis is the appropriate statistical method to assess which factors affect the persistence of fiscal consolidations. This method is superior, as it allows for a multivariate analysis of the determinants of the persistence of fiscal adjustments and makes use of all the information available in the data, rather than constraining the analysis to consolidation episodes only.

We use survival analysis to assess the factors determining the duration of fiscal consolidations in a sample of low-income countries. We expand the analysis of Gupta and others (2002) by using both a semiparametric and a parametric approach (following Adam and Bevan, 2003) to modeling the risk of ending a fiscal adjustment spell. The results of this study confirm the previous findings for industrial countries. In particular, there is a strong link between public expenditure reform and fiscal adjustment sustainability. Fiscal adjustments that protect capital outlays are more sustainable—that is, less likely to be aborted. The persistence of fiscal adjustment is also influenced by a country's initial fiscal conditions and by the size of the consolidation effort.

Fiscal Adjustment and Survival Analysis

The composition of fiscal adjustment is critical for the persistence of consolidation episodes. Many studies have analyzed episodes of fiscal adjustment in industrial countries, including Alesina and Perotti (1995), Alesina and Ardagna (1998), and Alesina, Perotti, and Tavares (1998). These studies focused on episodes of successful and unsuccessful fiscal consolidations. The main conclusion of these studies is that fiscal adjustments that rely primarily on reducing outlays on transfers and the wage bill are more likely to be sustainable than those based on tax increases and cuts in capital spending. Ardagna (2001) replicates these empirical results using a dynamic general equilibrium model calibrated with averaged data from 10 European economies for 1965–95. Her results indicate that fiscal stabilizations that rationalize public employment can stimulate the economy, provided that public employment does not have a positive effect on the productivity of capital and labor.

This chapter follows a different approach, consistent with recent research on this subject. Following von Hagen and Strauch (2001) and others, we define fiscal adjustments as sustainable if they persist over an adequate period of time. This definition of sustainability is somewhat different from the more common use of the term. In general, the term "sustainability" refers to whether the current fiscal stance is consistent with a non-increasing ratio of public debt to GDP over time (see Ize, 1991).

Most empirical studies on the sustainability of fiscal consolidations have used a descriptive and indirect approach to measure the determinants of sustainable fiscal adjustments. The approach consists of a two-step procedure: first, the authors preselect consolidation episodes according to a predefined threshold; and second, they provide a description of their main characteristics. As noted earlier, survival analysis is the superior technique. As such, this technique can be seen as a generalization of the previous approaches, which are based on fiscal adjustment episodes.

A few studies have applied this analysis to a wide set of countries. Maroto and Mulas-Granados (2001) and von Hagen, Hughes Hallet, and Strauch (2002) defined fiscal adjustments as sustainable if they persist over an adequate period of time, and applied this methodology to a sample of industrial countries. Gupta and others (2002; 2004) used a duration analysis to assess the factors underlying sustainable fiscal adjustment in 39 low-income countries. Adam and Bevan (2003) expanded the duration analysis of fiscal adjustments to a sample of 127 countries, including industrial, emerging, and developing countries (with the exception of transition economies) for the period 1970–2001.

One paper (Adam and Bevan, 2003) also provides a useful typology of the definition of "fiscal consolidation" in applying survival analysis: (1) the "level" approach (a specified threshold for the deficit); (2) the "gradient" approach (reduction of the deficit at some specified minimum rate); and (3) the composite approach. Each approach has its own strengths and weaknesses. While Adam and Bevan prefer the level approach, we define consolidations based on the gradient approach, but we condition the estimates on the existing level of deficit in each adjustment period, thereby capturing in part the "level" effect.

Data

Data for the variables used in the empirical application were drawn from the World Economic Outlook database, as well as a database for 39 countries supported by the Enhanced Structural Adjustment Facility (ESAF) or the Poverty Reduction Growth Facilty (PRGF) during the period 1990–2000.[1] The fiscal policy stance is measured by the general government budget balance on a cash basis. This is defined as total revenues and grants minus total expenditures and net lending.[2] A positive change in the budget balance can be interpreted as a consolidation, and a negative change as an expansion. Deficits were generally reduced during the period, with an average annual improvement of approximately ½ percentage point of GDP.

Fiscal deficits are also used to identify "post-stabilization" countries. Post-stabilization countries are defined as those that had an average budget deficit (after grants) below 2.5 percent of GDP in the 1990–2000 period.[3] Based on this criterion, only seven countries can be considered post-stabilizers (Benin, The Gambia, Lesotho, Macedonia, FYR, Mauritania, Senegal, and Tanzania).

Fiscal adjustment periods are based on the observed change in the fiscal deficit as a share of GDP. Based on annual budget balance data, we generate a dummy variable called *failure*, which takes a value of zero when the annual variation of the budget balance is above 1½ percentage points of GDP (years of fiscal consolidation), and takes a value of one when the annual change is equal or lower than this threshold (lack of adjustment). Note that this criterion is arbitrary. One could define as a fiscal consolidation any year when a positive change in the budget balance is observed. One reason to use the threshold mentioned above, however, is to avoid labeling as "fiscal consolidations" years in which minor improvements of the budget balance took place, reflecting unintended variations of the budget, or measurement errors.[4]

This definition makes our results broadly comparable with previous empirical studies. For example, Alesina and Perotti (1995); Perotti (1998); and von Hagen and Strauch (2001) define episodes of fiscal consolidation as those periods in which the fiscal impulse (measured by the average cyclically adjusted primary balance) falls by at least 1¼ percent of GDP over two consecutive years, or when it increases by more

---

[1]The countries are Albania, Armenia, Benin, Bolivia, Burkina Faso, Cambodia, Cameroon, the Central African Republic, Chad, Djibouti, Ethiopia, The Gambia, Ghana, Georgia, Guinea, Guinea-Bissau, Guyana, Honduras, Kenya, the Kyrgyz Republic, Laos, Lesotho, Macedonia (FYR), Madagascar, Malawi, Mali, Mauritania, Moldova, Mozambique, Nicaragua, Niger, Rwanda, São Tomé and Príncipe, Senegal, Tajikistan, Tanzania, Vietnam, Yemen, and Zambia.

[2]The difference between revenues and expenditures can be different from the cash deficit in those countries that measure expenditures on a commitment basis.

[3]This roughly corresponds to the low-deficit country group identified in Abed and others, 1998.

[4]As a robustness check, the analysis was also conducted using an alternative threshold of ½ percentage point of GDP, with broadly similar results being obtained.

than 1½ percent of GDP in one year. A successful adjustment is defined by two alternative conditions: (1) the fiscal impulse in the three years after the consolidation remains on average 2 percent of GDP above the level achieved in the last year of consolidation; or (2) the ratio of public debt to GDP three years after the consolidation is at least 5 percent of GDP below the level observed in the last year of consolidation.

Using the dates in which a failure event occurs, we create a new variable called *duration*, which counts the intervening years between two consecutive failures—that is, the time span that the fiscal consolidation lasts. Under the definition of consolidation described above, the minimum length of an adjustment is one year, while the maximum length is five years. The average probability of ending a consolidation is 47 percent and the average duration of a fiscal adjustment is slightly above one year.

Survival Analysis Methodology

The duration data used in this study can be summarized using three variables: the hazard rate, the survival rate, and the cumulative failure rate. The unconditional hazard function expresses the relative risk that a fiscal consolidation ends at time t, provided it was still ongoing in the previous period. The hazard function (Kaplan and Meier, 1958) is calculated as follows:

$$\hat{h}(t) = \frac{d_t}{n_t}, \tag{1}$$

where d_t represents the number of failures registered in moment t, and n_t is the surviving population in moment t, before the change in status (e.g., the end of the consolidation) takes place. Intuitively, this is the failure ratio. From the hazard function, it is possible to obtain the cumulative hazard function with an estimation procedure proposed by Aalen (1978). This hazard function is given by the following expression:

$$\hat{H}(s) = \sum_{s=1}^{t} \hat{h}(s). \tag{2}$$

The Kaplan-Meier survivor function for duration t is calculated as the product of one minus the existing risk until period t:

$$\hat{S}(t) = \prod_{j|t_j \leq t} \left(\frac{n_j - d_j}{n_j} \right). \tag{3}$$

In the context of a non-parametric analysis, Equation (1) is sufficient to construct a life table where the initial sample of individuals at risk of experiencing the event under study is subject to the duration-specific fail-ure rate. From the life table, summary information can be obtained of the survival process, such as the number of fiscal adjustment episodes that persist after a given number of years, the associated failure probability, and the cumulative survivor ratio up to that point. The equality of two or more survival functions across groups of countries can be formally tested using an extension of the Mantel-Haenszel test or the generalized Wilcoxon test (Cleves, Gould, and Gutierrez, 2002).[5]

Although non-parametric analysis is usually informative of the dura-tion process, it cannot help assess the factors underlying the persistence of fiscal adjustments. To analyze these factors one has to link a set of covariates to the hazard function. In the literature, two different classes of models have been used: semi-parametric and parametric. Semi-parametric models do not require specific assumptions on the form of the underlying baseline hazard ratio, while parametric models usually require the advance knowledge of the shape of the hazard function.

A semi-parametric model that has been widely used in empirical studies to estimate the effects of covariates on the hazard function is the Model of Proportional Hazard (PH), which assumes that the hazard function can be described as follows:

$$h(t, X) = h_0(t) * g(X), \qquad (4)$$

where $h_0(t)$ is the baseline hazard function and $g(X)$ is a function of in-dividual covariates. This is usually defined as $g(X) = exp(X'\beta)$. Note that in this proportional specification, regressors rescale the conditional probability of ending the period of fiscal consolidation. This model can be estimated without imposing any specific functional form to the base-line hazard function, following Cox (1972).[6]

A fundamental property of Cox's model is that when comparing two individuals with a different set of covariates the ratio of their hazard function is independent from the baseline hazard rate, which does not need to be specified. Model (6) can be estimated by a maximum likeli-hood estimator. Once the parameter is estimated, the model's propor-tional hazard assumption can be tested using a generalization of the

---

[5]The tests are based on the comparison across groups of the expected survival under the assumption that the failure rate is the same for each group, using an appropriate weighting matrix. Under the null hypothesis, the test is distributed as a χ^2 with $r - 1$ de-grees of freedom, where r is the number of groups.

[6] Mathematically, the baseline hazard function $ho(t)$ is defined for all time t in which a change has taken place, and is not defined for other moments of time. But the survivor function $So(t)$ is defined for all values of t. It follows that $h(t, X) = h_0(t) * exp(X'\beta)$.

Grambsch and Therneau test involving the calculation of Schoenfeld residuals (Cleves, Gould, and Gutierrez, 2002).[7]

An alternative specification can be obtained by imposing one specific parametric form to the baseline hazard function $h_0(t)$. When there is sufficient deductive information on the shape of the hazard function, a parametric specification yields more efficient estimates than the Cox's proportional hazard model. If, however, the information of the hazard function is such that the misspecification error could be large, results from a semi-parametric model would be more robust.

In the case of parametric models, the functional form most commonly assumed for the hazard function is the Weibul distribution. The baseline hazard function under this model is

$$h_0(t) = p t^{p-1} \exp(\beta_0), \tag{5}$$

where p is a parameter to be estimated and β_0 is a constant parameter. The hazard functions can be written as follows, assuming a proportional hazard specification:

$$h(t, X) = h_0(t) * \exp(X'\beta_0). \tag{6}$$

When $p=1$, this specification is equal to the exponential distribution that assumes the absence of any dependency on duration. The conditional probability of failure in a given interval is the same, regardless of when the observation is made. When $p > 1$, there is a positive duration dependency, and a negative one when $p < 1$. Therefore, by estimating p, it is possible to test the hypothesis of duration dependency during fiscal consolidations. An additional parametric function that has been widely used in biomedical studies is the Gompertz distribution. This distribution is suitable for modeling data with monotone hazard rates. Under this distribution, the baseline hazard function is $h_0(t) = \exp(\gamma t)\exp(\beta_0)$ and the baseline hazard function is increasing if γ is positive. Estimates of the parameters can be obtained by maximizing the corresponding log-likelihood function. Comparisons among

---

[7]This test is based on the assumption that if the model is correctly specified, the Schoenfeld residuals would not be correlated with time. Although a general goodness of fit statistic can be easily calculated as

$$pseudoR^2 = 1 - \left\{ \exp\left[\frac{2}{n}\right](L_0 - L_p) \right\},$$

its interpretation is not straightforward as it depends on the number of censored events in the sample. An alternative approach is based on the analysis of the residual as suggested in Hosmer and Lemeshow (1999).

nested models can be carried out using likelihood ratio test statistics.[8] An additional advantage of this class of duration models is that frailty models describing heterogeneity can be built in this formulation (Hosmer and Lemeshow, 1999).

Empirical Results

Non-Parametric Analysis

In Table 1 we report the survival function, the hazard function, and the cumulative failure function for our sample, together with the corresponding standard errors and confidence intervals. According to the results, only 43 percent of the fiscal adjustment periods last up to the end of first year. The confidence interval puts this risk in the range between 37 percent and 48 percent owing to the presence of large dispersion in the episodes. The relative risk that a consolidation episode is discontinued at the end of the first period (the hazard rate) is only 10 percent, but it increases rapidly to 71 percent at the beginning of the second period. Finally, in the third period more than 80 percent of the adjustment episodes have already been reversed. The cumulative hazard function increases rapidly from the first to the second period, it stabilizes between the second and the third period, and it increases steadily in the remaining intervals. These results can be visually summarized in Figure 1, which shows a large share of the consolidation episodes lasting about a year, with the hazard rate peaking at the end of the first year and then rapidly declining toward zero.

Semi-Parametric Analysis

This subsection reports the results of the semi-parametric analysis on the determinants of fiscal adjustment persistence. We use Cox's proportional hazard model described in the previous section to estimate the factors affecting the duration of fiscal adjustment efforts. In doing so we need not formulate any assumption on the functional form of the baseline hazard rate. This is allowed to vary freely with time. The actual hazard rate is thus dependent on the vector of covariates and on the estimated parameters. These can be interpreted similarly to a standard

---

[8]Non-nested models can be compared using the Akaike Information Criterion (AIC) based on the value of the maximized log-likelihood L as follows:

$$AIC = -2\ln L + 2(k+c),$$

where k is the number of covariates and c is the number of model-specific distribution parameters.

Table 1. Sustainability of Fiscal Consolidations in Low-Income Countries: Descriptive Results

Interval		Estimate	Standard error	95% confidence interval	
			Survival Function		
0	1	0.903	0.015	0.869	0.928
1	2	0.428	0.027	0.374	0.481
2	3	0.197	0.026	0.148	0.250
3	4	0.063	0.021	0.030	0.112
4	5	0.000			
			Cumulative Failure		
0	1	0.097	0.015	0.072	0.131
1	2	0.572	0.027	0.519	0.626
2	3	0.804	0.026	0.750	0.852
3	4	0.937	0.021	0.888	0.970
4	5	1.000			
			Hazard Function		
0	1	0.102	0.016	0.070	0.134
1	2	0.713	0.054	0.608	0.818
2	3	0.742	0.102	0.543	0.941
3	4	1.032	0.221	0.599	1.466
4	5	2.000	0.000	2.000	2.000

Source: Authors' calculations.

regression analysis as the effects of a unit change in the regressor on the logarithm of the probability of ending a fiscal consolidation spell. An alternative way to interpret the estimated coefficients is in terms of hazard ratios. For a given categorical variable, the hazard ratio represents the relative risk of experiencing the failure event.[9]

We regress the probability of interrupting a fiscal adjustment on a set of variables that, according to the literature, are likely to have an effect on the duration of the adjustment. The fiscal variables are as follows.

- The size of the adjustment, measured as the cumulative change in the budget balance during the entire period of analysis. The larger the size of the consolidation, the longer the effort is hypothesized to

---

[9]For example, we can assume that the sample is split into lower-income and higher-income countries, and a dummy variable having value equal to unity for the lower-income countries is used as a regressor. In this case the hazard ratio coefficient on this variable will measure the risk of ending a fiscal adjustment spell for a country that is in the lower-income group relative to the average risk in the higher-income group.

Figure 1. Sustainability of Fiscal Conditions in Low-Income Countries: Hazard and Survival Functions

All Countries

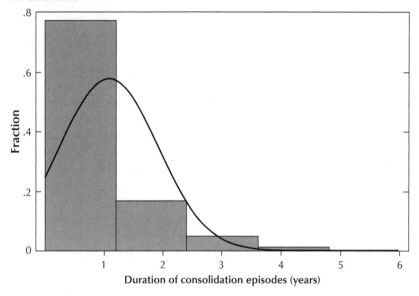

Kaplan-Meier Survival Estimate, All Countries

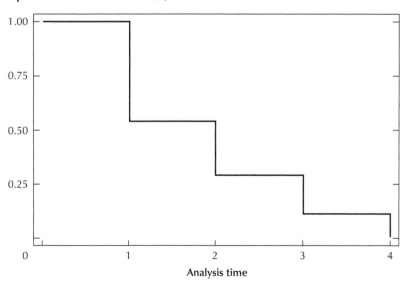

Source: Authors' calculations.

last. In fact, a larger adjustment size signals a willingness to bring fiscal policy onto a sustainable path.

- The composition of government spending, including both the share of current spending in total government spending and the share of transfers in current spending. The composition of the adjustment is assumed to have a critical role in the persistence of the consolidation. Fiscal adjustments based on curtailing current expenditure have been found to be more sustainable than those based on reduced capital outlays in the empirical literature on industrial countries.

- The initial level of the fiscal deficit and the change in tax revenues and social spending, all expressed as ratios to GDP. These variables control for initial fiscal conditions and the contributions of investment in human capital and accelerated improvements in tax collection to the consolidation effort. In particular, the social spending variable is a proxy for how willing the government is to support pro-poor spending and garner broad support for the adjustment process. As such, these variables account for the possible trade-off between fiscal consolidation and the need to protect the poor from the possibly negative effect of government spending cuts.

- We also include in the regression the change in per capita GDP growth and the previous number of failures in the adjustment process in the period considered; this is meant to control for the effect of exogenous growth shocks and past adjustment performance at the country level.

We use this model to estimate three alternative specifications: (1) we include the effect of the change in external financing as a share of GDP to take into account the effect of mostly concessional borrowing on the probability of ending an adjustment period (Model 1); (2) we omit any variable related to the composition of financing (Model 2); and (3) we include the change in the ratio of domestic financing to GDP (Model 3).

Results are reported in Table 2. The overall fit of the three models is good, although the goodness of fit indicator ranges between 21 percent for Model 1 to 16 percent for Model 3 owing to the large share of censored observations. The specification test rejects the hypothesis of omitted regressors at the 10 percent critical level and the generalized Grambsch and Therneau test based on Schoenfeld residuals confirms that the proportional hazard assumption is valid for the models presented here.

Table 2. Sustainability of Fiscal Consolidations and Budget Composition in Low-Income Countries: Results from Cox Proportional-Hazard Model, 1990–2000[1]

	Model 1		Model 2		Model 3	
	Coefficient	z-test	Coefficient	z-test	Coefficient	z-test
Size of adjustment	−0.04	−3.06***	−0.03	−3.67*	−0.04	3.68***
Initial deficit	0.01	1.20	0.01	1.60	0.02	1.74*
Change in growth	−0.02	−1.99**	−0.02	−2.42**	−0.02	−1.95*
Change in social spending/GDP	−0.04	−1.07	0.01	0.08	0.02	0.47
Number of previous failures	0.01	3.75***	0.01	4.46***	0.01	4.01***
Change in tax revenues/ GDP	−0.08	−2.51**	−0.11	−4.71***	−0.06	1.82*
Change in transfers/ current spending	0.03	2.18**	0.02	1.72*	0.02	1.79*
Change in current/ total spending	0.12	3.92***	0.12	5.05***	0.11	3.13***
Change in external financing/GDP	0.07	4.22***				
Change in domestic financing/GDP					0.01	0.07
Number of episodes	167		188		167	
Number of failures	107		118		107	
Time at risk	239		272		239	
Log likelihood	−467.43		−532.03		−472.07	
Wald test	86.62		75.66		65.24	
Probability	0.00		0.00		0.00	
Pseudo-R^2	0.21		0.17		0.16	
Omitted variables test	−0.03	−0.21	−0.21	−1.01	−0.22	−0.95
Grambsh-Therneau test χ^2	6.29		1.29		1.36	

Note: Significance at 10, 5, and 1 percent levels is indicated by *, **, and ***, respectively.
[1]Maximum likelihood estimates with robust standard errors.

The reallocation of current expenditures to capital outlays is positively related to the persistence of the adjustment in all models. Large levels of wages and salaries, transfers, and subsidies increase the probability of ending a fiscal adjustment. At the same time, allocating more public spending on capital outlays is not harmful for the sustainability of adjustment. This may be due to the positive effects of these expenditure reallocations on growth (Chu and others, 1995). Reallocating current spending away from transfers and subsidies has a positive impact on the probability of continuing the fiscal consolidation effort, while spending more on health and education is not harmful to the persistence of the adjustment.

The size of the fiscal adjustment effort also matters. The coefficient for the size of the adjustment is negative and highly significant. Thus, there appears to be little evidence of "adjustment fatigue": countries with larger cumulative reductions in the deficit are less likely to abandon their adjustment efforts than others. This may reflect the fact that larger fiscal adjustments—including those secured in the past—signal the commitment of the authorities to continue the fiscal consolidation process.

Initial fiscal conditions are also important for the persistence of fiscal consolidations. A country with unfavorable initial fiscal conditions is more likely to end a fiscal consolidation; furthermore, a history of past failures at fiscal consolidation also foreshadows failure. This result is consistent with the findings for a sample of low-income countries with ESAF-supported programs (Abed and others, 1998), which showed that countries that experienced a high number of interruptions of IMF-supported programs tended to have higher levels of current expenditures and lower capital outlays (relative to program targets) than countries with few or no interruptions.

When fiscal consolidations are supported by more buoyant tax revenues, the probability of ending an adjustment is lower. The results in Table 2 show that accelerated tax revenue collection increases the probability that the consolidation effort will be sustained. This result is at variance with the findings for industrial countries, where adjustments based on higher tax revenue were found to be less successful. However, in the context of low-income countries—where revenue ratios to GDP are generally modest—higher tax revenue collection can be triggered by improvements in tax administration, elimination of exemptions, and curbing of tax evasion, rather than an increase in tax rates. These factors are likely to have a positive effect both on the fiscal stance and on growth, thereby increasing the probability that an adjustment will last longer.

The availability of external financing tends to reduce the probability of continuing a fiscal consolidation in Model 1, while there is no evidence that this is true for domestic financing in Model 3. The coefficient for external financing is significant at the 5 percent level, even though including the share of either external or domestic financing in total deficit financing fails to lead to significant coefficients.

Finally, we find moderate empirical support in favor of an independent effect of economic growth on the duration of the fiscal adjustment. The probability of ending a fiscal consolidation effort is negatively related to per capita growth, as expected, but the coefficient is significantly different from zero only at the 10 percent level in Model 3.

Table 3. Sustainability of Fiscal Consolidations in Low-Income Countries by Group of Countries: Survival Function

Interval		Estimate	Standard error	95% confidence interval	
			Pre-stabilization Countries		
0	1	0.903	0.016	0.865	0.930
1	2	0.441	0.030	0.381	0.499
2	3	0.194	0.029	0.141	0.254
3	4	0.061	0.023	0.027	0.116
4	5	0.000			
			Post-stabilization Countries		
Interval		Estimate	Standard error	95% confidence interval	
0	1	0.903	0.035	0.808	0.953
1	2	0.373	0.062	0.254	0.492
2	3	0.207	0.061	0.103	0.336
3	4	0.069	0.050	0.010	0.209
4	5	0.000			

Source: Authors' calculations.

These results hold for all countries in the sample, independently of the degree of macroeconomic stability achieved during the period. To test the assumption of homogenous survival functions between countries, we split the sample into two groups: post-stabilization and pre-stabilization countries. Fiscal deficits are used to identify "post-stabilization" countries.[10] In Table 3, we compare the life tables for the two groups and report the survival functions. Results show that fiscal adjustments in post-stabilization countries have a slightly lower probability of survival after two periods. In fact, the survival rate is 37 percent compared with 44 percent in the pre-stabilization group. However, the difference between these two estimates cannot be considered significant as the confidence intervals for the post-stabilization groups is very large, ranging from 25 percent to 49 percent. This range includes the range of estimated survival probabilities for pre-stabilization countries (from 38 percent to 50 percent). To carry out a formal assessment of the equality of the survival functions in the two subsamples, we perform a Wilcoxon rank test. The χ^2 for this test is equal to 0.92 with one degree of freedom. The level of probability associated to this value is 0.34 and does not allow rejection of the null hypothesis that the two group-specific survival curves are equal.

---

[10]This roughly corresponds to the low-deficit country group identified in Abed and others, 1998. Based on this criterion, only seven countries can be considered post-stabilizers (Benin, The Gambia, Lesotho, Macedonia, FYR, Mauritania, Senegal, and Tanzania).

Table 4. Sustainability of Fiscal Consolidations and Budget Composition in Low-Income Countries: Results from Stratified Cox Proportional-Hazard Model, 1990–2000[1]

	Model 1		Model 2		Model 3	
	Coefficient	z-test	Coefficient	z-test	Coefficient	z-test
Size of adjustment	−0.04	−3.12***	−0.03	−3.77***	−0.04	3.71***
Initial deficit	0.21	1.60	0.02	2.17**	0.02	2.15**
Change in growth	−0.02	−2.17**	−0.02	−2.61***	−0.02	−2.06**
Change in social spending/GDP	−0.01	−1.00	0.01	0.25	0.02	0.53
Number of previous failures	0.01	3.58***	0.01	4.38***	0.01	3.91***
Change in tax revenues/GDP	−0.09	−2.94***	−0.11	−5.03***	−0.07	−2.19**
Change in transfers/ current spending	0.03	2.24**	0.02	1.82*	0.02	1.87*
Change in current/ total spending	0.13	4.01***	0.12	5.19***	0.11	3.17***
Change in external financing/GDP	0.07	4.54***				
Change in domestic financing/GDP					0.01	0.02
Number of episodes	167		188		167	
Number of failures	107		118		107	
Time at risk	239		272		239	
Log likelihood	−418.3		−477.8		−423.1	
Wald test	87.34		77.13		67.29	
Probability	0.00		0.00		0.00	
Pseudo-R^2	0.22		0.17		0.17	

Note: Significance at the 10, 5, and 1 percent levels is indicated by *, **, and ***, respectively.
[1]Maximum likelihood estimates with robust standard errors.

An alternative robustness analysis to assess the effect of macroeconomic stability on the duration of fiscal adjustments is based on a stratified Cox proportional hazard regression. This consists of assuming that the baseline hazard rate is allowed to be different between post-stabilization and pre-stabilization countries. Results are reported in Table 4, which shows almost identical coefficients for Models 1–3 compared to the baseline regressions in Table 2. A final Wald test has been carried out for each model to test the significance of the inclusion of the post-stabilization dummy in the baseline regression. The results of these tests do not allow rejection of the hypothesis that the effect of the post-stabilization dummy is zero.

Parametric Analysis

This section reports the results of the parametric analysis on the determinants of fiscal adjustment duration. In these models, we assumed that the hazard function has a predefined shape based on the prior knowledge of the event to be studied. In the case of the analysis of fiscal consolidation spells, the economic theory does not predict the distribution of the baseline hazard rate. The instantaneous probability of ending a fiscal consolidation may increase with time if fiscal adjustments become more costly the longer they last. However, fiscal consolidation efforts may also be self-reinforcing because the adjustment episodes based on non-permanent measures tend to be reversed sooner than deficit reduction based on structural policies. The latter tend to be a selected subsample of the total number of spells. Furthermore, the baseline probability of ending a fiscal consolidation may fall with time as a result of intrinsic adjustment fatigue not modeled in the covariates vector.

Since the choice of the distribution governing the duration process is unknown, it is recommended to minimize the assumptions regarding the shape of the baseline hazard function. This is in fact what we have done in the semi-parametric analysis discussed in the subsections above where the form of the hazard function was not restricted deductively. In this subsection, we compare the results of Cox's proportional hazard model with two flexible parametric models based on the Weibul and the Gompertz distribution. The only assumption made using these distributions is that the baseline hazard function is monotonic. Whether the failure rate falls or increases with time is based on the sign of the estimated ancillary parameter. In the case of a monotonically increasing baseline hazard function, the Weibul distribution's ancillary parameter is higher than unity, while it has to be positive in the case of the Gompertz function.

Results in Table 5 report the estimated hazard ratios based on the Cox's proportional hazard model and the two parametric models described above. To facilitate the comparison in terms of goodness of fit between the parametric models we also calculate the AIC statistic, which shows that the model based on the Weibul distribution should be preferred to the model based on the Gompertz function. The ancillary parameters for both models point to a positively sloped, monotonically increasing baseline hazard function. This means there could be some empirical evidence that the baseline risk of ending a fiscal consolidation is increasing with time. It does not, however, mean that the total hazard is also increasing with time.

The results of the regression coefficients (hazard ratios) of the two parametric models can be compared with the baseline regression. In general, results are fairly consistent across the different models. In particular, although the distribution of the baseline hazard function was found to be positively sloped with respect to time, the results confirm that the size of the adjustment is positively correlated with the duration of the fiscal consolidation spells.

Table 5. Sustainability of Fiscal Consolidations and Budget Composition in Low-Income Countries: Results from Parametric Models, Model 1, 1990–2000[1]

	Cox Proportional Model		Weibul		Gompertz	
	Coefficient	z-test	Coefficient	z-test	Coefficient	z-test
Size of adjustment	0.96	−3.06***	0.94	−3.59***	0.94	3.57***
Initial deficit	1.01	1.20	1.02	1.13	1.01	0.79
Change in growth	0.98	−1.99**	0.97	−1.99**	0.97	−1.93*
Change in social spending/GDP	0.96	−1.07	1.00	−0.08	0.98	−0.40
Number of previous failures	1.01	3.75***	1.02	7.74***	1.00	6.98***
Change in tax revenues/GDP	0.92	−2.51**	0.90	−1.86**	0.91	−1.73*
Change in transfers/ current spending	1.03	2.18**	1.04	1.76*	1.04	2.09**
Change in current/ total spending	1.13	3.92***	1.11	1.99**	1.12	2.17***
Change in external financing/GDP	1.07	4.22***	1.08	3.22***	1.08	3.90***
Ancillary parameter			3.65	18.81***	1.50	10.52***
Number of episodes	167		188		167	
Number of failures	107		118		107	
Time at risk	239		272		239	
Log likelihood	−467.43		−61.77		−91.41	
Wald test	86.62		114.77		106.60	
Probability	0.00		0.00		0.00	
AIC statistic			145.54		204.82	

Note: Significance at the 10, 5, and 1 percent levels is indicated by *, **, and ***, respectively.
[1]Hazard ratios. Maximum likelihood estimates with robust standard errors.

Conclusions

In this chapter, we have used survival analysis to assess the factors underlying the duration of fiscal adjustment episodes in a sample of 39 low-income countries during the period 1990–2000. The results show that tilting the overall composition of public expenditure toward more productive uses is particularly important for achieving more sustained fiscal adjustments.

Fiscal consolidations achieved by cutting selected current expenditures tend to last longer than adjustments based on cuts in more productive spending. According to the results of our analysis, protecting capital expenditures during a fiscal adjustment leads to a longer fiscal consolidation episode, as does an increase in the share of current spending on nonwage goods and services.

The size of the fiscal adjustment effort and economic growth conditions are important for the persistence of fiscal consolidations.

Countries with larger cumulative reductions in the deficit are less likely to abandon their adjustment efforts than others. Furthermore, the probability of ending a fiscal consolidation effort is negatively related to per capita growth.

Our results depart from the empirical literature on industrial countries in one significant aspect. When fiscal consolidations are supported by an accelerated pace of revenue collection, the probability of ending an adjustment is lower, while expenditure reductions play a minor role. This contrasts with findings in the literature on industrial countries, where expenditure reductions dominate the sustainability of fiscal adjustment. This result has important policy implications. As revenue-to-GDP ratios are particularly low in these countries, in part because of weak administration, narrow tax bases, and tax avoidance, there is scope to mobilize revenue without raising tax rates.

Finally, we find that having achieved macroeconomic stability does significantly affect the probability of ending a fiscal consolidation. Recent studies have found that the effects of fiscal policy on growth tend to be nonlinear (Adam and Bevan, 2001; Gupta and others, 2002). However, we do not find sufficient evidence that countries that have not yet achieved stable macroeconomic conditions behave significantly differently from post-stabilization economies with regard to the duration of fiscal adjustments. Nonetheless, a country with unfavorable initial fiscal conditions is more likely to end a fiscal consolidation.

References

Aalen, Olivier, 1978, "Nonparametric Inference for Family of Counting Processes," *Annals of Statistics*, Vol. 6, pp. 701–26.

Abed, George, and others, 1998, *Fiscal Reforms in Low-Income Countries: Experience Under IMF-Supported Programs*, IMF Occasional Paper No. 160 (Washington: International Monetary Fund).

Adam, Christopher, and David Bevan, 2001, "Nonlinear Effects of Public Deficits on Growth," paper prepared for the Cornell/ISPE Conference on Public Finance and Development, September 7–9, New York.

———, 2003, "Staying the Course: Maintaining Fiscal Control in Developing Countries," paper prepared for the Brookings Institution Trade Forum Conference, May 15–16, Washington.

Alesina, Alberto, and Silvia Ardagna, 1998, "Tales of Fiscal Adjustment," *Economic Policy*, Vol. 27 (October), pp. 487–546.

Alesina, Alberto, and Roberto Perotti, 1995, "Fiscal Expansions and Adjustments in OECD Countries," *Economic Policy*, Vol. 21 (October), pp. 205–48.

————, and Jose Tavares, 1998, "The Political Economy of Fiscal Adjustments," *Brookings Papers on Economic Activity: 1*, Brookings Institution.

Ardagna, Sylvia, 2001, "Fiscal Policy Composition, Public Debt, and Economic Activity," *Public Choice*, Vol. 109 (December), pp. 301–25.

Chu, Ke-young, and others, 1995, *Unproductive Public Expenditure: A Pragmatic Approach to Policy Analysis*, IMF Pamphlet No. 48 (Washington: International Monetary Fund).

Cleves, Mario, William Gould, and Roberto Gutierrez, 2002, *An Introduction to Survival Analysis Using Stata* (College Station, Texas: Stata Press).

Cox, D., 1972, " Regression Models and Life Tables," *Journal of the Royal Statistical Society*, Series B, Vol. 34, pp. 187–220.

Gupta, Sanjeev, Benedict Clements, Emanuele Baldacci, and Carlos Mulas-Granados, 2002, "Expenditure Composition, Fiscal Adjustment, and Growth in Low-Income Countries," IMF Working Paper No. 02/77 (Washington: International Monetary Fund).

————, 2004, "Fiscal Policy, Expenditure Composition, and Growth in Low-Income Countries," Chapter 2 in *Helping Countries Develop: The Role of Fiscal Policy*, ed. by Sanjeev Gupta, Benedict Clements, and Gabriela Inchauste (Washington: International Monetary Fund). Also published in the *Journal of International Money and Finance*, Vol. 23, 2004.

————, forthcoming, "The Persistence of Fiscal Adjustment in Developing Countries," *Applied Economics Letters*.

Hosmer, David W., and Stanley Lemeshow, 1999, *Applied Survival Analysis: Regression Modeling of Time to Event Data* (New York: John Wiley and Sons).

Ize, Alain, 1991, "Measurement of Fiscal Performance in IMF-Supported Programs: Some Methodological Issues," in *How to Measure the Fiscal Deficit: Analytical and Methodological Issues*, ed. by Mario I. Blejer and Adrienne Cheasty (Washington: International Monetary Fund).

Kaplan, E.I., and P. Meier, 1958, "Nonparametric Estimation from Incomplete Observations," *Journal of the American Statistical Association*, Vol. 53, pp. 457–81.

Maroto, Reyes, and Carlos Mulas-Granados, 2001, "The Duration of Fiscal Consolidations in the European Union," Fundación de Estudios de Economia Aplicada (FEDEA) Working Paper No. 2001/19 (Madrid, Spain).

Perotti, Roberto, 1998, "The Political Economy of Fiscal Consolidations," *Scandinavian Journal of Economics*, Vol. 100, No. 1, pp. 367–94.

von Hagen, Jürgen, and Rolf Strauch, 2001, "Fiscal Consolidations: Quality, Economic Conditions, and Success," *Public Choice*, Vol. 109 (December), pp. 327–46.

von Hagen, Jürgen, Andrew Hughes Hallett, and Rolf Strauch, 2002, "Budgetary Consolidation in Europe: Quality, Economic Conditions, and Persistence," *Journal of the Japanese and International Economies*, Vol. 16 (December), pp. 512–35.

4

Growth, Governance, and Fiscal Policy Transmission Channels in Low-Income Countries

EMANUELE BALDACCI, ARYE L. HILLMAN, AND NAOKO C. KOJO

1. Introduction

"Expansionary fiscal contractions" occur when sustained reductions in government budget deficits increase GDP or growth of real income. Evidence of expansionary fiscal contractions for high-income countries, following reductions in public spending rather than increases in government revenues, is reported by Giavazzi and Pagano (1990), Bertola and Drazen (1993), Alesina and Perotti (1995), and Alesina (1997); Drazen (2001) reviews the evidence regarding high-income countries. Evidence indicating the presence of expansionary fiscal contractions in low-income countries is reported by Gupta et al. (2002, 2004).

Increased private investment appears to be the principal explanation for expansionary fiscal contractions in high-income countries.

This chapter is reprinted from the *European Journal of Political Economy*, Vol. 20, Emanuele Baldacci, Arye L. Hillman, and Naoko C. Kojo, "Growth, Governance, and Fiscal Policy Transmission Channels in Low-Income Countries," ©2004, with permission from Elsevier.

The views expressed in this paper are those of the authors and do not necessarily represent those of the IMF or IMF policy. We thank Sanjeev Gupta for directing attention to the topic of the paper and for helpful subsequent observations. Benedict Clements and Philipp Harms provided very useful comments. Helpful comments were also received from Matt Davis, Michael Lav, Davide Lombardo, Paulo Medas, and Antonio Spilimbergo, and participants at the 2003 Silvaplana Workshop in Political Economy, the faculty seminar in economics at the University of Freiburg, and the Fiscal Affairs Department seminar at the International Monetary Fund. Qiang Cui provided excellent research assistance.

Sustained reductions in government budget deficits increase private investment through reduced real interest rates and enhanced price and external stability.

There is no corresponding evidence available indicating why expansionary fiscal contractions occur in low-income countries. The objective of the study reported in this paper is to investigate the reasons for expansionary fiscal contractions in low-income countries. This requires identifying the transmission channels through which fiscal policy affects growth in these countries.

In low-income countries, as in high-income countries, investment is a channel prospectively linking fiscal policy and growth. An alternative channel is factor productivity. We shall investigate the relative effectiveness of investment and factor productivity as fiscal-policy transmission channels in low-income countries.

Considerations that we shall set out suggest that, in low-income countries, factor productivity and not investment is predicted to be the primary channel linking fiscal policy to growth. This prediction is based prominently on governance characteristics of public sector spending and administration in low-income countries. Governance in these countries is often poor (see, for example, the studies reported in Abed and Gupta, 2002). This poor governance is predicted to diminish the effectiveness of the investment channel while increasing the effectiveness of the factor-productivity channel in the link between fiscal policy and growth.

The paper is organized as follows. Section 2 describes the transmission channels linking fiscal policy and growth in high- and low-income countries and sets out the basis for the prediction regarding the effectiveness of the investment and factor-productivity channels. Section 3 describes the specification for estimation. Section 4 describes the data. Section 5 reports the empirical results. Section 6 summarizes the conclusions. The principal policy conclusion is that, although increased investment is not a channel through which low-income countries might expect substantial benefit from fiscal adjustment, high-deficit low-income countries can expect to benefit from expansionary fiscal contractions through factor productivity, which can be expected to increase for governance-related reasons.

2. Transmission Channels

High-Income Countries

In the standard Keynesian macroeconomic model, fiscal policy fosters private sector investment by sustaining or increasing domestic demand. The positive effect on growth of fiscal expansions can be (partially or entirely) offset by adverse effects of deficit financing on investment through higher interest rates, inflationary pressures, and external sector instability. The decline in private investment following fiscal expansions—often referred to as a "crowding out" effect because public spending displaces private investment—can also occur because increases in interest rates affect perceptions of fiscal sustainability. The intertemporal budget constraint requires that the present value of obligations to repay government borrowing and to pay interest on government debt does not exceed the present value of future budgetary primary surpluses. Excessive deficits and the associated increased public debt reduce market confidence in a government's ability to satisfy this constraint. Conversely, deficit reductions or fiscal contractions can increase investment, and thereby increase growth. This in general requires that deficit reductions occur through lower current government expenditure rather than through tax increases or reduced public investment (see von Hagen et al., 2002).

Reduced government deficits may also increase investment through more stable exchange rates that restore investor confidence and moderate or eliminate capital flight (Hjelm, 2002).[1] Reduced deficits can also preempt financial crises by signaling changed policies and thereby positively affecting expectations of future budgetary viability (Bertola and Drazen, 1993).

A supply-side link between fiscal policy and investment has been suggested through wage levels (Alesina et al., 1999). Investment is a function of the shadow value of capital, which depends on the present discounted marginal product of capital, and falls as wage rates increase (because the capital/labor ratio is an increasing function of wage in a competitive market). Higher current or expected taxes on labor result in higher post-tax equilibrium wages, lower expected profits, and lower investment.

Reduced deficits can also increase private consumption and investment through a wealth effect, as emphasized by Giavazzi and Pagano (1990). Lower deficits imply reduced future taxes to service government debt. The reduced future taxes increase the present value of perceived private permanent income or wealth, and increase growth through increases in private spending on investment and consumption.[2]

---

[1] Hjelm (2002) finds that real exchange rate depreciations preceding fiscal contractions increase growth. Nominal depreciations reduce domestic supply prices and increase domestic demand. However, these beneficial effects can be reversed through higher prices unless fiscal policy reduces budget deficits. Hjelm concludes that fiscal contractions preceded by exchange rate depreciations have been expansionary in industrial countries.

[2] The perceived reduction in future taxes also increases the present value of utility through reduced deadweight losses associated with lower taxation. If public spending and private spending were perfect substitutes, changes in bond-financed public spending would be subject to the Ricardian equivalence (that is, subject to limitations and qualifications, the private sector would internalize and offset the intertemporal changes associated with the change in government policy).

Private investment can also increase because of a perception that deficit reductions signal political stability through agreement within the government on reduced spending. That is, the deficit reduction is a signal that discord within the government has come to an end, and that a period of political stability is to follow (Drazen, 2001).[3]

Low-Income Countries

The fiscal-policy transmission channels described above are not expected to be similarly effective in low-income countries. Wealth effects require the presence of adequately developed financial markets to facilitate increased private expenditures in response to perceived higher permanent income. Financial markets may not be sufficiently developed to facilitate such responses in poorer countries, where wealth is also often not principally held in the form of financial assets. When intertemporal exchange through financial markets cannot take place, current private spending cannot increase growth in response to perceived future increases in private-sector income.

In low-income countries, the investment channel for increased growth is impeded by low interest rate insensitivity of private investment. Interest rates do not respond to lower deficits if there is financial repression.[4] Independently of financial repression, insufficiently developed domestic credit and government bond markets may, in any event, not allow a role for interest rates in affecting private investment. Government policies of directed credits to designated enterprises (that may be owned by the state) may replace or override the role of financial and capital markets.

Restricted economic freedom also makes private investment unattractive in low-income countries (see De Haan and Sturm, 2000; Bengoa and Sanchez-Robles, 2003).[5] Private investment is discouraged when rights of

---

[3] In high-income countries the relation between fiscal policy and growth can also be a basis for political motives to influence election outcomes (see Economides et al., 2003). In low-income countries the motive of electoral influence is often absent because elections in which an opposition can be expected to replace the incumbent government do not take place.

[4] In financially repressed economies a government sets a lower than competitive market interest rate for domestic savers. The government legislates a state monopoly on receiving deposits at the low interest rate and thereby benefits from the low interest that it has set for itself as sole borrower. The benefit to the government from financial repression is directly expressed as the difference between the domestic interest rate and a higher interest rate available in international capital markets. On financial repression as a source of government revenue, see Hillman (2003), Chapter 7.

[5] The absence or limited presence of democratic institutions in many low-income countries adversely affects economic freedom and thereby private investment incentives. See De Haan and Sturm (2003).

ownership are compromised by inadequate protection of private property rights, when international remittances of profits are not allowed, and when exchange controls inhibit purchase of imported inputs.

While fiscal contractions reduce a government's reliance on inflationary financing in the presence of financing gaps, private investment in low-income countries tends to be insensitive to price stability. With domestic bond markets absent or rudimentary and access to foreign capital markets restricted or unavailable, domestic financing of deficits takes place principally through inflationary financing. In these circumstances, reduced deficits can improve incentives for private investment through enhanced price stability. Yet, because investment in low-income countries is often principally undertaken by the public sector, it is insensitive to price stability. Because public investment is financed largely through concessionary loans provided by international agencies and bilateral donors, investment is generally quite insensitive to the market incentives that affect private investment decisions.[6]

The above considerations taken together suggest that, although private investment is the primary channel for expansionary fiscal contractions in high-income economies, a similar role should not be expected for private investment in low-income countries.

Factor Productivity and Public Sector Governance

An aggregate production function can be represented in the form:

$$Y = AV_i^{\alpha_i}, \tag{1}$$

where Y is aggregate output, V_i indicates factor inputs, α_i indicates the elasticity of output for input i, and A is an index of total factor productivity. Growth of real output is given by the combined components of increased factor productivity through changes in A and increased availability of factors of production through increases in a factor-input quantity V_i, with the linkage emphasized by the endogenous growth theory that investment, particularly in human capital, increases factor productivity and so staves off decreasing returns.[7] Beyond increased investment (and the productivity consequences of increased investment), higher growth can occur if changes take place that directly increase factor productivity.

---

[6]Donors can, however, be influenced by social and political instability. See Chauvet (2002).

[7]See, for example, Barro and Sala-i-Martin (1995).

The aggregate production function Eq. (1) does not distinguish factors of production by sectoral location of employment or production. With competitive markets, intersectorally mobile factors, and only private profit-maximizing production, the value of the marginal product of a factor of production is the same in all uses, so that location of employment or use of a particular factor does not matter for factor productivity. However, the public sector is not necessarily subject to competitive conditions.[8]

Because of the absence of competitive conditions, public-sector wages can include a rent component. Incomes may then be higher in the public sector, whereas labor productivity can be higher in the private sector.[9] If resources are more productive in the private sector than in the public sector, average factor productivity will increase whenever reduced public expenditure shifts resources from the public sector to the private sector. In that case, the index of factor productivity A declines with the share of labor or resources employed in the public sector.

Factor productivity expressed in the index A also reflects externalities imposed on the private sector by the state sector. Effectively implemented government spending on needed infrastructure increases private sector productivity by providing complementary public inputs (for example, through spending on roads and bridges that facilitate trade in rural areas). The public sector can, however, also impose negative externalities on factor productivity in the private sector. One source of such negative externality is the deadweight loss from taxes that finance public spending, and the associated adverse factor-supply effects of taxation.[10] Poor governance has additionally been observed, particularly in low-income countries, as a source of negative externality imposed by the public sector. Poor governance has been reported to reduce the effectiveness and productivity of public spending (see, for

---

[8]See, for example, Hillman (2003), Chapter 3.

[9]The rent available in the public sector as a component of remuneration is, by definition, a payment beyond that available in the alternative of employment in the private sector (or through the alternative of unemployment). The rent in public-sector employment is a tax-financed transfer from the private sector or is financed through other internal means or through externally available funds. With incomes (including the rent component) in employment in the state sector exceeding incomes in the private sector (and exceeding income if unemployed), there is excess demand for employment in the public sector. Persons seeking the higher incomes available from employment in the public sector are blocked by entry barriers, which also preserve the public sector rents. That is, employment is described by an insider-outsider theory of rent preservation. See Lindbeck and Snower (1989).

[10]The magnitude of this effect is more than usually difficult to assess in low-income countries, where capital and labor supply are often influenced by considerations beyond marginal factor prices.

example, Mauro, 1998; Gupta, Davoodi, and Tiongson, 2001; and other papers in Abed and Gupta, 2002).

Unproductive public spending can take various forms, including spending on wages and salaries of unproductive employees or ghost workers.[11] Public spending is also unproductive when government expenditures do not reach designated spending objectives. This happens, for example, when government officials are corrupt and seek bribes for preferentially selecting beneficiaries of government programs, for authorizing private investment projects, for allowing participation of government enterprises in joint ventures with private investors, or for allowing access to inputs provided through state enterprises.[12]

Rent seeking also decreases factor productivity. When personal benefits from government employment or public spending take the form of rents, lower government deficits may decrease the values of the contestable rents. Incentives to use time, effort, and initiative in seeking to become a state-sector employee or to benefit from government programs are then reduced.[13] When resources for rent-seeking activities are redirected to productive activities, factor productivity increases, thereby increasing growth.

The seeking of rents through government employment or through personal benefit from public spending may not be equally contestable by all members of the population. Rather, educational achievements may be required to be able to compete for employment in government positions or to be able to attempt to influence designation of the beneficiaries of public spending. Rent-seeking incentives then reduce growth by diverting higher human capital away from productive activities.[14]

---

[11] Evidence on ghost workers (who are fictitious, duplicate, or otherwise erroneous entries in the public employment rolls) is provided in reports of public sector reform in low-income countries. An example of public spending on ghost workers is provided in a report (The Jakarta Post, September 17, 2003) of payments by the Indonesian government of more than Rp 111.7 billion per month (US$13 million) in salaries to absentee public employees. The payments were revealed following implementation of a government-initiated program to update the data on civil servants, as part of a policy of reform of the government bureaucracy. Public sector censuses undertaken by other governments have likewise identified ghost workers. On ghost workers and civil service reform in low-income countries, see http://www1.worldbank.org/publicsector/civilservice/common.htm (World Bank, 2001).

[12] On the relation between economic freedom and corruption in rich and poor countries, see Graeff and Mehlkop (2003), who identify restrictions on economic freedom with opportunities for corruption.

[13] In general, the value of the resources unproductively used in seeking rents declines when the value of a contested rent declines. On the different influences that can affect social costs when rent-seeking incentives are present, see, for example, Hillman (2003), Chapter 6.

[14] On the diversion of productive abilities, see Gelb et al. (1998), Acemoglu and Verdier (1998), and Dabla-Norris and Wade (2002).

The above governance-related considerations imply that it is increased factor productivity rather than private investment that is the principal transmission channel for expansionary fiscal contractions in low-income countries.

The Composition of Public Spending and Factor Productivity

For any level of budget deficit, the composition of public spending is expected to affect factor productivity. If public sector employees engage in bribe-seeking and rent-seeking activities, a change in the composition of public spending away from wages to more productive uses is predicted to increase factor productivity and thereby increase growth.

However, reductions in some categories of public spending on wages such as in education and health sectors can, of course, hamper growth. In addition, in poor-governance economies, lower levels of wages for public-sector employees may increase corruption. Lower public-sector wages may increase incentives to find sources of supplemental illegal income (see Van Rijckeghem and Weder, 2001), thereby increasing corruption and reducing factor productivity and growth. A reduction in the share of government spending on wages therefore need not always be beneficial for growth.

Increased public spending on some types of capital projects is not necessarily beneficial for growth. In poor-governance economies, corruption has been reported to reduce the effectiveness of capital spending. Through corruption, biases are imparted toward spending on types of capital equipment and infrastructure that are amenable to solicitation of bribes and to private appropriation of government budgetary allocations (Mauro, 1998; Gupta et al., 2001a).

Because of governance-related effects, increases in unproductive categories of public spending can therefore hamper growth.[15] We shall accordingly investigate the role of the composition of public spending in affecting growth.

---

[15] When the public sector imposes net negative externalities on the private sector, the overall adverse effect of higher public spending more than offsets the positive contributions to growth of other categories of public expenditure. In addition, in this case, the size of government spending (and not only the amount of deficit spending) is a determinant of growth. However, at the margin, reductions in deficit-financed public spending are reductions in overall public spending. Hence our estimates will apply equally for the consequences of a reduction in the deficit and a reduction in public spending.

Governance and Investment

We have proposed that, because of governance-related considerations, increased factor productivity is anticipated to be the principal transmission channel for expansionary fiscal adjustments in low-income countries. Governance-related considerations also affect the role of investment as a fiscal policy transmission channel in low-income countries. Because when governance is poor or inadequate, corruption creates adverse incentives for private investment.

The Fundamental Role of Governance

Governance therefore has a fundamental role in affecting both prospective fiscal policy transmission channels. Poor governance underlies the hypothesized prominence of factor productivity in expansionary fiscal contractions in low-income countries. At the same time, poor governance lowers the effectiveness of investment as a transmission channel linking fiscal policy to growth.

3. The Specification for Estimation

To investigate whether expansionary fiscal contractions are present, and to assess the roles of investment and factor productivity as fiscal policy transmission channels, we estimate a recursive system consisting of:

(i)   a growth equation;

(ii) a gross investment equation;

(iii) an equation linking fiscal policy to inflation; and

(iv) an equation linking fiscal policy to exchange rate movements.

This specification allows direct and indirect channels for the effects of fiscal policy on growth to be distinguished in a system that remains sufficiently tractable to be estimated using standard econometric methods.

The direction of causality in this system runs from fiscal policy to exchange rate movements that in turn affect inflation. These variables are expected to have an impact on gross investment, which is a component of growth.

The model corresponds to a system of equations with restrictions on the feedbacks among the endogenous variables. We also estimate an unrestricted system of equations allowing feedbacks between endogenous variables. The feedbacks were not statistically significant, confirming the empirical validity of the recursive model.[16]

---

[16] See Duncan (1975) on the advantage of using a recursive system.

With **y** a vector of endogenous variables and **x** a vector of exogenous variables, the recursive system is expressed as:

$$y = By + \Gamma x + \xi, \tag{2}$$

where **B** is an upper triangular matrix containing for each pair of endogenous variables i and j with elements $\beta_{ji} \neq 0$ and $\beta_{ij} = 0$, Γ is a matrix of direct effects of the exogenous variables on the endogenous variables, and ξ is a vector of the equations' error terms. With the error covariance matrix of the system diagonal (i.e., so that the disturbance terms are not correlated across equations), Eq. (2) can be estimated using standard least squares techniques with parameter estimates that are unbiased and efficient. If the error covariance matrix is not diagonal, the above system can be estimated simultaneously allowing for feedbacks among the error terms of the different equations.

A feature of this system is that total effects on **y** of each exogenous and endogenous variable can be estimated using the reduced form $y = \Pi x + \varsigma$. The total effect of **x** on **y** is given by $\Pi = (I - B)^{-1}\Gamma$ and the total effect of **y** on **y** is given by $\Theta = (I - B)^{-1} - I$.[17]

The Growth Equation

The form of the growth equation is:

$$g_{it} = \beta_{11}\log(y_{i0}) + \beta_{12}I_{it} + \beta_{13}n_{it} + \beta_{14}X_{it}$$
$$+ \beta_{15}def_{it} + \sum_{1}^{q}\alpha_{1j}e_{jit} + \sum_{1}^{p}\varphi_{1k}r_{kit} + \beta_{16}dhi_{it} + \beta_{17}trans_{it} + n_{1i} + v_{it}, \tag{3}$$

where $g_{it} = \log(y_{it}) - \log(y_{it-1})$ is growth of per capita income, with $y_{it} = Y_{it}/P_{it}$ and where P_{it} is the total population size. Growth is here specified as a function of standard covariates used in the endogenous growth literature:[18]

- The logarithm of initial per capita income $\log(y_{i0})$, which accounts for convergence, that is, the potential for growth depends on the level of per capita income that has been attained. The coefficient, which represents the rate of convergence, is negative if there is (conditional) convergence and is positive if poor countries are caught in a poverty trap.

---

[17] The indirect effects can be calculated by subtracting the direct effects matrices **B** and Γ from the respective total effects of **y** and **x**.

[18] See, for example, Kneller et al. (1999).

- Gross investment as a share of GDP (y_{it}): gross investment here includes private and public investments. The coefficient is expected to be positive.

- The population growth rate (n_{it}) is part of the definition of per capita income growth, but also affects growth through domestic market size and domestic demand. The coefficient could be positive or negative.

The vector X consists of:

- The initial primary and secondary school enrollment rates (pe_{i0} and se_{i0}): human capital is a main component of endogenous growth, although in the countries that we consider human capital was not overall well developed during the sample period. We use the data on school enrollment to proxy for the stock of human capital, although the proxy is of course imperfect and reflects more the development of human capital rather than human capital in place.[19]

- The terms of trade index (tot_{it}) appears in the growth equation to account for possible exogenous shocks in international commodity prices that may have an impact on growth.

- Time-invariant specific attributes of the country, such as institutions characterizing governance, are reflected in η_i.

Fiscal policy variables that affect growth are:

- The overall fiscal deficit as a ratio to GDP (def_{it}): expansionary fiscal contraction is indicated if the coefficient is negative.

- The share of the j-th expenditure category in total public spending (e_{jit}) to test for the effects through the composition of public spending.[20]

---

[19]School enrollment is subject to gender biases and also governance considerations through the provision of quality publicly financed schooling and abilities of parents to organize schooling based on self-financed user prices when provision by the state is ineffective or missing (see, for example, Hillman and Jenkner, 2002, for an overview of these issues). In addition, education or available human capital is not an input for growth if there are other impediments to productive employment of qualified people, as expressed in low or absent social mobility.

[20]It would be useful to be able to disaggregate capital spending into foreign and domestically financed components. Foreign-financed capital spending can be expected to be more productive than spending on domestically financed projects because of the monitoring of the former projects by the international community. However, data availability has constrained us to use aggregate capital expenditure. The disaggregation is not expected to have significant effects in this sample because: (1) the major share of capital spending is foreign-financed and (2) part of domestically financed capital spending is tied to foreign financing through counterpart funds.

- The share of the k-th revenue item in total budget revenue (r_{kit}), which allows us to consider how revenue sources affect growth.[21]

Also included in the growth equation are:

- The interaction of fiscal balance with a low-deficit dummy ($defpost_{it}$), to control for the effect of deficit reduction (or expansion) on growth in countries that have already achieved a modicum of fiscal stability.[22] We define low-deficit countries as countries that had an average fiscal deficit below 2.5% of GDP during the sample period.

- Following Khan and Senhadji (2001), a dummy is included for countries with annual inflation exceeding 20% (dhi_t) to test for a (nonlinear) negative effect on growth of high inflation.[23]

- A dummy for transition economies ($trans_i$): we expect the transition countries to have different average growth rates as a result of the collapse of GDP at the onset of the transition to market economies.

The Investment Equation

The investment equation is for gross investment (as defined in the growth equation, combining public and private investment). Investment appears in the growth equation and is endogenous to fiscal policy and other influences, including governance through corruption. To identify the *indirect effect* of fiscal policy on growth through investment, we estimate:[24]

$$I_{it} = \beta_{21}\log(y_{i0}) + \beta_{22}n_{it} + \beta_{23}X_{it} + \beta_{24}def_{it} + \beta_{25}defpost_{it} \\ + \beta_{26}i_{it} + \beta_{27}dhi_{it} + \beta_{28}trans_i + \beta_{29}ext_{it} + \eta_{2i} + v_{it}, \tag{4}$$

---

[21] See Kneller et al. (1999) for inclusion of budget composition in augmented growth models. Expenditure categories consist of wages and salaries, transfers and subsidies, interest on domestic and external debt, purchase of goods and services and other current expenditure, and capital outlays. Revenue categories include tax revenues and nontax revenues and grants. Other current expenditure and nontax and grant revenues are not included to avoid multicollinearity.

[22] $defpost_{it}$ is the interaction between deficit and a dummy for low-deficit countries. These are also called post-stabilization countries and fiscal policy is expected to have different effects in these countries. See Adam and Bevan (2000, 2001), Gupta et al. (2003).

[23] The empirical study by Khan and Senhadji (2001) suggests a 20% inflation rate as a threshold for developing countries, beyond which inflation exerts a negative effect on growth.

[24] See also Fischer (1993) and de la Fuente (1997).

where all variables are defined as in the growth equation. The initial value of per capita income reflects the link between income levels and profit expectations, which are determinants of private investment.

We have noted that corruption can be anticipated to discourage private investment and reduce the effectiveness of public investment.[25] To capture a nonlinear effect of government size on the level of investment, we include the change in the ratio of government spending to GDP interacted with a corruption index (ext_{it}). This variable is 0 for countries that have an index of corruption below a given threshold, and takes the value of the change in government size, measured by the share of government outlays to GDP, for the other observations.

The fiscal policy variables included in the equation are the overall fiscal deficit as a ratio to GDP and its interaction with the low-deficit dummy. We also control for transition economies in the sample using a dummy variable ($trans_i$) that takes the value of unity for these countries. Because we expect inflation to be a major determinant of investment,[26] we include both the level of annual inflation (i_{it}) and the dummy for countries with inflation higher than 20% per year (dhi_t) to express non-linearities in the effects of inflation on investment.

Inflation

Fiscal policy is a determinant of inflation, which appears in the growth and investment equations.[27] We regress the logarithm of one plus the inflation rate on the fiscal deficit and its interaction with the low-deficit dummy.[28] Other exogenous variables included are initial per capita income [$\log(y_{i0})$], as well as the terms of trade (tot_{it}), the currency depreciation rate ($excd_{it}$), the degree of openness ($open_{it}$)[29], the employment rate (emp_{it}), and two dummies for transition and low-deficit countries, all of which are included in vector Z_{it}:

$$\log(1 + i_{it}) = \beta_{31}\log(y_{i0}) + \beta_{32}def_{it} + \beta_{33}defpost_{it} + \beta_{34}Z_{it} + \eta_{3i} + \xi_{it}. \quad (5)$$

---

[25] See Del Monte and Papagni (2001) and Gupta et al. (2001a). Rajkumar and Swaroop (2002) similarly consider the efficacy of public spending on health care in developing countries and find that corruption reduces the effectiveness of public health expenditure on child mortality and other health status indicators in a sample of developed and developing countries.

[26] See, for example, Fischer (1993).

[27] See, for example, Catao and Terrones (2003).

[28] See also Fischer et al. (2002).

[29] For a review of the contribution of trade openness on growth in empirical and theoretical studies, see Berg and Krueger (2003).

The External Sector

Apart from effects on inflation, high budget deficits may have adverse effects on growth through unsustainable balance of payment positions. Fiscal policies that contribute to perceptions that fiscal or external policy is unsustainable may trigger capital flight and reduced foreign direct investment, thereby slowing output growth. Large fiscal deficits may also lead governments to use financial repression including restrictions on international capital flows.

It is difficult to estimate a proper exchange rate equation in a cross-country study with a static specification. Nonetheless, we include the exchange rate equation to capture the direct effect of fiscal policy on the external position (Fischer, 1993). This is done by regressing the fiscal deficit and its interaction with the low-deficit dummy on the annual change in the nominal exchange rate $excd_{it}$. Additional variables included in the equation are represented by vector Z_{it}, which consists of the terms of trade index, the low-deficit and transition economies dummies, the trade openness indicator, and the employment ratio. Vector W_{it} consists of the ratio of external debt to GDP, the interaction between change in government size and corruption, and the composition of government spending and revenue in percent of GDP. The external sector equation is:

$$excd_{it} = \beta_{41}def_{it} + \beta_{42}defpost_{it} + \beta_{43}Z_{it} + \beta_{44}W_{it} + \eta_{4i} + \vartheta_{it}. \tag{6}$$

4. Endogeneity of Fiscal Policy

In this recursive system of equations, endogeneity of fiscal policy implies that decisions about the level of the deficit and the composition of the budget precede decisions or realizations concerning other variables. To account for fiscal policy not being exogenous and to rule out reverse causality, we use a Generalized Method of Moments (GMM) estimator that also allows residuals to be heteroscedastic. The fiscal balance is instrumented using the lagged fiscal deficit and a variable representing the degree of democracy.[30]

The Country Sample

Our data set covers 39 low-income countries that had IMF-supported programs for the period 1999–2001. The sample of countries, which includes transition economies, is determined by data availability for all

---

[30]Democracy is a good instrument for fiscal deficit since it captures the link between fiscal policy and governance, which is significant in low-income countries.

variables used in the analysis, and the objective of having a broad range of low-income countries across regions and institutional characteristics. While our sample excludes low-income countries that did not have IMF-supported programs during the 1990s, the sample covers the majority of low-income countries for which requisite data for this study are available. The list of countries in the empirical estimation is provided in Appendix A, along with descriptions of variables and data sources.

All countries included in the sample have obtained concessional loans from the Fund since 1987 under the Enhanced Structural Adjustment Facility (ESAF) or since 1999 under the Poverty Reduction and Growth Facility (PRGF) that replaced the ESAF. Countries remain in the sample even if the Fund-supported program was interrupted because performance targets under the program were missed.[31]

Both ESAF-supported programs and PRGF-supported programs envisaged concessional budget assistance from the World Bank and other multilateral and bilateral donors.[32] In many cases, in the absence of a Fund program, external aid from other multilateral and bilateral donors would also be frozen, although this is not a rule. The programs are intended to ensure macroeconomic stability through implementation of sound economic policies and structural reforms that would enhance limited technical capacities in low-income countries.

There are differences between ESAFs and PRGFs. For example, for ESAF-supported programs over the 1986–1995 period, the deficit was targeted, on average, to decrease by about one percentage point of GDP relative to the preprogram year (see Abed et al., 1998), while the more recent PRGF-supported programs, on average, targeted relatively small increases in budget deficits to allow for higher poverty-reduction public spending. A basic tenet of the PRGF is that a stable macroeconomic position is critical for promoting growth and reducing poverty. The elimination of budget imbalances was not the sole aim of these Fund-supported programs, which also sought, inter alia, to improve the composition of public expenditure and revenues.

Table 1 reports descriptive statistics for the variables used in the study. Fiscal deficits were reduced on average by more than 1.5% of

---

[31] Typically performance targets envisaged under the programs include ceilings on the overall fiscal deficit and the change in net domestic assets of the banking sector and a floor on reserves. Occasionally, more specific targets specifying revenue performance or expenditure floors in specific sectors are also included.

[32] Budget assistance in the form of project loans (for specific projects, usually capital and development projects) and programs loans (based on specific policy-related conditionality) is classified as external financing in the fiscal accounts. However, direct assistance in the form of grants is classified above the line as a revenue source, thereby contributing to the reduction in the fiscal deficit.

GDP during the sample period of 1990–2001. The average fiscal deficit in the sample was 6.2% of GDP. Financing for the deficits came mostly from external concessional sources (4.6% of GDP). Real per capita GDP growth was not significantly different from zero during the period (the point estimate was –0.3% per year).[33] Between 1990 and 2001, the fiscal deficit fell from 7.6% of GDP to 5.4% of GDP, both as a result of the increase in the revenue to GDP ratio and a fall in the ratio of total government spending to GDP.

5. Econometric Results

Results for the estimations are set out in Tables 2–5. Each table contains a column with the baseline GMM estimation for each equation using both the overall fiscal balance and its financing components as regressors. We also present a set of alternative results based on different estimators to check the robustness of the baseline results. These estimators include the fixed effects least square dummy variable estimator (LSDV), a feasible generalized least square estimator (FGLS), and a robust regression estimator (Hamilton, 1991) that eliminates the influence of outliers on the results. We also estimate Eqs. (3)–(6) by relaxing the assumption that the error term is not correlated across equations, thereby allowing feedbacks among the equations. We use an error component two-stage least-square estimator (EC2SLS) and fixed-effect instrumental variable estimator (Baltagi, 1995).

Baseline Analysis

The Growth Equation

Table 2 shows the results of the estimation of the growth equation.[34] A fiscal surplus is positively related to growth, but not for countries with low deficits, for which increased deficits are found to have no significant effect on growth. That is, expansionary fiscal contractions arise only for initially high-deficit countries. For these countries, a reduction in the fiscal deficit by one percentage point of GDP raises the per capita GDP growth rate by around 0.2 percentage points. If a country has a low deficit, the positive effect on growth of deficit reductions is offset

---

[33]In the subsample of nontransition economies the deficit ratio was lower than for the whole sample, at 5.5% of GDP, while per capita GDP grew on average by 0.4% per year.

[34]Note that sample size differs depending on the availability of explanatory variables in each equation.

Table 1. Descriptive Statistics
(In percent, unless otherwise specified)

Variables	Mean	Median	Standard Deviation	Kurtosis	Skewness	Observations
Capital expenditure (percent of GDP)	9.02	7.4	7.25	11.89	3.01	457
Corruption dummy	0.07	0	0.25	9.82	3.43	468
Corruption index	2.70	3	1.06	0.77	–0.65	300
Democracy index	2.97	3	1.32	–0.10	–0.43	300
Domestic financing (percent of GDP)	1.65	0.7	4.78	9.29	1.96	407
Exchange rate appreciation	–15.31	–8.01	23.20	3.99	–1.41	468
External financing (percent of GDP)	4.57	3.58	5.98	8.94	2.30	407
Fiscal deficit (percent of GDP)	6.20	4.61	7.65	10.19	–2.68	468
Inflation	130.11	9.7	893.87	206.97	13.26	468
Initial gross primary enrollment	77.42	84.1	26.38	–1.00	–0.42	456
Initial gross secondary enrollment	32.45	23.5	29.64	0.13	1.22	456
Initial per capita GDP (national currency)	145,809.02	76,125.80	308,191.23	21.63	4.48	468
Interest payment (percent of GDP)	3.37	2.4	3.22	20.53	3.18	430
Investment (percent of GDP)	18.98	17.1	9.55	5.22	1.90	429
Labor ratio	45.88	47	5.68	1.51	–0.97	442
Low-deficit dummy	0.25	0	0.43	–0.66	1.16	468
Openness index	0.77	0.64	0.69	104.87	8.53	443
Population growth	2.35	2.56	2.59	72.61	–2.57	468
Tax revenue (percent of GDP)	15.05	13.6	7.37	1.28	1.13	459
Terms of trade	102.26	100	35.04	161.68	9.94	468
Total external debt (billions of U.S. dollars)	2.98	1.72	2.92	1.47	1.37	468
Transfer and subsidies (percent of GDP)	3.28	2.2	3.55	13.36	3.24	370
Transition economies dummy	0.21	0	0.40	0.15	1.47	468
Wages and salaries (percent of GDP)	6.64	5.6	3.73	7.58	2.48	410

Source: See Appendix A.

Table 2. Growth Regression: Dependent Variable—Average Per Capita Real GDP Growth Rate[a]

	Baseline GMM 1	GMM 2	LSDV 3	FGLS 4	Robust Regression 5	EC2SLS 6	2SLS 7
Fiscal deficit (in percent of GDP)	−0.188 (1.70)*		−0.202 (5.49)***	−0.201 (5.21)***	−0.142 (7.17)***	−0.227 (2.71)***	−0.183 (1.80)*
Fiscal deficit in low-deficit countries (in percent of GDP)	0.219 (1.83)*	0.134 (0.71)*	0.301 (2.40)**	0.352 (2.52)**	0.144 (2.16)**	0.397 (2.30)**	0.215 (1.19)
Initial per capita GDP level	0.0000014 (3.93)***	0.000001 (1.66)*	0.0000016 (3.84)***	0.00000035 (0.18)	0.0000014 (6.24)***	−0.0000048 (1.80)	0.0000023 (0.00)
Population growth rate	−0.248 (2.06)**	−0.187 (1.16)	−0.064 (0.95)	−0.145 (1.94)*	−0.01 (0.29)	−0.238 (1.95)*	−0.251 (1.90)*
Terms of trade	−0.028 (6.66)***	−0.025 (6.05)***	−0.022 (4.29)***	−0.011 (1.99)**	−0.002 (0.45)	−0.026 (5.65)***	−0.028 (6.15)***
Investment (in percent of GDP)	0.087 (1.73)*	0.066 (1.17)	−0.013 (0.32)	0.015 (0.59)	0.016 (0.74)	0.101 (2.52)**	0.088 (1.92)*
Initial gross primary enrollment rate	0.075 (1.88)*	0.071 (1.86)*	0.018 (0.64)	0.014 (1.34)	0.064 (4.20)***	0.003 (0.22)	
Initial gross secondary enrollment rate	−0.068 (1.99)**	−0.089 (1.42)	0.053 (2.03)**	0.046 (2.87)***	0.064 (4.61)***	0.027 (1.17)	
Wages and salaries (in percent of total expenditure)	−0.102 (2.20)**	−0.044 (0.94)	−0.066 (1.69)*	−0.091 (3.24)***	−0.053 (2.54)**	−0.035 (0.96)	−0.102 (2.10)**
Transfers and subsidies (in percent of total expenditure)	−0.022 (0.44)	0.005 (0.08)	−0.205 (5.40)***	−0.163 (4.86)***	0.061 (3.03)***	−0.053 (1.00)	−0.021 (0.37)
Interest payment (in percent of total expenditure)	−0.032 (0.62)	−0.059 (0.95)	0.032 (0.83)	−0.02 (0.65)	0.047 (2.17)**	−0.057 (1.50)	−0.03 (0.61)
Capital spending (in percent of total expenditure)	0.081 (1.99)**	0.075 (1.65)*	0.061 (1.92)*	0.021 (0.91)	0.012 (0.68)	0.051 (1.75)	0.082 (2.14)**
Tax revenue (in percent of total expenditure)	0.042 (1.73)*	0.041 (0.92)	0.027 (1.01)	−0.046 (2.98)***	0.027 (1.86)	−0.012 (0.61)	0.043 (1.38)
Transition economies dummy	9.122 (4.44)***	10.282 (3.55)***	8.716 (4.17)***	−1.74 (1.38)	8.484 (7.60)***	5.285 (2.81)***	
High-inflation dummy	−1.205 (2.11)**	−0.737 (1.20)	−2.082 (4.05)***	−2.194 (4.31)***	−0.892 (3.26)***	−0.911 (1.68)*	−1.23 (2.16)**
Domestic financing (in percent of GDP)		−0.373 (2.49)**					
External financing (in percent of GDP)		−0.062 (0.17)					
Constant			0.876 (−0.24)	8.238 (3.43)***	−9.909 (4.99)***	4.269 (−1.35)	3.557 0.00
Number of observations	193	172	332	332	331	193	193
R^2	0.63[b]	0.59[b]	0.56		0.79		
Hansen J	0.074	1.598					

Source: Authors' calculations.
[a] Robust z statistics in parentheses.
[b] Uncentered R^2.
* Significant at 10%.
** Significant at 5%.
*** Significant at 1%.

by the negative effect of the interaction between the fiscal deficit and the low-deficit dummy.[35]

Initial per capita GDP is positively related to growth. There is therefore absence of (conditional) convergence. Population growth is negatively related to growth of per capita income; domestic market expansion due to population growth does not lead to higher growth. The terms of trade have little direct effect on growth. An improvement in the terms of trade does not significantly increase per capita income growth, although an improvement in the terms of trade will increase national income. The initial gross primary school enrollment rate, a proxy for human capital, shows a positive effect on per capita growth but secondary school enrollment is not associated with higher per capita growth.

Gross investment is a determinant of growth: the growth rate of per capita GDP increases by almost 1% when the gross investment-to-GDP ratio increases by 10%.

The composition of government spending also affects growth. An increase by 1% in the ratio of total spending on wages to total expenditure reduces growth by 0.1%, ceteris paribus. A 1% increase in capital spending in total government outlays increases per capita GDP growth by less than 0.1%.

Decomposition into domestically and externally financed components of the deficit shows that the composition of deficit financing affects growth. Reduced deficits financed from domestic sources increase growth: a reduction in domestic deficit financing by 1% increases per capita GDP growth by 0.4%. That is, expansionary fiscal contraction is associated with reductions in domestic deficit financing. Changes in external deficit financing, however, do not have a significant effect on growth.

The composition of government revenue affects growth. Achieving fiscal consolidations by increasing the share of tax revenues to total revenue including grants is beneficial for growth. In addition, grants and non-tax revenue tend to be negatively correlated with tax revenue collection.[36]

The direct effect of inflation on growth is nonlinear: high-inflation countries grow less than low-inflation countries. Countries with inflation above 20% have lower per capita growth by more than one percentage point.

---

[35]The Wald test of the joint significance of the two coefficients rejects the hypothesis that fiscal consolidations increase growth in low-deficit countries.

[36]See Gupta et al. (2003).

The Investment Equation

The results for the growth equation show that investment affects growth. However, when investigating transmission channels, we ask whether fiscal contractions increase investment. The answer to this question is provided by the estimation of the investment equation. The results for the investment equation are reported in Table 3, which shows that, overall, fiscal contractions *do not* affect investment. Neither the overall fiscal deficit variable nor its interaction with a dummy for low-deficit countries is significantly different from zero.

However, when the deficit financing components are examined separately, reduced domestic deficit financing increases investment: a reduction in domestic deficit financing ratio by 1% increases the investment ratio by half a percentage point.[37] Both initial primary and secondary school enrollment ratios appear statistically significantly correlated with the investment ratio, whereas the terms of trade have no effects on investment.

Inflation reduces investment. The effect is nonlinear. A 10% increase in the rate of inflation reduces the investment ratio by 0.01%. The nonlinear effect of inflation on investment is larger: if the annual inflation rate exceeds 20%, the investment ratio is lower by 2.5% than in countries with low inflation.

Weak governance affects investment through corruption. In countries with high levels of corruption, an increase of 10% in the growth of the product of government spending and the index of corruption reduces the investment ratio by 1.5% of GDP. This confirms previously reported observations that provision of government-supplied goods and services in poor-governance countries is associated with wasteful spending that reduces investment.

The Inflation Equation

By reducing reliance on inflationary financing, fiscal contractions can reduce inflation, which can increase growth directly and indirectly through increased investment. The results of the estimate of the inflation equation are reported in Table 4. Large fiscal deficits are associated with higher inflation. An increase in the fiscal deficit by 1% of GDP in high-deficit countries increases inflation by 0.1%. However, when budget deficits are low, increasing the fiscal deficit has no significant effect

---

[37] It appears that fiscal consolidations that reduce domestic deficit financing may stimulate private investment through a change in the composition of credit in the economy.

Table 3. Investment Equation Regression: Dependent Variable—Average Investment
(In percent of GDP) [a]

	Baseline GMM 1	GMM 2	LSDV 3	FGLS 4	Robust Regression 5	EC2SLS 6	2SLS 7
Fiscal deficit (in percent of GDP)	0.068 (0.64)		0.035 (0.80)	0.013 (0.18)	−0.056 (2.24)**	0.084 (0.88)	0.070 (0.70)
Fiscal deficit in low-deficit countries (in percent of GDP)	0.025 (0.17)	0.342 (1.44)	−0.143 (1.00)	−0.496 (2.08)**	−0.049 (0.60)	0.02 (0.11)	0.025 (0.14)
Initial per capita GDP level	0.0000059 (4.38)***	2.0E-06 (0.77)	−4.1E-06 (−3.19)***	1.6 E-06 (0.98)	6.2E-06 (8.37)***	5.0E-06 (1.26)	1.4E-06 0.00
Population growth rate	−0.111 (0.95)	0.138 (0.55)	0.055 (0.65)	−0.077 (0.55)	0.039 (0.81)	−0.154 (0.96)	−0.121 (0.74)
Terms of trade	−0.0002 (0.03)	0.011 (1.83)*	−0.001 (0.23)	0.005 (0.49)	−0.002 (0.49)	0.0004 (0.06)	0.0003 (0.05)
Initial gross primary enrollment rate	0.191 (9.04)***	0.316 (6.22)***	0.418 (17.53)***	0.09 (5.06)***	0.483 (35.08)***	−0.014 (0.26)	
Initial gross secondary enrollment rate	0.15 (4.61)***	−0.045 (0.51)	−0.21 (7.69)***	0.038 (1.48)	−0.304 (19.23)***	0.089 (1.15)	
Change in the product of total expenditure* corruption	−0.149 (2.21)**	0.182 (0.65)	−0.128 (1.91)*	−0.148 (1.26)	0.01 (0.24)	−0.153 (2.18)**	−0.147 (2.07)**
Inflation rate	−0.001 (2.17)**	−0.0002 (0.33)	−0.00004 (0.09)	−0.0008 (0.11)	−0.0007 (0.25)	−0.001 (1.60)	−0.001 (1.48)
High-inflation dummy	−2.38 (3.19)***	−2.007 (2.00)**	−1.917 (3.38)***	−2.648 (3.08)***	−1.888 (5.76)***	−2.332 (3.68)***	−2.362 (3.68)***
Transition economies dummy	−14.911 (8.59)***	−7.835 (3.31)***	−16.409 (8.87)***	−9.098 (5.03)***	−14.229 (13.30)***	−11.015 (2.06)**	
Domestic financing (in percent of GDP)		−0.619 (2.06)**					
External financing (in percent of GDP)		0.247 (0.36)					
Constant			8.274 (4.43)***	12.41 (7.36)***	8.197 (7.59)***	18.772 (5.37)***	19.169 0.00
Number of observations	272	241	413	413	413	272	272
R^2	0.97[b]	0.96[b]	0.77		0.93		
Hansen J	0.098	3.006					

Source: Authors' calculations.
[a] Robust *z* statistics in parentheses.
[b] Uncentered R^2.
* Significant at 10%.
** Significant at 5%.
*** Significant at 1%.

Table 4. Inflation Equation Regression: Dependent Variable—Rate of Annual Inflation[a]

	Baseline GMM 1	GMM 2	LSDV 3	FGLS 4	Robust Regression 5	EC2SLS 6	2SLS 7
Fiscal deficit	0.106		0.025	0.023	0.004	0.048	0.096
(in percent of GDP)	(3.46)***		(6.41)***	(6.36)***	(4.15)***	(6.38)***	(6.23)***
Fiscal deficit in low-deficit	−0.114	−0.096	−0.029	−0.027	−0.006	−0.052	−0.103
countries (in percent of GDP)	(3.38)***	(3.36)***	(2.44)**	(2.36)**	(2.03)**	(3.25)***	(4.26)***
Initial per capita GDP level	4.0E-07	4.2E-07	−6.7E-08	8.3E-09	−2.7E-08	4.5E-09	−1.9E-06
	(2.55)**	(1.54)	(0.79)	(0.13)	(1.37)	(0.07)	0.00
Terms of trade	−0.001	−0.001	−0.0002	−0.001	0.001	−0.001	−0.001
	(1.31)	(1.02)	(0.32)	(1.94)*	(9.49)***	(2.42)**	(1.07)
Low-deficit dummy	0.534	0.387	0.087	0.085	0.008	0.261	0.484
	(3.29)***	(2.79)***	(1.63)	(1.86)*	(0.65)	(4.02)***	(4.54)***
Transition economies dummy	−0.989	−0.163	−0.05	0.112	0.087	0.116	
	(2.25)**	(0.21)	(0.30)	(1.97)**	(2.21)**	(1.58)	
Exchange rate fluctuation	−0.011	−0.008	−0.013	−0.014	−0.004	−0.013	−0.011
	(3.45)***	(3.54)***	(14.23)***	(16.76)***	(19.05)***	(11.49)***	(7.09)***
Openness index	−0.385	−0.289	−0.004	0.015	−0.004	−0.043	−0.341
	(2.26)**	(1.49)	(0.12)	(0.60)	(0.61)	(1.03)	(3.61)***
Labor ratio	−0.008	0.002	−0.004	−0.002	0.005	−0.004	−0.012
	(0.36)	(0.04)	(0.28)	(0.61)	(1.54)	(1.06)	(0.54)
Domestic financing		0.107					
(in percent of GDP)		(2.06)**					
External financing		0.088					
(in percent of GDP)		(1.29)					
Constant	0.686	−0.669	0.051	0.048	−0.339	0.042	0.672
	(0.59)	(0.27)	(0.07)	(0.31)	(2.08)**	(0.24)	0.00
Number of observations	275	241	417	417	417	275	275
R^2	0.50[b]	0.55[b]	0.59		0.76		
Hansen J	0.12	2.13					

Source: Authors' calculations.
[a] Robust z statistics in parentheses.
[b] Uncentered R^2.
* Significant at 10%.
** Significant at 5%.
*** Significant at 1%.

on inflation. The degree of trade openness, currency depreciation,[38] and a transition economy dummy reduce inflation.[39]

The Exchange Rate Equation

Results for the exchange rate equation are presented in Table 5. Fiscal deficits are associated with nominal exchange rate depreciation in both high- and low-deficit countries. A 1% increase in the deficit ratio leads to an exchange rate depreciation of 2.5%, irrespective of whether the country has a high deficit. Expenditure composition also affects the exchange rate. While higher wages and capital expenditures lead to exchange rate appreciation, spending on transfers is associated with currency depreciation. We also find that receiving a large share of overall revenue in the form of grants is associated with a negative effect on exchange rate stability. Increasing government size in a high-corruption country is also detrimental for exchange rate stability and leads to a more depreciated currency. These results should however be taken with caution, as variables possibly omitted from the equation could be important. However, these variables should not affect the significance and the sign of the fiscal deficit variable, which is robust to alternative specifications of this equation.

Transition Economies

We have controlled for the different initial conditions and experiences in the transition economies in our sample. Growth was higher over the sample period (1990–2001) in transition economies but

---

[38] The correlation between low inflation and currency depreciations is high in the sample (the correlation coefficient is 0.67). This can be attributed to the absence of a dynamic specification in the model. The results in both the exchange rate and inflation equations need to be qualified in this respect. At the same time, an overvalued exchange rate reduces exports, which can undermine fiscal stability and lead to inflationary financing of the budget if external deficit financing is limited. On the other hand, depreciation enhances fiscal stability through increased exports, and inflation declines when the need for inflationary financing is reduced. Another reason why exchange rate depreciation is associated with lower inflation is that, if the currency depreciates for external reasons, the authorities have incentives to bring inflation under control in order to gain in real terms from the depreciation. Otherwise the nominal depreciation would be offset by inflation and the real exchange rate could continue to appreciate. Aside from these considerations, we use data on the official exchange rate, which may deviate from an unofficial exchange rate that may be pertinent for a substantial part of foreign transactions.

[39] The net effect of being a transition economy becomes negative once we include the fiscal balance. It seems that in these countries, which had a higher average deficit (8% as opposed to the average 6%), it is the fiscal deficit that caused the high inflation. Once this effect is taken out, the consequence of being a transition economy is not negative for inflation. Perhaps this is because core inflation (defined as inflation not caused by fiscal policy) was lower than in other countries with more market rigidities.

Table 5. Exchange Rate Equation Regression: Dependent Variable—Exchange Rate Appreciation[a]

	Baseline GMM 1	GMM 2	LSDV 3	FGLS 4	Robust Regression 5	EC2SLS 6	2SLS 7
Fiscal deficit (in percent of GDP)	-2.350 (1.82)*		-0.361 (1.38)	-0.254 (1.07)	-0.528 (2.92)***	-0.932 (1.59)	-3.968 (2.61)***
Fiscal deficit in low-deficit countries (in percent of GDP)	1.871 (1.63)	2.743 (1.50)	0.078 (0.12)	0.019 (0.03)	0.323 (0.71)	0.470 (0.48)	3.250 (1.90)*
Terms of trade	-0.065 (2.28)**	-0.036 (0.91)	-0.095 (3.39)***	-0.074 (2.89)***	-0.094 (4.86)***	-0.075 (2.66)***	-0.068 (1.88)*
Low-deficit dummy	-3.828 (0.66)	-8.41 (0.99)	-1.185 (0.33)	2.082 (0.75)	-5.409 (2.15)**	1.353 (0.31)	-8.788 (1.05)
Transition economies dummy	-26.848 (0.84)	76.209 (3.01)***	-39.922 (2.37)**	3.43 (0.89)	-24.632 (2.11)**	27.199 (3.47)***	
Openness index	-25.985 (1.93)	-5.75 (0.30)	-24.099 (2.92)***	-2.457 (0.83)	-15.874 (2.78)***	-2.167 (0.59)	-15.909 (1.22)
Labor ratio	4.338 (3.52)***	2.391 (1.09)	2.013 (2.54)**	0.652 (2.99)***	0.351 (0.64)	0.288 (0.94)	3.505 (2.25)**
Debt to GDP	0.052 (0.52)	-0.049 (0.29)	-0.041 (0.31)	-0.226 (1.81)	-0.404 (4.42)***	-0.101 (0.79)	0.042 (0.27)
Change in the product of total expenditure (in percent of GDP) and the corruption control index	0.708 (1.86)*	1.681 (2.00)**	0.103 (0.62)	-0.012 (0.08)	0.089 (0.77)	0.207 (1.03)	1.295 (2.71)***
Wages and salaries (in percent of GDP)	0.878 (2.24)**	0.934 (1.91)	0.464 (2.01)**	0.607 (3.84)***	0.495 (3.10)***	0.968 (4.54)***	1.081 (2.83)***
Transfers and subsidies (in percent of GDP)	-0.998 (2.41)**	-1.587 (1.86)	-0.726 (2.65)***	-0.239 (1.45)	-0.182 (0.96)	-0.887 (2.89)***	-1.51 (3.10)***
Capital spending (in percent of GDP)	0.691 (2.18)**	0.358 (0.76)	0.382 (2.24)**	0.384 (3.28)***	0.411 (3.50)***	0.687 (4.40)***	0.741 (2.59)***
Interest payment (in percent of GDP)	0.147 (0.47)	-0.136 (0.38)	-0.21 (0.87)	0.008 (0.05)	-0.222 (1.34)	0.317 (1.74)	-0.104 (0.26)
Grants (in percent of GDP)	-0.248 (2.56)**	-0.242 (2.54)**	-0.252 (4.08)***	-0.151 (3.52)***	-0.12 (2.80)***	-0.153 (2.39)**	-0.316 (2.76)***
Domestic financing (in percent of GDP)		-5.027 (2.07)**					
External financing (in percent of GDP)		-1.747 (0.52)					
Constant	-158.023 (2.22)**	-139.121 (1.17)	-29.269 (0.78)	-51.756 (3.35)***	21.614 (0.83)	-51.892 (2.57)**	-158.026 (2.09)**
Number of observations	199	178	317	317	317	199	199
R^2	0.65[b]	0.43[b]	0.42		0.59		
Hansen J	2.46	1.06					

Source: Authors' calculations.
[a] Robust z statistics in parentheses.
[b] Uncentered R^2.
* Significant at 10%.
** Significant at 5%.
*** Significant at 1%.

investment was lower (Fig. 1). Other things being equal, the direct effect of being a transition economy increased growth sufficiently to more than offset the lower growth attributable to lower investment and inflation. Being a transition economy was therefore on average beneficial for growth, while the effect of fiscal policy on growth was not statistically different between transition and nontransition economies.[40]

Robustness Analysis

Alternative Estimation Methods

We assessed the robustness of the empirical results using alternative estimators. These include the standard fixed effects estimator based on dummy variable least squares, a feasible FGLS estimator that takes into account the possibility that the residual distribution departs from normality, a robust last absolute distance (LAD) estimator, the error component two-stage least-squares estimator, and a fixed effect instrumental variable estimator.[41] The latter two methods allow the correlation of the error terms across equations to be nonzero, so there can be feedbacks between growth and the other macroeconomic variables. Results from the alternative estimation methods confirm the previous findings and are presented in Tables 2–5.

The results of the robustness analysis confirm the finding of the baseline specification. We continue to find that fiscal consolidations are beneficial for growth in high-deficit countries. The main channel through which fiscal policy affects growth remains increased total factor productivity, including effects through a more productive composition of government spending. Good governance affects the total investment-to-GDP ratio. Government size becomes negatively related to investment when corruption is widespread. Inflation has an independent negative effect on growth and private investment, besides the indirect effect through fiscal deficits.

---

[40]We tested the significance of the introduction into the growth equation of the interaction between fiscal policy and the transition economies dummy, and the associated coefficient was found to be not significant.

[41]Robust regression is used to correct for large outliers and observations with large leverage values in the regression. The robust regression method adopted in this paper uses iteratively reweighted least squares to obtain robust estimation of both the regression coefficients and the standard errors by assigning lower weights to observations with higher influences.

Figure 1. Fiscal Balance, Growth, Investment, Inflation, and Exchange Rate Appreciation, 1990–2001

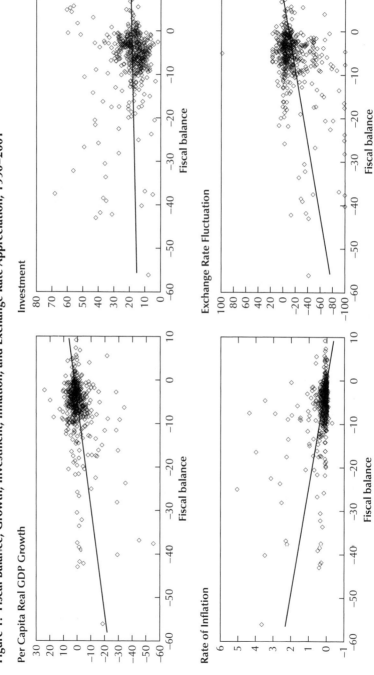

Alternative Definition of High-Deficit Countries

We also carried out an alternative robustness analysis by using a different definition for the low-deficit dummy and its interaction with the fiscal deficit. In the baseline regression the definition of this variable is based on the overall deficit (countries with an average fiscal deficit below 2.5% of GDP are classified as low-deficit countries). The advantage of using the overall deficit rather than a decomposition of its domestic and externally financed components is that this is a better proxy for public debt sustainability. Large fiscal deficits, no matter how they are financed, can become unsustainable when reflected in high levels of the net present value of public debt relative to GDP.[42] The sustainability of public debt is expected to be a major influence underlying the effects of fiscal policy on growth, with countries benefiting most from fiscal contractions when their debt positions are not sustainable (see also Giavazzi and Pagano, 1990).

However, besides the fiscal deficit size, the composition of fiscal deficit financing sources is also relevant for fiscal sustainability—as the results above have shown. Deficits mostly financed from domestic sources tend to be inflationary and to increase real interest rates, while concessionary external financing of the deficit has more limited negative macroeconomic consequences, except regarding exchange rate appreciation. Thus, high levels of domestic financing of the deficit as a share of GDP are more inhibiting for growth than the overall fiscal deficit.

We accordingly reestimated the recursive system Eqs. (3)–(6) using a dummy that reflects low levels of *domestic* financing of the fiscal deficit as a share of GDP. As in the baseline regression, this variable is interacted with the fiscal deficit to gauge the nonlinear effect of fiscal policy on growth. Results from the revised estimates largely confirm the findings of the baseline model.[43] The main difference from the findings of the baseline regressions is that the effect of domestic financing of the deficit on gross investment becomes less significant. The results suggest that fiscal contractions increase growth in countries with large domestic deficit financing, confirming the nonlinear relationship between fiscal policy and growth as reported in Gupta et al. (2002, 2004).

---

[42] In principle, one should use the net present value of public debt as a share of GDP to identify countries with initial fiscal vulnerabilities. However, this information is not available for many of our sample countries.

[43] These results are not presented in the paper but are available upon request from the authors.

Analysis of Total Effects

The above results for the different equations estimated can be combined using the properties of a recursive system (path analysis). The total effects can be reported for each variable, with the total contribution of each variable to the change in the dependent variable decomposed into direct effects and indirect effects that are mediated by other variables. Following the path of each effect allows identification of the channels through which fiscal policy affects growth.

Table 6 presents the total effects of the exogenous variables on the four endogenous variables: growth, investment, inflation, and exchange rate movements. Overall, deficit reductions increase growth in countries with high initial deficits and do not significantly affect growth in other countries. That is, expansionary fiscal contractions occur when deficits are initially large.

The total effect of fiscal deficits on growth (the sum of the direct and indirect effects) is larger than the direct effect of fiscal deficit on growth, although the additional indirect effect is small. The largest indirect effects on growth are related to high-inflation and transition countries. Primary and secondary enrollment both have a direct positive effect on investment, which, through the growth equation, increases per capita GDP growth (that is, there is an indirect positive effect of education to growth).

Table 7 presents direct and indirect effects of endogenous variables on the other dependent variables in the system. We see that indirect effects are small in size. The indirect effects of inflation on growth and investment and of exchange rate movements on inflation are negative. The total effect of inflation and exchange rate movements on the level of investment and total factor productivity growth is slightly higher than the direct negative effect.[44]

Finally, we have noted that the investment transmission channel is present, with a reduction in the ratio of domestic deficit financing to GDP of 1% increasing the corresponding investment ratio by half a percentage point. The total effect of fiscal policy on growth through the investment channel, measured by the product of the coefficient of the fiscal deficit in the investment equation and the coefficient of investment in the growth equation as $(0.61 \times 0.09) = 0.05$, compares, however, with the effect of fiscal policy on growth through the direct factor productivity channel, as measured by the coefficient of the fiscal deficit in the growth equation of 0.19. That is, the factor productivity channel is some four times more effective than the investment channel.

---

[44]This result is consistent with previous findings for industrial countries that point to the importance for growth and fiscal sustainability of combined fiscal tightening and real exchange rate depreciations (Lambertini and Tavares, 2001; Hjelm, 2002).

Table 6. Total Effects Decomposition: Exogenous Variables[a]

	Fiscal Deficit	Fiscal Deficit in Low-Deficit Countries	Initial Per Capita Real GDP	Population Growth	Terms of Trade	Primary Enrollment	Secondary Enrollment	Wages and Salaries	Transfer and Subsidies	Interest Payment
Total effects										
Per capita GDP growth	-0.19	0.22	0.00	-0.25	-0.03	0.09	-0.05	-0.10	0.00	0.00
Investment[b]	-0.10	0.07	0.01	0.00	-0.20	190.00	150.00	0.01	0.01	0.00
Inflation	0.14	-0.10	0.00	0.00	0.00	0.00	0.00	-0.01	-0.01	0.00
Exchange rate appreciation	-2.30	0.00	0.00	0.00	-0.06	0.00	0.00	0.87	0.99	0.00
Direct effects										
Per capita GDP growth	-0.19	0.22	0.00	-0.25	-0.03	0.08	-0.07	-0.10	0.00	0.00
Investment[b]	0.00	0.00	0.01	0.00	-0.20	190.00	150.00	0.00	0.00	0.00
Inflation	0.12	-0.10	0.00	0.00	0.00	0.00	0.00	0.00	0.00	0.00
Exchange rate appreciation	-2.30	0.00	0.00	0.00	-0.06	0.00	0.00	0.87	0.99	0.00
Indirect effects										
Per capita GDP growth	0.00	0.00	0.00	0.00	0.00	0.02	0.01	0.00	0.00	0.00
Investment[b]	-0.10	0.07	0.00	0.00	0.00	0.00	0.00	0.01	0.01	0.00
Inflation	0.03	0.00	0.00	0.00	0.00	0.00	0.00	-0.01	-0.01	0.00
Exchange rate appreciation	0.00	0.00	0.00	0.00	0.00	0.00	0.00	0.00	0.00	0.00

Table 6 (concluded)

	Capital Expenditure	Tax Revenue	Transition Dummy	Excessive Inflation	Exchange Rate Appreciation	Low-Deficit Dummy	Openness Index	Labor Ratio	Debt to GDP
Total effects									
Per capita GDP growth	0.08	0.04	7.80	-1.41	-0.01	0.00	0.00	0.00	0.00
Investment[b]	0.01	0.00	-14899.56	-2380.00	-147.99	-0.50	0.02	0.03	0.00
Inflation	-0.01	0.00	-0.62	0.00	-0.01	0.70	-0.03	-0.05	0.00
Exchange rate appreciation	0.69	0.24	0.00	0.00	0.71	0.00	-25.90	4.30	0.00
Direct effects									
Per capita GDP growth	0.08	0.04	9.10	-1.20	0.00	0.00	0.00	0.00	0.00
Investment[b]	0.00	0.00	-14900.00	-2380.00	-148.00	0.00	0.00	0.00	0.00
Inflation	0.00	0.00	-0.62	0.00	0.00	0.70	-0.32	0.00	0.00
Exchange rate appreciation	0.69	0.24	0.00	0.00	0.71	0.00	-25.90	4.30	0.00
Indirect effects									
Per capita GDP growth	0.00	0.00	-1.30	-0.21	-0.01	0.00	0.00	0.00	0.00
Investment[b]	0.01	0.00	0.44	0.00	0.01	-0.50	0.02	0.03	0.00
Inflation	-0.01	0.00	0.00	0.00	-0.01	0.00	0.28	-0.05	0.00
Exchange rate appreciation	0.00	0.00	0.00	0.00	0.00	0.00	0.00	0.00	0.00

Source: Authors' calculations.
[a] Matrix coefficients are from baseline regressions.
[b] Coefficients are multiplied by a factor of 1,000.

Table 7. Total Effects Decomposition: Endogenous Variables[a]

	Per Capita GDP Growth	Investment	Inflation	Exchange Rate Appreciation
Total effects				
Per capita GDP growth	0.000	87.000	–0.062	0.001
Investment	0.000	0.000	–0.709	0.008
Inflation	0.000	0.000	0.000	–11.000
Exchange rate appreciation	0.000	0.000	0.000	0.000
Direct effects				
Per capita GDP growth	0.000	87.000	0.000	0.000
Investment	0.000	0.000	–0.709	0.000
Inflation	0.000	0.000	0.000	–11.000
Exchange rate appreciation	0.000	0.000	0.000	0.000
Indirect effects				
Per capita GDP growth	0.000	0.000	–0.062	0.001
Investment	0.000	0.000	0.000	0.008
Inflation	0.000	0.000	0.000	0.000
Exchange rate appreciation	0.000	0.000	0.000	0.000

Source: Authors' calculations.

[a] Matrix coefficients are from baseline regressions. All coefficients are multiplied by a factor of 1,000.

6. Conclusions and Policy Implications

The empirical results that we have reported reveal the presence of expansionary fiscal contractions in high-deficit, low-income countries. Using different procedures, we have thereby confirmed the conclusions regarding fiscal policy and growth in low-income countries of Gupta et al. (2002, 2004).

Our objective has been to identify the transmission channels between fiscal policy and growth that underlie the expansionary fiscal contractions observed in low-income countries. We have proposed that, contrary to the case of high-income countries where investment is the primary channel linking fiscal policy to growth, in low-income countries factor productivity is expected to be the principal fiscal policy transmission channel for increased growth. The expectations of a diminished role for investment and a primary role for factor productivity have been based on poor governance attributes that have been characteristic of low-income countries. Poor governance is expected to discourage private investment, although other considerations as well suggest that in low-income countries investment is expected to be a relatively ineffective channel linking fiscal policy to growth. For reasons that we have set out, another consequence expected from poor governance is that when public expenditure, particularly on wages, declines, factor productivity will increase.

We find, as predicted, that although investment affects growth, investment is not the primary channel for expansionary fiscal contraction in low-income countries. Factor productivity is the primary fiscal policy transmission channel, expressed directly in a positive effect on growth when deficits are initially high. Increased factor productivity is also particularly related to reductions in the wage component of public spending.

The results support a governance-related explanation as the reason for expansionary fiscal contractions in low-income countries. The outcome that increased factor productivity and not investment is the primary transmission channel in high-deficit low-income countries is consistent with the evidence on poor governance in these countries with respect to public spending and public administration.

The expansionary fiscal contractions occur when the domestically financed component of the deficit is reduced. This implies that high levels of fiscal deficits financed from domestic sources are counterproductive for growth. Reductions in deficits financed through external concessionary budgetary support have no significant direct effect on growth.[45]

Because expansionary fiscal contractions in high-income countries occur principally through increased private investment, and because investment in low-income countries is not a primary transmission channel from fiscal policy to growth, governments in low-income countries might believe that benefits from increased growth achieved through fiscal contractions are not available. However, while the channel for growth through increased investment may be absent or minor in low-income countries, the results reported in this study show that governance attributes introduce a scope for expansionary fiscal contractions through the channel of increased factor productivity. Consequently, sound fiscal policies can promote growth in low-income countries that have high budget deficits.

---

[45] There may be an indirect positive effect on growth through an increased share of capital spending in total government expenditure. The finding that concessionary budget support did not appear to significantly affect growth in the 1990s raises issues that are not our major concern here. For an overview of these issues, see Easterly (2001). International-agency surveillance procedures have been a response to the ineffectiveness of external assistance in increasing growth (see, for example, Hillman, 2002).

Appendix A. Data Sources, Description of Variables, and Country Sample

Variable	Description	Source[a]
Terms of trade	Terms of trade index. Annual.	WEO
Growth rate	Growth rate of real per capita GDP (PPP). To avoid cyclically related fluctuations, the growth rate of per capita GDP is the average growth rate over the 3-year period.	WEO
Initial per capita GDP	Real GDP per capita in 1900.	WEO
Exchange rate fluctuations	Percentage changes in nominal exchange rates. Annual.	WEO
Openness	Sum of exports and imports in percent of GDP.	WEO
Labor ratio	Labor force in percent of total population. Annual data.	WDI
Inflation	Annual percentage changes in CPI.	WEO
Fiscal deficit	Fiscal deficit in percent of GDP (negative if in surplus). Note that grants are classified as part of government's revenue. Thus, receipt of a grant reduces the overall fiscal deficit. Annual data.	SR
Low-deficit countries	Countries with an average fiscal deficit below 2.5% of GDP during the sample period.	SR
Total revenue	General government's total revenue including grants.	WDI
Initial primary school enrollment	Gross primary school enrollment rate in 1990.	WDI
Initial secondary school enrollment	Gross secondary school enrollment rate in 1990.	WDI
Population	Total population.	WDI
Investment	Gross investment (public and private) in percent of GDP.	WEO

Appendix A (concluded)

Variable	Description	Source[a]
Composition of expenditure	Wages and salaries, transfers and subsidies, interest payments, and capital spending. Expressed in percent of total expenditure in the growth equation, and in percent of GDP in the exchange rate equation.	SR
Tax revenue	Tax revenue in percent of GDP.	SR
Transition economy dummy	1 for transition economies; 0 for nontransition economies.	WEO
High inflation dummy	1 for countries with the average annual inflation rate over 20%, otherwise 0.	
Domestic financing	Domestic financing includes domestic bank and nonbank financing. Expressed in percent of GDP.	SR
External financing	External financing includes concessional loans from multilateral and bilateral donors, and nonconcessional loans and bond issuance. Expressed in percent of GDP.	SR
Corruption	We use an indicator based on the International Country Risk index of corruption. This is defined in terms of excessive patronage, nepotism, job reservation, secret party funding, and suspiciously close ties between politics and business. Countries with highest levels of corruption have a score of zero while countries with no corruption have a score of six. We choose a threshold of two for constructing the corruption dummy variable. This threshold is consistent with additional existing information on high corruption countries in our sample. Robustness analysis is carried out using alternative thresholds with no significant change.	ICR
Debt to GDP	Stock of external debt in percent of GDP.	WEO
Democracy	This variable is based on scores of how governments are responsible to people. The highest score (6 points) is for countries that have alternating parties in democratic government and the lowest score is for autocratic regimes. In between, governance ranges from dominated democracy to a one-party state.	ICR

[a]Data are taken from IMF staff reports (SR), IMF World Economic Outlook (WEO) database, World Bank World Development Indicator (WDI) database, and the International Country Risk (ICR) index by the PRS Group.

List of Countries in the Sample

Albania, Armenia, Benin, Bolivia, Burkina Faso, Cambodia, Cameroon, the Central African Republic, Chad, Djibouti, Ethiopia, The Gambia, Ghana, Georgia, Guinea, Guinea-Bissau, Guyana, Honduras, Kenya, the Kyrgyz Republic, Laos, Lesotho, Macedonia (FYR), Madagascar, Malawi, Mali, Mauritania, Moldova, Mozambique, Nicaragua, Niger, Rwanda, São Tomé and Príncipe, Senegal, Tajikistan, Tanzania, Vietnam, Yemen, and Zambia.

References

Abed, G.T., Gupta, S. (Eds.), 2002. Governance, Corruption, and Economic Performance. International Monetary Fund, Washington, DC.

Abed, G.T., et al., 1998. Fiscal reform in low-income countries: experience under IMF-supported programs. IMF Occasional Paper No. 160. International Monetary Fund, Washington, DC.

Acemoglu, D., Verdier, T., 1998. Reward structures and the allocation of talent. American Economic Review 39, 17–33.

Adam, C.S., Bevan, D.L., 2000. Fiscal policy design in low-income countries. Paper prepared for UNU/WIDER research project on New Fiscal Policies for Poverty Reduction and Growth, Helsinki.

Adam, C.S., Bevan, D.L., 2001. Nonlinear effects of public deficits on growth. Paper prepared at Cornell/ISPE Conference, Ithaca, NY.

Alesina, A., 1997. Fiscal adjustments in OECD countries: composition and macroeconomic effects. IMF Staff Papers 44, 210–248.

Alesina, A., Perotti, R., 1995. Fiscal expansion and fiscal adjustments in OECD countries. Economic Policy: A European Forum 21, 205–248.

Alesina, A., Ardagna, S., Perotti, R., Schiantarelli, F., 1999. Fiscal policy, profits, and investment. NBER Working Paper No. W7207. National Bureau of Economic Research, Cambridge, MA.

Baltagi, B., 1995. Econometric Analysis of Panel Data. Wiley, Chichester, NY.

Barro, R., Sala-i-Martin, X., 1995. Economic Growth. McGraw-Hill, NY.

Bengoa, M., Sanchez-Robles, B., 2003. Foreign direct investment, economic freedom, and growth: new evidence from Latin America. European Journal of Political Economy 19, 529–545. Special Issue on Economic Freedom.

Berg, A., Krueger, A., 2003. Trade, growth and poverty: a selective study. IMF Working Paper No. 03/30. International Monetary Fund, Washington, DC.

Bertola, G., Drazen, A., 1993. Trigger points and budget cuts: explaining the effects of fiscal austerity. American Economic Review 83, 11–26.

Catao, L., Terrones, M., 2003. Fiscal deficits and inflation. IMF Working Paper No. 03/65. International Monetary Fund, Washington, DC.

Chauvet, L., 2002. Socio-political instability and the allocation of international aid by donors. European Journal of Political Economy 19, 33–59.

Dabla-Norris, E., Wade, P., 2002. Production, rent seeking and wealth distribution. In: Abed, G.T., Gupta, S. (Eds.), Governance, Corruption, and Economic Performance. International Monetary Fund, Washington, DC, pp. 439–457.

de Haan, J., Sturm, J.-E., 2000. On the relationship between economic freedom and economic growth. European Journal of Political Economy 16, 215–241.

de Haan, J., Sturm, J.-E., 2003. Does more democracy lead to greater economic freedom? New evidence for developing countries. European Journal of Political Economy 19, 547–563. Special Issue on Economic Freedom.

de la Fuente, A., 1997. Fiscal policy and growth in the OECD. CEPR Discussion Paper No. 1755. Centre for Economic Policy Research, London.

Del Monte, A., Papagni, E., 2001. Public expenditure, corruption and economic growth: the case of Italy. European Journal of Political Economy 17, 1–16.

Drazen, A., 2001. Political Economy in Macroeconomics. MIT Press, Cambridge, MA.

Duncan, O.D., 1975. Introduction to Structural Equations Model. Academic Press, New York.

Easterly, W., 2001. The Elusive Quest for Growth: Economists' Adventures and Misadventures in the Tropics. MIT Press, Cambridge, MA.

Economides, G., Philippopoulos, A., Price, S., 2003. How elections affect fiscal policy: revisiting the mechanism. European Journal of Political Economy 19, 777–792.

Fischer, S., 1993. Role of macroeconomic factors in growth. Journal of Monetary Economics 32, 485–512.

Fischer, S., Sahay, R., Végh, C., 2002. Modern hyper- and high inflations. Journal of Economic Literature 40, 837–890.

Gelb, A., Hillman, A.L., Ursprung, H.W., 1998. Rents as distractions: why the exit from transition is prolonged. In: Baltas, N.C., Demopoulos, G., Hassid, J. (Eds.). Economic Interdependence and Cooperation in Europe. Springer, Berlin, 21–38.

Giavazzi, F., Pagano, M., 1990. Can severe fiscal contractions be expansionary? Tales of two small European countries. NBER Macroeconomic Annual 1990. National Bureau of Economics Research, Cambridge, MA, 75–110.

Graeff, P., Mehlkop, G., 2003. The impact of economic freedom on corruption: different patterns for rich and poor countries. European Journal of Political Economy 19, 605–620. Special Issue on Economic Freedom.

Gupta, S., Davoodi, H.R., Tiongson, E.R., 2001a. Corruption and the provision of health care and education services. In: Arvind, K., Jain, A.K. (Eds.), The Political Economy of Corruption. Routledge, London, pp. 111–141. Reprinted in 2002 in: Abed, G.T., Gupta, S. (Eds.), Governance, Corruption, and Economic Performance. International Monetary Fund, Washington, DC, pp. 245–279.

Gupta, S., de Mello, L., Sharan, R., 2001b. Corruption and military spending. European Journal of Political Economy 17, 749–777. Reprinted in 2002 in: Abed, G.T., Gupta, S. (Eds.), Governance, Corruption, and Economic Performance. International Monetary Fund, Washington, DC, pp. 300–332.

Gupta, S., Clements, B., Baldacci, E., Mulas-Granados, C., 2002. Expenditure composition, fiscal adjustment, and growth in low-income countries. IMF Working Paper No. 02/77. International Monetary Fund, Washington, DC. [Chapter 2 in this volume—Ed.]

Gupta, S., Clements, B., Baldacci, E., Mulas-Granados, C., 2004. Fiscal policy, expenditure composition, and growth in low-income countries. Journal of International Money and Finance (in press).

Gupta, S., Clements, B., Pivovarsky, A., Tiongson, E.R., 2003. Foreign aid and revenue response: does the composition of aid matter? IMF Working Paper No. 03/176. International Monetary Fund, Washington, DC. [Chapter 14 in this volume—Ed.]

Hamilton, L.C., 1991. How robust is robust regression? Stata Technical Bulletin 2, 21–26. Reprinted in Stata Technical Bulletin Reprints 1, 169–175.

Hillman, A.L., 2002. The World Bank and the persistence of poverty in poor countries. European Journal of Political Economy 18, 783–795.

Hillman, A.L., 2003. Public Finance and Public Policy: Responsibilities and Limitations of Government. Cambridge University Press, New York.

Hillman, A.L., Jenkner, E., 2002. User payments for basic education in low-income countries. IMF Working Paper No. 02/182. Also published as Chapter 10 in: Gupta, S., Clements, B., Inchauste, G. (Eds.), Helping Countries Develop: The Role of Fiscal Policy. International Monetary Fund, Washington, DC.

Hjelm, G., 2002. Effects of fiscal contractions: the importance of preceding exchange rate movements. Scandinavian Journal of Economics 104, 423–441.

Khan, M., Senhadji, A., 2001. Threshold effects in the relationship between inflation and growth. IMF Staff Papers 48, 1–21.

Kneller, R., Bleaney, M., Gemmell, N., 1999. Fiscal policy and growth: evidence from OECD countries. Journal of Public Economics 74, 171–190.

Lambertini, L., Tavares, J., 2001. Exchange rates and fiscal adjustments: evidence from OECD and implications for EMU. Unpublished paper, Department of Econmics, University of California, Los Angeles.

Lindbeck, A., Snower, D., 1989, The Insider-Outsider Theory of Employment and Unemployment. MIT Press, Cambridge, MA.

Mauro, P., 1998. Corruption and the composition of government expenditure. Journal of Public Economics 69, 263–279. Reprinted 2002 in: Abed, G.T., Gupta, S. (Eds.), Governance, Corruption, and Economic Performance. International Monetary Fund, Washington, DC, 225–244.

Rajkumar, A., Swaroop, V., 2002. Public spending and outcomes: does governance matter? World Bank Policy Research Working Paper No. 2840. World Bank, Washington, DC.

Van Rijckeghem, C., Weder, B., 2001. Bureaucratic corruption and the rate of temptation: do wages in the civil service affect corruption and by how much? Journal of Development Economics 65, 307–331. Reprinted 2002 in: Abed, G.T., Gupta, S. (Eds.), Governance, Corruption, and Economic Performance. International Monetary Fund, Washington, DC, pp. 59–88.

von Hagen, J., Hughes Hallett, A., Strauch, R., 2002. Budgetary consolidation in Europe: quality, economic conditions, and persistence. Journal of the Japanese and International Economies 16, 512–535.

World Bank, 2001, "Administrative and Civil Service Reform" (Washington: World Bank). Available via the Internet: http://www1.worldbank.org/publicsector/civilservice/common.htm.

5

External Debt, Public Investment, and Growth in Low-Income Countries

BENEDICT CLEMENTS, RINA BHATTACHARYA, AND TOAN QUOC NGUYEN

The relationship between external debt and growth continues to attract considerable interest from policymakers and academics alike. A large number of heavily indebted poor countries (HIPCs) are now receiving debt relief under the HIPC and enhanced HIPC Initiatives. This, in turn, has revived the debate over the impact of a high external debt burden on economic growth. Indeed, one of the principal motivations for debt-relief initiatives stems from the presumed deleterious impact of a heavy debt burden on per capita income growth.

Although there is a substantial literature on the impact of external debt on growth, relatively few studies have focused on low-income countries. Because most low-income countries do not have access to international capital markets, the impact of external debt on growth can be different in low-income countries than in emerging market countries. Furthermore, the channels through which debt affects growth may differ, given differences in the structure of the economy and the public sector across these two country groups. In addition, low-income countries are usually net recipients of resource transfers from donors, even when debt service is high. Under these circumstances, the adverse effects of debt service on real activity are mitigated.

The authors would like to thank Emanuele Baldacci, Sanjeev Gupta, Tim Lane, Cathy Pattillo, Alex Segura, and Antonio Spilimbergo for helpful comments on an earlier draft. Toan Quoc Nguyen was a summer intern in the Fiscal Affairs Department in the summer of 2002.

In light of these considerations, the vast majority of the literature on the debt-growth nexus—developed in the context of emerging market economies—must be interpreted with caution in assessing the debt-growth relationship in a low-income context. These considerations also suggest that empirical estimates of *how much* debt affects growth across these two country groups are likely to differ. A separate empirical analysis of the debt-growth relationship in low-income countries would be especially useful in assessing the growth-enhancing effects of recent debt-relief initiatives.

This paper assesses the impact of external debt on growth in low-income countries and the channels through which these effects are realized. Special attention is given to the indirect effects of external debt on growth via its impact on public investment. After providing an overview of the theoretical and empirical literature on external debt and growth, we present the results from estimating reduced-form equations for growth and public investment in low-income countries, and discuss the policy implications of the results.

Summary of the Literature on External Debt and Growth

The theoretical literature on the relationship between the stock of external debt and growth has largely focused on the adverse effects of "debt overhang." Krugman (1988) defines debt overhang as a situation in which the expected repayment on external debt falls short of the contractual value of debt. If a country's debt level is expected to exceed the country's repayment ability with some probability in the future, expected debt service is likely to be an increasing function of the country's output level. Thus, some of the returns from investing in the domestic economy are effectively "taxed away" by existing foreign creditors, and investment by domestic and foreign investors—and thus economic growth—is discouraged. In its original formulation, the debt overhang theory centered on the adverse effects of external debt on investment in physical capital. The scope of the theory is, however, much broader: a high level of external debt can also reduce a government's incentive to carry out structural and fiscal reforms, since any strengthening of the fiscal position (including that generated indirectly through structural reforms) could intensify pressures to repay foreign creditors. These disincentives for reform are of special concern in low-income countries, where an acceleration of structural reforms is needed to sustain higher growth to meet the Millennium Development Goals (MDGs).

Debt overhang also depresses investment and growth by increasing uncertainty. As the size of the public debt increases, there is growing uncertainty about actions and policies that the government will resort to in order to meet its debt-servicing obligations, with adverse effects on investment. In particular, as the stock of public sector debt increases, there may be expectations that the government's debt-service obligations will be financed by distortionary measures (the inflation tax, for example), as in Agénor and Montiel (1996). The extensive literature on uncertainty and investment suggests that in these circumstances, potential private investors will prefer instead to exercise their option of waiting (Serven, 1997). Moreover, any investment that takes place is likely to be diverted to activities with quick returns rather than to long-term, high-risk, irreversible projects. Rapid accumulation of debt can also be accompanied by increasing capital flight if the private sector fears imminent devaluation and/or increases in taxes to service the debt (Oks and van Wijnbergen, 1995).

The theoretical literature suggests that foreign borrowing has a positive impact on investment and growth up to a certain threshold level; beyond this level, however, its impact is adverse. As indicated in Cohen (1993), the relationship between the face value of debt and investment can be represented as a kind of "Laffer curve": as outstanding debt increases beyond a threshold level, the expected repayment begins to fall as a consequence of the adverse effects mentioned above. The implication is that an increase in the face value of debt leads to an increase in repayment up to the "threshold" level; along the "wrong" side of the debt Laffer curve, on the other hand, increases in the face value of debt reduce expected payments. Given the positive effects of capital accumulation on economic activity, a similar type of Laffer curve between external debt and growth could also be expected.[1]

The empirical literature has found mixed empirical support for the debt overhang hypothesis. Relatively few studies have econometrically assessed the direct effects of the debt stock on investment. In most studies, reduced-form equations for growth are employed, under which the stock of debt is presumed to affect growth both directly (by reducing the incentives to undertake structural reforms) and indirectly (via its effects on investment). In middle-income countries, Warner (1992) concludes that the debt crisis did not depress investment, while Greene and Villanueva (1991), Serven and Solimano (1993), Elbadawi, Ndulu, and Ndung'u (1997), Deshpande (1997), and Chowdhury (2001), on

---

[1] This analysis assumes that the capital stock increases as more debt is incurred, provided that at least part of the debt is used to finance investment. Thus, as external debt increases, so does the capacity to repay, but subject to diminishing returns to capital. Beyond a certain level of debt, repayment capacity declines, owing to these diminishing returns and the debt overhang considerations described in the text.

the other hand, find evidence in support of the debt overhang hypothesis. Fosu (1999), in his empirical study of 35 sub-Saharan African countries, also finds support for the debt overhang hypothesis. In contrast, Hansen (2002) finds that in a sample of 54 developing countries (including 14 HIPCs), the inclusion of three additional explanatory variables (the budget balance, inflation, and openness) leads to rejection of any statistically significant negative effect of external debt on growth. In a similar vein, Savvides (1992) finds that the ratio of debt to GNP has no statistically significant effect on growth. Dijkstra and Hermes (2001) review a number of studies on the debt overhang hypothesis and conclude that the empirical evidence is inconclusive. Furthermore, few studies give a clear idea of the level of the debt-to-GDP ratio at which debt overhang effects come into play.

A recent study finds strong support for a nonlinear, Laffer-type relationship between the stock of external debt and growth. Using a large panel data of 93 developing countries over the period 1969–98, Pattillo, Poirson, and Ricci (2002) find that the average impact of external debt on per capita GDP growth is negative for net present value of debt levels above 160–170 percent of exports and 35–40 percent of GDP. These results are robust across different estimation methodologies and specifications, and suggest that doubling debt levels slows down annual per capita growth by about ½ to 1 percentage point.

High debt stocks appear to affect growth through their dampening effects on both physical capital accumulation and total factor productivity growth. In a follow-up paper, Pattillo, Poirson, and Ricci (2003) apply a growth accounting framework to a group of 61 developing countries in sub-Saharan Africa, Asia, Latin America, and the Middle East over the period 1969–98. Their results suggest that, on average, doubling debt reduces by almost 1 percentage point both growth in per capita physical capital and growth in total factor productivity. Moreover, the policy environment also affects the debt-growth relationship.

External debt service (in contrast to the total debt stock) can also potentially affect growth by crowding out private investment or altering the composition of public spending. Other things being equal, higher debt service can raise the government's interest bill and the budget deficit, reducing public savings; this, in turn, may either raise interest rates or crowd out credit available for the private investment, dampening economic growth. Higher debt service payments can also have adverse effects on the composition of public spending by squeezing the amount of resources available for infrastructure and human capital, with negative effects on growth. Indeed, in the view of some nongovernmental organizations, high external debt service is one of the key obstacles to meeting basic human needs in developing countries.[2]

Relatively few empirical studies have assessed the effects of debt service on private investment or the composition of public spending. Greene and Villanueva (1991) find that external debt service dampens private investment, while Serieux and Samy (2001) find a similar link between debt service and total investment. For a large sample of developing countries, including some HIPCs, Savvides (1992) finds that debt service crowds out public investment spending. Using a panel of 24 African HIPCs, Stephens (2001) finds that each additional $1 in debt service results in (1) a $0.33 decrease in education spending; (2) a $0.14–0.23 fall in government wage expenditure; and, surprisingly, (3) a $0.12–0.23 *increase* in health spending. Hence, his results indicate that an increase in debt service may not necessarily lead to a decline in investment in human capital (in this case, health spending). Reduced-form equations have also been employed to assess the impact of debt service on growth, under the presumption that debt service affects growth via its consequences on the composition of spending or the crowding out of private investment. The empirical evidence in this regard is mixed: Elbadawi, Ndulu, and Ndung'u (1997), for example, find a statistically significant relationship between debt service (as a share of exports) and growth in sub-Saharan Africa, while Fosu (1999) finds no such relationship for countries of that region. Using a broader set of countries, Pattillo, Poirson, and Ricci (2002) also find no statistically signficant relationship between debt service and growth.

In sum, the existing empirical literature provides limited evidence on how the stock of external debt and debt service affect growth, particularly in low-income countries. In particular, there is scope for additional work to clarify the size of these effects, especially for low-income countries that are benefiting from debt relief. Furthermore, more work is needed to explore the channels through which debt affects growth. This study attempts to fill this gap in the literature, with special attention being paid to the effects of external debt service on public investment.

Empirical Analysis

Methodology

Our empirical analysis attempts to shed light on the channels through which external debt affects per capita income growth in low-

---

[2] See, for example, Oxfam International (1999).

income countries. Following the earlier literature—and to assist in comparing our results with other studies—we begin by estimating reduced-form growth equations for these countries. This does not identify the channels through which external debt affects growth, but provides helpful insights into potential channels. We then go on to examine in more detail the potential channels through which external debt might affect growth.

Growth Model

Following earlier studies, the standard growth model is augmented with debt variables to assess the impact of external debt on growth. We use four widely used indicators of the external debt stock burden: the face value of the stock of external debt as a share of GDP; the net present value of the stock of external debt as a share of GDP; the face value of the stock of external debt as a share of exports of goods and services; and the net present value of debt as a share of exports of goods and services. In principle, the net present value of debt should reflect the degree of concessionality of loans, and thus more accurately measure the expected burden of future debt-service payments. However, as all four measures have been used in previous studies, we also follow this convention.

The following reduced-form growth model is estimated as follows:

$$GRPCY_{it} = \alpha_r + \alpha_1 LYRPC(-1)_{it} + \alpha_2 TOTGR_{it} + \alpha_3 POPGR_{it} +$$
$$\alpha_4 GSEC_{it} + \alpha_5 GROINV_{it} + \alpha_6 FISBAL_{it} + \alpha_7 OPEN_{it} +$$
$$\alpha_8 DEBTSERX_{it} + \alpha_9 EXTDEBT_{it} + \alpha_{10} EXTDEBT_{it}^2 + \mu_{it}, \quad (1)$$

where $GRPCY$ is the growth of real per capita income (GDP); $LYRPC(-1)$ is real per capita income (GDP per capita in constant 1995 U.S. dollars) lagged one period, measured in natural logs; $TOTGR$ is the percentage change in the terms of trade; $POPGR$ is the population growth rate, in percent; $GSEC$ is the gross secondary school enrollment rate; $GROINV$ is the gross domestic investment in percent of GDP; $FISBAL$ is the central government fiscal balance in percent of GDP; $OPEN$ is the openness indicator (exports plus imports as a share of GDP); $DEBTSERX$ is total debt service in percent of exports of goods and services; $EXTDEBT$ is one of four indicators of the stock of external debt (see below), measured in natural logs; and μ_{it} is the usual error term. The subscript (it) for the main explanatory variables refers to country and time period, respectively.

Lagged per capita income is included as an explanatory variable, as in the standard Barro growth model, to test for convergence across countries over time toward a common level of real per capita income. Population growth and gross investment are proxies for the rates of growth of factor inputs (labor and capital) in the production process, while the secondary school enrollment rate is typically used as a proxy for the quality of human capital. The terms of trade variable is intended to capture external shocks to the economy; many of the countries in our sample are heavily dependent on exports of primary commodities, and are therefore especially vulnerable to these shocks. The central government fiscal balance is included to control for the impact of fiscal balances on growth. The openness indicator takes account of the substantial literature arguing that economies that are more open to trade enjoy higher long-term rates of growth of per capita real income (see Sachs and Warner, 1995). Finally, to distinguish between debt overhang and the crowding-out effect mentioned earlier, both contemporaneous debt service and a measure of the stock of external debt are included in the regression analysis.

We estimate the model using both fixed effects and system generalized method of moments (GMM). The advantage of a fixed-effects model is that it provides consistent estimates in the presence of country-specific effects that are correlated with the explanatory variables in the model. In a traditional fixed-effects formulation, however, the estimate of the lagged income variable may be biased downward. To overcome this problem, we follow Pattillo, Poirson, and Ricci (2002) and also provide estimates based on the system GMM methodology of Blundell and Bond (1998). A further advantage of this method is that it addresses the potential endogeneity of the variables (for example, investment). This method involves the joint estimation of equation (1) in levels and first differences, imposing the restriction that the coefficients in the level and differenced equations are equal. The instruments used in our model in the level equation are lagged first differences of the variables, while the instruments for the differenced equation are the lagged levels of the variables.[3]

Data

The empirical analysis in this paper uses data for 55 low-income countries that are classified as eligible for the IMF's Poverty Reduction and Growth Facility (PRGF). The data cover the period 1970–99. To net out the effects of short-term fluctuations, three-year averages have been used

---

[3] Data were first de-meaned before applying system GMM, rather than directly applying the individual country dummy option for system GMM under the Blundell and Bond routine available in the PC-Give econometric software package.

for the panel regressions. External debt and gross domestic investment data (total, private, and public) were drawn from the World Bank's Global Development Network Growth database. Data on debt-service payments as a share of exports and as a share of GDP were taken from the World Bank's Global Development Finance database, supplemented with data from the World Bank's World Development Indicators (WDI) database. Data on the net present value of debt are taken from the website of William Easterly.[4] The terms of trade and the central government balance as a share of GDP were calculated using data drawn from the World Economic Outlook database. All other data came from the WDI.

Econometric Results

The fixed effects and system GMM estimates yield broadly similar results. In all cases the F-tests reject the null hypothesis of a common intercept term across countries, and the Hausman tests consistently reject random effects in favor of fixed effects. The system GMM estimates all pass the Sargan test for validity of the instrument set. Only in the case where the growth equation is formulated with gross investment and the net present value of external debt as a share of exports do the two methodologies yield notably different results (Table 1).

The empirical estimates provide some support for the debt overhang hypothesis. They suggest that, beyond a certain threshold, higher external debt is associated with lower rates of growth of per capita income (independent of any impact it may have on gross domestic investment). Depending on which estimation method is used, the results indicate a threshold level of about 30–37 percent of GDP, or about 115–120 percent of exports.

Debt service has no direct effect on real per capita GDP growth. As argued below, one reason that debt service may be insignificant is that its effect is realized through its impact on investment, which is included as an explanatory variable in the model and is thus held constant.

Both fixed effects and system GMM show that gross investment has a significant positive impact on real per capita GDP growth.[5] Lagged income and the central government fiscal balance are also always statistically significant, with lagged income having a negative coefficient

---

[4]Data are available at http://www.nyu.edu/fas/institute/dri/index.html.

[5]Pattillo, Poirson, and Ricci (2002) also find that investment has a significant impact on growth. However, their results on the impact of debt on growth were largely unchanged when total investment was excluded from the model; they interpret this as suggesting that it is the impact of debt on the quality (rather than the quantity) of investment that matters.

Table 1. Gross Investment and Impact of External Debt on Per Capita Income Growth

	Fixed Effects	System GMM	Fixed Effects	System GMM	Fixed Effects	System GMM	Fixed Effects	System GMM
Log (income)$_{-1}$	-13.149*** (-8.471)	-13.133*** (-6.750)	-12.733*** (-8.063)	-12.471*** (-5.600)	-12.128*** (-8.159)	-12.883*** (-7.230)	-11.896*** (-7.886)	-11.934*** (-5.710)
Terms of trade growth	-0.009 (-1.331)	-0.012 (-1.500)	-0.01 (-1.429)	-0.01 (-1.210)	-0.012* (-1.724)	-0.015* (-1.720)	-0.012* (-1.706)	-0.014 (-1.590)
Population growth	-1.178** (-2.133)	-0.65 (-1.380)	-1.366** (-2.391)	-1.205** (-2.480)	-0.834 (-1.489)	-0.947* (-1.830)	-1.064* (-1.885)	-1.091** (-2.210)
Secondary school enrollment	-0.005 (-0.154)	-0.04 (-0.947)	0.005 (-0.146)	-0.046 (-1.010)	0.012 (-0.329)	-0.01 (-0.237)	0.015 (-0.412)	-0.041 (-0.911)
Gross investment ratio	0.206*** -4.644	0.176*** -3.58	0.206*** -4.561	0.186 -3.63	0.223*** -5.031	0.192*** -3.72	0.22*** -4.839	0.189*** -3.81
Fiscal balance	0.248*** -4.967	0.251*** -3.4	0.238*** -4.637	0.243*** -3.41	0.272*** -5.39	0.241*** -3.39	0.26*** -4.997	0.228*** -3.09
Openness	-1.069 (-0.580)	0.105 (-0.067)	-2.148 (-1.206)	-1.466 (-0.752)	-2.248 (-1.212)	-0.27 (-0.168)	-2.562 (-1.412)	-1.392 (-0.771)
Debt service/exports	-0.006 (-0.246)	0.011 (-0.382)	0.004 (-0.147)	0.031 (-0.04)	-0.018 (-0.726)	0.029 (-0.871)	-0.006 (-0.249)	0.033 (-1.15)
Log (debt/GDP)	3.862*** -3.209	4.26*** -2.61	⋮	⋮	⋮	⋮	⋮	⋮
(Log (debt/GDP))^2	-0.535*** (-3.375)	-0.617*** (-3.010)	⋮	⋮	⋮	⋮	⋮	⋮
Log (debt/exports)	⋮	⋮	3.854* -1.876	4.855** -2.18	⋮	⋮	⋮	⋮
(Log (debt/exports))^2	⋮	⋮	-0.406** (-2.120)	-0.508** (-2.300)	⋮	⋮	⋮	⋮

Table 1 *(concluded)*

	Fixed Effects	System GMM	Fixed Effects	System GMM	Fixed Effects	System GMM	Fixed Effects	System GMM
Log (NPV(debt)/GDP)	...	...	...	...	4.292***	3.866**	...	...
					−3.202	−2.55		
(Log (NPV(debt)/GDP))²	...	...	...	...	−0.593***	−0.699***	...	...
					(−2.837)	(−3.220)		
Log (NPV(debt)/exports)	...	...	...	...	...	...	5.023**	1.219
							−2.285	−0.478
(Log (NPV(debt)/exports))²'²	...	...	...	...	...	...	−0.51**	−0.193
							(−2.261)	(−0.748)
Constant	...	−0.104	...	0.05	...	−4.404	...	−0.935
	...	(−0.344)	...	−0.157	...	(−1.570)	...	(−0.144)
Number of observations	272	261	272	261	272	261	272	261
Number of countries	55	49	55	49	55	49	55	49
Adjusted R²'²	0.526	0.295	0.512	0.260	0.523	0.320	0.512	0.260
Common intercept test (fixed effects)[1]	0.000	...	0.000	...	0.000	...	0.000	...
Hausman test (random vs. fixed effects)[1]	0.000	...	0.000	...	0.000	...	0.000	...

Notes: Statistical significance at the 10 percent, 5 percent, and 1 percent level is indicated by *, **, and ***, respectively. The panels are constructed as averages over three-year periods. The numbers in parentheses are *t*-ratios.

[1] *p*-values.

[2] 1 − *RSS/TSS* reported for system GMM.

and the fiscal balance having a positive coefficient. This is consistent with recent works showing the positive effects of good fiscal policy on growth (see Gupta and others, 2004a). The coefficients on population growth and terms of trade growth are, in some cases, statistically significant and negative. Openness is found to be statistically insignificant.

Secondary school enrollment has no statistically significant impact on per capita income growth. This contrasts with the finding of Pattillo, Poirson, and Ricci (2002) for a sample that included middle-income countries.[6] Our results suggest that within the modest range of educational attainment levels in low-income countries, it is not possible to identify a positive relationship between education and growth—although such a relationship may exist for developing countries as a whole. Given the difficulty of identifying an empirical relationship between variables measuring human capital and growth, however, it is not possible to quantify how external debt might depress growth via this channel in low-income countries.

Reestimating the growth equations with gross investment disaggregated into private and public investment suggests that it is the latter that has an impact on growth. This applies for all four debt stock indicators and for both estimation methodologies (Table 2). The results imply that for each 1 percentage point of GDP increase in public investment, annual per capita growth rises by 0.2 percentage point. However, higher public investment that leads to larger budget deficits will not have a salutary effect on growth, given the adverse effects of deficits on economic activity. Changes in the terms of trade, population growth, and openness have no statistically significant effect on growth. As before, the coefficient on the debt-service variable is, in all cases but one, statistically insignificant. With respect to the debt stock, the results are once again consistent with the debt overhang hypothesis, and indicate that the marginal impact of debt on growth becomes negative beyond a certain threshold level. This threshold level is estimated at about 50 percent of GDP for the face value of external debt, and at about 20–25 percent of GDP for its estimated net present value. These values are much higher than the estimated ones of 11 percent and 9–14 percent, respectively, in Pattillo, Poirson, and Ricci (2002). One reason for the difference in results could be that our country sample only includes low-income, PRGF-eligible countries, whereas the study by Pattillo, Poirson, and Ricci (2002) includes emerging market countries in their sample. The results with the external debt indicators expressed as a ratio

---

[6]The same model was estimated using various proxies for human capital, including illiteracy rates and growth rates of secondary school enrollment. In all cases the human capital variables were statistically insignificant, including when measured in logs.

Table 2. Private/Public Investment and Impact of External Debt on Per Capita Income Growth

	Fixed Effects	System GMM	Fixed Effects	System GMM	Fixed Effects	System GMM	Fixed Effects	System GMM
Log (income)[1]	-12.420*** (-7.408)	-12.275*** (-5.910)	-12.726*** (-7.494)	-11.863*** (-5.100)	-12.279*** (-7.566)	-12.865*** (-7.280)	-12.153*** (-7.315)	-12.058*** (-5.350)
Terms of trade growth	-0.002 (-0.254)	-0.002 (-0.210)	-0.004 (-0.482)	-0.003 (-0.399)	-0.002 (-0.274)	-0.004 (-0.519)	-0.003 (-0.374)	-0.002 (-0.313)
Population growth	-0.594 (-0.909)	-0.080 (-0.148)	-0.613 (-0.913)	-0.279 (-0.446)	-0.689 (-1.070)	-0.638 (-1.110)	-0.741 (-1.103)	-0.581 (-0.971)
Secondary school enrollment	0.013 (0.280)	-0.031 (-0.727)	0.049 (1.032)	0.003 (0.064)	-0.011 (-0.243)	0.001 (0.004)	0.022 (0.488)	0.008 (0.198)
Private investment ratio	-0.025 (-0.410)	0.008 (0.247)	0.010 (0.164)	0.011 (0.269)	-0.030 (-0.504)	-0.001 (-0.031)	0.002 (0.039)	0.011 (0.235)
Public investment ratio	0.207*** (2.748)	0.167** (2.130)	0.222*** (3.061)	0.184** (2.480)	0.214*** (2.978)	0.181*** (2.600)	0.242*** (3.389)	0.194*** (2.880)
Fiscal balance	0.211*** (3.647)	0.226*** (3.450)	0.188*** (3.182)	0.190*** (2.850)	0.246*** (4.212)	0.233*** (4.190)	0.226*** (3.681)	0.189*** (3.570)
Openness	3.762 (1.490)	0.972 (0.638)	2.665 (1.060)	0.254 (0.147)	3.403 (1.356)	2.509 (1.530)	2.427 (0.952)	0.973 (0.579)
Debt service/exports	-0.039 (-1.630)	-0.037 (-1.380)	-0.033 (-1.386)	-0.021 (-0.740)	-0.044* (-1.755)	-0.017 (-0.631)	-0.037 (-1.496)	-0.008 (-0.279)
Log (debt/GDP)	3.465* (1.894)	6.731*** (3.250)	... ...	... ...	... ...	... ...	... ...	... ...

	(1)	(2)	(3)	(4)	(5)	(6)	(7)	(8)
(Log (debt/GDP))^2	-0.458** (-1.972)	-0.863*** (-3.290)	...	...	...	...	...	...
Log (debt/exports)	...	...	3.187 (0.966)	6.872* (1.840)	...	...	...	...
(Log (debt/exports))^2	...	...	-0.344 (-1.157)	-0.677** (-1.970)	...	...	...	...
Log (NPV(debt)/GDP)	...	...	...	...	6.827*** (3.009)	7.804*** (3.250)	...	...
(Log (NPV(debt)/GDP))^2	...	...	...	...	-0.923*** (-2.853)	-1.250*** (-4.200)	...	...
Log (NPV(debt)/exports)	...	...	...	...	...	...	6.888* (1.731)	6.550** (2.030)
(Log (NPV(debt)/exports))^2	...	...	...	...	...	...	-0.674* (-1.761)	-0.706** (-2.190)
Constant	-0.121 (-0.363)	...	-0.011 (-0.034)	...	-11.050** (-2.320)	...	-14.591* (-1.750)	...
Number of observations	211	204	211	204	211	204	211	204
Number of countries	40	38	40	38	40	38	40	38
Adjusted R^2[2]	0.465	0.252	0.461	0.221	0.481	0.258	0.462	0.199
Common intercept test (fixed effects)[1]	0.000	...	0.000	...	0.000	...	0.000	...
Hausman test (random vs. fixed effects)[1]	0.000	...	0.000	...	0.000	...	0.000	...

Notes: Statistical significance at the 10 percent, 5 percent, and 1 percent level is indicated by *, **, and ***, respectively. The panels are constructed as averages over three-year periods. The numbers in parentheses are t-ratios.

[1] p-values.

[2] 1 – RSS/TSS reported for system GMM.

to exports (rather than GDP) are somewhat weaker, but still indicate a statistically significant relationship, with a threshold level for the net present value of external debt at about 100–105 percent of exports.

This study uses various econometric tests to assess whether debt affects growth through its effect on the level of private investment. As noted in Pattillo, Poirson, and Ricci (2002), the formulation above understates the potential effect of debt on growth via its effect on investment, given the simultaneous inclusion of investment and debt variables in the re-duced-form equation. To assess whether debt might be affecting growth through its effect on private investment, we ran the growth regression without the private investment variables for all the model formulations reported in Table 2.[7] The debt variables remained statistically significant, but indicated that a reduction of debt would generally have a *smaller* ef-fect on growth than indicated in Table 2. In addition, Hausman tests under the fixed-effects formulation of the model revealed there were no systematic differences in coefficient values whether private sector invest-ment was included or excluded.[8] Finally, we ran the growth equations in Table 2 without the external debt variables, and found that private in-vestment remained statistically insignificant.[9] In sum, these results sug-gest that debt affects growth through its impact on the efficiency of resource use, rather than through the level of private investment.

The overall results have important implications for the impact of debt relief on growth in the HIPCs. The weighted average net present value (NPV) of external debt to GDP for the 27 decision point HIPCs is projected to decline from 60 percent prior to debt relief at the deci-sion point to 30 percent by 2005, when most HIPCs are expected to have reached their completion points. Based on our estimates from the second column of Table 2 (the system GMM results), this debt reduc-tion would, ceteris paribus, directly add 0.8–1.1 percent to their annual per capita GDP growth rates.

---

[7]A similar method was used by Pattillo, Poirson, and Ricci (2002) to assess the effect of debt on growth, albeit in a model that included total investment (rather than both private and public investment).

[8]The Hausman test could not be used in the model formulation when the net present value (NPV) of debt to exports was used. Results are available from the authors upon re-quest. The model was also estimated with an interaction variable, based on the multiple of the NPV of the debt to GDP (or to exports) and the level of private investment to GDP. This variable was also found to be statistically insignificant or incorrectly signed.

[9]Relatively few studies have assessed the impact of private investment on growth in developing countries; in most studies, total investment, rather than private investment, has been included in the empirical analysis. Two exceptions are Khan and Kumar (1997) and Gupta and others (2004). The weak relationship between private investment and growth merits further research.

The results imply a more powerful relationship between debt and growth than recent research focusing on developing countries as a whole. Assuming a reduction in the NPV of debt to GDP from 60 percent to 30 percent, and using the quadratic system GMM results presented in Table 6 of Pattillo, Poirson, and Ricci (2002), growth would increase by 0.4 percentage point a year—about half the figure reported above. Using the quadratic fixed-effects results from Table 6 of their paper, however, growth would rise by a figure similar to our estimates noted above.

The effects of debt on growth could be even higher when indirect effects are taken into account. Our results indicate that both the central government balance and public investment influence growth. We explore in greater detail below the effect of one of these indirect channels (public investment).

Public Investment Model

Relatively little research has been done on the determinants of *public* investment (as opposed to *total* or *private* investment) in developing countries. Tanzi and Davoodi (1997) model the public investment ratio for a wide range of countries as a function of corruption (proxied by the *International Country Risk Guide* Corruption Index), real per capita income, and the government revenue to GDP ratio. Their empirical results suggest that corruption increases public investment while reducing its productivity. Sturm (2001) focuses on developing countries and models public investment using three sets of explanatory variables: structural variables, such as urbanization and population growth; economic variables, such as real GDP growth, government debt, budget deficits, and foreign aid; and political-institutional variables, such as political stability and political business cycles. Sturm finds that political-institutional variables do not seem to be important in explaining public investment in developing economies, in contrast to structural and economic variables.

In our empirical analysis of public investment we exclude institutional variables for two reasons. The first is that recent work has not found these variables to be of significance in explaining public investment in developing countries. The second—and more important—is that given the lack of available data, inclusion of these variables would significantly reduce the number of observations in our sample.

More specifically we estimate the following public investment equation:

$$PUBINV_{it} = \beta_r + \beta_1 LYRPC_{it} + \beta_2 AIDGNI_{it} + \beta_3 URBAN_{it} + \beta_4 OPEN_{it} + \\ \beta_5 DEBTSERY_{it} + \beta_6 EXTDEBT_{it} + \beta_7 EXTDEBT^2_{it} + \upsilon_{it}, \quad (2)$$

where *PUBINV* represents public investment in percent of GDP; *AIDGNI* is foreign aid in percent of gross national income; *URBAN* is the urbanization ratio; *DEBTSERY* is total debt service in percent of GDP; *LYRPC, OPEN,* and *EXTDEBT* are as defined earlier for equation (1); and v_{it} is the standard error term. As before, the subscript (*it*) for the main explanatory variables refers to country and time period, respectively. The model is estimated using fixed effects.[10]

The real per capita income variable is used as a proxy for the level of economic development, as in Tanzi and Davoodi (1997). The impact of the urbanization ratio on public investment is ambiguous. On the one hand, it could be argued that as a society becomes urbanized, there is a shift from the family to the government with regard to the provision of services like education and health care; thus, one might expect the coefficient on urbanization to be positive.[11] On the other hand, most public capital spending concerns physical infrastucture, the need for which is relatively greater in rural areas. It is plausible that increasing urbanization leads to less demand for physical infrastructure and perhaps more demand for public consumption spending, giving rise to a negative coefficient. It is also expected that higher foreign aid enables governments to spend more on public investment. The openness indicator is included as an explanatory variable because more open economies often compete for foreign direct investment by, among other things, trying to invest more in infrastructure; thus, there is likely to be a positive relationship between openness and the public investment ratio.

We report results using total debt service as a percent of GDP (rather than as a share of exports). This appears to be the most intuitively appealing measure of how debt affects general government decisions regarding the appropropriate level of public investment. These are presented in columns 1 and 5 of Table 3. However, there is no reason to expect a *linear* relationship between debt service and public investment; it is plausible that the crowding-out effect of debt service on public investment becomes increasingly more important as debt service absorbs a growing share of national output. We thus rerun equation (2) replacing the ratio of debt service to GDP with the square of its value. These results are presented in columns 2 and 6 of Table 3.

---

[10] A system GMM approach is not necessary in this context, given that all the explanatory variables are exogenous and the absence of a lagged dependent variable.

[11] Wagner's law also suggests that public investment spending might increase with urbanization. Writing at the end of the nineteenth century, Wagner posited that the development of an industrialized society would increase pressures to supply public services. For more on Wagner's law, see Wagner (1958).

It is also plausible that low levels of debt-service payments have no perceptible impact on public investment. Rather, it could be the case that crowding out only occurs after a certain "threshold" of high levels of debt service. To test this, we experimented with various dummies for the ratio of debt service to GDP, which took a value of zero below a specified threshold level and the percent of GDP absorbed by debt-service payments beyond this threshold. Separate regressions were also run with the square of this dummy variable to allow for an increasingly stronger crowding-out effect as the ratio of debt service to GDP rises. Since the adjusted R^2 did not vary much across the different specifications, the Schwartz Information Criterion was used to distinguish between the various specifications. The best results were obtained at a threshold level of 5 percent of GDP.[12] These results are presented in columns 3, 4, 7, and 8 of Table 3.

Econometric Results

The fixed-effects estimates of the public investment equation yield a number of interesting results (Table 3).[13] The overall goodness of fit of the model is satisfactory, as over half of the variation in public investment is explained by the model. With respect to individual coefficients, the openness indicator is always highly significant and positive, while the urbanization ratio is always highly significant and negative, as in Sturm (2001). Foreign aid is statistically significant and positive in most formulations of the model. The coefficient on real per capita income is *positive* and statistically significant, in direct contrast to Tanzi and Davoodi (1997), whose empirical results show a *negative* and statistically significant coefficient. This may be because the Tanzi and Davoodi results cover a wider range of countries, including middle- and high-income countries, and the negative coefficient may reflect long-run convergence across countries of the ratio of public investment to GDP. By contrast, our sample is limited to low-income countries, and the positive coefficient may reflect the fact that, within this sample, countries with higher real per capita income can generate greater tax revenues and can afford higher levels of public investment.

The empirical estimates indicate that the stock of external debt has no significant impact on public investment. This implies that prospective debt-servicing payments for the public sector (as indicated by the

---

[12] Of the 44 countries included in the regressions in Table 2, 24 had ratios of debt service to GDP above 5 percent.

[13] As with the growth equations, in all cases the F-tests reject the null hypothesis of a common intercept term across countries, and the Hausman tests consistently reject random effects in favor of fixed effects.

Table 3. Public Investment and External Debt/Debt Service

	(1)	(2)	(3)	(4)	(5)	(6)	(7)	(8)
				Dependent Variable: Ratio of Public Investment to GDP Estimation Method: Fixed Effects				
Log (income)	4.729*** (3.355)	4.587*** (3.331)	4.607*** (3.270)	4.575*** (3.323)	5.112*** (3.774)	4.806*** (3.607)	4.960*** (3.667)	4.773*** (3.584)
Foreign aid as a percentage of GNI	0.085** (2.339)	0.091** (2.532)	0.082** (2.261)	0.090** (2.512)	0.056 (1.542)	0.063* (1.755)	0.052 (1.431)	0.062* (1.743)
Urbanization ratio	−0.216*** (−4.589)	−0.222*** (−4.769)	−0.216*** (−4.571)	−0.222*** (−4.764)	−0.209*** (−4.768)	−0.215*** (−5.026)	−0.211*** (−4.802)	−0.215*** (−5.015)
Openness	7.985*** (5.020)	7.763*** (4.946)	7.955*** (4.990)	7.764*** (4.947)	13.434*** (7.116)	12.828*** (7.024)	13.209*** (7.031)	12.824*** (7.025)
Debt service/GDP	−0.167* (−1.932)	...	...	...	−0.197** (−2.526)	...	...	...
(Debt service/GDP)^2	...	−0.010*** (−3.345)	...	...	...	−0.011*** (−3.646)	...	...
Debt service threshold dummy	...	...	−0.106 (−1.577)	...	...	...	−0.14** (−2.325)	...
(Debt service threshold dummy)^2	...	...	...	−0.01*** (−3.354)	...	...	...	−0.011*** (−3.677)

Log (NPV(debt)/GDP)	2.297 (1.457)	1.732 (1.109)	2.202 (1.360)	1.630 (1.039)	...	...	...	...
(Log (NPV(debt)/GDP)^2	−0.150 (−0.569)	−0.079 (−0.312)	−0.162 (−0.605)	−0.065 (−0.255)	...	...	...	...
Log (NPV(debt)/exports)	...	...	...	...	1.771 (0.721)	1.272 (0.524)	1.529 (0.622)	1.204 (0.496)
(Log (NPV(debt)/exports))^2	...	...	...	...	−0.033 (−0.133)	−0.006 (−0.002)	−0.021 (−0.084)	0.005 (0.022)
Number of observations	338	338	338	338	336	336	336	336
Number of countries	44	44	44	44	44	44	44	44
Adjusted R^2	0.519	0.531	0.517	0.531	0.540	0.551	0.539	0.551
Schwartz Information Criterion	990.457	986.180	991.183	986.144	978.432	974.493	978.994	974.366
Common intercept test (fixed effects)[1]	0.000	0.000	0.000	0.000	0.000	0.000	0.000	0.000
Hausman test (random vs. fixed effects)[1]	0.000	0.000	0.000	0.000	0.000	0.000	0.000	0.000

Notes: Statistical significance at the 10 percent, 5 percent, and 1 percent level is indicated by *, **, and ***, respectively. The panels are constructed as averages over three-year periods. The numbers in parentheses are t-ratios.

[1] p-values.

NPV of debt) do not deter public investment in the short run. This sug-gests that public investment is driven more by the current fiscal posi-tion and the availability of resources than by factors that affect fiscal sustainability over the longer term.

The results provide support for the hypothesis that higher debt ser-vice crowds out public investment, and that this effect becomes stronger as debt service absorbs a growing share of GDP. Under most formulations of the model, debt service has a statistically significant ef-fect on public investment. The relationship is nonlinear, with the crowding-out effect intensifying as the ratio of debt service to GDP rises. The Schwartz Information Criterion suggests that the results with the threshold dummies are marginally better than those using the ratio of debt service to GDP or its square. The better performance of the threshold dummies is indicative of the underlying nonlinearity in the relationship between debt service and public investment.

How significant is the crowding-out effect? Under the linear formula-tions of the model, the results indicate that for every 1 percentage point of GDP increase in debt service, public investment declines by about 0.2 percent of GDP. In some sense, the modest size of this coefficient is sur-prising, indicating that high debt burdens have not had a very large ef-fect on public investment in low-income countries. More importantly, this implies that, ceteris paribus, debt relief per se cannot be expected to lead to large increases in public investment. Instead, in most cases it ei-ther leads to greater public consumption, or—if used for deficit reduction or lower taxes—higher private consumption or investment.

If only a small share of debt relief is channeled into public invest-ment, the corresponding impact on growth will also be modest. For ex-ample, assume a reduction in the ratio of debt service to GDP from 8.7 percent (the average in 2000 of the seven most heavily indebted HIPCs) to 3.0 percent (roughly the average ratio of debt service to GDP for all HIPCs in 2002).[14] Table 4 presents the results of this exer-cise. The calculations from the best-fitting regression results suggest that a reduction in debt-service payments from 8.7 to 3.0 percent of GDP would increase public investment by 0.7–0.8 percent of GDP, and indirectly raise real per capita GDP growth by 0.1–0.2 percent annually. While this boost to growth would be small in absolute terms, it is roughly equivalent to the actual growth in per capita incomes achieved

---

[14]Some caution is needed in interpreting these results, as our debt-service variable captures both private and public debt service on long-term debt, while HIPC debt relief is provided for public and publicly guaranteed external debt. Since about three-fourths of the long-term external debt service in low-income countries is public and publicly guaranteed, this is unlikely to have a significant effect on our results.

Table 4. Impact on Public Investment and Indirect Impact on Real Per Capita Income Growth of Reducing the Debt Service to GDP Ratio from 8.7 Percent to 3.0 Percent

	Impact on Public Investment (percent of GDP)	Impact on Annual GDP Growth Rate	
		Fixed Effects	System GMM
Results with net present value of debt in percent of GDP			
Debt service/GDP	0.95	0.20	0.17
(Debt service/GDP)^2	0.70	0.15	0.13
Debt service threshold dummy	0.92	0.20	0.17
(Debt service threshold dummy)^2	0.78	0.17	0.14
Results with net present value of debt in percent of exports			
Debt service/GDP	1.12	0.27	0.22
(Debt service/GDP)^2	0.71	0.17	0.14
Debt service threshold dummy	1.22	0.29	0.24
(Debt service threshold dummy)^2	0.79	0.19	0.15

by HIPCs in the 1990s. Morever, if half of this debt service were channeled to higher public investment (instead of one-fifth), annual growth would rise quite significantly (about 0.5 percentage point a year). Under all scenarios, greater public investment only bolsters growth if it is matched by other revenue and expenditure measures that do not lead to higher budget deficits.

Conclusions

High levels of debt can depress economic growth in low-income countries. Debt appears to affect growth via its effect on the efficiency of resource use, rather than through its depressing effect on private investment. As indicated by the debt overhang hypothesis, however, debt has a deleterious effect on growth only after it reaches a threshold level. This threshold level is estimated at about 50 percent of GDP for the face value of external debt, and at about 20–25 percent of GDP for its estimated net present value. The results with the external debt indicators expressed as a ratio to exports are somewhat weaker, but indicate a threshold level for the net present value of external debt at about 100–105 percent of exports. Our results imply that the substantial reduction in external debt projected for the HIPCs by the time most of them reach their completion points in 2005 would, ceteris paribus, directly add 0.8–1.1 percent to their per capita GDP growth rates. Indeed, the positive effects of debt relief may already be reflected in some of the healthier growth experienced by HIPCs in the past few years relative to their poor performance of the 1990s.[15]

External debt also has indirect effects on growth through its effects on public investment. While the stock of public debt does not appear to depress public investment, debt service does. The relationship is nonlinear, with the crowding-out effect intensifying as the ratio of debt service to GDP rises. On average, every 1 percentage point increase in debt service as a share of GDP reduces public investment by about 0.2 percentage point. This implies that a reduction in debt service of about 6 percentage points of GDP would raise investment by 0.75–1 percentage point of GDP, raising growth modestly by about 0.2 percentage point. However, if a more sizeable share of this debt relief were channeled into public investment—say about half—growth could increase by 0.5 percentage point a year. While the use of debt relief is determined by each country in the context of its poverty reduction strategy paper (PRSP), our results here suggest that one viable option for country authorities to raise growth and combat poverty would be to allocate a substantial share of debt relief for public investment. To reap these positive effects of debt relief on investment and growth, higher spending on capital outlays would need to be matched by spending cuts, higher external grants, or increases in domestic revenues to prevent an increase in the budget deficit.

These results have important implications for the design of adjustment programs in countries receiving debt relief. Reducing the stock of debt alone—rather than an immediate reduction in debt service—is unlikely to induce governments to increase their spending on public investment. And while cutting debt-service obligations can provide breathing space to raise public investment, debt relief per se is likely to lead to just a modest rise in public investment spending. In practice, most HIPCs have been raising public investment in the context of their PRGF-supported programs; on average, these countries have targeted an increase of 0.5 percentage point of GDP in this spending, relative to the pre-PRGF year.[16]

Additional research could further evaluate other indirect channels through which external debt affects growth. In particular, our reduced-

---

[15] GDP per capita grew by an average of 1.2 percent a year in 2000–02, compared with 0.2 percent during the 1990s.

[16] Drawn from an update on the database on fiscal targets in PRGF-supported countries in Gupta and others (2002).

form equation suggests that stronger central government fiscal balances contribute to growth, suggesting that the relationship between debt and public sector deficits merits further examination. These linkages are complex and beyond the scope of the present paper; from a theoretical standpoint, the impact of aid on both revenues and expenditures is ambiguous (see Gupta and others, 2004b). Further research could also fruitfully assess how debt interfaces with other macroeconomic determinants of growth.

Appendix I: List of Countries

Albania	Congo, Democratic	Macedonia,	Solomon
Angola	Republic of	FYR of	Islands
Armenia	Congo, Republic of	Madagascar	Sri Lanka
Bangladesh	Côte d'Ivoire	Malawi	Tanzania
Benin	Djibouti	Mali	Togo
Bhutan	Eritrea	Mauritania	Uganda
Bolivia	Ethiopia	Mozambique	Vanuatu
Burkina Faso	Gambia, The	Nepal	Vietnam
Burundi	Ghana	Nicaragua	Yemen
Cambodia	Guinea	Niger	Zambia
Cameroon	Haiti	Nigeria	Zimbabwe
Cape Verde	Honduras	Pakistan	
Central African	India	Rwanda	
Republic	Kenya	Samoa	
Chad	Kyrgyz Republic	Senegal	
Comoros	Lao PDR	Sierra Leone	

References

Agénor, Pierre-Richard, and Peter Montiel, 1996, *Development Macroeconomics* (Princeton, New Jersey: Princeton University Press).

Blundell, Richard, and Stephen Bond, 1998, "Initial Conditions and Moment Restrictions in Dynamic Panel Data Models," *Journal of Econometrics*, Vol. 87 (November), pp. 115–43.

Chowdhury, Abdur R., 2001, "Foreign Debt and Growth in Developing Countries: A Sensitivity and Causality Analysis," paper presented at WIDER Conference on Debt Relief (Helsinki: United Nations University).

Cohen, Daniel, 1993, "Low Investment and Large LDC Debt in the 1980s," *American Economic Review*, Vol. 83 (June), pp. 437–49.

Deshpande, Ashwini, 1997, "The Debt Overhang and the Disincentive to Invest," *Journal of Development Economics*, Vol. 52 (February), pp. 169–87.

Dijkstra, Geske, and Niels Hermes, 2001, "The Uncertainty of Debt Service Payments and Economic Growth of Highly Indebted Poor Countries: Is There a Case for Debt Relief?" (unpublished; Helsinki: United Nations University).

Elbadawi, Ibrahim A., Benno J. Ndulu, and Njuguna Ndung'u, 1997, "Debt Overhang and Economic Growth in Sub-Saharan Africa," Chapter 5 in *External Finance for Low-Income Countries*, ed. by Zubair Iqbal and Ravi Kanbur (Washington: International Monetary Fund), pp. 49–76.

Fosu, Augustin K., 1999, "The External Debt Burden and Economic Growth in the 1980s: Evidence from Sub-Saharan Africa," *Canadian Journal of Development Studies*, Vol. 20, No. 2, pp. 307–18.

Greene, Joshua, and Delano Villanueva, 1991, "Private Investment in Developing Countries: An Empirical Analysis," in *Staff Papers* (International Monetary Fund), Vol. 38 (March), pp. 33–58.

Gupta, Sanjeev, and others, 2002, *Is the PRGF Living Up to Expectations? An Assessment of Program Design*, IMF Occasional Paper No. 216 (Washington: International Monetary Fund).

———, 2004a, "Fiscal Policy, Expenditure Composition, and Growth in Low-Income Countries," Chapter 2 in *Helping Countries Develop: The Role of Fiscal Policy* (Washington: International Monetary Fund).

———, 2004b, "Foreign Aid and Revenue Response: Does the Composition of Aid Matter?" Chapter 14 in *Helping Countries Develop: The Role of Fiscal Policy* (Washington: International Monetary Fund).

Hansen, Henrik, 2002, "The Impact of Aid and External Debt on Growth and Investment: Insights from Cross-Country Regression Analysis," CREDIT Research Paper No. 02/26 (Nottingham, United Kingdom: University of Nottingham, Centre for Research in Economic Development and International Trade).

Khan, Mohsin S., and Manmohan S. Kumar, 1997, "Public and Private Investment and the Growth Process in Developing Countries," *Oxford Bulletin of Economics and Statistics*, Vol. 59 (February), pp. 69–88.

Krugman, Paul, 1988, "Financing vs. Forgiving a Debt Overhang: Some Analytical Issues," *Journal of Development Economics*, Vol. 29, pp. 253–68.

Oks, Daniel, and Sweder van Wijnbergen, 1995, "Mexico After the Debt Crisis: Is Growth Sustainable?" *Journal of Development Economics*, Vol. 47 (June), pp. 155–78.

Oxfam International, 1999, "Debt Relief and Poverty Reduction: Meeting the Challenge," Oxfam Briefing Paper. Available via the Internet: http://www.oxfam.org/eng/pdf/pp9908_debt_relief_and_poverty_reduction.pdf.

Pattillo, Catherine, Hélène Poirson, and Luca Ricci, 2002, "External Debt and Growth," IMF Working Paper 02/69 (Washington: International Monetary Fund).

———, 2003, "What Are the Channels Through Which External Debt Affects Growth?" (unpublished; Washington: International Monetary Fund).

Sachs, Jeffrey, and Andrew Warner, 1995, "Economic Reform and the Process of Global Integration," *Brookings Papers on Economic Activity: 1*, pp. 1–118.

Savvides, Andreas, 1992, "Investment Slowdown in Developing Countries during the 1980s: Debt Overhang or Foreign Capital Inflows," *Kyklos*, Vol. 45, No. 3, pp. 363–78.

Serieux, John, and Yiagadeesen Samy, 2001, "The Debt Service Burden and Growth: Evidence from Low-Income Countries," North-South Institute Working Paper (Ottawa: North-South Institute).

Serven, Luis, 1997, "Uncertainty, Instability, and Irreversible Investment: Theory, Evidence and Lessons for Africa," World Bank Policy Research Working Paper No. 1722 (Washington: World Bank).

————, and Andres Solimano, 1993, "Debt Crisis, Adjustment Policies, and Capital Formation in Developing Countries: Where Do We Stand?" *World Development*, Vol. 21 (January), pp. 127–40.

Stephens, Marc, 2001, "External Debt, Human Capital, and Growth in Heavily Indebted Poor Countries" (unpublished Ph.D. thesis; New York: New York University).

Sturm, Jan-Egbert, 2001, "Determinants of Public Capital Spending in Less-Developed Countries," CCSO Centre for Economics Research Working Paper No. 200107 (Munich: University of Groningen).

Tanzi, Vito, and Hamid Davoodi, 1997, "Corruption, Public Investment, and Growth," IMF Working Paper 97/139 (Washington: International Monetary Fund).

Wagner, Adolf, 1958, "Three Extracts on Public Finance," in *Classics in the Theory of Public Finance*, ed. by Richard A. Musgrave and Alan T. Peacock (New York: Macmillan), pp. 1–15.

Warner, Andrew M., 1992, "Did the Debt Crisis Cause the Investment Crisis?" *Quarterly Journal of Economics*, Vol. 107 (November), pp. 1161–86.

6

A Framework for Fiscal Debt Sustainability Analysis in Low-Income Countries

EMANUELE BALDACCI AND KEVIN FLETCHER

Assessing fiscal debt sustainability is an important element of fiscal policy analysis. It aids in evaluating the appropriateness of a country's macroeconomic policies in both the short and long run by helping to determine whether current and future fiscal policies are sustainable or whether a period of fiscal adjustment is needed.

To perform debt sustainability analysis, it is first necessary to define debt sustainability. While debt sustainability can be defined in several ways, this paper considers a country's debt to be sustainable if the country can meet its debt-service obligations without recourse to debt relief, rescheduling of debt, or the accumulation of arrears and without unduly compromising growth.[1] While the last element of this definition is admittedly somewhat vague, it is meant to capture the notion that fiscal sustainability cannot be predicated on assumed future fiscal adjustments and growth that are so large as to be unrealistic. In other words, fiscal debt sustainability requires that governments be not just able, but also politically willing, to repay their debt.

A variety of methodologies can be used to assess fiscal debt sustainability. In countries with significant access to private capital markets, market signals (such as interest rate spreads) can be useful indicators of the probability of debt default. However, such market signals are typically absent in low-income countries (at least for external debt, which may be almost entirely noncommercial). In these countries, debt sus-

---

[1] Alternative definitions of debt sustainability have been presented in the literature. See, for example, IMF (2003) and Chalk and Hemming (2000).

tainability must be assessed more directly by examining whether a government has sufficient resources to meet its debt-service obligations. In theory, this can be determined by calculating whether a government's debt (D) is less than or equal to the present value of the primary surpluses (P) that will be used to pay the debt:

$$D_t \leq \sum_{j=1}^{\infty} \frac{P_{t+j}}{\left(1+i\right)^j}, \tag{1}$$

where t denotes the time period and i is the nominal interest rate.[2] However, such calculations are very sensitive to the assumed long-run interest rate and primary balance, which are typically not known with much certainty. Moreover, such a simple budget constraint approach may not adequately account for factors that make debt unsustainable even when the government is technically solvent. For example, debt crises could also be triggered by liquidity constraints, constraints on the degree to which domestic revenue can be converted into foreign currency for debt service, and political constraints on the share of revenue that the public is willing to use for debt service. Thus, a more holistic approach to debt sustainability analysis requires that debt dynamics be assessed under a variety of scenarios to allow for variability in the underlying assumptions and incorporate a variety of indicators to allow for the different types of constraints that could lead to debt crises.

This paper presents one such framework for debt sustainability analysis that is meant to be both pragmatic and accessible to a wide range of policy analysts.[3] The framework has the following key features: (1) it allows analysts to break down the evolution of debt into various factors (for example, effects of primary balances, effects of GDP growth); (2) it provides a simple mechanism for clarifying the key underlying assumptions in a baseline scenario and for assessing their realism in light of historical experience; (3) it suggests the use of various indicators to examine the multiple constraints on debt sustainability; and (4) it suggests several "stress tests" to debt sustainability that are aimed to capture the major risks facing most low-income countries.

---

[2] For expositional simplicity, it is assumed that the interest rate is constant over time. This condition also assumes that the present value of the government's debt in the indefinite future converges to zero, so that no "Ponzi game" is possible. See Cuddington (1997) for further discussion.

[3] The framework is based largely on an approach that has been developed primarily by the IMF's Policy Development and Review Department (PDR) for emerging market countries (IMF, 2002). However, the framework in this chapter is modified somewhat to address some specific issues that are common in low-income countries, and the authors take responsibility for any errors.

The framework is intended primarily to be a "toolkit" for analyzing the main factors and risks affecting debt sustainability and is not a complete guide to medium-term macroeconomic programming. The framework provides a check on whether the underlying policies assumed in a baseline scenario would lead to, or maintain, debt sustainability and on how robust they are to shocks. It also provides the means to test the realism of the base case projections as well as whether alternative policies may be more appropriate. The results of this framework should be supplemented by additional work that identifies the links between government policies, debt dynamics, and economic growth. Thus, analysts should take care to try to specify these links as accurately as possible, drawing on both the general economic growth literature and country-specific factors, and to carefully consider both the policy choices that are implicit in their baseline scenarios and the policy implications that should be derived from it.

The Framework

This section describes in detail the framework's specific features, including the definition of public debt, the time frame of the debt sustainability analysis, the key indicators used in the framework, the assessment of the macroeconomic assumptions, and the stress tests used.

Time Frame

To conduct debt sustainability analysis, it is first necessary to determine the time frame over which debt dynamics will be examined. In this regard, one must consider whether a country is in a "steady state" in regard to its fiscal policies or whether major changes in the fiscal policy environment are expected in the future. In the former case, a relatively short time frame could be used on the assumption that current trends will continue more or less indefinitely. The latter assumption, however, requires that debt sustainability analysis be carried out long enough to capture the effects of major changes, such as the effects of large demographic shifts on pension systems.[4]

In the case of low-income countries, an important future shift in the fiscal environment that may need to be considered is a country's future "graduation" from highly concessional assistance. Currently, many low-income countries finance their deficits primarily through borrowing from official lenders on concessional terms, meaning that the interest

---

[4]See Heller (2003) for a discussion of the importance of framing fiscal policy in a long-run context.

rates are low (1–2 percent) while the maturities are long (10–40 years), with long grace periods (5–10 years) during which no principal payments are due. Because of this relatively cheap source of financing, many low-income countries may currently be able to maintain their current debt levels despite running significant deficits.[5] In the long run, however, one of the goals of concessional financing is for the recipient countries to substantially reduce their reliance on external official flows. Accordingly, it is generally envisaged that low-income countries will eventually graduate from concessional assistance, implying that the rate of interest they pay on their debt will gradually approach market rates as access to concessional financing is phased out.

For most low-income countries, graduation from concessional borrowing is expected to occur only in the long run. In the process, these countries will have to shift their primary balances from deficits in the near and medium terms to significant surpluses in the long run in order to remain solvent while repaying maturing concessional loans and financing any current overall deficits. Moreover, the necessary adjustments in the primary balance will have to reflect any loss in grants that these countries might suffer, placing greater pressure to increase their own revenue and decrease expenditure. To reflect these circumstances, the time frame of the analysis should, if possible, extend to the point of the country's expected graduation from concessional assistance.[6] In most low-income countries, it is envisaged that this will be at least 20 years.

On the other hand, there are costs to using an excessively long time frame for debt sustainability analysis. In particular, projections very far into the future are typically highly sensitive to very small changes in long-run assumptions, which typically are highly uncertain. As a result, a very long timeframe risks diverting attention away from near-term policy needs and instead allows debt sustainability to be predicated on highly uncertain long-run macroeconomic assumptions or on changes in fiscal policy in the distant future that current policymakers cannot credibly commit to. In addition, long time frames increase the computational costs. Thus, even if graduation is not expected after 20 years, analysts may wish to cap the exercise at this point to keep it manageable. In these cases, the analysis will at least indicate how far the country may be from graduation in 20 years.

---

[5] Indeed, it is often a condition of concessional financing that a country *increase* its social spending, reducing or eliminating (increasing) any fiscal surplus (deficit) that it may have been running.

[6] This is the point at which all *new* debt is on commercial terms, although some existing debt may still be on concessional terms.

Defining Public Debt

Another important preliminary issue in fiscal debt sustainability analysis is determining how public debt should be defined. In this regard, there are choices to be made regarding coverage (which could range from a narrow focus on central government to a very broad focus on total public sector), as well as type of debt (gross versus net).

In our framework, we suggest that, in most cases, debt statistics should be compiled for the entire public sector as well as its major subcomponents. The definition of public debt should in principle include both domestic and external debt of the central government, regional or state governments, and local governments. The liabilities of extrabudgetary funds, such as social security funds, and public enterprises, such as publicly owned airlines and utilities, should, if possible, be included in the definition of public debt in most cases (see caveats below). However, it is recognized that in many cases limits on data availability may allow coverage only for a smaller subsector, such as the central government.

In principle, it is useful to focus most public debt sustainability analyses on net debt concepts (liabilities minus the value of assets), since it is important to look at not just the debt a government owes but also the assets that a government has to repay its debt. In practice, however, the value of government assets is difficult to establish in many low-income countries. As a result, rough estimates of net debt may have to be made in many cases. In this regard, it is worth noting that the assets of the general government in most countries are either small or not readily sellable in the market (e.g., a public monument). Thus, in these cases, gross debt may be an acceptable proxy for net debt for the general government sector. Similarly, gross debt may be a good proxy for net debt for public enterprises that are known to have weak financial positions, perhaps due to the quasi-fiscal activities that these enterprises often undertake. However, in cases where public enterprises or extrabudgetary funds (such as social security institutions) are known to have substantial assets, it may often be necessary to take account of these assets in the sustainability analysis. For example, if an enterprise is known to have substantial assets (such as a financial institution) or to operate on a sound commercial basis, analysts might decide to estimate the net debt of these enterprises to be zero, effectively excluding them from the analysis.

Another exception to using broad coverage may be cases in which subnational governments do not contract debt and their revenues cannot be used (either directly or indirectly) to pay central government debt. In these cases, it may be sensible to exclude these subnational governments from both measures of debt and measures of public sector balances, so that, for example, debt-to-revenue ratios are more meaningful.

In any event, care should be taken to ensure that the definition of the public sector is consistent across stocks and flows, so that changes in the flows, such as a larger primary balance, can be reconciled with changes in the stock of debt. To allow reconciliation between stocks and flows, contingent liabilities of the public sector should be excluded from debt stocks until the liabilities are officially recognized. However, if the value of contingent liabilities is known, these can be shown in output tables of the debt sustainability analysis as a memorandum item, as recommended by the *Government Finance Statistics Manual 2001* (IMF, 2001). Such contingent liabilities may include government loan guarantees, the expected costs of bank recapitalization, or unfunded pension liabilities. In such cases, the contingent liabilities should be valued at the option price that a financial institution would charge to take responsibility for the government's potential liability. For example, if the coverage of public sector stocks and flows extends only to the general government, then general government guarantees on debt contracted by public enterprises should be included in the memo items as a contingent liability, valued at the present value of the expected cost of the government's liability.[7] On the other hand, if the coverage of public sector stocks and flows includes public enterprises, then the gross value of such debt will already be included in the public sector debt stock and need not be listed as a contingent liability.

Key Indicators

A third key issue in debt sustainability analysis is to determine which indicators one will use to assess debt sustainability. In this regard, we suggest using multiple indicators to capture the various economic and political constraints on debt sustainability, as discussed in this chapter's introduction. In particular, the following indicators may be especially useful in the low-income country context.

Nominal level of debt as a share of GDP: This is one of the most commonly quoted debt sustainability statistics, since it compares the level of indebtedness with a measure of a country's capacity to pay (GDP) in a manner that is easily understood and straightforward to calculate. However, its simplicity also entails at least two important drawbacks: (1) it ignores the terms on which debt is denominated, which can have a major impact on sustainability; and (2) it ignores the pattern of debt-service payments, which can create debt-service problems owing to liquidity or political constraints, even at low debt-to-GDP ratios.

---

[7]This assumes that the general government has not yet officially assumed the liability, in which case it would become part of general government debt and not be shown as a contingent liability.

Net present value (NPV) of debt as a share of GDP: The NPV of debt (debt service discounted at the market interest rate) can be another useful summary indicator of indebtedness since, unlike the nominal value of debt, it takes account of the terms on which the debt is denominated—that is, low-interest-rate debt will have a lower NPV while high-interest-rate debt will have a higher NPV. This is especially important in low-income countries, where much of the debt is concessional. As a result, comparisons of these countries' nominal debt ratios to those in countries with low levels of concessional financing may be misleading.[8] In the case of concessional financing, the total amount of debt service is lower and farther in the future, when a country's capacity to pay will be higher relative to current GDP, if this variable's growth is positive. Thus, to reflect these effects of concessional lending, a time series for the NPV of debt ratios can be useful.

The NPV concept may be most useful in low-income countries for external debt, since a large portion of external debt is often concessional. Ideally, consistent methods should be used for calculating the NPV of domestic debt by, for example, transforming future domestic debt-service payments into U.S. dollars using exchange rate projections and then using the same U.S. dollar discount rate for domestic debt as for external debt. However, the NPV of domestic debt may not differ significantly from the nominal value since most domestic debt is on market terms and is often very short-term debt. Moreover, in many cases, analysts may have insufficient detail on domestic debt-service payments to calculate the NPV. Thus, it may be necessary to make the simplifying assumption that the NPV of domestic debt equals the nominal value (so that the NPV of total fiscal debt is the NPV of external debt plus the nominal value of domestic debt). In the following discussion, it is assumed that this approach is taken.

Foreign currency–denominated public debt as a share of GDP: Foreign currency debt as a share of GDP can be another useful indicator of fiscal debt sustainability, since countries with a high degree of foreign currency debt may encounter problems generating a sufficient amount of foreign exchange to service this debt, even when total indebtedness is not excessively high.[9]

---

[8]Similarly, NPV calculations may facilitate comparisons of indebtedness across time within the same country when the terms on which the debt is denominated are changing.

[9]In this regard, it is useful to complement fiscal debt sustainability analyses with external debt sustainability analyses, in which the focus is on the evolution of the balance of payments, and total external debt (both public and private) as a share of exports is typically a key indicator of vulnerabilities in generating sufficient foreign exchange. However, this chapter restricts its focus to fiscal debt sustainability issues.

Gross financing needs as a share of GDP: Gross financing need is defined as the public sector deficit plus amortization of medium- and long-term debt plus the stock of short-term debt at the end of the previous period.[10] This statistic is important because it indicates whether liquidity constraints may become problematic.

Debt-to-revenue ratio: The debt-to-revenue ratio is useful because it gives a further indication of a country's ability to finance its debt and, unlike the debt-to-GDP ratio, takes account of constraints that may exist in converting national income into public revenue.[11] In addition, this ratio is likely to be less sensitive to the definition of the public sector than the debt-to-GDP ratio.[12] As a result, the debt-to-revenue ratio may be more useful for cross-country comparisons. One issue in calculating the debt-to-revenue ratio is whether one should include grants in revenue, and the answer to this question may depend largely on the purpose of the analysis. If the goal is to determine the ability of a country to pay its debt obligations given its current and projected level of grants, then it seems reasonable to include grants in revenue; but if the goal is to assess whether a country is able to graduate from external assistance and still service its debts, then it may be reasonable to exclude grants from revenue.

Ratio of debt service to revenue: Debt service is typically defined as interest payments plus amortization of medium- and long-term debt. Debt service as a ratio to revenue is another useful indicator of potential liquidity problems, as well as the degree to which debt may become "politically unsustainable," in the sense that high levels of debt service relative to other types of spending may create political pressure to renege on debt payments.

Primary deficit that stabilizes the debt-to-GDP ratio: The primary deficit that stabilizes the debt-to-GDP (or NPV of debt) ratio is useful as a measure of the amount of adjustment that is needed to stabilize the debt dynamics. In our framework, we define the debt-stabilizing primary

---

[10] Short-term debt is debt with a maturity of one year or less.

[11] On the other hand, some may argue that GDP is better than current revenue at approximating the potential revenue that a country could raise in the event of a debt-servicing crisis.

[12] The coverage of public sector debt in debt sustainability analysis should be consistent with the coverage of public sector flows; for example, if public sector debt is defined for the general government, then revenue should also be defined for the general government. As a result, when the definition of the public sector differs across countries, the debt-to-revenue ratio is more likely to be similar across countries than is the debt-to-GDP ratio; for example, the ratio of general government debt to general government revenue in Country X may be somewhat comparable to the ratio of central government debt to central government revenue in Country Y, whereas the ratio of general government debt to GDP in Country X is likely to differ significantly from the ratio of central government debt to GDP in Country Y simply because of the different coverage.

balance as the sum of the actual primary balance (as a share of GDP) and the actual change in the debt ratio in each period of the baseline scenario. Note that, in this case, this estimated primary deficit only stabilizes the debt ratio in the period in question, assuming that all previous periods followed the path of the baseline scenario.

Decomposing Fiscal Debt Dynamics

To better analyze debt dynamics, it is also useful to decompose the evolution of the debt-to-GDP ratio in order to determine the main factors driving the evolution of the debt ratio. In this regard, the change in the debt-to-GDP ratio between any two periods can be described by the following equation:

$$d_{t+1} - d_t = \frac{\left[\left(1-\alpha_1\right)r^d_{t+1} + \alpha_t r^f_{t+1} - g + \alpha_t \varepsilon_{t+1}\left(1+r^f_{t+1}\right)\right]d_t}{\left(1+g_{t+1}\right)} - p_{t+1} + \eta_{t+1}, \quad (2)$$

where d_t is the nominal value of public debt at time t expressed as a ratio to GDP, α is the share of debt held in foreign currency, r^f is the average real interest rate on foreign currency debt,[13] r^d is the average real interest rate on domestic debt, g is the real GDP growth rate, ε is the percentage change in the real exchange rate,[14] p is the primary balance as a share of GDP, and η represents other balance sheet changes that affect debt as a share of GDP. This equation is derived in the Appendix.

Equation (2) can be used to calculate the change in the public debt ratio and to separate the different channels that contribute to its evolution: (1) the primary deficit effect ($-p$); (2) the real foreign-currency interest rate effect ($\alpha dr^f/(1+g)$); (3) the real domestic interest rate effect ($(1-\alpha)dr^d/(1+g)$); (4) the real GDP growth effect ($-gd/(1+g)$); and (5) the real exchange rate effect ($\alpha d\varepsilon(1+r^f)/(1+g)$). The separation of the different factors allows an assessment of their relative importance for the evolution of the debt ratio. It also serves as the basis for stress tests in which the key assumptions are varied (see the subsection on

---

[13] $r^f = (1+i^f)/(1+\pi^f)-1$, where i^f = the average nominal interest rate on foreign currency debt and π^f = the GDP deflator in the country in whose currency the foreign currency debt is denominated. If the debt is denominated in several currencies, this could reflect an average of partner country inflation or, as a simplifying approximation, inflation in the country of the most important partner (e.g., the United States or the euro area).

[14] A real depreciation of the local currency ($\varepsilon > 0$) leads to an increase in foreign currency debt, expressed in local currency terms. If the debt is denominated in several currencies, this could reflect the average real depreciation against these currencies or, as a simplifying approximation, real depreciation against the most important currency could be used as a proxy (e.g., the U.S. dollar or the euro).

stress tests below). In addition to these terms, there are other factors (η) that may increase or decrease debt; for example, from recognition of contingent liabilities, debt relief operations, or privatization receipts. Gross debt can also change as a result of other below-the-line operations (such as repayment of debt financed by a reduction in financial assets) as well as cross-currency movements. Finally, factors that cannot be identified are counted as a residual that is equal to the difference between the actual change in debt and the identified factors. Large residuals might indicate problems in the data and/or projections.

The evolution of the NPV of debt can also be decomposed through an analogous equation:

$$n_{t+1} - n_t = \frac{\left[\alpha_t r^\delta_{t+1} + \left(1 - \alpha_t\right) r^d_{t+1} - g_{t+1} + \alpha_t \varepsilon_{t+1}\left(1 + r^\delta_{t+1}\right)\right] n_t}{1 + g_{t+1}} - p_{t+1} - \lambda_{t+1} b^f_{t+1} + \eta_{t+1}, \quad (3)$$

where n_t is the NPV of public debt at time t expressed as a ratio to GDP, r^δ is the real discount rate on foreign currency debt,[15] λ is the grant element of new debt (expressed as a percentage), and b^f is new foreign currency borrowing as a share of GDP. This equation is also derived in the Appendix.

This equation can be used to separate the different channels contributing to the evolution of the NPV: (1) the primary deficit effect ($-p$), (2) the real discount rate effect ($\alpha n r^\delta/(1+g)$), (3) the real domestic interest rate effect ($(1-\alpha)n r^d/(1+g)$), (4) the real GDP growth effect ($-ng/(1+g)$), (5) the real exchange rate effect ($\alpha n \varepsilon (1+r^\delta)/(1+g)$), (6) the impact of grants that are effectively given via the grant element of new borrowing (λb^f), and (7) the other balance sheet changes, including a residual for unidentified factors (η).

Assessing Key Macroeconomic Assumptions

Projections of debt sustainability are typically highly sensitive to the underlying assumptions regarding the evolution of real GDP growth, interest rates, exchange rate appreciation, primary balances, and other macroeconomic variables. Thus, it is critical to analyze how realistic these assumptions are in the baseline scenario. A simple check that can be made on the assumptions is simply to compare them to their historic averages. In general, it is probably imprudent to assume that key variables will differ markedly from their historic averages, unless there are clear and specific reasons for doing so.

---

[15] If δ is the nominal, time-invariant U.S. dollar discount rate, then $(1+\delta) = (1+\pi^f_t)(1+r^\delta_t)$, where π^f_t = the U.S. GDP deflator inflation rate.

Stress Tests

Because of the importance of and uncertainty regarding key macro-economic variables, it is also useful to perform several "stress tests" to assess the sensitivity of the baseline scenario to major departures from the assumed trends in macroeconomic variables.

In choosing the most appropriate stress tests, it is useful to first con-sider which factors typically have the largest effects on debt sustain-ability. Important factors that are often cited are real GDP growth,[16] exchange rate depreciation, real interest rates, primary balances, and the recognition of previously contingent liabilities. Thus, the following are some suggested stress tests for low-income countries.

- Real GDP growth and the primary balance in each period are equal to the historical averages over the past 10 years (or latest years available);[17] if the results of this stress test differ markedly from the baseline scenario, this might indicate excessively optimistic or pes-simistic assumptions in the baseline.

- The primary balance remains at last year's level for all future years; this might be a "no-reform" scenario.[18]

- Real GDP growth in each of the first two periods is below the his-torical average by one standard deviation (standard deviations for key variables can be calculated using historical data); this simu-lates the effects of a severe recession.

- The primary balance in each of the first two periods is below the historical average by one standard deviation; this simulates the ef-fects of a significant policy slippage.

- Both real GDP growth and the primary balance in each of the first two periods are below their historical averages by one-half a stan-dard deviation.

- The real GDP growth rate in each period is below the baseline scenario by one standard deviation of the average real GDP growth rate for the entire projection period.[19]

---

[16]For example, Easterly (2001) finds that a slowdown in growth rates was a primary determinant of the debt crises in Heavily Indebted Poor Countries (HIPCs).

[17]For countries where exceptional noneconomic episodes (e.g., wars) have severely af-fected economic performance in the recent past, the period covered by such episodes may have to be excluded when computing historical averages. Alternatively, historical averages for similar countries could be used.

[18]Unless, for example, there has already been a substantial adjustment that the base-line scenario predicts will be difficult to sustain.

[19]If the standard deviation of the one-period growth rate is SD, then the standard de-viation of the average growth rate over n periods is $SD/\sqrt{n}$. This is to test the sensitiv-ity of the results to a lower-than-expected long-run growth rate.

- There is a permanent 30 percent depreciation in the first projection period.

- There is a 10 percent of GDP increase in other debt-creating flows in the first projection period; this simulates the potential effects of having to assume contingent liabilities such as a bank recapitalization.

- There is a permanent, one-standard-deviation shock to the most important commodity price in the first projection period.

Of course, this list is only meant to be suggestive; the number and type of stress tests should be tailored to the particular risks facing each country.[20]

Note that one easy method of performing these stress tests is to use the decomposition in equations (2) and (3) to estimate the effect on debt of changing a particular macroeconomic variable in each period. However, for shocks that have many pass-through effects (e.g., exchange rate depreciation may be associated with higher interest rates and also affect growth), more complicated modeling may be required. In general, the need for more complicated modeling will depend on how important the pass-through effects are judged to be in each case.

Note also that, to perform stress tests, it is necessary to make assumptions about the terms of marginal borrowing. In other words, if a change in macroeconomic assumptions results in more borrowing, then one must make assumptions about the terms on which this borrowing is contracted. Since these assumptions may have a substantial impact on the outcome of the stress tests, it is important that the terms of marginal borrowing be specified realistically. In particular, it may be that, while many low-income countries' debt is, on average, highly concessional, these countries' access to concessional financing at the margin may be more limited (especially in the event of policy slippages).

Bringing the Elements Together

The elements of this debt sustainability analysis framework—the key indicators of the baseline scenario, the decomposition of the evolution of debt, the highlighting of key macroeconomic assumptions, and the results of the stress tests—are all brought together in Tables 1 and 2, which show how one might present these elements for a particular country (the details of this particular case study are discussed in the next section). Table 1 shows how the decomposition of nominal debt

---

[20]It may also be useful, in some cases, to assess the favorable impact on debt sustainability of substituting grants for loans.

Table 1. Public Sector Debt Sustainability Framework, 2000–2023, Nominal Debt
(Percent of GDP, unless otherwise indicated)

	Actuals			Estimate	Projections	
	2000	2001	2002	2003	2004	2005
I. Baseline Projections						
Public sector debt[1]	222.2	171.1	171.9	125.3	113.6	105.6
of which, foreign currency–denominated	217.1	150.2	152.9	105.9	97.8	91.8
Change in public sector debt	39.3	–51.1	0.9	–46.6	–11.7	–8.1
Change in public sector debt	39.3	–51.1	0.9	–46.6	–11.7	–8.1
Identified debt-creating flows	28.5	–45.3	2.4	–45.5	–10.3	–7.1
Primary deficit	2.8	4.7	1.6	0.5	–1.5	–1.0
Revenue and grants	25.1	24.8	26.3	25.5	25.5	24.5
of which, grants	5.7	5.7	8.3	7.1	7.4	6.3
Primary (noninterest) expenditure	27.9	29.5	27.8	25.9	24.0	23.5
Automatic debt dynamics	33.5	–62.5	0.8	–12.8	–8.8	–6.1
of which, contribution from average real interest rate	–1.1	–3.0	–0.8	–0.2	0.6	0.1
of which, contribution from real GDP growth	–6.3	–10.4	–5.0	–7.4	–5.4	–5.4
of which, contribution from real exchange rate depreciation	40.9	–49.1	6.6	–5.3	–4.0	–0.8
Other identified debt-creating flows	–7.9	12.5	0.0	–33.1	0.0	0.0
Privatization receipts (negative)	0.0	0.0	0.0	0.0	0.0	0.0
Recognition of implicit or contingent liabilities	0.0	0.0	0.0	0.0	0.0	0.0
Debt relief (HIPC and other)	–7.9	0.0	0.0	–33.1	0.0	0.0
Bank recapitalization	0.0	12.5	0.0	0.0	0.0	0.0
Residual, including asset changes	10.9	–5.9	–1.5	–1.1	–1.4	–0.9
Other sustainability indicators						
NPV of public sector debt	140.2	115.0	123.1	61.1	55.4	52.4
Ratio of NPV of public sector debt to revenue and grants (percent)	558.8	463.2	468.2	240.0	217.1	214.4
Gross financing need	7.0	8.0	6.4	8.6	10.9	8.9
Ratio of public sector debt to revenue and grants (percent)	885.5	689.0	654.1	492.1	445.6	431.7
Ratio of debt service to revenue and grants (percent)	12.1	10.1	15.5	32.0	31.4	25.2
Primary deficit that stabilizes the debt-to-GDP ratio	–36.5	55.8	0.7	47.1	10.2	7.1
Key macroeconomic and fiscal assumptions						
Real GDP growth (percent)	3.6	4.9	3.0	4.5	4.5	5.0
Average real interest rate on domestic debt (percent)	16.3	12.8	0.1	1.6	3.3	4.6
Average real interest rate on foreign exchange debt (percent)	–1.1	–1.8	–0.6	–0.3	–0.1	–0.7
Real exchange rate depreciation (percentage change, + = depreciation)	24.0	–24.1	4.6	–3.6	–3.9	–0.9
Inflation rate (GDP deflator; percent)	30.0	24.3	19.7	19.9	13.7	7.9
Growth of real primary spending (deflated by GDP deflator; percent)	9.2	10.9	–2.9	–2.7	–3.2	2.6
Major commodity price: copper $/lb	0.8	0.7	0.7	0.8	0.8	0.9

	Projections				10-Year Standard Deviation	10-Year Historical Average	Projected Average 2004–08	Projected Average 2009–23
2006	2007	2010	2015	2023				
97.9	92.2	79.6	66.3	42.6	. . .	. . .	. . .	. . .
85.5	80.8	71.1	60.9	40.0	. . .	. . .	. . .	. . .
–7.7	–5.8	–3.5	–3.7	–3.2	. . .	. . .	. . .	. . .
–7.7	–5.8	–3.5	–3.7	–3.2	. . .	. . .	. . .	. . .
–5.7	–5.8	–4.3	–3.7	–2.8	. . .	. . .	. . .	. . .
–0.4	–0.9	0.0	0.3	0.0	3.9	–1.1	–0.9	0.1
24.0	23.0	22.4	21.3	20.0	2.0	26.2	23.9	21.2
5.9	4.8	4.3	3.2	1.9	3.7	3.4	5.8	3.1
23.6	22.0	22.5	21.6	20.1	3.8	25.1	23.1	21.3
–5.2	–4.9	–4.4	–4.0	–2.8	. . .	. . .	. . .	. . .
–0.2	–0.4	–0.5	–0.7	–0.6	. . .	. . .	. . .	. . .
–5.0	–4.2	–3.6	–3.0	–2.0	. . .	. . .	. . .	. . .
0.0	–0.3	–0.3	–0.3	–0.3	. . .	. . .	. . .	. . .
0.0	0.0	0.0	0.0	0.0	. . .	. . .	. . .	. . .
0.0	0.0	0.0	0.0	0.0	. . .	. . .	. . .	. . .
0.0	0.0	0.0	0.0	0.0	. . .	. . .	. . .	. . .
0.0	0.0	0.0	0.0	0.0	. . .	. . .	. . .	. . .
0.0	0.0	0.0	0.0	0.0	. . .	. . .	. . .	. . .
–2.0	0.1	0.8	0.0	–0.4	. . .	. . .	. . .	. . .
47.3	43.9	38.4	34.0	21.5	. . .	. . .	. . .	. . .
197.3	191.4	171.1	163.6	114.8	. . .	. . .	. . .	. . .
8.3	7.0	5.0	2.7	1.3	. . .	. . .	. . .	. . .
408.0	401.4	355.1	310.8	212.7	. . .	. . .	. . .	. . .
22.4	21.1	14.8	9.8	6.5	. . .	. . .	. . .	. . .
7.2	4.8	3.6	4.0	3.2	. . .	. . .	. . .	. . .
5.0	4.5	4.5	4.5	4.5	5.6	0.6	4.7	4.5
5.5	5.4	5.0	4.8	4.3	8.5	9.8	4.8	4.6
–1.1	–1.2	–1.3	–1.5	–1.6	0.6	–1.1	–0.9	–1.5
0.1	–0.4	–0.5	–0.5	–0.7	. . .	. . .	–1.1	–0.5
5.2	5.0	5.0	5.0	5.0	44.2	43.7	7.4	5.0
5.4	–2.2	4.4	3.3	3.6	17.0	3.9	1.6	3.8
0.9	0.9	0.9	0.9	0.9	0.2	0.9	0.9	0.9

Table 1 *(concluded)*
(Percent of GDP, unless otherwise indicated)

	2000	2001	2002	2003	2004	2005
	Actuals			Estimate	Projections	
				II. Stress Tests for Public Debt Ratio		
Alternative scenarios						
A1. Real GDP growth and primary balance are at historical averages				125.3	114.0	106.3
A2. Primary balance is unchanged from 2002 (no reform)				125.3	116.7	111.1
A3. Long-run real GDP growth is at baseline minus one standard deviation				125.3	115.2	108.8
Bounds tests						
B1. Real GDP growth is at baseline minus one standard deviation in 2004–05				125.3	121.2	121.2
B2. Primary balance is at baseline minus one standard deviation in 2004–05				125.3	117.5	113.3
B3. Combination of B1 and B2 using one-half-standard-deviation shocks				125.3	118.8	115.5
B4. One-time 30 percent real depreciation in 2004				125.3	177.0	165.1
B5. 10 percent of GDP increase in other debt-creating flows in 2004				125.3	123.6	115.5
B6. A permanent, one-standard-deviation negative shock to the major commodity price in 2004				125.3	116.0	109.2

Sources: Country authorities; and IMF staff estimates and projections.
[1]Central government; gross debt.

Projections					10-Year Standard Deviation	10-Year Historical Average	Projected Average 2004–08	Projected Average 2009–23
2006	2007	2010	2015	2023				
98.4	92.4	77.1	57.4	25.4	. . .	. . .	. . .	. . .
105.4	102.1	94.5	86.6	71.1	. . .	. . .	. . .	. . .
102.9	99.0	93.1	94.8	102.4	. . .	. . .	. . .	. . .
114.7	110.4	102.5	97.0	83.5	. . .	. . .	. . .	. . .
105.6	99.7	86.9	72.8	48.1	. . .	. . .	. . .	. . .
107.1	100.8	86.7	71.2	44.9	. . .	. . .	. . .	. . .
154.1	145.1	124.2	100.2	65.2	. . .	. . .	. . .	. . .
107.7	101.9	88.9	74.6	49.6	. . .	. . .	. . .	. . .
102.9	98.5	89.9	82.6	67.1	. . .	. . .	. . .	. . .

evolution could be presented, while Table 2 shows the decomposition of the NPV of debt.

Once one has projected the indicators and run the stress tests, the key remaining question is what do they imply for the prospects for debt sustainability? In this regard, a few econometric studies have tried to map indicators such as the debt-to-GDP ratio into probabilities of experiencing a debt crisis or a period of low growth.[21] However, most of these studies either focus on emerging markets or on external debt; the analysis of total public sector debt indicators (external plus domestic debt) in low-income countries has been more problematic. To some degree this should not be surprising, given the wide differences across low-income countries in the quality and coverage of public sector data.

Thus, while acknowledging that the literature on external debt and emerging markets can provide some useful guideposts, our framework eschews a purely formulaic approach to mapping various public debt indicators into a specific probability of default, given the still early stage of the literature and the heterogeneity in conditions across countries. Rather, some judgment is required on the part of the analyst, taking into account his or her knowledge of country-specific details,[22] to assess whether the indicators suggest that debt sustainability is a sufficiently low risk or whether corrective action is needed, given the path of the key variables under the baseline scenario and stress tests. In this regard, scenarios that show rapidly rising debt or debt-service ratios should raise warning flags. Similarly, projections that show debt-service or gross financing need spiking in a particular period may signal a need to restructure debt payments to reduce the risk of liquidity crises.

Case Study

In this section we present simulation results illustrating the use of the debt sustainability analysis framework for a typical low-income country with a large stock of debt. We use the framework described in the previous sections to decompose the factors underlying the trends in the nominal value and NPV of public debt under the baseline scenario. We then analyze the range of risks to the baseline projection by using the results derived from the stress tests.

---

[21] See, for example, Cohen (1997), Patillo, Poirson, and Ricci (2002), Hemming, Kell, and Schimmelpfennig (2003), and Kraay and Nehru (2004).

[22] In this regard, Kray and Nehru (2004) find that the quality of a country's policies is a key factor affecting the relationship between debt indicators and the likelihood of a debt crisis.

Data used for the simulation are based on a typical low-income country. Parameters of the simulation are calibrated to replicate the case of a highly indebted country that reaches the completion point under the HIPC Initiative during 2003. In this year, the country benefits from substantial debt relief. The policy issue in this country is whether the post-relief profile of debt will be sustainable or not under a set of economic policies aimed at achieving macroeconomic stability and poverty reduction. From 2004 onward this country is expected to start a gradual process toward graduation from exceptional financing. This process will not be finished by the time of the end of the simulation. The simulation period spans between 2004 and 2023, with model calibration based on historical data referring to the 1993–2002 period. The first projection period in the simulation is 2004. Results are presented on an annual basis for the 2004–07 period, for 2010, 2015, and 2023 (Tables 1 and 2).

The coverage of public debt is critical to the interpretation of the results. In this country, public debt is defined as the sum of the gross liabilities of the central government, as local government debt is generally not significant and data on state-owned enterprises are usually incomplete in a typical low-income country. With incomplete data on the broader definition of public sector, the results of the simulation have to be assessed with caution. Other fiscal risks reflect the presence of institutions outside the coverage of the public sector chosen in this analysis that can engage in important quasi-fiscal operations. The simulation results have to be analyzed in combination with a broader analysis of the possible risks to fiscal sustainability stemming from quasi-fiscal operations of off-budgetary units and contingent liabilities.

At the start of the simulation, the country has a high level of public debt (Table 1). In 2003, the NPV of public debt was above 60 percent. The nominal value of public debt reached 125 percent of GDP, a level well above that of emerging and industrial countries (IMF, 2003). The large stock of debt also implied large flows of payments for debt service. Gross financing needs were high, at nearly 9 percent of GDP, and debt service represented 32 percent of overall revenue collection. Although approximately 85 percent of the debt was contracted from external lenders, the share of domestic debt was substantial for a low-income country. Domestic debt represented almost 20 percent of GDP at the beginning of the simulation period, reflecting a large reliance on domestic sources of deficit financing in the past in the absence of sufficiently large inflows of foreign aid.

In this country, the NPV of public debt has been on a downward trend since 2000 when it reached 140 percent of GDP. The subsequent fall in the ratio was a result of improved macroeconomic conditions and

Table 2. Public Sector Debt Sustainability Framework, 2000–2023, NPV of Debt
(Percent of GDP, unless otherwise indicated)

	Actuals			Estimate	Projections	
	2000	2001	2002	2003	2004	2005
I. Baseline Projections						
NPV of public sector debt[1]	140.2	115.0	123.1	61.1	55.4	52.4
of which, foreign currency–denominated	135.1	94.1	104.0	41.7	39.5	38.7
Change in NPV	−0.5	−25.2	8.1	−62.0	−5.8	−3.0
Identified debt-creating flows	6.4	−19.4	4.0	−58.9	−6.1	−3.7
Primary deficit	2.8	4.7	1.6	0.5	−1.5	−1.0
Revenue and grants	25.1	24.8	26.3	25.5	25.5	24.5
of which, grants	5.7	5.7	8.3	7.1	7.4	6.3
Primary (noninterest) expenditure	27.9	29.5	27.8	25.9	24.0	23.5
Grant element of new concessional loans	−4.7	−3.1	−3.0	−2.4	−2.8	−2.1
Automatic debt dynamics	33.7	−33.6	5.4	−4.3	−1.8	−0.7
of which, contribution from real discount rate on foreign-currency debt	5.0	4.6	4.4	4.4	1.9	1.6
of which, contribution from real interest rate on domestic debt	0.7	0.6	0.0	0.3	0.6	0.7
of which, contribution from real GDP growth	−4.9	−6.6	−3.4	−5.3	−2.6	−2.6
of which, contribution from real exchange rate depreciation	32.8	−32.2	4.4	−3.7	−1.6	−0.3
Other identified debt-creating flows	−25.4	12.5	0.0	−52.7	0.0	0.0
Privatization receipts (negative)	0.0	0.0	0.0	0.0	0.0	0.0
Recognition of implicit or contingent liabilities	0.0	0.0	0.0	0.0	0.0	0.0
Debt relief (HIPC and other)	−25.4	0.0	0.0	−52.7	0.0	0.0
Bank recapitalization	0.0	12.5	0.0	0.0	0.0	0.0
Residual, including asset changes	−6.9	−5.8	4.1	−3.0	0.3	0.8
Other sustainability indicators						
Nominal value of public sector debt	222.2	171.1	171.9	125.3	113.6	105.6
NPV of contingent liabilities (not yet officially recognized in public sector debt)	...	...	...	...	...	...
Ratio of NPV of public sector debt to revenue and grants (percent)	558.8	463.2	468.2	240.0	217.1	214.4
Gross financing need	7.0	8.0	6.4	8.6	10.9	8.9
Ratio of public sector debt to revenue and grants (percent)	885.5	689.0	654.1	492.1	445.6	431.7
Ratio of debt service to revenue and grants (percent)	12.1	10.1	15.5	32.0	31.4	25.2
Primary deficit that stabilizes the NPV of debt-to-GDP ratio	3.4	30.0	−6.5	62.4	4.3	2.0

	Projections				10-Year Standard	10-Year Historical	Projected Average	Projected Average
2006	2007	2010	2015	2023	Deviation	Average	2004–08	2009–23
47.3	43.9	38.4	34.0	21.5	...	...	...	...
34.9	32.6	29.8	28.6	19.0	...	...	...	...
−5.1	−3.4	−1.3	−1.2	−1.6	...	...	...	...
−2.1	−2.5	−1.4	−0.9	−0.7	...	...	...	...
−0.4	−0.9	0.0	0.3	0.0	3.9	−1.1	−0.9	0.1
24.0	23.0	22.4	21.3	20.0	2.0	26.2	23.9	21.2
5.9	4.8	4.3	3.2	1.9	3.7	3.4	5.8	3.1
23.6	22.0	22.5	21.6	20.1	3.8	25.1	23.1	21.3
−1.4	−1.3	−1.2	−0.9	−0.5	...	...	...	...
−0.3	−0.3	−0.3	−0.3	−0.3	...	...	...	...
1.4	1.3	1.1	1.1	0.8	...	...	...	...
0.7	0.6	0.5	0.3	0.1	...	...	...	...
−2.5	−2.0	−1.7	−1.5	−1.0	...	...	...	...
0.0	−0.1	−0.1	−0.1	−0.1	...	...	...	...
0.0	0.0	0.0	0.0	0.0	...	...	...	...
0.0	0.0	0.0	0.0	0.0	...	...	...	...
0.0	0.0	0.0	0.0	0.0	...	...	...	...
0.0	0.0	0.0	0.0	0.0	...	...	...	...
0.0	0.0	0.0	0.0	0.0	...	...	...	...
−3.0	−0.9	0.1	−0.3	−0.9	...	...	...	...
97.9	92.2	79.6	66.3	42.6	...	...	...	...
...	...	...	...	...	...	...	...	...
197.3	191.4	171.1	159.2	107.5	...	...	...	...
8.3	7.0	5.0	2.7	1.3	...	...	...	...
408.0	401.4	355.1	310.8	212.7	...	...	...	...
22.4	21.1	14.8	9.8	6.5	...	...	...	...
4.6	2.5	1.4	1.5	1.7	...	...	...	...

Table 2 *(concluded)*
(Percent of GDP, unless otherwise indicated)

	Actuals			Estimate	Projections	
	2000	2001	2002	2003	2004	2005
I. Baseline Projections						
Key macroeconomic and fiscal assumptions						
Real GDP growth (in percent)	3.6	4.9	3.0	4.5	4.5	5.0
Average nominal interest rate on						
foreign exchange debt (in percent)	1.0	0.6	0.6	1.1	1.1	1.0
Average real interest rate on						
domestic debt (in percent)	16.3	12.8	0.1	1.6	3.3	4.6
Real exchange rate depreciation						
(percentage change, + = depreciation)	24.0	–24.1	4.6	–3.6	–3.9	–0.9
Inflation rate (GDP deflator, percent)	30.0	24.3	19.7	19.9	13.7	7.9
Growth of real primary spending						
(deflated by GDP deflator, percent)	9.2	10.9	–2.9	–2.7	–3.2	2.6
Major commodity price: copper $/lb	0.8	0.7	0.7	0.8	0.8	0.9
Grant element of new external borrowing						
(share of total external borrowing, percent)	62.3	62.3	62.3	62.3	62.3	62.3
II. Stress Tests for NPV						
Alternative scenarios						
A1. Real GDP growth and primary balance						
are at historical averages				61.1	55.7	52.9
A2. Primary balance is unchanged						
from 2002 (no reform)				61.1	58.3	57.7
A3. Long-run real GDP growth is at baseline						
minus one standard deviation				61.1	56.3	54.3
Bounds tests						
B1. Real GDP growth is at baseline minus one						
standard deviation in 2004–2005				61.1	59.5	61.6
B2. Primary balance is at baseline minus one						
standard deviation in 2004–2005				61.1	59.1	59.7
B3. Combination of B1 and B2 using						
one-half-standard-deviation shocks				61.1	58.8	59.2
B4. One-time 30 percent real depreciation in 2004				61.1	81.1	77.6
B5. 10 percent of GDP increase in other						
debt-creating flows in 2004				61.1	65.0	61.7
B6. A permanent, one-standard-deviation						
negative shock to the major						
commodity price in 2004				61.1	57.2	55.5

Sources: Country authorities; and IMF staff estimates and projections.
[1]Central government; gross debt.

		Projections			10-Year Standard Deviation	10-Year Historical Average	Projected Average 2004–08	Projected Average 2009–23
2006	2007	2010	2015	2023				
5.0	4.5	4.5	4.5	4.5	5.6	0.6	4.7	4.5
0.9	0.9	0.7	0.4	0.3	0.3	0.7	0.9	0.5
5.5	5.4	5.0	4.8	4.3	8.5	9.8	4.8	4.6
0.1	−0.4	−0.5	−0.5	−0.7	...	...	−1.1	−0.5
5.2	5.0	5.0	5.0	5.0	44.2	43.7	7.4	5.0
5.4	−2.2	4.4	3.3	3.6	17.0	3.9	1.6	3.8
0.9	0.9	0.9	0.9	0.9	0.2	0.9	0.9	0.9
62.3	62.3	62.3	62.3	62.3	18.2	88.7	62.3	62.3
47.4	43.8	35.6	25.6	5.7	...	...	...	...
54.4	53.2	51.8	52.3	47.4	...	...	...	...
50.4	48.2	47.7	55.9	71.5	...	...	...	...
57.9	56.0	55.2	58.7	56.6	...	...	...	...
54.4	50.8	44.8	39.9	26.6	...	...	...	...
53.4	49.5	42.7	36.9	22.7	...	...	...	...
70.7	65.6	56.0	46.6	30.1	...	...	...	...
56.3	52.7	46.6	41.5	27.9	...	...	...	...
51.7	49.5	47.5	48.5	43.6	...	...	...	...

the beneficial impact of debt relief (nearly 80 percent of GDP). The reduction in the stock of debt did not necessarily, however, lead to a more manageable debt-service burden, for the ratio of debt service to revenue increased from 12 percent to 32 percent in the same period, reflecting higher reliance on more costly domestic debt and a decline in domestic revenue collection that largely offset higher grant flows.[23] The latter suggests that the volatility of revenue collection may be an important source of vulnerability for debt sustainability in this country.

For the projections, the baseline scenario is one in which tight fiscal policy is assumed to be conducive to a noninflationary environment that would maintain moderate real interest rates and foster growth.[24] Thus, real GDP growth is projected to be buoyant, averaging 4.7 percent a year in the first five years of the simulation and stabilizing at 4.5 percent a year in the following period. These buoyant growth rates compare with the poor performance in the previous decade when GDP growth was limited to 0.6 percent a year with large annual fluctuations.[25] The average real interest rate on domestic debt is expected to fall from an average 10 percent in 1993–2002 to 4–5 percent in the projection period. Inflation, as measured by the GDP deflator, is projected to subside, reaching 5 percent by the end of the simulation period from high initial values (20 percent a year in 2003).

The improved macroeconomic framework is expected to be sustained by a prudent fiscal policy that would maintain a small primary surplus during the initial part of the simulation period. Maintaining this fiscal stance is achieved by reductions in primary expenditure, since grants are projected to fall while domestic revenue collection is projected to remain broadly constant over the projection period.

The reduction in primary expenditure consistent with this scenario is large. The ratio of public spending to GDP is projected to fall by almost 6 percentage points of GDP from 26 percent in 2003 to slightly more than 20 percent at the end of the simulation period. This implies that the growth rate of real primary spending will be limited to 3.8 percent a year (the historical average growth rate) in the period 2009–23, while real spending is projected to grow only slightly in the initial years of the simulation. Given the projected growth of the population in the same period, the assumed growth rate of primary spending will reflect

---

[23] For more on the relationship between domestic revenue and grants, see Clements and others (2004).

[24] On the relationship between fiscal policy and growth and its determinants in low-income countries, see Baldacci, Hillman, and Kojo (2003).

[25] The standard deviation of GDP growth rates in the period 1992–2002 is estimated at 5.6 percent, or more than nine times the average growth rate in the same period.

only a moderate increase in real per capita primary spending. To achieve this target and make progress to reduce poverty in the medium term would entail enhancing the effectiveness of public expenditure and improving its composition in favor of poverty reduction programs that benefit the vulnerable groups in the population. However, this level of expenditure compression may not be politically sustainable in this country, giving rise to risks of political instability that could affect the persistence of the fiscal consolidation effort and highlighting a possible need for more grant aid.

Debt dynamics are projected to improve markedly under the baseline scenario, with the NPV of public debt projected to fall steadily as a share of GDP from 61 percent in 2003 to 22 percent in 2023. Gross financing requirements would be dramatically reduced from 9 percent of GDP in 2003 to less than 2 percent in 2023. Debt service as a share of total revenue is also projected to fall to more sustainable levels—about 6.5 percent at the end of the simulation. However, debt-service indicators are expected to remain relatively high in the next few years. This result highlights the vulnerability of the country adjustment if it does not succeed in stabilizing the domestic revenue base.[26]

The decline in the NPV of public debt to GDP projected under the baseline scenario primarily reflects the maintenance of prudent fiscal policies, buoyant economic growth, and continued access to concessional financing. In the absence of large primary deficits (as in recent years) and high real interest rates, robust real GDP growth drives a continuous reduction in the NPV of public debt to GDP, as can be seen in the decomposition in Table 2. Exchange rate dynamics are conducive to a lower stock of public debt in the first period of the simulation, while the contribution of exchange rate dynamics to debt stabilization becomes marginal thereafter.

The results of the "no-reform" alternative scenario highlight the importance of achieving the targeted fiscal consolidation to maintain the NPV of debt-to-GDP ratio on a declining path. This scenario, which is based on the assumption that the primary fiscal deficit remains unchanged at the level of 1.6 percent of GDP observed in 2002, does not lead to a large reduction in the debt stock. Rather, the ratio of the NPV of public debt to GDP remains significant at 47 percent of GDP at the end of the projection period.

The stress tests show that growth and exchange rate assumptions have a large impact on public debt projections. Under many alternative simulations, results for both the ratio of public debt to GDP and the

---

[26] For more on the persistence of fiscal adjustment, see Baldacci and others (2004).

ratio of NPV of debt to GDP depart significantly from the baseline (Figure 1). Results are very sensitive to a fall in the real GDP growth rate in both the short term and long run. Debt levels are also sensitive to changes in the exchange rate, especially in the short run. The stress tests also show that excessive debt service continues to be a source of risk for this country despite the large debt relief received in 2003. In the event of negative shocks, debt service could remain at high levels indefinitely (Figure 1).

The fiscal stance projected under the baseline scenario at the end of the simulation (no primary deficit) is consistent with a sustainable path of public debt, which is defined in this case as a nonincreasing ratio of the NPV of public debt to GDP. If, however, long-run growth rates fall below the real interest rate, a tighter fiscal stance would be required.

In sum, achieving fiscal sustainability will be a challenge for this country. Even though the fiscal stance projected under the baseline scenario is consistent with a declining debt-to-GDP ratio, there is great vulnerability to depreciation and income growth shocks. This is especially pertinent in light of the relatively optimistic assumptions for growth relative to the historical record. Furthermore, the success of the adjustment is predicated on cuts in spending (relative to GDP), which will pose a challenge as the government simultaneously attempts to reallocate the budget toward poverty-reducing activities. In this context, an adjustment strategy that relies on raising the revenue effort might be politically more viable. In addition, higher external grants could help alleviate the pressure to cut spending.

Policy Implications of Debt Sustainability Analysis

Debt sustainability analysis can be an important aid in determining the appropriate policy stance to achieve a country's policy objectives. The policies underlying the baseline scenario are critical, since alternatives can lead to substantially different debt dynamics by affecting growth and other key macroeconomic variables. Debt sustainability results should be assessed in light of the policy options that are available to low-income countries to correct possibly unsustainable paths of public and external debt. In this context, the stress tests can help shed light on the robustness of these baseline scenarios. For example, while the baseline scenario could indicate that debt would remain sustainable, stress tests may indicate that the country would be unduly vulnerable to lower growth or adverse exogenous developments. Debt sustainability analysis could also facilitate an assessment of the extent to which the policies are consistent with the country's broader development agenda.

Figure 1. Indicators of Public Debt Under the Baseline Scenario and Selected Stress Tests, 2003–23
(Percent)

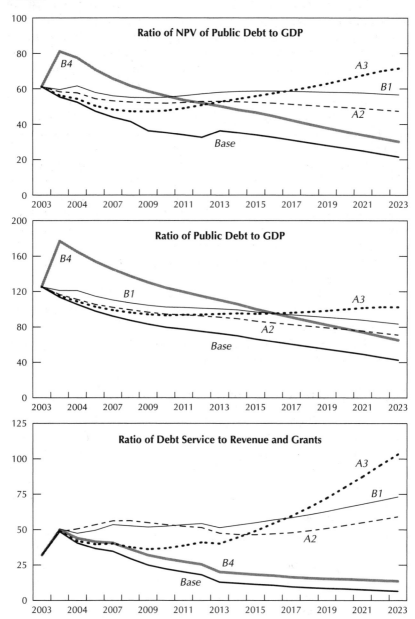

Source: IMF staff projections and simulations.

For example, countries may need higher public spending to achieve the United Nations' Millennium Development Goals. In these cases, debt sustainability analysis can be useful in highlighting the additional resources that may be needed for countries to achieve the Millennium Development Goals while maintaining a sustainable debt position.

An unsustainable debt position can be addressed in a number of ways—for example, through increased foreign grants, higher domestic revenue mobilization, or lower public spending. As such, an assessment that debt is rising over time, or that a higher primary surplus must be obtained to achieve debt sustainability in the future, does not necessarily imply that public expenditures must be reduced. The feasibility and desirability of the alternative options would need to be judged on a case-by-case basis.

In this regard, it is important to keep in mind that growth is an important determinant of debt sustainability in low-income countries; thus, options to reduce the fiscal debt burden must be assessed in light of their effects on growth, which makes a thorough analysis of the determinants of growth in each country essential.

Nonetheless, many countries may find that debt sustainability requires the implementation of more prudent fiscal policies. Fiscal prudence can contribute to debt sustainability directly, through a sufficiently large primary surplus, and indirectly, through the beneficial effect of low fiscal deficits on growth and macroeconomic stability.

In this regard, the composition of fiscal policy also has an important role. Fiscal consolidations based on expenditure savings stemming from efficiency-enhancing reforms, such as the reduction of subsidies, tend to be more effective at fostering growth than fiscal adjustments based on curtailing productive outlays. In fact, protecting the capital budget is associated with higher growth in low-income countries.[27] Over the long run, expanding basic social services and investing in human development and infrastructure are also likely to promote growth. In cases where such investments cannot be funded by cuts in less productive spending, analysts may need to carefully weigh the possible trade-offs between the growth-enhancing effects of such investments and the costs of the borrowing needed to finance them.

Conclusion

In this paper, we have presented a simple, pragmatic, and flexible framework that analysts might use to assess debt sustainability in low-

---

[27] See, for example, Gupta and others (2004).

income countries. The framework allows one to analyze the main determinants of debt dynamics, takes account of multiple constraints on debt sustainability via multiple indicators, examines the main risks to debt sustainability via stress tests, and emphasizes the importance of clarifying the underlying assumptions behind debt projections. This framework is simply meant to be suggestive, and it can and should be adjusted and tailored to the specific issues in the country of interest. Similarly, the framework is not intended to yield a simple "yes" or "no" answer to the question of whether a country's debt is sustainable; rather, it provides the basic building blocks for formulating an assessment of the balance or risks, taking into account both the empirical literature on key determinants of debt crises[28] and the analyst's knowledge of country-specific factors. In doing so, it is hoped that such a framework can assist in formulating appropriate macroeconomic policies.

Technical Appendix

Derivation of Fiscal Debt Equations

We model public debt dynamics as follows:

$$D_{t+1} = \left(1 + r_{t+1}^d\right)\left(1 + \pi_{t+1}^d\right)D_t^d + \left(1 + \varepsilon_{t+1}\right)\left(1 + r_{t+1}^f\right)\left(1 + \pi_{t+1}^d\right)D_t^f - P_{t+1} + H_{t+1}. \quad \text{(A1)}$$

The debt stock is composed of debt instruments denominated in both domestic and foreign currencies. Domestic currency debt (D_t^d) evolves according to the real interest rate in the domestic market (r^d) and the change in the domestic GDP deflator (π^d), while the evolution of the foreign currency debt (D_t^f), expressed in domestic currency, is affected not just by the foreign real interest rate (r^f) and inflation rate,[29] but also by changes in the real exchange rate (ε).[30] Finally, H is a residual that captures all other debt-creating flows, such as cross-currency movements.

The analysis looks at debt stocks relative to GDP. Therefore, defining lower-case variables as upper-case variables expressed as a proportion of nominal GDP (e.g., $d_{t+1} = D_{t+1}/Y_{t+1}$) and dividing both sides of equation (A1) by nominal GDP, Y_{t+1} yields the following:

---

[28] See the studies cited in footnote 21.

[29] See footnote 13.

[30]
$$\left(1 + \varepsilon_{t+1}\right) = \frac{e_{t+1}}{e_t}\left(\frac{1 + \pi_{t+1}^f}{1 + \pi_{t+1}^d}\right),$$

with e defined as the nominal exchange rate in units of local currency per unit of foreign currency.

$$d_{t+1} = \frac{\left(1 + r_{t+1}^d\right)d_t^d + \left(1 + \varepsilon_{t+1}\right)\left(1 + r_{t+1}^f\right)d_t^f}{\left(1 + g_{t+1}\right)} - p_{t+1} + \eta_{t+1}, \qquad (A2)$$

where g = the real GDP growth rate. Letting $d_t^f = \alpha_t d_t$ (where α_t is the share of debt held in foreign currency) and $d_t^d = (1-\alpha_t)d_t$, subtracting d_t from both sides, and rearranging yields equation (2) in the main text:

$$d_{t+1} - d_t = \frac{\left[\left(1 - \alpha_t\right)r_{t+1}^d + \alpha_t r_{t+1}^f - g_{t+1} + \alpha_t \varepsilon_{t+1}\left(1 + r_{t+1}^f\right)\right]d_t}{\left(1 + g_{t+1}\right)} - p_{t+1} + \eta_{t+1}. \qquad (A3)$$

The fiscal template uses this equation to calculate the change in debt and to separate the different channels that contribute to the evolution of the debt-to-GDP ratio.

To see how the equation for the evolution of the NPV of debt-to-GDP ratio is derived (equation (3) in the main text), note first that the NPV of foreign currency debt at the end of time period t is equal to the following:

$$N_t^f = \left(\frac{DS_{t+1}^{f*}}{\left(1+\delta\right)} + \frac{DS_{t+2}^{f*}}{\left(1+\delta\right)^2} + \frac{DS_{t+3}^{f*}}{\left(1+\delta\right)^3} + \ldots + \frac{DS_{\infty}^{f*}}{\left(1+\delta\right)^{\infty}}\right)e_t, \qquad (A4)$$

where N_t^f = the NPV of foreign currency debt (expressed in units of local currency), DS^{f*} is the foreign currency debt service (* denotes a value denominated in foreign currency) in each period on the stock of *existing debt* as of time period t, δ is the foreign-currency discount rate, and e is the nominal exchange rate (expressed in local currency per unit of foreign currency).

In time period $t+1$, DS_{t+1}^f will be paid off and new debt will be contracted, so that the NPV of foreign currency debt at the end of $t+1$ will be the following:

$$N_{t+1}^f = \left(\frac{DS_{t+2}^{f*}}{\left(1+\delta\right)} + \frac{DS_{t+3}^{f*}}{\left(1+\delta\right)^2} + \frac{DS_{t+4}^{f*}}{\left(1+\delta\right)^3} + \ldots + \frac{DS_{\infty}^{f*}}{\left(1+\delta\right)^{\infty}}\right)e_{t+1} + \left(1 - \lambda_{t+1}\right)B_{t+1}^f, \qquad (A5)$$

where the NPV of new debt contracted in time period $t+1$ is equal to nominal gross new borrowing (B^f) times one minus the grant element (λ) of this borrowing. Inserting equation (A4) in (A5), one can see that there is a clear relationship between N_t^f and N_{t+1}^f:

$$N_{t+1}^f = N_t^f\left(1+\delta\right)\left(\frac{e_{t+1}}{e_t}\right) - DS_{t+1}^f + \left(1 - \lambda_{t+1}\right)B_{t+1}^f. \qquad (A6)$$

(Note that debt service is now expressed in local currency units). Gross new foreign currency borrowing will equal foreign currency debt service minus the portion of the primary balance that is funded via foreign currency borrowing:

$$B_{t+1}^f = DS_{t+1}^f - P_{t+1}^f. \tag{A7}$$

Combining equation (A6) with equation (A7) and rearranging yields

$$N_{t+1}^f = N_t^f (1+\delta)\left(\frac{e_{t+1}}{e_t}\right) - P_{t+1}^f - \lambda_{t+1} B_{t+1}^f. \tag{A8}$$

It is assumed that all domestic debt is nonconcessional, so that the present value of domestic debt equals the nominal value,[31] which evolves as follows:

$$N_{t+1}^d = D_{t+1}^d = D_t^d (1+i_{t+1}^d) - P_{t+1}^d, \tag{A9}$$

where N^d is the NPV of domestic debt, D^d is the nominal value of domestic debt, i^d is the nominal interest rate on domestic debt, and P^d is the portion of the primary surplus financed by domestic debt.

Combining equation (A8) with (A9) and letting α equal the share of the NPV of debt held in foreign-currency yields the following expression for the evolution of the NPV of total debt:

$$N_{t+1} = N_{t+1}^f + N_{t+1}^d = \alpha_t N_t (1+\delta)\left(\frac{e_{t+1}}{e_t}\right) + (1-\alpha_t) N_t (1+i_{t+1}^d) - P_{t+1} - \lambda_{t+1} B_{t+1}^f. \tag{A10}$$

Dividing both sides of the equation by GDP in $t+1$ and letting smaller case symbols indicate amounts as a share of GDP yields:

$$n_{t+1} = \frac{\alpha_t n_t (1+\delta)\left(\frac{e_{t+1}}{e_t}\right) + (1-\alpha_t) n_t (1+i_{t+1}^d)}{(1+g_{t+1})(1+\pi_{t+1}^d)} - p_{t+1} - \lambda_{t+1} b_{t+1}^f. \tag{A11}$$

Now define the "real discount rate," r^δ, the real domestic interest rate, r^d, and the rate of real exchange rate depreciation, ε, as follows:

$$(1+\delta) = (1+r_t^\delta)(1+\pi_t^f) \tag{A12}$$

$$(1+i_t^d) = (1+r_t^d)(1+\pi_t^d) \tag{A13}$$

---

[31] See the subsection in the main text on key indicators.

$$\frac{e_{t+1}}{e_t} = \frac{\left(1 - \pi_{t+1}^d\right)\left(1 + \varepsilon_{t+1}\right)}{\left(1 + \pi_{t+1}^f\right)}. \tag{A14}$$

Inserting these expressions into equation (A11), subtracting n_t from both sides, and adding a residual term, η, to capture all other effects on the NPV yields equation (3) in the main text:

$$n_{t+1} - n_t = \frac{\left[\alpha_t r_{t+1}^\delta + \left(1 - \alpha_t\right)r_{t+1}^d - g_{t+1} + \alpha_t \varepsilon_{t+1}\left(1 + r_{t+1}^\delta\right)\right]n_t}{1 + g_{t+1}} - p_{t+1} - \lambda_{t+1}b_{t+1}^f + \eta_{t+1}. \tag{A15}$$

Intuitively, equation (A13) states that the NPV grows at the difference between the real interest rate and the real growth rate (with the real interest rate defined as a weighted average of the real discount rate on foreign-currency debt and the real interest rate on domestic debt), plus real exchange rate depreciation, minus the primary balance, and minus the grant that is implicit in new concessional borrowing.

References

Baldacci, Emanuele, Benedict Clements, Sanjeev Gupta, and Carlos Mulas-Granados, 2004, "Persistence of Fiscal Adjustments and Expenditure Composition in Low-Income Countries," Chapter 3 in *Helping Countries Develop: The Role of Fiscal Policy*, ed. by Sanjeev Gupta, Benedict Clements, and Gabriela Inchauste (Washington: International Monetary Fund).

Baldacci, Emanuele, Arye Hillman, and Naoko Kojo, 2003, "Growth, Governance, and Fiscal Policy in Low-Income Countries," Chapter 4 in *Helping Countries Develop: The Role of Fiscal Policy*, ed. by Sanjeev Gupta, Benedict Clements, and Gabriela Inchauste (Washington: International Monetary Fund).

Chalk, Nigel, and Richard Hemming, 2000, "Assessing Fiscal Sustainability in Theory and Practice," IMF Working Paper 00/81 (Washington: International Monetary Fund).

Cohen, Daniel, 1997, "Growth and External Debt: A New Perspective on the African and Latin American Tragedies," CEPR Discussion Paper No. 1753 (London: Centre for Economic Policy Research).

Cuddington, John, 1997, "Analyzing the Sustainability of Fiscal Deficits in Developing Countries," World Bank Policy Research Working Paper No. 1784 (Washington: World Bank).

Easterly, William, 2001, "Growth Implosions, Debt Explosions, and My Aunt Marilyn: Do Growth Slowdowns Cause Public Debt Crises?" World Bank Policy Research Working Paper, No. 2531 (Washington: World Bank).

Gupta, Sanjeev, Benedict Clements, Emanuele Baldacci, and Carlos Mulas-Granados, 2004, "Fiscal Policy, Expenditure Composition, and Growth in Low-Income

Countries," Chapter 2 in *Helping Countries Develop: The Role of Fiscal Policy*, ed. by Sanjeev Gupta, Benedict Clements, and Gabriela Inchauste (Washington: International Monetary Fund).

Gupta, Sanjeev, Benedict Clements, Alexander Pivovarksy, and Erwin Tiongson, 2004, "Foreign Aid and Revenue Response: Does the Composition of Aid Matter?" Chapter 14 in *Helping Countries Develop: The Role of Fiscal Policy*, ed. by Sanjeev Gupta, Benedict Clements, and Gabriela Inchauste (Washington: International Monetary Fund).

Heller, Peter, 2003, *Who Will Pay? Coping with Aging Societies, Climate Change, and Other Long-Term Fiscal Challenges* (Washington: International Monetary Fund).

Hemming, Richard, Michael Kell, and Axel Schimmelpfennig, 2003, *Fiscal Vulnerability and Financial Crises in Emerging Market Economies*, IMF Occasional Paper No. 218 (Washington: International Monetary Fund).

International Monetary Fund, 2001, *Government Finance Statistics Manual* (Washington).

———, 2003, *World Economic Outlook, September 2003: Public Debt in Emerging Markets*, Chapter 3, World Economic and Financial Surveys (Washington: International Monetary Fund).

———, 2002, "Assessing Sustainability," prepared by the Policy Development and Review Department (Washington: IMF). Available via the Internet: http://www.imf.org/external/np/pdr/sus/2002/eng/052802.htm.

Kraay, Aart, and Vikram Nehru, 2004, "When Is Debt Sustainable?" World Bank Policy Research Working Paper No. 3200.

Patillo, Catherine, Helen Poirson, and Luca Ricci, 2002, "External Debt and Growth," IMF Working Paper 02/69 (Washington: International Monetary Fund).

7

Experience with Budgetary Convergence in the WAEMU

OUSMANE DORÉ AND PAUL R. MASSON

The viability of any economic integration plan depends upon its ability to ensure that the economic and financial policies defined by individual member countries of the union are consistent with those of the other members and guarantee sustained convergence of the members' economic performance. This is especially true for a monetary union in which a common currency and common monetary policy exerts even more stringent constraints on national economic policies. In the West African Economic and Monetary Union (WAEMU),[1] where the CFA franc is pegged to the euro and the autonomy of monetary policy and the ability to use the interest rate as an instrument are therefore limited, fiscal policies are of prime importance. They must be coordinated and be consistent with the maintenance of a fixed exchange rate over

A version of this chapter was presented at the fortieth anniversary Conference of the Central Bank of West African States (BCEAO), May 13–14, 2002. It was earlier presented at an IMF African Department lunchtime seminar; the authors are grateful for comments received from their colleagues.
[1]Established in 1994, the WAEMU consists of eight countries: Benin, Burkina Faso, Côte d'Ivoire, Guinea-Bissau, Mali, Niger, Senegal, and Togo. These countries have a common stable and convertible currency—the CFA franc—which has been pegged to the French franc since 1948 and to the euro since 1999. In addition to the common central bank (BCEAO), the WAEMU institutions include the WAEMU Commission, the Banking Commission, and the regional stock exchange. In recent years, WAEMU countries have taken important steps toward greater regional integration and coordination of macroeconomic policies by adopting convergence criteria, establishing a common external tariff, and harmonizing taxes.

the medium term, even if they reflect differences in economic conditions over the short term. Lack of economic policy coordination can lead to negative externalities and therefore to policy changes in response to shocks that could jeopardize the common monetary policy.

Since the devaluation of their currency in 1994, member states of the WAEMU have collectively become aware that fiscal consolidation is essential to their adjustment process. To mitigate the risks posed by uncoordinated fiscal policies, they established in 1994 a multilateral surveillance system aimed at ensuring greater economic policy cohesiveness among the member states. As a community mechanism for economic policy control in the WAEMU member states, multilateral surveillance is based on a set of core rules and standards for national economic policies to encourage economic convergence, defined as a reduction of the differences between the economic performances of member states.

The following criteria were established within the framework of the Convergence, Stability, Growth, and Solidarity Pact adopted by WAEMU governments in 1999:

- an average annual inflation rate of no more than 3 percent, based on the objective of keeping the inflation differential small between the WAEMU and the euro area;
- a basic fiscal balance (defined as nongrant revenue minus expenditure excluding foreign-financed investment) to GDP ratio that is zero or positive, based on the need to strengthen fiscal sustainability;
- an overall debt-to-GDP ratio less than 70 percent, based on the need to prevent public debt in the Union from disrupting the proper functioning of financial markets; and
- no change or a decrease in domestic and external payment arrears, based on the need to avoid alternative nonmarket financing of public deficits.

These so-called first-order criteria are supplemented with second-order indicators related to the wage bill (less than 35 percent of tax receipts), the ratio of domestically financed investment with respect to tax receipts (over 20 percent), the ratio of tax receipts to GDP (over 17 percent), and the external current account deficit, excluding grants (less than 3 percent of GDP).

The convergence criteria applied since 1999 pay special attention to the public deficit and public debt sustainability, because unsustainable budget deficits and excessive indebtedness can increase the pressure for monetary financing and undermine the viability of the common currency. The setting of budgetary norms was also predicated on the belief that fiscal consolidation will lead to sustainable growth by freeing up resources for the private sector. Indeed, pegging the CFA franc to the euro at a fixed exchange rate considerably reduces the risk of capital loss for investors. With such a peg, an asset's yield depends on the size of the borrower's default risk and the intrinsic profitability of the asset in question. Lenders will therefore pay particular attention to the basic indicators of internal balance—namely, the stock of debt and the borrowing requirements of the government.

While the regional convergence pact reinforces fiscal discipline in the zone, the question arises whether it might also constrain the scope for countercyclical fiscal policy. In addition to the effect of cycle, a number of other factors, such as terms of trade fluctuations in developing countries, could explain why fiscal reference values may be breached. This chapter assesses how cyclical variations and terms of trade fluctuations may have affected the WAEMU's experience with the convergence mechanism since 1994. The analysis of the factors underlying fiscal slippages in the zone is particularly important now, when the Council of Ministers of the WAEMU is proposing to eliminate the monetary financing of public deficits. We estimate that, on average, a 1 percent shortfall of output from potential worsens the fiscal balance by 0.3 percent of GDP in the WAEMU; for the terms of trade, the effect would be on the order of 0.08 percent.

Assessment of the Convergence Mechanism

Experience suggests that the convergence criteria and associated regional surveillance process have contributed to fiscal consolidation in the WAEMU (Table 1). However, while substantial progress was made during an initial period (1994–97), there has been a marked slowdown in fiscal convergence among member states since 1998. An examination of developments in the overall fiscal balance (excluding grants) in member states of the Union shows that the standard deviation around the unweighted mean tended to decline up to 1997 before starting to increase once again in recent years (Figure 1), which tends to confirm a greater divergence in the degree of fiscal performances among countries recently. This observation is corroborated by developments in the unweighted average deficit for the seven WAEMU countries; after a sharp improvement up to 1997, the deficit once again widened during 1998–2001.

Considerable efforts were made toward fiscal consolidation in the WAEMU during 1994–97, as illustrated by performance. The key criterion—basic fiscal balance—improved considerably over this period,

Table 1. WAEMU: Budgetary Convergence Criteria, 1995–2001

	1995	1996	1997	1998	1999	2000	2001
Basic fiscal balance (≥ 0)[1]							
Benin	–0.8	1.4	1.5	3.8	2.8	2.0	0.6
Burkina Faso	8.6	0.6	0.1	–0.3	–0.4	–1.4	–1.2
Côte d'Ivoire	–1.2	0.5	–0.6	–0.3	–1.5	–0.2	1.7
Guinea Bissau	–2.8	–5.3	–1.0	–16.3	–8.6	–0.7	–3.6
Mali	0.1	2.2	1.0	1.2	0.1	–0.8	–1.3
Niger	–3.7	–1.7	–3.6	–3.1	–5.1	–1.3	–1.2
Senegal	–0.1	1.7	2.2	2.6	1.5	1.4	1.4
Togo	–4.3	–2.5	–1.4	–3.8	–1.9	–3.4	–1.9
WAEMU	**–0.3**	**0.6**	**0.0**	**0.2**	**–0.6**	**–0.1**	**0.3**
Wages and salaries/fiscal revenue (≥ 35 percent)							
Benin	43.8	40.8	39.0	35.4	33.2	32.0	31.8
Burkina Faso	48.1	43.4	40.7	39.2	41.7	42.9	38.8
Côte d'Ivoire	32.0	37.4	36.7	36.4	37.0	41.6	42.8
Guinea Bissau	40.4	46.7	39.1	126.7	53.9	60.0	56.5
Mali	36.5	28.9	28.9	27.4	27.8	31.3	29.3
Niger	80.1	48.8	56.6	49.8	46.9	43.8	35.2
Senegal	47.7	44.0	40.0	37.0	33.9	32.7	32.1
Togo	59.0	54.6	50.3	51.2	51.2	54.9	52.0
WAEMU	**42.9**	**40.5**	**38.4**	**37.2**	**36.8**	**38.7**	**37.9**
Domestically financed investment/ fiscal revenue (≥ 20 percent)							
Benin	10.7	5.1	7.5	8.2	11.0	15.0	21.5
Burkina Faso	8.2	11.3	23.9	25.3	20.8	23.7	25.3
Côte d'Ivoire	14.7	15.9	21.7	26.7	17.6	9.7	4.9
Guinea Bissau	3.2	16.7	16.1	80.0	64.8	20.6	17.6
Mali	14.1	14.1	16.3	20.2	22.2	25.7	23.7
Niger	3.9	5.3	7.2	9.1	15.8	6.9	13.9
Senegal	10.8	11.3	14.3	17.9	22.7	19.8	20.1
Togo	9.6	4.4	2.9	6.3	1.8	3.1	3.2
WAEMU	**11.8**	**12.1**	**17.6**	**21.3**	**18.2**	**14.6**	**13.9**
Fiscal revenue/GDP (≥ 17 percent)							
Benin	12.3	12.6	12.6	13.3	13.6	14.6	14.5
Burkina Faso	10.8	11.5	12.1	12.4	12.8	12.8	13.8
Côte d'Ivoire	18.0	19.0	17.9	16.9	16.8	16.2	16.5
Guinea Bissau	6.9	6.8	7.7	3.7	8.6	10.9	9.5
Mali	11.1	13.1	13.8	13.9	14.1	12.9	14.8
Niger	6.6	6.7	8.2	9.1	9.9	10.6	11.9
Senegal	14.8	15.6	15.7	16.0	16.8	17.3	17.1
Togo	13.6	13.1	13.0	13.8	12.8	12.0	12.2
WAEMU	**14.4**	**15.2**	**15.1**	**14.9**	**15.1**	**14.9**	**15.4**

Sources: Data provided by the WAEMU Commission, national authorities, and staff projections
[1]Total revenue excluding grants minus total expenditures, excluding foreign financed investment outlays.

Figure 1. WAEMU: Unweighted Average Deficit and Standard Deviation
(Percent of GDP)

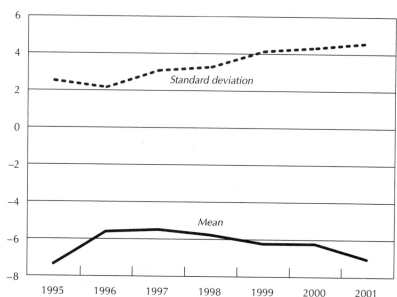

even though it generally remained negative for all member states. The public expenditure structure improved because of better control of current primary expenditure, especially that related to the wage bill, which declined from 55.5 percent of tax revenue for the WAEMU as a whole in 1994 to 37.2 percent in 1998. During 1994–98, all the countries recorded a sharp decline in the share of the wage bill in terms of tax receipts, and only two countries (Niger and Togo) were above the regional norm set at 40 percent in 1998. The control of the wage bill had a positive impact on the contribution of domestic resources to investment. For the Union as a whole, the ratio of investment spending to tax revenues rose from 11 percent in 1994 to about 21 percent in 1998, compared with a regional norm of 20 percent. Domestic and external payment arrears were also reduced.

Since 1998, there has been a sharp reversal of these trends. The performances of the Union's member states during 1998–2001 shows a worsening in the unweighted average for the overall fiscal deficit (excluding grants), from –3.9 percent in 1998 to –4.8 percent for the Union as a whole. Although this development occurred during a slowdown in real growth in the area, it is also clear that expenditure controls were relaxed. This is evidenced by developments related to the

Figure 2. WAEMU: Deviations from Targets for Secondary Criteria

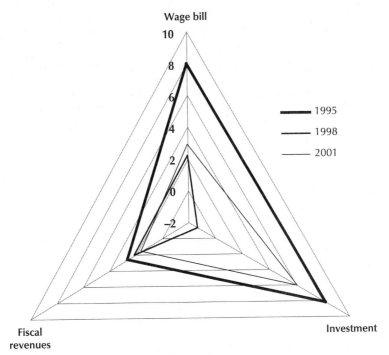

three secondary fiscal criteria during 1998–2001 (see Figure 2). As regards the wage bill, not only did the average for the Union grow from 37.2 percent of tax receipts in 1998 to 37.9 percent in 2001, but only three countries (Benin, Mali, and Senegal) were in compliance with the regional norm at end-2001, compared with five at end-1998. The ratio of domestically financed investment to tax receipts improved slightly for the Union as a whole during the period, but this general trend masks sizable disparities from one country to the next. Indeed, only Burkina Faso and Mali were in conformity with the regional norm of 20 percent throughout the period. There was no perceptible improvement in the tax ratio during the period: it averaged about 15 percent and divergence increased among countries.

In light of the above, the cause of divergences among the countries still needs to be clarified. A number of factors make it difficult to distinguish between convergence effects and those that encourage divergence among economies in the process of integration. Historical experience and recent theoretical research highlight the observation that regional arrangements among developing countries (south-south integration) tend to widen the gap between the poorest and the least poor countries, unlike north-north arrangements, where the relatively less developed countries (e.g., Spain, Greece, Ireland, and Portugal, in the case of the European Union) tend to converge toward the income levels of their richer partners such as France and Germany. But it is difficult to ascertain to what extent convergence is the result of underlying economic forces or the consequence of policies, including compensatory assistance from the richer states (no such mechanism exists in the WAEMU).

Why Have the Criteria Not Been Met?

As noted above, an examination of economic developments in the WAEMU countries seems to reveal two adjustment phases. During 1995–97, growth was strong and fiscal balances improved; by contrast, from 1998 onward there was far less progress or indeed a reversal on the fiscal side, while growth was slower. Figure 2 shows that this observation also applies to two of the three secondary criteria when considering the WAEMU as a whole: for investment and the wage bill, deviations from the target were limited in the first period but have expanded since 1999.[2] More lasting progress was achieved with the ratio of tax revenue to GDP: receipts climbed from 14 percent of GDP in 1995 to about 15 percent in 1999 on average, but this figure is still well below the target of 17 percent. Since 1994, there has also been a decline in the stock of public debt, which however remained above the ceiling of 70 percent of GDP. In sum, the deterioration in the fiscal balance is attributable to a series of slippages in the primary criteria (debt) and secondary criteria (revenue and wages). Paradoxically, the real progress made in boosting investment also contributed to the worsening of the fiscal balance.

This issue can be analyzed more thoroughly by attempting to link these slippages to economic or political causes. Were there factors external to the region that could explain the poor fiscal performance? Were there political factors in some countries that may have influenced developments related to the criteria?

A standard approach to the calculation of structural deficits is to correct for the cyclical position of the economy; this is routinely done for industrial countries using an "output gap" concept. We therefore first establish the correlation, country by country, between the fiscal balance and the GDP growth rate (or, corresponding to an output gap, the cumulative growth rate, net of the average for the period 1995–2001).

---

[2] In Figure 2, the deviations from the criteria have been calculated such that a positive deviation indicates a worse outcome (e.g., for investment, it indicates an investment level below the target, while for the wage bill, it corresponds to a level in excess of the target).

This leads to a distinction between those countries for which the correlation is strong and positive (Benin, Mali) and those for which, on the contrary, it is decidedly negative (Côte d'Ivoire)—that is, goes in the wrong direction. These results suggest that correcting for the output gap is insufficient in the case of these developing countries. Indeed, instead of using the output gap, we examined the correlations between the terms of trade and the fiscal balance, using both the rates of growth and the levels of the terms of trade (the latter variable gave the most satisfactory results). These correlations are much stronger than for the output gap: there are large positive correlations for all the countries (ranging up to 0.81 and 0.94 for Benin and Burkina Faso, respectively), except Côte d'Ivoire and Togo. A further advantage of using the terms of trade is that they are closer to being exogenous than is GDP in the case of small open economies. The countries of the region certainly have limited power over their terms of trade, since typically their exports are primary commodities priced on world markets and their imports are manufacturing goods produced by industrial countries. When the two variables are included together in a regression, both are significant (see below).

It therefore seems that much of the change in fiscal balances results from movements in the terms of trade, over which the countries of the region have little control (see Figure 3). The two exceptions, in contrast, can be explained by political events that strongly influenced the macroeconomic performances of the countries concerned. The political crisis in Côte d'Ivoire in 1999–2000 curtailed growth and cut off access to external financing, and this had the effect of shrinking the budget deficit. Paradoxically, this allowed Côte d'Ivoire to remain below the deficit ceiling but explains why a normal correlation between the fiscal balance and growth or the terms of trade does not apply to that country. Togo has also experienced a political crisis since 1998, leading to the curtailment of external financial assistance as a result of which it could not generate a higher deficit despite the slow economic growth.

Tables A1, A2, and A3 in the Appendix show the results of an estimation with fixed effects, based on panel data for the seven countries (excluding Guinea-Bissau) over 1995–2001. The observations covering 1999–2001 for Côte d'Ivoire and Togo were excluded from the data because of political factors, for the reasons mentioned above. The regression of the overall balance (OB) on the output gap (difference between potential GDP and actual GDP, expressed as a percentage) and the terms of trade (TOT) provides the following results (t-statistics in parentheses):

$$OB = -6.3 + 0.293 \ YGAP + 0.075 \ TOT. \tag{1}$$
$$(2.24) \qquad (2.68)$$

Figure 3a. Budget Balance, GDP Growth, and Changes in the Terms of Trade
(Percent)

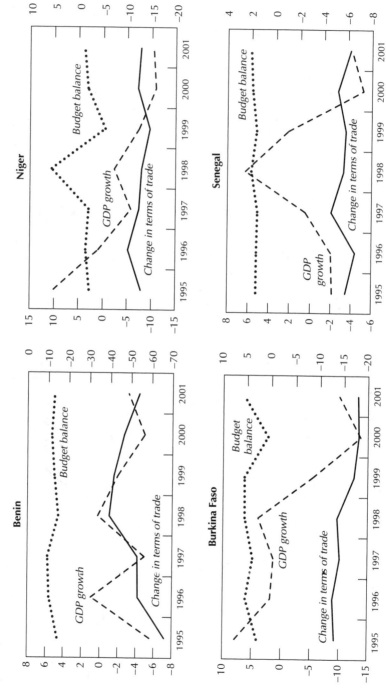

Figure 3b. Budget Balance, GDP Growth, and Changes in the Terms of Trade
(Percent)

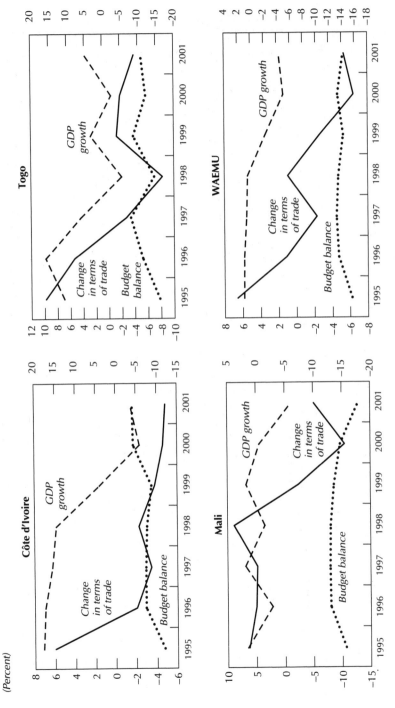

These estimates show that the fiscal slippages observed are partly attributable to changes in the deficit related to the economic cycle and partly to fluctuations in the terms of trade. On average, a 1 percentage point decline in growth, compared with the rate of potential growth, would widen the deficit by about 0.3 percent of GDP, which is not negligible. For the terms of trade, this effect would be on the order of 0.08 percent. However, as we shall see below, the variability of the terms of trade for most countries is much larger than for the output gap. The magnitude of these automatic stabilizers, which varies from one country to the next, points to the need to have a minimum degree of flexibility for adapting fiscal policy to take account of exogenous shocks. In the event of an asymmetric temporary shock (affecting the dollar rate, the prices of raw materials, etc.), fiscal accommodation of these short-term developments may be necessary through the free play of a countercyclical fiscal policy, and fiscal norms should allow for that possibility. What this means—especially for countries whose public revenue is particularly volatile because of their heavy reliance on one or two raw materials—is that the government should make every effort to generate large fiscal surpluses in years when positive shocks occur and use them to dampen the restrictive effects of periods of economic downturn.

The analysis can be taken further by arguing that the imposition of strict fiscal rules in the WAEMU context is inimical to the smoothing of business cycles fluctuations. This is true insofar as monetary policy cannot absorb asymmetric shocks to the various economies, the mobility of factors is limited, and the Union does not yet have a system of taxes and transfers for mitigating shocks.

We therefore propose that the structural deficit concept, borrowed from industrial countries, be extended from cyclical adjustment to include a correction for the terms of trade. In light of the estimated effects on developments in the countries' fiscal positions, the correlations calculated above can be used to "adjust" the fiscal balance to take account of both of these factors. The resulting estimates of structural deficits suggest that member countries' performance did not deteriorate as much as indicated previously. Figure 4 shows that there were sizable movements in the terms of trade in the WAEMU over the period 1995–2001, with a tendency toward deterioration, whereas the cyclical effect was less strong. Developments in the context of a deficit that has been adjusted to take account of cyclical effects and the terms of trade are more positive than those of an unadjusted deficit.

Moreover, in the calculation of the fiscal balance for the WAEMU as a whole, weighted to take account of the GDP level for each member country, the overall budget deficit, excluding grants, seems to have

Figure 4. WAEMU: Cyclical Position and Terms of Trade
(Percent deviation from 1994 level)

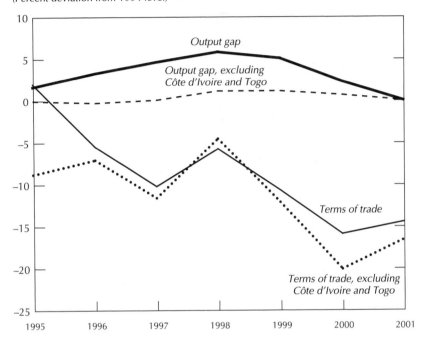

shrunk during 1995–2001. An adjustment to take account of cyclical conditions and the terms of trade gives an even more positive picture of convergence. But this picture is misleading and is caused by the large share of Côte d'Ivoire, which, as we have seen, should be excluded from the study for the period 1999–2001, along with Togo. As was the case with an unweighted average, a weighted average covering all the countries except Côte d'Ivoire and Togo shows a deterioration over 1995–2001, despite the adjustment made to take account of cyclical conditions and the terms of trade (Figure 5).

The source of cyclical changes in fiscal balances is another important issue. In the industrial countries, it is assumed that cyclical effects are primarily the result of revenue changes. Indeed, observations show that in positive economic circumstances that boost earnings from capital and labor, tax revenues increase while expenditure rises less (or falls, for example because of the decline in unemployment benefits). For developing countries in general, however, Talvi and Végh (2000) provide some evidence that fiscal deficits may vary countercyclically, not procyclically. For the WAEMU countries, our evidence given above—see equation (1)—suggests that deficits vary procyclically, but

Figure 5. WAEMU: Effects of Cycle and Terms of Trade on Budget Balance
(Percent of GDP)

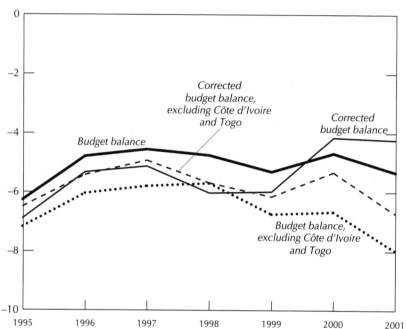

this does not seem to come from the revenue side, as instead we find a negative coefficient when regressing revenue on the output gap.[3] By contrast, there are strong cyclical effects on expenditure, which rises when the cycle is negative and the terms of trade are favorable. Indeed, a regression with panel data provides the following results:

$$EXP = 20.6 - 0.339\,YGAP - 0.112\,TOT. \tag{2}$$
$$\quad\quad\quad\quad (2.05) \quad\quad\quad (3.12)$$

Therefore, cyclical effects and terms of trade shocks seem to have a sizable impact on public expenditure. However, a country-by-country examination is needed to identify the source of these correlations—automatic stabilizers or discretionary expenditure. It would also be important to observe what expenditure components are affected by the cycle and the terms of trade. Cyclical changes are not completely independent of economic policies. In addition, if changes in the terms

---

[3] A positive correlation may have been skewed by the tax and customs reforms that were made within the Union and that pushed revenue downward over this period. Also, specific rather than ad valorem taxes on primary commodities may cause the revenue ratio to decline in booms and increase in slumps.

of trade are permanent rather than temporary, a fiscal adjustment will be needed.

Does the Elimination of Monetary Assistance Have Implications for the Maintenance of Fiscal Discipline Within the Union?

It is difficult to determine whether the planned elimination of monetary financing from the BCEAO to the national treasuries will have a noticeable impact on fiscal adjustment efforts within the WAEMU. The answer depends, to a certain extent, on the direction of the causality between financing and adjustment efforts. Studies on the WAEMU[4] show that the causality is unidirectional, moving from resources to expenditure (Burkina Faso and Senegal) and from expenditure to resources (Benin and Togo), and bidirectional for Côte d'Ivoire and Mali. The implication of this analysis is that for some countries of the Union, a constraint on financing may well lead to expenditure adjustments, but that this may not be the case for others.

Clearly, the countries concerned do not have direct control over the external financing of their deficits, which tends to be concessionary rather than commercial. Financing based on the accumulation of payment arrears is not allowed in the context of the regional Convergence Pact, because the nonaccumulation of payment arrears is a first-order criterion that must be met by member countries. In addition, the use of this form of financing would curtail economic development and should in any case be avoided because it jeopardizes confidence in the ability of the economic players to fulfill their obligations. External payment arrears are also generally penalized through the suspension of financial disbursements by donors and lenders, as shown in the case of Côte d'Ivoire over the past two years.

Finally, with the current monetary policy guidelines aimed at fully eliminating monetary assistance from the BCEAO, the governments now only have the financial markets as alternative financing sources, through public issues. Such a financing method will require the governments to establish their creditworthiness by sustained adjustment efforts. In light of the savings constraint in the Union and because the regional financial market is not an emerging market that is able to attract foreign investors, the financing of public deficits in this manner will certainly have a crowding-out effect on private investment—hence

---

[4]See Doré and Nachega (2000).

the need to monitor this financing method.[5] Also, problems of access to the various financing methods can often lead to fiscal adjustments of lesser quality.[6] The example of Côte d'Ivoire in 2001 illustrates this point. Following its sociopolitical crisis, Côte d'Ivoire was unable to obtain external financing and alternative financing (monetary or nonmonetary) since it was required both by regional surveillance and by its interim arrangement with the IMF (staff-monitored program) to accumulate no new arrears; it was therefore forced to adjust by substantially reducing its capital expenditure.

What Leeway Is There for Achieving the Deficit Objective in the Future?

Breaking down the deficit into its various components helps determine what can be done to remedy the slippages observed. The breakdown of the basic fiscal balance is also instructive because it allows for a link to be established between this first-order criterion and the secondary criteria. In practice, this balance has largely mirrored the overall balance, excluding grants, since 1994. The basic fiscal balance as a percentage of GDP (B) can be written as follows:

$$B = R + N - SR - IR - rD_{-1} - A, \tag{3}$$

where R = tax revenue as a percentage of GDP; N = nontax revenue as a percentage of GDP; S = the ratio of wages and salaries to tax receipts; I = the ratio of domestically financed investment to tax receipts; r = the interest rate on government debt; D = government debt as a percent of GDP; and A = other expenditure, as a percentage of GDP. Changes in the stock of debt, as a percentage of GDP, depend on the fiscal balance (in the absence of valuation effects, including those resulting from debt reduction agreements):

$$\Delta D = -B - g * D_{-1}, \tag{4}$$

where g is the GDP growth rate. The evolution of the debt ratio is therefore largely determined by the government's success in containing the deficit and enhancing growth. Moreover, the ceilings on revenue, wages, and the level of public debt clearly help the government to

---

[5]One approach could be to establish ceilings on bond issues by governments, as performance criteria in country programs.

[6]Alesina and Perotti (1996) have shown that fiscal adjustments of good quality are those based on cuts in primary current expenditure (transfers and the wage bill) rather than in capital expenditure.

remain below the deficit ceiling. By contrast, the floor on domestically financed investment as a percentage of GDP can have negative effects on the objective sought: if a government keeps its investment high, it will have to make greater efforts on the other criteria to remain below the deficit ceiling.

During the stability phase of the WAEMU convergence process begun in 2003, member states are expected to observe all the fiscal norms set in the Convergence Pact. With the ratio of the wage bill to tax revenue at 35 percent, the ratio of domestically financed investment to tax revenue at 20 percent, and the tax to GDP ratio at 17 percent, the wage bill would have to total less than 5.9 percent of GDP (0.35 x 0.17 x 100), and the level of domestically financed investment would represent at least 3.4 percent of GDP (0.20 x 0.17 x 100). Based on equation (3) and assuming that interest payments as a percentage of GDP could be reduced to a level equal to the average nontax revenue to GDP ratio over the past three years (i.e., about 2 percent),[7] observance of the key criterion on the basic fiscal balance (i.e., a nonnegative basic fiscal balance) would imply that other expenditure (A) should represent at most 7.7 percent of GDP. This level includes social expenditure and all other nonpersonnel operating expenditure (transfers, subsidies, equipment, etc.).

For most of the WAEMU countries, investment spending and social expenditure are items that can hardly be cut. In addition, the interest on public debt is a variable largely beyond government control. For investment, as stressed previously, there is a (second-order) criterion that tends to push this item upward (or at least to keep it from declining), which is also a reflection of the WAEMU countries' real infrastructure needs. And the objective of poverty reduction, to which governments, international institutions, and donor countries are giving increasing importance, would make a reduction in social expenditure highly unlikely. Capital and operating expenditure in the social sectors can be made more efficient, but not to the point of justifying cuts in the budget amounts allocated to them.

The government wage bill and the "compressible" component of other operating expenditures (subsidies and transfers, other government current expenditure) thus seem to be the only fiscal adjustment variables. Although wage bill adjustments are possible, it is not entirely clear that there is room for sufficient reductions. Indeed, if the countries

---

[7]This assumption can be made, given that all the countries involved are eligible for the HIPC Initiative. The size of the relief is of no relevance to our analysis, for it can be assumed that any reduction larger than that envisaged here would contribute to a related increase in social expenditure.

maintained their wage ceilings at the current levels, all the countries except Togo and Guinea-Bissau would be in conformity with the regional convergence norms, if the efforts made to raise revenue resulted in the observance of the norm on the ratio of tax revenue to GDP. As we have already stressed, few countries are currently able to meet the wage bill criterion because of the low level of their tax receipts (denominator). This underscores the need to increase tax revenue, which currently averages about 15 percent of GDP, compared with the convergence norm of 17 percent.

In light of the difficulties of reducing other expenditure items, the only possible approach is to ensure that other operating expenditure is limited to 7.7 percent of GDP. This item could be used as an adjustment indicator whenever there is a decline in revenue as a result of exogenous shocks. Alternatively, it seems clear that priority should be given to reducing the share of government wages and salaries to no more than 7.7 percent of GDP.

Although this model does not reveal the sensitivity of revenue to cyclical conditions and other exogenous shocks, the substantial change in revenue over time is evidence that a mechanism is needed to stabilize revenue, to reduce the vulnerability of government finance to external shocks in the medium term. Such a mechanism would encourage fiscal discipline and strengthen the multilateral surveillance exercise while reserving a portion of fiscal resources for use in economic downturns.

Summary

Despite considerable progress, the WAEMU's experience in the area of fiscal convergence has produced mixed results since the 1994 devaluation. After an initial period of robust growth and fiscal consolidation, a marked deterioration of the fiscal balance was observed in most of the countries after 1997. Unfavorable terms of trade developments have undoubtedly had a negative impact on growth and budget balances, but in several countries economic policies have been the main cause of the fiscal slippages, which have hindered the achievement of strong, sustained growth within the Union.

The elimination of statutory advances by the BCEAO, already approved more than three years ago by the WAEMU Council of Ministers, makes it all the more necessary to pursue adjustment, with a view to reducing budget deficits to levels consistent with the regional convergence norms. The above analysis suggests that the credibility of multilateral surveillance would be further strengthened if the deficit were adjusted to take account of the effects of temporary changes in cyclical conditions and in the terms of trade. This would provide governments with a minimum of elbow room to adapt their fiscal policy to take account of exogenous shocks. However, the effects on growth brought about by economic policies themselves should be taken into account, as should the fact that some changes in the terms of trade are not temporary and should therefore lead to fiscal policy adjustments. The analysis also suggests that for governments to meet the fiscal convergence standards, they will have to pay more attention to reducing the share of public wages and monitoring other operating expenditure. In light of the limited scope for reducing expenditure in a context of poverty reduction efforts, it would be helpful to focus on the quality of fiscal adjustments and on the fiscal revenue ratio. This would mean streamlining expenditure (for instance, better redeployment of civil service staff) and engaging in sustained revenue-raising efforts.

Appendix. Panel Regressions for WAEMU's Fiscal Adjustment

Cyclical and Terms of Trade Adjustment

To adjust for the cycle, an estimate of the output gap was calculated for each country by cumulating (from zero in 1994) its annual rate of real GDP growth minus its average over 1995–2001. Similarly, the changes in the terms of trade were cumulated from zero in 1994 (but the mean was not subtracted).

The actual overall deficits were regressed on measures of the cycle and the terms of trade for seven of the countries of WAEMU (all except Guinea-Bissau), from 1995–2001, using a panel with fixed effects. The observations for Côte d'Ivoire and Togo for 1999–2001 were omitted from the regressions because of political turmoil in those countries. The deficit was regressed on both the change in GDP and terms of trade, and their cumulated values (described above). The cumulated variables were most significant. Fixed effects are equivalent here to including separate country intercepts.

The result of the estimation is given in Table A1. Both the cycle and the terms of trade are significant. The relative importance in explaining the deficit varies from country to country. For instance, for Benin the terms of trade movements have been very large, and hence that variable dominates the cyclical correction. For Côte d'Ivoire, the opposite is true.

Effect on Expenditure and Revenues

In industrial countries, revenues vary with the cycle and explain most of the countercyclical variation in the deficit, which reflects the role of fiscal policy as an automatic stabilizer. In principle, expenditures can

Table A1. WAEMU: Panel Regression of Fiscal Balance (Ratio to GDP) on Output Gap and Terms of Trade, 1995–2001[1]
(Fixed effects regression within estimator)

Variable	Coefficient	Standard Error	t	$P > |t|$	95% Confidence Interval
YGAP	0.2939564	0.1313383	2.24	0.032	0.027045 – 0.5608679
TOT	0.0758493	0.0283099	2.68	0.011	0.183166 – 0.133382
_CONS	–6.305955	0.4116946	–15.32	0.000	–7.142619 – –5.469291

$sigma_u$	3.7979959
$sigma_e$	1.498465
rho	0.86530447 (fraction of variance due to u_i)

Memorandum:
F test that all $u_i = 0$: $F(6, 34) = 26.15$
Prob > F   0.0000
Number of observations   43
Number of groups   7
R^2: within   0.2218
      between   0.0026
      overall   0.0046

Number of observations
   per group: minimum   4
           average   6.1
           maximum   7

Correlation (u_i, Xb)   –0.5662

$F(2,34)$ 4.85
Probability > F   0.0141

[1]WAEMU, excluding Guinea-Bissau. Observations for 1999–2001 exclude Côte d'Ivoire and Togo.

also vary countercyclically, since such items as unemployment insurance payments increase in times of recession, but the cyclical behavior of revenues is the main driving force behind movements in the deficit.

Some literature suggests that such fiscal policy has a very different role for developing countries (e.g., Talvi and Végh, 2000). Table A2 reports panel regressions of government total revenues on the cycle and the terms of trade. Contrary to industrial countries, these do not seem to vary procyclically: higher activity or positive terms of trade shocks do not, over this sample period, produce significantly higher revenues. Instead, the countercyclical variation of the deficit (see above) comes from a countercyclical variation of government expenditures: in bad times, the government spends more (Table A3), which produces a widening of the deficit. This may be explained by transfers that vary with the cycle or with the terms of trade—for instance, subsidies to the

Table A2. WAEMU: Panel Regression of Government Revenues (Ratio to GDP) on Output Gap and Terms of Trade, 1995–2001[1]

(Fixed effects regression within estimator)

Variable	Coefficient	Standard Error	t	$P > \lvert t \rvert$	95% Confidence Interval
YGAP	–0.0452888	0.0917907	–0.49	0.625	0.23183 – 0.1412524
TOT	–0.0356357	0.0197855	–1.80	0.081	–0.0758446 – 0.0045732
CONS	14.30594	0.2877284	49.72	0.000	13.7212 – 14.89067

sigma$_u$	4.2033001
sigma$_e$	1.0472589
rho	0.94155175 (fraction of variance due to u_i)

Memorandum:

F test that all $u_i = 0$:	F(6, 34) =	65.76
Probability > F	0.0000	
Number of observations	43	
Number of groups	7	
R^2: within	0.0871	
between	0.0433	
overall	0.0054	

Number of observations per group: minimum	4
average	6.1
maximum	7

Correlation (u_i, Xb)	–0.2629

$F(2,34)$	1.62
Prob > F	0.2124

[1]WAEMU, excluding Guinea-Bissau. Observations for 1999–2001 exclude Côte d'Ivoire and Togo.

cotton sector. More detailed data would be needed to identify the sources of the fiscal role in countering shocks.

Correlation Between Real GDP and the Terms of Trade

Since many of the countries in the region are strongly dependent on one or several primary commodities, it is interesting to see whether GDP growth is primarily driven by the terms of trade. Table A4 shows that this is not the case. These results suggest that over 1995–2001 (excluding certain observations for Côte d'Ivoire and Togo for reasons given above), there is no significant effect of changes in the terms of trade on the rate of GDP growth, nor from the level of the terms of trade on the output gap. Thus it is justified to include both variables in equations for the fiscal balance.

Table A3. WAEMU: Panel Regression of Government Expenditures (Ratio to GDP) on Output Gap and Terms of Trade, 1995–2001[1]

(Fixed effects regression within estimator)

Variable	Coefficient	Standard Error	t	$P > \lvert t \rvert$	95% Confidence Interval
YGAP	–0.3393732	0.1657104	–2.05	0.048	–0.6761373 – –0.0026091
TOT	–0.1116187	0.0357188	–3.12	0.004	–0.1842081 – –0.0390293
CONS	20.61155	0.5194381	39.68	0.000	19.55593 – 21.66718

$sigma_u$	5.1421178
$sigma_e$	1.8906241
rho	0.88091421 (fraction of variance due to u_i)

Memorandum:
F test that all $u_i = 0$:	$F(6, 34) = 19.34$
Probability > F	0.0000
Number of observations	43
Number of groups	7
R^2: within	0.2505
between	0.2321
overall	0.0703

Number of observations per group: minimum	4
average	6.1
maximum	7

Correlation (u_i, Xb)	–0.7483

$F(2,34)$	5.68
Probability > F	0.0074

[1]WAEMU, excluding Guinea-Bissau. Observations for 1999–2001 exclude Côte d'Ivoire and Togo.

Table A4. WAEMU Correlation Between Rate of Change of Output and Rate of Change of Terms of Trade, 1995–2001

Country	Correlation Coefficient
Benin	0.023
Burkina Faso	0.221
Côte d'Ivoire	0.061
Mali	–0.552
Niger	0.510
Senegal	0.225
Togo	0.179
WAEMU (weighted)[1]	–0.064

[1]Excluding Guinea-Bissau.

References

Alesina, Alberto, and Roberto Perotti, 1996, "Fiscal Adjustment in OECD Countries: Composition and Macroeconomic Effects," IMF Working Paper 96/70 (Washington: International Monetary Fund).

Doré, Ousmane, and Jean-Claude Nachega, 2000, "Budgetary Convergence in the WAEMU: Adjustment Through Revenue or Expenditure?" IMF Working Paper 00/109 (Washington: International Monetary Fund).

Talvi, Ernesto, and Carlos A. Végh, 2000, "Tax Base Variability and Procyclical Fiscal Policy," NBER Working Paper No. 7499 (Cambridge, Massachusetts: National Bureau of Economic Research).

8

The Effectiveness of Government Spending on Education and Health Care in Developing and Transition Economies

SANJEEV GUPTA, MARIJN VERHOEVEN, AND ERWIN R. TIONGSON

1. Introduction

Policy makers are interested in the composition of public spending.[1] This attention stems in part from the belief that government spending on education and health care can increase economic growth, promote income equality, and reduce poverty (Barro, 1991; Chu et al., 1995; and Tanzi and Chu, 1998). International financial institutions, donors, and NGOs therefore call for increased government spending on education and health care.[2] In addition, an increasing number of studies have documented the adverse

---

This chapter is reprinted from the *European Journal of Political Economy*, Vol. 18, Gupta et al., "The Effectiveness of Government Spending on Education and Health Care in Developing and Transition Economies," pp. 717–37, © 2002, with permission from Elsevier.

The views expressed in this paper are those of the authors and do not necessarily represent those of the IMF. The authors wish to thank Benedict Clements, Hamid Davoodi, Luiz de Mello, Robert Gillingham, Henry Ma, Edgardo Ruggiero, Christian Schiller, Gustavo Yamada, and two anonymous referees for their helpful comments on the earlier drafts.

[1] Amartya Sen (1999) has correspondingly proposed that "since premature mortality, significant undernourishment, and widespread illiteracy are deprivations that directly impoverish human life, the allocation of economic resources as well as arrangements for social provision must give some priority to removing these disadvantages for the affected population." This typically requires improvement in the provision of basic education and primary health care.

[2] Increasing education and health care spending in the poorest countries is a central element of the recently launched initiative granting debt relief to Heavily Indebted Poor Countries (Andrews et al., 1999).

economic consequences of corruption; in particular, studies have shown that corruption is associated with higher military spending (Gupta et al., 2001) and lower government spending on education and health care (Mauro, 1998). These studies provide evidence that policies aimed at reducing corruption lead to increased spending on more productive outlays, such as education and health spending.

The justification for public spending on basic education is based on the social rate of return. Studies have found that the social rate of return is highest for primary education, followed by secondary and tertiary education (Psacharopoulos, 1994; and World Bank, 1995).[3] At the same time, evidence suggests that spending on tertiary education in many countries is excessively high (see, for example, Sahn and Bernier, 1993; Gupta et al., 1998; and World Bank, 1995).

Public spending on primary health care is justified by disease reduction during the productive years of life. The burden of disease in developing countries could be reduced if governments were to make available a minimum package of essential, cost-effective clinical services (World Bank, 1993). In this respect, secondary health care has been found to provide little health gain. Many studies have concluded that the most cost-effective interventions are often preventive in character, and that in many developing countries public allocations for secondary or curative services are excessive (see, for example, Sahn and Bernier, 1993; and Pradhan, 1996).

Although the studies that focus on social rates of return to education and on the burden of disease provide a compelling reason for policy makers to shift public resources toward basic education and primary health care, they do not yield conclusive evidence that such a reallocation would improve education attainment and health status. It may well be that public spending crowds out private spending on primary and secondary education and primary health care, or that public resources are used inefficiently and inequitably. In fact, the evidence on whether aggregate education and health spending has a beneficial impact on relevant social indicators—taken as a proxy for outputs of public spending on social sectors—is mixed. Many studies show that the relationship between public spending for education and measures of education attainment is weak (Landau, 1986; Noss, 1991; Mingat and Tan, 1992, 1998; and Flug et al., 1998). Instead, other variables have been found to be important in explaining

---

[3] The methodological basis of studies estimating social rates of return of education has however been questioned. For example, Bennell (1995, 1996) does not find support for the proposition that basic education has a higher social return than other levels of education. See also Appleton et al. (1996) and Cassen (1996).

education attainment. These include per capita income (Flug et al., 1998; Mingat and Tan, 1992), the age distribution of the population (Mingat and Tan, 1992), parental perceptions of costs and benefits, and family background or parental education (Appleton et al., 1996). In contrast, Gallagher (1993) shows that, after correcting for its quality and efficiency, spending on education has a positive impact on indicators of education attainment.

Similarly, many studies find that the contribution of public health outlays to health status as measured by infant mortality or child mortality is either small or statistically insignificant (Kim and Moody, 1992; McGuire et al., 1993; Aiyer et al., 1995; Musgrove, 1996; Filmer and Pritchett, 1997; and Filmer et al., 1998). Carrin and Politi (1995) conclude that poverty and income are crucial determinants of health status indicators but fail to find that public health spending has a statistically significant effect on these indicators. Similarly, Filmer and Pritchett (1997) find that cross-country differences in income alone account for 84% of the variation in infant mortality, with socioeconomic variables accounting for 11%, and public spending for less than ⅙ of 1%. These results are confirmed by Demery and Walton (1998), who note that "the conclusion that public spending is a poor predictor of good health is a common one" (p. 26). In contrast, Anand and Ravallion (1993) and Hojman (1996)—with relatively small sample sizes of 22 observations and 10–20 observations, respectively—do find that public health spending has a statistically significant effect on health status. Similarly, Bidani and Ravallion (1997) find for a larger sample of 35 countries that public spending has a beneficial impact on the health condition of the poor.

Although the evidence presented in the above-mentioned studies in general goes against the presumption that higher public spending on education and health is effective in improving social indicators, some relevant issues are overlooked in these studies. As noted earlier, allocations within the sectors are widely believed to be important in explaining changes in social indicators, but these studies typically sidestep this issue.[4] In fact, Ogbu and Gallagher (1991) infer from a study of five African countries that enrollment rates are affected by the composition of public education spending. And in a survey of 10 country studies, Mehrotra (1998) concludes that high education attainment is associated with relatively high public spending on edu-

---

[4] Also, the absence of a measurable impact of public spending on indicators could be due to a differential effect on poor and nonpoor groups, which is not captured by aggregated social indicators (Bidani and Ravallion, 1997).

cation and a relatively high share of primary education in total education expenditures. Unfortunately, neither paper supports its claim about the efficacy of public spending on basic education with statistical analysis.

Filmer et al. (1998) attempt to address the issue of allocations within the health sector by including a measure of government spending on primary health care in their cross-section analysis of the causal factors of infant mortality. As it turns out, they fail to find a statistically significant impact of primary health care spending on infant mortality rates. But their aggregate health sector data are not necessarily consistent with either the overall fiscal or the intrasectoral data. Measurement errors may have been further exacerbated by the use of statistical techniques to create imputed values for missing observations.

Against the background of these empirical results, this paper reassesses whether increased public spending on education and health matters by using a comprehensive, internally consistent, and up-to-date cross-section data set of public spending and social indicators for 50 developing and transition countries. The statistical results indicate that, in education, both the overall level of public spending and intrasectoral allocation matter; in particular, shifting spending toward primary and secondary education is associated with improvements in widely used measures of education attainment. In the health sector, increased overall health spending is associated with reduced infant and child mortality rates. We do not, however, prove that higher spending causes such improvements—although the results that we present provide some, but indefinite, evidence of causality. We also address the issue of the appropriate functional form of the relationship between social indicators and public spending.

The paper is organized as follows. Section 2 discusses the model and the data set; Section 3 presents the results; and Section 4 sets out the policy implications.

2. Model and Data

We use the following equation to evaluate the impact of public spending on education and health care:

$$Y_i = f(X_{1i}, X_{2i}, Z_i),$$ (1)

where Y_i is a social indicator reflecting education attainment or health status for a country i, which is a function of aggregate public spending on education or health care as a share of GDP,[5,6] X_{1i}; allocations to different programs within the sector (i.e., primary education and primary health care) as a share of total sectoral spending,[7] X_{2i}; and a vector of socioeconomic variables, Z_i.

A range of social indicators is available to gauge performance of education and health care spending by the government. Three considerations guided the choice of indicators. First, to facilitate a comparison of results, indicators used by other authors were selected where possible. Second, because many indicators are collected infrequently and with a lag, the indicators used were those for which the most up-to-date values were available. Finally, as many as possible of the core indicators proposed by the Development Assistance Committee (DAC) of the OECD, the World Bank, and the UN to measure development performance were used.[8]

Education attainment is proxied by the gross enrollment ratio in primary and secondary education (the number of enrolled students in percent of the total number of school-age persons), the persistence through grade four (percent of children reaching that grade), and the primary-school drop-out rates. Two indicators are used to gauge health status: infant (aged 0 to 1 year) mortality rates and child (aged 0 to 5 years) mortality rates.[9]

---

[5] A consequence of measuring education spending as a share of GDP is that the associated spending per student can vary greatly among countries depending on the level of GDP. The results presented in this paper also hold, however, when education and health care spending is expressed in per capita terms. To capture the impact of income, GDP per capita was included as a control variable (see below). Thus, the effect of per capita spending can be gauged from the coefficients for spending as a percent of GDP and GDP per capita (since the product of these variables equals spending per capita). See also footnote 6.

[6] A simple "production function" for health should yield the same point estimate and significance for the effect of public spending on health outcomes, regardless of which measure of public spending on health is used (Filmer et al., 1998). The difference is the coefficient on income. For example, suppose the production function for health is of the following form: $Y = (H/N)^{\alpha} (NH/N)^{\beta} (e)^{A}$, where Y is a measure of health status; H is public spending on health; and NH is the "rest of GDP." Dividing the numerators and denominators by GDP and taking logs gives the following equation: $\ln Y = \alpha^* \ln H/GDP + \beta^* \ln NH/GDP + (\alpha + \beta)^* \ln GDP/N + A$.

[7] It should be noted that an increase in public allocations for, say, primary education, while holding all other spending constant, has an effect on education indicators both directly through X_{2i}, and indirectly through the overall level of education spending X_{1i}.

[8] The list of core indicators for education and health includes: net enrollment in primary education, persistence through grade four, literacy rate of 15- to 24-year-olds, adult literacy rate, infant mortality rate, child mortality rate, maternity mortality ratio, births attended by skilled health personnel, contraceptive prevalence rate, HIV infection rate in 15- to 24-year-old pregnant women, and life expectancy at birth. See http://www.oecd.org/dac/Indicators/index.htm.

[9] The relevant descriptive statistics are provided in Appendix B.

In addition to two expenditure variables, the education regressions include the following control variables.

- *Percent of population in the age group 0–14.* It is difficult and costly to expand enrollment rates in countries with low enrollment when the population is relatively young (Mingat and Tan, 1992). A high share of young in the population would be expected to be negatively correlated with enrollment rates.

- *Per capita income.* As household incomes rise, the relative cost of enrolling children in school is reduced, suggesting that increasing income would be associated with rising enrollments. Furthermore, at higher income levels, the demand for education increases, if education is a normal good. This effect is captured by GDP per capita in purchasing power parity (PPP) terms.

- *Urbanization.* Households in urban areas are more likely to send their children to school, because, among other reasons, access to education is typically better in urban areas (Plank, 1987). In addition, the private cost of education (e.g., transportation costs) may be lower for urban households.

- *Child nutrition.* Better nutrition for children makes it easier for enrolled school-age children to continue in school, thereby affecting enrollment and persistence (Glewwe and Jacoby, 1995). This variable is proxied by child mortality.[10]

Control variables in the health regressions include the following.

- *Per capita income.* Empirical evidence suggests that the population's health status improves as per capita incomes rise.

- *Adult illiteracy rates.* As for education, many studies show a strong inverse relationship between adult illiteracy and infant mortality rates (e.g., Tresserras et al., 1992). A number of studies indicate that female literacy affects the health status of infants and children (see, for example, Schultz, 1993). However, due to data limitations, the overall—rather than the female—adult illiteracy rate is used.[11]

- *Access to sanitation and safe water.* A sanitary environment, as reflected by increased access to sanitation and safe water, improves health status. Access to safe water, for example, has a significant effect on infant and child mortality (Kim and Moody, 1992; and Hojman, 1996). Because of data limitations, access to sanitation is used in the regressions.

---

[10] Other proxies of child nutrition, such as indicators of malnourishment and birth weight, were not available.

[11] In fact, female illiteracy was found to have a weaker effect than overall illiteracy.

- *Urbanization.* Schultz (1993) finds that mortality is higher for rural, low-income, agricultural households, suggesting that increased urbanization is associated with improved health status of the population.

Data limitations prevent adding other controls for socioeconomic characteristics that may affect indicators of education attainment and health status. In particular, private spending on both education and health is omitted due to a lack of data (evidence on the importance of private spending is provided by Psacharopoulos and Nguyen, 1997). Similarly, data limitations prevent including control variables that capture the factors adversely affecting children's caregivers (for example, the impact of the AIDS epidemic in Africa).[12]

Some authors (Bredie and Beeharry, 1998; and Filmer et al., 1998) propose including other demand factors, such as income distribution, in the regressions for both education and health. While data are available for only a small subsample, the regression results are tested for robustness by including the Gini coefficient.

Finally, Mingat and Tan (1998) point to the importance of teachers' salaries in increasing the cost of education in low-income countries. They estimate that 50% of the difference in education attainment between high-income and low-income countries can be attributed to lower teachers' salaries in relation to the rest of the economy in high-income countries that release resources for nonwage inputs, such as textbooks. Data on teacher salaries are not available for a sufficient number of countries to use as a control variable. However, as relative teacher salaries are highly correlated with illiteracy and child mortality rates,[13] the latter control variables are expected to pick up much of the effect of differences in salary levels.

Data on education and health spending are drawn from a number of sources, including various issues of the IMF's *Government Finance Statistics* (GFS) and *Recent Economic Development* reports. These expenditure data, in general, exclude local government spending. This can be a major deficiency in countries that have devolved expenditure responsibilities to lower levels of government.

For around 50 developing and transition countries, the intrasectoral allocation for education spending (primary, secondary, and tertiary) and

---

[12] An attempt was made to circumvent the problem of missing control variables by adding dummies for regions, under the assumption that the variation of omitted controls within regions is dominated by the variance among regions. The results are robust to the inclusion of these dummy variables.

[13] The correlation coefficient between illiteracy rates and average teacher salaries as a multiple of GDP per capita was –0.80 for 24 countries for which data were available (data on teachers' salaries are from Mehrotra and Buckland, 1998). The correlation coefficient with child mortality rates was –0.72. The correlation coefficient between income per capita in PPP terms and the relative teacher salaries was also relatively high at –0.48.

health care spending (primary, secondary, and other) are taken from GFS and UNESCO databases, the World Bank's *Poverty Assessments*, and *Public Expenditure Reviews*.[14] Most spending and other data are for 1993–1994. The intrasectoral data have been taken from the same source as aggregate allocations to that sector where possible and were checked for consistency with aggregate spending.[15] Available data on education spending typically do not distinguish between primary and secondary education. Consequently, spending on these two levels is analyzed as a single item.

A universally accepted definition of primary health care does not exist. As a result, intrasectoral data for health care are not strictly comparable across sources. Primary health care is defined as public spending on clinics and practitioners according to the GFS categorization.[16] For countries for which this classification is not available, public spending on primary health care or preventive care, as defined in the World Bank's *Poverty Assessments* and *Public Expenditure Reviews*, is used. Secondary health care is defined as hospital services and curative treatments by medical specialists.

Data for control variables and the indicators of education attainment and health status were drawn mostly from the *World Development Indicators* database. Data on primary drop-out rates are from Barro and Lee (1996) and Gini coefficients are from Deininger and Squire (1996). To the extent possible, the data for the health and education indicators and control variables were matched with the year of the spending data.[17]

Figs. 1–3 present average public spending levels and intrasectoral shares of education and health care spending in the sample countries. These figures show that in the sample countries, the share of education expenditures allocated to primary and secondary education is 79%, whereas the share of health care spending allocated to primary care is 16%. These numbers are broadly consistent with average intrasectoral allocations previously observed by others (World Bank, 1993; Sahn and Bernier, 1993).

---

[14] The list of countries is included in Appendix A.

[15] If the deviation between the sum of intrasectoral spending and total sectoral spending exceeded 10%, the observation was dropped.

[16] This measure of primary health care, which includes services provided by clinics and medical, dental, and paramedical practitioners, appropriately captures primary-level health care, as it is the "first point of contact" between clients and a facility in a health system (e.g., Shaw and Griffin, 1995). The GFS disaggregation of health spending—into hospitals, clinics and practitioners, and other spending—is also used by others to examine priorities in the health sector (e.g., Appleton and Mackinnon, 1996).

[17] For example, intrasectoral education data for 1994 were matched with enrollment data for 1994, if available. If enrollment data for 1994 were not available, observations in the range of three years before and after the year of spending were used (1991–1997). Potential problems of measurement error were addressed by running two-stage least squares regressions.

Figure 1. Total Education and Health Care Spending
(Percent of GDP)

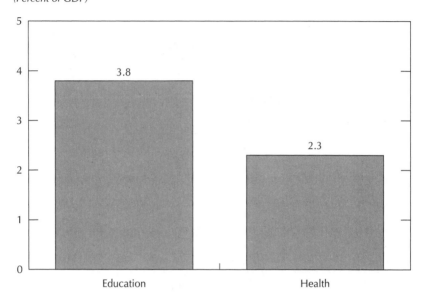

Sources: UNESCO database; World Bank, *Public Expenditure Review* (Washington, various issues); World Bank, *Poverty Assessment* (Washington, various issues); IMF, GFS database; and IMF staff estimates.

Figure 2. The Intrasectoral Shares of Education Spending
(In 50 selected countries)

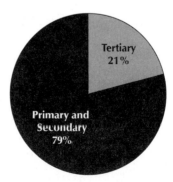

Sources: UNESCO database; World Bank, *Public Expenditure Review* (Washington, various issues); World Bank, *Poverty Assessment* (Washington, various issues); IMF, GFS database; and IMF staff estimates.

Figure 3. The Intrasectoral Shares of Health Care Spending
(In 40 selected countries)

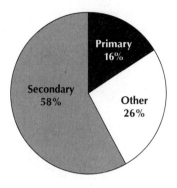

Sources: UNESCO database; World Bank, *Public Expenditure Review* (Washington, various issues); World Bank, *Poverty Assessment* (Washington, various issues); IMF, GFS database; and IMF staff estimates.

Empirical Results

Eq. (1) is estimated using OLS (correcting for heteroskedasticity) and two-stage least squares (2SLS) regressions. In the first instance, we follow functional forms used previously in the literature—that is, linear and log-log specifications—for ease of comparison of our results with those previously obtained. For example, Hojman (1996) previously tested a linear specification. Pritchett and Summers (1996) use log-log specifications to estimate the nonlinear relationship between income and health. The log-log specification provides the added convenience of yielding ready elasticity estimates. We employ statistical tests to assess the appropriateness of the functional forms.

This section is set up as follows. The appropriate functional form— whether linear or log-log—for Eq. (1) is tested using both the Mackinnon, White, and Davidson (MWD) and Ramsey's RESET test of up to three fitted terms. As it turns out, the issue of functional form is difficult to resolve in some cases. In addition, stylized facts pertaining to social indicators, such as diminishing returns to increased spending, suggest alternative specifications in addition to the linear and log-log specifications. In particular, Anand and Ravallion (1993) created an index of health status to reflect diminishing returns to scale. A similar index has been proposed by Kakwani (1993). This issue is taken up in the section on robustness tests.

The 2SLS technique is used primarily to address the problem of reverse causality. For instance, higher spending on primary education may have a positive effect on enrollment, but a higher demand for primary education, reflected in higher enrollment rates, may also provide a push for higher spending. A similar dual relationship may exist between public spending on primary health care, on the one hand, and child and infant mortality rates, on the other. In addition, 2SLS regressions address potential problems of measurement errors in variables.[18]

However, it is difficult to find the appropriate instruments because it is also not clear a priori which variables determine social expenditures but do not affect social indicators. The literature on the determinants of social spending (for example, Looney and Frederiksen, 1996; Gbesemete and Gerdtham, 1992) suggest that foreign aid and military spending may explain some of the variance in the share of public spending on education and health. These variables are tested as potential instruments, along with other variables, in the 2SLS regression. The results should not be interpreted as providing strong evidence for the existence of a causal relationship between spending and social indicators because this study relies on cross-section data.

In evaluating the regression results, it should be borne in mind that multicollinearity among variables affects the standard errors of coefficients on the control variables. The literature on the determinants of social spending, for example, suggests that per capita income is a significant predictor of social spending.

A final note of caution is related to the number of observations. This can vary, depending on the availability of data for a specific variable. The number of observations for the health care regressions is relatively low.

Education Regressions

Table 1 reports results of the education attainment regressions for the linear specification. Four measures of education attainment are used: gross enrollment in primary and secondary education, gross enrollment in secondary education, persistence through Grade 4, and primary school drop-out rates. The MWD test of functional forms suggests that the linear form is appropriate for regressions for drop-out rates and persistence through Grade 4 (therefore, we do not present results for the log-log specification in the table). This is supported by Ramsey's RESET test of up to three fitted terms. However, both tests are agnostic as to

---

[18]The data set includes some outlying observations (for example, Papua New Guinea). However, these outliers did not critically affect the regression results after corrections for heteroskedasticity were made.

the preferred functional form for the regressions on secondary enrollment, while the linear form is weakly preferred for the regression on primary plus secondary enrollment. The explanatory variables account for 40–83% of cross-country variation in education attainment. The F-statistic for all regressions is statistically significant at the 1% level.[19]

Total education spending in relation to GDP is significant in all but the regressions for persistence through Grade 4 at the conventional levels of significance. On the other hand, the share of spending on primary plus secondary education in total education spending is statistically significant for the OLS specifications, but not the 2SLS specification, possibly reflecting the weakness of the instruments. Sargan's test suggests, however, that the 2SLS specifications for all regressions are correct, except possibly for persistence through Grade 4, at the 10% level of significance. The first-stage adjusted R-squared for overall education spending and the intrasectoral spending are 0.51 and 0.29, respectively; the F-statistics are significant at the 1% level.[20] Finally, results from regressions with gross primary enrollment and net secondary enrollment (not reported) also suggest that the intrasectoral allocation and total level of education spending matter.[21] This contrasts with the findings of a positive but insignificant correlation between spending and enrollment (Flug et al., 1998).

The results show that socioeconomic variables, such as urbanization, the percent of the population in age group 0–14, and per capita income, are important in explaining variances in enrollment rates. Except for percent of population aged 0–14, all the other variables have signs that

---

[19] To address heteroskedasticity, White's (1980) corrected covariance and standard errors are used, except for the equation with gross primary plus secondary enrollment as the dependent variable. The latter regression was estimated using the weighted-least-squares (WLS) technique, with adult illiteracy used as a weight. This weight can be interpreted as a scaling factor, indicative of the challenge of achieving targeted levels of education attainment, and yields better results than White's corrected regression. The use of a consistent set of instruments in the 2SLS regressions was checked for validity using Sargan's (1964) general misspecification test.

[20] Foreign aid as a proportion of government expenditure is strongly correlated with the endogenous variables; military spending is negatively correlated with the overall level of public spending on education.

[21] The coefficient estimate of the share of spending on primary plus secondary education from the WLS regression with gross primary enrollment as the dependent variable is 0.21. The coefficient estimate from an OLS regression with net secondary enrollment as the dependent variable is 0.19. Both are significant at the 5% level. OLS regressions with the spending and education attainment variables in logs yield similar results for gross primary and secondary enrollment and gross secondary enrollment as dependent variables, but the statistical significance of the intrasectoral spending variable for persistence through Grade 4 regression is reduced.

Table 1. Regression Results for Education Indicators: Linear Regressions[a]

| | Enrollment Rates | | | |
| | Gross primary and secondary | | Gross secondary | |
	OLS (weighted) (1)	2SLS (weighted) (2)	OLS (3)	2SLS (4)
Constant	45.94*** (6.55)	47.44*** (5.92)	32.60** (3.42)	41.79*** (2.70)
Primary and secondary education spending (percent of total education spending)	0.17** (2.31)	0.08 (0.82)	0.28*** (3.34)	0.20 (0.21)
Education spending (percent of GDP)	1.68* (1.86)	3.20** (2.46)	2.26** (2.18)	2.62** (2.16)
Population aged 0–14 (percent of population)	0.29** (2.25)	0.32** (2..10)	−0.98*** (−4.93)	−1.03*** (−5.22)
Child mortality rate (per thousand of children 0–5 years)	−0.16** (−2.54)	−0.18** (−2.47)	−0.05 (−1.47)	−0.05 (−1.42)
Income per capita in PPP terms[b]	0.34 (0.69)	0.61 (−0.55)	0.15** (1.98)	0.16** (2.00)
Urbanization (percent of population)	0.27*** (3.01)	0.35*** (3.17)	0.41*** (3.50)	0.37*** (3.28)
Adjusted R-squared	0.67	0.64	0.82	0.83
Number of observations	42	39	45	42
F-statistic	15.39***	12.02***	35.64***	34.14***
Sargan's P-value	0.22		0.25	

Source: Authors' calculations.

The instruments used are aid per capita, aid in percent of government expenditures, military spending in percent of government expenditures, share of unallocated education spending, and total government spending.

[a]Except for columns (1) and (2), where regular t-statistics are shown in parentheses, White's heteroskedasticity-corrected statistics are shown.

[b]Multiplied by 100.

* Indicates significance at the 10 percent level.

** Indicates significance at the 5 percent level.

*** Indicates significance at the 1 percent level.

Persistence Through Grade 4		Primary Drop-Out Rates	
OLS	2SLS	OLS	2SLS
(5)	(6)	(7)	(8)
71.72***	62.78***	34.46*	25.58
(10.78)	(8.11)	(1.86)	(1.25)
0.17**	0.25**	−0.43*	−0.21
(2.19)	(2.14)	(−1.89)	(−0.68)
1.59	2.73	−5.19**	−6.49**
(1.29)	(1.57)	(2.06)	(−2.45)
−0.07	−0.19	1.16***	1.13***
(−0.32)	(−0.59)	(3.93)	(3.58)
−0.10*	−0.08	0.03	0.04
(−1.73)	(−1.40)	(0.44)	(0.52)
0.10	−0.25	−0.98	−0.55
(0.21)	(−0.43)	(−0.69)	(−0.43)
0.11	0.16	0.07	0.00
(1.04)	(1.56)	(0.25)	(0.00)
0.50	0.45	0.42	0.39
24	23	38	38
4.90***	4.56***	5.49***	4.33***
0.10			0.15

are consistent with our expectations. Significance varies across indicators. Urbanization is a strong predictor of enrollment rates. Because of multicollinearity, however, the level of significance of the control variables should be interpreted with caution; nevertheless, findings presented here are broadly consistent with the empirical literature on determinants of education attainment.

Robustness Tests

The literature suggests a nonlinear relationship between individual incomes and social indicators.[22] This relationship can be taken into account by including a measure of within-country income distribution in the regression of aggregate indicators. When the Gini coefficient is added to the linear education regressions, the sample size drops by about a third and the spending variable loses significance. When added to the log-log regressions, however, the spending variables remain significant.

We also added dummy variables for regions. This addresses, to some extent, the lack of data on some important control variables, such as a proxy for the impact of the AIDS epidemic in Africa. In general, the inclusion of dummy variables for regions did not improve the explanatory power of the regression models, nor did it affect the coefficient estimates and significance levels. Similarly, the results are robust to the inclusion of adult illiteracy rates which are a proxy for parental education. As expected, illiteracy is negatively correlated with educational attainment.

Running the regressions in log-log form yields results similar to those of the linear form (not reported in the paper). The share of spending in primary plus secondary education is significant at the 5% confidence level or better across all education indicators, whereas total education spending in percent of GDP is significant in two of four indicators (gross secondary enrollment regressions and in the primary school drop-out rates). Per capita income and urbanization are significant in the primary school drop-out rates but not in other regressions.

Finally, we estimated an ad hoc system of four equations, to allow for the "production" of multiple goods with increased spending, including gross primary enrollment rates, gross secondary enrollment rates, persistence to Grade 4 and primary drop-out rates. Following Barro and Lee (1997) and Wenger (2000), we estimated this system using the seemingly unrelated regression (SUR) technique. We allowed for

---

[22] Deaton (2001) and Wagstaff and van Doorslaer (2000) review the theoretical and empirical literature on the nonlinear relationship at the individual level. See also Ravallion (1992). The literature is based on micro studies of the determinants of health, although a nonlinear relationship has been suggested in education as well (see, for example, Behrman et al., 1998).

different intercepts and slope coefficients for each independent variable.[23] Both the share of spending on primary and secondary education and total education spending are significant at conventional levels of significance in all education regressions, except gross primary enrollment rate where the adjusted R-squared itself is low. The other control variables vary in significance; in cases where they are significant, however, the direction is as expected. The results are in Appendix B, Table B2.

Several conclusions can be drawn from the education regressions. First, despite the lack of data on some control variables, the regressions explain a large part of the cross-country variation in enrollment rates. Second, the intrasectoral distribution of public spending for education generally has a statistically significant effect on indicators of both access and education attainment. Third, the overall level of education spending has a statistically significant impact on all indicators except for persistence through Grade 4.[24]

Table 2 reports the results of an analysis of partial variances. For selected regressions, the adjusted R-squared of models of education attainment, with and without the spending variables, are compared. This analysis indicates that including the spending variables increases the explained cross-country variation in education attainment by between 4% and 15%.[25]

The magnitude of the impact of education spending on education attainment can be put in perspective by examining some of the relevant coefficient estimates. For instance, based on the estimates of the OLS regression in column (3) of Table 1, a 5 percentage point increase in the share of outlays for primary and secondary education in total public

---

[23] A Wald test of equality of the slope coefficients indicates that they are different.

[24] The regressions do not permit drawing up of conclusions about the effect of changes in the *level* of spending on primary and secondary education—as opposed to the *share* of such spending in total education expenditure. This issue was addressed by re-estimating the education regressions including spending on primary and secondary education as a percentage of GDP and omitting the variables for intrasectoral spending and the overall spending. In the four regressions for enrollment, this newly defined spending variable was significant at the 1% level; the coefficient estimated ranges between 3.0 and 4.0. In the two regressions for persistence through Grade 4, spending on primary and secondary education as a percent of GDP was only significant at the 10% level, with a coefficient of 2.7 for the OLS regression and 5.5 for the 2SLS regression. These results suggest that, irrespective of the specification, spending for the two sectors matters.

[25] Partial variance analysis only yields accurate results if the underlying assumption on the ordering of casual effects is correct (i.e., partial variance analysis assumes here that public spending affects social indicators only after all other variables have taken effect). Alternatively, the results of partial variable analysis would be correct if spending were to have an effect independent of the other explanatory variables. These are demanding assumptions, and the results presented here should be interpreted with caution.

Table 2. Adjusted *R*-Squared of the OLS Education Attainment Regressions

	Gross Secondary Enrollment	Persistence Through Grade 4	Primary Drop-Out Rate
Excluding spending variables	0.78	0.41	0.27
Including total education spending	0.80	0.45	0.37
Including share of primary and secondary education	0.82	0.50	0.42

Source: Authors' calculations.

expenditures for education increases gross secondary enrollment by over one percentage point. A 1 percentage point of GDP increase in spending on education increases gross secondary enrollment by more than 3 percentage points. Although this shows that spending and its intrasectoral allocation have an important impact on education attainment, it also indicates that increasing attainment through shifting intrasectoral allocations or increasing total spending on education alone may be very difficult. This illustrates the importance of control variables in explaining education attainment.

Mingat and Tan (1998) suggest another reason why the marginal costs of increasing indicators of education attainment are so high. They demonstrate for a sample of 125 countries that, as primary enrollment increases, resources earmarked for primary education are shifted toward decreasing pupil-teacher ratios (this shift in focus begins to occur at primary enrollment rates as low as 50%). Consequently, these additional resources do not significantly increase enrollment rates or persistence.

Health Regressions

Table 3 reports the results of log-log regressions with infant and child mortality rates as dependent variables. The MWD test of functional forms as well as Ramsey's RESET test of up to three fitted terms suggests that the log-log form is the appropriate functional form. The log-log form follows the Cobb-Douglas production function described by Filmer et al. (1998). In addition, the empirical literature has used mainly the log-log specification (see, for example, Pritchett and Summers, 1996; Filmer and Pritchett, 1997; Filmer et al., 1998; and Wang, 2001).

Table 3. Regression Results for Health Indicators: Log-Log Regressions[a]

	Infant Mortality		Child Mortality	
	OLS (1)	2SLS (2)	OLS (3)	2SLS (4)
Constant	5.38*** (5.56)	5.34* (5.89)	6.07*** (4.61)	6.03*** (4.83)
Primary health care spending (percent of total health care spending)	0.02 (0.50)	0.06 (0.24)	0.04 (0.85)	0.09 (0.31)
Health spending (percent of GDP)	−0.31*** (−3.65)	−0.26* (−1.91)	−0.30*** (−3.73)	−0.29** (−2.11)
Adult illiteracy rate (percent of population 15 years or older)	0.31*** (4.18)	0.31** (2.26)	0.32*** (3.75)	0.30** (2.08)
Income per capita in PPP terms	−0.31*** (−2.60)	−0.33** (2.26)	−0.36** (−2.31)	−0.37* (−1.97)
Urbanization (percent of population)	−0.24* (−1.77)	−0.24 (1.43)	−0.28** (−2.43)	−0.27 (−1.62)
Access to sanitation (percent of population)	0.20 (1.69)	0.20* (1.73)	0.21 (1.35)	0.20 (1.31)
Adjusted R-squared	0.84	0.83	0.83	0.82
Number of observations	22	22	22	22
F-statistic	19.98***	18.40***	18.14***	17.30***
Sargan's P-value		0.79		0.86

Source: Authors' calculations.
The instruments used are aid per capita, aid in percent of government expenditures, military spending in percent of government expenditures, and total government spending.
[a]Except for columns (1) and (2), where regular t-statistics are shown in parentheses, White's heteroskedasticity-corrected statistics are shown in parentheses.
* Indicates significance at the 10 percent level.
** Indicates significance at the 5 percent level.
*** Indicates significance at the 1 percent level.

On average, the explanatory variables account for more than 80% of cross-country variation in infant and child mortality rates. The F-statistic for all regressions is statistically significant at the 1% level. Sargan's specification test suggests that the instruments are correctly specified.

Total health spending is statistically significant in all regressions, but the share of primary health spending is not.[26] As in the education regressions, control variables are important in explaining variances in health care status. For example, both adult illiteracy rate and income per capita are consistently significant in all the regressions. In addition, the income elasticities are comparable with previous estimates. For example, Pritchett and Summers (1996) estimate that the long-run income elasticity of infant and child mortality in developing countries lies between –0.2 and –0.4. The results in Table 1 indicate that the income elasticity in our sample is about –0.3. The elasticity of infant and child mortality with respect to health spending in percent of GDP is thrice that of Filmer and Pritchett (1997). On the other hand, Filmer et al. (1998) estimated higher income elasticities.

Robustness Tests

The health regressions are robust to various specifications. When dummy variables for regions are added, total health spending remains significant, with estimated elasticity of health status with respect to spending roughly about the same. The signs of the dummy variables also suggest that other regions have better health status than sub-Saharan Africa, on average.

While our test of functional form suggests that the log-log specification is appropriate, Anand and Ravallion (1993) have suggested that the proper specification should take into account deceasing returns to scale in the improvement of health. This was noted by Kakwani (1993) as well. This can be done using an index that transforms mortality rates into a new variable that reflects decreasing rates of mortality reduction.[27] We replicate this index for our sample and find that overall health care

---

[26] These results should be interpreted with caution. First, because of the above-noted lack of a uniform definition of primary health care, the intrasectoral distribution is not measured consistently across the sample. Second, the sample size is relatively small. Third, the sample used for the health regressions includes eight observations that have zero spending on primary health care, which could reflect institutional differences in these countries (e.g., all primary health care could be private), or simply measurement error. Finally, in the case of 2SLS regressions, the results may reflect the weakness of the instruments. The test for over identifying restrictions suggests that the chosen instruments are appropriate; however, while the F-statistic for the first-stage regression is significant at the 1% level for overall health spending, the F-statistic for the share of primary health spending is not. In particular, foreign aid is strongly correlated with overall level of health spending. The adjusted R-squared for the first-stage regression is 0.67.

[27] This index is defined for a given country i as $[\ln(Max - Min) - \ln(MR_i - Min)]/\ln(Max - Min)$, where Max is the maximum of observed mortality rate, Min is the minimum of observed mortality rate, and MR_i is the mortality rate observed in country i. As the mortality rate in country i approaches the minimum of observed mortality rates, the index for country i approaches 1.

spending remains a significant determinant of infant and child mortality, but with higher elasticities than those reported in Table 3. The estimated elasticities are also higher than those of income. Primary health care spending is not statistically significant.

In order to account for the concave relationship between health attainment and individual incomes, a control for income distribution was added. The results are robust to the inclusion of the Gini coefficient. Owing the lack of Gini data, however, the sample size drops significantly.

An ad hoc system of two equations using the SUR technique accounts for the multiple production of health output with increased spending. The relevant results are in Appendix B, Table B3. We considered different intercept and slope coefficients and also the same intercepts and slope coefficients.[28] The results remain essentially unchanged. Total health spending, adult illiteracy, and per capita income are significant at the 1% level. The estimated elasticities are approximately the same as those reported in Table 3.

Table 4 reports the results of partial variances for health regressions. These suggest that the health spending variable may explain as much as an additional 6–9% of cross-country variation in health status. This contrasts with the results of Filmer and Pritchett (1997), who found that the contribution of health outlays to health care status as measured by child mortality rates was almost negligible (less than ⅙ of 1%).

Taking the results reported in columns (1) and (3) of Table 3, the coefficient estimates suggest that increasing the share of total health care spending in GDP by 1 percentage point decreases child and infant mortality rates by about 3 death per 1,000. This suggests significant gains from increased health spending.

Conclusions and Policy Implications

We have provided evidence supporting the proposition that increased public spending on education and health care matter for education attainment and health status, although definitive evidence for a causal relationship is lacking. The evidence is strongest for education. The relationship is weaker for health.[29]

---

[28] However, the null hypothesis that the slope coefficients are equal was rejected in a Wald test.

[29] Research using panel data (Guin-Sui et al., 1999) suggests that there are no apparent gains from longitudinal analysis in terms of stronger or more robust results. As regards the functional form, we find that of the specifications used hitherto in the literature (linear and log-log), there is evidence that linear specification is more appropriate for the education regressions and the log-log specification for the health regressions. The results are robust to alternative functional forms, such as the nonlinear specification for health indicators following Anand and Ravallion (1993) and Kakwani (1993).

Table 4. Adjusted _R_-Squared of the OLS Health Status Regressions

	Infant Mortality	Child Mortality
Excluding spending variables	0.75	0.77
Including health spending	0.84	0.83

Source: Authors' calculations.

Greater public spending on primary and secondary education has a positive impact on widely used measures of education attainment, and increased health care spending reduces child and infant mortality rates. For example, a 5 percentage point increase in the share of outlays for primary and secondary education increases gross secondary enrollment by over one percentage point. A 1 percentage point increase in health care spending decreases infant and child mortality rates by about 3 per 1,000 live births. If expenditure allocations for education and health care are to boost economic growth and promote the well-being of the poor, policy makers in many developing and transition economies need to pay greater attention to allocations within these sectors. These allocations—both their size and efficiency—are an important vehicle for promoting equity and furthering second-generation reforms.

Some caution, however, is required in using these results for estimating the budgetary resources needed for achieving objectives.[30] Education and health are also affected by per capita income, urbanization, adult illiteracy, and access to safe sanitation and water. Private sector spending also matters.

---

[30] The Development Assistance Committee (DAC) of the OECD, building on the results of the 1995 Social Summit in Copenhagen, has established goals that include reaching universal enrollment in primary education and reducing infant and child mortality by two-thirds in all developing countries by 2015 (OECD/DAC, 1996).

Appendix A

Countries with Intrasectoral Education Spending Data

Algeria	Ghana	Panama
Bahrain	Grenada	Papua New Guinea
Belize	Guatemala	Paraguay
Bolivia	Guyana	Philippines
Botswana	Hungary	Romania
Brazil	Iran, Islamic Republic	Sierra Leone
Bulgaria	Jamaica	St. Vincent and the
Cameroon	Jordan	Grenadines
Chile	Korea	Syrian Arab Republic
Colombia	Lao PDR	Thailand
Congo	Madagascar	Togo
Croatia	Malaysia	Tunisia
Czech Republic	Maldives	Turkey
Ecuador	Malta	Uruguay
El Salvador	Mauritania	Vanuatu
Ethiopia	Mongolia	Vietnam
Fiji	Myanmar	Zambia

Countries with Intrasectoral Health Spending Data

Armenia	Honduras	Paraguay
Bahamas	Hungary	Philippines
Barbados	Jamaica	Poland
Belize	Jordan	Romania
Bolivia	Korea	St. Vincent and the
Botswana	Latvia	Grenadines
Bulgaria	Lithuania	Syrian Arab Republic
Croatia	Malawi	Tanzania
Egypt	Maldives	Thailand
El Salvador	Mali	Trinidad and Tobago
Ethiopia	Malta	Tunisia
Fiji	Morocco	Turkey
Grenada	Netherlands Antilles	Vietnam
Guinea	Papua New Guinea	

Appendix B

Table B1. Summary Statistics

(Individual samples as indicated)

	Mean	Median	Minimum	Maximum	Standard Deviation	Observations
Education						
Gross primary enrollment	96.9	100.0	27.0	130.0	19.9	45
Gross secondary enrollment	50.3	49.0	11.0	99.0	24.8	45
Gross primary and secondary	75.2	80.0	20.0	105.0	18.8	44
Drop-out rates, primary	28.7	21.5	1.0	80.0	23.2	38
Persistence to Grade 4	89.8	92.7	63.7	100.0	9.8	24
Primary and secondary education spending	78.9	80.2	19.8	95.5	12.8	50
Education spending	3.8	3.6	1.0	7.5	1.6	50
Income per capita in PPP terms	3,982	3,633	144	13,370	2,964	50
Population aged 0–14	37.6	39.7	18.1	51.6	9.5	50
Adult illiteracy rate	21.4	16.9	1.1	79.3	18.2	48
Urbanization (percent of population)	49.7	51.2	14.6	89.8	19.9	50
Child mortality rate	65.3	51.5	9.1	269.0	56.2	50
Health Care						
Infant mortality	42.0	35.5	9.1	137.0	35.6	40
Child mortality	60.9	42.0	11.0	233.0	59.6	39
Primary health care spending	16.3	12.7	0.0	50.6	15.1	40
Health care spending	2.3	1.9	0.1	7.5	1.6	40
Immunization against measles	82.2	86.0	22.0	100.0	15.7	39
Access to sanitation	69.2	70.0	10.0	100.0	26.1	33
Adult illiteracy rate	19.1	11.6	0.5	68.0	19.8	38
Income per capita in PPP terms	4,258	3,170	156	15,181	3,377	39
Urbanization (percent of population)	50.1	52.0	11.2	88.6	20.4	40

Sources: See text.

Table B2. SUR Regression Results for Education Indicators
(t-statistics in parentheses)

	Gross Primary (1)	Gross Secondary (2)	Primary Drop-out (3)	Grade 4 (4)
Constant	85.77*** (4.16)	33.03*** (2.62)	35.13 (1.58)	70.76***
Primary and secondary education spending (percent of total education spending)	0.09 (0.46)	0.29*** (2.61)	-0.46** (-2.34)	0.18** (2.13)
Education spending (percent of GDP)	0.70 (0.42)	2.24** (2.30)	-5.44*** (-2.91)	1.65* (1.72)
Income per capita in PPP terms[a]	0.026 (0.19)	0.15** (2.01)	-0.71 (-0.47)	0.13 (0.19)
Population aged 0–14 (percent of population)	0.35 (1.00)	-1.00*** (-4.66)	1.19*** (3.07)	-0.09 (-0.52)
Urbanization (percent of population)	0.02 (0.14)	0.41*** (3.65)	0.06 (0.29)	0.11 (1.13)
Child mortality rate (per thousand children 0–5 years)	-0.21*** (3.59)	-0.05 (-1.39)	0.04 (0.66)	-0.10** (-2.11)
Adjusted R-squared	0.24	0.82	0.42	0.50
Number of observations	45	45	38	24

Source: Authors' calculations.
* Indicates significance at the 10% level.
** Indicates significance at the 5% level.
*** Indicates significance at the 1% level.
[a] Coefficient estimates in linear regressions are multiplied by 100.

Table B3. SUR Regression Results for Health Indicators: Log-Log Regressions
(t-statistics in parentheses)

	Different Slopes		Same Slopes	
	Infant mortality (1)	Child mortality (2)	Infant mortality (1)	Child mortality (2)
Constant	5.38*** (8.40)	6.07*** (8.45)	5.66*** (8.64)	5.66*** (8.64)
Primary health spending (percent of total health spending)	0.02 (0.42)	0.04 (0.59)	0.03 (0.51)	0.03 (0.51)
Health spending (percent of GDP)	−0.31*** (−3.71)	−0.30*** (−3.22)	−0.30*** (−3.58)	−0.30*** (−3.58)
Access to sanitation (percent of population)	0.20 (1.31)	0.21 (1.22)	0.20 (1.30)	0.20 (1.30)
Adult illiteracy rate (percent of population 15 years or older)	0.31*** (4.84)	0.32*** (4.37)	0.31*** (4.75)	0.31*** (4.75)
Income per capita in PPP terms	−0.31*** (−3.13)	−0.36*** (−3.18)	−0.33*** (−3.24)	−0.33*** (−3.24)
Urbanization (percent of population)	−0.24 (−1.18)	−0.28 (−1.23)	−0.26 (−1.23)	−0.26 (−1.23)
Adjusted R-squared	0.84	0.83	0.81	0.77
Number of observations	22	22	22	22

Source: Authors' calculations.
*** Indicates significance at the 1% level.

References

Aiyer, S., Jamison, D.T., Londoño, J.L., 1995. Health policy in Latin America: Progress, problems, and policy options. Cuadernos de Economía 32, 11–28.

Anand, S., Ravallion, M., 1993. Human development in poor countries: On the role of private incomes and public services. Journal of Economic Perspectives 7, 133–50.

Andrews, D., Boote, A.R., Rizavi, S.S., Singh, S., 1999. Debt relief for low-income countries. IMF Pamphlet Series No. 51, International Monetary Fund, Washington, DC.

Appleton, S., Hoddinott, J., Mackinnon, J., 1996. Education and health in sub-saharan Africa. Journal of International Development 8, 307–39.

Appleton, S., Mackinnon, J., 1996. Enhancing human capacities in Africa. In: Ndulu B. and others (Eds.), Agenda for Africa's Economic Renewal. Overseas Development Council, Washington, DC, 109–49.

Barro, R.J, 1991. Economic growth in a cross-section of countries. Quarterly Journal of Economics 106, 407–44.

Barro, R.J., Lee, J.W., 1996. International measures of schooling years and schooling quality. American Economic Review 86, 218–23.

Barro, R.J., Lee, J.W., 1997. Schooling quality in a cross section of countries. NBER Working Paper No. 6198, National Bureau of Economic Research, Cambridge, MA.

Behrman, J. R., Birdsall, N., Szekely, M., 1998. Intergenerational schooling mobility and macro condition and schooling policies in Latin America. IDB Office of the Chief Economist working paper no. 386, Inter-American Development Bank, Washington, DC.

Bennell, P., 1995. Rates of return to education in Asia: a review of the evidence. Working paper no. 24, Institute of Development Studies, Oxford.

Bennell, P., 1996. Rates of return to education: does the conventional pattern prevail in sub-Saharan Africa. World Development 24, 183–200.

Bidani, B., Ravallion, M., 1997. Decomposing social indicators using distributional data. Journal of Econometrics 77, 125–39.

Bredie, J.W.B., Beeharry, G.K., 1998. School enrollment decline in sub-Saharan Africa: Beyond the supply constraint. World Bank discussion paper no. 395, Washington, DC.

Carrin, G., Politi, C., 1995. Exploring the health impact of economic growth, poverty reduction, and public health expenditure. Tijdschrift voor Economie en Management 40, 227–246.

Cassen, R., 1996. Human development: research and policy choices, ODC occasional paper no. 3, Overseas Development Council, Washington, DC.

Chu, K. et al., 1995. Unproductive public expenditures: a pragmatic approach to policy analysis. IMF pamphlet series no. 48, International Monetary Fund, Washington, DC.

Deaton, A., 2001. Health, inequality, and economic development. WHO Commission on Macroeconomics and Health (CMH) working paper no. WG1:3, World Health Organization, Geneva.

Deininger, K., Squire, L., 1996. A new data set measuring income equality. World Bank Economic Review 3, 565–591.

Demery, L., Walton, M., 1998. Are Poverty Reduction and Other 21st Century Social Goals Attainable? World Bank, Washington, DC.

Filmer, D., Hammer, J., Pritchett, L., 1998. Health policy in poor countries: weak links in the chain. Policy research working paper no. 1874, World Bank, Washington, DC.

Filmer, D., Pritchett, L., 1997. Child mortality and public spending on health: how much does money matter? Policy research working paper no. 1864, World Bank, Washington, DC.

Flug, K., Spilimbergo, A., Wachtenheim, E., 1998. Investment in education: do economic volatility and credit constraints matter? Journal of Development Economics 55, 465–81.

Gallagher, M., 1993. A public choice theory of budgets: implications for education in less developed countries. Comparative Education Review 37, 90–106.

Gbesemete, K. P., Gerdtham, U.G., 1992. Determinants of health care expenditure in Africa: a cross-sectional study. World Development 20, 303–308.

Glewwe, P., Jacoby, H.G., 1995. An economic analysis of delayed primary school enrollment in a low-income country: the role of early childhood nutrition. Review of Economics and Statistics 77, 156–69.

Guin-Sui, M.T., Yamada, G., Corbacho, A., 1999. The effects of public spending on education and health on social development indicators: a panel data analysis. Mimeo, International Monetary Fund, Washington, DC.

Gupta, S., Clements, B., Tiongson, E., 1998. Public Spending on Human Development. Finance and Development 35, 10–13.

Gupta, S., de Mello, L., Sharan, R., 2001. Corruption and military spending. European Journal of Political Economy 17, 794–77.

Hojman, D.E., 1996. Economic and other determinants of infant and child mortality in small developing countries: the case of Central America and the Caribbean. Applied Economics 28, 281–90.

Kakwani, N., 1993. Performance in living standards: an international assessment. Journal of Development Economics 41, 307–36.

Kim, K., Moody, P.M., 1992. More resources better health? a cross-national perspective. Social Science & Medicine 34, 837–42.

Landau, D., 1986. Government and economic growth in the less developed countries: an empirical study for 1960–80. Economic Development and Cultural Change 35, 35–75.

Looney, R.E., Frederiksen, P.C., 1996. Defense expenditures and budgetary patterns in selected Middle Eastern and Mediterranean countries: an assessment. Public Budgeting and Financial Management 8, 93–105.

Mauro, P., 1998. Corruption and the composition of government expenditure. Journal of Public Economics 69, 263–79.

McGuire, A., Parkin, D., Hughes, D., Gerard, K., 1993. Econometric analyses of national health expenditures: can positive economics help answer normative questions? Health Economics 2, 113–26.

Mehrotra, S., 1998. Education for all: Policy lessons from high-achieving countries. UNICEF staff working papers, Evaluation, Policy and Planning Series No. 98-005, UNICEF, New York, NY.

Mehrotra, S., Buckland, P., 1998. Managing teacher costs for access and quality. UNICEF staff working papers, Evaluation, Policy and Planning Series No. 98-004, UNICEF, New York, NY.

Mingat, A., Tan, J.-P., 1992. Education in Asia: A Comparative Study of Cost and Financing. World Bank, Washington, DC.

Mingat, A., Tan, J.-P., 1998. The mechanics of progress in education: evidence from cross-country data. Policy research working paper no. 2015, World Bank, Washington, DC.

Musgrove, P., 1996. Public and private roles in health: theory and financing patterns. World Bank discussion paper no. 339, Washington, DC.

Noss, A., 1991. Education and adjustment: a review of the literature. Policy Research and External Affairs working paper WPS 701, World Bank, Washington, DC.

OECD (Organisation for Economic Co-operation and Development)/DAC (Development Assistance Committee), 1996. Shaping the 21st century: the contribution of development cooperation. Paris.

Ogbu, O.M., Gallagher, M., 1991. On public expenditures and delivery of education in sub-Saharan Africa. Comparative Education Review 35, 295–318.

Plank, D.N., 1987. The expansion of education: a Brazilian case study. Comparative Education Review 31, 361–76.

Pradhan, S., 1996. Evaluating public spending: a framework for public expenditure reviews. World Bank discussion paper no. 323, Washington, DC.

Pritchett, L., Summers, L.H., 1996. Wealthier is healthier. Journal of Human Resources 31, 841–68.

Psacharopoulos, G., 1994. Returns to investment in education: a global update. World Development 22, 1325–43.

Psacharopoulous, G., Nguyen, N.X., 1997. The role of government and the private sector in fighting poverty. World Bank technical paper no. 346, Washington, DC.

Ravallion, M., 1992. Does undernutrition respond to incomes and prices? Dominance tests for Indonesia. World Bank Economic Review 6, 109–24.

Sahn, D., Bernier, R., 1993. Evidence from Africa on the intrasectoral allocation of social sector expenditures. Cornell Food and Nutrition Policy Program working paper no. 45, Cornell University, Ithaca.

Sargan, J.D., 1964. Wages and prices in the United Kingdom: a study in econometric methodology. In: Hart, P.E., Mills, G., Whitaker, J.K. (Eds.), Econometric Analysis for National Economic Planning. Butterworth, London, 25–63.

Schultz, T.P., 1993. Mortality decline in the low income world: causes and consequence. Economic Growth Center discussion paper no. 681, Yale University, New Haven, CT.

Sen, A., 1999. Economic policy and equity: an overview. In: Tanzi, V., Chu, K., Gupta, S. (Eds.), Economic Policy and Equity. International Monetary Fund, Washington, DC, 28–42.

Shaw, R.P., Griffin, C.C., 1995. Financing Health Care in Sub-Saharan Africa Through User Fees and Insurance. World Bank, Washington, DC.

Tanzi, V., Chu, K., (Eds.), 1998. Income Distribution and High-Quality Growth. MIT Press, Cambridge, MA.

Tresserras, R.J.C., Alvarez, J., Sentis, J., and Salleras, L., 1992. Infant mortality, per capita income, and adult illiteracy: an ecological approach. American Journal of Public Health 82, 435–37.

Wagstaff, A., van Doorslaer, E., 2000. Income inequality and health: what does the literature tell us? Annual Review of Public Health 21, 543–67.

Wang, L., 2001. Health outcomes in poor countries and policy options: a summary of empirical findings from DHS data. Mimeo, World Bank, Washington, DC.

Wenger, J.W., 2000. What do schools produce? Implications of multiple outputs in education?" Contemporary Economic Policy 18, 27–36.

White, H., 1980. A heteroskedasticity-consistent covariance matrix and a direct test for heteroskedasticity. Econometrica 48, 817–38.

World Bank, 1993. World Development Report 1993: Investing in Health. Oxford University Press, New York, NY.

World Bank, 1995. Priorities and Strategies for Education: A World Bank Review. World Bank, Washington, DC.

9

Public Spending on Health Care and the Poor

Sanjeev Gupta, Marijn Verhoeven, and Erwin R. Tiongson

Introduction

A number of national and international initiatives aim to increase pro-poor public spending, particularly in education and health care. A key international program for poverty reduction is the Heavily Indebted Poor Countries (HIPC) Initiative launched in 1996. The resources freed up by this debt relief initiative will be significant relative to current levels of expenditure on health care and education (see Gupta et al., 2001). The question is whether the increase in public outlays on health care as a result of new initiatives will necessarily benefit the poor and contribute to significant improvements in health status.

Empirical evidence concerning the impact of public spending on the health status of a country's population is mixed (see Jack, 1999; Filmer and Pritchett, 1999; and Gupta, Verhoeven, and Tiongson, forthcoming in the *European Journal of Political Economy*). Because data on the distribution of indicators by income classes are rarely available, existing studies have typically relied on aggregate health indicators. As a result, these

Reprinted from *Health Economics*, Vol. 12, Issue 8 (August 2003), pp. 685–96. "Public Spending on Health Care and the Poor," by Sanjeev Gupta, Marijn Verhoeven, and Erwin R. Tiongson, © 2002 John Wiley & Sons Limited. Reproduced with permission.

The authors wish to thank Emanuele Baldacci, Benedict Clements, Hamid Davoodi, Emmanuela Gakidou, Robert Gillingham, Gabriela Inchauste, Dean Jamison, Gary King, and Martin Ravallion, and three anonymous referees for helpful comments and I-Lok Chang for technical assistance. The authors are especially indebted to P.A.V.B. Swamy for his generous advice and assistance. The usual disclaimer applies.

studies do not necessarily reveal anything about the impact of spending on the poor. This issue has been raised by Bidani and Ravallion (1997), who found that the poor have worse health status than others and that public spending on health care matters more to them. They suggest that the poor rely more on public health spending while the nonpoor are better able to substitute private for public spending.

This paper uses new cross-country data to assess the relationship between public spending on health care and the health status of the poor. Data are drawn from two sources: (i) existing data on health status by income quintile tabulated from demographic health surveys in 44 countries; and (ii) our estimates of the health status of the poor in over 70 countries drawn from a new technique in decomposing social indicators. Our estimates confirm that the poor have significantly worse health status than the nonpoor and the regression results provide new evidence that public spending on health care matters more to them.

Review of the Literature

As noted earlier, cross-country studies estimating the relationship between public health spending and health status have typically used data on aggregate indicators of health status. Aggregate data on indicators often mask important variations in health status and health service use by income groups within developing and transition countries. Studies have found, for example, that

- the poor are significantly less healthy than the rich (see Wagstaff, 2000; Gwatkin, 2000; and Wagstaff and Watanabe, 2000);

- the rich are more likely to obtain medical care when sick (see Makinen et al., 2000; and Castro-Leal et al., 1999); and

- the poor are more likely than the rich to obtain health care from publicly provided facilities (see Gwatkin, 2000).

These suggest that public spending on health may matter more to the poor, because they rely more on public health resources while the nonpoor are able to substitute private spending for public spending. However, few studies assess the impact of spending on the poor. For example, the World Bank (1995) reports that public expenditure on health in the Philippines contributes to a reduction in infant mortality rates in poorer regions, but not in richer regions. Deolalikar (1995) finds that the marginal impact of public health spending on the incidence and duration of children's illness is slightly larger among the poor than the nonpoor, in a sample of Indonesian households. Finally, the widely cited study by Bidani and Ravallion (1997) finds that public spending on health care does indeed affect the poor more favorably.

Until recently, limited data on health were available by household income or expenditure, and rarely did existing disaggregated data allow for cross-country comparisons. In the absence of actual data on variations in health status by income, Bidani and Ravallion use the two-dollar-a-day poverty line to decompose aggregate health indicators into subgroup averages for 35 countries using a random coefficients model.

They use the following accounting identity:

$$Y_i = \sum_{j=1}^{M} Y_{ij} n_{ij},\tag{1}$$

where Y_i is the health indicator for country i; Y_{ij} is the mean indicator for the jth subgroup in country i; n_{ij} is the population share of subgroup j in i, and

$$\sum_{j=1}^{M} n_{ij} = 1,\tag{2}$$

where $j = 1, \ldots, M$ denotes the number of subgroups; and $i = 1, \ldots, N$ denotes the number of countries. A vector of explanatory variables for country i, X_i, and a vector of explanatory variables for group j in country i, Z_{ij} is observed:

$$Y_{ij} = \alpha_j + \beta_j' X_i + \gamma_j' Z_{ij} + \varepsilon_{ij}.\tag{3}$$

Substituting (3) into (1) gives

$$Y_i = \sum_{j=1}^{M} \left(\alpha_j + \beta_j' X_i + \gamma_j' Z_{ij} \right) n_{ij} + u_i,\tag{4}$$

where

$$u_i = \sum_{j=1}^{M} \varepsilon_{ij} n_{ij}.\tag{5}$$

Bidani and Ravallion estimate (4) using international poverty lines as the cutoff for two subgroups: the poor and nonpoor. They use aggregate health indicators and cross-country data on the distribution of consumption, public spending on health care at the country level, initial primary school enrollment ratio at the country level, and mean consumption per capita of subgroup j. This allows them to estimate health outcomes by subgroups, the Y_{ij}'s, as well as test some of their possible determinants.

Bidani and Ravallion's approach has some methodological weaknesses. It does not take into account available information on the reasonable range of values for the relevant health indicators. As originally implemented, their approach reports the average health indicators for the poor and nonpoor, using the means of the explanatory variables, without retrieving the country-level estimates. In general, when restrictions are not properly specified in regressions of this form, the estimated country-level subgroup means may lie beyond their reasonable range. Bidani and Ravallion's approach also uses a specific model of health status to estimate the distribution of aggregate health indicators. While there are certainly gains from including a model of health status in the estimation process, the accuracy of the estimates, in practice, is sensitive to the particular model of health status adopted. Ravallion (1996) shows that, after trial and error, the inclusion of the appropriate control variables in a regression similar to Bidani and Ravallion's model improves the estimates of subgroup means. In practice, however, it is difficult to identify what these control variables should be.

Our reproduction of their results for 68 countries shows that in as many as 35 percent of the underlying country-level estimates, the nonpoor could have higher child mortality rates than the poor, an unlikely scenario (see Gupta, Verhoeven, and Tiongson, forthcoming). But more importantly, 7–16 percent of the countries in the sample are estimated to have a negative figure for child mortality—a physical impossibility.

Alternative methods for decomposing aggregate indicators have evolved in political science in the context of the analysis of voting behavior. The problem of inferring characteristics at the individual level from aggregate voting data is called "the ecological inference problem" and is represented by the following accounting identity:

$$Y_i = Y_{i,n}(n_i) + Y_{i,p}(1 - n_i),$$ (6)

where Y_i is the aggregate indicator (e.g., voter turnout), n_i is the population share ($0 < n < 1$) of the subgroup of interest (e.g., the poor), and $Y_{i,n}$ and $Y_{i,p}$ are the unknown subgroup characteristics. $Y_{i,n}$ and $Y_{i,p}$ are equivalent to Y_{ij} in equations (1) and (3) for subgroup j.

King (1997) develops a methodology for estimating disaggregated data that addresses weaknesses of existing solutions to the ecological inference problem. It assumes random coefficients, allowing the distribution of health status to vary from country to country. It restricts the disaggregated data (which are specified as proportions) to the appropriate intervals, in particular, the [0,1] interval or narrower. In particular, equation (6) is used to solve for one unknown in terms of the other:

$$Y_{i,p} = \left(\frac{Y_i}{1-n_i}\right) - \left(\frac{n_i}{1-n_i}\right)Y_{i,n}. \tag{7}$$

Equation (7) shows that $Y_{i,p}$ is a linear function of $Y_{i,n}$, where the intercept and the slope are known. This indicates that the Y's must fall within the following bounds:

$$\max\left(0, \frac{Y_i - n_i}{1-n_i}\right) \le Y_{i,p} \le \min\left(\frac{Y_i}{1-n_i}, 1\right) \tag{8}$$

$$\max\left(0, \frac{Y_i - (1-n_i)}{n_i}\right) \le Y_{i,n} \le \min\left(\frac{Y_i}{n_i}, 1\right). \tag{9}$$

King uses Bayesian statistics to determine the probabilistic values of Y_p and Y_n in i within the permissible bounds. In particular, King assumes a truncated bivariate normal distribution from which $Y_{i,p}$ and $Y_{i,n}$ are drawn. First, a maximum likelihood function is used to estimate the parameters that define the shape of this distribution. Second, King uses this hypothetical distribution as a priori for simulating values of Y_p and Y_n in every i within the known permissible bounds. The point estimates are the means of the simulated distribution and the standard error is the degree of variation in the simulated values.

In estimating Y_p and Y_n in i , King does not assume an explicit production function. An extension of his model allows for the inclusion of control variables (see King, 1997, pp. 169–184) to address aggregation bias or the information loss due to aggregation, though he strongly cautions against the inclusion of such variables to avoid problems such as those associated with misspecification. To explain the variation in subgroup averages across i's as a function of measured explanatory variables, he recommends performing instead a second-stage analysis, such as regression analysis, with the estimated subgroup averages as dependent variables.[1]

---

[1]King distinguishes between two possibilities: first, the addition of covariates to address aggregation bias in the first stage, and second, the use of explanatory variables in a second-stage analysis (King, 1997, pp. 170, 280). Variables that are candidates for inclusion in the second stage can be used as covariates in the first stage *only if* they are applied to data with aggregation bias and do not create other problems. For example, King shows that the erroneous inclusion of covariates in the absence of aggregation bias may degrade the quality of data. An extensive discussion of aggregation bias and measures for avoiding it is presented in Chapters 3 and 9 (King, 1997, pp. 38–73, 186–184).

Our simulations show that King's method provides a good approximation of actual, disaggregated social indicators data (see Gupta, Verhoeven, and Tiongson, forthcoming in *Applied Economics Letters*). As with all other methods of ecological inference, however, King's method is not guaranteed to work perfectly. For example, some information is still lost in the aggregation. In addition, King's method, in practice, readily allows for only two subgroups while the Bidani-Ravallion method allows for any number of subgroups. Notwithstanding these limitations, we use King's method to generate new disaggregated data of health status for over 70 developing and transition economies.

Data and Analysis

This paper estimates the impact of public spending on the health status of the poor. In particular, the following regression equation is estimated:

$$Y_{ij} = \alpha_j + \beta_j' X_i + \gamma_j' Z_{ij} + \varepsilon_{ij}, \tag{10}$$

where Y_{ij} is the mean indicator for the jth subgroup in country i; X_i is a vector of explanatory variables for country i; and Z_{ij} is a vector of explanatory variables for group j in country i.

Data on Y_{ij} are drawn from two sources: First, we use quintile data for 44 developing and transition economies for the mid-1990s tabulated by Gwatkin et al. (2000) from *Demographic Health Surveys* (DHS). Table 1 reports selected summary statistics. If it is assumed that the lowest quintile or the bottom 20 percent of the population proxies the poor, the data suggest that, indeed, the health status of the poor is significantly worse than that of the nonpoor. But this measure of poverty is relative. The "poor" in one country are not necessarily comparable with the "poor" in another country. As we are interested in the absolute poor across countries—those who are least able to substitute private for public spending—a distribution of health status based on an internationally comparable cutoff point, such as an international poverty line, would be a more suitable measure of the health status of the poor across countries.

We modify the quintile data accordingly, using DHS quintile data and the poverty headcount based on the 2-dollar-a-day poverty line. For example, given a 40 percent poverty headcount, the average child mortality rate of the lowest two quintiles would proxy the health status of the poor. For all observations for which poverty headcount is over 20 percent, we take the weighted average of the relevant quintiles. For a poverty headcount below 20 percent, we simply let the mortality rate of

Table 1. Social Indicators by Quintiles, 1995[a]
(Number of countries in parentheses)

	All[b] (44)		Sub-Saharan Africa (22)		Asia (7)		Western Hemisphere (9)		Transition Economies (3)		Other[c] (3)	
	Q1	Q5	Q1	Q5	Q1	Q5	Q1	Q5	Q1	Q5	Q1	Q5
Births attended by skilled staff (%)	31	84	25	82	16	68	40	94	96	100	23	88
Mortality rate (per thousand births)												
Infant mortality rate	91	51	107	67	80	41	69	29	56	41	96	31
Child mortality rate	148	74	192	105	118	53	97	37	68	45	128	35
Malnutrition												
Children stunted (%)	41	18	41	23	57	30	36	6	35	16	38	11
Children underweight (% moderate)	32	14	36	18	57	29	19	4	16	8	19	5
Immunization rate (%)												
Immunization rate, DPT	49	76	43	79	47	81	52	75	70	76	61	95
Immunization rate, measles	55	78	47	80	50	82	65	82	80	80	69	93

Source: Gwatkin et al. (2000).
[a] Q1 is the poorest 20 percent of the population, Q5 is the richest. The survey years range from 1990 to 1998. On average, they are for 1995.
[b] Unweighted average.
[c] Egypt, Morocco, and Turkey.

the bottom quintile proxy the health status of the poor. This is admittedly a crude approach, and makes two strong assumptions: first, that the asset index proxies living standards; and second, that there is linearity in the relationship between living standards and mortality. The results should therefore be interpreted with caution.

Second, we follow King's methodology to construct disaggregated data for the health status of the poor and nonpoor in over 70 countries, using aggregate country-level data on health indicators and the poverty headcount based on the 2-dollar-a-day poverty measure. Data on aggregate health indicators are drawn from the *World Development Indicators* (WDI) database (World Bank, 2001) while data on poverty headcount for 82 developing and transition economies are drawn from Ravallion and Chen (1997). We employ the statistical procedure used by King as programmed in *EzI* version 2.3 (see King, 1997; and Benoit and King, 1996). Using this procedure, Gakidou et al. (1999) generated estimates of the probability of dying and tuberculosis prevalence among the poor and nonpoor for the *World Health Report 1999*.

The baseline model uses the following explanatory variables: initial (1980) primary school enrollment ratio at the country level, public spending on health per capita at the country level, and mean consumption per person of subgroup *j*. To test the robustness of the results of the initial regressions and to allow for a more complete model specification, a number of other known determinants of health, such as private spending, urbanization, and others, are added to the baseline model.

Data on public spending on health care per capita are drawn from national authorities and IMF staff estimates. These have the advantage of being taken from a consistent set of fiscal data. An alternative data source for health spending per capita in U.S. dollars is the *World Health Report 2000* (World Health Organization, 2000). Although not necessarily consistent with overall budget data, data on both private and public spending are available from this source, mostly for 1997. We use them in the section on robustness tests. Data from the two sources are strongly correlated, with a correlation coefficient of 0.8.

Per capita health spending is measured in PPP terms. This is calculated as the product of health spending as a share of GDP in local currency and GDP per capita expressed in PPP terms, following Gupta and Verhoeven (2001). Data on the enrollment ratio and urbanization are drawn from the WDI database. Data on mean consumption per person are calculated using data from Ravallion and Chen (1997). Data on private spending are from the *World Health Report 2000* (WHO, 2000). Unless otherwise indicated, the variables are the country averages for the 1990–1999 period. This is due to the unavailability of annual data, particularly for health indicators, for a number of countries. Therefore, this paper does not attempt to distinguish between lagged and current impact of public health spending on health indicators.

We use two functional forms to estimate the relationship between health status and its determinants: (1) log-log specification, where all the variables are logarithmic, and (2) linear-log (lin-log) specification, where the dependent variable is linear and the regressors are logarithmic. These functional forms have the added convenience of providing parameter estimates that are the implied elasticities and the absolute change in health status associated with a percent change in spending, respectively. All the regression results described in this paper also hold for linear regressions.

Results

To start with, we run an OLS regression of equation (10) using DHS quintile data on the child mortality rate. The regression results of the baseline model are reported in columns (1), (2), (5), and (6) in Table 2, where child mortality is a function of public spending on health per capita, initial primary school enrollment, and mean consumption per capita for the relevant subgroup. In the absence of data on consumption or expenditure in DHS, mean consumption per capita by subgroup is proxied by multiplying data on quintile expenditure share by the average per capita GDP. Data on quintile income shares are from the WDI. This measure of quintile expenditure or income follows several antecedents in the literature, including Deininger and Squire (1998) and Dollar and Kraay (2001). It should be kept in mind, however, that these are income quintiles while DHS quintile data are based on asset or wealth quintiles. Therefore, the regression results should be interpreted with caution.

Columns (3), (4), (7), and (8) in Table 2 add private health spending per capita to the baseline model. The results suggest that public spending on health is a consistent, significant determinant of the child mortality rate among the poor. In contrast, there is some evidence that the nonpoor rely more on private resources.

However, as noted earlier, the quintile measures of the poor and nonpoor are not necessarily comparable across countries. The baseline model is run again using the modified quintile data (described above) as a function of public spending on health per capita, initial primary school enrollment for the country as a whole, and mean consumption per capita for the relevant subgroup. The results are reported in Table 3. While public spending on health per capita is a significant determinant of the health status of the nonpoor, it has a slightly larger impact on the health

Table 2. Public Health Spending and Child Mortality: Evidence from Quintile Data, 1990–1999
(Heteroskedastic-consistent t-statistics in parentheses)

	Poor (Q1)				Nonpoor (Q5)			
	(1) Log-log	(2) Lin-log	(3) Log-log	(4) Lin-log	(5) Log-log	(6) Lin-log	(7) Log-log	(8) Lin-log
Constant	9.23*** (17.24)	745.85*** (9.37)	9.17*** (17.10)	735.75*** (9.29)	10.65*** (19.87)	546.29*** (10.41)	10.29*** (21.46)	520.24*** (10.58)
Public health spending per capita	-0.32*** (-4.10)	-37.01*** (-3.71)	-0.30*** (-3.64)	-33.54*** (-3.23)	-0.02 (-0.22)	-5.27 (-0.81)	-0.02 (-0.24)	-5.39 (-0.78)
Initial primary enrollment ratio	-0.23*** (-2.69)	-37.69** (-2.35)	-0.23*** (-2.78)	-37.82* (-2.41)	-0.37*** (-4.26)	-38.95*** (-3.86)	-0.38*** (-5.34)	-40.24*** (-4.35)
Quintile income per capita	-0.13* (-1.85)	-31.16** (-2.85)	-0.12 (-0.99)	-24.48* (-1.85)	-0.69*** (-5.59)	-38.17*** (-4.21)	-0.52*** (-3.75)	-25.91** (-2.31)
Private health spending per capita			-0.07 (-0.63)	-13.13 (-1.08)			-0.19*** (-2.53)	-14.44 (-2.23)
Adjusted R-squared	0.65	0.69	0.64	0.69	0.81	0.75	0.83	0.78
Number of observations	32	32	32	32	32	32	32	32
F-statistic	20.27***	24.35***	15.13***	18.72***	45.18***	33.68***	39.57***	28.68***

Source: See text.
***, **, and * denote significance at the 1, 5, and 10% levels, respectively.

Table 3. Public Health Spending and Child Mortality: Evidence from Modified Quintile Data, 1990–1999
(Heteroskedastic-consistent t-statistics in parentheses)

	Poor[a]				Nonpoor[a]			
	(1) Log-log	(2) Lin-log	(3) Log-log	(4) Lin-log	(5) Log-log	(6) Lin-log	(7) Log-log	(8) Lin-log
Constant	9.52*** (13.07)	794.71*** (7.96)	9.17*** (10.56)	744.17*** (7.07)	10.31*** (10.38)	634.24*** (6.38)	8.49*** (8.67)	431.15*** (4.21)
Public health spending per capita	-0.32*** (-3.61)	-34.02*** (-3.21)	-0.26** (-2.46)	-25.17** (-2.30)	-0.30** (-3.26)	-31.60*** (-3.37)	-0.23** (-2.77)	-23.48*** (-3.20)
Initial primary enrollment ratio	-0.39*** (-3.60)	-62.23*** (-3.52)	-0.38*** (-3.87)	-61.34*** (-3.71)	-0.43*** (-3.18)	-0.52** (-2.77)	-0.41*** (-4.21)	-50.53*** (-3.50)
Mean consumption per person	-0.13 (-0.55)	-34.31 (-1.21)	-0.05 (-0.19)	-23.22 (-0.76)	-0.30 (-1.25)	-11.25 (-0.55)	0.12 (0.45)	36.30 (1.29)
Private health spending per capita			-0.12 (-1.11)	-17.73 (-1.56)			-0.28*** (-3.37)	-31.41*** (-2.84)
Adjusted R-squared	0.58	0.65	0.59	0.67	0.64	0.61	0.71	0.70
Number of observations	29	29	29	29	29	29	29	29
F-statistic	14.41***	19.06***	11.40***	15.61***	17.72***	15.73***	18.58***	17.36***

Source: See text.
***, **, and * denote significance at the 1, 5, and 10% levels, respectively.
[a] These are estimated using DHS data and the poverty headcount as described in the text.

status of the poor, both in terms of the implied elasticities and in absolute terms. Similarly, the initial primary enrollment ratio has a higher marginal impact on the poor in the lin-log regressions. As in Table 2, the nonpoor are able to rely more on private resources. Mean consumption per capita is insignificant and in some cases has the "wrong" sign, but this is driven in part by collinearity. Mean consumption per capita is highly correlated with public health spending per capita and private health spending per capita. In a bivariate regression of health status on mean consumption per capita, the implied elasticity is about 0.8. The results should be interpreted with caution: as noted earlier, this is a rough approximation of the health status of the absolute poor based on quintile averages for a relatively small sample of countries (29 countries).

The baseline model is rerun once again using estimates of health indicators generated from ecological inference. These estimates provide twice as many country observations for three health indicators: infant and child mortality rates and births attended by skilled staff. Estimates of the health status of the poor and nonpoor using ecological inference are presented in Table 4. As expected, across all country groups, the poor have significantly worse health status than the nonpoor.[2]

Table 5 reports the log-log and lin-log regression results for child mortality rates and births attended by skilled staff. The results for infant mortality rates (not shown) are similar to those of child mortality rates. For births attended by skilled staff, a measure of service provision, in columns (3), (4), (7) and (8), the patterns follow those reported in Table 2 and Table 3: public health spending matters more to the poor. Similarly, initial primary school enrollment affects the poor more favorably, with a comparable elasticity (about 0.50). Mean consumption per person in each subgroup is not significant and, in some cases, has the "wrong" sign but this seems to be driven largely by collinearity with health spending and enrollment ratio. In a bivariate regression, for example, births attended by skilled staff have an elasticity with respect to mean consumption per capita of about 0.7 among the poor and about 0.3 among the nonpoor. This is significant at the 1 percent level. Given the absolute definition of the poor, there could also be limited cross-country variation in mean consumption per capita of the poor.

For the child mortality rate in the log-log regression results reported in columns (1) and (5), public spending on health care is a significant determinant of health status of both the poor and nonpoor. A higher elasticity of the child mortality rate with respect to public health spending is observed among the nonpoor. However, as reported in Table 4,

---

[2] It should be kept in mind, however, that the nonpoor are defined to also include those that are very close to the poverty line, i.e., the nonpoor are not just the rich.

Table 4. Health Status of the Poor and Nonpoor, 1990–1999

(In units as indicated)

	All	Sub-Saharan Africa	Asia	Western Hemisphere	Other[a]	Transition Economies	Sample Size
Child mortality rate (per 1,000 live births)	81.0	162.9	71.4	42.1	60.3	35.1	76
Poor	136.8	206.8	101.0	92.1	170.3	105.9	76
Nonpoor	23.4	28.7	31.3	18.9	31.0	13.9	76
Infant mortality rate (per 1,000 live births)	54.9	98.4	53.2	33.7	50.0	26.7	76
Poor	88.6	120.9	71.1	67.4	109.0	73.5	76
Nonpoor	23.2	32.0	26.4	16.8	33.4	13.0	76
Births attended by health staff (% of total)	61.5	44.3	52.7	77.2	61.0	90.6	58
Poor	50.2	34.8	45.1	64.6	37.1	86.4	58
Nonpoor	80.2	75.9	74.0	88.3	68.1	95.9	58

Sources: World Development Indicators database; and authors' calculations.
[a] Middle Eastern and North African countries.

Table 5. Public Spending and Health Status: Evidence from Ecological Inference, 1990–1999

(Heteroskedastic-consistent t-statistics in parentheses)

	Poor				Nonpoor			
	Child mortality rate		Births attended by skilled staff		Child mortality rate		Births attended by skilled staff	
	Log-linear (1)	Lin-log (2)	Log-linear (3)	Lin-log (4)	Log-linear (5)	Lin-log (6)	Log-linear (7)	Lin-log (8)
Constant	7.95*** (10.27)	635.93*** (4.92)	−1.79 (−1.49)	−173.64*** (−4.91)	4.01*** (3.41)	5.79 (0.12)	3.53*** (4.54)	20.09 (0.49)
Public health spending per capita	−0.19*** (−2.68)	−26.65*** (−2.95)	0.50*** (4.33)	18.49*** (6.61)	−0.32*** (−4.37)	−9.17** (−2.33)	0.22*** (2.93)	13.04*** (3.54)
Initial primary enrollment ratio	−0.48*** (−3.66)	−64.60*** (−3.84)	0.51** (2.13)	13.73** (2.37)	0.01 (0.09)	5.22 (0.68)	0.05 (0.47)	2.28 (0.42)
Mean consumption per person	0.16 (0.60)	4.14 (0.10)	−0.26 (−0.78)	3.39 (0.31)	0.33 (1.24)	14.25 (1.43)	−0.25 (−1.38)	−11.12 (−1.07)
Adjusted R-squared	0.24	0.35	0.50	0.49	0.39	0.24	0.29	0.38
Number of observations	67	67	52	52	67	67	52	52
F-statistic	8.19***	13.09***	18.14***	17.68***	15.38***	8.00***	7.97***	11.42***

Source: See text.

***, **, and * denote significance at the 1, 5, and 10% levels, respectively.

the poor and nonpoor have widely divergent average child mortality rates per 1,000 live births. This implies that in absolute terms (in terms of number of deaths per 1,000 live births), spending has a larger impact on the poor. This is confirmed by the results of the lin-log regressions in columns (2) and (6), where the parameter estimates are the implied absolute change in the child mortality rate associated with a percent increase in the independent variables. A 1 percent increase in public spending on health reduces child mortality by almost thrice as many deaths among the poor. Infant mortality rates follow this same pattern.

The results in Table 5 present separate regressions for the poor and nonpoor. When the two samples are pooled to run the Chow break-point test, the result suggests that the coefficients of the two sets of regressions are significantly different. This provides evidence that pooling is not appropriate and that, as indicated by the coefficient estimates, public spending matters more to the poor.

There is evidence that the elasticities are not constant across countries. Kakwani (1993) has previously suggested that the income elasticity of health status varies with per capita income at the country level. In his analysis, the income elasticity of infant mortality rate is observed to decrease monotonically with income. Similarly, Gakidou and King (2000) find that the impact of both income and expenditure on health status is stronger at low levels of income.

To examine the impact of spending on the poor among low-income countries, the sample is divided into low-income and other countries, using the 1999 GDP per capita of $885 as a cutoff point. This is consistent with eligibility for assistance under the International Development Association (IDA). Table 6 provides the new regression results for these groups.

The implied elasticities in Table 6 indicate that in low-income countries, public health spending has a higher impact on the health status of the poor. Given the prevailing higher levels of child mortality in low-income countries, the effect of public spending is more pronounced when measured in absolute terms. This result is robust to the inclusion of other control variables. However, the results show the absence of a statistically significant association between public spending on health care and the health status of the poor among countries with higher per capita income. This could be due, in part, to inefficiencies in the provision of services and poor targeting in these countries that weaken the impact of public spending on health. In addition, the sample of countries with higher income, as expected, has a much lower share of the absolute poor, thus limiting cross-country variation. On average, the poverty headcount in this sample is less than 10 percent, or one-fourth that of low-income countries.

Table 6. Coefficient Estimates from Log-Log Regressions, 1990–1999[a]

(Elasticity of child mortality rates with respect to public spending on health)

	Model 1		Model 2		Model 3	
	Low income	Other	Low income	Other	Low income	Other
Poor	−0.32***	−0.06	−0.36***	−0.03	−0.28***	−0.07
	(−3.30)	(−0.58)	(−2.94)	(−0.33)	(−2.78)	(−0.69)
Nonpoor	−0.29***	−0.29***	−0.32***	−0.28***	−0.27**	−0.33***
	(−2.63)	(−2.39)	(−2.69)	(−2.63)	(−2.49)	(−3.10)
Sample size	29	38	29	38	29	38

Source: See text.

***, **, and * denote significance at the 1, 5, and 10% levels, respectively.

[a] Model 1 is the baseline model; model 2 is the baseline model plus controls for private spending and urbanization; and model 3 is the baseline model plus private spending, urbanization, and a dummy for sub-Saharan Africa.

Robustness Tests

The results in the preceding section are robust to various specifications. For example, using public health spending data drawn from the WHO (2000) yields similar results though the implied elasticities are higher. The results also hold when controlling for other known determinants of health status. First, individuals may protect themselves against health risks by relying on out-of-pocket expenditure on health care. A suitable test would be the addition of a control variable for private spending on health care. Second, studies report that mortality is higher for rural, low-income, agricultural households, suggesting that increased urbanization is associated with improved health status of the population (Schultz, 1993). Urban areas may also provide better access to health facilities (Prescott and Jamison, 1985). Third, HIV infection is generally thought to have a significant impact on child mortality rates in developing countries (Stanton, 1994).

Adding these new control variables yields patterns similar to those in the previous section. The absolute impact of public health spending on the health status of the poor is more than twice that of the nonpoor, across all models. Private spending on health care is also a significant determinant of the health status of the poor. The magnitude, however, is small: it is less than half the impact of public health spending. This confirms, to some extent, previous findings in the literature that the poor rely more on publicly provided services. Meanwhile, urbanization is not statistically associated with child and infant mortality rates, though it is significantly associated with more births attended by skilled staff. Adult HIV prevalence has a significant impact on health status, as expected. A percentage point increase in adult HIV prevalence, for example, is associated with about three more deaths per 1000 live births. The regression results are robust to the inclusion of dummy variables for regions (see listing of countries in sub-Saharan Africa, Asia, Latin America and the Caribbean, and others; Table 7).

It can also be argued that the impact of public spending on the poor reflects the incidence of such spending or the share of spending received by the poor. Deolalikar (1995) suggests that the marginal impact of *total* government health spending is smaller for the poor when increased government spending benefits the nonpoor more than the poor. Conversely, a higher marginal impact of spending on the health status of the poor may reflect a progressive distribution of health subsidies.[3] Testing the robustness of the results to the inclusion of a measure of benefit incidence is hampered by two major difficulties. First, benefit incidence is typically measured for quintiles, without the use of absolute poverty lines. Second, data on benefit incidence, as compiled by Davoodi, Tiongson, and Asawanuchit (2003), are available for only a small sample of developing and transition economies. Notwithstanding these difficulties, the results are robust to the inclusion of the share of health expenditures received by the poorest quintile. Benefit incidence itself has the "right" sign, i.e., a higher incidence is associated with lower mortality rates, but is not significant. Public spending, however, is consistently significant. This provides some preliminary evidence that the marginal benefit of public spending on health is higher among the poor, regardless of the observed share of total public spending on health received by different income groups.[4]

Conclusion and Policy Implications

This paper finds evidence in over 70 developing and transition economies that the poor have significantly worse health status than the nonpoor and that the poor are more strongly affected by public spending on health care in comparison with the nonpoor. The regression results suggest that the difference in the impact of spending between the poor and nonpoor could be substantial. For child mortality rates, a

---

[3] Over the last 25 years, a large volume of literature has emerged on the benefit incidence of government expenditure. A recent review of 29 developing and transition countries over the period 1978–1995 finds that, on average, government spending on health care is progressive but poorly targeted in sub-Saharan Africa and in transition economies (Chu, Davoodi, and Gupta, 2000).

[4] This result is similar but stronger than the claim that given a *uniform* distribution of public spending on health across income groups, the impact on health status of public spending should still be larger for the poor.

Table 7. Countries in the Sample

Algeria	Gambia, The	Mexico	Senegal
Bangladesh	Ghana	Moldova	Sierra Leone
Bolivia	Guatemala	Mongolia	Slovak Republic
Botswana	Guyana	Morocco	South Africa
Brazil	Honduras	Mozambique	Sri Lanka
Bulgaria	Hungary	Namibia	Tanzania
Burkina Faso	Indonesia	Nepal	Thailand
Cambodia	Jamaica	Nicaragua	Trinidad and Tobago
Central African	Jordan	Niger	Tunisia
Republic	Kazakhstan	Pakistan	Turkey
Chile	Kenya	Panama	Turkmenistan
Colombia	Kyrgyz Republic	Paraguay	Uganda
Costa Rica	Latvia	Peru	Ukraine
Côte d'Ivoire	Lesotho	Philippines	Uruguay
Dominican Republic	Lithuania	Poland	Uzbekistan
Ecuador	Madagascar	Romania	Venezuela, RB
Egypt	Malaysia	Russian Federation	Yemen, Republic of
El Salvador	Mali	Rwanda	Zambia
Estonia	Mauritania	St. Lucia	Zimbabwe
Ethiopia			

1 percent increase in public spending on health reduces child mortality by twice as many deaths among the poor. Infant mortality rates follow a similar pattern. In addition, there is some evidence that the returns to public spending on health are higher among the poor regardless of the benefit incidence. The estimates of the elasticity of health status of the poor to health spending suggest that projected increases in health spending due to international initiatives such as debt relief may, on average, lead to a reduction in child mortality rates by 5 deaths out of 1,000 live births among the poor between 1999 and 2000/2001. A similar reduction may be expected for infant mortality rates.

While these reductions are not trivial, they are by themselves not enough for countries to achieve better health outcomes. The averages also hide potentially significant variations across countries. Additional complementary policies are needed. For example, governments also need to make sure that health interventions reach their intended beneficiaries. Our empirical results suggest a number of areas where progress is needed. First, primary school enrollment is a significant determinant of health status, particularly among the poor. Second, economic growth that translates into increased private resources for health care may also have a large pay-off. Finally, there is evidence that adult HIV prevalence has a large impact on child mortality rates, for both the poor and the nonpoor.

References

Benoit K, King G. A preview of EI and EzI: programs for ecological inference. *Soc Sci Comput Rev* 1996; **14**: 433–438.

Bidani B, Ravallion M. Decomposing social indicators using distributional data. *J Econometrics* 1997; **77**: 125–139.

Castro-Leal F et al. Public social spending in Africa: do the poor benefit? *World Bank Res. Observer* 1999; **14**: 49–72.

Chu Ke-y, Davoodi H, Gupta S. Income distribution and tax and government social spending policies in developing countries. *WIDER Working Paper No. 214.* World Institute for Development Economics Research: Helsinki, 2000.

Davoodi H, Tiongson ER, Asawanuchit SS. How useful are benefit incidence analyses of public education and health spending? *IMF Working Paper No. 03/227.* International Monetary Fund: Washington, 2003.

Deininger K, Squire L. New ways of looking at old issues: inequality and growth. *J Dev Econ* 1998; **57**: 259–287.

Deolalikar AB. Government health spending in Indonesia: impacts on children in different economic groups. In *Public Spending and the Poor: Theory and Evidence,* van de Walle D, Nead K (eds.). Johns Hopkins University Press: Baltimore, 1995.

Dollar D, Kraay A. Growth is good for the poor. *World Bank Policy Research Working Paper No. 2587.* World Bank: Washington, 2001.

Filmer D, Pritchett LH. The impact of public spending on health: does money matter? *Soc Sci Med* 1999; **49**: 1309–1323.

Gakidou E, Jamison D, King G, Spohr C. *Health Status and Access to Health Services: How Different are the Poor?* WHO Economics Advisory Service: Geneva, 1999, unpublished.

Gakidou E, King G. An individual-level approach to health inequality: child survival in 50 countries. *Global Programme on Evidence for Health Policy Discussion Paper No. 18.* World Health Organization: Geneva, 2000, available via the Internet: http://www-nt.who.int/whosis/statistics/discussion papers/pdf/paper18.pdf.

Gupta S, Verhoeven M. The efficiency of government expenditure: experiences from Africa. *J Policy Modeling* 2001; **23**(4): 433–467. [Chapter 11 in this volume—Ed.]

Gupta S et al. Debt relief and public health spending in heavily indebted poor countries. *Finance Dev* 2001; **38**: 10–13.

Gupta S, Verhoeven M, Tiongson E. The effectiveness of government spending on education and health care in developing and transition economies. *Eur J Pol Economy,* forthcoming. [Chapter 8 in this volume—Ed.]

————. Decomposing social indicators using ecological inference. *Applied Economics Letters,* forthcoming.

Gwatkin DR. Health inequalities and the health of the poor: what do we know? what can we do? *Bull WHO* 2000; **78**(1): 3–18.

Gwatkin DR et al. *Socio-Economic Differences in Health, Nutrition, and Population, Health, Nutrition, and Population Series*, various issues. World Bank: Washington, 2000.

Jack W. *Principles of Health Economics for Developing Countries*. World Bank: Washington, 1999.

Kakwani N. Performance in living standards: an international comparison. *J Dev Econ* 1993; **41**: 307–336.

King G. A *Solution to the Ecological Inference Problem: Reconstructing Individual Behavior from Aggregate Data*. Princeton University Press: Princeton, NJ, 1997.

Makinen M et al. Inequalities in health care use and expenditures: empirical data from eight developing countries and countries in transition. *Bull WHO*, 2000; **78**(1): 55–65.

Prescott N, Jamison DT. The distribution and impact of health resource availability in China. *Inter J Health Planning Manage* 1985; **1**: 45–56.

Ravallion M. How well can method substitute for data? five experiments in poverty analysis. *World Bank Res Observer* 1996; **11**: 199–221.

Ravallion M, Chen S. What can new survey data tell us about recent changes in distribution and poverty? *World Bank Econ Rev* 1997; **11**(2): 357–382.

Schultz TP. Mortality decline in the low income world: causes and consequence. *Economic Growth Center Discussion Paper No. 681*. Yale University: New Haven, 1993.

Stanton B. Child health: equity in the non-industrialized countries. *Soc Sci Med*, 1994; **38**(10): 1375–1383.

Wagstaff A. Socioeconomic inequalities in child mortality: comparisons across nine developing countries. *Bull WHO* 2000; **78**(1): 19–29.

Wagstaff A, Watanabe N. Socioeconomic inequalities in child malnutrition in the developing world. *World Bank Policy Research Working Paper No. 2434*. World Bank: Washington, 2000.

World Bank. Philippines: public expenditure management for sustained and equitable growth. *World Bank Report No. 14680–PH*. World Bank: Washington, 1995.

World Bank. *World Development Indicators 2001*. World Bank: Washington, 2001.

World Health Organization. *World Health Report 2000: Health Systems: Improving Performance*. World Health Organization: Geneva, 2000.

10

User Payments for Basic Education in Low-Income Countries

ARYE L. HILLMAN AND EVA JENKNER

Basic education combined with social mobility is a prerequisite for successful economic development. Basic education improves productivity through investment in human capital, and also through beneficial externalities when more educated people complement one another in productive activities. Basic education also improves the quality of life by allowing people to read, write, and do arithmetic calculations. It is a responsibility of government to ensure that children have quality basic education independently of their parents' social and economic circumstances. Ideally, therefore, all children should have access to free-access, publicly financed, quality schools.[1] Yet, in many poor countries, education of children is not free; rather, parents pay fees or user payments for the education of their children. The user payments in some cases supplement public spending on schools. In other cases, where no public financing is available, user payments self-finance community schools that are organized and funded by communities and parents independently of government.

User payments can be voluntary or compulsory, and can take different forms. School fees might pay for salaries of teachers and administrative staff, learning and teaching materials (such as pencils and textbooks), and maintenance of schools. In many low-income countries, user payments take the form of payments-in-kind, such as food for

---

[1] We stress quality because simply being present at school does not ensure an adequate basic education. On determinants of the effectiveness of spending in education in a sample of poor countries, see Michaelowa (2001).

the teacher or labor provided for construction or refurbishment of the school. Compulsory school uniforms are also a form of user payment, since parents are obliged to buy the uniform. User payments can also be used to improve the quality of education financed through public spending. Supplements to the teacher's government-financed salary may improve the motivation of teachers and allow the recruitment of better-qualified staff.

It has been proposed that user payments for basic education should be forbidden or, where already present, abolished. For example, the nongovernmental organization Oxfam declares that "The evidence is indisputable. Success in achieving universal basic education depends on education becoming affordable to the poor, and this requires the abolition of education charges" (Oxfam, 2001, p. 15).

User payments are indeed regressive payments that place a burden on poor parents. The only difference between compulsory and voluntary user payments is that if parents choose not to pay voluntary fees, their children are excluded from school. Moreover, in low-income countries primary schooling may be compulsory and financed by compulsory fees but payment and attendance at school may not be enforced, so that officially compulsory payments become for practical purposes voluntary payments and exclusion from schooling takes place.

The purpose of this chapter is to assess the policy recommendation that user prices for basic education in poor countries should be disallowed or abolished. We accept without qualification that, ideally, parents should not have to pay to send their children to school and that governments should provide quality free-access education through publicly financed schools. As in richer countries, high-income households in poor countries can often afford and choose to send their children to expensive private schools financed through user payments. We are concerned here with the education of children from poorer households who would attend quality free-access government schools if the schools were available.

Enrollment and Primary School Completion in Low-Income Countries

School attendance in low-income countries is far from universal. There is also a clear gender bias: two-thirds of the children not attending school are girls. Primary completion rates are low and educational standards are often inadequate: teachers are poorly trained and paid and, as a result, are often insufficiently motivated. Classrooms are overcrowded and basic teaching resources such as textbooks, blackboards,

Table 1. Primary Enrollment Rates
(Percent)

	Net		Gross	
	1980	1997	1980	1996
East Asia and Pacific	86	99	111	116
East Europe and Central Asia	92	100	99	100
Latin America and Caribbean	86	95	105	113
Middle East and Northern Africa	74	87	87	95
South Asia	64	77	77	100
Sub-Saharan Africa	54	—	81	78
Developing countries	78	89	96	107
OECD countries	97	100	102	104

Source: World Bank, *World Development Indicators* (2002).

pens, and paper are lacking.[2] The need to address these inadequacies is reflected in the Millennium Development Goals of eliminating the gender gap in primary and secondary education by 2005, and achieving universal primary education worldwide by 2015.[3]

Table 1 shows changes in net and gross primary school enrollment rates between 1980 and 1996/97.[4] The data highlight significant regional disparities, with the lowest enrollment rates in sub-Saharan Africa and South Asia. Primary completion rates are an even more accurate indicator of educational attainment than enrollment, since enrollment does not guarantee completion. Furthermore, literacy surveys demonstrate that many adults who have completed fewer than five or six years of schooling remain functionally illiterate and innumerate.[5] Table 2 provides an overview of primary completion rates by region in 1990 and 1999.

The geographic profile of differences in educational attainment is accompanied by large income and gender disparities. Table 3 shows the proportion of children aged 6–14 years in school for a sample of low-income countries, distinguishing between children from poor and well-off families.[6]

---

[2]See the World Bank (2002).

[3]The Millennium Development Goals were originally set out in the United Nations Millennium Declaration, adopted by all 189 member states at the Millennium Summit in September 2000.

[4]Net enrollment rates are enrollments based on the age cohort that should be at the level of a class. Gross enrollment rates take into account children who are not in the age cohort for a class: gross enrollment rates can therefore exceed 100 percent.

[5]The primary completion rate is defined as the total number of students successfully completing the last year of the primary cycle, as defined for the country, in a given year, divided by the total number of children of official graduation age in the population.

[6]This dichotomy can be used because the distribution of income or wealth in these countries is in general bimodal; that is, the countries lack a significant middle class.

Table 2. Primary Completion Rates by Region

Regions	1990	1999[1]
Sub-Saharan Africa	49	55
East Asia and Pacific	80	81
Europe and Central Asia	86	93
Latin America and the Caribbean	79	83
Middle East and North Africa	73	74
South Asia	511	56
All developing countries	68	73

Source: World Bank, *World Development Indicators* (2002).
[1]Data are generally for 1999, or most recent year available.

Table 3. Percentage of Poor Children Aged 6–14 in School

Country	Year	Poor 6–14-Year-Olds in School (percent)	Rich 6–14-Year-Olds in School (percent)	Rich-Poor Gap
West Africa				
Senegal	1992–93	14.1	65.6	51.5
Ghana	1993	69.3	90.8	21.5
East Africa				
Madagascar	1997	46.8	90.0	43.2
Malawi	1996	87.0	93.3	6.3
North Africa				
Morocco	1992	26.7	89.5	62.8
Egypt	1995–96	67.6	95.5	27.9
South Asia				
Pakistan	1990–91	36.6	85.6	49.0
Bangladesh	1996–97	66.8	83.4	16.6
East Asia				
Philippines	1993	70.0	86.3	16.3
Indonesia	1997	80.5	95.0	14.5
South America				
Colombia	1995	80.9	97.6	16.7
Peru	1996	85.8	94.6	8.8
Central America and the Caribbean				
Guatemala	1995	46.4	90.8	44.4
Dominican Republic	1996	88.7	97.8	9.1
Eastern Europe and Central Asia				
Turkey	1993	61.0	80.1	19.1
Uzbekistan	1996	80.2	81.1	0.9

Source: Filmer (1999); poverty is defined with respect to ownership of assets.

The rich-poor gap varies across countries and is considerable in all cases with the exception of Uzbekistan, the only transition economy in the sample. The data confirm that low enrollment in low-income countries is a problem for children of poor families: there is high or near universal school enrollment for the children of rich families.

Table 4 illustrates the gender bias in education in a number of low-income countries. The bias is shown to be especially prevalent in the regions of North, Western, and Central Africa, and in South Asia.[7] In some countries, on the other hand, the bias against girls is insignificant, or there is marginal favoritism toward girls.

A World Bank study (2002) has identified 89 countries that are not on track to meet the Education for All goals incorporated in the Millennium Development Goals. Of these countries, 29 are "seriously off track" and will require significant and unprecedented increases in school enrollment and retention rates to achieve the objectives of universal primary education and gender balance. Sahn and Stifel (2003) present the same discouraging picture of lack of progress toward the Millennium Development Goals.

Influences on School Attendance

The above circumstances raise the question of how educational improvement can be achieved. But before we address this question, we must identify the reasons underlying low educational attainment, which are both demand- and supply-side related.

Influences Through the Demand for Schooling

Low school enrollment can be the consequence of low demand for schooling. Poverty is often singled out as the main impediment to universal enrollment rates in low-income countries. The very poor may be unable to pay voluntary user fees for schooling of their children or may be burdened by the requisites of compulsory payments.

Even when access to schools is free, parents face opportunity costs of children attending school that the very poor cannot afford to incur. The opportunity cost can take the form of forgone income from child labor. The loss may also be through contributions by children to the household. Children may, for example, perform the household tasks of gathering and preparing food and tending to fields and animals. A high incidence of AIDS also reduces the demand for schooling as orphaned children take

---

[7]The gender bias underlies a case for investing more educational resources in girls because of the greater marginal gains: see Schultz (2002).

Table 4. Percentage of 6–14-Year-Old Girls in School

Countries	Survey Year	6–14-Year-Old Girls in School (percent)	6–14-Year-Old Boys in School (percent)	Male-Female Gap
High female disadvantage				
Nepal	1996	55.5	76.1	20.6
Benin	1993	32.6	53.1	20.5
Pakistan	1990–91	44.3	64.7	20.4
Morocco	1992	45.8	63.9	18.1
Central African Republic	1994–95	48.9	65.9	17.0
India	1992–93	59.1	75.7	16.6
Côte d'Ivoire	1994	41.7	55.8	14.1
Turkey	1993	63.7	74.5	10.8
Egypt	1995–96	75.7	85.6	9.9
Burkina Faso	1992–93	22.1	31.9	9.8
Mozambique	1997	51.7	61.0	9.3
Comoros	1996	48.3	57.2	8.9
Senegal	1992–93	27.4	35.8	8.4
Mali	1995–96	22.3	30.4	8.1
Niger	1997	18.9	26.7	7.8
Low/No female disadvantage				
Kenya	1998	87.0	87.9	0.9
Haiti	1994–95	73.4	73.7	0.3
Zambia	1996–97	60.4	60.1	–0.3
Brazil	1996	93.8	93.4	–0.4
Indonesia	1997	86.6	86.0	–0.6
Madagascar	1997	58.6	58.0	–0.6
Kazakhstan	1995	85.3	84.6	–0.7
Malawi	1996	89.7	88.9	–0.8
Bangladesh	1996–97	73.8	72.6	–1.2
Dominican Republic	1996	94.2	92.8	–1.4
Colombia	1995	89.7	87.9	–1.8
Tanzania	1996	48.6	45.8	–2.8
Uzbekistan	1996	82.9	80.0	–2.9
Namibia	1992	87.1	83.6	–3.5
Philippines	1998	88.4	83.5	–4.9

Source: Filmer (1999).

on the tasks of tending younger siblings, or children stay home to attend to their incapacitated parents and other family members.

The demand for education may also be low because parents expect or perceive low returns from education for their children. There may be information failures, with parents being unaware of opportunities available to educated children. Parents may believe (or be aware) that social mobility is low because family or tribal connections are more important than education in finding jobs and in personal advancement. Lack of social mobility, therefore, constrains the demand for education.

Distance from urban labor markets also decreases demand for education. Missing or inadequate credit markets prevent parents from borrowing to pay for their children's education. This is so for the usual moral hazard reasons associated with borrowing for education (see, for example, Chapter 10 of Hillman, 2003). Also, the low social mobility decreases the likelihood that children of poor parents will be able to increase their future incomes as a consequence of education.

Social norms influence the demand for education of children. A convention that children do not attend school may be adhered to because of social disapproval for acting inconsistently with norms.[8] In particular, the role of social norms in influencing community education decisions regarding girls is highlighted by the regional gender bias illustrated in Table 4. Investment in girls' education is discouraged when the social norm is that girls marry young and when marriage markets do not provide a return to girls' education.

Parents who personally place a low value on girls' education are unwilling to pay either direct or opportunity costs to send girls to school. In addition, the opportunity costs of girls' schooling tend to be higher than for boys when the social norm is for girls to contribute more labor to the household than boys (McGee, 2000).

Supply-Side Influences on Enrollment

Low school enrollment and low educational attainment can also be the result of supply-side influences, with governments supplying insufficient resources for primary education. Total government revenue may be inadequate because the tax base is constrained by a significant shadow economy and ineffective tax administration and collection.[9] Reflecting these considerations, many countries that have been identified as unlikely to meet the goal of universal primary completion have low ratios of government revenue to GDP.[10]

Due to resource limitations, public education may be rationed or only selectively provided. For example, government-financed schools may be available in urban areas but not in rural areas, or they may vary in quality.

---

[8]The role of social norms in influencing the decision whether to send children to school has been studied by Katav-Herz (2003).

[9]Inflationary financing is of course undesirable.

[10]For example, government tax revenue as a percentage of GDP is 9.6 percent in the Central African Republic, 8 percent in Chad, 9.3 percent in Haiti, 9.1 percent in Niger, and 9.8 percent in Rwanda. However, low tax revenues and expenditure do not necessarily have to lead to low education indicators if spending is efficient (see Gupta and Verhoeven, 2001).

Ineffective public expenditure management systems can also limit the resources available for basic education.[11] Significant parts of budget allocations may leak from the expenditure disbursement system. In one example, tracking surveys in Uganda revealed that between 1991 and 1995 on average only 13 percent of nonwage recurrent expenditures allocated for primary education actually reached primary schools (Reinikka and Svensson, 2001).[12]

Corruption also introduces a bias against social spending (see Gupta, Davoodi, and Tiongson, 2000; and Gupta, Davoodi, and Alonso-Terme, 2002). Corrupt officials tend to prefer spending allocations for defense or road construction, for example, rather than for education, because of the greater ease of arranging the payment of illegal commissions and greater flexibility in siphoning off funds for personal benefit (Mauro, 1997). This preference for budget allocations for capital spending rather than for the recurring expenses in schools, such as salaries or textbooks, is compounded by a similar bias in donor financing, which tends to cover a significant part of low-income countries' budgets. Such imbalances within education budgets can depress the quality of education because schools are not maintained or adequately heated in winter, and basic educational materials are lacking. One impediment to the schooling of girls that has been identified is inadequately separated latrine facilities.

The list of the impediments to public spending on education includes political-economy motives. Quality public schools that are broadly available may not be of interest to political and economic elites in low-income countries, who tend to send their children to private schools. Moreover, ruling groups may not have an interest in the emergence of an educated middle class that would, in the future, insist on more accountable and democratic government and upset the status quo (see Easterly, 2001).

Conditions Determining Whether User Payments Can Increase Enrollment

When demand-side influences—through opportunity costs, low returns due to social and geographic immobility, and social norms, in particular

---

[11]On problems of low productivity of public expenditures, see Chu and others (1995). For a study that confirms that public expenditures on education can be productive, see Gupta, Verhoeven, and Tiongson (2002). On the role of political culture in determining the effectiveness of public policy and public spending, see Hillman and Swank (2000).

[12]Conditions in Uganda have improved, and recent surveys showed that leakage has fallen substantially. In the context of the Enhanced Initiative for Highly Indebted Poor Countries (HIPCs), the World Bank and the IMF are helping countries to track poverty-reducing spending (including that financed from debt relief) through improved public expenditure management systems. See http://www.imf.org/external/np/hipc/2001/track/index.htm.

biases against girls—are the reasons for low school attendance, user payments are an ineffective way to finance basic education, because ability or willingness to pay is absent. At the same time, free access to publicly financed education might not induce parents to send their children to school either. That is, if more education brings no advantage in the local job market, families will not incur the opportunity costs of sending children to school, even if education is free.

User payments, whether voluntary or compulsory, can, however, provide resources that increase the quality of education (see also the section below in which we consider benefits from user payments). In turn, the increased quality can increase the demand for schooling by overcoming opportunity-cost impediments that are present when the quality of education is low. The relation between user payments and demand can therefore be positive, because of the intervening effect of quality improvement.

Where there is demand for schooling but enrollment and educational achievement are low due to supply-side limitations, user payments are a means of removing the supply-side constraints. Compulsory user payments oblige parents to provide resources for schools; with voluntary user fees, parents can choose to pay to provide improved education for their children.

There are, however, fundamental problems that make the financing of children's education through user payments undesirable. These problems underlie the objections to user prices and the recommendations that user prices be disallowed or abolished. The following section reviews these problems.

Problems with User Payments for Basic Education

Various problems make user financing for education for children inferior to free-access publicly financed schools. User payments are regressive, whether they are voluntarily paid or compulsory. It is preferable that schools be financed through general budgetary spending with progressive taxation or taxation that appropriately trades off equity and efficiency (on the trade-off between efficient and socially just taxation, see, for example, Chapter 7 of Hillman, 2003).

Exclusion is the main problem. Voluntary user fees, like all prices, exclude people who are unwilling or unable to pay the market price. When parents are unwilling or unable to pay, financing schools through voluntary user payments can prevent children from receiving a basic education. The evidence confirms a negative price elasticity of demand (other things being equal) for children's education by poor households in low-income countries (see, for example, Birdsall and Orivel, 1996; and Gertler and Glewwe, 1989). In Ghana and Côte d'Ivoire, primary school enrollment declined after the introduction of school fees (World Bank, 1993). Primary school enrollment increased after the abolition of fees in Indonesia, Ghana, Kenya, Malawi, Uganda, and Tanzania (World Bank, 1995a; Lockheed and Verspoor, 1991; Bray and Lillis, 1988; and Oxfam, 2002).

The price elasticity of demand is related to parents' incomes. Studies have shown that the price elasticity is considerably higher for poor people than it is for the rich (see, for example, Morrisson, 2002). Even seemingly low user fees can be significant for poor households in low-income countries. For example, user fees in Tanzania of between US$8 and US$16 a year (depending on the grade) are equivalent to one to two months of agricultural wages (Oxfam, 2002). For a household with several children, such user fees are unaffordable. Parents are then placed in a position of having to choose which of their children will go to school, or they may not be able to afford to send any children to school at all and exclusion from schooling takes place.

The gender biases to which we have referred affect the price elasticity of demand for education. The elasticity is greater for girls than for boys (Gertler and Glewwe, 1989, 1992). In Kenya, for example, girls were twice as likely to be taken out of school than boys when school fees increased (World Bank, 1995b).

Social benefits from externalities call for subsidies for education. The costs imposed on parents through user payments are the precise opposite of the subsidies appropriate for achieving socially desirable enrollment and educational attainment. Thus, not only does exclusion because of user fees deny children their personal educational entitlement, but also broader social benefits are lost when children do not go to school because parents do not pay (Jimenez, 1989; Birdsall and Orivel, 1996).

The problem of exclusion when voluntary user payments finance schools is illustrated in Figure 1, which is taken from Chapter 8 of Hillman (2003). In the absence of outside funding, user payments need to cover educational costs so that schools can be self-financing. In Figure 1, DD shows demand by parents for education of children. As parents decide whether or not to send children to school, parents of n children are ranked along the demand function by declining ability or willingness to pay for schooling. As the user fee falls along DD, more parents pay and send their children to school.

The total costs of schooling are shown in Figure 1 as fixed (the costs are for the class requirements of the blackboard, the salary of the

Figure 1.   A Self-Financing User-Pricing Solution for Education

Valuation and cost

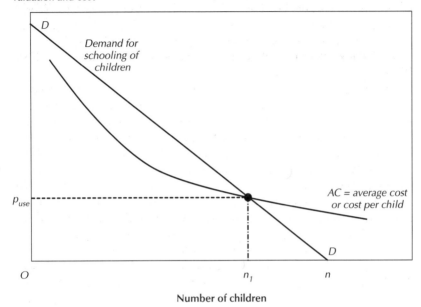

Number of children

teacher, maintenance of the school building, etc).[13] The function AC shows the declining average cost as the number of children in the class increases (AC is a rectangular hyperbola given by C/n, where C is the fixed cost).

In Figure 1 there are n children who potentially would attend school. A zero user fee is however required for all parents to choose to send their children to school. A zero user fee would, of course, provide no funding for a school. In the case shown in Figure 1, if revenue is to be provided for a school through user fees, there will necessarily be exclusion of some children.

The lowest self-financing (or cost-covering) user fee in Figure 1 is P^{use}. At this user fee, the number of children attending school is n_1. This number of children is smaller than the total number of children n who would attend school if compulsory school attendance were financed through public expenditure. User payments, therefore, result in the exclusion of $(n - n_1)$ children from school because parents of this number of children are unable or unwilling to pay a user fee that covers average cost.

---

[13] Allowing for only fixed costs is a simplification because some costs are per student (textbooks, pencils, etc.). Major costs can, however, be viewed as fixed and independent of the number of children in the classroom (up to the ceiling for effective learning).

With costs fixed, the marginal cost of admitting an additional child to the class is zero. The variable costs of sending an additional child present in a class are low compared with the fixed costs. Hence, for purposes of exposition, Figure 1 assumes only fixed costs. *Efficiency* then requires that no child be excluded from school. But excluding children from school is also *socially unjust*.

Exclusion can be avoided through exemptions or personalized payments to accommodate parents who would otherwise not pay for the schooling of their children (see Chu and Hemming, 1991). Discriminatory user-fee schemes are, however, costly to administer and often are not administratively feasible in low-income countries. There are also moral hazard problems: some parents might declare unwillingness or inability to pay for their children knowing that the community will not allow the children to be excluded from school. In practice, attempts to implement discriminatory user fees to avoid exclusion have not been successful (for a survey of the evidence, see Reddy and Vandemoortele, 1996).

A Case Where User Financing Is Not Feasible

Self-financing through user payments may simply not be feasible (see Chapter 8 of Hillman, 2003). In Figure 2, the combination of demand and costs provides no user fee that can cover costs. Willingness or ability to pay (shown by HR) of any group of parents is always below average cost AC. There is therefore no user fee that, if paid by some groups of parents, allows costs to be covered. Yet in Figure 2, the total benefit from providing schooling for all n children (and so excluding nobody), measured by the parents' personal valuation of the education to the children, exceeds total cost. The total benefit is the area HRO. The total benefit exceeds the total fixed cost, which is equal to OJER (because the area JAH exceeds the area REA). A cost-benefit calculation based on parents' own evaluations of the benefits of education of their children therefore calls for schooling to be provided for everybody. Since no user fee can cover costs, the only way to finance schooling is through government expenditure financed through general revenue taxation.

Figures 1 and 2 demonstrate the fundamental theoretical problems with voluntary user payments. (1) A voluntary self-financing user fee will, in all likelihood, exclude some children from schooling, which is neither efficient nor socially just. (2) Even if the intention is to finance education through user payments, there is also no assurance that a self-financing user fee will always be feasible.

Figure 2. No Self-Financing User-Payments Solution Exists, but the Project Satisfies the Test of Cost-Benefit Analysis

Valuation and cost

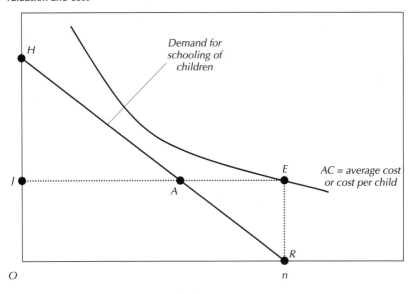

Number of users

Special Education

It is estimated that in Africa only 5 percent of children with learning disabilities requiring special education attend school, whereas 70 percent of these children could attend school. In high-income countries, governments acknowledge social obligations toward children with learning disabilities and provide for children's special needs through public spending. In low-income countries, the children in poor households who require special education may not attend school because there are no schools provided by the government for them to attend. That is, supply-side problems that affect schooling in general are compounded for children who may require special resources and suitable access to classrooms. Society and parents in richer societies face beneficial incentives to pay for education of children with learning disabilities, since there are employment opportunities consistent with such children's attainments and abilities. In low-income countries, the personal incentives of parents are, unfortunately, often different. Disabled children may be sent out to beg.[14]

---

[14] In some poor societies children are, unfortunately, purposely disabled to allow income to be earned as disabled beggars. On abuses of disabled people's rights, see Disability Awareness in Action (2002).

The opportunity cost of educating a disabled child, through the loss of income from begging, is a demand-side constraint to educating disabled children. User payments can only make the education of disabled children even more unattractive.

User Payments as Preempting Public Spending

Once schooling is financed through voluntary or compulsory user payments, a government may feel that it has been absolved of its responsibility to provide free-access basic schooling financed through public expenditure. Problems can therefore arise in transition to government responsibility for schooling when user payments successfully self-finance children's schooling. User payments should, of course, not preempt the transition to free-access publicly financed schools. User payments are a temporary, stop-gap means of providing resources for schooling, until tax revenue, public expenditure management, and governance allow governments to fulfill the responsibility of providing quality free-access education for children through general-purpose taxation or through effective management and use of donor resources.

Benefits of User Payments

We have outlined the disadvantages of user payments for basic education, but there are also benefits when user payments finance children's schooling.

Availability of Resources for Education

The most direct benefit of user payments is that resources are mobilized for education when government resources are unavailable or inadequate. We have noted that for spending by government to be effective, expenditure management capacities, political will, and good governance are required. When these conditions are not present and adequate resources from governments do not reach schools, user payments allow parents themselves to provide the necessary resources (see Jimenez, 1987, 1989).

Inadequate quality of education can leave children illiterate after years of schooling and depress parents' demand for schooling for their children because of low expected returns. Inadequate education may be the consequence of unqualified and unmotivated teachers, and teacher absenteeism. As we have noted, resources mobilized through user payments can be expected to improve school quality, which can be expected to increase demand for schooling.

Monitoring Incentives

Government spending is ineffective when funding intended for schools is appropriated or diverted. However, in the absence of monitoring and supervision, the funds that *do* reach schools or teachers may not have beneficial effects either.[15] User payments address this problem because parents who pay directly tend to be actively involved to ensure that they receive benefits in return for their payments. The monitoring by parents that accompanies user payments can thereby improve both the quality and cost-effectiveness of education.[16] While the amounts that parents can afford to pay through user payments may be low, supervision, monitoring, and the sense of ownership by parents increase, which enhances the productivity of resources provided. Evidence from low-income countries supports the presence of a link between user payments and enhanced quality and cost-effectiveness of education. Jimenez and Paqueo (1996) studied 586 primary schools in the Philippines and concluded that schools relying more heavily on local funding from municipal government and parent-teacher associations tended to be more cost-effective. A study of El Salvador's EDUCO program similarly confirms that decentralized administration improves the quality of schooling and enhances educational outcomes (Jimenez and Sawada, 1999). Gershberg (1999) concluded that increased accountability by teachers and administrators to parents, with associated financial incentives, was instrumental in the implementation of Nicaragua's Autonomous School Program (ASP).

In general, parents have also shown a willingness to pay for improved education. Mingat and Tan (1986) found that parents in Malawi were prepared to pay user payments in return for higher-quality education. Birdsall and Orivel (1996) studied rural Mali and found that, although fees for primary schools (other things being equal) reduced demand, improvements in quality, and proximity to schools more than offset the negative effect of user payments on school enrollment. Gertler and Glewwe (1989) report that in rural Peru, households were willing to pay sufficient user payments to cover the operating costs of new local schools that would reduce travel time for their children.

---

[15]Some evidence suggests that private schools in richer countries that require user payments are generally more efficient than pubic schools, which are free of charge. Again, parents sending children to private schools are making a market purchase as opposed to receiving benefits from government, and they therefore put more effort into evaluating and monitoring benefits.

[16]Parental involvement does not necessarily require user fees, as evident in some developed countries.

The direct involvement of parents that accompanies user payments can also result in quality improvements that increase school attendance by girls. For example, the construction of separate latrines increased enrollment of girls in African primary schools.

Effects on Norms of Willingness to Pay

The personal benefits from taxes paid to a central government may not be clear, and the absence of a direct link between tax payments and benefits can be the reason for a social norm of tax evasion. Voluntary payment for children's schooling can create social norms that result in the vast majority of (or all) children attending school. This occurs when norms of evasion of tax payments to the central government are replaced by conventions of voluntarily paying for children's schooling, because of the directly perceived benefits. A demonstration effect can affect behavior through changed norms. Parents who do not pay confront questions from their children who do not attend school about why *other* parents are prepared to pay for their children to attend school. The norm or convention of sending children to school (because others do) can thereby influence the decisions of parents who are not sending children to school. Once a social norm of educating children is in place, the norm can continue if, in the future, the government provides free-access public education.

Governance and Political-Economy Problems

Decentralized financing and administration through user payments can also help overcome problems of exclusion and governance. Although moral hazard makes it difficult to implement schemes to avoid exclusion through personalized payments, information available to members of a small community—and the repeated personal interactions within the community—can make personalized user payments and rudimentary community-insurance schemes feasible. For example, it will be evident within a community if a particular household has fallen on hard times, and fees can be adjusted accordingly. Mechanisms of local collective action may therefore spontaneously arise to deal with the problem of exclusion and overcome moral hazard problems. Anecdotal evidence from Chad confirms such outcomes. On the other hand, Oxfam (2001) points to studies of partially user-financed government schools where children are excluded from schools and from exams owing to inability to pay, and parents are confronted with court proceedings because of non-payment or insufficient payment of school fees.

User payments save the cost of disbursement through government bureaucracies and avoid leakages through corruption in the central bureaucracies. User payments may however attract the attention of local government officials, who may view the local organization of parents to pay user payments as part of their domain of governance. The problems of central-government governance (that is, corruption) that gave rise to the need for community organization and user payments in the first place can then recur at the local government level. If the local education providers themselves are corrupt, user charges simply become a means of rent extraction by local public sector employees, without improving education. Therefore, for user payments to be beneficial, the local mechanisms for organizing collective action by parents have to be able to withstand such local governance problems.[17] There is some evidence that governance issues are less severe at local levels than at central levels of government (Fisman and Gatti, 2000). This is not necessarily the case in all circumstances, however. As we shall see below in the case study of Mexico's Progresa program, when the central government wished to ensure that funds targeted to local communities were properly disbursed, the central government took measures to ensure that local government officials could not access the funds and local disbursement officers were rotated to avoid development of long-term local relationships.

An advantage of user payments is the proximity of parents to local officials. When user payments are voluntary, parents can also choose not to pay. The threat of withdrawal of payment can act as a disciplining mechanism for governance problems. When a committee of parents and teachers takes responsibility for collecting and allocating payments, problems of political intrusion are either more limited or do not arise at all.

User payments are also a means of allowing parents to overcome the political-economy problems that we have noted can impede public spending for education or can result in public spending selectively favoring certain groups. User payments through voluntary collective action in organizing and financing schools allow children in marginalized groups or peripheral areas to receive entitlements to basic education; the voluntary collective action by parents to organize and finance schools is, of course, a response to governments' *not* providing adequate resources for schools.

Over the longer term, democratic institutions should ideally emerge to enfranchise poorer parts of the population and to put a check on corruption, or—even better—ethics of governance should change (see

---

[17]We are not in this chapter concerned with transition economies. Illegal or informal local user charges imposed by teachers and local officials have been reported in some of these countries.

Hillman, 2000). Eventually, democratic institutions should result in the replacement of user payments by parents with public spending. When ethical governance has prevailed and corruption has been eliminated or relegated to a marginal phenomenon, the bias against public spending on education and in favor of capital-intensive projects (such as defense and construction) will also diminish. Until such institutional change takes place, user payments allow self-financing so that the children of the poor can receive an education that would not otherwise be available to them.

The education made possible by user payments is in itself an impetus for democratic institutional change. As part of the beneficial externalities from education, a more educated population will seek greater democratic participation and greater accountability from the government, and will also insist on more benefits through public spending. We have observed that one reason why governments may be reluctant to provide public spending for children's education is precisely to avoid such future calls for democracy and political openness by a more educated population.

User Payments in Practice

The question of whether user payments should finance the basic education of children in low-income countries would be hypothetical if user payments were in fact uncommon. However, a World Bank study by Burnett and Bentaouet Kattan (2002) revealed that user payments were present in some form or other in 77 out of 79 countries surveyed. Often payments by parents supplemented government spending or took on the form of uniform requirements or payments-in-kind. For example, in Kenya in 1992, user payments by parents financed 34 percent of the cost for primary education, 66 percent of the cost for secondary education, and about 20 percent of the cost for higher education, with the remainder financed through public spending (Van Adams and Hartnett, 1996). In neighboring Tanzania, user payments covered about one-third of the cost of schooling prior to their abolition (Oxfam, 2001). In some cases the payments by parents are compulsory; in other cases schooling for children is based on "voluntary" payments that are nonetheless a precondition for school admission.

The prevalence of user payments is influenced by the demand- and supply-side effects that we have noted. The demand-side influences inhibit financing of schooling through user payments. The opportunity costs confronting parents can affect government decisions regarding how schools are financed. For example, in Ghana, schooling has been free in the north when children are valuable to parents in tending grazing animals, whereas in the south, where this opportunity cost is not present, parents have been obliged to pay school fees.

The supply-side influences are evident in the fact that parents are willing to pay for their children's education, and for improved quality or closer proximity of schools (Gertler and Glewwe, 1989; Mingat and Tan, 1986; Birdsall and Orivel, 1996; Morrisson, 2002). The prevalence of cases where poor parents are willing to pay voluntary user fees for schooling confirms problems with government supply. In Haiti—the poorest country in the Western Hemisphere—for example, some 65 percent of children are enrolled in the fee-paying private sector, since there are few public alternatives.[18] Community schooling based on voluntary user payments also occurs in rural areas in parts of Africa and Latin America (e.g., El Salvador, Honduras, Chad, and Somalia). User payments in these cases allow parents to exercise their right to voluntarily finance schooling for their children when governments have not provided schools or when resources provided by governments have been inadequate.

We shall now consider case studies that illustrate different circumstances associated with user payments for schools. Evidence from Chad shows how voluntary community involvement provides resources for education when public resources are inadequate. Mexico's Progresa program demonstrates a case where government has paid parents to send their children to school so that user payments were in fact negative. Experiences in Uganda, Malawi, and Tanzania show the consequences of replacing user payments with free-access, publicly financed schools.

Spontaneous Community Organization and User Payments in Chad

Chad has an estimated per capita GNP of US$215.[19] Although public spending on education is 20 percent of the total domestic revenue, the total domestic revenue is only 8 percent of GDP, and the government has had only limited success in providing free-access, publicly financed universal basic education.[20] Net primary school enrollment is about 50 percent; the primary completion rate is 20 percent; and the illiteracy rate is in excess of 60 percent, and is high even among school graduates. There are also wide disparities in schooling among regions and along gender lines. The case of Chad nonetheless demonstrates the value that poor parents in low-income countries can attach to education. Schooling has been financed by user payments collected through spontaneous community organization when government spending has been ineffective.

---

[18] Interview with Nick Burnett, Chief Executive, Burnett International LLC.
[19] Nagy, Karangwa, and Dauphin (2002).
[20] From Mingat and Winter (2002); and Nagy, Karangwa, and Dauphin (2002).

Parental involvement in primary education, both administrative and financial, has a long history in Chad. Community-managed schools emerged during the colonial period. Against the background of political and economic instability, and the inability of the central government to provide even the most basic education for the majority of children in rural areas, parents' associations took full responsibility for the management of schools, including schools abandoned by the government as well as for the construction and operation of new schools. Some 20 percent of students are currently enrolled in community schools that are run without governmental involvement.

Government schools, where 75 percent of children are enrolled, are also significantly supported by parents, who hire and pay the salaries of many teachers.[21] Excluding in-kind expenditure, such as the supply of books and volunteer time, parents in Chad spend the equivalent of US$2 a child annually. Reports from the field suggest that children are not excluded from attending school even if parents cannot afford to pay this moderate user-price. Cooperation through mutual insurance prevents exclusion.

Regional and ethnic divisions have affected education in Chad. Centrally trained teachers refuse to teach in remote regions; furthermore, when and where they do teach, the teachers are poorly supervised by the government. Currently only 46 percent of teachers are government civil servants. The rest are community teachers, who are literate volunteers teaching in their own communities after minimal training. With support from the World Bank, the government covers 80 percent of the salary these teachers receive (about one-third of "civil service" teachers' salaries), with the community paying the additional 20 percent. Parent-teacher associations are responsible for hiring and supervising the teachers.

Consistent with the earlier observations on local accountability, there are close ties between parents and the community teacher. The close ties are less likely when civil service teachers instruct in the schools, because ties are also affected by Chad's ethnic diversity and civil service teachers tend to be of a different ethnicity than their students.

However, poor qualifications of teachers, combined with poorly supplied schools, have kept educational attainments low.[22] Only

---

[21] Strategies to enhance education developed by the government and the World Bank, along with other donors, have taken into account Chad's history of parental participation and community involvement, and rely on parent-teacher associations, formalizing the role of these associations in education (Chad, 2002).

[22] The World Bank education project and the government are trying to address this issue by improving training for community teachers. Also, teachers are being trained in areas where none are currently present.

47 percent of adults in Chad can read fluently after six or more years of schooling, in contrast to 90 percent in Rwanda or Burundi (Mingat and Rakotomalala, 2002).

The government has expressed its intention to increase public spending for education, as resources will become available through debt relief under the HIPC Initiative. Also, revenue from new oil discoveries will be available in the future. In the meantime, however, financial and human resource constraints make user payments the only means of financing schooling for many children. Thus, eliminating user payments in Chad under prevailing institutional conditions would deprive a large part of the school-age population of the opportunity to go to school.

An Incentive-Based Welfare Program in Mexico

Under the Progresa incentive-based welfare program in Mexico, poor families receive income transfers from the central government, conditional on the regular school attendance of their children.[23] In villages targeted by Progresa, schooling increased from 6.8 years on average to 7.5 years (Schultz, 2001). Transitions to secondary school increased by nearly 20 percent, with a more significant increase for girls, who were targeted through higher transfers.

Two features of the program merit special attention. First, cash transfers are given only to the female head of household.[24] Second, to circumvent corruption, resources are channeled from the central administrative office directly to Progresa officers in eligible villages without the involvement of local government officials. These program officers are moreover rotated regularly, to minimize the familiarity that may become the basis for collusion with local beneficiaries.

In the case of Progresa, user payments for basic education are negative. In principle, the income subsidies could change social norms regarding education and child labor decisions. While average schooling duration has increased, demand for schooling has been quite inelastic: the school subsidy has cut the cost of attending school by more than half, but enrollment has increased by only 10 percent (Schultz, 2001). The limited response indicates demand-side constraints.

---

[23] The families are also obliged to obtain preventive health care, participate in growth monitoring and nutrition-supplement programs, and learn about health and hygiene. Gertler and Boyce (2001) report that the outcome has been a significant improvement in the health of both children and adults. On how households were chosen, see Skoufias, Davis, and de la Vega (2001).

[24] Thomas (1990) shows that giving money to women increases the likelihood that money will be spent on children.

Progresa in Mexico benefited from generous funding and commitment from the federal government. The poorest households in a politically unstable region were targeted. There was strong political will for the program to succeed—hence the payments to female heads of households and the concerted measures against corruption by ensuring that local government officials were not involved in the program.

The Progresa program has been replicated elsewhere. The special circumstances of the program in Mexico may however limit the success of such replication. Resource considerations apart, if inadequate public spending for education is due to political-economy problems, governments may lack the political will to counter corruption and to target resources effectively.

Experiences with Abolition of User Payments: Uganda, Malawi, and Tanzania

Malawi, Uganda, and Tanzania (in 1994, 1997, and 2001, respectively) implemented universal education initiatives that included the abolition of user payments for children's education. Tanzania's experience remains too recent to draw conclusions, while the experiences of Malawi and Uganda do provide some insights.

User payments were abolished in Malawi and replaced by a policy of Free Primary Education. In 1994, the incoming government made primary education a priority: 65 percent of spending in 1997 was for primary education and total spending on education was 24 percent of the total current expenditure (see Kadzamira and Rose, 2001). A democratic election had therefore resulted in more public spending focused on the poor (Castro-Leal, 1996). The higher budgetary allocations for education nonetheless proved inadequate. Although school enrollment increased by over 60 percent, the quality of education declined and dropout rates increased. In 1999, the primary completion rate was only 50 percent, despite a gross enrollment rate of 117 percent.

Quality deteriorated because of crowding: classrooms were inadequate and teachers had to be trained for an additional one million students. Also, it appears that teacher performance deteriorated as a result of reduced accountability vis-à-vis parents, who felt less compelled to monitor teachers, given the parents' reduced personal financial involvement (Kadzamira and Rose, 2001). Donor funding, which had previously provided for about 40 percent of the total primary education budget, was delayed (Bernbaum and others, 1998). Low educational attainment increased the effective cost of schooling for parents, and reduced the perceived returns from education. Moreover, although school fees were abolished along with school uniform requirements, parents were still expected to contribute labor and materials to school construction and to buy school supplies and clothes. These costs were additional to the opportunity cost through loss of income from child labor, resulting in a significant total cost of education for some parents. Gender biases persisted, and some teachers continued to regard girls as less intelligent than boys.

In Uganda, tuition fees for primary schools were waived for four children from each household under the Universal Primary Education initiative in 1997. Education did not, however, become "free." While tuition fees were waived, households were still responsible for paying for uniforms and school materials, and for contributing to school construction and maintenance, and there were also fees for primary final exams (McGee, 2000). In contrast to the experience of Malawi, the government in Uganda was careful to prepare for the anticipated increase in enrollment rates. An increase of 70 percent in school enrollment was matched by a doubling of the share of recurrent spending targeted to primary education in the government budget. External aid also assisted in training additional teachers, building classrooms, and providing teaching materials.

The shift of resources to social sectors and infrastructure projects continues in Uganda under the Poverty Action Fund. Nonetheless, between 1997 and 2000, net school enrollment declined from 85 percent to 77 percent, despite the increases in gross enrollment rates. Regional gender biases also persist (Uganda, 2001a; and McGee, 2000). The low quality of education owing to high pupil-teacher and pupil-classroom ratios and the inadequate educational materials has tended to depress demand for schooling (Uganda, 2001b).[25]

In Tanzania, the abolition of user payments in 2001 appears to have substantially increased the demand for schooling (Oxfam, 2002). School enrollment rates had been low, with net enrollment below 50 percent between 1994 and 1997 and gross enrollment in 1999 below 66 percent. In cooperation with various donors, the government developed a comprehensive basic education strategy to enhance service delivery, in conjunction with efforts to also improve the public expenditure management system. Total spending on education increased from 2.6 percent of GDP in 1999 to 3.3 percent in 2000, and to 4.1 percent in 2001. While it is too early to judge the consequences of abolishing user payments in Tanzania, evidence suggests that the public education system is experiencing difficulties coping with the large increase in demand. There are claims that user payments are being reintroduced through the back door (Oxfam, 2002).

---

[25]On Uganda, see also Appleton (1999).

While the circumstances and outcomes in these three African coun-tries vary, general conclusions can be drawn. First, universal primary completion rates and true improvements in educational attainment cannot be achieved through higher gross enrollment rates alone, as the case of Malawi in particular demonstrates. Quality standards are criti-cal and depend not only on spending levels but also on policy planning, implementation, and monitoring. Second, even when user payments are eliminated, primary education is still far from free. Substantially greater commitments of resources are required in these countries, per-haps with Progresa-style income transfers, to relieve poor parents of all costs associated with education. To illustrate this point, World Bank simulations have shown that sub-Saharan African countries alone face a financing gap of US$2.1 billion to achieve universal primary educa-tion (World Bank, 2002).[26] The experiences of Uganda and Malawi ap-pear, moreover, to indicate that universal primary completion rates and gender equality cannot be achieved solely by reducing the costs of schooling. Although the evidence in these countries is weaker than in the case of Progresa, where even opportunity costs were offset to a de-gree, observers have noted that other complementary and targeted poli-cies are needed to improve educational attainment. Cultural barriers remain, prejudices have to be overcome, and higher opportunity costs for girls than for boys have to be addressed (McGee, 2000).

Should User Prices Be Allowed?

We return now to our focal question: should user prices be allowed? The evidence in the first section of this chapter showed that enrollment and primary completion rates are low in many low-income countries. Children are not attending school because of the supply- or demand-side influences that we outlined. At the same time, as noted in the pre-vious section, user payments of different types for financing schooling are prevalent in poor countries. Financing by user payments is undesir-able for the reasons that were outlined in the section on influences on school attendance. However, while ideally governments should provide quality educational opportunities for all children in free-access publicly financed schools, user financing for schools is nonetheless prevalent. User financing has associated benefits, including local monitoring and accountability, which increase the quality of—and thereby demand for—schooling, and circumvent political-economy and governance

---

[26] These simulations imply benchmarks for average teacher salaries, pupil-teacher ra-tios, nonsalary recurrent spending, average repetition rates, private enrollment rates, and budgetary allocations to primary education.

impediments to education of poor children, as set out in the section on problems with user payments for basic education.

Notwithstanding these benefits associated with user payments, free-access publicly financed schools remain the ideal. Because this ideal based on government responsibility is not being achieved in many poor countries, does this imply, as Oxfam and others would recommend, that user prices should be disallowed and abolished where present?

When user payments are voluntary, parents have taken upon themselves the responsibility of financing and providing education for their children, as illustrated by our case study of Chad. In general, voluntary payment outcomes are efficient.[27] A conflict can however be present between efficiency and the objective of social justice, defined as equality of outcomes (see, for example, Chapter 1 of Hillman, 2003).

We can consider an example in which voluntary user fees result in 45 children attending school and 5 children are excluded because of parents' unwillingness or inability to pay. The outcome through user prices is therefore socially inequitable. Equality may however result in none of the 50 children attending school. Usual criteria of efficiency and social welfare suggest that the more children in school the better, and that exclusion of some children is preferable to an outcome where there is equality but no children attend school. A strong preference for equality could nonetheless lead to a recommendation that financing of schools through voluntary user payments be disallowed.

All the children would then be treated equally in being excluded from schooling and the children would await the substitute ideal: free-access schooling that government should but does not (yet) provide. Equality would be achieved at the expense of all children being denied an education.[28]

---

[27]Exceptions include strategic situations such as arise in the voluntary financing of public goods (see, for example, Chapter 2 of Hillman, 2003) but such strategic interactions are not present here.

[28]By the criterion of Pareto efficiency (some persons are better off while no one is worse off), 45 attending school is better than none attending. Usual specifications of social welfare rank the outcome in which some children are attending school (and others not) ahead of the situation in which no child is attending school. For example, a Bentham specification of social welfare calls for maximizing the expected utility of children who do not know who they are going to be (that is, whether they will have parents who are willing or unwilling to pay the user price). Under such a view of social welfare, society is better off (expected utility is higher) when some children are educated although others are excluded. Using the alternative social welfare specification of Rawls requires identifying and sequentially maximizing the well-being of the worst-off person. The worst-off is an excluded child. The logic of Rawls is that, if the excluded child cannot be helped, no improvement takes place in social welfare by educating other children. This is an extreme view of social welfare that gives prominence to an objective of equal outcomes without regard for efficiency. On these different views of social welfare, see, for example, Chapter 5 of Hillman, 2003).

The equality would also require extensive monitoring to ensure that parents were not violating equality by themselves teaching their children or by hiring private tutors. This outcome of illegality of private user-based education is not what the proponents of disallowing user prices for basic education have in mind. They rather hope for the replacement of user payments with the ideal of free-access publicly financed schools.

The case studies of Uganda, Tanzania, and Zambia show that prerequisites have to be in place for successful transition from user pricing to public financing for schools, even when governments display the will to make the change. The replacement of user payments with public finance requires careful planning and preparation to ensure that resources are available to meet increased demand without quality deterioration, which reduces the value of schooling to children and parents. The case studies show that if additional resources are not available to match increased enrollment, reduced quality of education decreases demand for schooling even when education is free, because of the opportunity costs of sending children to school.

In other cases, as in the example of Chad, governments have not attempted to provide budgetary resources for adequate basic education. In these cases abolishing user prices would eliminate available educational opportunities.

We have noted that, when demand-side constraints are present, user prices are an additional impediment to education. There is then no assurance that parents will send children to school when education is free. The case of the Progresa program in Mexico has illustrated how demand-side constraints discourage universal school attendance even when parents are paid to send their children to school. When impediments to education reside in social norms and are cultural, in particular with regard to girls, or there are high opportunity costs of sending children to school, user prices are not the problem—or the only problem. Norms regarding education of children need to change in some countries.

Alternatively, social mobility needs to be enhanced to increase the returns to education to make education of poor children worthwhile. William Easterly (2001), in summarizing the empirical literature on education and growth, has concluded that the evidence shows no positive link between education and growth because of the absence of opportunities in poor countries for productive benefit from education. That is, so long as privilege through family and connections remains the principal determinant of employment opportunities rather than merit judged by educational achievement, increased education will not have a positive private (or social) return.

Conclusion

We now summarize our conclusions. Box 1 provides an overview of the conditions that may or may not make user payments feasible or successful.

Our assessment of user payments as a means of financing basic education has accepted as a given that user payments by parents are inferior to quality free-access publicly financed schooling. However, through financing of children's education by voluntary user prices, parents have taken responsibility for the education of their children in the face of ineffective public expenditure management, problems of political will, or problems of governance. Compulsory user prices can also reflect administrative and governance impediments to replacing regressive benefit taxation with broadly based taxation or donor funding as a means of financing schools. When poor parents pay or contemplate user prices for education of children, the problem is therefore in the domain of government. As Box 1 indicates, user payments are not required when governments provide adequate resources for effective public spending for basic education (so the means is available); educating poor children is a priority of government (so the political will is present); and governance problems do not impede resources from

---

Box 1. User Payments

Circumstances in which user payments can be expected to arise and be beneficial:
- Inadequate public resources are available for education;
- Public expenditure management systems are inadequate;
- Governance/political-economy problems impede resources from reaching schools;
- Education through government is of poor quality because of inadequate monitoring.

Circumstances hindering user payments:
- Governance problems extend to those administering user payments;
- Poverty, high opportunity costs, or social norms are impediments to enrollment;
- Low social mobility makes education unattractive.

Circumstances in which user payments will not be required:
- Resources available to the budget, from both domestic and external sources, are sufficient to finance quality education;
- Education of children from poor households is a priority of government;
- Minor governance problems still allow resources to reach the schools.

reaching the schools. Focusing on and resolving these problems of government will naturally end the financing of schools through user prices without decrees to prohibit or abolish user payments.

Low enrollment and low educational achievement are independent of the form of school financing if demand-side influences—such as biases against education of children, in particular against girls—are prevalent. In such cases, user payments discourage schooling but publicly financed schooling may not increase school enrollment without changes in social norms regarding education. In these circumstances, societal attitudes are impediments to increasing enrollment and improving educational achievement. User prices if present are a problem, but not necessarily the principal problem.

In other cases, where opportunity costs combine with low returns from education to deter parents from sending children to school, improvements in enrollment and educational attainment require social mobility to increase the returns from education. As with social norms, when personal incomes are based on privileged relations and the society is some distance from being a market economy in which incomes are determined according to personal productive contributions, children may not attend school even if education is free or subsidized. In such circumstances, absence of incentives for education of the children of the underprivileged poor is the fundamental problem. User prices if present supplement opportunity costs in the face of low returns from education but user prices are not necessarily the fundamental problem.

We conclude that proposals to disallow or abolish user prices for basic education in poor countries should be made with caution and with detailed reference to the case-by-case circumstances that underlie the existence of user prices.

Postscript

In a special initiative, donors have decided to grant resources to 23 "fast-track" countries that are at serious risk of not achieving the Education for All Millennium Development Goals. The donor community pledged an additional US$12 billion a year to help achieve universal primary completion rates by 2015 at the UN Conference on Financing for Development in Monterrey. However, as this chapter has emphasized, constraints on education need not be only of a financial nature. In addition to improved expenditure capacities and mechanisms ensuring minimum quality standards, political commitment to effective implementation and resolution of governance problems is also required, as is possible change in social norms regarding education and social mobility.

References

Appleton, Simon, 1999, "Education, Incomes and Poverty in Uganda in the 1990s," CREDIT Research Paper No. 01/22 (Nottingham, England: Centre for Research in Economic Development and International Trade, University of Nottingham).

Bernbaum, Marcia, and others, 1998, *Evaluation of USAID/Malawi Girls' Attainment in Basic Literacy and Education (GABLE) Program* (Washington: Academy for Educational Development).

Birdsall, Nancy, and François Orivel, 1996, "Demand for Primary Schooling in Rural Mali: Should User Fees Be Increased?" *Education Economics*, Vol. 4 (December), pp. 279–96.

Bray, Mark, and Kevin Lillis, eds., 1988, *Community Financing of Education: Issues and Policy Implications in Less Developed Countries* (New York: Pergamon Press).

Burnett, Nicholas, and Raja Bentaouet Kattan, 2002, *User Fees in Primary Education* (unpublished; Washington: World Bank).

Castro-Leal, Florencia, 1996, "Who Benefits from Public Education Spending in Malawi? Results from the Recent Education Sector Reform," World Bank Discussion Paper No. 350 (Washington: World Bank).

Chad, Ministry of Education, 2002, "Education Sector Policy Statement: Support Program for Education Sector Reform in Chad" (unpublished; N'Djamena).

Chu, Ke-young, and Richard Hemming, eds., 1991, *Public Expenditure Handbook: A Guide to Public Expenditure Policy Issues in Developing Countries* (Washington: International Monetary Fund).

———, and others, 1995, *Unproductive Public Expenditures: A Pragmatic Approach to Policy Analysis*, IMF Pamphlet No. 48 (Washington: International Monetary Fund).

Disability Awareness in Action, 2002, *A Real Horror Story: The Abuse of Disabled People's Human Rights* (London).

Easterly, William Russell, 2001, *The Elusive Quest for Growth: Economists' Adventures and Misadventures in the Tropics* (Cambridge, Massachusetts: MIT Press).

Filmer, Deon, 1999, "The Structure of Social Disparities in Education: Gender and Wealth," World Bank Policy Research Report on Gender and Development Working Paper No. 5 (Washington: World Bank).

Fisman, Raymond, and Roberta Gatti, 2000, "Decentralization and Corruption: Evidence Across Countries," World Bank Policy Research Working Paper No. 2290 (Washington: World Bank).

Gershberg, Alec Ian, 1999, "Fostering Effective Parental Participation in Education: Lessons from a Comparison of Reform Processes in Nicaragua and Mexico," *World Development*, Vol. 27 (April) pp. 753–71.

Gertler, Paul, and Simon Boyce, 2001, "An Experiment in Incentive-Based Welfare: The Impact of Progresa on Health in Mexico," paper prepared for the Royal Economic Society Annual Conference 2003, Warwick, England, April 7–9. Available via the Internet: http://ideas.repec.olg/p/ecj/ac2003/85.html.

Gertler, Paul, and Paul Glewwe, 1989, "The Willingness to Pay for Education in Developing Countries: Evidence from Peru," World Bank Living Standards Measurement Study Working Paper No. 54 (Washington: World Bank).

————, 1992, "The Willingness to Pay for Education for Daughters in Contrast to Sons: Evidence from Rural Peru," World Bank Economic Review, Vol. 6 (January), pp. 171–88.

Gupta, Sanjeev, Hamid Davoodi, and Rosa Alonso-Terme, 2002, "Does Corruption Affect Income Inequality and Poverty?" Economics of Governance, Vol. 3 (March), pp. 23–45.

Gupta, Sanjeev, Hamid Davoodi, and Erwin Tiongson, 2000, "Corruption and the Provision of Health Care and Education Services," IMF Working Paper 00/116 (Washington: International Monetary Fund).

Gupta, Sanjeev, and Marijn Verhoeven, 2001, "The Efficiency of Government Expenditure: Experiences from Africa," Chapter 11 in Helping Countries Develop: The Role of Fiscal Policy (Washington: International Monetary Fund).

————, and Erwin Tiongson, 2002, "The Effectiveness of Government Spending on Education and Health Care in Developing and Transition Economies," Chapter 8 in Helping Countries Develop: The Role of Fiscal Policy (Washington: International Monetary Fund).

Hillman, Arye L., 2000, "Poverty, Inequality, and Unethical Behavior of the Strong," IMF Working Paper 00/187 (Washington: International Monetary Fund).

————, 2003, Public Finance and Public Policy: Responsibilities and Limitations of Government (New York: Cambridge University Press).

————, and Otto Swank, 2000, "Why Political Culture Should Be in the Lexicon of Economics," European Journal of Political Economy, Vol. 16 (March), pp. 1–4.

Jimenez, Emmanuel, 1987, Pricing Policy in the Social Sectors: Cost Recovery for Education and Health in Developing Countries (Baltimore, Maryland: Johns Hopkins University Press for the World Bank).

————, 1989, "Social Sector Pricing Policy Revisited: A Survey of Some Recent Controversies," in Proceedings of the World Bank Annual Conference on Development Economics (Washington: World Bank).

————, and Vincent Paqueo, 1996, "Do Local Contributions Affect the Efficiency of Public Primary Schools?" Economics of Education Review, Vol. 15, No. 4, pp. 377–86.

Jimenez, Emmanuel, and Yasuyuki Sawada, 1999, "Do Community Managed Schools Work? An Evaluation of El Salvador's EDUCO Program," World Bank Economic Review, Vol. 13 (September), pp. 415–41.

Kadzamira, Esme, and Pauline Rose, 2001, "Educational Policy Choice and Policy Practice in Malawi: Dilemmas and Disjunctures," IDS Working Paper No. 124 (Brighton, England: Institute of Development Studies, University of Sussex).

Katav-Herz, Shirit, 2003, "A Model of Parental Demand for Child Labor with High Fertility Norms," *Review of Economics of the Household*, Vol. 1, Issue 3, pp. 219–33.

Lockheed, Marlaine E., and Adriaan M. Verspoor, 1991, *Improving Primary Education in Developing Countries* (Washington: World Bank).

Mauro, Paolo, 1997, *Why Worry About Corruption?* Economic Issues No. 6 (Washington: International Monetary Fund).

McGee, Rosemary, 2000, "Meeting the International Poverty Targets in Uganda: Halving Poverty and Achieving Universal Primary Education," *Development Policy Review*, Vol. 18 (March), pp. 85–106.

Michaelowa, Katherina, 2001, "Primary School Education Quality in Francophone Sub-Saharan Africa: Determinants of Learning Achievements and Efficiency Considerations," *World Development*, Vol. 29 (October), pp. 1699–1716.

Mingat, Alain, and Jee-Peng Tan, 1986, "Expanding Education Through User Charges: What Can Be Achieved in Malawi and Other LDCs?" *Economics of Education Review*, Vol. 5, No. 3, pp. 273–86.

Mingat, Alain, and R. Rakotomalala, 2002, "Coverage of Primary Education in Chad: Analysis of the Multiple Indicator Cluster Survey (MICS 2000) of Households and Demographic Data of Education" (unpublished; Washington: World Bank).

Mingat, Alain, and Carolyn Winter, 2002, "Education for All by 2015," *Finance & Development*, Vol. 39 (March), pp. 32–35.

Morrisson, Christian, ed., 2002, "Education and Health Expenditure and Poverty Reduction in East Africa: Madagascar and Tanzania," OECD Development Centre Studies (Paris: OECD)

Nagy, Piroska Mohácsi, Joseph Karangwa, and Jean-François Dauphin, 2002, "Chad: Statistical Appendix," IMF Country Report No. 02/28 (Washington: International Monetary Fund).

Oxfam, 2001, "Education Charges: A Tax on Human Development," Oxfam Briefing Paper No. 3 (Oxford, England).

———, 2002, "Every Child in School: A Challenge to Finance and Development Ministers," Oxfam Briefing Paper No. 20 (Oxford, England).

Reddy, Sanjay, and Jan Vandemoortele, 1996, "User Financing of Basic Social Services: A Review of Theoretical Arguments and Empirical Evidence," UNICEF Staff Working Papers Series (New York: United Nations International Children's Emergency Fund).

Reinikka, Ritva, and Jacob Svensson, 2001, "Explaining Leakage of Public Funds," World Bank Policy Research Working Paper No. 2709 (Washington: World Bank).

Sahn, David E., and David C. Stifel, 2003, "Progress Toward the Millennium Development Goals in Africa," *World Development*, Vol. 31 (January), pp. 23–52.

Schultz, T. Paul, 2001, "School Subsidies for the Poor: Evaluating the Mexican Progresa Poverty Program," Economic Growth Center Discussion Paper No. 834 (New Haven, Connecticut: Yale University).

———, 2002. "Why Governments Should Invest More to Educate Girls," *World Development*, Vol. 30 (February), pp. 207–25.

Skoufias, Emmanuel, Benjamin Davis, and Sergio de la Vega, 2001, "Targeting the Poor in Mexico: An Evaluation of the Selection of Households into PRO-GRESA," *World Development*, Vol. 29 (November), pp. 1769–84.

Thomas, Duncan, 1990, "Intra-Household Resource Allocation: An Inferential Approach," *Journal of Human Resources*, Vol. 25 (Fall), pp. 635–64.

Uganda, Ministry of Finance, Planning, and Economic Development, 2001a, *Poverty Status Report* (Kampala).

———, 2001b, *Poverty Reduction Strategy Paper: Progress Report 2001* (Kampala). Available via the Internet: http://www.imf.org/external/NP/prsp/2001/uga/01/index.htm.

Van Adams, Arvil, and Teresa Hartnett, 1996, "Cost Sharing in the Social Sectors of Sub-Saharan Africa: Impact on the Poor," World Bank Discussion Paper No. 338 (Washington: World Bank).

World Bank, 1993, "Ghana: Primary School Development Project," Staff Appraisal Report No. 11760 (Washington).

———, 1995a, *Priorities and Strategies for Education: A World Bank Review*, (Washington).

———, 1995b, "Kenya Poverty Assessment," Sector Report No. 13152 (Washington).

———, 2002, "Achieving Education for All by 2015: Simulation Results for 47 Low-Income Countries," Human Development Network: Africa Region and Education Department (unpublished; Washington).

11

The Efficiency of Government Expenditure: Experiences from Africa

SANJEEV GUPTA AND MARIJN VERHOEVEN

1. Introduction

Governments provide a host of goods and services to their populations, to achieve various economic and social objectives. The efficiency with which these goods and services are provided is important, not only in the debate on the size of the government and the possible role of the private sector,[1] but also in macroeconomic stabilization and economic growth. The purpose of this paper is to assess the efficiency of government spending on education and health in 37 countries in Africa, both in relation to each other and in comparison with countries in Asia and the Western Hemisphere. Besides ranking countries within Africa for

Reprinted with permission of Elsevier from "The Efficiency of Government Expenditure: Experiences from Africa," by Sanjeev Gupta and Marijn Verhoeven, *Journal of Policy Modeling*, Vol. 23, pp. 433–467, © 2001, by the Society for Policy Modeling.

This paper was prepared with the assistance of Keiko Honjo. We wish to thank Henry Tulkens for introducing us to the technique used in the paper, and Irma Adelman, Željko Bogetić, Benedict Clements, Ke-young Chu, Hamid Davoodi, Jörg Decressin, Edgardo Ruggiero, Christian Schiller, and Gerd Schwartz for many helpful comments on an earlier draft. In addition, we would like to thank James Condie and Prem Pillai for computational assistance. The usual disclaimer applies.

[1]Using a regression that relates government consumption to the rate of economic growth, Karras (1996) estimates the optimal size of the government at an average of 23% of GDP. He also finds that government services are overprovided in Africa, underprovided in Asia, and optimally provided elsewhere. Tanzi and Schuknecht (1997) find that the increase in public spending in many industrial countries since 1960 has been excessive in relation to its impact on social welfare, as measured by certain social and economic indicators.

their efficiency during a given time period and over time, this paper assesses changes in efficiency in the three regions.

Governments can be viewed as producers, engaged in the production of different outputs by combining labor with other inputs. For instance, governments finance teachers and books to reduce illiteracy, and pay for medical facilities and personnel to increase their populations' life expectancy. Governments that produce more of these outputs while spending less on inputs can be viewed as more efficient than governments that produce less outputs and use more inputs, other things being equal.

This paper shows that governments in some African countries are relatively inefficient in the provision of education and health services, in relation both to other countries in Africa and to those in Asia and the Western Hemisphere. This implies that higher budgetary allocations to the social sectors in these countries will not necessarily translate into an improvement of their social outcomes, unless specific measures are implemented to correct the underlying inefficiency in spending.

This paper is structured as follows. Section 2 provides a selective overview of the literature on the efficiency of government expenditure and lays out the paper's methodology. Section 3 tests the statistical relationship between government spending and output indicators; it also provides an analysis of the efficiency of government spending of African countries relative to each other and to those in Asia and the Western Hemisphere, and over time. Section 4 summarizes the results and the policy implications.

2. Measuring the Efficiency of Government Expenditures

Several approaches for measuring the efficiency of government expenditure have been proposed in the literature. In general, these approaches either do not allow for easy comparison of efficiency among countries or use proxies to gauge efficiency. The main advantage of the technique employed in this paper is that it allows for a direct measurement of the relative efficiency of government spending among countries.

Measuring the Efficiency of Government Expenditure: A Selective Overview

Studies of the efficiency of government spending have developed broadly along four lines. First, some studies have concentrated on gauging and enhancing efficiency in practical applications, often focusing on certain types of government spending in a specific country. Second, the efficiency of governments has been addressed in quantitative terms, using data on inputs of government spending but not on outputs. Third, some studies have assessed the efficiency of public spending using outputs but not inputs. Finally, a number of studies have looked at both inputs and outputs; these studies, however, typically have not made a consistent comparison of the efficiency of government spending across countries.

The issue of gauging and enhancing government efficiency continues to interest policymakers and researchers alike (Chu and Hemming, 1991; Chu et al., 1995). This interest received a boost with the initiation of wide-ranging institutional reforms by the Government of New Zealand in the late 1980s, aimed at improving the efficiency of the public sector (Scott, 1996). The central elements of these reforms were to separate policy formulation from policy implementation, create competition between government agencies and between government agencies and private firms, and develop output-oriented budgets using a wide array of output indicators. One reform objective was to transform government institutions to reflect the distinction between outputs—the goods or services produced by the government—and outcomes—the goals that the government wants to achieve with the outputs. Elements of this approach have been adopted by many countries, and the theory and practice of result-oriented public expenditure management has generated a wealth of information on how to control production processes within the government and how to enhance their efficiency (OECD, 1994; Oxley, Maher, Martins, and Nicoletti, 1990).

Other studies have assessed inefficiency in government spending with the help of regression analysis, focusing on inputs. For example, a study of OECD member countries covering 20 years (Gerdtham, Jönsson, MacFarlan, and Oxley, 1995) analyzed the efficiency of health care systems. They show that public-reimbursement health systems, which combine private provision with public financing, are associated with lower public health expenditures and higher efficiency than publicly managed and financed health care systems.[2] This is traced to the high incidence of relatively expensive in-patient care and the lack of a mechanism to restrain demand for specialized health care. Countries without ceilings on in-patient care were also found to have higher public health expenditure.

Another strand of literature has focused on differences in social indicators among countries (used as indicators of government outputs) after netting out the effect of economic development on these indicators. For example, a number of studies have found that when differences

---

[2]Gerdtham et al. (1995) gauge efficiency by looking at the level of spending associated with a high degree of inefficiency, such as in-patient care and specialized care.

in income levels and rates of economic growth are taken into account, Sri Lanka's social indicators outperform those of Pakistan (Aturupane, Glewwe, and Isenman, 1994; Isenman, 1980; Sen, 1981). Kakwani (1993) conjectures that this difference in performance reflects variation in the level and efficiency of public expenditure between Pakistan and Sri Lanka. However, these studies do not explicitly analyze the relationship between government spending and social indicators.

Instead of concentrating on either inputs or outputs, the analysis of efficiency should use information contained in both inputs and outputs, and address the question of whether the same level of output could be achieved with less input—or, equivalently, whether more output could be generated with the same level of input. Indeed, a final strand of quantitative analyses looks at both inputs and outputs. Harbison and Hanushek (1992) give an overview of 96 studies of education production functions in developing countries, and 187 studies of education production functions in the United States, and investigate the relation between education inputs and outputs. Typically, the studies sampled by Harbison and Hanushek specify a functional form of the production function, and use data from different schools in a region or country to estimate the coefficients for a regression of the production function. The output of the education production process is usually measured by test scores, whereas input use is gauged by indicators, such as the pupil-teacher ratio, teacher education, teacher experience, teacher salary, expenditure per pupil, and the availability of facilities. In most studies of developing countries, it is found that teacher education, teacher experience, and the availability of facilities have a positive and significant impact on education output; the effect of expenditure per pupil is significant in half the studies. The pupil-teacher ratio and teacher salary have no discernable impact on education output.

Jimenez and Lockheed (1995) assess the relative efficiency of public and private education in several developing countries by taking into account both inputs and outputs. They compare for each country the ratio of test scores to the average cost per pupil. This ratio measures the cost per pupil in the two education systems corrected for test score differences, and is in all cases lower for private education than for public education—in some instances, by a large margin.[3] However, this type of analysis only allows for establishing the efficiency of public education relative to that of private education within a country.

More recently, Tanzi and Schuknecht (1997) assessed the incremental impact of public spending on social and economic indicators (for

---

[3] In Thailand, for example, the cost per pupil of public education is almost seven times as high as in private education, taking into account the differences in test scores.

example, real growth and the mortality rate) in industrial countries. From a comparison of social indicators in countries with varying income levels, they conclude that higher public spending does not significantly improve social welfare.

Free Disposal Hull (FDH) Analysis

The FDH analysis method used in this paper has been developed to empirically assess the relative efficiency of production units in a market environment.[4] FDH analysis is based on the concept of X-efficiency (Leibenstein, 1966), and its central premise is, loosely speaking, that a producer is relatively inefficient if another producer uses less or an equal amount of inputs to generate more or as much output.[5] FDH analysis consists of, first, establishing the production possibility frontier representing a combination of best-observed production results within the sample of observations (the "best practices"), and, second, measuring the relative inefficiency of producers inside the production possibility frontier by the distance from the frontier. The contribution of this paper lies in applying FDH analysis to measuring efficiency of government spending in over 80 developing countries.[6,7]

The major advantages of FDH analysis are that it imposes only weak restrictions on the production technology, and that it still allows for a comparison of efficiency levels among producers. The only assumption made is that inputs and/or outputs can be freely disposed of, so that it is possible with the same production technology to lower outputs while

---

[4] FDH analysis was first proposed in a study of the relative efficiency of post office operations in Deprins, Simar, and Tulkens (1984). An overview of the methodology can be found in Tulkens (1993); a discussion of advanced issues such as technological change and shifts in the production possibility frontier can be found in Tulkens and Vanden Eeckhaut (1995).

[5] There are several approaches toward assessing production possibility frontiers and X-efficiency that can be distinguished into parametric and non-parametric techniques. Parametric techniques postulate a functional form for the production possibility frontier, and then select a set of parameters that best fit the sample data. Non-parametric techniques include FDH analysis and Data Envelopment Analysis (DEA). The latter technique was developed by Charnes, Cooper, and Rhodes (1978), and assumes that the production possibility set is convex. Tulkens and Vanden Eeckhaut (1995) provide a more comprehensive overview of the differences between FDH analysis and these alternative techniques. The advantage of FDH over these alternatives is that FDH imposes the least a priori restrictions on the production technology (see Bauer, 1990; Lewin and Lovell, 1990; and Seiford and Thrall, 1990 for further discussions of the merits of FDH and DEA over parametric estimation techniques).

[6] Throughout this paper, the term "producer" is meant to include governments.

[7] Fakin and de Crombrugghe (1997) have applied the FDH analysis in assessing the efficiency of government spending in a study of a limited number of Central European and OECD member countries (see below).

maintaining the level of inputs and to increase inputs while maintaining outputs at the same level.[8] This assumption guarantees the existence of a continuous FDH, or production possibility frontier, for any sample of production results. Thus, FDH analysis provides an intuitive tool that can be used to identify best practices in government spending and to assess how country governments are faring in comparison with these best practices.

A producer is relatively efficient if there is no other producer that uses less or an equal amount of input to generate as much or more output (with either one input being strictly lower or one output being strictly higher). Producers that are not relatively efficient are relatively inefficient. In Fig. 1, this is illustrated for the case of one input and one output. Producer B uses more input to produce less output than producer A, and is therefore relatively inefficient in comparison with producer A. Producer A, C, and D are relatively efficient; there is no producer in the sample that uses less input and generates more output. The set of all production results that are inefficient relative to a given set of results is bounded from above by the production possibility frontier. In Fig. 1, this is indicated by the step-form solid line connecting A, C, and D.

It should be noted that a producer can be relatively efficient, even though no producer is inefficient in relation to it (i.e., there is no producer in the rectangular area to the southeast of and below the relatively efficient producer). Such producers are assumed to be on the production possibility frontier, and will be called *independently efficient*.[9]

Production results can be ranked using the efficiency score, which represents the distance of individual production results from the production possibility frontier. In Fig. 1, producer B's efficiency in input terms is given by the distance by the line bB, that is, the Fig. 1 quotient of inputs used by producer A over inputs used by producer B, $x(A)/x(B)$. This measure of efficiency is referred to as the input efficiency score. For all observations in the interior of the production possibility set, the input efficiency score is smaller than 1. For all observations on the production possibility frontier (producers A, C, and D), the efficiency score equals 1. The input efficiency score indicates the excess use of inputs by the inefficient producer, and therefore the extent to which this producer allocates its resources in an inefficient manner. On the output side, the efficiency score of producer B is given by the line b'B, that is, the output quotient $y(B)/y(A)$. This score indicates the loss of output relative to the most efficient producer with an equal or lower level of

---

[8]Note that the production possibility set is not assumed to be convex, as in DEA.

[9]Examples of independently efficient production results are producers C and D in Fig. 1. Producer A is not independently efficient, as producer B is inefficient in relation to A.

Figure 1. Free Disposable Hull (FDH) Production Possibility Frontier

Output

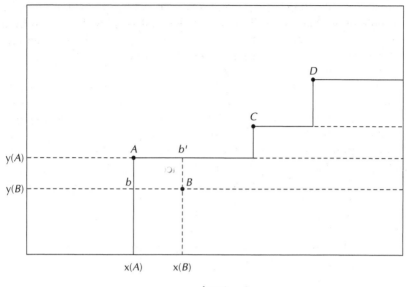

Input

inputs. As in the case of the input efficiency score, the output efficiency score is smaller than 1 for observations in the interior of the production possibility set (producer B) and equal to 1 for observations on the production possibility frontier (producers A, C, and D).

In the one-input one-output case depicted in Fig. 1, formulation of an efficiency score is relatively straightforward. With multiple inputs and outputs, a score of efficiency can be formulated for every input and output. The overall input (output) efficiency score is defined as the score of the input (output) that is closest to the production possibility frontier. This input (output) efficiency score indicates by how much the efficiency of the use of inputs (production of outputs) should increase for the production result to become relatively efficient, assuming that the efficiency in all inputs (outputs) is increased by the same percentage.

The step-by-step procedure of calculating the input efficiency score in the case of multiple inputs is as follows. First, a producer is selected (let us denote that producer as A). Then all producers that are more efficient than A are identified.[10] For every pair of producers comprising A and a more efficient producer, scores are calculated for each input by

---

[10] As in the one-input one-output case, if a more efficient producer cannot be identified, producer A would be assigned input and output efficiency scores of 1.

dividing that producer's input use by A's use of that input. The result is
an M × N matrix, where M is the number of inputs and N is the number of producers who are more efficient than A. The technique then involves selecting for every more efficient producer the input that brings
producer A closest to the production possibility frontier. In other words,
from each column of the matrix, the largest score, one for each more efficient producer, is taken, yielding a 1 × N vector of scores. Then, the
score relative to the most efficient producer is selected—that is, the
smallest score in the 1 × N vector. This is the input efficiency score.[11]

	x_1	x_2
B/A	0.80	0.83
D/A	0.70	0.32

From the above matrix, the maximum score in each of the two rows—(0.70, 0.83)—is
taken. The smallest of these scores is the input efficiency score: 0.70.

If $f(x;y)$ is the production set where x and y are inputs and outputs, respectively, and where $x_m(n)$ denotes use of the mth type of input by producer n, then the input efficiency score of producer A is:

$$\min_{n\in N}\max_{m\in M}\frac{x_m(n)}{x_m(A)}.$$

The output efficiency score can be calculated in a similar manner using:

$$\min_{n\in N}\max_{p\in P}\frac{y_p(A)}{y_p(n)},$$

where P denotes the set of outputs.

It should be noted that in the case of multiple inputs (outputs), FDH
analysis does not rely on some weighing of inputs (outputs) in order to
obtain a unit-dimensional indicator of efficiency. Calculating the input
efficiency score involves selecting the quotient of inputs that most accurately captures the distance to the production possibility frontier, which
is quite different from a weighted average of input quotients. This sets

---

[11] The calculation of the input efficiency score can be illustrated with an example of a
2-input 3-output case. Assume four producers, A through D, with production sets A(50,
72.5; 29.6, 4.2, 35.2), B(40, 60; 35, 4.3, 37), C(55, 70; 33.3, 5, 38), and D(35, 23.4; 43.5,
5.6, 44.5). The first two numbers in the sets denote use of inputs, the last three numbers the
yield of outputs. Producer A is less efficient than B and D—A uses more of both inputs
while its outputs are smaller—but is not less efficient than C. To calculate the input efficiency score, a comparison is made of A's use of inputs with those of the countries that are
more efficient—that is, B and D. The following matrix of input quotients (or scores) is used:

FDH analysis apart from most economic performance indices, such as the "Misery Index," an often-used negative measure of macroeconomic performance, and the "Magic Diamond" developed by the OECD.

FDH analysis has not yet been widely used in the empirical analysis of efficiency. An application to post offices in Belgium can be found in Deprins, Simar, and Tulkens (1984); FDH analyses of Belgian retail banking, courts, and urban transit are presented in Tulkens (1993). Lovell (1995) uses FDH analysis to establish the relative efficiency of 10 countries in Asia in engendering high economic growth, low inflation, low unemployment, and a favorable trade balance during 1970–1988. He assumes one fixed input (the policymaker) and takes four proxies for the output of economic policy (economic growth, employment, the trade balance, and price stability). He finds that Taiwan and Japan outperform other countries, while the Philippines and Australia are at the bottom of the efficiency ranking.

Several studies have used FDH analysis to assess the efficiency of government spending, as this paper attempts to do. Vanden Eeckhaut, Tulkens, and Jamar (1993) have sought to establish relative efficiency of spending by municipalities in Belgium. They use the total population, length of roads maintained by the municipality, number of senior citizens, number of welfare recipients, number of registered crimes, and number of students enrolled in primary education as indicators of output. They compare results of FDH analysis with results from DEA, and conclude that the convexity assumption imposed by DEA distorts the results of efficiency analysis. Moreover, they find a relationship between the degree of efficiency and the political party that governs the municipality. Finally, Fakin and de Crombrugghe (1997) use FDH analysis to assess the efficiency of government spending in OECD member countries and countries in Central Europe. They use total aggregate government spending as input, and the number of patents, the number of university entrants, the rates for infant mortality and life expectancy, the dependency ratio, and the number of telephone mainlines as outputs. They find that Belgium, Hungary, Italy, Poland, Slovenia, the Czech Republic, Greece, and Portugal are relatively inefficient, and that the inefficiencies are larger for transition countries than for OECD member countries.

Empirical Results

FDH analysis is used here to determine the relative efficiency of government spending on education and health. Per capita education and health spending by the government in purchasing power parity (PPP) terms is taken as a measure of input.[12] This allows for a more accurate cross-country comparison of the domestic shadow costs of the resource allocation for education and health than conventional U.S. dollar measures and GDP shares.[13] Output is measured by relevant social indicators, the choice of which is determined by their availability in a wide range of countries over many years. In addition, an attempt was made to include as many as possible of the core indicators recently proposed by the Development Assistance Committee (DAC) of the OECD, the World Bank, and the UN to measure development performance.[14] In particular, health output is measured by life expectancy, infant mortality, and immunizations against measles and diphtheria-pertussis-tetanus (DPT);[15]

---

[12] Per capita PPP public spending on education and health for the countries in the sample is calculated as the product of the respective shares of education and health spending in GDP in local currency, and GDP per capita expressed in PPP terms. Data on education and health spending are taken from IMF databases, whereas indicators of educational attainment and health output are from the World Bank's World Development Indicators database.

[13] The meaning of cross-country comparisons of inputs, and thus the efficiency measure calculated using FDH analysis, varies with the way the input is measured. For example, comparing education and health spending as a share of GDP captures relative national priorities; if a country spends more as a share of GDP on health, it can be said to attach more priority to health care spending than a country which has a lower spending-to-GDP ratio. However, GDP is not very reliable as a denominator; if GDP falls or is revised downwards, the spending ratio would go up, even though nominal spending remains unchanged. Using a U.S. dollar measure would accurately capture the shadow cost of education and health care spending measured in terms of internationally traded goods. But, similar to the case of GDP ratios, large short-term swings in exchange rates can obscure underlying spending trends. Finally, we agree with a referee's suggestion that it is more appropriate to compare the cost of providing education and health services across countries after adjusting for differences in wage cost. This is especially relevant for the social sectors, where such costs predominate. However, attempts to follow this approach were thwarted by lack of consistent data on public sector wages. For instance, ILO (1996) provides data for only 12 countries on government salaries, and that too for only a few years.

[14] The list of core indicators for education and health includes: net enrollment in primary education, persistence through grade four, literacy rate of 15- to 24-year-olds, adult literacy rate, infant mortality rate, child mortality rate, maternal mortality rate, births attended by skilled health personnel, contraceptive prevalence rate, HIV infection rate in 15- to 24-year-old pregnant women, and life expectancy at birth. [These have since in part been integrated into the much wider set of targets for the Millenium Development Goals—Ed.]

[15] Some caution needs to be exercised in the use of mortality indicators, because few developing countries report the cause of death and even when they do, the quality of information provided is often poor. Furthermore, mortality indicators are typically derived from a common model that projects mortality for all age groups; hence, the mortality rates from the model may not necessarily reflect differences in underlying trends in health status among population groups. Finally, there is some interaction between education and health indicators; for instance, female education has a favorable impact on infant mortality. Lack of data prevents use of other relevant indicators of health status, such as morbidity rates.

and educational attainment by primary school enrollment, secondary school enrollment, and adult illiteracy.[16] It could be argued that some of these indicators, such as the adult illiteracy rate, actually measure the outcome of government spending rather than output. However, in practice, the distinction between the concepts of output and outcome is imprecise, and although the selected variables may not directly measure output, they are indicative of the level of government output.

Data on educational attainment, health output, and public spending on education and health are available for 37 African countries, and for pooled data of 85 countries in Africa, Asia, and the Western Hemisphere (Appendix A lists the countries in the sample). Data on government spending and output indicators have been averaged over time periods because of the unavailability of complete annual data particularly for output indicators for many countries. The data for education spending are averaged over three periods (1984–1987, 1988–1991, and 1992–1995); the data on health spending are averaged over two periods (1984–1989 and 1990–1995). The averages for these periods are treated as separate observations. Therefore, for education expenditure, a maximum of three observations are available for each country; and for health expenditure, a maximum of two observations.

It should be noted that government spending is not the only variable that impacts on indicators of education and health output. Private expenditures, including activities of NGOs, the general level of economic and social development, the manner in which government expenditure for education and health is targeted, and other factors such as the incidence of AIDS, also have a bearing on output indicators.

The existence of a statistical relationship between public spending and indicators of output in the sample was checked with a log-linear regression, using robust OLS, which corrects standard errors for heteroskedasticity of unknown form using White's (1980) method. Separate regressions were run for indicators of educational attainment (primary school enrollment, secondary enrollment, and adult illiteracy) and health output (life expectancy, infant mortality, measles immunization,

---

[16]Performance in the education sector should be assessed in terms of access, completion of schooling, and achievement level. For the purposes of monitoring performance, two indicators are critical: net (i.e., age-specific) enrollment and completion rates. In accordance with the proposed set of core indicators, the reliance in this paper is on (gross) enrollment rates in primary and secondary schools (only for a few countries data on net enrollment rates are available). Unfortunately, data on completion rates were not available for a wide enough sample. Barro and Lee (1996) provide data on education attainment for a large number of countries, but these data could not be used because they measure attainment for persons 25 years of age and older, and their most recent observations are for 1990. By contrast, the period covered in this study is 1984–1995. Thus, these attainment data cover the period preceding the spending data on this study.

and DPT immunization), with the level of education and health spending, respectively, as independent variables. In all cases, the coefficients of education and health spending were statistically significant at the 5% confidence level and have the right sign (similar results are found by Anand and Ravallion, 1993; Commander, Davoodi, and Lee, 1997; Gupta, Verhoeven, and Tiongson, 1999—see the last paper for a critical assessment of the existing analyses of the relationship between public spending and social indicators). Introducing GDP per capita in PPP terms as an explanatory variable reduced the significance of government spending; however, GDP per capita and government spending on education and on health per capita are highly correlated (for African countries, the correlation coefficient between education spending and per capita GDP is 0.76; between health spending and initial per capita GDP, the correlation coefficient is 0.78). A dummy for African countries had a negative coefficient and was statistically significant in all cases except immunization for measles and DPT, suggesting that the efficiency of public education and health spending is lower in Africa than in Asia and the Western Hemisphere.[17]

Linking health spending in the current time period to contemporaneous adult illiteracy and life expectancy rates raises the issue of lags. Illiteracy is measured for the population over 15 years of age, and therefore partly reflects the impact of past schooling. Life expectancy is measured as the current expected life span of a newborn. To the extent that current mortality patterns reflect health care in previous years, life expectancy will be historically determined and unaffected by current health spending. Data limitations, particularly missing observations, preclude the use of stock-adjustment methods to gauge which part of these output indicators are historically determined. Less sophisticated methods of circumventing the problem of lags, such as taking first differences or estimating the historic component by regressing output indicators on past values, fail to eliminate the effect of lags. The change in the adult illiteracy rate, for example, reflects the difference in illiteracy of those who have just turned 15 years of age and those who recently died, and is therefore in part driven by past schooling and lags. An alternative would be to regress output indicators on past values and take the error terms as indicators of output that is instantaneously affected by government spending. This option is also not without problems, as output indicators as well as public spending on education and health turn out to be strongly autoregressive. The fact that output indicators and government spending are autoregressive makes it virtually impossible to differentiate between lagged and current effects of

---

[17]Gupta, Honjo, and Verhoeven (1997) present detailed regression results.

spending by using the regression approach. Therefore, in this paper, no attempt has been made to distinguish between the lagged and current impact of government spending on output indicators.[18]

As noted above, regression analysis indicates that the level of economic development has a relatively large impact on output indicators, suggesting that differences in economic development should be taken into account when assessing the efficiency of government spending (see also Anand and Ravallion, 1993; Carrin and Politi, 1997; and Musgrove, 1996). This paper uses the Adelman-Morris index of socio-economic development, and follows their ranking of developing countries into three levels: lowest, intermediate, and highest (Adelman and Morris, 1967). This index is based on a large number of economic, social, and political variables that are associated with long-run economic development.[19] Using FDH analysis on country groups separately mitigates considerably the impact on the results of differences in economic development. Most African countries (the only exception is Mauritius) are in the lowest and intermediate groups. This paper focuses on these groups.

An alternative way of dealing with the impact of differences in economic development would be to control for such differences in measuring both government expenditure and output indicators. Unfortunately, netting out the effect of the level of economic development on government spending on education and health is anything but straightforward. Barro (1990), for example, argues that education spending has a positive impact on economic growth through its effect on the accumulation of human capital.[20] Isolating the effect of economic development on government spending for education and health would thus require the formulation of an economic model capturing the causal links between these variables. The development of such a model lies outside the scope of this paper. Netting out the effect of economic development on output indicators, but not on public spending on education and health, would distort the analysis. The relatively high level of economic development of countries such as Mauritius and Korea would imply a large downward adjustment of their output indicators, while their corresponding high spending levels remain unadjusted. This would leave them with low efficiency scores and at the bottom of the efficiency ranking.

---

[18] The implications of this will be discussed in the concluding section.

[19] For 42 out of the 87 countries in our sample, the socio-economic development level can be found in Adelman and Morris (1967). For the other countries, the level was assigned based on a calculation using data on the most important variables in their analysis for which information was available—size of the agricultural sector, literacy rate, urbanization, and the degree of cultural and ethnic homogeneity—and the weights of these factors.

[20] Levine and Renelt (1992), on the other hand, dispute the existence of a relationship between public spending and economic growth.

Government Spending and Social Indicators: Initial Results

In the initial analysis of the efficiency of government spending, the level of spending is compared separately with each output indicator. This is equivalent to the one-input one-output case shown in Fig. 1. For each time period and each output indicator, a production possibility frontier is calculated that indicates the relatively efficient way ("the best practices") of achieving educational attainment. Relative efficiency can be measured by the distance of a country's spending result from the production possibility frontier.[21] This distance can be measured horizontally (in which case the input efficiency score would be obtained), vertically (i.e., by the output efficiency score), or by some combination of these measures. In the analysis below, both the horizontal and vertical distances have been taken into account.

In at least two time periods government spending on education in The Gambia, Guinea, Malawi, Niger, and Tanzania—with an average annual spending of 2.4% of GDP in the most recent time period (1992–1995)— is relatively efficient in impacting on primary school enrollment rates;[22] however, Côte d'Ivoire, Senegal, and Zimbabwe—with an average annual spending of 5.9% of GDP—are not as efficient. By the same measure, The Gambia, Ghana, Namibia, and Zimbabwe—where yearly government spending on education averages 6.0% of GDP—achieve relatively high secondary school enrollment, whereas Burundi, Côte d'Ivoire, Niger, and Senegal—with annual government spending of on average 4.3% of GDP—do not. In Madagascar, Niger, and São Tomé and Príncipe—with an average annual government spending of 4.0% of GDP—public spending facilitates relatively high rates of literacy;[23] however, Côte d'Ivoire, Gabon, and Kenya—where annual government spending averages 5.4% of GDP—do not fare as well.

The analysis also can be used to track the development in the productivity of education spending over time. It should be noted that the concept of productivity is different from the concept of efficiency. Efficiency is a measure of how far an individual country is from the production possibility frontier, whereas productivity measures the maximum output associated with different levels of spending, that is, the position of the production possibility frontier. In the case of all three output indicators,

---

[21] The results of the FDH analysis presented here, particularly the cross-country comparisons, should be interpreted with some caution, as the coverage of education and health expenditures may vary among countries. Although spending is measured in per capita PPP terms for the FDH analysis, expenditure as a share of GDP is given for comparison.

[22] Nigeria also has high primary school enrollment rates considering the level of government spending. However, data on government spending for Nigeria do not cover substantial expenditures by lower levels of government.

[23] Defined as 100 minus the adult illiteracy rate.

the production possibility frontier shifts outward, suggesting that the productivity of government spending in terms of different measures of educational attainment has increased in Africa. However, the outward shift in the production possibility frontier is not necessarily attributable to better use of inputs due to changes in production technology; it could also be the result of economic growth and private spending.

An analysis of the relationships between per capita government spending on health expressed in PPP terms and life expectancy shows that Botswana and São Tomé and Príncipe—with an average annual government spending of 2.1% of GDP in the most recent time period (1990–1995)—have relatively high life expectancy, whereas Côte d'Ivoire, Lesotho, and Zimbabwe—where yearly public spending averages 2.7% of GDP—are not faring as well. With respect to the infant survival rate,[24] Botswana, Ethiopia, Guinea, Lesotho, and São Tomé and Príncipe—with an average yearly spending of 1.8% of GDP—are achieving better results than Côte d'Ivoire and Mozambique, where annual spending averages 1.4% of GDP. Yearly government spending on health in The Gambia and Guinea—averaging 0.5% of GDP—engenders relatively high rates of immunization, but it does not do so in Mauritania, Togo, and Zambia—where annual spending averages 1.3% of GDP. Over time, the productivity of health spending in Africa has generally increased, as evidenced by the outward shift of the production possibility frontier over most of its range (except for the frontier for life expectancy).[25]

The Efficiency of Health and Education Spending: Combining Output Indicators

Analyzing the efficiency of government spending separately for each output indicator does not give a definitive answer to the question of which countries spend their public resources relatively efficiently, as this would require taking into account all indicators of output. For example, although Niger attains high primary school enrollment, it performs relatively badly in secondary school enrollment. The reverse is true for Zimbabwe. To establish whether Niger and Zimbabwe efficiently spend their government resources for education (and health care), all indicators of education output and health output need to be combined.

Tables 1 and 2 present results from FDH analyses of education and health spending of African countries in the sample, taking account all output indicators separately for each of the time periods. The analysis

---

[24] Defined as 1000 minus the infant mortality rate.
[25] A World Bank (1997) study, however, finds that since 1900 worldwide life expectancy has increased by 25 years at similar income levels.

excludes Mauritius, which is in the group of countries with the highest socio-economic development. Results are shown for the groups of countries at lowest and intermediate development separately, as well as for all these countries together.

The country ranking is a lexicographic ordering based on: (1) the relative input efficiency scores, and (2) the number of countries relative to which the country in question is more efficient.[26] Country observations that cannot be compared because they are neither more nor less efficient than any other country in any time period—the independently efficient cases—are identified with a "*", and are omitted from the rankings.

The analysis in this section focuses on input efficiency scores rather than output efficiency scores, as the former have a straightforward interpretation and more relevance for policymaking. The input efficiency score indicates the amount of spending that would be needed to achieve the same or a higher level of each output at the same level of efficiency as the most efficient country. In other words, if the input efficiency score is 0.1%, 90% of education spending does not contribute in an efficient manner to educational attainment in that country. As the expenditure allocations (rather than outputs) are under the control of the policymakers, a focus on input efficiency scores is more meaningful.[27]

Comparing Efficiency within Africa

Table 1 shows that in at least two time periods the efficiency of education spending is relatively high in Togo—with an average annual spending of 4.3% of GDP in the last time period (1992–1995);[28] Burkina Faso, Côte d'Ivoire, and Mauritania, however, where yearly government spending averages 4.0% of GDP, have relatively low efficiency. For example, Côte d'Ivoire used only 35–45% of its education spending efficiently when judged against the best-practice benchmark set by Ghana.

---

[26]The method of ranking proposed here allows for a distinction among countries on the production possibility frontier, which would not be possible if the efficiency scores were used as the sole argument for ranking the countries (as noted earlier, all countries on the production possibility frontier are assigned an efficiency score of 1). The number of observations relative to which a country is more efficient is an indication of the robustness of the efficiency result; the greater the number of countries that are less efficient than a given country on the production possibility frontier, the smaller the chance that this country will shift into the interior of the production possibility set if the sample were to change slightly or if measurement errors were corrected.

[27]Results of output efficiency scores for education and health spending (not presented here) tend to be higher and more evenly distributed than input efficiency scores.

[28]For Togo, this result partly reflects that capital expenditures are not covered in the education spending data.

The relative efficiency of education spending improved significantly in a number of countries (Burkina Faso and Mauritania), as shown by an improvement in ranking and an increase in efficiency scores in Table 1. In Burkina Faso, the input efficiency score in the sample that includes all African countries in the lowest and intermediate development groups increased from 0.29 during period 2 (1988–1991) to 0.56 during period 3 (1992–1995), which is reflected in an improvement of its ranking from last to a better-than-median position, with annual government spending on education increasing from 2.7% of GDP to 3.0% of GDP. Education spending in Burundi, on the other hand, became relatively less efficient between periods 1 and 3, even when yearly government education spending remained unchanged at 4.4% of GDP.

Table 2 presents results for health spending. It shows that Ethiopia, Tanzania, and Zimbabwe—with an average annual spending of 2.1% of GDP in the last time period (1990–1995)—perform relatively well in two time periods, whereas the ranking and input efficiency scores for Malawi, Mali, Mauritania, Mozambique, and Niger—with an average annual spending of 1.8% of GDP—are lower. Finally, the relative efficiency of health spending improved between periods 1 (1984–1989) and 2 (1990–1995) in Madagascar and Mali, as average yearly government spending remained about constant at 1.0% and 1.6% of GDP, respectively. At the same time, the relative efficiency of health expenditure declined in Malawi and Mozambique, where annual government spending was broadly unchanged at about 1.6% of GDP.

Comparing Efficiency in Africa with That in Asia and the Western Hemisphere

In the previous section, separate production possibility frontiers were derived for each time period. It was thus assumed that the production technology differs between time periods, and that changes in productivity may occur. Alternatively, it can be assumed that the production technology is constant and that the production possibility frontier does not shift over time. This would be captured in the FDH analysis by pooling observations for all time periods, and by deriving production possibility frontier and efficiency scores from pooled observations. This pooling of observations enables a direct comparison of efficiency scores for different time periods.

Table 3 presents input efficiency scores for education spending for countries at the lowest and intermediate level of socio-economic development in Africa, Asia, and the Western Hemisphere. In addition, all time periods are pooled in the sample. Results are sorted by time period and region. They show that Africa has, on average, the lowest ef-

Table 1. Africa Education Input Efficiency Scores During 1984–1995 Using Literacy, Primary Enrollment, and Secondary Enrollment as Output Indicators[a]

	Period 1 (1984–1987)			
	Ranking in lowest and intermediate development groups separately		Ranking in lowest and intermediate development groups combined	
	Efficiency Score	Ranking	Efficiency Score	Ranking
Countries with lowest socio-economic development				
Burkina Faso	—	—	—	—
Cameroon	1.00	*	1.00	*
Chad	—	—	—	—
Côte d'Ivoire	0.70	5	0.35	8
Ethiopia	—	—	—	—
Gambia, The	—	—	—	—
Guinea	—	—	—	—
Kenya	1.00	1	0.69	7
Malawi	1.00	*	1.00	*
Mali	1.00	*	1.00	*
Mozambique	1.00	*	1.00	*
Niger	—	—	—	—
Nigeria	1.00	*	1.00	4
Rwanda	—	—	—	—
Senegal	0.72	4	0.71	6
Togo	1.00	1	1.00	4
Zambia	1.00	1	1.00	3
Average[b]	0.88	2.4	0.79	5.3
Variance[b]	0.02	3.0	0.06	3.2
Total number of countries	10		10	
Number of countries not independently efficient	5		6	
Countries with intermediate socio-economic development				
Botswana	1.00	*	1.00	*
Burundi	—	—	—	—
Cape Verde	—	—	—	—
Congo, Democratic Republic of	—	—	—	—
Ghana	1.00	1	1.00	1
Lesotho	1.00	*	1.00	1
Mauritania	0.94	2	0.10	9
Swaziland	1.00	*	1.00	*
Zimbabwe	1.00	*	1.00	*
Average[b]	0.97	1.5	0.70	3.7
Variance[b]	0.00	0.3	0.18	14.?
Total number of countries	6		6	
Number of countries not independently efficient	2		3	

Source: authors' calculations.

[a] The efficiency scores and rankings are based on separate FDH analyses of education spending for all three time periods for countries in Africa. For each time period, the first column includes the results for separate FDH analyses for countries in the lowest and in the intermediate socio-economic development groups, while the second column presents the ranking of countries if the analysis is run for the two country groups combined. The classification of countries follows Adelman and Morris (1967).

[b] Independently efficient outcomes are indicated with "*" and are excluded from the calculation of average and median input efficiency scores.

Period 2 (1988–1991)				Period 3 (1992–1995)			
Ranking in lowest and intermediate development groups separately		Ranking in lowest and intermediate development groups combined		Ranking in lowest and intermediate development groups separately		Ranking in lowest and intermediate development groups separately	
Efficiency Score	Ranking	Efficiency Score	Ranking	Efficiency Score	Ranking	Efficiency Score	Ranking
0.29	7	0.29	13	1.00	*	0.56	3
1.00	2	1.00	4	—	—	—	—
—	—	—	—	1.00	*	0.47	4
0.56	5	0.43	11	0.45	2	0.45	5
—	—	—	—	1.00	*	1.00	*
1.00	1	1.00	2	—	—	—	—
0.51	6	0.51	10	—	—	—	—
1.00	*	1.00	*	—	—	—	—
—	—	—	—	—	—	—	—
1.00	*	1.00	*	—	—	—	—
0.73	4	0.73	8	—	—	—	—
1.00	*	1.00	*	—	—	—	—
1.00	*	1.00	4	—	—	—	—
1.00	2	1.00	2	—	—	—	—
1.00	*	0.85	6	—	—	—	—
1.00	7	0.82	7	1.00	1	1.00	2
—	—	—	—	—	—	—	—
0.76	4.3	0.76	6.7	0.73	1.5	0.62	3.5
0.07	4.9	0.06	13.0	0.07	0.3	0.05	1.3
13		13		5		5	
7		9		2		3	
1.00	*	1.00	*	1.00	*	1.00	*
1.00	*	0.64	9	0.38	2	0.38	6
—	—	—	—	0.13	3	0.13	7
—	—	—	—	1.00	1	1.00	1
1.00	*	1.00	1	—	—	—	—
—	—	—	—	—	—	—	—
1.00	*	0.29	12	—	—	—	—
—	—	—	—	—	—	—	—
1.00	*	1.00	*	1.00	*	1.00	*
—	—	0.64	7.3	0.50	2.00	0.50	4.67
—	—	0.08	21.6	0.13	0.67	0.13	6.89
5		5		5		5	
0		3		3		3	

Table 2. Africa: Health Input Efficiency Scores During 1984–1995 Using Life Expectancy, Infant Survival, and DPT and Measles Immunizations as Output Indicators[a]

	Period 1 (1984–1989)				Period 2 (1990–1995)			
	Ranking in lowest and medium development groups separately		Ranking in lowest and medium development groups combined		Ranking in lowest and medium development groups separately		Ranking in lowest and medium development groups combined	
	Efficiency Score	Ranking	Efficiency Score	Ranking	Efficiency Score	Ranking	Efficiency Score	Ranking
Countries with lowest socio-economic development								
Burkina Faso	1.00	4	0.75	10	1.00	5	0.88	12
Cameroon	0.99	5	0.99	7	1.00	8	1.00	10
Chad	—	—	—	—	0.38	9	0.38	14
Côte d'Ivoire	1.00	*	1.00	*	1.00	*	1.00	*
Ethiopia	0.96	7	0.96	8	1.00	3	1.00	4
Gambia	1.00	*	1.00	*	1.00	5	1.00	6
Guinea	1.00	*	1.00	*	1.00	*	1.00	*
Kenya	1.00	3	1.00	3	1.00	3	1.00	*
Madagascar	0.99	6	0.72	11	1.00	3	1.00	4
Malawi	0.52	10	0.52	13	0.35	11	0.35	16
Mali	0.40	11	0.40	15	1.00	5	0.72	13
Mozambique	0.80	8	0.58	12	0.35	12	0.34	17
Niger	0.68	9	0.49	14	0.36	10	0.36	15
Nigeria	1.00	2	1.00	3	1.00	2	1.00	3
Tanzania	1.00	1	1.00	2	1.00	1	1.00	1
Togo	1.00	*	1.00	*	1.00	*	1.00	6
Zambia	1.00	*	1.00	*	1.00	*	0.90	11
Average[b]	1.00	6.0	0.76	8.91	0.79	6.17	0.78	9.43
Variance[b]	0.00	10.0	0.05	19.72	0.09	12.64	0.08	26.39
Total number of countries	16		16		17		17	
Number of countries not independently efficient	11		11		12		14	

Countries with intermediate
socio-economic development

Country	Score	Rank	Score	Rank	Score	Rank	Score	Rank
Botswana	1.00	*	1.00	*	—	—	—	—
Burundi	—	—	—	—	1.00	*	1.00	1
Central African Republic	—	—	—	—	1.00	*	1.00	6
Congo, Republic of	1.00	*	1.00	*	0.31	2	0.06	19
Ghana	0.89	4	1.00	*	1.00	*	1.00	*
Guinea Bissau	1.00	2	0.89	9	—	—	—	—
Lesotho	0.34	6	1.00	5	—	—	—	—
Mauritania	1.00	1	0.34	17	0.31	18	0.31	18
São Tomé and Principe	0.45	5	1.00	1	—	—	—	—
Swaziland	1.00	2	0.35	16	—	—	—	—
Zimbabwe	1.00	3	1.00	5	1.00	1	1.00	6
Average[b]	0.78	3.33	0.76	8.83	0.66	1.50	0.81	8.00
Variance[b]	0.08	3.22	0.09	34.81	0.12	0.25	0.14	44.50
Total number of countries	8		8		6		6	
Number of countries not independently efficient	6		6		3		5	

Source: authors' calculations.

[a] The efficiency scores and rankings are based on separate FDH analyses of education spending for the two time periods, using data for countries in Africa. For each time period, the first column includes the results for countries in the lowest and in the intermediate socio-economic development groups, while the second column presents the ranking of countries if the analysis is run for the two country groups combined. The classification of countries follows Adelman and Morris (1967).

[b] Independently efficient outcomes are indicated with "*" and are excluded from the calculation of average and median input efficiency scores.

Table 3. Countries with Lowest and Intermediate Socio-economic Development in Africa, Asia, and the Western Hemisphere: Input Efficiency Scores and Ranking[a]

	Number of Observations	Input Efficiency Score	Number of More Efficient Country Observations	Number of Less Efficient Country Observations	Rank
Education expenditures					
Overall sample	88	0.27 (0.08)	7.9 (7.0)	7.9 (3.0)	44.5 (44.5)
Period 1 (1984–1987)	28	0.24 (0.08)	8.7 (7.0)	5.9 (2.0)	46.8 (41.5)
Period 2 (1988–1991)	33	0.21 (0.06)	8.9 (8.0)	7.5 (2.5)	49.2 (50.0)
Period 3 (1992–1995)	27	0.38 (0.12)	5.9 (3.0)	10.6 (5.0)	36.1 (30.0)
Africa	43	0.08 (0.04)	11.5 (10.0)	1.9 (0.0)	56.9 (59.0)
Period 1 (1984–1987)	16	0.09 (0.03)	10.6 (9.0)	1.7 (0.0)	58.6 (64.5)
Period 2 (1988–1991)	17	0.06 (0.04)	11.8 (9.5)	1.2 (0.0)	58.3 (59.0)
Period 3 (1992–1995)	10	0.10 (0.06)	9.8 (8.5)	3.6 (0.0)	51.6 (53.0)
Asia	36	0.50 (0.30)	3.9 (1.5)	15.7 (13.5)	29.3 (24.0)
Period 1 (1984–1987)	10	0.44 (0.11)	3.8 (2.5)	12.7 (12.0)	29.6 (32.5)
Period 2 (1988–1991)	12	0.39 (0.11)	5.7 (2.5)	17.3 (16.0)	37.3 (33.0)
Period 3 (1992–1995)	14	0.62 (0.90)	2.6 (0.5)	16.6 (10.0)	22.3 (17.0)
Western Hemisphere	9	0.30 (0.05)	6.2 (8.0)	6.1 (6.0)	45.8 (56.0)
Period 1 (1984–1987)	2	0.52 (0.52)	4.5 (4.5)	5.0 (5.0)	38.5 (38.5)
Period 2 (1988–1991)	4	0.29 (0.06)	5.5 (6.0)	6.8 (8.0)	46.8 (51.5)
Period 3 (1992–1995)	3	0.17 (0.05)	8.3 (8.0)	6.0 (5.0)	49.3 (56.0)

Health expenditures

Overall sample	83	0.18 (0.07)	6.1 (4.0)	6.1 (1.0)	42.0 (30.0)
Period 1 (1984–1989)	42	0.17 (0.08)	5.9 (4.5)	4.1 (1.0)	42.1 (38.5)
Period 2 (1990–1995)	41	0.18 (0.06)	6.2 (3.0)	8.1 (2.0)	41.9 (45.0)
Africa	47	0.08 (0.06)	8.0 (6.0)	2.4 (1.0)	45.6 (45.0)
Period 1 (1984–1989)	24	0.08 (0.07)	7.3 (6.0)	2.7 (1.0)	44.8 (41.0)
Period 2 (1990–1995)	23	0.07 (0.06)	8.7 (6.0)	2.3 (1.0)	46.5 (46.0)
Asia	27	0.30 (0.09)	3.5 (2.0)	13.8 (8.0)	33.0 (30.0)
Period 1 (1984–1989)	14	0.29 (0.09)	3.7 (2.5)	7.3 (2.0)	34.4 (31.5)
Period 2 (1990–1995)	13	0.32 (0.15)	3.3 (1.0)	20.9 (14.0)	31.5 (21.0)
Western Hemisphere	9	0.31 (0.03)	3.8 (2.0)	1.8 (2.0)	50.0 (67.0)
Period 1 (1984–1989)	4	0.27 (0.03)	5.3 (4.0)	2.0 (1.5)	53.3 (66.5)
Period 2 (1990–1995)	5	0.35 (0.02)	2.6 (2.0)	1.6 (2.0)	47.4 (71.0)

Source: authors' calculations.

Numbers outside brackets refer to averages, numbers in parenthesis are medians. The observation for Niger during period 2 (1988–1991) for education spending is independently efficient, and is excluded from the table.

[a] The input efficiency scores are based on a production possibility frontier for all observations for countries with lowest and intermediate socio-economic development and for all time periods. For example, the average input efficiency score is 0.27 for all country observations, with 7.9 countries being more (and less) efficient than the average country observation. The input efficiency score 0.24 for period 1 (1984–1987) refers to the performance of countries in this period relative to the production possibility frontier derived for the overall sample.

ficiency of education spending, with an average input efficiency score of 0.08 in all three time periods. Asia performs the best with an average input efficiency score of 0.50, whereas the countries in the Western Hemisphere are between countries in the other two regions with an average score of 0.30. Countries in Africa score relatively low in terms of efficiency while, on average, spending more on education as a share of GDP than countries in Asia and the Western Hemisphere. In the last time period (1992–1995), education spending in Africa averaged 4.0% of GDP, against 3.2% of GDP in Asia and 3.4% of GDP in the Western Hemisphere.

The results for efficiency scores are consistent with averages of the results also presented in Table 3 for the number of more efficient countries, for the number of less efficient countries, and for the ranking of countries in the sample. For instance, in reflection of low-average input efficiency scores for all time periods, the countries in Africa are, on average, less efficient than 11.5 countries in the overall sample, and more efficient than only 1.9 countries. It is interesting to note that the average efficiency score for period 1 (1984–1987) is higher for the Western Hemisphere than for the Asian countries, but that since then the relative performance in the Western Hemisphere has declined and that of Asia improved.

The observed inefficiency of education spending in Africa cannot be explained by differences in private spending on education. Jimenez and Lockheed (1995) find that in 1985 the average share of government schools in primary enrollment in the African countries varied from 80% in East Africa to 84% in West Africa. In both Asia and the Western Hemisphere, the government share in primary enrollment averaged 88% in 1985. In that same year, the government share in secondary enrollment averaged 52% in East Africa and 72% in West Africa, against 78% in Asia and 75% in the Western Hemisphere. Furthermore, James (1991) finds that in the African countries a relatively low share of funding of private education is from public sources, such as government subsidies. These findings suggest that the share of private spending in total education spending is higher in the African than in the Asian and Western Hemisphere countries. And as a relatively large part of educational attainment in Africa is produced with private inputs, the African countries should come out of the FDH analysis as being more—not less—efficient than those in Asia and the Western Hemisphere, all other things being equal.[29]

---

[29] Using a limited dataset by Psacharapoulos and Nguyen (1997) on private education spending, a statistically significant relationship could not be found between private spending on education and input efficiency scores.

Table 3 also shows median values for the input efficiency scores. These are generally lower than the average scores, indicating that the majority of countries are clustered at relatively low efficiency scores, and that the average is pulled up by a few countries with high efficiency scores.

An analysis of the input efficiency scores of individual countries reinforces the conclusion that African countries, on average, are less efficient with their education spending than countries in Asia and Western Hemisphere. No African country in the sample has an efficiency score of 1, and the highest efficiency score for a recent time period is 0.34 for Zimbabwe. Relatively high efficiency scores were also achieved by The Gambia, Malawi, and the Democratic Republic of Congo (formerly Zaire).[30] Many of the African countries are at the lower end of the efficiency score distribution, particularly Botswana, Cameroon, Côte d'Ivoire, and Kenya. Of the Asian countries, China, India, the Philippines, and Vietnam record high efficiency scores.[31] Papua New Guinea, on the other hand, does not perform as well. Apart from relatively high scores for Ecuador and Guyana, most Western Hemisphere countries perform around the average for the sample. Education spending in Guatemala, Honduras, and Nicaragua is relatively less efficient.

The results show that high efficiency scores for education spending are clustered at low levels of expenditure in per capita PPP terms. No country spending more than US$150 per capita on education has an input efficiency score greater than 0.4, suggesting that over half their spending is not allocated efficiently. It also suggests that increased government spending would have to be accompanied by improved targeting of such spending if a discernible impact on attainment indicators is to be felt.

This inverse relationship between government spending and relative efficiency suggests that at advanced levels of educational attainment it becomes harder to emulate examples of best practices. As a result, differences between high-performing countries and poor performers become larger. A further explanation could be that as spending and education attainment increase, governments shift resources away from productive uses. For example, Mingat and Tan (1998) demonstrate for a sample of 125 countries that as primary enrollment goes up, resources in primary education are shifted toward decreasing pupil-teacher ratios (this shift in

---

[30] For Malawi, this is partly due to the fact that total education spending does not cover capital expenditure.

[31] The results for China and India are influenced by partial coverage of government spending; in both countries, a significant part of government spending on education and health is undertaken at lower levels of government, which is not captured in the data used in this paper.

focus begins to occur at primary enrollment rates of as low as 50%). But smaller pupil-teacher ratios do not tend to have a substantial impact on measures of education attainment, and therefore these additional resources do not yield significant increases in enrollment or literacy rates. Furthermore, the observed pattern may reflect the inability of the analysis to capture the differential impact of private spending on social indicators. Finally, higher spending on education may reflect the higher cost of tertiary education with rising per capita incomes; in that case, spending differences partly reflect cost differences among countries. However, the impact of such differences is minimized in this study by using a PPP measure of spending and by distinguishing between countries at different levels of socioeconomic development.

The cost of tertiary education can be large. In sub-Saharan Africa in 1990, government spending per student on higher education was 44.1 times as large as government spending per primary school student (in 1980, it was 65.3 times; see World Bank, 1997). That same year in Asia, a higher education student was 7.4 times as costly; in the Western Hemisphere, 8.2 times. This higher cost of tertiary education for African countries is reflected in the social rate of return of different levels of education (the impact of education on lifetime income in relation to total government and private spending per pupil). The annual social rate of return to primary education in sub-Saharan African countries is 24.3%, against only 11.2% for tertiary education. In Asian countries, these rates of return are 19.9% and 11.7%, respectively; in Western Hemisphere countries, 17.9% and 12.3%, respectively (Psacharapoulos, 1994). In terms of social indicators, such as illiteracy, the rate of return to primary education is even higher and the rate of return to higher education lower. It can thus be concluded that, when compared with the cost of primary education, the cost of higher education is high and the rate of return low, particularly in Africa. An inordinately high level of government spending on tertiary education would therefore exact a high price in terms of efficiency loss.[32]

Turning to health spending in Table 3, Asian and Western Hemisphere countries again have higher average input efficiency scores (an average of 0.31 and 0.30, respectively, during both time periods, against 0.08 for Africa). Government spending on health as a percent of GDP was on average the highest in the last time period (1990–1995) in the Western Hemisphere countries (2.6% of GDP), followed by the

---

[32] In a sample of eight African countries, the share of tertiary education in total government education spending around 1994 varied from 9.1% in Mauritania to 32.8% in the Republic of Congo, with an average of 19.7%. See Gupta et al. (1999) for more information on the intrasectoral distribution of spending and the relation with social indicators.

African countries (1.6% of GDP) and the Asian countries (1.4% of GDP). The median efficiency scores vary less between regions than the average scores, and are higher for Africa than for the Western Hemisphere. If the median score is interpreted as the score of a "typical" country, it would imply that a typical country in Africa is more efficient than a typical country in the Western Hemisphere.

Analysis of the input efficiency scores of individual countries reveals that, as in the case of education, a negative relationship can be identified between input efficiency scores and the level of health spending in per capita PPP terms. The efficiency scores for health spending of relatively well-performing countries in Africa—Guinea, Ethiopia, and The Gambia—vary from 0.15 to 0.20. Congo, Côte d'Ivoire, Ghana, Kenya, and Zimbabwe have lower scores. Of the Asian countries, China, Sri Lanka, and Vietnam have relatively high efficiency scores, whereas Papua New Guinea is among those with the lowest. Of the Western Hemisphere countries, Panama and St. Vincent and the Grenadines have been performing well, whereas Honduras, Nicaragua, Bolivia, and Guatemala have relatively low efficiency scores.

No trend consistent with the efficiency results is discernable from the relative shares of government and private spending on health in the three regions. In Africa, private per capita spending on health is on average US$10.7, and government spending is US$13.3.[33] In Asia, private spending on health averages US$36.7 per capita, and government expenditure amounts to US$24.5. In the Western Hemisphere, private spending averages US$42.0 per capita, against US$63.1 for government spending. Therefore, whereas per capita private spending on health in Asia and the Western Hemisphere is larger than in Africa, it is smaller as a share of total health spending in the Western Hemisphere, and larger in Asia.

As noted above, the differences in efficiency levels could reflect differences in the cost of providing education and health services. It could be, for example, that the relatively poor performance of some countries is due to relatively high wages of teachers and medical personnel. As a result, too few resources would be available for teaching materials, medical equipment, and other types of inputs, resulting in a distorted input mix and a loss of efficiency. To test this hypothesis, two OLS regressions were run for a sample of 23 countries in Africa, Asia, and the Western Hemisphere with average government wages as a percent of per capita GDP as the explanatory variable and the efficiency ranking for education and health spending as the explained variables.[34] In the case of

---

[33] The figures refer to 1990 and are based on Psacharapoulos and Nguyen (1997).

[34] Wage data were obtained from Kraay and Van Rijckeghem (1995) and authors' calculations.

health spending, no statistically significant relationship could be found, but a negative and statistically significant relationship was found between the degree of efficiency of education spending and relative government wages.[35] This suggests that in the case of education spending, part of the inefficiency due to cost differences is traceable to wage level differentials. This result is not surprising in light of the study by Harbison and Hanushek (1992), who conclude on the basis of a sample of education production functions that teacher wages have no significant effect on education output. In other words, consistent with the finding in this paper, their study suggests that countries with relatively high teacher salaries incur larger costs, but not significantly higher education output than countries with relatively low teacher salaries.

The Development of Efficiency Over Time

Table 3 shows that the average input efficiency score of education expenditure for all observations between periods 1 (1984–1987) and 3 (1992–1995) rose from 0.24 to 0.38. This implies that countries during period 1 were less efficient than during period 3. In period 2 (1988–1991), however, the average efficiency score dropped to 0.21. The efficiency scores for the African countries show the same pattern—a decrease in period 2 followed by a marked increase in period 3—as do countries in Asia. In Western Hemisphere countries, the average efficiency score has steadily declined over time. Similar trends are reflected in the development of the average number of more efficient countries, the average number of less efficient countries, and the average rankings.

Increases in the efficiency score over time indicate that the relative efficiency of government spending has improved, that is, that the country or region has moved closer to the production possibility frontier. This does not imply that individual countries have become more efficient in the latter time periods. As explained above, for a country to become more efficient requires constant or increasing output indicators and falling spending levels. Such an increase in efficiency can only be observed for education spending in India and Togo between periods 2 (1988–1991) and 3 (1992–1995), and for health spending in Cameroon, The Gambia, and Myanmar between periods 1 (1984–1989) and 2 (1990–1995).

Figs. 2 and 3 provide further illustration of the developments of the input efficiency scores of education and health spending over time in countries at the lowest and intermediate level of socio-economic

---

[35] The coefficient of government wages as a percent of per capita GDP is 0.7, with a t-statistic of 1.9. The adjusted R^2 of the regression is 0.10.

development in different regions.[36] The charts showing the frequency distribution of the input efficiency scores of education spending (the three panels on the left-hand side of Fig. 2) confirm that efficiency scores of the African countries tend to be relatively low, whereas those of the Asian countries are relatively high. The three charts in the right-hand side of Fig. 2 show the cumulative frequency distribution of the input efficiency scores.[37] The unevenness of the frequency distribution of input efficiency scores is reflected by the deviation from the diagonal line shown. In the first period (1984–1987), the frequency distributions for Asia and the Western Hemisphere are mostly below and to the right of the diagonal line, indicating that efficiency scores are clustered around relatively high values near 1. In the second period (1988–1991), the frequency distribution for Africa shows the opposite pattern, with a clustering of efficiency scores at relatively low levels. The frequency distributions for the Western Hemisphere and Asian countries, on the other hand, show a clustering both at relatively low and at relatively high levels, with few countries scoring intermediate values. In the third period (1992–1995), the pattern for Western Hemisphere countries moves toward the African pattern, while the distribution for Asian countries becomes more skewed toward higher efficiency scores.

Fig. 3 shows the frequency of input efficiency scores for health spending. In period 1 (1984–1989), all regions show a similar clustering of scores at relatively low and relatively high values. In the next period (1990–1995), the distribution of efficiency scores is concentrated at low levels, particularly in Africa and the Western Hemisphere.

Sensitivity of FDH Analysis

The FDH analysis results for the African countries, as presented in Tables 1 and 2, include a number of independently efficient observations. Because little can be gauged from the classification of a country as independently efficient, this limits the information from the FDH analysis. One way of decreasing the number of independently efficient results is to reduce the number of output indicators. The FDH analysis was repeated using two output indicators each for education

---

[36] The figures illustrate results of FDH analyses for separate time periods. As noted above, efficiency scores generated by such separate FDH analyses are not directly comparable across time because the production possibility frontier relative to which efficiency is measured is different for each period.

[37] The surface above the line depicting the frequency distribution reflects the average efficiency scores. For example, if the frequency distribution were along the 45° line (shown in the charts), the average efficiency score would be 0.5.

Figure 2. Education Expenditures in Countries at the Lowest and Intermediate Level of Socio-Economic Development: A Cross-Regional Comparison of Input Efficiency Scores

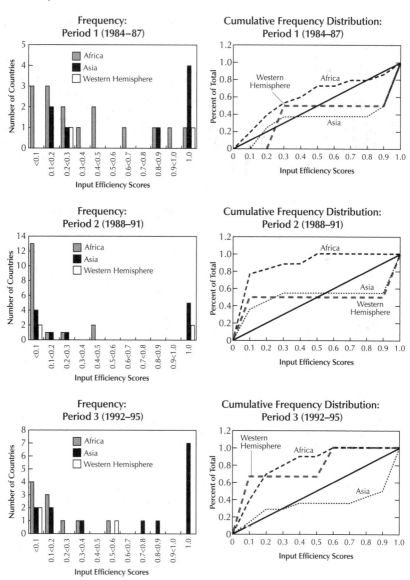

Source: Authors' calculations.
Note: Reflects the results of FDH analyses of education expenditures in countries at the lowest and intermediate levels of socio-economic development for the three periods of 1984–87, 1988–91, and 1992–95 separately. Independently efficient observations are excluded from the samples.

Figure 3. Health Expenditures in Countries at the Lowest and Intermediate Level of Socio-Economic Development: A Cross-Regional Comparison of Input Efficiency Scores

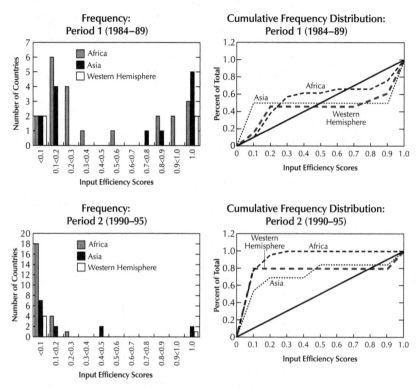

Source: Authors' calculations.
Note: Reflects the results of FDH analyses of health expenditures in countries at the lowest and intermediate levels of socio-economic development for the two periods of 1984–89 and 1990–95 separately. Independently efficient observations are excluded from the samples.

and health instead of three and four, respectively (literacy and primary enrollment were used for education, and life expectancy and infant survival for health).

In the analysis with fewer output indicators, the number of independently efficient observations is greatly reduced; the results for education spending include only three independently efficient cases, and no independently efficient cases for health spending. The results also suggest that education spending in São Tomé and Príncipe and Zambia is relatively efficient, which is not obvious from Table 1. The efficiency of education spending in Ghana, Senegal, and Togo seems lower with two output indicators than when three output indicators are used. Reducing the number of output indicators from four to two for health spending does not seem to have such a large effect on the results. Overall, this analysis shows that FDH analysis is impacted strongly by changes in the number of output indicators, underscoring the sensitivity of the FDH analysis results to variations in the dataset.

Conclusions and Policy Implications

With the help of a technique used in production theory, this paper attempts to assess the efficiency of government spending on health and education in sample countries in Africa, relative both to each other and to sample countries in Asia and the Western Hemisphere. The results are revealing. There is a wide variation in the way government spending in the African countries impacts on measurable output indicators. For instance, in comparison with other countries in Africa and countries in Asia and the Western Hemisphere, health and education spending in The Gambia, Guinea, Ethiopia, and Lesotho is associated with relatively high educational attainment and health output. This is not the case in countries such as Botswana, Cameroon, Côte d'Ivoire, and Kenya.

The results further indicate that, on average, governments in the African countries are less efficient in the provision of health and education services than the countries in Asia and the Western Hemisphere, with those in Asia appearing as most efficient. The results suggest that the inefficiencies observed in Africa are unrelated to the level of private spending, but may be the result of relatively high government wages (in the case of education spending) and the intrasectoral allocation of government resources. Furthermore, the results suggest no apparent relationship between input efficiency scores and public spending as a share of GDP.

There is some evidence that suggests that productivity of government spending on education and health in the African countries has improved since the mid-1980s, as evidenced by the outward shift of the production possibility frontier. However, in a sample that combines country observations for all time periods, the average level of efficiency in Africa since the mid-1980s has remained largely unchanged relative to countries in Asia and the Western Hemisphere.

Due to the lagged impact of government spending on some output indicators (particularly literacy and life expectancy),[38] caution needs

---

[38] In the case of investment, government spending would have an additional lagged impact on output indicators.

to be exercised in interpreting the efficiency results. In the absence of such lags, input efficiency scores would indicate the extent of expenditure reallocation that could be achieved, without affecting the level of output. In the presence of lags, the observed inefficiencies could be the result of past spending decisions. Reducing inefficiencies and government expenditures may therefore only be achieved gradually and over time.

The FDH analysis of the efficiency of government spending on education and health provides important insights not revealed by more traditional regression analysis (see Gupta, Honjo, and Verhoeven, 1997). The regression analysis shows a positive relationship (with a constant elasticity) between government spending on education and health and indicators of educational attainment and health output, respectively. This suggests that an increase in spending generates benefits in the form of improved output, independent of the level of government spending. However, the efficiency analysis shows that the degree of inefficiency increases rapidly with the level of government spending. In contrast to the regression analysis, this implies that governments should carefully consider expanding government expenditure on education and health when the initial level of spending is already high.

The above results suggest that improvements in educational attainment and health output in Africa and the Western Hemisphere are feasible by correcting inefficiencies in government spending on education and health. For instance, relatively low allocations for primary education, or relatively high allocations for curative health care, or directing most benefits of such government spending to high-income groups is symptomatic of expenditure inefficiencies.[39] This suggests that caution needs to be exercised in increasing budgetary allocations for education and health, and that proper attention should be given to improving the efficiency of existing expenditure.

---

[39] For instance, outlays on wages and salaries in Bolivia between 1980 and 1995 accounted for 95–98% of primary and secondary current expenditure compared with the Latin American average of 75%. Furthermore, budgetary allocations for curative care in Bolivia are excessive and there is a high concentration of health facilities in higher-income regions. Similarly, wages accounted for 95% of current costs in Ghana in the early 1990s. The bottom 20% of the population received 16% of the benefits of education spending in 1992. Only 11% of health spending went to the poorest 20%, and urban Ghana received 49% of the health budget, despite the fact that only 33% of the population lived in urban areas. Primary education in Togo received 41% of the 1995 education budget, even though primary school enrollment accounted for 83% of the school population.

Appendix A. Sample Countries

Africa
Lowest level of socio-economic development (21)

Burkina Faso	Malawi
Cameroon	Mali
Chad	Mozambique
Côte d'Ivoire	Niger
Ethiopia	Nigeria
Gabon	Rwanda
The Gambia	Senegal
Guinea	Tanzania
Kenya	Togo
Liberia	Zambia
Madagascar	

Intermediate level of socio-economic development (15)

Botswana	Ghana
Burundi	Guinea-Bissau
Cape Verde	Lesotho
Central African Republic	Mauritania
Republic of Congo	Namibia
Democratic Republic of Congo	São Tomé and Príncipe
(formerly Zaïre)	Swaziland
Equatorial Guinea	Zimbabwe

Highest level of socio-economic development (1)
Mauritius

Asia
Lowest level of socio-economic development (6)

Bangladesh	Nepal
Cambodia	Papua New Guinea
Lao People's Democratic Republic	Vietnam

Intermediate level of socio-economic development (16)

Bhutan	Myanmar
China	Pakistan
Fiji	Philippines
India	Solomon Islands
Indonesia	Sri Lanka
Malaysia	Thailand
Maldives	Tonga
Mongolia	Vanuatu

Highest level of socio-economic development (2)

Korea	Singapore

Western Hemisphere
Intermediate level of socio-economic development (5)

Bolivia	Honduras
Ecuador	St. Vincent and the Grenadines
Guatemala	

Highest level of socio-economic development (19)

Argentina	Guyana
The Bahamas	Mexico
Barbados	Nicaragua
Belize	Panama
Brazil	Paraguay
Chile	Peru
Colombia	St. Kitts and Nevis
Costa Rica	Uruguay
Dominican Republic	Venezuela
El Salvador	

References

Adelman, I., & Morris, C. T. (1967). *Society, politics, and economic development.* Baltimore: The Johns Hopkins Press.

Anand, S., & Ravallion, M. (1993). Human development in poor countries: on the role of private incomes and public services. *Journal of Economic Perspectives, 7* (1), 133–150 (Winter).

Aturupane, H., Glewwe, P., & Isenman, P. J. (1994). Poverty, human development and growth: an emerging consensus? Human Resources Development and Operations Policy Working Paper No. 36. Washington, DC: The World Bank, Human Resources and Operations Policy Department.

Barro, R. J. (1990). Government spending in a simple model of endogenous growth. *Journal of Political Economy, 98* Part 2, s103–s125 (October).

Barro, R. J., & Lee, J. W. (1996). International measures of schooling years and schooling quality. *American Economic Review, 86* (2), 218–223 (May).

Bauer, P. W. (1990). Recent developments in the econometric estimation of frontiers. *Journal of Econometrics, 46* (1), 39–56 (October–November).

Carrin, G., & Politi, C. (1997). Poverty and health: an overview of the basic linkages and public policy measures. Health Economics Technical Briefing Note. Washington, DC: World Bank.

Charnes, A., Cooper, W. W., & Rhodes, E. (1978). Measuring the efficiency of decision making units. *European Journal of Operational Research, 2* (6), 429–444.

Chu, K., Gupta, S., Clements, B., Hewitt, D., Lugaresi, S., Schiff, J., Schuknecht, L., & Schwartz, G. (1995). *Unproductive public expenditures: A pragmatic approach to policy analysis.* IMF Pamphlet Series No. 48. Washington, DC: International Monetary Fund.

Chu, K., & Hemming, R. (Eds.) (1991). *Public expenditure handbook: a guide to public expenditure policy issues in developing countries.* Washington, DC: International Monetary Fund.

Commander, S., Davoodi, H., & Lee, U. J. (1997). The causes and consequences of government for growth and well-being. Washington, DC: World Bank (unpublished).

Deprins, D., Simar, L., & Tulkens, H. (1984). Measuring labor-efficiency in post offices. In: M. Marchand, P. Pestieau, and H. Tulkens (Eds.), *The performance of public enterprises: concepts and measurement.* Amsterdam: North-Holland.

Fakin, B., & de Crombrugghe, A. (1997). Fiscal adjustment in transition economies: social transfers and the efficiency of public spending: a comparison with OECD countries. Policy Research Working Paper No. 1803. Washington, DC: World Bank.

Gerdtham, U., Jönsson, B., MacFarlan, M., & Oxley, H. (1995). New directions in health care policy. *OECD Health Policy Studies* (Vol. 7). Paris: Organization for Economic Cooperation and Development.

Gupta, S., Honjo, K., & Verhoeven, M. (1997). The efficiency of government expenditure: experiences from Africa. IMF Working Paper No. 97/153. Washington, DC: International Monetary Fund.

Gupta, S., Verhoeven, M., & Tiongson, E. (1999). Does higher government spending buy better results in education and health care? IMF Working Paper No. 99/21. Washington, DC: International Monetary Fund.

Harbison, R. W., & Hanushek, E. A. (1992). *Educational performance of the poor: lessons from rural northeast Brazil.* Oxford: Oxford Univ. Press.

International Labour Office (ILO). (1996). *Yearbook of Labor Statistics.* Geneva: International Labour Office.

Isenman, P. J. (1980). Basic needs: the case of Sri Lanka. *World Development,* 8 (3), 237–258 (March).

James, E. (1991). Public policies toward private education: an international comparison. *International Journal of Educational Research, 15,* 359–376.

Jimenez, E., & Lockheed, M. E. (1995). Public and private secondary education in developing countries: A comparative study. World Bank Discussion Paper No. 309. Washington, DC: World Bank.

Kakwani, N. (1993). Performance in living standards: an international comparison. *Journal of Development Economics, 41* (2), 307–336 (August).

Karras, G. (1996). The optimal government size: further international evidence on the productivity of government services. *Economic Inquiry, 34* (2), 193–203 (April).

Kraay, A., & Van Rijckeghem, C. (1995). Employment and wages in the public sector: A cross-country study. IMF Working Paper No. 95/70. Washington, DC: International Monetary Fund.

Leibenstein, H. (1966). Allocative efficiency vs. X-efficiency. *American Economic Review,* 56 (3), 392–415 (June).

Levine, R., & Renelt, D. (1992). A sensitivity analysis of cross-country growth regressions. *American Economic Review, 82* (4), 942– 963 (September).

Lewin, A. Y., & Lovell, C. A.K. (1990). Editors introduction. *Journal of Econometrics,* 46 (1), 3–5 (October–November).

Lovell, C. A. K. (1995). Measuring the macroeconomics performance of the Taiwanese economy. *International Journal of Production Economics, 39,* 165–178.

Mingat, A., & Tan, J.-P. (1998). The mechanics of progress in education: evidence from cross-country data. *Policy Research Working Paper* No. 2015. Washington, DC: World Bank.

Musgrove, P. (1996). Public and private roles in health: theory and financing patterns. World Bank Discussion Paper No. 339. Washington, DC: World Bank.

Organization for Economic Cooperation and Development. (1994). Performance management in government: performance measurement and results-oriented management. *Public Management Occasional Paper* No. 3. Paris: Organization for Economic Cooperation and Development.

Oxley, H., Maher, M., Martins, J.P., & Nicoletti, G. (1990). The public sector: issues for the 1990s. OECD Working Paper No. 90, Paris: Organization for Economic Cooperation and Development.

Psacharapoulos, G. (1994). Returns to investment in education: a global update. *World Development, 22* (9), 1325–1343 (September).

Psacharapoulos, G., & Nguyen, N. X. (1997). The role of government and the private sector in fighting poverty. World Bank Technical Paper No. 346, Washington, DC: World Bank.

Scott, G. C. (1996). *Government reform in New Zealand.* IMF Occasional Paper No. 140. Washington, DC: International Monetary Fund.

Seiford, L., & Thrall, R. M. (1990). Recent developments in DEA: the mathematical programming approach to frontier analysis. *Journal of Econometrics, 46* (1), 7–38 (October–November).

Sen, A. K. (1981). Public action and the quality of life in developing countries. *Oxford Bulletin of Economics and Statistics, 43* (4), 287–319 (November).

Tanzi, V., & Schuknecht, L. (1997). Reconsidering the fiscal role of government: the international perspective. *American Economic Review, 87* (2), 164–168 (May).

Tulkens, H. (1993). On FDH analysis: some methodological issues and applications to retail banking, courts and urban transit. *Journal of Productivity Analysis, 4,* 183–210.

Tulkens, H., & Vanden Eeckaut, P. (1995). Non-parametric efficiency, progress and regress measures for panel data: methodological aspects. *European Journal of Operational Research, 80,* 474–499.

Vanden Eeckhaut, P., Tulkens, H., & Jamar, M. A. (1993). Cost-efficiency in Belgian municipalities. In: H. Fried, C. A. Knox Lovell, and S. Schmidt (Eds.), *The Measurement of Productive Efficiency: Techniques and Applications.* New York: Oxford Univ. Press.

White, H. (1980). A heteroskedasticity-consistent covariance matrix and a direct test for heteroskedasticity. *Econometrica, 48,* 817–838 (May).

World Bank. (1997). Health, nutrition and population. Sector Strategy Paper Series. Washington, DC: World Bank.

12

Tax Policy in Developing Countries: Some Lessons from the 1990s and Some Challenges Ahead

MICHAEL KEEN AND ALEJANDRO SIMONE

One of the central challenges facing low-income and developing countries is to mobilize sufficient tax revenue to sustainably finance, when combined with whatever aid is available, the expenditures needed for growth and poverty relief—and to do so in a way that does not itself undercut those objectives by unduly worsening preexisting distortions or inequities. This chapter seeks to describe and assess the way in which developing countries were addressing these problems at the turn of the century. More particularly, it focuses on the experience of the 1990s—roughly the period since the major survey of taxation in developing countries by Burgess and Stern (1993). While experiences have naturally varied quite significantly across countries over this decade, and although 10 years is a relatively short period in the life of a tax system—indeed, that may be one of the central lessons to be drawn from the analysis in this chapter—some common themes nevertheless emerge. And some of them are troubling.

Many of the characteristics of developing countries, some of which are displayed in Tables 1 and 2 (with countries grouped by income range and region, respectively),[1] make the problem of revenue mobilization particularly difficult. Informal activities are extensive (as proxied, for instance, by the low degree of monetization in the second column),[2] tending to

---

[1] Data and definitions are discussed in the next section.

[2] The survey by Schneider and Este (2000) of empirical work on the shadow economy—which they define as legal but untaxed/unregistered activities—tends to confirm that this is substantially larger in developing countries than in developed.

imply a relatively narrow potential tax base; the agricultural sector—
hard to tax in all countries, for both practical and, in many cases,
political reasons—is large; the capacity of potential taxpayers to com-
ply with tax rules, and of the authorities to administer them, is likely to
be relatively low (as suggested by relatively high rates of illiteracy); and
corruption is often pervasive (final column). All these features constrain effective taxation. Moreover, many of them are themselves likely
to be affected by the tax system in force. Heavy taxation of the formal
sector will tend to encourage growth of the informal sector, for instance, and inappropriate tax design may provide further opportunities
for corruption. While similar concerns arise in developed countries,
they are an order of magnitude more significant in the developing
world—posing problems for tax design in these countries to which the
public finance literature has paid scant attention.

One implication of these distinctive concerns is that the link between tax policy and tax administration is especially intimate in developing countries. It has been famously claimed, indeed, that in
developing countries "tax administration *is* tax policy" (Casanegra de
Jantscher, 1990). This may be going too far[3]—any administration op-
erates within the broad confines of some policy framework, even if only
to abuse and even misrepresent it. But it is clear that the disconnect between what tax rules say and what actually happens can be especially
great in the developing world, and that this needs to be taken into account in designing tax policy. While the distinction between tax policy
and administration is particularly blurred in developing countries, it is
the broad policy design that sets the stage for implementation. And it
is this that is the focus of this paper.

Our coverage is necessarily selective. For instance, we shall not address the tax treatment of small and medium-sized enterprises—not because it is unimportant (indeed, the considerations above suggest that
the taxation of those at the margin of formality is likely to be a key issue
in many developing countries), but because it does not seem to be an
area in which the 1990s saw much change. Nor do we discuss in any detail the experiences of transition countries over the 1990s (though we
do include them in our data analysis, treating them in our regional
analyses as a separate group): these are so distinctive as to require separate treatment (for a recent study, see Summers and Baer, 2003). This
indeed is a reminder that while our focus is on broad and emerging
trends, tax design must ultimately be attuned to countries' divergent
circumstances.

---

[3]As President Clinton even more famously remarked, "it depends what you mean by
'is'." (We owe this happy remark to Joel Slemrod.)

Table 1. Economic Indicators by Income Range, Early 1990s and Early 2000s

	Nominal GDP Per Capita (U.S. dollars, average)	Money and Quasi-Money (M2)	Absolute Value Capital and Financial Account	Trade = Value of Exports and Imports of Goods and Services (Open)	Measure of Debt	Agriculture, Value Added	Illiteracy Rate, Adult Total (Percent of people aged 15 and above)	Transparency Index, Transparency International (1996)
				(Percent of GDP)				
Early 2000s								
Low-income countries	614	42.2	5.5	74.2	79.0	29.6	25.4	2.8
Lower-middle-income countries	1,642	56.5	6.6	84.4	49.7	15.4	20.6	3.6
Upper-middle-income countries	4,142	50.3	6.0	93.4	37.0	9.9	7.7	4.1
High-income countries	21,387	72.7	5.4	98.2	25.4	3.4	8.4	7.7
Unweighted average[2]								
Developing countries[3]	2,269	49.2	6.0	84.5	54.3	18.3	17.5	3.6
High-income countries	21,387	72.7	5.4	98.2	25.4	3.4	8.4	7.7
Total unweighted average	7,756	53.3	5.8	88.3	53.6	14.6	16.4	5.1
Memorandum								
PRGF-eligible countries[4]	617	36.3	7.3	80.8	81.0	29.7	29.2	2.4

Early 1990s

Low-income countries	445	32.0	6.1	54.9	103.7	31.1	32.4	2.4
Lower-middle-income countries	1,194	54.4	6.6	72.4	61.7	18.3	27.4	3.3
Upper-middle-income countries	3,747	43.0	6.7	62.6	27.8	14.4	11.2	4.4
High-income countries	18,418	62.1	4.1	80.0	6.3	4.5	11.5	7.7
Unweighted average[2]								
Developing countries[3]	1,936	42.4	6.5	62.7	61.6	21.1	23.1	3.6
High-income countries	18,418	62.1	4.1	80.0	6.3	4.5	11.5	7.7
Total unweighted average	6,667	45.8	5.8	67.5	60.1	16.7	21.8	5.6
Memorandum								
PRGF-eligible countries[5]	856	33.4	8.1	62.3	98.0	31.3	37.2	2.3

Sources: IMF, Government Finance Statistics, International Financial Statistics, and World Economic Outlook; and World Bank, World Development Indicators database.

[1]Data used for early 1990s and early 2000s are averages for two years 1990–91 and 2000–01 for most countries. For countries for which these averages could not be calculated, some flexibility in the years taken to represent the early 1990s and early 2000s was used to avoid a significant sample size reduction.

[2]For each indicator, only countries for which data are available are included in the calculation.

[3]Developing countries are defined to be low- and middle-income countries, closely following the World Bank income classification of economies.

[4]Averages were calculated for PRGF-eligible countries for which data were available (see Appendix Table A6 for details).

Table 2. Economic Indicators by Region, Early 1990s and Early 2000s

	Nominal GDP Per Capita (U.S. dollars, average)	Money and Quasi-Money (M2)	Absolute Value Capital and Financial Account	Trade = Value of Exports and Imports of Goods and Services (Open)	Measure of Debt	Agriculture, Value Added	Illiteracy Rate, Adult Total (Percent of people aged 15 and above)	Transparency Index, Transparency International (1996)
				(Percent of GDP)				
Early 2000s								
Americas[2]	3,301	38.0	6.4	63.7	51.6	12.0	11.7	3.8
Sub-Saharan Africa	765	29.2	6.7	69.7	90.5	27.9	28.9	3.0
Central Europe and BRO[3]	2,420	33.7	6.6	104.2	40.2	15.1	2.0	3.7
North Africa and Middle East	2,486	76.4	5.0	71.0	46.8	14.2	29.1	4.4
Asia and Pacific	1,447	63.1	3.8	92.6	47.1	23.7	19.7	3.1
Small islands[4]	4,673	97.6	9.7	150.7	30.4	10.9	5.4	...
Unweighted average[5]								
Developing countries[6]	2,269	49.2	6.0	84.5	54.3	18.3	17.5	3.6
High-income countries	21,387	72.7	5.4	98.2	25.4	3.4	8.4	7.7
Memorandum								
PRGF-eligible countries[7]	617	36.3	7.3	80.8	81.0	29.7	29.2	2.4

Early 1990s

Americas[2]	2,026	27.6	4.4	55.2	83.6	14.2	15.5	3.6
Sub-Saharan Africa	831	27.7	3.2	63.0	88.7	27.1	38.5	3.5
Central Europe and BRO[3]	3,470	45.0	9.8	34.3	17.2	22.4	3.1	4.6
North Africa and Middle East	1,951	70.8	8.2	68.1	68.4	17.0	39.4	3.8
Asia and Pacific	1,061	41.5	6.7	66.3	56.9	27.9	24.9	3.1
Small islands[4]	3,221	77.9	9.8	146.5	24.0	12.3	8.2	...
Unweighted average[5]								
Developing countries[6]	1,936	42.4	6.5	62.7	61.6	21.1	23.1	3.6
High-income countries	18,418	62.1	4.1	80.0	6.3	4.5	11.5	7.7
Memorandum								
PRGF-eligible countries[7o]	856	33.4	8.1	62.3	98.0	31.3	37.2	2.3

Sources: IMF, *Government Finance Statistics*, *International Financial Statistics*, and *World Economic Outlook*; and World Bank, World Development Indicators database.

[1] Data used for early 1990s and early 2000s are averages for two years 1990–91 and 2000–01 for most countries. For countries for which these averages could not be calculated, some flexibility in the years taken to represent the early 1990s and early 2000s was used to avoid a significant sample size reduction.

[2] Regional breakdown averages include only developing countries.

[3] Baltics, Russia, and other countries of the former Soviet Union.

[4] Island economies with population of under 1 million.

[5] For each indicator, only countries for which data are available are included in the calculation.

[6] Developing countries are defined to be low- and middle-income countries, closely following the World Bank income classification of economies.

[7] Averages were calculated for PRGF-eligible countries for which data were available (see Appendix Table A6 for details).

The chapter is organized as follows. The next section seeks to develop some broad stylized facts to guide further analysis, providing a broad overview of revenue structures in developing countries, both at the turn of the century and as they changed (or not) over the past decade. The remaining sections then focus on three particular issues that emerge as having been prominent in the 1990s, and, perhaps, likely to be important in the coming years: the continued move away from trade taxes, the spread of the VAT to the developing world, and the apparent erosion of corporate tax revenues. The final section concludes.

Levels and Composition of Revenue—Some Stylized Facts

Data

Any analysis of taxation in developing countries faces the fundamental problem that reliable and comparable information is scant, both on revenues and, still more, on details of tax structure. So it is appropriate to begin with a word—and a warning—about the data that we are about to use.

The account of revenue developments in this section is based on information from *Government Finance Statistics* (GFS), which, though the best source, suffers from a number of serious deficiencies. In particular, the breadth of coverage of the government sector varies across countries, and many countries provide information for some years, but not for others.[4] Here, we focus on central government revenues; this will be too narrow a definition for countries with significant revenue-raising at lower levels of government, but alternative approaches produce unusably small samples. The incompleteness and variability of coverage in the GFS is especially troublesome for the purposes of this paper, given the focus on identifying trends. In all the tables below, we take the same sample of countries throughout the period so as to minimize spurious compositional effects from a changing sample (such as finding a large apparent increase in reliance on total revenues by including a resource-rich country at the end of the 1990s, but not at the beginning).[5] The price paid for maintaining a reasonably large sample in this way is some

---

[4] There are other difficulties too. For instance, a number of countries appear to record as trade tax revenue the receipts from other taxes (notably, VAT and excises) collected at their borders.

[5] Such effects are eliminated with respect to overall and total tax revenue (since countries are included in the sample if and only if data on these are available at both start and end of the decade), but not for the various components of tax revenue (since some countries do not report a complete breakdown of their revenues).

flexibility in the years taken to represent the early 1990s and early 2000s—our (informal) sense being that biases from any consequent time-specific effects are likely to be less significant than those from country-specific ones.[6] There are, thus, many caveats to be borne in mind in interpreting the figures to which we now turn.

Where Are We Now?

The upper panel of Table 3 shows the level and composition of central government revenues (relative to GDP) at the end of the 1990s; the lower panel shows level and composition at the start. Countries here are grouped into four categories by their income level at the start of the 1990s,[7] the categorization corresponding broadly to that used by the World Bank income classification of countries. Roughly speaking, the category "high-income countries" corresponds to developed countries. Appendix Table A1 shows the same figures relative to total tax revenue, with countries again grouped by income range. Appendix Table A2 shows the same information but with countries grouped regionally,[8] with Appendix Table A3 again reexpressing the same figures relative to total tax revenue.

The snapshot picture at the end of the century is relatively straightforward and familiar. As is well known, tax ratios—sometimes referred to, for no very good reason, as "tax effort"—decrease, all else equal, with the level of GDP. Although it is not shown here, they also increase with the level of openness.[9]

In terms of structure, developing countries rely heavily on indirect taxes (about 40 percent of their tax revenue, as a rule of thumb), and derive about one-fourth of their tax revenue from income taxes (personal and corporate), one-fifth from trade taxes, and about one-sixth from payroll and social security. Property taxes are insignificant. For developed countries, indirect taxes are less important and income

---

[6] Details of the country coverage and regional grouping are provided in Appendix Table A5.

[7] Thus, a country classified as "low-income" at the start of the 1990s is included in the low-income group at the end of the 1990s even if, by the World Bank standards of the time, it would then have been classified as being "lower-middle-income." This is to avoid biases that would otherwise arise from excluding the experience of "successful" low-income countries in evaluating the performance of the group as a whole.

[8] Details of the country groups are also in Appendix Table A5.

[9] There is a large empirical literature on tax effort, to which we refrain from adding. See, for instance, Tanzi (1987) and, with a particular focus on the role of openness—the question being why it is that openness is associated with high revenues—Rodrik (1998). Some broad hint of these robust empirical findings can be seen from Tables 1 and 3.

Table 3. Central Government Revenues by Income Group, Early 1990s and Early 2000s[1]

(Percent of GDP)

	Nominal GDP per Capita (U.S. dollars, average)	Total Revenue	Tax Revenue	Other Revenue
Early 2000s				
Low-income countries	614	18.0	14.9	3.1
Lower-middle-income countries	1,642	22.0	16.0	6.1
Upper-middle-income countries	4,142	25.6	21.0	4.6
High-income countries	21,387	32.8	27.5	5.3
Unweighted average[3]				
Developing countries[4]	2,269	22.1	17.6	4.5
High-income countries[5]	21,387	32.8	27.5	5.3
Total unweighted average	7,756	25.1	20.4	4.7
Early 1990s				
Low-income countries	445	17.7	14.5	3.1
Lower-middle-income countries	1,194	21.4	16.3	5.1
Upper-middle-income countries	3,747	26.9	21.9	5.0
High-income countries	18,418	31.9	26.6	5.2
Unweighted average[3]				
Developing countries[4]	1,936	22.3	17.9	4.4
High-income countries[5]	18,418	31.9	26.6	5.2
Total unweighted average	6,667	25.0	20.4	4.6

Sources: IMF, *Government Finance Statistics, International Financial Statistics,* and *World Economic Outlook.*

[1] Data used for early 1990s and early 2000s are averages for two years—1990–91 and 2000–01 for most countries. For countries for which these averages could not be calculated, some flexibility in the years taken to represent the early 1990s and early 2000s was used to avoid a significant sample size reduction.

[2] European Union countries do not report statistics on international trade taxes to *Government Finance Statistics.*

[3] For each revenue classification, only countries for which data are available are included in the calculation.

[4] Developing countries are defined to be low- and middle income countries, closely following the World Bank income classification of economies.

[5] See Table A5 for details.

| Taxes on Income, Profits, and Capital Gains | | | Social Security Taxes | Payroll Taxes | Domestic Taxes on Goods and Services | | | International Trade Taxes[2] | | | Property Taxes |
| | of which: | | | | | of which: | | | of which: | | |
Total	Individual	Corporate			Total	General sales, turnover, or VAT	Excises	Total	Import duties	Export duties	
3.9	1.9	2.0	1.0	0.0	5.9	3.5	2.0	3.7	2.4	0.2	0.2
3.9	1.8	2.2	1.3	0.1	6.4	4.9	2.1	3.6	3.5	0.1	0.3
5.3	2.6	2.6	4.5	0.1	8.2	5.3	2.4	2.5	2.4	0.2	0.3
8.9	7.4	2.5	7.3	0.3	9.1	6.7	2.8	1.3	1.3	0.0	0.7
4.4	2.1	2.3	2.5	0.1	6.9	4.5	2.2	3.2	2.7	0.2	0.3
8.9	7.4	2.5	7.3	0.3	9.1	6.7	2.8	1.3	1.3	0.0	0.7
5.7	3.7	2.3	3.9	0.1	7.5	5.1	2.3	2.9	2.5	0.2	0.4
3.8	1.3	2.6	0.7	0.0	5.3	2.8	2.1	4.3	3.8	0.6	0.3
4.3	1.5	2.9	1.4	0.2	5.0	2.9	2.0	4.4	4.1	0.2	0.4
5.9	2.2	3.3	4.3	0.2	6.5	3.7	2.4	4.3	3.9	0.6	0.3
8.5	7.6	1.9	7.2	0.3	8.6	6.3	2.4	1.9	2.0	0.0	0.7
4.7	1.7	2.9	2.3	0.1	5.7	3.2	2.2	4.3	3.9	0.5	0.3
8.5	7.6	1.9	7.2	0.3	8.6	6.3	2.4	1.9	2.0	0.0	0.7
5.8	3.5	2.6	3.7	0.2	6.5	4.0	2.3	3.9	3.6	0.4	0.4

taxes more important (each about one-third of total tax revenue); social security and payroll is far more important (rather less than one-third), trade taxes are much less important; and property taxes, though more important than in developing countries, make only a very modest contribution.

What Happened in the 1990s?

This chapter is less concerned with the snapshot just given, however, than with developments over the 1990s. Consider first the experience of developing countries as a whole.

In terms of overall revenue performance—total revenues and total tax revenues relative to GDP—the story is of the dog that didn't bark. This was a period in which the general objective of (or at least conventional advice to) many low-income countries was to increase their tax collections in order to finance growth-enhancing and poverty-reducing expenditures. There were exceptions, of course: Kenya, for example, has deliberately sought to encourage development by reducing its tax ratio. And certainly the efficiency and growth-friendliness of a tax system can be enhanced without necessarily increasing revenue (by, for instance, shifting away from more distortionary taxes (such as those on trade) to less (perhaps a clean VAT). Nevertheless, it is striking that there was no general increase in tax ratios for developing countries as a whole: indeed, the average tax ratio for these countries fell slightly, though the safer characterization is one of stagnation.

There are, however, some clear general changes in the composition of tax revenues. One is a shift away from trade taxes and (to a lesser extent) toward indirect taxation, especially general sales taxes (of which the VAT is the leading but not the only type). This would no doubt have been widely predicted at the start of the 1990s as a continuation of the process of trade liberalization. Even more intriguing, however, is the reduction in revenues from the corporate income tax—these fell, for developing countries as a whole, by about one-fifth. Here the contrast with the developed countries in the sample is especially marked: despite widespread concern at the erosion of corporate taxes as a result of intensified international tax competition, developed countries actually experienced an increase in corporate tax revenues both relative to GDP and as a share of total tax revenue.

This overall picture masks, however, rather different experiences at different levels of development and in different regions. The tax ratio in the poorest countries was essentially stagnant: the average increased by 0.4 point of GDP, but this is both small and largely owing to an outstanding measured increase in Estonia, a single country in unusual economic (and statistical) circumstances.[10] In the two poorest regions (sub-Saharan Africa and Asia-Pacific), and in our sample of PRGF-eligible countries, the picture is again one of stagnation, but with tax ratios, if anything, falling (see Appendix Table A2). The effects in some countries were quite marked: in Côte d'Ivoire, for example, tax revenue fell by about 3 percentage points,[11] and in Sri Lanka it fell by about 5 percentage points (with total revenue also falling in both cases, so that this does not simply reflect an offset to increased nontax revenues). Experience has thus been very variable among the poorest countries—but with no very clear overall tendency to enhanced domestic revenue collection. It is also in these poorest countries that some of the compositional changes mentioned above (the shift away from trade and toward indirect taxes) are least marked. It is also noticeable, however, that these countries did experience a significant loss of corporate tax revenues: relative to GDP, they fell by about one-fourth.

In contrast, while tax ratios changed relatively little among lower-middle-income countries, they tended, if anything, to fall. This masks a striking compositional change. In these countries, a spectacular increase in indirect tax revenues (by about 25 percent)—especially from sales taxes—more than offset a marked reduction in revenue from trade taxes. Revenue from the personal income tax (PIT) also tended to rise. Yet total tax revenues fell as a result of reduced revenue from the corporate income tax. The experience in upper-middle-income countries—such as Brazil—was broadly the same, except that there the reductions in trade taxes were matched by increases in indirect taxes (increasing revenue presumably being less of a concern in these countries).

One other potentially significant source of revenue should also be considered, though it is not recorded in the standard statistics used above. This is seignorage: the command over resources that governments enjoy by virtue of their ability to issue base money. Table 4 shows that this was indeed an important source of revenue for developing countries in the early 1990s: about 4 percent of GDP, or 22 percent of (seignorage-exclusive) tax revenue. By the end of the decade, the widespread reduction in inflation rates was associated with a reduction in seignorage of more than one-third.[12] This fall is large enough to produce a significant overall reduction in revenues in developing countries. There are certainly considerable macroeconomic benefits from this reduction in inflation rates. But the important point here is that

---

[10]The tax ratio in Estonia increased by about 5 percentage points of GDP between 1990–01 and 2000–01, but the accuracy of the figure for the start of the decade is questionable.

[11]The sample period predates the current troubles in Côte d'Ivoire.

[12]For completeness, Appendix Table A4 shows the same data by region.

Table 4. Seignorage as a Share of GDP by Income Group, Early 1990s and Early 2000s[1]

	Nominal GDP per Capita (U.S. dollars, average)	Seignorage (Percent of GDP)
Early 2000s		
Low-income countries	614	3.0
Lower-middle-income countries	1,642	2.0
Upper-middle-income countries	4,142	2.2
High-income countries	21,387	1.7
Unweighted average[2]		
Developing countries[3]	2,269	2.4
High-income countries[4]	21,387	1.7
Total unweighted average	7,756	2.3
Early 1990s		
Low-income countries	445	4.4
Lower-middle-income countries	1,194	3.7
Upper-middle-income countries	3,747	3.9
High-income countries	18,418	1.4
Unweighted average[2]		
Developing countries[3]	1,936	4.0
High-income countries[4]	18,418	1.4
Total unweighted average	6,667	3.5

Sources: IMF, *Government Finance Statistics, International Financial Statistics, World Economic Outlook;* and staff calculations.

[1]Data used for early 1990s and early 2000s are average for two years—1991–92 and 2000–01 for most countries. For countries for which these averages could not be calculated, some flexibility in the years taken to represent the early 1990s and early 2000s was used to avoid a significant sample size reduction. Seignorage is calculated as the money growth rate multiplied by money stock (M1) divided by nominal GDP. The hyperinflation episodes of Brazil and Nicaragua in the early 1990s are ignored, and replaced by estimates from normal times.

[2]For each region, only countries for which data are available are included in the calculation.

[3]Developing countries are defined to be low- and middle-income countries, closely following the World Bank income classification of economies.

[4]Comparable measures of M1 were not available for most European countries.

seignorage can be seen as a tax like any other, in that it creates inefficiencies and inequities to be weighed against the revenue it yields—and, whatever the efficiency gains, that revenue has fallen noticeably over the past decade.

Summing up, experiences differ greatly when one looks behind the group averages to the experience of individual countries. Nevertheless, four general conclusions seem to characterize the experience of developing countries in the 1990s:

- revenue has been essentially stagnant, at best, in the poorest countries and regions of the developing world—taking seignorage into account, it has generally fallen;

- revenues from general sales taxes (in practice often meaning the VAT) have increased markedly, albeit less in the poorest countries and regions than elsewhere;

- trade tax revenues have fallen significantly, though least in the poorest countries; and

- corporate tax revenues have declined, except in the Americas (where, especially given the relatively high average level of income, receipts from this source have long been noticeably low) and in small island economies (perhaps reflecting to some extent tax haven activities).[13]

We do not attempt a full explanation of the first of these observations, which would need to be rooted in the diversity of country experiences. Instead, the rest of the chapter considers in more detail the last three of these developments, which are likely to prove important in future tax design—and which may also hold some clues for explaining, and starting to escape, the stagnancy of total revenues.

The Spread of the VAT

The most significant change in the tax structure of the typical developing country during the 1990s has been the adoption, under a variety of names, of the VAT.[14] Having swept through Latin America and Western Europe from the late 1960s, the tax made remarkable inroads into the developing world over the past decade. In 1990, about 30 percent of developing countries in our sample had a VAT; by the end of the century, this figure had risen to about 75 percent. More detail on the rise of the VAT in the developing world is shown in Table 5. Among both low-income and lower-middle-income countries, the number of countries with a VAT more than doubled. To some extent, this reflects the unusual experience of the CIS countries, almost all of which adopted the VAT very quickly at independence. But there is much

---

[13] Six of the eight small island economies in our sample were included in the OECD's descriptive list of tax havens.

[14] The essence of the VAT is that, in principle (from which practice often departs in important ways), tax is charged on all sales (including imports, but excluding exports), whether to consumers or producers, but producers are effectively refunded (whether explicitly or by way of a credit against the tax due on their own sales) taxes charged on their inputs. The tax thus becomes one on final domestic consumption.

Table 5. Number of Countries with VAT, by Region and Income[1]

	By Region						
	Americas[2]	Sub-Saharan Africa	Central Europe and BRO[3]	North Africa and Middle East	Asia and Pacific	Small Islands[4]	Total Number of Developing Countries with VAT in Sample
Early 2000s	16	9	14	5	11	2	57
Early 1990s	13	2	1	3	4	0	23

	By Income[1]			
	Low-Income	Lower-Middle-Income	Upper-Middle-Income	High-Income
Early 2000s	17	17	23	26
Early 1990s	7	6	10	18

Sources: International Bureau of Fiscal Documentation, 2003, and PricewaterhouseCoopers, *Corporate Taxes 2003–04, Worldwide Summaries.*
[1] Developing countries are defined to be low- and middle-income countries, closely following the World Bank income classification of economies.
[2] Regional breakdown averages include only developing countries.
[3] Baltics, Russia, and other countries of the former Soviet Union.
[4] Island economies with population of under 1 million.

more to it than that. In sub-Saharan Africa, in particular, the number of countries with a VAT increased from two to nine; by the end of the 1990s, only 40 percent of the sub-Saharan African countries in our sample for the region did not have a VAT. These figures somewhat overdramatize the effective change: many pre-VAT sales tax systems had VAT-like features (for instance, some limited degree of crediting, perhaps among a "ring" of firms), and all VATs fall short, in practice, of the textbook ideal (perhaps excluding the retail stage, or providing only imperfect credits for purchases of capital goods). Nevertheless, the structural change is clearly profound.

This remarkable spread of the VAT to the developing world has been little studied—indeed, the same is true of its spread in the developed world. Little is known, for instance, of the political economy behind the adoption of what is often an extremely unpopular tax—though there is some evidence[15] that, apart from possible efficiency gains (discussed below), an important role has been played both by regional demonstration effects (whether as mere fashion, or the consequence of yardstick competition as influential groups observe the functioning of

---

[15] See Keen and Lockwood (2003).

VATs nearby), and by participation in IMF programs (which may, in turn, proxy a deeper fiscal malaise).

Much better understood are the arguments of principle deployed by the advocates and critics of the VAT. Broadly speaking, the principal merits claimed for the VAT are the prospect of securing revenue—as a consequence of tax being levied on all transactions—more securely than do retail sales taxes (under which all tax is lost if there is evasion at the final stage) and without the distortion of production decisions and non-transparency associated with cascading turnover taxes. Critics, on the other hand, have argued that the VAT imposes unreasonable bookkeeping requirements on small traders, tends to have adverse distributional effects, and—a concern heard increasingly loudly—is, by virtue of its allowing for substantial tax refunds, worryingly vulnerable to fraud.

This is not the place to enter the detail of these debates, which are discussed at length in Ebrill and others (2001) and, with a more skeptical view of the VAT, by Stiglitz (2003). It should be noted, however, that the important question is whether the concerns of critics can be adequately addressed by proper design of the VAT rather than by its wholesale rejection in favor of some (often unspecified) alternative. In some respects, the design issues raised by critics of the VAT are relatively straightforward to address. For example, small traders can be kept out of the VAT system with relatively little loss of revenue—given the apparently ubiquitous concentration of potential tax base among a relatively small number of traders—by setting a reasonably high threshold, though the distortions that this in itself creates by placing small traders at a tax advantage further complicates the design issue (Keen and Mintz, 2004). Other trade-offs are more difficult.

In particular, as noted by Ebrill and others (2001) and stressed by Stiglitz (2003), the limited effectiveness of personal income taxes in developing countries implies a stronger case for differentiating rates of indirect taxation across commodities in developing than in developed countries. At the same time, however, the administrative and compliance problems associated with differential rates of VAT—including the increased likelihood that traders will become entitled to refunds (using highly taxed inputs to produce lightly taxed outputs)—points in exactly the opposite direction, toward a stronger case for a single VAT rate in developing countries than in developed. It may also be that the governance weaknesses of developing countries make them more vulnerable to lobbying for reduced rates against which adherence to a single rate provides some protection.[16] And, indeed, a feature of the VATs

---

[16] See, for instance, Panagariya and Rodrik (1993).

adopted by developing countries over the past decade is that they had, by and large, a single positive rate.[17] While that suggests that the administrative and compliance arguments have, in practice, won the day, the degree of differentiation in indirect tax rates is far greater in developing countries than the appearance of a single rate VAT might imply. Considerable differentiation is, in practice, generally achieved by the exemption of basic commodities under the VAT,[18] a compromise between setting a differentially low statutory rate and the collection difficulties that would create. Moreover, excise taxes on particular commodities directly introduce some differentiation, often to a larger extent—by imposing such taxes on a wider range of items—than is common in developed countries.

Whether the VAT has reduced or increased the progressivity of the overall tax systems in developing countries is ultimately an empirical question (and one that encounters the wide range of conceptual issues associated with any such question of incidence).[19] A number of studies, including Younger and Sahn (1998) and the analysis for Ethiopia by Muñoz and Cho (2004), conclude that the impact of the VAT is often moderately progressive, and sometimes more so than the taxes it replaces.

Other aspects of the spread of the VAT are even harder to quantify. While there is some evidence on the administration and compliance costs of the VAT in developed countries, for instance (such as Cnossen, 1994), there is almost no hard empirical evidence on this or on the costs associated with alternative taxes in developing countries. Moreover, while such collection costs are fairly straightforward to measure,[20] the main administrative argument for the VAT is so fundamental as to defy precise definition or measurement. For, caricaturing somewhat, the (often unspoken) response to the complaint that developing countries find the VAT hard to implement is "good, they are supposed to." This is because adoption of the VAT is often intended to spearhead a fundamental change in how taxes are collected, in particular by introducing

---

[17]See Table 7.2 of Ebrill and others (2001).

[18]"Exemption" means that tax is not charged on sales but (in contrast to zero-rating) tax paid on inputs is irrecoverable.

[19]Concerning, for instance, the extent to which indirect tax increases are passed on to consumers through higher prices rather than borne by profits or payments to labor; whether progressivity is better assessed relative to consumption rather than income (on the grounds that the former is a better indicator of lifetime welfare); and what the appropriate counterfactual is in assessing the impact of the VAT. These and other issues in assessing the distributional impact of the VAT are discussed in Chapter 10 of Ebrill and others (2001).

[20]There are real difficulties (for instance, in the treatment of costs shared between implementation of the VAT and other taxes), but of an order commonplace in empirical work.

methods of self-assessment—that is, self-declaration of liability by the taxpayer supplemented by risk-based audits—that can then be applied to other taxes. In particular, the income tax might in this way be transformed into something more than a glorified withholding tax on employees of the public sector and large enterprises. Tax collection thus moves away from the face-to-face contact that is so conducive to bribery and extortion. More generally, the VAT can serve as a catalyst for broader changes in the way countries conduct their tax business, for instance, with a move away from tax-based organizational structures to functional- (or taxpayer-segment-) based ones. This perspective can change the way one thinks about the VAT. Rather than a distraction from strengthening the income tax, for example, the VAT becomes a strategy for its ultimate improvement. While there are relatively few signs of such strengthening happening yet, moving to this second stage of reform has always been seen as a task for years rather than months. Whether this strategy for wider tax reform—and, indeed, for governance reform more broadly—succeeds or not may in time be the most important question to be asked about the spread of the VAT to the developing world.

In the meantime, there are some simpler empirical questions that can and should be addressed. The most basic of these is whether the VAT has, in fact, delivered the efficiency gains claimed by its advocates. It is a telling observation that only a handful of countries have ever removed a VAT, and of these only one—Grenada—appears adamantly opposed to its reintroduction in any guise. Revealed preference thus suggests that adoption of the VAT has, at the least, not been widely perceived as a serious mistake.

A more systematic approach to this issue is developed by Ebrill and others (2001) and Keen and Lockwood (2003). This is to exploit the prediction of theory that if adoption of the VAT reduces the marginal social cost of raising tax revenue (this cost taking into account both efficiency and distributional effects), then—assuming, as is commonly supposed, that the income elasticity of public expenditure exceeds unity—countries with a VAT should have a higher ratio of total tax revenue to GDP, all else equal, than do countries without. Empirically, this boils down to including in a standard "tax effort" regression—relating the tax ratio to GDP per capita, openness, and other usual suspects—a dummy representing the presence or absence of a VAT.[21]

---

[21] The purpose of this exercise is not, it should be stressed, to judge the VAT by whether it increased revenue (even if revenue is increased, national welfare could fall because the additional revenue is spent in a corrupt or wasteful manner), but rather to use any increase in revenue to infer an increase in the efficiency of the overall tax system.

The broad empirical conclusions are the same for both the cross-section analysis in Ebrill and others (2001) and (though less marked) the panel data used by Keen and Lockwood (2003). Broadly speaking, the revenue gain associated with a VAT increases with the level of real income and decreases with the level of openness (the former effect, perhaps, proxying the lesser importance of hard-to-tax sectors, such as agriculture, in more developed economies; the latter perhaps reflecting the ease of raising trade taxes, an alternative source of revenue).

The results leave open the possibility that in very open developing countries, adoption of the VAT may actually have been associated with a reduction in overall revenues, implying—given the maintained assumption on the demand for public expenditure—that adoption increased rather than reduced the marginal social cost of public funds. In principle, it is possible to make this calculation for any particular country. In practice, however, the coefficients are not well enough determined to do so with great confidence. What these results do suggest, however, is that it is not as easy for poor and open economies to show clear efficiency gains from the VAT as its advocates might have hoped.

For reasons touched on above, thinking of the VAT as an all-or-nothing matter—while a reasonable (and, in practice, inescapable) simplification for statistical analysis—is not a good basis for policymaking. Indeed, experience in developing countries has demonstrated the need to think of a VAT as work in progress. Many countries still struggle, in particular, to find an appropriate balance between providing speedy refunds to exporters—essential if the tax is not to function in part as a de facto export tax—and ensuring adequate protection against fraud (Ebrill and others, 2001). This, in turn, is but the most obvious example of the more general control problem implied by the observation that ". . . a supplier's invoice (or export certificate) in effect constitutes a check drawn on government [and so] constitutes a tempting target for those who would loot the treasury" (Bird, 1993).

Policy and administrative improvements for the VAT are closely aligned. In policy terms, for instance, exemptions are anathema to the logic of the VAT—in a way that multiple rates of VAT, in particular, are not—since they imply a potential for production inefficiencies. Yet removing those exemptions would amplify the control difficulties. In pure policy terms too, understanding of what can be achieved under the VAT continues to improve. More has been learned, for instance, of how financial services can be brought properly into the tax net (though whether one wants to is a different issue),[22] and how the VAT might be

---

[22] This issue is surveyed in Boadway and Keen (2003).

made to function as a lower-level tax within a federal system.[23] In developed countries, such structural improvements are likely to dominate the VAT agenda in the coming years; in the developing world, in contrast, the primary tasks continue to be unwinding inappropriate exemptions and ensuring proper functioning of the refund and credit mechanisms—a key part of the wider reform of ways of doing tax business that, as mentioned above, was a primary motive for its introduction.

Shifting Away from Trade Taxes

The 1990s saw a continuation in the shift away from trade taxes as a source of revenue in developing countries. But the shift was particularly modest in the poorest of countries. In sub-Saharan Africa, most noticeably, there was effectively no change in the reliance on trade taxes, which continued to account for about one-third of all tax revenues. In all other regions, the decline was marked. This decline in reliance on trade tax revenues seems to have been the product of deliberate trade liberalization policies. Table 6 shows that collected rates of trade taxation—the ratio of tariff and export tax revenue to the value of imports plus exports[24]—fell in all income groups and regions, though least in sub-Saharan Africa, North Africa, and the Middle East. While openness increased over the 1990s, as can be seen from Table 1—perhaps partly in response to these and other measures of trade liberalization—it did not do so by enough to actually increase revenues.

Despite the setback to the Doha Round, it seems likely that trade liberalization will continue in the years ahead. This raises important challenges for tax policy. Trade liberalization does not, of course, always reduce revenue from trade taxes. The reduction of tariffs set, for protective purposes, above revenue-maximizing levels, the tariffication of quotas, elimination of exemptions, reduction of tariff peaks, and improvement of customs procedures can all liberalize trade—in the sense of reducing policy-induced distortions to trade flows—while actually increasing revenues. The point is argued forcefully, and shown to be more than a theoretical nicety, by Ebrill, Stotsky, and Gropp (1999). But fully free trade means no trade-related taxes. Thus, there must come a point at which further liberalization does reduce revenue from trade taxes. Whether that point has been met can only be answered on

---

[23] See, for instance, the symposium on this issue in *International Tax and Public Finance*, December 2000.

[24] Export taxes are still important in a few cases (such as forestry exports from West Africa), though, as Table 3 and Appendix Tables A1–A3 show, these have been far less significant than import tariffs throughout this period.

Table 6. Effective Rate of Trade Taxation, Early 2000s and Early 1990s[1]
(Percent of GDP unless noted otherwise)

	Early 2000s	Early 1990s
Low-income countries	5.6	8.1
Lower-middle-income countries	4.5	5.9
Upper-middle-income countries	2.6	5.4
High-income countries	1.3	3.1
Unweighted average		
Developing countries[2]	4.2	6.5
High-income countries	1.3	3.1
Region		
Americas	2.8	4.9
Sub-Saharan Africa	8.1	9.0
Central Europe and BRO[3]	1.4	4.7
North Africa and Middle East	3.3	5.9
Asia and Pacific	2.7	6.3
Small islands	6.9	10.1
Unweighted average		
Developing countries[2]	4.2	6.5
High-income countries	1.3	3.1

Sources: IMF, *Government Finance Statistics, International Financial Statistics, World Economic Outlook;* and World Bank, World Development Indicators database.

[1]Trade tax revenue divided by the value of exports plus imports.

[2]Developing countries are defined to be low- and middle-income countries, closely following the World Bank income classification of economies.

[3]Baltics, Russia, and other countries of the former Soviet Union.

a country-specific basis.[25] Nevertheless, the evidence cited above suggests that in many developing countries it has.

One kind of trade reform that is becoming increasingly important in developing countries, though not necessarily one to be welcomed as liberalizing trade,[26] is the entry into bilateral and regional integration agreements. Many such agreements have already been entered into, but with effects phased in over the coming years (and the most revenue-costly measures back-loaded). This is the case, for instance, with the series of

---

[25]Ebrill, Stotsky, and Gropp (1999) report regressions of trade tax revenue against (inter alia) the collected tariff that imply that revenue is maximized (for their full sample of countries) at a little over 20 percent. Khattry and Rao (2002) arrive at the higher figure of 40 percent. As these authors recognize, however, the collected tariff is such an amalgam of distinct policy instruments (reflecting exemptions, rate structures, and administrative effectiveness), that these figures—even leaving aside some nonrobustness—should be taken as only very broadly suggestive of the likely impact of further tariff reductions.

[26]In particular, such selective tariff reductions can lead to inefficient trade diversion, with imports being sourced from countries charging higher prices before tariff but lower prices inclusive of the tariff; moreover, the formation of trading blocs may impede rather than facilitate multilateral liberalization. For a taste of the issues, see the symposium on this topic in the July 1998 issue of the *Economic Journal.*

association agreements reached between the European Union and countries of North Africa and the Middle East. The formation of regional customs unions among developing countries (such as the East African Community (EAC) of Kenya, Uganda, and Tanzania) can also have significant revenue effects even when trade between the participating countries is limited; the loss of revenue from the removal of internal tariffs may be modest, but that from the agreed common external tariff (affecting revenue derived from third-country imports) may be more substantial.[27]

The loss of revenue from trade taxes raises an obvious and critical question for tax policy: how is it to be recovered? While some countries may be prepared to absorb this loss as a permanent reduction in the size of government, the need for revenue in developing countries, especially the poorest of them, makes the issue a real one. Indeed, without a coherent strategy to compensate for this revenue loss, the process of trade liberalization in developing countries—widely, if not quite universally, seen as key to enhancing their growth prospects, and, in any event, likely to be the quid pro quo for the reduction of protection in the developed world that they need even more urgently—may be jeopardized.

In principle, recovering revenue from alternative sources should not be difficult. One conceptually simple strategy is to match tariff reductions by exactly offsetting increases in taxes on domestic consumption. This preserves the gain in production efficiency from the closer alignment of prices faced by producers to world prices as a consequence of the tariff reduction; leaves prices faced by consumers unchanged so that the combined reform has no effect on their welfare; and increases the government's total revenue, since this is now collected not only on imports but also on the wider base of domestic consumption. This increase in public revenues could, in turn, be used to compensate those producer groups that lose as a consequence of the tariff reduction, and/or to reduce consumption taxes, and so ensure that consumers also end up strictly better off as a consequence of the reform. For a small, competitive economy importing only final goods, this simple strategy thus has extremely attractive welfare properties.[28]

Matters are less straightforward when, for instance, the importation of intermediate goods or the exercise of domestic market power—both important features in developing countries—are recognized. Nevertheless, the basic consequence of effective trade liberalization is an increase in the value of national output at world prices and, hence, an increase in the potential tax base. In that sense, successful trade reform itself creates

---

[27]Indeed, low-tariff countries entering a customs union may find that their trade tax revenue increases, as seems likely for Uganda in the case of the EAC.

[28]The arguments in this paragraph are spelled out and explored further in Keen and Ligthart (2001).

additional resources from which it should be possible to more than re-cover any reduction in revenue from trade taxes. Moreover, it seems clear that there is a potentially important role here for indirect taxation, both general sales and excise taxes, in doing this. These instruments have both the theoretical attractions just described and the practical advantage that they are largely collected at the border—it is not uncommon for more than half of all VAT revenue to be collected at the border[29]—and so can be enforced by exactly the same machinery that is used to collect trade tax revenues. So far as borders provide an attractive tax handle, this can be applied to indirect taxes as well as to customs revenues.

The theory is straightforward. What about practice? Have countries in fact managed to recover reductions in trade tax revenues from other sources? The figures in Table 3 show that, on average, all income groups among the developing countries indeed managed to raise indirect tax revenue by about as much as trade tax revenue fell—but, as seen in the earlier section on levels and composition of revenue, many ended up with reduced total revenue because of a decline in corporate tax receipts.

It is important, however, to look behind these group averages, which may reflect the exceptional performance in a few countries or the im-pact on the level and composition of revenues of other developments (such as a growth in real incomes) over the decade. Analysis of panel data paints a gloomy picture. Using panel data for 125 countries for the period 1975–2000 (corrected to some degree for the tendency, men-tioned earlier, of some developing countries to record as trade taxes other taxes), Baunsgaard and Keen (2003) find that while developed countries rarely had difficulty recovering lost trade tax revenues, devel-oping countries did.[30] Dividing the latter into two groups, they find that for each US$1 of trade tax revenue forgone, the better-off developing countries tended to recover, eventually, about 40 cents. For the less well-off, however, the recovery tended to be effectively zero.

There is significant cause for concern in these results. It seems that developing countries, especially the poorest and those in Africa, have not found it easy to deal with the revenue consequences of past trade liberal-ization. This is not to say that they have been harmed by such liberaliza-tion, since there are potential efficiency and growth gains to offset any revenue loss. It does suggest, however, that from the fiscal perspective more attention needs to be paid to the sequencing of trade reform and the strengthening of the domestic tax system. Here, for the reasons described above, improving the design and administration of indirect taxes is likely to be particularly important. Jordan, for instance, managed a significant

---

[29]See Table 4.3 of Ebrill and others (2001).

[30]For a smaller sample of countries, using uncorrected data and focusing on simple cross-tabulations, Khattry and Rao (2002) reach broadly similar conclusions.

switch away from trade taxes (about 4 percentage points of GDP) and toward indirect tax revenues during the 1990s, while maintaining overall tax revenue broadly constant; in Egypt, on the other hand, the overall tax ratio has for the past 20 years or so tracked a decline in trade taxes—except for one episode of reform in the early 1990s (when it moved its sales tax significantly in the direction of a VAT). But the issue is not simply one of introducing a VAT: statistically, Baunsgaard and Keen (2003) find that the presence of a VAT makes only a slight difference (if any) to the ease with which countries adjust to the loss of trade tax revenue. This may well reflect the heterogeneity of VATs stressed earlier, and there is, no doubt, more to be learned by studying the experiences of individual countries. What does seem clear, however, is that many developing countries have reached a point at which further trade liberalization would likely have significant revenue consequences, and that the domestic tax system needs to do a better job of coping with this than, in too many cases, it has done in the past.

Decline of the Corporate Income Tax

One of the most striking conclusions to emerge from the overview in the second section was the sharp contrast in the performance of corporate tax revenues in developed and developing countries: in the former, these rose noticeably, both relative to GDP and as a share of total tax revenues, while in the latter, they fell in both senses (Tables 3 and A1). In regional terms, the decline was most marked in the countries of central and eastern Europe, but it was also evident in sub-Saharan Africa and Asia-Pacific (whereas the share of corporate tax revenues rose in the Americas and among small islands) (Tables A1 and A2).

The development of corporate tax revenues in the developed world, especially in the OECD, has received much attention in recent years, reflecting the concern, which began to emerge in the latter 1980s, that increased ease of capital movements would intensify international tax competition to such an extent that revenue from capital income taxation—of which corporate tax is a prominent (and relatively easily measured[31]) component—would be reduced. A comprehensive review of the OECD experience is provided, for example, by Devereux,

---

[31]The main difficulty is that imputation forms of corporate tax (which alleviate the double taxation of dividends by providing credit at a personal level with respect to taxes paid at the corporate level) in effect record as corporate tax receipts what are more accurately shareholder-level taxes on dividends. This is unlikely to be a serious concern for the analysis here, since most countries retained the same system throughout this period (the move away from integration in many developed economies—including the United Kingdom, Germany, Ireland, and Italy—generally being more recent than our data).

Figure 1. **Average Statutory Corporate Rates, 1990–2002**
(Percent)

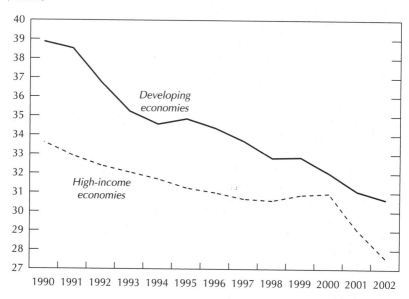

Source: World Tax Database (Ann Arbor, Michigan: University of Michigan).

Griffith, and Klemm (2002). Figure 1 shows that statutory rates of corporation tax in developed economies have fallen substantially over this period, a trend that shows no sign of stopping. There is, moreover, increasing evidence (beyond the anecdotal, which abounds) that these developments have reflected not merely fashion but strategic interaction in tax-setting: that is, international tax competition (see, for instance, Besley, Griffith, and Klemm, 2001). As statutory rates have fallen, however, corporate tax revenues in the OECD have, broadly speaking, held up—or, at least, not declined precipitately. Thus, the reduction in statutory rates has generally been offset by an expansion of the tax base, with the latter, in turn, seen as reflecting a range of base-broadening measures (limiting depreciation and other allowances against corporation tax). From the 1984 U.K. reform through to the German tax reform of 2001, the archetypal corporate tax reform in developed countries has been one of rate reduction accompanied by base broadening. This has posed the theoretical challenge of explaining why international tax competition might take the form of a simultaneous reduction in statutory reduction and expansion of the base, one argument being that this is a way to attract highly mobile paper transactions—using transfer pricing and financial structuring—while continuing to extract surplus from relatively immobile domestic investments (Devereux, Griffith, and Klemm, 2001).

Figure 1 also shows that, as in the developed world, developing countries saw quite marked reductions in statutory rates of corporation tax in the 1990s. Tables 7 and 8 provide more information on developments in corporate taxation over this period (the former by income group, the latter by region). The reduction in statutory rates of corporation tax is typically greatest in the better-off developing countries (about 8 points, or one-fourth of the initial level), and quite moderate in the poorest developing countries (about 4 percentage points, or one-tenth of the initial level). Figure 2 shows that average statutory rates have fallen in all regions of the developing world, with especially noticeable reductions in sub-Saharan Africa and in North Africa and the Middle East. The downward pressure on statutory tax rates, much remarked on in the developed world, has thus been just as marked—perhaps more so—in the developing world. The dispersion of statutory tax rates[32] has also fallen within all regions. Interestingly, while the dispersion of rates within regions has fallen within regions, it has not fallen across them (as can be seen from Figure 1). This dispersion, combined with both still-high statutory taxation and the prospect of continued reductions in developing countries, suggests that the process of rate reduction in the developing world is likely to continue.

This reduction in statutory rates in developing countries—which has been little noted in the literature—partly accounts for the reduced revenue yield of corporate tax in developing countries. This could, in principle, have been offset to some degree by expansion of the base, whether due to supply-side effects or to policy measures to limit allowances. But, in fact—and in complete contrast to developed countries—Table 7 shows that the exact opposite has happened: the corporate tax base, which increased in the developed world (by enough, as we have already seen, to more than offset rate reductions), has fallen, and noticeably so, in developing countries. The regional breakdown in Table 8 shows that much of the action here comes from central and eastern Europe, where, under circumstances that were clearly exceptional (at least in the first half of the decade or so), the corporate tax base fell by more than 50 percent. In the Americas and in North Africa and the Middle East, the corporate tax base has actually risen. In all other regions—including sub-Saharan Africa, Asia, and the Pacific—the impression is of stagnation at best. Thus, while corporate tax reform among developed countries has been (to use the unavoidable cliché) rate reducing and

---

[32] As measured by either the standard deviation or (except in North Africa and the Middle East) the coefficient of variation.

Figure 2. Statutory Corporate Tax Rates of Developing Economies by Region, 1990–2002

(Percent)

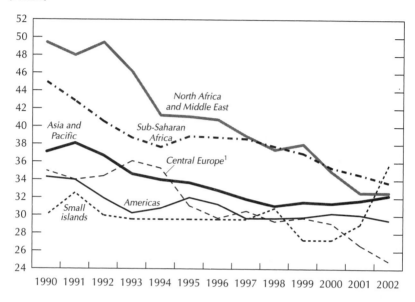

Source: World Tax Database (Ann Arbor, Michigan: University of Michigan).
[1]Including Russia, the Baltic countries, and other countries of the former Soviet Union.

base broadening, in the developing world it has been rate reducing but also base reducing (or, at best, base neutral).

The poor performance of the corporate tax base in developing countries could reflect wider structural changes in the income share of the corporate sector, or simply the weakness of hoped-for supply-side effects. But there is also evidence that it reflects quite widespread base-narrowing policy reform. Figure 3 shows the spread of a variety of tax incentives, for a sample of 40 developing countries for which sufficient information can be gleaned (from tax guides) for both the start and end of the decade: tax holidays (widely regarded as the most pernicious form of incentive[33]), reduced statutory rates for particular sectors or regions, direct tax breaks for exporters (WTO-inconsistent for all but the poorest countries) and free-trade zones.[34] All become more common. The

---

[33]For reasons spelled out, for example, in Zee, Stotsky, and Ley (2002).

[34]There is an important distinction between free-trade zones that offer only customs and indirect tax remission to exporters within the zone (this being essentially a particular way of implementing standard procedures), and those that also offer zone firms direct tax advantages of various kinds. Available information does not allow us to distinguish between these, so that the figures are for free-trade zones of all types.

Table 7. Corporate Tax Revenues, Rates, and Bases by Income Group, Early 2000s and Early 1990s[1]

(Percent of GDP unless noted otherwise)

	Corporate Tax Revenues	Average Statutory Corporate Rate[2] (Percent)	Average Corporate Tax Base
Early 2000s			
Low-income countries	2.0	34.6	5.8
Lower-middle-income countries	2.2	31.7	7.4
Upper-middle-income countries	2.6	29.8	8.7
High-income countries	2.5	32.6	8.3
Unweighted average[3]			
Developing countries[4]	2.3	31.8	7.5
High-income countries	2.5	32.6	8.3
Total unweighted average	2.3	32.1	7.7
Early 1990s			
Low-income countries	2.6	38.5	7.7
Lower-middle-income countries	2.9	37.0	8.6
Upper-middle-income countries	3.3	37.7	8.6
High-income countries	1.9	35.8	5.5
Unweighted average[3]			
Developing countries[4]	2.9	37.8	8.3
High-income countries	1.9	35.8	5.5
Total unweighted average	2.6	37.1	7.4

Sources: IMF, *Government Finance Statistics, International Financial Statistics, World Economic Outlook;* and University of Michigan, World Tax Database.

[1] Data used for early 1990s and early 2000s are average for two years—1990–91 and 2000–01 for most countries. For countries for which these averages could not be calculated, some flexibility in the years taken to represent the early 1990s and early 2000s was used to avoid a significant sample size reduction.

[2] Since average corporate rates and corporate tax revenues are from different sources, this resulted in a reduction of the effective sample size.

[3] For each revenue classification, only countries for which data are available are included in the calculation.

[4] Developing countries are defined to be low- and middle-income countries, closely following the World Bank income classification of economies.

proportion of the sample offering tax holidays rose from 45 percent to about 60 percent, for instance, while the growth of the other incentives was even more dramatic: reduced rates were available in about 40 percent of the sample at the start of the period, for example, and in 60 percent by the end; tax breaks for exporters and free-trade zones increased from 33 percent and 18 percent of the sample, respectively, to about 45 percent. In short, and with the exception of free-trade zones and tax breaks for exporters, each of these incentives was initially offered only by a minority of countries in the sample, but by a majority at the end.

Table 8. Corporate Tax Revenues, Rates, and Bases by Region, Early 2000s and Early 1990s[1]

(Percent of GDP unless noted otherwise)

	Corporate Tax Revenues	Average Statutory Corporate Rate[2] (Percent)	Average Corporate Tax Base
Early 2000s			
Americas[3]	1.9	29.2	6.4
Sub-Saharan Africa	1.6	36.5	5.1
Central Europe and BRO[4]	1.8	28.2	6.8
North Africa and Middle East	3.2	35.6	10.1
Asia and Pacific	2.9	31.8	9.9
Small islands[5]	3.7	35.0	9.6
Unweighted average[6]			
Developing countries[7]	2.3	31.8	7.5
High-income countries	2.5	32.6	8.3
Memorandum			
PRGF-eligible countries[8]	1.8	34.9	5.6
Early 1990s			
Americas[3]	1.2	32.7	4.6
Sub-Saharan Africa	2.0	43.6	5.3
Central Europe and BRO[4]	4.8	33.0	14.3
North Africa and Middle East	3.1	47.1	7.0
Asia and Pacific	3.4	35.5	10.2
Small islands[5]	3.4	35.0	11.1
Unweighted average[6]			
Developing countries[7]	2.9	0.4	8.3
High-income countries	1.9	37.8	5.5
Memorandum			
PRGF-eligible countries[8]	2.2	0.4	7.1

Sources: IMF, *Government Finance Statistics, International Financial Statistics, World Economic Outlook;* and University of Michigan, World Tax Database.

[1]Data used for early 1990s and early 2000s are average for two years—1990–91 and 2000–01 for most countries. For countries for which these averages could not be calculated, some flexibility in the years taken to represent the early 1990s and early 2000s was used to avoid a significant sample size reduction.

[2]Since average corporate rates and corporate tax revenues are from different sources, this resulted in a reduction of the effective sample size.

[3]Regional breakdown averages include only developing countries.

[4]Baltics, Russia, and other countries of the former Soviet Union.

[5]Island economies with population of under 1 million.

[6]For each revenue classification, only countries for which data are available are included in the calculation.

[7]Developing countries are defined to be low- and middle-income countries, closely following the World Bank income classification of economies.

[8]See Table A5 for details.

[9]Averages were calculated for PRGF-eligible countries for which data were available (see Appendix Table A6 for details).

Figure 3. The Spread of Tax Incentive in Developing Countries, 1990 and 2001
(Percent of developing countries in sample)

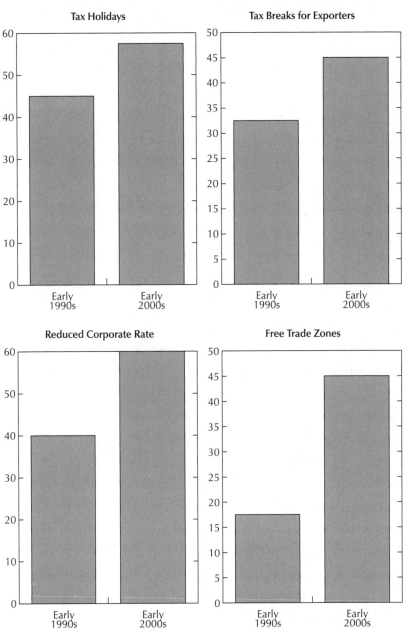

Source: *Corporate Taxes, 2003–04, Worldwide Summaries* (PricewaterhouseCoopers).

Moreover, Table 9 shows that the spread of tax incentives has been especially marked in the poorest of the developing countries. Among the very lowest-income countries, in particular, the proportion offering tax holidays increased by 75 percent, to about 78 percent of countries. In the lower-middle-income countries, on the other hand, the incidence of holidays remained broadly the same, while that of tax breaks for exporters and free-trade zones increased particularly noticeably. There are also important differences in experience across regions, as can be seen by the transition matrices—by region and incentive type—shown in Appendix Table A7. In sub-Saharan Africa, although a small sample size (seven countries) limits the firmness of any conclusion, it is striking that whereas only one country offered tax holidays at the start of the decade, all did by its end.[35] And, in the Americas, although two countries (from a more respectable sample size of 15) introduced holidays during the 1990s, rather more (four) removed them. In North Africa and the Middle East, in contrast, there was only a very slight increase in incentives.

It is by no means clear why the thrust of corporate tax policy reform has been to broaden the base in developed countries but to narrow it in the developing world, especially in the poorest regions. Certainly the standard advice to developing countries has been against the kind of base erosion seen above. In terms of the explanation for the trend in developing countries above, perhaps they have a smaller immobile base, offering less of a counterweight to the incentive to narrow the base to attract mobile inward investment. However, this is somewhat difficult to reconcile with the observation (from Table 7) that, at the start of the 1990s, the corporate tax base (relative to GDP) was actually higher in developing countries than in developed. Perhaps the explanation of a greater proclivity toward corporate tax incentives in developing countries lies in institutional structures more vulnerable to the exercise of influence by interest groups, including, not least, foreign multinationals. Why international tax competition appears to be taking such different forms in developed and developing countries—with a stronger adverse effect on revenue in the latter—thus remains something of a puzzle, clearly in need of explanation.

Should the apparent erosion of the corporate tax in developing countries be regretted or welcomed? It is a fairly robust result of optimal tax theory that economies that are small in world capital markets should set a marginal effective corporate tax rate—that is, a rate on the investment that just breaks even after tax—of zero. This is essentially a production efficiency argument, an intertemporal analogue to that for

---

[35]However, Uganda (not in the sample) withdrew tax holidays (grandfathering those already granted) in 1997.

the absence of trade taxes in developing countries:[36] small economies should trade at world prices for capital, just as they should for atemporal commodities. This suggests that the developing world may simply be moving toward what is now (even if it was not when capital was less mobile) an efficient tax structure.

That, however, seems too optimistic a view. To the extent that the corporate tax bears on rents, it does not distort investment decisions, and so is not optimally zero. It may be that part of the reduction in base and revenues simply represents a loss of rents, either (through bad policy) location-specific rents that could in principle be taxed at up to 100 percent without driving investment abroad or rents (through competition for footloose firms) that can be taken in any of a variety of countries. In either case, the result is the loss of an attractive source of revenue. The corporate tax is also traditionally seen as playing an important role as a backup to the income tax, preventing avoidance by accumulating earnings subject only to capital gains tax (often absent or ineffective in developing countries). There is little evidence in Tables 3 and A1–A3, however, that the personal income tax has been subject to significant erosion in the developing world, especially bearing in mind that there has in general been a marked reduction in personal income tax rates over this period—at least in the highest marginal rate[37]—in tandem with the reduction in statutory rates of corporation tax. Perhaps most troubling is the simple fact that developing countries have traditionally relied more heavily on corporate tax revenues than have developed: at the end of the 1990s, they still accounted for 12 percent of tax revenue in PRGF-eligible countries. This, in turn, seems likely to reflect the relative administrative ease of collecting corporate tax revenue, which is typically highly concentrated in a relatively small number of large (and perhaps also relatively honest) firms. Like the decline of trade tax revenues, the erosion of the corporate tax may thus jeopardize a convenient tax handle.

What then is the proper policy response to these pressures, apparently from intensified international tax competition, on corporate tax revenue in developing countries? Some take the view that downward pressure on tax revenues from tax competition should be welcomed as a further means of disciplining governments prone to spend wastefully, and this has indeed been an influential view in the formation of policy

---

[36] As such, the production efficiency argument is subject to a range of qualifications: it presumes that pure profits are fully taxed, and that there are no constraints on the other tax instruments that can be deployed. Further, qualifications arise in the international context: see Keen and Wildasin (2004). Nevertheless, this remains an important benchmark for policy design.

[37] This is documented in Appendix Table A8.

Table 9. Tax Incentives in Developing Countries[1]
(Percent of total number of countries in category)

Countries	Tax Holidays		Reduced Corporate Rate		Investment Allowance		Tax Breaks for Exporters		Free-trade Areas	
	Early 1990s	Early 2000s	Early 1990s	Early 2000s	Early 1990s	Early 2000s	Early 1990s	Early 2000s	Early 1990s	Early 2000s
Low-income										
Sub-Saharan Africa	44.4	77.8	44.4	66.7	11.1	11.1	44.4	77.8	33.3	55.6
Kenya										
Zambia										
Zimbabwe										
Central Europe and BRO[2]										
Asia and Pacific										
Estonia										
China										
India										
Indonesia										
Pakistan										
Philippines										
Lower-middle-income										
Americas	58.3	58.3	33.3	33.3	0.0	0.0	33.3	50.0	16.7	41.7
Guatemala										
Dominican Republic										
Ecuador										
Colombia										
Paraguay										
Peru										
Sub-Saharan Africa										
Cameroon										
Congo, Rep. of										
North Africa and Middle East										
Morocco										
Egypt										
Asia and Pacific										
Papua New Guinea										
Thailand										

Upper-middle-income Americas	36.8	42.1	42.1	68.4	26.3	21.1	26.3	21.1	10.5	42.1
Jamaica										
Costa Rica										
Panama										
Venezuela, Rep. Bol.										
Chile										
Brazil										
Uruguay										
Mexico										
Argentina										
Sub-Saharan Africa										
Mauritius										
South Africa										
Central Europe and BRO[2]										
Hungary										
Russia										
Lithuania										
Latvia										
North Africa and Middle East										
Iran, I.R. of										
Oman										
Asia and Pacific										
Malaysia										
Small islands[3]										
Malta										
All developing countries	45.0	57.5	40.0	60.0	15.0	15.0	32.5	45.0	17.5	45.0
Total number of countries in sample	40.0	40.0	40.0	40.0	40.0	40.0	40.0	40.0	40.0	40.0
Total number of low-income countries	9.0	9.0	9.0	9.0	9.0	9.0	9.0	9.0	9.0	9.0
Total number of lower-middle-income countries	12.0	12.0	12.0	12.0	12.0	12.0	12.0	12.0	12.0	12.0
Total number of upper-middle-income countries	19.0	19.0	19.0	19.0	19.0	19.0	19.0	19.0	19.0	19.0

Source: Pricewaterhouse Coopers, *Corporate Taxes, 2003–2004, Worldwide Summaries;* and IMF staff compilation.

[1] For transition countries data are for 1993 instead of 1990.

[2] Baltics, Russia, and other countries of the former Soviet Union.

[3] Island economies with population of under 1 million.

in the OECD. In the context of low-income and developing countries, however, the most common prescription, as noted earlier, is for an increase in revenues (even while recognizing that some would doubtless be wasted). This implies that there would then be merit in measures of cooperation intended to bolster corporate tax revenues.

Such cooperation might take a number of forms. One (fairly minimalist) possibility, for instance, is agreement on a code of conduct, proscribing and seeking to roll back particular forms of tax incentive: this might include a prohibition, for example, on the issuing of new tax holidays. A code of this sort—enforced not legally, but by peer pressure—has been adopted, for example, by the European Union[38] and proposed for the West African Economic and Monetary Union and for the South African Development Community. This strategy may be particularly appealing for emerging customs unions, since the elimination of internal tariff barriers can be expected to enhance firms' mobility between participating countries, and so increase the incentive of each country to offer more favorable tax treatment than do the others. The difficulty with this and any other form of coordination, however, is that by increasing their levels of corporate taxation those countries party to the agreement may find themselves more vulnerable to tax competition from those outside it.[39] Nor is it even clear that a wide regional coverage will deal with this problem, since potential competitor countries may be geographically far removed from one another: Mauritius may compete for investment with Fiji, for example. Only a genuinely global arrangement, which remains far from political reality, avoids this problem. How vulnerable more limited regional agreements would be to competition from third countries, and (a related issue) how much political will can be mustered to enter and abide by such arrangements, are likely to prove important issues for the future of corporate taxation not only in developed but also, perhaps especially, in developing countries. Experience with agreements of this kind, for example with the CARICOM agreement on fiscal incentives, has not been wholly encouraging.

Concluding Remarks

Experiences with tax policy varied widely across developing countries in the 1990s. Nepal, for instance, managed to increase its tax ratio by over 3 percentage points while modestly reducing its reliance on trade taxes and offsetting this with increased revenue from sales taxation. In

---

[38]There it is also supplemented by binding state-aid rules, which are proving even more effective in unwinding tax practices containing incentive elements.

[39]Konrad and Schelderup (1999) establish conditions under which tax coordination among a subset of countries is welfare improving for the participants.

Burundi, on the other hand, the tax ratio fell by about 4 percentage points, even though trade tax revenue remained broadly constant.

While generalizations are, thus, dangerous, the overall picture that emerges is certainly not comforting. Tax ratios in the developing world have been stagnant at best (and tending to fall once seignorage is taken into account), when the most common objective was actually to mobilize more domestic revenue. That in itself does not imply unmitigated failure: a number of countries have succeeded in keeping revenue broadly unchanged while reducing their reliance on distortionary trade taxes, which would generally be regarded as a worthwhile improvement in the efficiency of the overall tax system. There are also some clear achievements. In particular, there is evidence that the adoption of the VAT has improved the effectiveness of the tax systems of many developing countries. Nevertheless, there is cause for concern in the lackluster performance of overall revenues in low-income countries.

What also stands out is the prospect of significant challenges ahead. With the VAT now so widespread, the emphasis is likely to shift from the introduction of this tax (except, perhaps, in parts of the Middle East, where it has only recently begun to make its appearance) toward the improvement of its design and administration, tasks that may require more time than originally supposed. Other challenges are even more fundamental. Experience suggests, in particular, that better sequencing of domestic and trade-tax reform is necessary if developing countries, especially the poorest of them, are to preserve their revenues in the face of further trade reforms. And the erosion of corporate tax revenues in developing countries over the past decade suggests that international tax competition may have a far more significant impact on revenues for them than it does (or, at least, has yet had) for developed countries. This raises issues of international tax coordination that have proved both conceptually and politically thorny. There are other issues too, beyond those addressed in this chapter, likely to require attention in the coming years—not least, improving the tax treatment of small and medium-sized enterprises.

The past decade has been one of some successes. But trade reform and tax competition may provide another twist of the fiscal knife for many low-income and other developing countries, posing continuing and, in some respects, deepening problems for tax design in the years ahead.

Appendix

The appendix provides details regarding the sample of countries (region classification, income classification, PRGF sample of countries), the results discussed in the text, and the tables and figures of the chapter.

Table A1. Central Government Revenues by Income Group, Early 2000s and Early 1990s[1]

(Percent of total tax revenues)

	Nominal GDP per Capita (U.S. dollars, average)	Total Revenue	Tax Revenue	Other Revenue
Early 2000s				
Low-income countries	614	121.2	100.0	21.2
Lower-middle-income countries	1,642	137.9	100.0	37.9
Upper-middle-income countries	4,142	122.1	100.0	22.1
High-income countries	21,387	119.3	100.0	19.3
Unweighted average[3]				
Developing countries[4]	2,269	125.8	100.0	25.8
High-income countries	21,387	119.3	100.0	19.3
Total unweighted average	7,756	123.3	100.0	23.3
Early 1990s				
Low-income countries	445	121.4	100.0	21.4
Lower-middle-income countries	1,194	131.1	100.0	31.1
Upper-middle-income countries	3,747	122.7	100.0	22.7
High-income countries	18,418	119.7	100.0	19.7
Unweighted average[3]				
Developing countries[4]	1,936	124.4	100.0	24.4
High-income countries	18,418	119.7	100.0	19.7
Total unweighted average	6,667	122.7	100.0	22.7

Sources: IMF, *Government Finance Statistics, International Financial Statistics,* and *World Economic Outlook.*

[1] Data used for early 1990s and early 2000s are averages for two years—1990–91 and 2000–01 for most countries. For countries for which these averages could not be calculated, some flexibility in the years taken to represent the early 1990s and early 2000s was used to avoid a significant sample size reduction.

[2] European Union countries do not report statistics on international trade taxes to *Government Finance Statistics.*

[3] For each revenue classification, only countries for which data are available are included in the calculation.

[4] Developing countries are defined to be low- and middle-income countries, closely following the World Bank income classification of economies.

| Taxes on Income, Profits, and Capital Gains | | | Social Security Taxes | Payroll Taxes | Domestic Taxes on Goods and Services | | | International Trade Taxes[2] | | | Property Taxes |
| | of which: | | | | | of which: | | | of which: | | |
Total	Indivi-dual	Corpo-rate			Total	General sales, turnover, or VAT	Excises	Total	Import duties	Export duties	
26.0	12.6	13.2	7.0	0.2	39.4	23.5	13.2	24.9	16.4	1.7	1.4
24.2	11.5	13.5	8.3	0.4	40.1	30.9	13.2	22.7	21.8	0.9	1.6
25.0	12.2	12.4	21.3	0.5	39.3	25.4	11.3	11.9	11.5	0.8	1.4
32.6	26.9	9.3	26.7	1.2	33.0	24.4	10.3	4.9	4.6	0.0	2.5
25.1	12.1	12.9	14.0	0.4	39.4	25.8	12.3	18.3	15.6	1.1	1.4
32.6	26.9	9.3	26.7	1.2	33.0	24.4	10.3	4.9	4.6	0.0	2.5
28.0	17.9	11.5	19.0	0.7	36.9	25.0	11.5	14.2	12.2	0.8	1.9
26.0	8.8	17.6	5.0	0.1	36.1	19.2	14.6	29.9	26.0	4.3	1.7
26.2	9.1	17.5	8.8	1.2	30.9	17.5	12.2	26.7	25.1	1.2	2.3
26.9	10.1	15.2	19.7	0.8	29.7	16.7	11.0	19.7	17.6	2.6	1.4
32.0	28.6	7.0	27.1	1.0	32.2	23.6	9.1	7.3	7.4	0.1	2.7
26.4	9.5	16.4	12.8	0.7	31.7	17.6	12.3	24.3	21.8	2.6	1.7
32.0	28.6	7.0	27.1	1.0	32.2	23.6	9.1	7.3	7.4	0.1	2.7
28.6	17.2	12.8	18.2	0.9	31.9	19.7	11.1	19.2	17.5	2.0	2.1

Table A2. Central Government Revenues by Region, Early 2000s and Early 1990s[1]
(Percent of GDP)

	Nominal GDP per Capita (U.S. dollars, average)	Total Revenue	Tax Revenue	Other Revenue
Early 2000s				
Americas[2]	3,301	20.0	16.3	3.7
Sub-Saharan Africa	765	19.7	15.9	3.8
Central Europe and BRO[3]	2,420	26.7	23.4	3.2
North Africa and Middle East	2,486	26.2	17.1	9.1
Asia and Pacific	1,447	16.6	13.2	3.4
Small islands[4]	4,673	32.0	24.5	7.6
Unweighted average[5]				
Developing countries[6]	2,269	22.1	17.6	4.5
High-income countries	21,387	32.8	27.5	5.3
Memorandum				
PRGF-eligible countries[7]	617	19.6	14.8	4.8
Early 1990s				
Americas[2]	2,026	18.3	14.9	3.4
Sub-Saharan Africa	831	19.3	16.3	2.9
Central Europe and BRO[3]	3,470	30.9	27.3	3.6
North Africa and Middle East	1,951	23.3	15.1	8.3
Asia and Pacific	1,061	17.6	13.6	4.0
Small islands[4]	3,221	33.4	25.5	7.9
Unweighted average[5]				
Developing countries[6]	1,936	22.3	17.9	4.4
High-income countries	18,418	31.9	26.6	5.2
Memorandum				
PRGF-eligible countries[7]	856	19.4	15.2	4.1

Sources: IMF, *Government Finance Statistics, International Financial Statistics,* and *World Economic Outlook.*

[1] Data used for early 1990s and early 2000s are averages for two years—1990–91 and 2000–01 for most countries. For countries for which these averages could not be calculated, some flexibility in the years taken to represent the early 1990s and early 2000s was used to avoid a significant sample size reduction.

[2] Regional breakdown averages include only developing countries.

[3] Baltics, Russia, and other countries of the former Soviet Union.

[4] Island economies with population of under 1 million.

[5] For each revenue classification, only countries for which data are available are included in the calculation.

[6] Developing countries are defined to be low- and middle-income countries, closely following the World Bank income classification of economies.

[7] Averages were calculated for PRGF-eligible countries for which data were available (see Table A6 for details).

Taxes on Income, Profits, and Capital Gains			Social Security Taxes	Payroll Taxes	Domestic Taxes on Goods and Services			International Trade Taxes[2]			Property Taxes
Total	of which:				Total	of which:		Total	of which:		
	Individual	Corporate				General sales, turnover, or VAT	Excises		Import duties	Export duties	
3.9	1.3	1.9	2.3	0.1	7.9	5.5	2.2	1.9	1.9	0.0	0.3
4.7	2.7	1.6	0.3	0.1	5.0	3.2	1.4	5.6	3.5	0.4	0.2
3.6	2.1	1.8	8.1	0.1	10.5	6.8	3.0	1.1	0.9	0.4	0.1
5.5	2.5	3.2	0.8	0.2	5.9	4.6	2.5	3.3	3.0	0.1	0.5
4.6	2.0	2.9	0.5	0.0	5.3	2.7	1.9	2.1	1.9	0.2	0.2
4.8	2.7	3.7	2.8	0.0	6.4	4.3	1.6	9.7	9.7	0.0	0.3
4.4	2.1	2.3	2.5	0.1	6.9	4.5	2.2	3.2	2.7	0.2	0.3
8.9	7.4	2.5	7.3	0.3	9.1	6.7	2.8	1.3	1.3	0.0	0.7
3.4	1.7	1.8	1.0	0.0	5.6	3.4	1.9	4.5	3.5	0.3	0.2
3.7	1.1	1.2	2.2	0.1	5.2	2.8	2.1	2.9	2.5	0.2	0.4
4.7	2.1	2.0	0.3	0.0	5.0	3.3	1.4	5.9	4.9	1.0	0.2
6.6	1.7	4.8	7.9	0.5	9.9	5.2	3.7	2.3	1.4	0.8	0.2
4.9	1.8	3.1	1.0	0.2	4.0	2.9	1.8	3.8	3.6	0.1	0.5
4.5	1.7	3.4	0.2	0.0	4.9	2.2	2.2	3.4	3.2	0.3	0.3
4.2	1.4	3.3	2.8	0.0	4.0	0.5	0.6	14.0	13.5	0.3	0.3
4.7	1.7	2.9	2.3	0.1	5.7	3.2	2.2	4.3	3.9	0.5	0.3
8.5	7.6	1.9	7.2	0.3	8.6	6.3	2.4	1.9	2.0	0.0	0.7
3.5	1.3	2.2	0.4	0.0	5.0	2.4	2.2	5.5	4.8	0.6	0.2

Table A3. Central Government Revenues by Region, Early 2000s and Early 1990s[1]
(Percent of total tax revenue)

	Nominal GDP per Capita (U.S. dollars, average)	Total Revenue	Tax Revenue	Other Revenue
Early 2000s				
Americas[2]	3,301	122.5	100	22.5
Sub-Saharan Africa	765	123.5	100	23.5
Central Europe and BRO[3]	2,420	113.8	100	13.8
North Africa and Middle East	2,486	153.7	100	53.7
Asia and Pacific	1,447	125.9	100	25.9
Small islands[4]	4,673	130.9	100	30.9
Unweighted average[5]				
Developing countries[6]	2,269	125.8	100	25.8
High-income countries	21,387	119.3	100	19.3
Memorandum				
PRGF-eligible countries[7]	617	132.3	100.0	32.3
Early 1990s				
Americas[2]	2,026	122.6	100	22.6
Sub-Saharan Africa	831	118.1	100	18.1
Central Europe and BRO[3]	3,470	113.1	100	13.1
North Africa and Middle East	1,951	155.0	100	55.0
Asia and Pacific	1,061	129.0	100	29.0
Small islands[4]	3,221	130.9	100	30.9
Unweighted average[5]				
Developing countries[6]	1,936	124.4	100	24.4
High-income countries	18,418	119.7	100	19.7
Memorandum				
PRGF-eligible countries[7]	5,624	127.2	100.0	27.2

Sources: IMF, *Government Finance Statistics, International Financial Statistics,* and *World Economic Outlook.*

[1]Data used for early 1990s and early 2000s are averages for two years—1990–91 and 2000–01 for most countries. For countries for which these averages could not be calculated, some flexibility in the years taken to represent the early 1990s and early 2000s was used to avoid a significant sample size reduction.

[2]Regional breakdown averages include only developing countries.

[3]Baltics, Russia, and other countries of the former Soviet Union.

[4]Island economies with population of under 1 million.

[5]For each revenue classification, only countries for which data are available are included in the calculation.

[6]Developing countries are defined to be low- and middle-income countries, closely following the World Bank income classification of economies.

[7]Averages were calculated for PRGF-eligible countries for which data were available (see Table A6 for details).

Taxes on Income, Profits, and Capital Gains			Social Security Taxes	Payroll Taxes	Domestic Taxes on Goods and Services			International Trade Taxes[2]			Property Taxes
	of which:					of which:			of which:		
Total	Indivi-dual	Corpo-rate			Total	General sales, turnover, or VAT	Excises	Total	Import duties	Export duties	
23.9	8.0	11.4	14.3	0.5	48.3	33.6	13.2	11.7	11.5	0.0	1.9
29.5	16.7	9.8	1.7	0.3	31.2	20.2	9.0	34.8	21.9	2.3	1.3
15.3	8.9	7.7	34.5	0.4	44.7	29.0	12.8	4.9	3.9	1.7	0.3
32.4	14.5	18.6	4.9	1.1	34.6	27.1	14.7	19.4	17.5	0.5	3.1
35.1	15.5	22.1	3.9	0.1	40.5	20.8	14.7	15.9	14.5	1.8	1.5
19.5	11.2	15.2	11.4	0.0	26.0	17.4	6.5	39.7	39.7	0.0	1.4
25.1	12.1	12.9	14.0	0.4	39.4	25.8	12.3	18.3	15.6	1.1	1.4
32.6	26.9	9.3	26.7	1.2	33.0	24.4	10.3	4.9	4.6	0.0	2.5
22.7	11.4	12.1	6.5	0.2	37.8	22.7	12.7	30.1	23.5	1.8	1.2
24.9	7.1	8.3	14.5	0.6	35.1	18.9	13.8	19.3	17.0	1.6	2.6
28.6	12.8	12.4	1.9	0.3	30.4	20.3	8.7	36.4	30.3	5.9	1.0
24.0	6.1	17.6	29.0	1.7	36.3	19.1	13.7	8.5	5.2	2.8	0.7
32.2	12.0	20.6	6.6	1.1	26.7	19.1	12.1	25.5	24.0	0.7	3.3
33.2	12.4	24.8	1.5	0.0	36.1	16.1	16.3	24.8	23.4	2.1	2.4
16.4	5.4	12.8	11.0	0.0	15.8	1.9	2.4	54.8	53.1	1.3	1.0
26.4	9.3	16.3	12.8	0.7	31.7	17.6	12.3	24.3	21.8	2.6	1.7
32.0	28.6	7.0	27.1	1.0	32.2	23.6	9.1	7.3	7.4	0.1	2.7
22.9	8.5	14.8	2.9	0.1	32.8	15.7	14.2	36.1	31.6	4.1	1.4

Table A4. Seignorage as a Share of GDP, by Region[1]

	Nominal GDP per Capita (U.S. dollars, average)	Seignorage (Percent of GDP)
Early 2000s		
Americas[2]	3,301	1.2
Sub-Saharan Africa	765	2.5
Central Europe and BRO[3]	2,420	3.1
North Africa and Middle East	2,486	3.3
Asia and Pacific	1,447	2.7
Small islands[4]	4,673	1.9
Unweighted average[5]		
Developing countries[6]	2,269	2.4
High-income countries[7]	21,387	1.7
Memorandum		
PRGF-eligible countries[8]	617	2.4
Early 1990s		
Americas[2]	2,026	3.5
Sub-Saharan Africa	831	2.5
Central Europe and BRO[3]	3,470	6.2
North Africa and Middle East	1,951	4.5
Asia and Pacific	1,061	4.0
Small islands[4]	3,221	2.5
Unweighted average[5]		
Developing countries[6]	1,936	4.0
High-income countries[7]	18,418	1.4
Memorandum		
PRGF-eligible countries[8]	856	4.0

Sources: IMF, *Government Finance Statistics, International Financial Statistics, World Economic Outlook,* and staff calculations.

[1] Data used for early 1990s and early 2000s are average for two years—1991–92 and 2000–01 for most countries. For countries for which these averages could not be calculated, some flexibility in the years taken to represent the early 1990s and early 2000s was used to avoid a significant sample size reduction. Seignorage is calculated as the money growth rate multiplied by money stock (M1) divided by nominal GDP. The hyperinflation episodes of Brazil and Nicaragua in the early 1990s are ignored, and replaced by estimates from normal times.

[2] Regional breakdown averages include only developing countries.

[3] Baltics, Russia, and other countries of the former Soviet Union.

[4] Island economies with population of under 1 million.

[5] In each region, only countries for which data are available are included in the calculation.

[6] Developing countries are defined to be low- and middle-income countries, closely following the World Bank income classification of economies.

[7] Comparable measures of M1 were not available for most European countries.

[8] Average were calculated for PRGF-eligible countries for which data were available (see Table A6 for details).

Appendix Table A5. List of Countries by Region and Income

	Americas	Sub-Saharan Africa	Central Europe and BRO[1]	North Africa and Middle East	Asia and Pacific	Small Islands[2]	European Union[3]
Low-income countries	Bolivia Nicaragua	Burundi Congo, Dem. Rep. of Côte d'Ivoire Ethiopia Guinea Kenya Lesotho Madagascar Sierra Leone Zambia Zimbabwe	Albania Estonia		Bhutan China India Indonesia Mongolia Myanmar Nepal Pakistan Philippines Sri Lanka Vietnam		
Lower-middle-income countries	Colombia Dominican Rep. El Salvador Guatemala Paraguay Peru Tunisia	Cameroon Congo, Rep. of	Bulgaria Romania	Egypt Jordan Lebanon Morocco Syria Yemen	Papua New Guinea Thailand	Maldives Vanuatu	
Upper-middle-income countries	Argentina Belize Brazil Chile Costa Rica Jamaica Mexico Panama Uruguay Venezuela	Mauritius South Africa	Azerbaijan Belarus Czech Republic Hungary Kyrgyz Republic Latvia Lithuania Moldova Poland Russian Federation	Iran Oman Turkey	Malaysia Korea	Malta St. Vincent & Grenadines Seychelles	

Appendix Table A5 *(concluded)*

	Americas	Sub-Saharan Africa	Central Europe and BRO[1]	North Africa and Middle East	Asia and Pacific	Small Islands[2]	European Union[3]
High-income countries	Canada United States		Croatia Slovenia	Bahrain Israel Kuwait United Arab Emirates	Australia New Zealand Singapore	Bahamas, The Cyprus Iceland	Austria Belgium Denmark Finland France Germany Greece Ireland Italy Luxembourg Netherlands Norway Portugal Spain Sweden Switzerland United Kingdom

Source: IMF staff compilation. The regional classification follows that in Ebrill and others (2001).
[1] Baltics, Russia, and other countries of the former Soviet Union.
[2] Island economies with population of under 1 million.
[3] Plus Norway and Switzerland.

Table A6. Sample of PRGF-Eligible IMF Members

Albania	Guinea	Nepal
Azerbaijan	India	Nicaragua
Bhutan	Kenya	Pakistan
Bolivia	Kyrgyz Republic	Papua New Guinea
Burundi	Lesotho	Sierra Leone
Cameroon	Madagascar	St Vincent and Grenadines
Congo, Dem. Rep. of	Maldives	Vanuatu
Congo, Rep. of	Moldova	Vietnam
Côte d'Ivoire	Mongolia	Yemen
Ethiopia	Myanmar	Zambia

Source: IMF staff compilation.

Table A7. Tax Incentive Transition Matrices, 1990 and 2001[1]

Region	Countries	Tax Holidays				Reduced Corporate Rates			
Asia and Pacific	China India Indonesia Malaysia Papua New Guinea Philippines Thailand		Early 2000s				Early 2000s		
				Yes	No	Total		Yes	No	Total
		Early 1990s	Yes	5	0	5	Early 1990s	Yes	3	0	3
			No	1	1	2		No	1	3	4
			Total	6	1			Total	4	3
Small islands[2]	Malta		Early 2000s				Early 2000s		
				Yes	No	Total		Yes	No	Total
		Early 1990s	Yes	1	0	1	Early 1990s	Yes	1	0	1
			No	0	0	0		No	0	0	0
			Total	1	0			Total	1	0
North Africa and Middle East	Egypt Iran Morocco Oman Pakistan		Early 2000s				Early 2000s		
				Yes	No	Total		Yes	No	Total
		Early 1990s	Yes	4	0	4	Early 1990s	Yes	2	0	2
			No	0	1	1		No	1	2	3
			Total	4	1			Total	3	2
Americas	Argentina Mexico Brazil Chile Colombia Costa Rica Dominican Rep. Ecuador Guatemala Jamaica Panama Paraguay Peru Uruguay Venezuela		Early 2000s				Early 2000s		
				Yes	No	Total		Yes	No	Total
		Early 1990s	Yes	0	4	4	Early 1990s	Yes	2	0	2
			No	2	9	11		No	5	8	13
			Total	2	13			Total	7	8
Central Europe and BRO[3]	Hungary Estonia Latvia Lithuania Russia		Early 2000s				Early 2000s		
				Yes	No	Total		Yes	No	Total
		Early 1990s	Yes	1	2	3	Early 1990s	Yes	3	1	4
			No	2	0	2		No	1	0	1
			Total	3	2			Total	4	1
Sub-Saharan Africa	Cameroon Congo Kenya Mauritius South Africa Zambia Zimbabwe		Early 2000s				Early 2000s		
				Yes	No	Total		Yes	No	Total
		Early 1990s	Yes	1	0	1	Early 1990s	Yes	3	1	4
			No	6	0	6		No	2	1	3
			Total	7	0			Total	5	2
Overall			Early 2000s				Early 2000s		
				Yes	No	Total		Yes	No	Total
		Early 1990s	Yes	12	6	18	Early 1990s	Yes	14	2	16
			No	11	11	22		No	10	14	24
			Total	23	17			Total	24	16

Sources: Pricewaterhouse Coopers, *Corporate Taxes, 2003–04, Worldwide Summaries;* and IMF staff compilation.

[1] For most countries early 1990s means 1990 and early 2000s means 2001. For transition countries data for 1993 are used instead of 1990 and 2001 instead of 2000.

[2] Island economies with population of under 1 million.

[3] Baltics, Russia, and other countries of the former Soviet Union.

		Investment Allowance Early 2000s					Tax Breaks for Exporters Early 2000s					Free-Trade Areas Early 2000s		
		Yes	No	Total			Yes	No	Total			Yes	No	Total
Early	Yes	2	0	2	Early	Yes	5	0	5	Early	Yes	3	0	3
1990s	No	0	5	5	1990s	No	2	0	2	1990s	No	2	2	4
	Total	2	5			Total	7	0			Total	5	2	

		Investment Allowance Early 2000s					Tax Breaks for Exporters Early 2000s					Free-Trade Areas Early 2000s		
		Yes	No	Total			Yes	No	Total			Yes	No	Total
Early	Yes	1	0	1	Early	Yes	1	0	1	Early	Yes	0	0	0
1990s	No	0	0	0	1990s	No	0	0	0	1990s	No	0	1	1
	Total	1	0			Total	1	0			Total	0	1	

		Investment Allowance Early 2000s					Tax Breaks for Exporters Early 2000s					Free-Trade Areas Early 2000s		
		Yes	No	Total			Yes	No	Total			Yes	No	Total
Early	Yes	0	0	0	Early	Yes	3	0	3	Early	Yes	0	1	1
1990s	No	0	5	5	1990s	No	1	1	2	1990s	No	1	3	4
	Total	0	5			Total	4	1			Total	1	4	

		Investment Allowance Early 2000s					Tax Breaks for Exporters Early 2000s					Free-Trade Areas Early 2000s		
		Yes	No	Total			Yes	No	Total			Yes	No	Total
Early	Yes	2	0	2	Early	Yes	2	1	3	Early	Yes	3	0	3
1990s	No	0	13	13	1990s	No	1	11	12	1990s	No	4	8	12
	Total	2	13			Total	3	12			Total	7	8	

		Investment Allowance Early 2000s					Tax Breaks for Exporters Early 2000s					Free-Trade Areas Early 2000s		
		Yes	No	Total			Yes	No	Total			Yes	No	Total
Early	Yes	0	1	1	Early	Yes	0	0	0	Early	Yes	0	0	0
1990s	No	0	4	4	1990s	No	0	5	5	1990s	No	3	2	5
	Total	0	5			Total	0	5			Total	3	2	

		Investment Allowance Early 2000s					Tax Breaks for Exporters Early 2000s					Free-Trade Areas Early 2000s		
		Yes	No	Total			Yes	No	Total			Yes	No	Total
Early	Yes	0	0	0	Early	Yes	1	0	1	Early	Yes	0	0	0
1990s	No	1	6	7	1990s	No	2	4	6	1990s	No	2	5	7
	Total	1	6			Total	3	4			Total	2	5	

		Investment Allowance Early 2000s					Tax Breaks for Exporters Early 2000s					Free-Trade Areas Early 2000s		
		Yes	No	Total			Yes	No	Total			Yes	No	Total
Early	Yes	5	1	6	Early	Yes	12	1	13	Early	Yes	6	1	7
1990s	No	1	33	34	1990s	No	6	21	27	1990s	No	12	21	33
	Total	6	34			Total	18	22			Total	18	22	

Table A8. Statutory Rates of Personal Income Tax in Developing Countries[1]

	Averages
Late 1990s[2]	
Low-income countries[3]	33.3
Lower-middle-income countries[4]	33.3
Upper-middle-income countries[5]	30.4
Early 1990s[2]	
Low-income countries[6]	41.3
Lower-middle-income countries[7]	42.6
Upper-middle-income countries[8]	35.9

Source: University of Michigan, World Tax Database.

[1]Top income tax rates for 2000 and 2001 are not available.

[2]Data used for countries of the former Soviet Union for the early 1990s are not from years 1990 and 1991, but the earliest available observation.

[3]Excluding Bhutan, Burundi, Ethiopia, Guinea, Lesotho, Madagascar, Malaysia, Moldova, Myanmar, Sierra Leone, Nepal, and Sri Lanka.

[4]Excluding Albania, Belarus, Jordan, Maldives, Tunisia, Turkey, St. Vincent and Grenadines, and Syria.

[5]Excluding Belize, Croatia, Czech Republic, Hungary, Lebanon, Mexico, Poland, and Seychelles.

[6]Excluding Albania, Bhutan, Burundi, Ethiopia, Guinea, Lesotho, Madagascar, Malaysia, Myanmar, Nepal, Sierra Leone, Slovenia, and Vietnam.

[7]Excluding Bulgaria, Cameroon, India, Jordan, Lebanon, Maldives, Morocco, Tunisia, Yemen, and Vanuatu.

[8]Excluding Azerbaijan, Belarus, Czech Republic, Hungary, Korea, Kyrgyz Republic, Mexico, Moldova, Poland, St. Vincent and Grenadines, Seychelles, and Turkey.

References

Baunsgaard, Thomas, and Michael Keen, 2003, "Tax Revenue and (or?) Trade Liberalization" (unpublished; Washington: International Monetary Fund).

Besley, Timothy, Rachel Griffith, and Alexander Klemm, 2001, "Empirical Evidence on Fiscal Interdependence in OECD Countries" (unpublished; London: Institute for Fiscal Studies).

Bird, Richard M., 1993, "Review of 'Principles and Practice of Value-Added Taxation: Lessons for Developing Countries,'" *Canadian Tax Journal*, Vol. 41, No. 6, pp. 1222–25.

Boadway, Robin, and Michael Keen, 2003, "Theoretical Perspectives on the Taxation of Capital Income and Financial Services," in *The Taxation of Financial Intermediation: Theory and Practice for Emerging Economies*, ed. by Patrick Honohan (World Bank and Oxford University Press), pp. 31–80.

Burgess, Robin, and Nicholas Stern, 1993, "Taxation and Development," *Journal of Economic Literature*, Vol. 31, pp. 762–830.

Casanegra de Jantscher, Milka, 1990, "Administering the VAT," in *Value-Added Taxation in Developing Countries*, ed. by Malcolm Gillis, Carl S. Shoup, and Gerardo P. Sicat (Washington: World Bank).

Cnossen, Sijbren, 1994, "Administrative and Compliance Costs of the VAT: A Review of the Evidence," *Tax Notes*, Vol. 63 (June 20), pp. 1609–26.

Devereux, Michael, Rachel Griffith, and Alexander Klemm, 2002, "Corporate Income Tax Reforms and International Tax Competition," *Economic Policy*, Vol. 35 (October), pp. 451–95.

Ebrill, Liam, Janet Stotsky, and Reint Gropp, 1999, *Revenue Implications of Trade Liberalization*, IMF Occasional Paper No. 180 (Washington: International Monetary Fund).

Ebrill, Liam, Michael Keen, Jean-Paul Bodin, and Victoria Summers, 2001, *The Modern VAT* (Washington: International Monetary Fund).

Keen, Michael, and Jenny E. Ligthart, 2001, "Coordinating Tariff Reduction and Domestic Tax Reform," *Journal of International Economics*, Vol. 56 (March), pp. 489–507.

Keen, Michael, and Ben Lockwood, 2003, "The Causes and Consequences of the Uptake of VAT: An Empirical Investigation" (unpublished; Washington: International Monetary Fund).

Keen, Michael, and Jack Mintz, 2004, "The Optimal Threshold for a Value-Added Tax," *Journal of Public Economics*, Vol. 88 (March), pp. 559–76.

Keen, Michael, and David Wildasin, 2004, "Pareto Efficient International Taxation," *American Economic Review*, forthcoming.

Khattry, Barsha, and Mohan Rao, 2002, "Fiscal Faux Pas? An Analysis of the Revenue Implications of Trade Liberalization," *World Development*, Vol. 30 (August), pp. 1431–44.

Konrad, Kai, and Guttorm Schelderup, 1999, "Fortress Building in Global Tax Competition," *Journal of Urban Economics*, Vol. 46 (July 1999), pp. 156–67.

Muñoz, Sonia, and Stanley Sang-Wook Cho, 2004, "Social Impact of a Tax Reform: The Case of Ethiopia," Chapter 13 in *Helping Countries Develop: The Role of Fiscal Policy*, ed. by Sanjeev Gupta, Benedict Clements, and Gabriela Inchauste (Washington: International Monetary Fund).

Panagariya, Arvind, and Dani Rodrik, 1993, "Political-Economy Arguments for a Uniform Tariff," *International Economic Review*, Vol. 34 (August), pp. 685–703.

Rodrik, Dani, 1998, "Why Do More Open Economies Have Bigger Governments?" *Journal of Political Economy*, Vol. 106 (October), pp. 997–1032.

Schneider, Freidrich, and Dominik Este, 2000, "Shadow Economies: Size, Causes, and Consequences," *Journal of Economic Literature*, Vol. 37 (March), pp. 77–114.

Stiglitz, Joseph, 2003, "Development Oriented Tax Policy," presentation at International Institute of Public Finance, Washington, November 6.

Summers, Victoria, and Katherine Baer, 2003, "Revenue Policy and Administration in the CIS-7: Recent Trends and Future Challenges" (unpublished; Washington: International Monetary Fund).

Tanzi, Vito, 1987, "Quantitative Characteristics of the Tax Systems of Developing Countries," in *The Theory of Taxation for Developing Countries*, ed. by David Newbery and Nicholas Stern (New York: Oxford University Press for the World Bank), pp. 205–41.

Younger, Stephen D., and David E. Sahn, 1998, "Fiscal Incidence in Africa: Microeconomic Evidence," CFNPP Working Paper No. 91 (Ithaca, New York: Cornell Food and Nutrition Policy Program).

Zee, Howell, Janet Stotsky, and Eduardo Ley, 2002, "Tax Incentives for Business Investment: A Primer for Policy Makers in Developing Countries," *World Development*, Vol. 30 (September), pp. 1497–1516.

13

Social Impact of a Tax Reform: The Case of Ethiopia

SÒNIA MUÑOZ AND STANLEY SANG-WOOK CHO

Ethiopia is one of the poorest countries in the world, with a per capita gross national income of less than one-fourth of the sub-Saharan average.[1] It also has some of the poorest human development indicators in the world[2] with a national poverty level at about 44 percent and more than 80 percent of the population living on less than U.S.$1 a day. It has experienced a war with neighboring Eritrea ending in 2000, as well as frequent natural disasters that have ravaged many parts of the country and hampered development plans. The economy of Ethiopia is very agrarian, focusing mainly on the production and export of commodities such as coffee. Consequently, the country is particularly vulnerable to drought and the adverse effects of fluctuations in the commodity prices.

Efforts by the Ethiopian government to reduce poverty are currently being supported by an IMF three-year Poverty Reduction and Growth

The authors are indebted to Sanjeev Gupta, Ben Clements, Shamsuddin Tareq, Robert Gillingham, and Gabriela Inchauste for their guidance, and to Amor Tahari, Louis Erasmus, Robert Powell, Dominique Simard, and Ayumu Yamauchi for their valuable comments. They are grateful to Jorge Baca-Campodónico for sharing the method to calculate cascading effects and Peter Wobst for the input-output table on Tanzania (see Wobst, 1998). They have also benefited from discussions with Isaias Coelho, Hyoung-Goo Kang, Tatsuyoshi Okimoto, and Erwin Tiongson.
[1]Based on the *World Bank Atlas* method, Ethiopia's per capita gross national income is $US100.
[2]According to the *Human Development Report* (World Bank, 2003), Ethiopia's human development index ranks 169th out of 175 countries.

Facility (PRGF) arrangement approved in March 2001. Over the past three years, public spending for poverty reduction has more than doubled as a percentage of GDP, rising from 8 percent in 1999/2000 to nearly 18 percent in 2002/03. This increase has been facilitated by a significant reduction in defense spending, as well as an increase in grants and government borrowing specifically targeted to fight poverty. Additional resources for fighting poverty are expected from the IMF and World Bank Heavily Indebted Poor Country (HIPC) debt relief initiative, amounting to US$1.9 billion (36 percent of the nominal debt stock). On the revenue side, the strategy calls for an increase in tax revenue as a share of GDP from 12.4 percent of GDP to 14.9 percent of GDP over the same period. Tax policy reforms focus on improving the efficiency and equity of the income tax system, modernizing tax administration by enhancing technical capacities, and reforming indirect taxation. The main reform to indirect taxation was the introduction of a value-added tax (VAT) in January 2003.

Poverty and Social Impact Analysis (PSIA) is currently at its incipient stage in Ethiopia. PSIA is meant to provide information on the trade-offs among different policy options for achieving both growth and poverty alleviation. It will also assess the timing and sequencing of possible reforms, estimate the risks involved, and consider appropriate compensatory and complementary measures. Currently, the U.K. Department for International Development is considering a PSIA on falling commodity prices and on civil service reform.

This chapter carries out a PSIA of the introduction of the VAT in Ethiopia. We first present the methodology used to analyze the incidence of the VAT using the Ethiopian Central Statistical Authority's *1999/2000 Household Income, Consumption and Expenditure Survey*. In the next section, we present (1) estimates of the incidence of the VAT, (2) a comparison of the progressivity of the VAT to the progressivity of the sales tax it replaced, (3) an examination of the distribution of expenditures on exempt goods and services to see whether these exemptions increase or decrease the progressivity of the VAT, and (4) separate evaluations of the incidence of VAT on food and nonfood items and on rural and urban consumers. Since the incidence of a tax should not be looked at in isolation, but rather in combination with the incidence of the government spending it finances, in the following section we summarize a benefit incidence study on spending on primary education and health in Ethiopia. This section also assesses the changing trend of public expenditure with a focus on poverty-reducing outlays and provides insights for future expenditure policies in Ethiopia. In the next section we estimate the net effect of introducing VAT on the poor, and we then conclude and summarize the policy implications of our analysis.

Tax Incidence Analysis of the VAT

As noted above, the VAT replaced the sales tax in Ethiopia as of January 1, 2003.[3] In comparison to the sales tax, the new VAT taxes services in addition to production, grants zero-rating to exports, and gives exemptions to fewer basic products. The VAT is expected to enhance revenue, improve economic efficiency, promote exports, and foster growth. However, the broadening of the tax base, the increase of the tax rate, and the choice of exemptions will have differential effects on the income/expenditures of different groups of the population. We are particularly interested in the impact on equity and the consequences for the poor and vulnerable.

In an important deviation from the basic logic of a VAT, most countries that have adopted a VAT exempt certain items or activities. In these cases, output is untaxed and the VAT paid on inputs is not recoverable. Exemptions complicate administration, erode the tax base, and distort input-choice decisions; consequently, they should be kept to a minimum. Some items are exempted to improve the distributional impact of the tax—a potentially reasonable trade-off. Others might be exempted for administrative or political reasons. In this section, we look at the current exemptions in Ethiopia to see if they are justified.

Description of the VAT

The sales tax, initially introduced in 1993,[4] underwent several amendments until its abolition at the end of 2002. Under the latest amendment (January 2001), the sales tax was levied on imports and domestically produced goods at a top rate of 15 percent. However, many goods—primarily agricultural products and food, pharmaceutical products, and printed books—were taxed at a lower rate (5 percent). A few specified services were taxed at the 15 percent rate, and financial services and work contracts were taxed at the lower 5 percent rate. Water, electricity, and medical and educational services were completely exempt. The tax paid on some inputs, including raw materials—narrowly defined to include materials embodied in the final product—was credited against the output tax. However, no credits were given to tax paid on capital equipment or on other inputs in the areas of distribution, warehousing, and administration. In summary, the sales tax base in Ethiopia was narrow because it was limited to imports, manufactured

---

[3] Proclamation No. 285/2002.

[4] The original sales tax law is Proclamation No. 68/1993. Our analysis is based on the last amendment made in January 2001, Proclamation No. 228/2001.

goods, and a few selected services. Because credit was given only for taxes paid on raw materials, the tax had a cascading effect, distorted efficient resource allocation, and thus likely impeded economic growth.

The newly introduced VAT has a uniform rate of 15 percent on most goods and services, with a zero rate on exports and exempted goods and services. The scope of exempted goods and services differs from that under the sales tax. Under the new VAT, the main exempt items are sales of used dwellings, financial services, medical and educational services, electricity, kerosene, water, and transportation. See Table 1 for a summary comparison of the sales tax and the VAT.

Methodology for Analyzing Tax Incidence

Data

This paper uses the *1999/2000 Household Income, Consumption and Expenditure Survey* (2001), published by the Central Statistical Authority of Ethiopia, to analyze the incidence of the VAT. This survey covers the settled areas of the country with a random sample of 17,332 households (8,660 from rural and 8,672 from urban areas). The data set includes basic demographic characteristics and household expenditures. The domestic expenditure items fall into the following categories: food; beverages; cigarettes and tobacco; clothing and footwear; housing, water, electricity, gas, and other fuels; furnishings, household equipment and operation; health; education; transport and communication; entertainment, religious, and cultural services; personal care and effects; miscellaneous goods and services; and nonconsumption expenditures (such as bank deposits, interest paid, and donations).

In constructing consumption aggregates for the tax incidence analysis, we exclude nonconsumption expenditures as well as lumpy and infrequent expenditures such as those on marriages and dowries, births, and funerals. Since we are interested in estimating the incidence of VAT in the year 2002/03, we inflated the expenditures proportionally, using the change in nominal GDP between 1999/2000 and 2002/03. Since the survey measures out-of-pocket expenses, the sales tax is already embedded in the reported expenses.

Estimation of Sales Tax and VAT Amounts

Since the observed expenditures are posttax values, we use the following formula to derive the net expenditure and tax paid on each expenditure item:

Table 1. Summary of Sales Tax versus VAT in Ethiopia

	Sales Tax		Value-Added Tax
	Goods	Services	

Tax rate	*15 percent* on the value of all goods and services other than specified below.
	
	5 percent on the following:
	  live animals, meat, and fish
	  fresh milk, cream, and eggs
	  honey
	  vegetables, fruits, and nuts
	  cereals
	  coffee, cocoa, and spices
	  milled products
	  pharmaceutical products
	  hides and skins
	  books and newspapers
	  cotton
	  sales of food in hotels and restaurants
	  sales of local food and beverages
	
	2 birr/kg on locally sold chat[1]
		15 percent, including:
		telecommunications
		garage, laundry
		tailoring, translation
		photography
		auditing, engineering
		lodging
		consultation
		cinema
		commission agents
		barber/beauty salon
		tourism
		hire of goods
		
		5 percent on the following:
		  work contracts
		  financial services
			15 percent on the value of all goods and services other than specified below.

Exempt items	bread, *injera*[2] fertilizer aviation fuel/kerosene railway/marine transport equipment for national defense	water electricity medical services educational services	sale/ transfer of used dwelling/lease financial services religious services medical services and goods educational/child-care services humanitarian goods and services electricity, kerosene, and water post-office supplies transportation printed books permits and license fees import of gold, currency
Zero rate			exports

Source: Sales tax proclamation (No. 228/2001) and VAT proclamation (No.285/2002) in Ethiopia.

[1] *Chat* is a leafy green shrub that contains stimulant properties. It has been chewed for many centuries in parts of East Africa and the Middle East.

[2] *Injera* is a common sour flatbread made of teff, which grows in the highlands of Ethiopia.

$$T_{i,j} = t_{VAT,j} p_j x_{i,j} = \frac{t_{VAT,j}}{1 + t_{SalesTax,j}} e_{i,j}, \tag{1}$$

where $T_{i,j}$ is household i's VAT payment on good j; $p_j x_{i,j}$ is net expenditure on good j; $t_{VAT,j}$ is the VAT rate; $t_{SalesTax,j}$ is the sales tax rate; and $e_{i,j}$ is post–sales tax gross expenditure on good j (observed expense).

The first step in the analysis is to estimate the sales tax applied to each item from the observed expense. To rigorously calculate the sales tax paid, we need to take into account the price-cascading effect of the sales tax, using an input-output table for Ethiopia as well as the total sales tax collection by each sector of the economy. Since an input-output table for Ethiopia is unavailable, we use the 1992 table for Tanzania, a neighboring country with a similar economic structure. After matching the expenditure items in the household survey with the industries in the input-output table and those in the sales tax revenue data,[5] we derive the degree of cascading for each individual item and then apply it to the statutory sales tax rates to get the actual sales tax embedded in the reported expenditures. After extracting the sales tax paid, we calculate the VAT that would have been paid by each household by multiplying the statutory VAT rate times the before-tax expenditure on each good, following equation (1). Because the VAT is a tax on final consumption, this method is an accurate approximation of the incidence.[6]

One characteristic of the Ethiopian economy is the high percentage of the population that consumes home-produced goods and therefore is not exposed to indirect taxes. For our purpose, the household survey asks consumers if the expenditure was made in the form of cash or in kind. In-kind payment broadly incorporates home-produced and -consumed goods and services as well as goods and services received free, in trade, or as gifts from outside the household. Therefore, we use in-kind goods as a proxy for home-produced goods and do not apply a tax on them.

Finally, we cross-check our simulation results with the available national data on tax revenues. Since the latest available sales tax revenue collection was for 2001/02, we inflate this figure to 2002/03 values using the nominal GDP growth rates between 2001/02 and 2002/03. From this adjusted figure and the aggregate sales tax revenue from our simulation, we subsequently derive a noncompliance rate of 26.6 percent, and we apply this share uniformly across all the households for our estimation of the VAT and sales tax amounts.

---

[5]The matching of items in the sales tax revenue data against the economic activities in the input-output table is described in Appendix I.

[6]For a description of a more sophisticated method for assessing the distributive effects of introducing a VAT—which includes a Linear Expenditure System to assess the impact on the expenditures of different income groups—see Hossain (2003).

Incidence Analysis

In carrying out our incidence analysis, we use household expenditure as our welfare measure and we divide the sample into deciles of total expenditure to estimate the distributional impacts of introducing the VAT. We first look into the effective tax rate for each decile and then examine the generalized Lorenz curve for expenditure and the concentration curve for the VAT. The Lorenz curve plots cumulative expenditure against population share, with the population ordered by expenditure level. The concentration curve is the same except that cumulative tax expenditure is plotted against cumulative population. If the concentration curve lies below the Lorenz curve, then the tax is progressive. We also perform rigorous tests of progressivity as described in Appendix II.

Analysis of Exempt Goods

To analyze the distributional characteristics of exempt goods and services, we rely on the methodology used by Gibson (1998) to measure consumption of the poor in Papua New Guinea. The distributional characteristic of a good i is defined by Newbery (1995) as

$$d_i \equiv \frac{\sum_n^H \beta^h q_i^h}{\bar{\beta} Q_i}, \tag{2}$$

where β^h is the "social weight," defined as the social marginal utility of transferring one unit of currency to household h. Assuming a constant elasticity of substitution social welfare function, the social weight is given by $\beta^h = (c^h)^{-\upsilon}$, where c^h is the consumption level of household h and υ is the inequality-aversion parameter. For our work, we take 0.5 as a low level of inequality aversion and 2 as a high level.[7] The consumption of the ith good by household h is defined as q_i^h, and $\bar{\beta}$ and Q_i are the average of the social weights over all the households and the aggregate consumption of food i, respectively. Given the definition of the distributional characteristic, we aggregate expenditure items into 95 goods and services, with a more detailed classification for food items, and rank them according to the low inequality aversion parameter.

---

[7] Inequality aversion parameters reflect judgments on the desirability of giving transfers or levying taxes to correct income inequality. For the high inequality aversion parameter, taxing one extra Birr from a poor household has four times the social cost of taxing a household with twice the income. For the low inequality aversion parameter, the ratio is 1.4.

Limitations

Finally, we outline the limitations of our approach. First, since the analysis does not take behavioral changes into account, it only provides a first-order approximation of the incidence. Second, inaccuracy inevitably results from our simple assumption of how statutory taxes translate into economic incidence. Furthermore, our approach does not take into account possible cascading effects from the existence of exempt goods and services—that is, we have no information on the differential *indirect* effects of exempt goods and services on taxes paid by different households. This would require not only complex models (primarily models of production by stage of processing) but also access to more detailed data on household-level consumption. Finally, simplifying assumptions had to be made in the absence of data. This includes the use of the Tanzania input-output table as a proxy for the Ethiopian economic structure, using an estimated share of home-produced consumption uniformly across households, and the approximation of tax revenue collections for 2002/03 based on the 2001/02 outturn.

Results

Progressivity of the VAT

As a baseline model, we look at the tax incidence of the VAT (Table 2). The national average of the effective VAT rate is 4.77 percent. Households in the sixth decile face the lowest effective rate at 4.22 percent, while the tenth decile—the richest expenditure group—faces the highest at 5.78 percent. Figure 1 shows the effective VAT rate by deciles, while Figure 2 depicts the generalized Lorenz curve and the concentration curve for the VAT. Since the concentration curve lies strictly below the Lorenz curve, we can conclude that the VAT is progressive. The statistical tests described in Appendix I also confirm this result.

The estimated progressivity of the VAT depends entirely on the shares of consumption of exempt items and items obtained in kind. Although the magnitude of these two groups taken together is higher for the lower deciles, the implications for each of the groups are different. Figure 3 shows that the percentage of in-kind transactions stays well above 50 percent for all but the last decile. This adds to the progressivity of the VAT. On the other hand, Figure 4 illustrates the distribution effects of exempt items. It is worth noticing that the exempt goods and services are consumed mostly by the households in the highest decile. This feature will be discussed in the subsection on the distributional characteristics of exempt items.

Table 2. Tax Incidence of VAT by Deciles

Decile	Average Expenditure (Birr)	Average VAT Payment (Birr)	Effective VAT Rate (Percent)
1	1,688.76	73.27	4.34
2	2,593.04	117.08	4.52
3	3,206.68	139.69	4.36
4	3,747.69	162.03	4.32
5	4,301.92	185.15	4.30
6	4,895.82	206.47	4.22
7	5,582.59	245.35	4.40
8	6,531.42	289.52	4.43
9	8,028.06	375.76	4.68
10	13,839.50	800.57	5.78
Average	5,442.49	259.54	4.77

Source: Authors' calculations based on Ethiopia, Central Statistical Authority (2001).

Figure 1. Effective VAT Rates

Percent

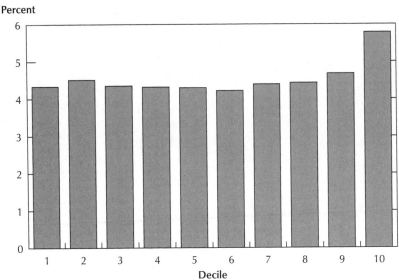

Source: Authors' calculations based on Ethiopia, Central Statistical Authority (2001).

Figure 2. Generalized Lorenz Curve and Concentration Curve for VAT

Cumulative expenditure/tax payment

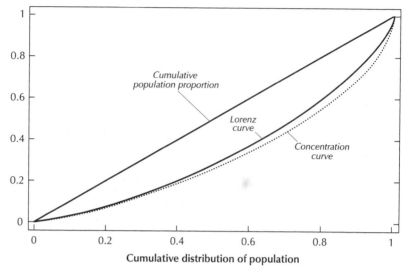

Cumulative distribution of population

Source: Authors' calculations based on Ethiopia, Central Statistical Authority (2001).

Figure 3. Share of "In-Kind" Transactions in All Transactions

Percent

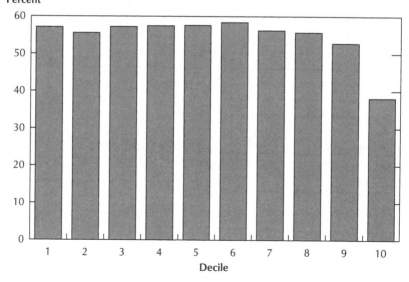

Decile

Source: Authors' calculations based on Ethiopia, Central Statistical Authority (2001).

Figure 4. Share of Exempt Goods and Services Consumption in All Consumption

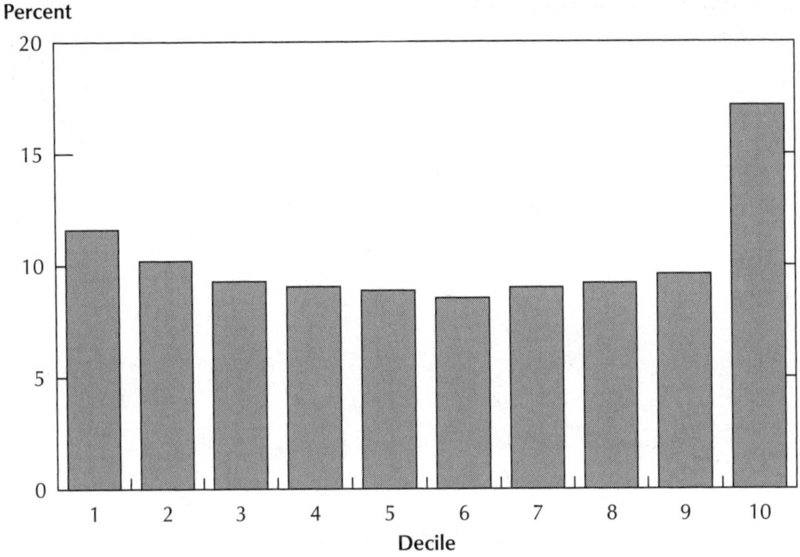

Percent

Source: Authors' calculations based on Ethiopia, Central Statistical Authority (2001).

Comparison with the Sales Tax

Next, we compare our results with the sales tax incidence. As Table 3 shows, the effective sales tax rates are lower than the effective VAT rates, since many goods and services had lower rates under the sales tax. On average, households faced an effective tax rate of 3.88 percent, which is 18.7 percent lower than the rate under the VAT (4.77 percent). In other words, the replacement of the sales tax by the VAT has increased the tax payment burden for the average household (see Figure 5 for the effective sales tax rate by decile). Figure 6 shows the increase in tax burden from the sales tax to the VAT as a percentage of household expenditure. We see that poorer households are harder hit from the shift in the tax regime because their increase in tax burden (1.36 percent of total expenditure for the lowest decile) is more than three times the portion of the highest decile (0.38 percent).[8] Figure 7, which compares the concentration curves for the VAT and the sales

[8] This is on top of the adverse cascading effect under the sales tax for the poorer households. The cascading effect of the sales tax creates an increase of 24.1 percent in the overall effective sales tax burden. The effect, however, varies among different expenditure categories, with the highest burden for the lowest decile (25.9 percent) and lowest burden for the highest decile (23.4 percent).

Table 3. Tax Incidence of Sales Tax by Decile

Decile	Average Expenditure (Birr)	Average Sales Tax Payment (Birr)	Effective Tax Rate (Percent)
1	1,688.76	50.22	2.97
2	2,593.04	81.41	3.14
3	3,206.68	99.73	3.11
4	3,747.69	118.44	3.16
5	4,301.92	137.29	3.19
6	4,895.82	154.43	3.15
7	5,582.59	189.92	3.40
8	6,531.42	228.31	3.50
9	8,028.06	306.87	3.82
10	13,839.50	747.33	5.40
Average	5,442.49	211.44	3.88

Source: Authors' calculations based on Ethiopia, Central Statistical Authority (2001).

tax, demonstrates that the sales tax is more progressive than the VAT. In sum, this is true because the VAT has fewer exempt items, and these items are not disproportionately purchased by the poor. The VAT is more efficient, but it does shift some of the relative burden of the tax on the poor. The result is that the replacement of the sales tax with the VAT has had an adverse impact on the poorest 40 percent of the population. Note, however that the impact is small (about 1 percent of their consumption). Moreover, this is of course only half of the story. If the additional revenue is spent primarily on the poor, the net incidence will be reversed (see the section below on the net effects on the poor of the move to VAT).

Distributional Characteristics of Exempt Goods

Table 4 shows the estimated distributional characteristics for exempt goods and services. The rankings reflect the degree to which the goods and services are disproportionately consumed by the poor. As Table 4 demonstrates, the current exempt goods and services are primarily goods that are disproportionately consumed by higher-income groups. Using the low inequality-aversion parameter, the highest-ranked among the exempt goods and services was utilities at 36, followed by rent at 54. Health expenditure was ranked at 73, whereas public transport was ranked at 80. Finally, education and financial services were the two categories of expenditures with the lowest relative consumption by the poor, ranking at 86 and 93 out of 95 items. The goods disproportionately consumed by the poor were primarily basic food items and

Figure 5. Effective Sales Tax Rates

Percent

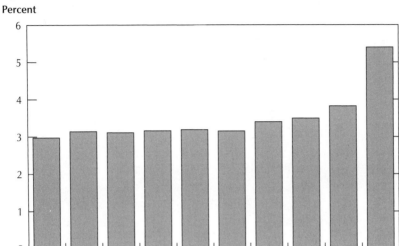

Source: Authors' calculations based on Ethiopia, Central Statistical Authority (2001).

Figure 6. Average Increase in Tax Burden from Sales Tax to VAT

Percentage of total expenditure

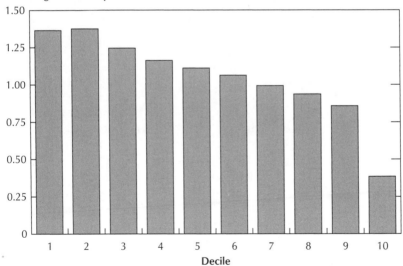

Source: Authors' calculations based on Ethiopia, Central Statistical Authority (2001).

Figure 7. Generalized Lorenz Curve and Concentration Curve (Sales Tax, VAT)

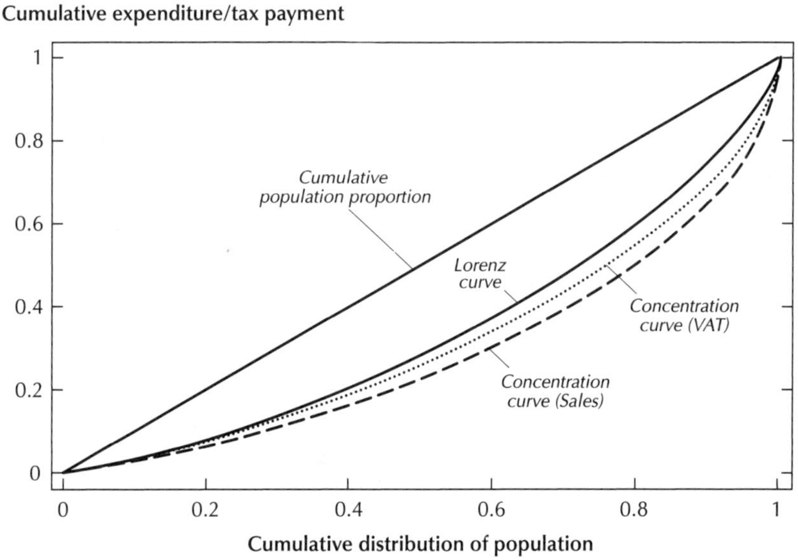

Cumulative expenditure/tax payment

Source: Authors' calculations based on Ethiopia, Central Statistical Authority (2001).

traditional fuel sources such as dung cakes and firewood. From this, we can conclude that the exempt goods and services do not properly serve the purpose of alleviating poverty or improving equity.

Disaggregated Results

In this section, we separately analyze food and nonfood items, and the urban and rural populations. More than 80 percent of Ethiopians live on less than U.S.$1 a day, and basic foodstuff takes a significant share of expenditure for most households. We compare the progressivity of the VAT for food—which is such an important expenditure component for the poor—to the progressivity of the VAT on nonfood items. Next, we do a regional decomposition into urban and rural areas and see how the degree of urbanization affects our results. Currently the urban population is only about 17 percent of the total population, but Ethiopia has experienced a huge flow of migration into urban areas, with the urban population growing by almost 70 percent between 1990 and 2000. As urbanization progresses, it is important to evaluate the impact of VAT on those—especially the poor—migrating to urban areas.

Table 4. Distributional Characteristics of Top 10 Goods versus Exempt Goods and Services

Rank	Expenditure Item	Low Aversion	High Aversion
1	Unmilled *durrah*[1]	1.011	0.950
2	Milled *durrah*	0.976	0.760
3	Bread traditional	0.946	0.782
4	Milled millet	0.939	0.665
5	Oilseed	0.937	0.647
6	Tobacco (local)	0.935	0.586
7	*Injera*[2]	0.931	0.713
8	Unmilled sorghum	0.930	0.659
9	Milled sorghum	0.927	0.614
10	Salt	0.927	0.649
36	Utilities	0.833	0.475
54	Rent	0.779	0.485
73	Health	0.733	0.314
80	Transport	0.660	0.247
86	Education	0.602	0.178
92	Other exempt items	0.502	0.044
93	Financial services	0.482	0.103

Source: Authors' calculations based on Ethiopia, Central Statistical Authority (2001).
[1] *Durrah* is a form of (wheat) flour.
[2] *Injera* is a common sour flatbread.

Food versus Nonfood

Table 5 displays the distributional analysis for food and nonfood items separately. The figures in brackets denote the share of food in the overall expenditure for each decile. Note that the share of food expenditure is above two-thirds for most of the households in the survey. Because the average proportion of in-kind expenditures is higher for food than for nonfood items, the effective VAT rate on food is lower. However, because the share of in-kind expenditures is not inversely related to income as one might expect it to be—at least through the first nine deciles—the effective VAT rate is higher for lower expenditure deciles. Those households in the first two deciles face especially high effective rates. On the other hand, the share of exempt and in-kind expenditures in the nonfood category does fall as income increases, so the effective tax rate increases monotonically from lower to higher deciles, with the national average at about 5.18 percent.

Based on the Lorenz curves and the concentration curves decomposed into food and nonfood categories, the VAT on nonfood is still progressive whereas the VAT on food is not. In fact, as shown in Appendix II, we fail to conclude the dominance of the VAT on food

Table 5. Tax Incidence of VAT by Deciles—Food versus Nonfood

	Food			Nonfood		
Decile	Expenditure	VAT paid	Effective rate	Expenditure	VAT paid	Effective rate
1	1,183.41 (0.701)	56.05	4.74	505.36	17.22	3.41
2	1,829.12 (0.705)	87.53	4.79	763.92	29.55	3.87
3	2,272.29 (0.709)	100.66	4.43	934.40	39.03	4.18
4	2,612.64 (0.697)	113.21	4.33	1,135.05	48.82	4.30
5	3,021.11 (0.702)	128.01	4.24	1,280.81	57.14	4.46
6	3,443.38 (0.703)	138.59	4.02	1,452.44	67.88	4.67
7	3,808.20 (0.682)	159.47	4.19	1,774.39	85.89	4.84
8	4,420.56 (0.677)	181.51	4.11	2,110.86	108.01	5.12
9	5,292.62 (0.659)	226.31	4.28	2,735.44	149.45	5.46
10	7,084.12 (0.512)	396.34	5.59	6,755.38	404.23	5.98
Average	3,497.34 (0.643)	158.79	4.54	1,945.15	100.74	5.18

Source: Authors' calculations based on Ethiopia, Central Statistical Authority (2001).

over food expenditure as the concentration curve and the Lorenz curve cross each other (see Figures 8 and 9). Not surprisingly, given the high share of expenditure on food by low-income households, we note that food expenditure is more regressive than nonfood expenditure (Figure 10). In addition, however, the VAT on food expenditure is not progressive like the VAT on nonfood expenditure (Figure 11). Combining the two factors, we can infer that while the poor spend more on food, they pay a disproportionately larger fraction of their expenditure on taxes on the food items they purchase.

Rural versus Urban

About 17 percent of Ethiopians lived in urban areas in 2002,[9] but this share has been growing rapidly since the 1990s. This fact is important, because the incidence of the VAT on rural households is very different from the incidence on urban households for two reasons: (1) income levels are higher in urban areas, and (2) the share of in-kind expenditures is much larger in rural areas. For example, the average expenditure in the richest decile is almost 2.5 times higher in the urban areas than in rural areas, but the incidence of the VAT is more than 3 times higher for urban households in this decile (Table 6). On average, urban dwellers face an effective VAT rate of 7.8 percent, while rural

---

[9]Currently, Ethiopia is one of the least urbanized countries in Africa, but with its urban population growing at about 6 percent annually, the level of urbanization is expected to reach about 30 percent by 2020.

Figure 8. Generalized Lorenz Curve and Concentration Curve (VAT on Food)

Cumulative expenditure/tax payment

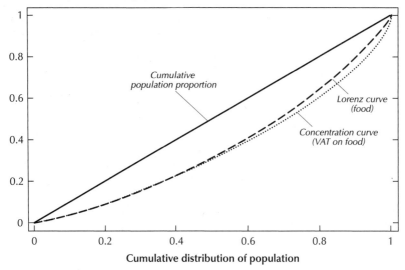

Cumulative distribution of population

Source: Authors' calculations based on Ethiopia, Central Statistical Authority (2001).

Figure 9. Generalized Lorenz Curve and Concentration Curve (VAT on Nonfood)

Cumulative expenditure/tax payment

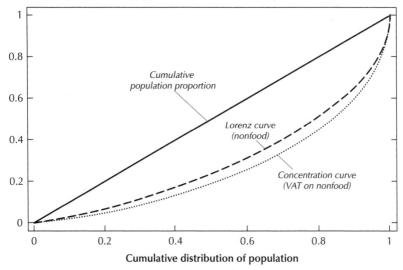

Cumulative distribution of population

Source: Authors' calculations based on Ethiopia, Central Statistical Authority (2001).

Figure 10. Comparison of Generalized Lorenz Curves

Cumulative expenditure

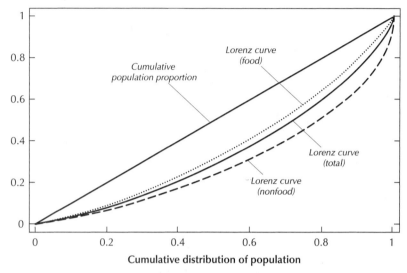

Source: Authors' calculations based on Ethiopia, Central Statistical Authority (2001).

Figure 11. Comparison of Concentration Curves (VAT on Food versus VAT on Nonfood)

Cumulative expenditure

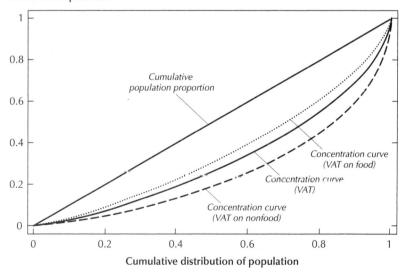

Source: Authors' calculations based on Ethiopia, Central Statistical Authority (2001).

Table 6. Tax Incidence of VAT by Deciles—Urban versus Rural

	Urban			Rural		
Decile	Expenditure	VAT paid	Effective rate	Expenditure	VAT paid	Effective rate
1	1,681.20	125.92	7.49	1,690.58	64.60	3.82
2	2,671.18	214.02	8.01	2,582.28	104.39	4.04
3	3413.89	281.97	8.26	3,182.00	125.60	3.95
4	4,184.70	353.83	8.46	3,699.39	142.92	3.86
5	4,971.05	418.23	8.41	4,220.34	155.88	3.69
6	5,869.94	488.02	8.31	4,789.68	183.41	3.83
7	7,084.93	581.75	8.21	5,418.57	204.40	3.77
8	8,729.87	708.08	8.11	6,281.35	241.95	3.85
9	11,716.63	947.88	8.09	7,566.72	296.42	3.92
10	25,192.19	1,765.06	7.01	11,405.07	517.12	4.53
Average	7,552.59	588.56	7.79	5,084.45	203.71	4.01

Source: Authors' calculations based on Ethiopia, Central Statistical Authority (2001).

dwellers pay 4.0 percent in VAT. Another noteworthy feature is that in the urban areas, households in the highest decile face the lowest effective tax rate. This, together with our earlier analysis on the exempt goods, confirms that the exempt goods are heavily used by the richer urban households in Ethiopia. Looking at the Lorenz curves and concentration curves (Figures 12 and 13), we have opposite results for urban and rural areas. For rural households, the VAT is even more progressive than it is for all households, but for urban households, the VAT is regressive. As urbanization in Ethiopia is expanding at a fast pace, this regressive nature of the VAT for urban households requires additional attention in defining exempt goods, administering the tax regime, and implementing expenditure policies oriented at addressing urban poverty and inequity.

Benefit Incidence of Spending on Primary Education and Health

As noted in the introduction, a comprehensive PSIA would evaluate not only the incidence of taxes, but also the benefits that they finance. Over the past three years, public spending for poverty reduction in Ethiopia has more than doubled as a percentage of GDP, rising from 8 percent in 1999/2000 to nearly 18 percent in 2002/03. This is in part due to the sharp decrease in defense outlays following the peace agreement with neighboring Eritrea, but also in line with the efforts by the government and the outside donors to fight poverty and

Figure 12. Generalized Lorenz Curve and Concentration Curve (VAT Urban)

Cumulative expenditure/tax payment

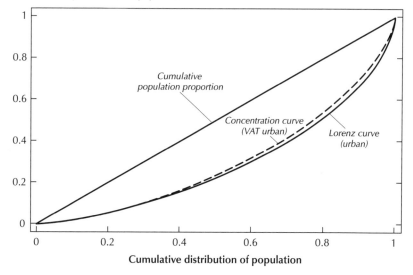

Source: Authors' calculations based on Ethiopia, Central Statistical Authority (2001).

Figure 13. Generalized Lorenz Curve and Concentration Curve (VAT Rural)

Cumulative expenditure/tax payment

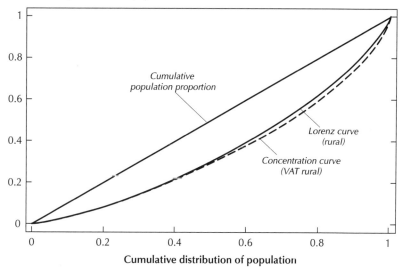

Source: Authors' calculations based on Ethiopia, Central Statistical Authority (2001).

finance pro-poor activities. The main areas of poverty-targeted public expenditure are health, education, infrastructure, and agricultural services. Of those, health and education are particularly important in the sense that not only do they address the well-being of the current population but they also play a significant role in investing for future human capital.[10]

In October 2001, Ethiopia reached a decision point for enhanced HIPC relief,[11] with the total amount of debt relief estimated at about US$1.9 billion, accounting for 36 percent of its nominal debt stock. This decision point was reached following Ethiopia's successful completion of the first annual review under the three-year PRGF arrangement and launching of a wide consultative process for the elaboration of the country's Poverty Reduction Strategy Paper (PRSP), which will serve as a basis for IMF and World Bank concessional lending. This debt relief is expected to assist in the federal and regional governments' own efforts to increase social spending by allocating more for poverty reduction. According to the estimates, the allocation of resources from the HIPC Debt Relief to education and health spending is expected to be about 520 million Birr and 156 million Birr, respectively, over the three years from 2002/03 to 2004/05.

Importance of Benefit Incidence Analysis

While the tax incidence analysis compares the relative tax burden for different expenditure groups, it provides only half the information necessary to assess the equity of budget policy. Benefit incidence analysis shows the distribution of benefits provided by the government and financed—at least in part—from tax receipts. Even if a tax turns out to be regressive, the overall impact on the poor can be neutralized or reversed if the public expenditure financed by that tax effectively targets the poor. Likewise, even if the tax revenues are collected in a progressive manner, the overall effect on the welfare of the poor can be reversed if the benefit from public expenditure falls disproportionately on

---

[10] Poverty-reducing spending is defined in Ethiopia's Poverty Reduction and Strategy Paper (PRSP). Strictly speaking, only a small share of poverty-reducing expenditure is used to fight current poverty—for instance, by providing direct aid to increase the consumption level of poor households. Rather, much of this expenditure takes the form of investment in human capital—health, education, sanitation infrastructure—which will only show up as poverty reduction some time in the future, and only if appropriately targeted.

[11] Once a country has made sufficient progress in meeting the criteria for debt relief, the Executive Boards of the IMF and World Bank formally decide on a country's eligibility, and the international community commits to reducing debt to a sustainable threshold. This is called the decision point.

the rich. Unfortunately, we do not have access to the data necessary to carry out a benefit incidence analysis for Ethiopia.[12] Consequently, we draw in this section on a recent benefit incidence analysis on health and education in Ethiopia by Seifu (2002) as illustrative of the information necessary for a comprehensive analysis of the impact of public policy on the poor. That paper uses 2000/01 Welfare Monitoring Survey data that cover limited consumption and asset information as well as health access and use, literacy, enrollment and dropout, and malnutrition information. Seifu analyzes both the average and marginal benefits of public expenditure on health and primary education across different income groups.[13] Furthermore, it undertakes urban-rural and gender decompositions and examines how the benefits vary by area and gender. For education service, the proxy used to estimate benefits was the enrollment ratio[14] for primary schools, while for health service it was utilization of different health facilities.[15]

Main Findings

The results of the analysis are mixed. For primary education, the average benefits of public expenditure accrue more heavily to the rich not only at the national level, but also in rural and urban areas. The divergence in benefits between the poor and nonpoor is especially great in the rural areas. Seifu argues that the lower enrollment ratio for the poor, especially the rural poor, is correlated with the high opportunity costs of sending a child to school. A similar result holds for marginal benefits. Given an increase in primary education access, the nonpoor are

---

[12] To carry out a benefit incidence analysis, it would be necessary to have data on which government services were consumed by which households. This is usually done in a crude fashion—as in the paper by Seifu—by using household surveys to determine if a household has access to a government service and implicitly assuming that all access is equal in terms of the quantity and quality of the service. A more rigorous analysis would analyze government provision of a service in more detail to determine if quantity and quality, as well as cost of provision, vary across demographic groups or by region.

[13] Average benefit incidence analysis estimates the incidence of all aggregate benefits, whereas marginal benefit incidence analysis measures the incidence of the last (or the next) unit of benefit.

[14] The methodology considers both gross and net enrollment ratios. The former is defined as the ratio of total number of pupils attending primary schools currently to total number of primary school age children, and the latter is defined as the ratio of number of primary school age children currently attending primary school to total number of primary school children.

[15] Benefit incidence analyses typically entail a number of assumptions that reduce their precision. For instance, in the Seifu analysis, all enrollments are assumed of equal value. To the extent that the quality of education services or attendance rates vary across income groups, the benefit incidence will vary in a manner that is not captured in the study.

expected to benefit considerably more than the poor.[16] In terms of regional decomposition, a marginal increase in education expenditure benefits the urban poor more than the rural poor.

For health expenditure, however, the opposite result holds. Public expenditure on health gives larger benefits to the poor than the nonpoor. In addition, for the urban-rural dichotomy, the same results hold and the poor take more advantage of public health facilities than do the nonpoor. Thus, public health outlays are well targeted. Finally, the results are the same for marginal benefits, as people in lower-income brackets reap more benefit from additional spending than do those in the upper brackets.

Changing Trend of Public Expenditure and Poverty-Reducing Outlays

The results of the Seifu benefit incidence analysis provide some insights into the effectiveness of public expenditure policy on education and health. The analysis, however, covers data prior to 2001, and given the more recent information on the trend of public expenditure and medium-term forecasts until 2004/05, it would be appropriate to assess the likely impact of these recent trends on poverty-reducing spending.

Table 7 summarizes the recent trend in poverty-reducing outlays from 2000/01. In addition, it provides revised projections under the Medium-Term Expenditure Fiscal Framework (MEFF) in the PRSP until 2005/06. Total poverty-reducing expenditure as a share of total expenditure is expected to jump from 41.4 percent in 2000/01 to 59.6 percent in 2005/06. As a percentage of GDP, expenditure for poverty-targeted sectors is projected to increase from 11.8 percent in 2000/01 to 18.2 percent in 2005/06. Education and health-related expenditures as a share of total expenditure are expected to rise from 14.2 percent and 6.3 percent in 2000/01 to 22.4 percent and 6.8 percent in 2005/06, respectively. As a percentage of GDP, these shares are projected to increase from 4.0 percent and 1.8 percent in 2000/01 to 6.8 percent and 2.1 percent in 2005/06, respectively. Finally, looking into the composition of expenditures on education and health, current expenditure in education is expected to rise from 2.8 percent in 2000/01 to 4.0 percent of GDP by 2005/06, whereas capital expenditure is forecast to increase from 1.2 percent to 2.8 percent of GDP. Current expenditure on health, on the other hand, is expected to have only a moderate increase from 0.9 percent of GDP to 1.1 percent of GDP

---

[16]Primary education spending is nonetheless progressive. That is, the distribution of benefits from primary education spending is more egalitarian than the distribution of private expenditure.

Table 7. Public Expenditure Trends and Forecasts

	2000/01	2001/02	2002/03 Estimate	2003/04 Forecast	2004/05 Forecast	2005/06 Forecast
			(In millions of birr)			
Total expenditure	15,382	16,680	21,063	22,563	22,521	23,357
of which:						
Poverty-reducing expenditure	6,375	7,553	9,941	11,287	12,443	13,911
Education	2,185	2,470	3,330	3,808	4,197	5,243
Current	1,513	1,777	2,172	2513	2,700	3,100
Capital	672	693	1,158	1,295	1,497	2,143
Health	972	1,046	1,448	1,472	1,332	1,592
Current	470	522	622	711	819	832
Capital	502	524	826	761	513	760
Other (water, road, agriculture)	3,218	4,037	5,164	6,006	6,915	7,076
			(In percent of total expenditure)			
Total expenditure	100.0	100.0	100.0	100.0	100.0	100.0
of which:						
Poverty-reducing expenditure	41.4	45.3	47.2	50.0	55.3	59.6
Education	14.2	14.8	15.8	16.9	18.6	22.4
Current	9.8	10.7	10.3	11.1	12.0	13.3
Capital	4.4	4.2	5.5	5.7	6.6	9.2
Health	6.3	6.3	6.9	6.5	5.9	6.8
Current	3.1	3.1	3.0	3.2	3.6	3.6
Capital	3.3	3.1	3.9	3.4	2.3	3.3
Other (water, road, agriculture)	20.9	24.2	24.5	26.6	30.7	30.3
			(In percent of GDP)			
Total expenditure	28.4	32.2	37.5	35.7	32.3	30.5
of which:						
Poverty-reducing expenditure	11.8	14.6	17.7	17.9	17.9	18.2
Education	4.0	4.8	5.9	6.0	6.0	6.8
Current	2.8	3.4	3.9	4.0	3.9	4.0
Capital	1.2	1.3	2.1	2.1	2.1	2.8
Health	1.8	2.0	2.6	2.3	1.9	2.1
Current	0.9	1.0	1.1	1.1	1.2	1.1
Capital	0.9	1.0	1.5	1.2	0.7	1.0
Other (water, road, agriculture)	5.9	7.8	9.2	9.5	9.9	9.2
Memorandum items:						
GDP (Current price, in million Birr)	54,211	51,761	56,192	63,139	69,681	76,582

Source: IMF Country Report No. 03/272 (September 2003) and IMF staff estimates.
Note: Capital spending in health and education is estimated on the basis of the most recent figures for aggregate poverty-reducing spending, current spending, and less recent data on the shares of these sectors in total capital spending. Projected expenditures may increase if more external finance is identified following the HIPC completion point.

within the same period, while capital expenditure is expected to remain at about 1.0 percent with only a peak at 1.5 percent in 2002/03.

This increase in expenditure is expected to be funded by the newly mobilized domestic tax revenue system, including the new VAT, donor support including HIPC debt relief, and restraint on expenditures of non-poverty sectors, especially defense outlays. Given the relatively poor targeting of education spending, at least some of these resources should be aimed at making social spending more pro-poor. The government plans to increase the gross enrollment ratio to 65 percent by the end of 2004/05. However, the government should also keep in mind how to provide better access to the poor in utilizing the benefits of primary education service. This would involve not only establishing building capacity in the rural and remote areas of the country, but also creating greater incentives for the poor families to send their children to school.

An example of this pro-poor policy would be to modify the school calendar so that classes do not overlap with the harvesting season. In addition to attaining its gross-enrollment-ratio target, the government should make efforts at reducing the dropout rates and minimizing the gender gap. As for the latter, efforts are under way to equip primary schools with grinding mills, separate toilets for girls, and more female teachers. One way to make health spending more pro-poor would be to reallocate more resources for preventive care against diseases such as malaria, HIV/AIDS, and tuberculosis, with the main emphasis on the rural population. Finally, it should be recognized that expenditure management will need to be improved to ensure that the additional resources obtained through taxes are being efficiently used. In this regard, institutional arrangements to supplement this pro-poor spending would include engaging with the civil society to track and monitor public expenditure, and the systematic application of a set of criteria to test whether the expenditure policy effectively targets the poor.

Net Effects on the Poor of Replacing the Sales Tax with VAT

The discussion above raises the question of whether the poor, on net, would benefit from the introduction of the VAT, provided the extra funds were used for education and health. To provide a rough estimate of this, we use the estimates of marginal odds of using primary education and health services from Seifu (2002) and the estimate of the increase in revenue from our VAT incidence analysis.[17] The net benefit

---

[17]For an example of a similar use of marginal odds estimates to describe the distribution of benefits to different income groups from additional public spending, see Lanjouw and Ravallion (1999).

to the poor depends on the assumption of how much of the extra funds are used on primary education and how much on health.

Table 8 illustrates the net effect of the VAT by quintile. The second column shows the gain in revenue from the introduction of VAT for the government (loss in expenditure for households) as a percentage of the average consumption of households. We use three different scenarios to estimate the benefit for households: (1) additional tax revenues are used for primary education and health equally; (2) additional tax revenues are used for primary education; and (3) additional tax revenues are used for health. Assuming that half of the spending goes for primary education and half for health, we estimate that the poorest 20 percent of the population would receive a net benefit equivalent to ¾ percentage point of its average consumption. For the poorest 40 percent of the population as a whole, the net benefit would be the equivalent of about ½ percentage point of its average consumption. Table 8 shows, however, that households in the richest quintiles would experience a net loss. Interestingly, if all spending goes for primary education, the poorest 20 percent of the population would receive a net benefit equivalent to ½ percentage point of its average consumption; if all spending goes for health, the poorest 20 percent of the population would receive a net benefit of a full percentage point of its average consumption. This difference in the net benefit for the poorest reflects the fact that spending in health is well targeted, while spending in primary education is not (as discussed in the previous section).

Some caution should be used in interpreting these results, given that the sources of data in the two studies are different. In addition, it should be noted that distribution of benefits to different quintiles for education and health are derived from these authors' estimates on the basis of the marginal odds data in Seifu (2002); for this purpose, the results across men and women, and urban and rural groups, were averaged. Nevertheless, the results are suggestive of the fact that the introduction of the VAT—coupled with an increase in poverty-reducing spending—has yielded net benefits to the poorest 40 percent of Ethiopia's population.

Conclusion

This chapter reports the results of a PSIA of the tax incidence of the new VAT in Ethiopia and compares it with the incidence of the sales tax that it replaced. We used the *1999/2000 Household Income, Consumption and Expenditure Survey* to evaluate the tax incidence of the VAT. The analysis shows that the VAT is progressive when we analyze total expenditure at the national level. This coincides with the findings

Table 8. Net Impact of VAT
(Percentage of Average Consumption)

Quintile	Loss	Gain			Net Effect		
		Extra Spending			Extra Spending		
		Divided equally between primary education and health	In primary education only	In health only	Divided equally between primary education and health	In primary education only	In health only
1	1.37	2.16	1.79	2.53	0.79	0.42	1.16
2	1.20	1.55	1.41	1.70	0.35	0.21	0.50
3	1.09	1.05	1.02	1.08	−0.04	−0.07	0.00
4	0.96	0.74	0.84	0.64	−0.22	−0.12	−0.32
5	0.56	0.43	0.51	0.35	−0.13	−0.05	−0.21
Average	1.04	1.19	1.11	1.26	0.15	0.08	0.22

Source: Authors' calculations based on Seifu (2002).

of Sahn and Younger (1999) on the progressivity of VAT in eight sub-Saharan African countries. However, because it has fewer exemptions and only one rate, the VAT is less progressive than the sales tax it replaced. Most of the exempt goods and services are disproportionately consumed by the relatively well-to-do, so the exemptions cannot be justified on the equity grounds.

The progressivity of the VAT comes mainly from the high ratio of in-kind transactions for poorer households, but this share is expected to decrease as the economy moves onto a stable growth track and becomes more market based. Therefore, the VAT in Ethiopia is likely to become less progressive in the future, even at the national level. Moreover, the VAT is regressive or at most neutral in urban areas. Considering the growing urbanization in Ethiopia and the fact that most urban immigrants are poor, this could have significant consequences for the poor. Thus, in the future, the authorities should look for ways to adjust the VAT that would both yield sufficient revenue and increase its progressivity. This may require a restructuring of the VAT exemptions.

The replacement of the sales tax with the VAT has had an adverse impact on the poorest 40 percent of the population. However, the impact is very small (about 1 percent of their consumption). Thus, this reform has not had a major adverse effect on the poor, especially in light of the higher expenditures on poverty-reducing activities that can be financed out of these revenues. Our estimates indicate that if the additional revenues from the VAT were allocated for higher spending on primary education and health, the poorest 40 percent of the population would be net beneficiaries.

Our benefit incidence analysis summarizes a recent paper on health and primary education in Ethiopia that uses the 2000/01 Welfare Monitoring Survey. The results from this analysis are mixed. For primary education, both average and marginal benefits accrue mostly to the rich, with the distribution of benefits being more inegalitarian in rural areas. On the other hand, health expenditures are well targeted, meaning that the poor benefit more, in absolute terms, from public expenditure on health. Recent and projected increases in poverty-reducing spending hold out the promise for even greater benefits for the poor. More comprehensive benefit incidence analyses are needed to help design and implement expenditure policies that focus more directly on the poor.

Appendix I. Harmonization of Data Sources

This appendix lists the classification of sales tax revenue collections and the corresponding economic activities from the input-output table.

Table A1. Classification of Sales Tax Revenue

Sales Tax Revenue Items	Activities in Input-Output Table
Goods	
Sugar	Processed food
Food	Growing of maize
	Growing of paddy
	Growing of sorghum/millets
	Growing of wheat
	Growing of beans
	Growing of cassava
	Growing of other cereals
	Growing of oil seeds
	Growing of other roots and tubers
	Growing of coffee
	Growing of tea
	Growing of cashew nuts
	Growing of fruits and vegetables
	Growing of other crops
	Operation of poultry and livestock
	Fishing and fish farms
	Hunting and forestry
	Processing of meat and dairy products
	Grain milling
	Processed food
Soft drinks	Beverages and tobacco products
Mineral water	Utilities
Alcohol and beverages/beer	Beverages and tobacco products
Tobacco/cigarettes	Growing of tobacco
	Beverages and tobacco products

Table A1 *(concluded)*

Sales Tax Revenue Items	Activities in Input-Output Table
Cotton, yarn, and fiber	Growing of cotton
	Growing of sisal fiber
Leather and products	Textile and leather products
Chemicals and products	Manufacture of basic and industrial chemicals
	Manufacture of fertilizers and pesticides
Iron and steel/nonmetallic products	Mining and quarrying
Vehicles	Transport and communication
Petroleum products	Petroleum refineries
Machineries	Iron, steel, and metal products
Building materials	Glass and cement
	Construction
Electrical equipment	Manufacture of all equipment
Household goods	Glass and cement
	Manufacture of all equipment
Films and musical equipment	Manufacture of all equipment
Personal goods	Rubber, plastic, and other manufacturing
Pharmaceutical equipment	Manufacture of all equipment
Textiles and clothing	Textile and leather products
Wood and products (stationery)	Wood, paper, and printing
Other goods	Rubber, plastic, and other manufacturing
	Manufacture of all equipment
Services	
Telecommunications	Transport and communication
Garages	Wholesale and retail trade
Laundries	Business and other service activities
Tailoring	Business and other service activities
Works contracts	Utilities
	Construction
	Hotels and restaurants
	Public administration, health, and education
	Business and other service activities
Advocates	Wholesale and retail trade
Auditing	Wholesale and retail trade
Consultancies	Business and other service activities
Commission agents	Wholesale and retail trade
Entertainment	Business and other service activities
Barbers and beauty salons	Business and other service activities
Rent of goods	Real estate
Advertisement	Wholesale and retail trade
Financial services	Financial intermediation
Other service (including pest control,	Hotels and restaurants
tourism, lodging, photography)	Business and other service activities

Sources: Ethiopia, Ministry of Finance; and International Food Policy Research Institute.

Appendix II. Statistical Tests

In accordance with Yitzhaki and Slemrod (1991) and Sahn and Younger (1999, 2000), we do "welfare dominance testing" to see if the VAT is regressive or progressive. This is done by comparing the concentration curve with the generalized Lorenz curve and the 45-degree line. If the concentration curve is below the Lorenz curve, we can say that the VAT is progressive, implying that the poorer households pay less in taxes than the richer households in relation to their expenditure. The dominance tests use statistical procedures to confirm this result. To implement the test, we measure the difference of the ordinates of the two curves at equally spaced abscissas of the x-axis to see if the difference of the ordinates of two curves is significantly larger than zero and of the same sign. Since the two curves need not be independent, we follow the method presented in Davidson and Duclos (1997) to derive distribution-free standard errors to test for the significance of the differences between the two curves. If so, we conclude that the progressivity of one of the curves with the smaller ordinates is significantly greater than the other—that is, it "dominates" the other. If we fail to reject the null hypothesis, however, we evaluate the extended Gini coefficients,[18] constructed by Yitzhaki (1983), and undertake statistical comparison of them. If all the pairs of difference in coefficients are significantly different from zero and have the same sign, then we conclude that one dominates the other.

Tables A2–A4 present the final results from the welfare dominance testing. Note that "dominance" indicates that the column item dominates the row item, which comes after we reject the null hypothesis of nondominance. To match with our intuitions, if VAT "dominates" expenditures, we have a statistical confirmation that the Lorenz curve for the expenditures lies above the concentration curve for the VAT. This implies that the VAT is more progressive. Further, the indication of "dominance" of the sales tax over the VAT shows that the concentration curve for the VAT is strictly above that for the sales tax. Thus, the sales tax is more progressive than the VAT.

---

[18]The extended Gini coefficient is defined as

$$G(v) = -v \left[\frac{\text{cov}\left\{x, \left(1 - F(y)\right)^{v-1}\right\}}{\bar{x}} \right],$$

where v is the weight parameter chosen from 1.01 to 10.01 with increments of 0.5; x is the amount of tax payment, with mean $\bar{x}$; and $F(y)$ is the cumulative distribution of all households in ascending order of expenditure.

Table A2. Dominance Results for the VAT and the Sales Tax

	VAT	Sales Tax
Expenditures	Dominance	Dominance
VAT		Dominance
Sales tax		

Table A3. Dominance Results for the VAT (Food versus Nonfood)

	VAT	VAT Food	VAT Nonfood
Expenditure, food		No dominance	
Expenditure, nonfood			Dominance
VAT (total)			Dominance
VAT (food)	Dominance		Dominance
VAT (nonfood)			

Table A4. Dominance Results for the VAT (Urban versus Rural)

	Expenditures Urban	Expenditures Rural	VAT Urban	VAT Rural
Expenditures, urban				
Expenditures, rural				Dominance
VAT, urban	Dominance			
VAT, rural				

References

Davidson, Russell, and Jean-Yves Duclos, 1997, "Statistical Inference for the Measurement of the Incidence of Taxes and Transfers," *Econometrica*, Vol. 65 (November), pp. 1453–65.

Ethiopia, Central Statistical Authority, 2001, *Report on the 1999/2000 Household Income, Consumption and Expenditure Survey* (Addis Ababa). Available via the Internet: http://www4.worldbank.org/afr/poverty/pdf/docnav/03502.pdf.

Gibson, John, 1998, "Indirect Tax Reform and the Poor in Papua New Guinea," *Pacific Economic Bulletin*, Vol. 13, No. 2, pp. 29–39.

Hossain, Shahabuddin M., 2003, "Poverty and Social Impact Analysis: A Suggested Framework," IMF Working Paper 03/195 (Washington: International Monetary Fund).

Jung, Hong-Sang, and Erik Thorbecke, 2001, "The Impact of Public Expenditure on Human Capital, Growth, and Poverty in Tanzania and Zambia: A General Equilibrium Approach," IMF Working Paper 01/106 (Washington: International Monetary Fund).

Lanjouw, Peter, and Martin Ravallion, 1999, "Benefit Incidence, Public Spending Reforms, and the Timing of Program Capture," *World Bank Economic Review*, Vol. 13 (May), pp. 257–74.

Newbery, David, 1995, "Distributional Impact of Price Changes in Hungary and the United Kingdom," *Economic Journal*, Vol. 105 (July), pp. 847–63.

Sahn, David E., and Stephen D. Younger, 1999, "Dominance Testing of Social Sector Expenditures and Taxes in Africa," IMF Working Paper 99/172 (Washington: International Monetary Fund).

———, 2000, "Expenditure Incidence in Africa: Microeconomic Evidence," *Fiscal Studies*, Vol. 21 (September), pp. 329–47.

Seifu, Michael, 2002, "Benefit Incidence Analysis on Public Sector Expenditures in Ethiopia: The Case of Education and Health," paper submitted to the Annual Conference on the Ethiopian Economy, Addis Ababa, December. Available via the Internet: http://www.addischamber.com/downloads/ pepdownloads.asp.

Wobst, Peter, 1998, "A 1992 Social Accounting Matrix (SAM) For Tanzania," Trade and Macroeconomics Division Discussion Paper No. 30 (Washington: International Food Research Policy Institute).

World Bank, 2003, "A User's Guide to Poverty and Social Impact Analysis" (Washington: World Bank, Poverty Reduction Group and Social Development Department). Available via the Internet: http://poverty.worldbank.org/files/ 12685_PSIA_Users_Guide_-_Complete_-_High_resolution_-_May_2003.pdf.

Yitzhaki, Shlomo, 1983, "On an Extension of the Gini Inequality Index," *International Economic Review*, Vol. 24 (October), pp. 617–28.

———, and Joel Slemrod, 1991, "Welfare Dominance: An Application to Commodity Taxation," *American Economic Review*, Vol. 81 (June), pp. 480–96.

14

Foreign Aid and Revenue Response: Does the Composition of Aid Matter?

SANJEEV GUPTA, BENEDICT CLEMENTS, ALEXANDER PIVOVARSKY, AND ERWIN R. TIONGSON

The debate on the effectiveness of foreign aid has revolved for some time around the relative efficiency of loans versus grants. Since the early 1960s, an often-repeated view has been that loans are used more efficiently than grants because they are expected to be repaid. Furthermore, the need for repayment motivates governments to select projects or programs whose benefits exceed costs (see Schmidt, 1964). Therefore, concessional loans are better for meeting the objectives underlying development assistance (see Singer, 1961).

This issue has reemerged with recent calls for a shift from loans to grants. In the view of some observers, excessive lending has led to massive debt accumulation in many developing countries while failing to reach intended development objectives. Therefore, it has been argued that aid should be motivated primarily by humanitarian objectives and come in the form of grants (see, for example, Rogoff, 2003). Such an approach would also avoid worsening the debt sustainability outlook of these countries. In 2000, the International Financial Institution Advisory Commission (IFIAC, also known as the Meltzer Commission) concluded that financial assistance from multilateral development banks should be provided exclusively in the form of grants (IFIAC, 2000). In addition, the United States has proposed converting a major

The authors thank Emanuele Baldacci, Tito Cordella, Kevin Fletcher, Arye Hillman, Michael Keen, Timothy Lane, Eric Le Borgne, Mark McGillivray, Oliver Morrison, Ratna Sahay, and Juan Zalduendo for helpful comments on earlier versions of this chapter.

share of international development assistance (IDA) lending to grants and called on the World Bank and other multilateral development banks to provide up to 50 percent of their funds to developing countries in this form. In a separate initiative, the U.S. administration announced in 2002 that it would provide US$5 billion in additional foreign aid annually by the fiscal year 2006. The increased aid would take the form of grants and be channeled through a new Millennium Challenge Account. This fund would finance initiatives in selected countries with good performance as gauged by 16 indicators.

Some donor countries and researchers have expressed reservations regarding the conversion of concessional lending to grants (see, for example, Kapur, 2002).[1] This proposal has important implications for the functioning of IDA, which relies on principal and interest repayments to finance new lending. In the absence of additional contributions from donors, a significant shift from loans to grants would limit IDA from maintaining existing lending over a period of time. In addition, some analysts are concerned that the switch to grants would diminish public support in donor countries for transfers to developing countries.[2] Finally, a massive increase in resource transfers could pose a host of macroeconomic and microeconomic challenges (Heller and Gupta, 2004). For many low-income countries, scaled-up aid could amount to up to *three times* the current levels of domestic revenue.

This debate has not sufficiently emphasized the fiscal implications of these proposals. In particular, an increase in grants could have ramifications for the domestic tax revenue of these countries. It has been argued that grants are free resources that substitute for domestic revenues, while the burden of future loan repayments induces policymakers to mobilize taxes or, at least, to protect current levels of revenue collection (Bräutigam, 2000).[3] The strength of this argument depends on how strongly policymakers perceive loans, in practice, as being different from grants. If a large share of these loans is frequently forgiven (e.g., through debt relief, such as that provided by the Heavily Indebted Poor Country (HIPC) Initiative), over time rational policymakers may come to view them as roughly equivalent to grants.

Whether the possibly dampening effect of grants on revenues is favorable or unfavorable for economic development must be judged on a

---

[1] Sanford (2002) reviews the main arguments and counterarguments on this issue. See also U.S. Treasury (2000). Bulow (2002) outlines the arguments in favor of converting loans to grants in the context of difficult debt negotiations.

[2] See the general discussion in Bulow (2002).

[3] Bräutigam (2000) also argues that aid creates enclaves in the economy when projects and consultants are exempted from import duties and other local taxes.

case-by-case basis. In some circumstances, a reduction in the tax burden can promote growth by freeing resources for the private sector. Furthermore, cutting marginal tax rates and eliminating taxes that distort private sector incentives may help spur economic activity. On the other hand, reduced revenues—and the resulting dependency on aid—may have adverse macroeconomic consequences. First, aid is much more volatile and unpredictable than revenues, and the volatility of aid grows with the degree of aid dependence (Bulíř and Hamann, 2001). This volatility has implications for macroeconomic stability in aid-dependent countries. Second, poverty-reducing spending becomes dependent on aid and could be cut should aid inflows decline or cease. Third, the growing dependence on aid reduces incentives for governments to adopt good policies and maintain efficient institutions (Azam, Devarajan, and O'Connell, 1999).[4] Furthermore, in many cases, low tax revenues are due to widespread tax exemptions for powerful interest groups and to weak tax compliance. Increased aid inflows could thus divert attention from addressing these weaknesses in governance.

A number of important issues remain unresolved in the empirical literature on the revenue response to foreign aid. Studies have also focused largely on individual country experiences or selected regions. They have yielded mixed results (see McGillivray and Morrissey, 2001, and World Bank, 1998, for summaries). In some countries, foreign aid is associated with higher domestic revenues, while in others it is associated with lower revenues.[5] Furthermore, a comprehensive and systematic study of how the revenue response differs for the separate components of aid (i.e., loans and grants) is yet to be undertaken. The few studies that have taken the composition of aid into account have either used a limited sample or estimated a very simple model of the determinants of tax revenues across countries. They have also offered inconclusive results. For example, Otim (1996) finds that in a pooled sample of three South Asian economies, grants are more likely to leak into consumption than loans. To stimulate domestic investment, he suggests that donors should extend loans to developing countries rather

---

[4]On the other hand, should donors condition their aid on good policies (e.g., as in proposed MCA), then aid-dependent countries could face increased pressure to maintain or improve the efficiency of their public institutions.

[5]For example, Pack and Pack (1990) find foreign aid had a positive effect on domestic revenues in Indonesia, while Franco-Rodriguez, Morrissey, and McGillivray (1998) find a negative relationship in Pakistan. McGillivray and Ahmed (1999) find that aid depressed tax revenues in the Philippines during 1960–92. The results from the Cashel-Cordo and Craig (1990) study suggest that aid has had a positive impact on revenue mobilization among African countries and a negative impact on non-African countries. Heller (1975) finds a negative effect of aid on revenue for 11 African countries.

than provide grants. He also finds that both grants and loans increase tax revenues. On the other hand, Khan and Hoshino (1992) provide some empirical evidence that grants reduce tax revenues while loans increase it, for a sample of five South and Southeast Asian countries over 1955–76. Odedokun (2003) provides preliminary evidence that grants reduce the level of taxation in low-income countries, using a simple model of tax revenue as a function of per capita income and the (lagged) ratio of grants to total aid in 72 developing countries.

This chapter fills the void in the literature by investigating the revenue response to foreign loans and grants separately in a sample of 107 developing countries over the period 1970–2000. The study builds on the empirical literature on the determinants of tax revenues and the literature on the fiscal response to aid. It augments regression equations for structural determinants of revenues and adds both grants and net concessional loans to the vector of explanatory variables. The chapter explores several variations and specifications using panel data regressions to test the robustness of the baseline specification. Going beyond the standard econometric procedures employed by most studies in this literature, the study also tests for nonlinearities in the relationship between foreign aid and fiscal response, examines the impact of corruption on the aid-revenue nexus, explores issues related to the endogeneity of the relationship between aid and revenue, and allows for the presence of serial correlation.

Analytical Framework

The relationship between foreign aid and revenues could be viewed in terms of the government's budget constraint in any given period, written as follows:

$$G = T + A + B, \tag{1}$$

where G is government expenditure, T is recurrent revenues, A is aid (comprising both grants and loans), and B is net domestic borrowing (countries are assumed to have no access to nonconcessional foreign borrowing).

Differentiating equation (1) with respect to A yields:

$$\frac{\partial G}{\partial A} = \frac{\partial T}{\partial A} + \frac{\partial A}{\partial A} + \frac{\partial B}{\partial A}. \tag{2}$$

Thus, in response to an exogenous increase in aid, a government could (1) reduce revenues; (2) increase expenditures; (3) adjust domestic borrowing downward to meet the budget constraint; or choose a combination of these options.

In the first scenario, the government chooses to pass the benefit of higher aid inflows to the private sector by reducing revenues. At the extreme, the government could decide to reduce revenues by the full amount of aid while holding aggregate public expenditures and borrowing constant.[6] This would imply the following:

$$\frac{\partial T}{\partial A} = -1 \text{ and } \frac{\partial G}{\partial A} = 0 \text{ and } \frac{\partial B}{\partial A} = 0.$$

A similar result would arise when higher aid inflows promote rent-seeking behavior by domestic vested interests that begin to clamor for tax exemptions or a weakening of efforts to collect taxes due.[7] In the extreme, this behavior can cause revenues to decline by the full amount of aid inflows.

Under the second scenario—where expenditures increase in response to increase in aid—revenue may either increase or decrease, depending on the form aid takes and on the magnitude of the response of expenditures to aid. If the increase in expenditures is smaller than the increase in aid (i.e., aid is "fungible"), or $0 < \partial G/\partial A < 1$, holding domestic borrowing unchanged (i.e., $\partial B/\partial A = 0$), revenues would decline.[8] If the expenditures' increase is greater than the increase in aid (i.e., $\partial G/\partial A > 1$), revenues should increase. This could happen if aid is provided primarily in the form of project assistance that requires matching government spending and when aid is not fungible.[9]

---

[6] The assumption is that the aid comes in the form of budget support. If aid is tied to projects, it would require generation of counterpart funds for implementation of projects. In that case, $\partial T/\partial A > -1$.

[7] Azam, Devarajan, and O'Connell (1999) find that when institutions are initially weak, foreign aid undermines institutional capacity building (i.e., revenue-raising capacity). As such, foreign aid eventually finances the whole public budget. There is some evidence that increased aid is associated with a higher level of rent-seeking activities (Knack, 2001, and Svensson, 2000), although Tavares (2003) presents evidence to the contrary.

[8] The fungibility of aid refers to a situation where recipients reallocate resources that would have been spent for purposes now financed by foreign aid.

[9] This is analogous to scenarios discussed by Feeny and McGillivray (2003), using a similar analytical framework (equations (1) and (2)), where aid inflows lead to additional spending. In their framework, however, additional spending leads to increased (nonconcessional) borrowing rather than to increased tax revenues. Catterson and Lindahl (1999) suggest that the mode of aid delivery, such as a "matching funds" system, can provide an incentive to boost domestic revenue generation. They find that in Tanzania this system has created a "strong incentive for revenue collection."

Finally, consider the implications of a third scenario, where aid induces a decrease in domestic borrowing. Here the government decides not to spend foreign aid (i.e., $\partial G/\partial A = 0$). This can happen when the government builds up deposits with the banking system, so as to release resources for the private sector.

Thus, viewed in terms of the government's budget constraint, the response of revenues to increased aid flows could be positive, negative, or zero.

Existing models of the fiscal response to foreign aid also find that taxes could either increase or decrease in response to higher aid. The first models developed in this area tend to conclude that the increase in government spending is likely to be smaller than the increase in aid (i.e., aid is fungible). Thus, assuming domestic borrowing does not decline, aid can lead to a reduction in taxes (see, for example, Heller, 1975, and Leuthold, 1991). More recent literature has considered the theoretical scenarios under which this assumption might not hold. For example, White (1993) finds that whether or not aid adversely affects tax revenues depends, among other things, on the impact of aid on private investment.

A shortcoming of the existing literature is the tendency to lump together loans and grants when considering the effects of aid on tax revenues (e.g., Leuthold, 1991). Even models that differentiate between the two make them enter the government's utility function either as a single variable (e.g., Ghura, 1998) or as separate terms (e.g., Otim, 1996), but without explicitly allowing a government to consider the fundamental difference between the two—in particular, that grants are unrequited transfers, but loans need to be repaid. In this light, it is plausible that the effects of loans and grants on revenues could differ. In the scenarios discussed above, for example, the first one is arguably more consistent with aid provided in the form of grants, where free resources substitute for domestic revenues.

As revealed in the existing literature, the direction of the relationship between grants and loans and revenues remains a fundamentally empirical question. In the following section we present our empirical model and data that will be used to investigate this relationship.

Empirical Model and Data

The econometric approach for the present study is based on the previous literature investigating determinants of cross-country variation in taxation. Lotz and Morss (1967, 1970) developed a model of tax ratios as a function of income and trade that has become the standard for subsequent studies. Other variables were added in subsequent studies to reflect the sectoral composition of income and variables that do not necessarily represent tax bases but which have been found to affect tax revenues (see, for example, Tanzi, 1992; Stotsky and WoldeMariam, 1997; and Ghura, 1998).[10]

Unlike in the previous empirical models, we distinguish between the effects of loans (L) and grants (F). Following the analytical framework, we test the hypothesis that grants are negatively related to revenues.[11] On the other hand, the relationship between concessional lending and revenues could be influenced by the fact that loans have to be repaid. Hence, we postulate that multilateral and bilateral borrowing would have a positive effect on revenues.

We thus model cross-country variations in revenue shares as a function of grant (F) and loan (L) flows in percent of GDP, controlling for the structure of the economy (agricultural value added (AGR) and industry value added (IND) in percent of GDP); openness (the sum of exports and imports in percent of GDP ($TRADE$)); and the level of economic development (real income per capita ($SIZE$)):

$$[T/GDP]_{i,t} = \beta_0 + \beta_1 AGR_{i,t} + \beta_2 IND_{i,t} + \beta_3 TRADE_{i,t} + \beta_4 SIZE_{i,t} \quad (3)$$
$$+ \beta_5 F_{i,t} + \beta_6 L_{i,t} + \varepsilon_{i,t}.$$

We estimate equation (3) using panel data regression analysis. As noted above, the analysis covers 107 countries over 1970–2000. We allow for nonlinearities by including the product variable generated by the squared aid variable. Because the dependent variable is nonnegative and positively skewed,[12] a log transformation of the dependent variable is used in estimating equation (1). This yields a semi-log quadratic regression equation, where the βs are an estimate of the impact of each independent variable on the growth rate of the dependent variable.

---

[10]Tanzi (1989) has emphasized that researchers need to look beyond the traditional determinants of tax revenue—that is, the tax bases—to get a better understanding of variations in taxation across countries.

[11]Unlike earlier studies, we assess the determinants of total revenues (tax and nontax revenues), not just taxes. The rationale for this approach is that in some countries, nontax revenue can be significant and a substitute for resources generated by taxation. As such, it is important to assess how aid might affect total revenues, and not just taxes.

[12]Both the Jarque-Bera and Shapiro-Wilk tests for nonnormal distributions are significant at the 1 percent level. The best equation fit was obtained using the semi-log specification. In addition, the log transformation of the dependent variable has the added benefit that predicted values, which are the exponential of the predicted log value, will always be positive.

Data on total domestic revenue are drawn from the IMF's *Government Finance Statistics*. They refer to a consolidated central government.[13] Data on *net* foreign aid are from the OECD's *Geographical Distribution of Financial Flows to Aid Recipients*. The data include official development assistance (ODA) from all donor countries. ODA includes grants by official agencies of the members of the Development Assistance Committee (DAC) and loans with a grant element of at least 25 percent, and value of technical cooperation and assistance, less any repayments of loan principal during the same period.[14] Data are expressed in percent of recipient country GDP.

Data on control variables are drawn from the World Bank's *World Development Indicators* (WDI) and the IMF's World Economic Outlook database (WEO). These include the agriculture and industry value added in percent of GDP; imports and exports of goods and services in percent of GDP; and per capita GDP in constant U.S. dollars.

We also test the robustness of the baseline results to the inclusion of other variables that have been found to be significantly related to cross-country variations in domestic revenues. These include corruption, inflation, debt, and dummy for oil-producing countries. Tanzi (1992) suggests that high public debt requires a higher revenue effort; however, a high debt burden could also create macroeconomic imbalances that tend to reduce tax levels. Ghura (1998) finds that variations in tax revenue in percent of GDP are significantly related to economic policies and the level of corruption in a sample of 39 countries over 1985–96.

Except for corruption, data on all the other control variables are drawn from the WEO database. Data on corruption are drawn from the *International Country Risk Guide* (ICRG) by Political Risk Services.[15] This corruption index reflects the assessment of foreign investors about the degree of corruption in an economy. In particular, investors are asked whether high government officials are likely to demand special

---

[13] Since most foreign assistance is routed through the central government budget, the nonavailability of data on revenue collected at the subnational level should not be a major handicap.

[14] It is difficult to quantify and separate out the value of nonmonetized aid in total aid flows. It could therefore be argued that the reported aid flows overestimate the level of resources actually at the disposal of governments. However, different components of nonmonetized aid do alleviate spending pressure on a government. As such, an attempt to exclude them would understate the impact of aid on a government's fiscal behavior. For example, commodity food aid—a large proportion of which is nonmonetized—requires a government to spend less on provision of food in response to shortfalls in domestic production. In any case, data limitations prevent disaggregation of aid flows into monetized and nonmonetized components.

[15] Data have been re-scaled such that higher values reflect weak institutions.

payments and whether illegal payments are generally expected throughout lower levels of government, especially those connected with import and export licenses, exchange controls, tax assessment, police protection, or loans. Thus, the index does not necessarily capture corruption in tax administration alone.

The final sample size varies depending on the specification. The list of countries in the sample and selected summary statistics are provided in Appendix Table A1.

Econometric Results

Baseline Results

Table 1 provides the results of the baseline regressions. The regression reveals that the effect of overall aid (defined as the sum of net loans and grants) on revenue is negative and statistically significant (column 1). When aid is separated into two components, loans have a positive effect on revenues while grants have a negative effect. The sign and magnitude of this effect is more or less similar when each variable is included in the regression separately and also when both variables are included. The results of a random effects regression in column (5) are also similar.[16]

Across all regressions, the impact of the standard set of regressors on the dependent variable is consistent with results of the previous studies. For example, agricultural value added is consistently significant and has a negative impact on revenues, as expected, while trade and industry value added both have a statistically significant and positive impact on revenues. Per capita income has an ambiguous effect on revenues. In our sample, a bivariate regression of revenue on income yields a positive and significant impact on revenue (not shown); this is consistent with the seminal regression models of the determinants of tax revenues across countries. However, when the baseline model controls for other factors, per capita income is negative and significant (or insignificant, in some of the regressions in the following section).

What do the coefficients imply with respect to projected increases in grants and/or concessional loans? Assume, for example, a doubling of foreign aid (both loans and grants) from its current average levels. This is not unreasonable, given the renewed calls for the donor community to meet the 0.7 percent of GNP target for ODA. Some of the increases in grants may also come from a conversion of concessional

---

[16]The Hausman test and the Breusch-Pagan specification test both indicate that the fixed-effects model is preferable.

Table 1. Foreign Aid and Domestic Revenue: Baseline Regressions
(t-statistics in parentheses; dependent variable is the log revenue in percent of GDP)

Estimation Technique	Fixed Effects (1)	Fixed Effects (2)	Fixed Effects (3)	Fixed Effects (4)	Random Effects (5)
Aid	−0.01*** (−3.91)	... ...	... ...	... ...	... ...
(Aid)²	0.0002 (4.76)	... ...	... ...	... ...	... ...
Loan	... ...	0.007** (2.15)	... ...	0.011*** (3.05)	0.009*** (2.59)
(Loan)²	... ...	−0.0001 (−0.63)	... ...	−0.0001 (−0.99)	−0.0001 (−1.03)
Grant	... ...	... ...	−0.013*** (−4.32)	−0.016*** (−5.00)	−0.014*** (−4.48)
(Grant)²	... ...	... ...	0.0004*** (4.56)	0.0004*** (5.07)	0.0004*** (4.16)
Agriculture value-added	−0.01*** (−9.56)	−0.01*** (−9.78)	−0.01*** (−9.68)	−0.01*** (−9.94)	−0.01*** (−10.89)
Industry value-added	0.007*** (6.62)	0.007*** (6.45)	0.007*** (6.51)	0.007*** (6.58)	0.006*** (6.09)
Per capita income	−0.00004*** (−12.12)	−0.00004*** (−11.56)	−0.00004*** (−12.16)	−0.00004*** (−12.03)	−0.00004*** (−13.00)
Trade[1]	0.002*** (8.19)	0.002*** (7.88)	0.002*** (8.51)	0.002*** (8.13)	0.003*** (9.39)
Adjusted R^2	0.87	0.87	0.87	0.87	0.35
F-statistic/Wald χ^2	121.76	120.51	121.62	120.24	540.19
P-value	0.00	0.00	0.00	0.00	0.00
Number of observations	1943	1943	1943	1943	1943
Number of groups	107	107	107	107	107

Source: See text.
Significance at the 10, 5, and 1 percent levels is indicated by *, **, and ***, respectively.
[1]Trade refers to exports plus imports in percent of GDP.

loans into grants, as recommended by the Meltzer Commission and the U.S. administration.

The coefficient estimates in column (4) suggest that a doubling of average loans (from an average of 1.5 percent of GDP, using the sample underlying this regression) leads to a 0.35 percentage point of GDP increase in revenue, while a doubling of grants (from an average of 4 percent of GDP) leads to a fall in revenue by about 1.1 percentage points of GDP.[17] This implies, then, that for each additional dollar of aid in the form of grants, 28 percent of it is offset by reduced domestic revenues. This increase in grants will also lead to higher aid dependence, as the ratio of grants to domestic revenues goes up from 18 percent to 39 percent.

Robustness Tests

Table 2 adds other control variables to the baseline model such as corruption (following Ghura, 1998), foreign debt (Tanzi, 1992), and others. The results are very similar to those of the baseline model: grants reduce revenues while loans increase it, even after taking into account the small offsetting effect of the debt stock on revenues. In addition, we find that corruption has a significant impact on domestic revenues. That is, in countries with weaker institutions, revenues are lower.

It might be argued that there is some endogeneity in the relationship between foreign aid and revenue, as foreign aid may respond to shortfalls in domestic revenue mobilization (see, for example, Ghura, 1998). However, a number of papers have modeled the allocation of aid based on foreign policy and commercial interests of the donor and economic and welfare needs of the recipient (see, for example, Alesina and Dollar, 2000). These models have generally used initial mortality rates or per capita income as proxies for recipient need, not tax revenue.[18] Furthermore, Bulíř and Hamann (2001) have argued that "shortfalls in aid tend to coincide with shortfalls in domestic revenue," suggesting that donors do not increase aid when there are shortfalls in domestic revenues. Nonetheless, to allow for the possibility of some endogeneity, Table 3 reruns the regression models in Table 2, using (one-period) lagged values of the loans and grants. The results are broadly similar.[19]

---

[17] These estimates are drawn from the regression coefficients reported in column (4) and use the average values of revenues (about 21 percent of GDP) and of loans and grants (about 1.5 and 4 percent of GDP, respectively). The estimates are based on the sample underlying this regression. Given a semi-log regression of the form $\ln Y = \beta_1 + \beta_2 * X + \beta_3 * (X^2)$, the slope is equal to $Y * (\beta_2 + 2\beta_3 X)$, while the elasticity is equal to $X * (\beta_2 + 2\beta_3 X)$.

[18] The other standard determinants of aid allocation are arms imports and total population.

[19] To further assess whether endogeneity affects the results, we also estimated an instrumental variable regression of the baseline model, using initial income and initial population of recipient countries as instruments for aid, along with lagged values of aid. The results (not shown) are similar. In addition, we employed other estimation techniques (not shown) such as robust regression and maximum likelihood. We tested both the relationship between revenue and contemporaneous aid as well as revenue and lagged aid. The results are consistent with the baseline estimates in the magnitude, direction, and significance of the aid variables.

Table 2. Foreign Aid and Domestic Revenue: Including Other Regressors
(t-statistics in parentheses; dependent variable is the log revenue in percent of GDP)

Estimation Technique	Random Effects (1)	Fixed Effects (2)	Random Effects (3)	Fixed Effects (4)	Random Effects (5)	Fixed Effects (6)
Loan	0.009**	0.01***	0.009**	0.01***	0.011***	0.014***
	(2.51)	(2.96)	(2.51)	(2.96)	(3.04)	(3.79)
(Loan)^2	–0.0001	–0.0001	–0.0001	–0.0001	–0.0002	–0.0002
	(–1.02)	(–0.98)	(–1.01)	(–0.98)	(–1.53)	(–1.57)
Grant	–0.015***	–0.016***	–0.015***	–0.016***	–0.008**	–0.010***
	(–4.59)	(–5.12)	(–4.63)	(–5.12)	(–2.38)	(–3.15)
(Grant)^2	0.0004***	0.0005***	0.0004***	0.0005***	0.0002***	0.0004***
	(4.36)	(5.28)	(4.39)	(5.28)	(2.84)	(4.54)
Inflation	–0.00001*	–0.00002*	–0.00001*	–0.00002*	–0.000003	–0.000008
	(–1.70)	(–1.89)	(–1.70)	(–1.89)	(–0.34)	(–0.80)
Dummy for oil exporter	...	...	–0.12	–0.21	0.19*	0.17*
	...	...	(–0.88)	(–1.57)	(1.69)	(1.79)
Foreign debt (percent of GDP)	...	...	...	...	–0.0005***	–0.0004***
	...	...	...	...	(–4.24)	(–4.40)
Corruption	...	...	...	...	–0.10**	–0.20***
	...	...	...	...	(–2.22)	(–4.77)
Other control variables[1]	Yes	Yes	Yes	Yes	Yes	Yes
Adjusted R^2	0.35	0.87	0.36	0.87	0.34	0.85
F-statistic/Wald χ^2	539.28	118.84	539.72	118.84	432.65	100.79
P-value	0.00	0.00	0.00	0.00	0.00	0.00
Number of observations	1923	1923	1923	1923	1426	1426
Number of groups	107	107	107	107	74	74

Source: See text.
Significance at the 10, 5, and 1 percent levels is indicated by *, **, and ***, respectively.
[1]Agriculture and industry value added in percent of GDP; real per capita income; and trade (exports plus imports in percent of GDP).

The analytical framework also suggests that the impact of foreign aid on revenue could be either magnified or mitigated by the quality of institutions. In countries with weaker institutions, for example, higher aid inflows may undermine efforts to raise revenue (Azam, Devarajan, and O'Connell, 1999). There could then be some heterogeneity in the relationship between revenues and foreign aid, depending on the quality of governance.

To test this possibility, we rank countries in the sample according to their average corruption index. We then identify the lower half and the bottom quartile of the sample based on the quality of institution. Table 4

Table 3. Foreign Aid and Domestic Revenue: Lagged Values of Loans and Grants
(t-statistics in parentheses; dependent variable is the log revenue in percent of GDP)

Estimation Technique	Random Effects (1)	Fixed Effects (2)	Random Effects (3)	Fixed Effects (4)	Random Effects (5)	Fixed Effects (6)
Loan	0.011***	0.012***	0.011***	0.012***	0.012***	0.014***
	(3.16)	(3.54)	(3.15)	(3.54)	(3.24)	(3.85)
$(Loan)^2$	–0.0001	–0.0001	–0.0001	–0.0001	–0.0001	–0.0001
	(–1.03)	(–0.99)	(–1.03)	(–0.99)	(–1.24)	(–1.22)
Grant	–0.015***	–0.016***	–0.015***	–0.016***	–0.010***	–0.011***
	(–4.88)	(–5.20)	(–4.90)	(–5.20)	(–2.88)	(3.41)
$(Grant)^2$	0.0004***	0.0004***	0.0004***	0.0004***	0.0003***	0.0004***
	(4.50)	(5.08)	(4.52)	(5.08)	(3.25)	(4.37)
Inflation	–0.00001	–0.00001	–0.00001	–0.00001	0.000001	0.000002
	(–1.29)	(–1.20)	(–1.29)	(–1.20)	(0.13)	(0.23)
Dummy for oil exporter	...	...	–0.08	–0.21	0.19	0.21
	...	...	(–0.60)	(–1.59)	(1.64)	(2.04)
Foreign debt (percent of GDP)	...	...	...	...	–0.0004***	–0.0004***
	...	...	...	...	(–4.07)	(–3.97)
Corruption (ICRG)	...	...	...	...	–0.10**	–0.22***
	...	...	...	...	(–2.30)	(–4.93)
Other control variables[1]	Yes	Yes	Yes	Yes	Yes	Yes
Adjusted R^2	0.37	0.88	0.37	0.87	0.34	0.85
F-statistic/Wald χ^2	515.68	113.04	515.68	113.04	432.83	99.09
P-value	0.00	0.00	0.00	0.00	0.00	0.00
Number of observations	1879	1879	1879	1879	1412	1412
Number of groups	107	107	107	107	74	74

Source: See text.
Significance at the 10, 5, and 1 percent levels is indicated by *, **, and ***, respectively.
[1]Agriculture and industry value added in percent of GDP; real per capita income; and trade (exports plus imports in percent of GDP).

reports the regression results based on the sample of relatively corrupt countries. The results indicate that in countries with weak institutions, the magnitude of the negative relationship between grants and revenue mobilization is substantially higher than for the sample as a whole. Concessional loans have some offsetting effect, because they are associated with higher revenues, but the impact is statistically insignificant in the most corrupt quartile.

The level of domestic revenue mobilization tends to persist over time. Previous empirical studies—with the exception of Leuthold (1991)—have

Table 4. Foreign Aid and Domestic Revenue: Fixed Effects with Sub-Sample of Corrupt Countries[1]

(t-statistics in parentheses; dependent variable is the log revenue in percent of GDP)

	Contemporaneous Aid		Lagged Aid	
	Lower Half (1)	Lowest Quartile (2)	Lower Half (3)	Lowest Quartile (4)
Loan	0.015*** (3.57)	0.001 (0.19)	0.013*** (3.04)	0.014 (1.62)
(Loan)²	−0.0003** (−2.41)	0.0006 (1.12)	−0.0003** (−2.54)	−0.001 (−1.64)
Grant	−0.037*** (−5.97)	−0.091*** (−8.10)	−0.033*** (−6.01)	−0.081*** (−7.29)
(Grant)²	0.002*** (8.94)	0.003*** (10.85)	0.002*** (9.27)	0.003*** (9.42)
Inflation	−0.0001 (−0.94)	0.003*** (2.67)	−0.002*** (−7.48)	−0.002*** (−3.38)
Dummy for oil exporter	0.3788 (2.37)	0.035 (0.26)	0.12 (1.55)	0.54*** (3.26)
Foreign debt (percent of GDP)	−0.001*** (−3.79)	−0.0001 (−0.40)	−0.0006*** (−2.40)	−0.0001 (−0.27)
Corruption (ICRG)	−0.08 (−1.53)	−0.12 (−1.44)	−0.02 (−0.53)	−0.031 (−0.32)
Other control variables[2]	Yes	Yes	Yes	Yes
Adjusted R^2	0.90	0.93	0.91	0.91
F-statistic	143.56	128.88	155.92	155.92
P-value	0.00	0.00	0.00	0.00
Number of observations	657	253	653	250
Number of groups	37	18	37	18

Source: See text.

Significance at the 10, 5, and 1 percent levels is indicated by *, **, and ***, respectively.

[1] The sub-samples are based on the ICRG index of corruption, averaged over 1984–2000. The lower half and lowest quartile refer to sub-samples of relatively corrupt countries.

[2] Agriculture and industry value added in percent of GDP; real per capita income; and trade (exports plus imports in percent of GDP).

not taken this into account.[20] A Durbin-Watson test suggests that there is evidence of the presence of first-order serial correlation in our sample. To estimate our regression model in the presence of serial correlation, we

---

[20] Leuthold (1991) estimated a feasible GLS (FGLS) to correct for serial correlation.

utilize several regression techniques: (1) feasible GLS (FGLS) with AR1 correlation, assuming both common and panel-specific AR1 processes; (2) the Baltagi-Wu estimator that allows for unbalanced panels with unequally spaced observations; and (3) panel-corrected standard error (PCSE) estimates using Prais-Winsten regression to correct for autocorrelation.[21]

Columns (1) to (6) in Table 5 report the regression results corresponding to these three regression techniques. The results are weaker than the baseline results; in particular, the PCSE results yield, as expected, larger standard errors. In general, the results still suggest that loans are associated with higher domestic revenue mobilization while grants are associated with lower revenue. A doubling of the current average level of grants, for example, is associated with a 0.35 percent of GDP decline in revenue. It also implies that for each additional dollar of aid in the form of grants, about 10 percent is offset by reduced revenue.

It might again be argued that some heterogeneity exists in the relationship between foreign aid and revenues, depending on the existing level of rent seeking. To allow for this possibility, we run the serial correlation-corrected regressions using the subsample of relatively corrupt countries (Table 6). The results indicate that the inflows of grants have a bigger, negative impact on revenues in countries with weak institutions. The positive impact of loans on grants mitigates this to some extent, but the impact is statistically insignificant among the most corrupt countries. The level of corruption in itself is also associated with lower revenues.

The coefficient estimates suggest that a doubling of grants as a share of GDP is associated with a 1.3 percentage point decline in revenues in percent of GDP among the relatively corrupt countries and as much as a 3.8 percentage point decrease in revenues among the most corrupt countries. This means that the additional inflow of grants, whether from an overall increase of foreign aid from donor countries or from a conversion of loans into grants, may be completely offset by reduced domestic revenues in countries where institutions are weakest.

Conclusions and Policy Implications

To meet the Millennium Development Goals (MDGs), including cutting global poverty in half by 2015, donor countries have been called upon to meet the goal of allocating 0.7 percent of their GNP for official development assistance. Some recent initiatives have called for a shifting of foreign aid away from loans to grants while increasing overall

---

[21] The use of the FGLS procedure in the estimation of time series cross-section models has been criticized for underestimating standard errors (see Beck and Katz, 1995). The PCSE procedure addresses this problem and assumes that disturbances are heteroscedastic and contemporaneously correlated across panels.

Table 5. Foreign Aid and Domestic Revenue: Accounting for Serial Correlation
(t-statistics in parentheses; dependent variable is the log revenue in percent of GDP)

	FGLS Common AR1 (1)	FGLS Panel-Specific AR1 (2)	Baltagi-Wu Estimator (3)	Baltagi-Wu Estimator (4)	Panel-Corrected Standard Errors Common AR1 (5)	Panel-Corrected Standard Errors Panel-Specific AR1 (6)
Loan	0.005** (2.08)	0.006** (2.27)	0.004 (1.48)	0.004 (1.53)	0.006* (1.67)	0.006* (1.83)
(Loan)²	−0.00005 (−0.60)	−0.00005 (−0.57)	−0.00003 (−0.35)	−0.00003 (−0.37)	−0.00006 (−0.80)	−0.00006 (−0.72)
Grant	−0.007** (−2.28)	−0.008*** (−2.77)	−0.007** (−2.21)	−0.007*** (−2.23)	−0.007 (−1.37)	−0.008* (−1.70)
(Grant)²	0.0004*** (6.20)	0.0004*** (6.70)	0.0004*** (5.38)	0.0004*** (5.48)	0.0004*** (2.57)	0.0004** (2.68)
Inflation	−0.00001* (−1.98)	−0.00001* (−1.96)	−0.00001 (−1.18)	−0.00001 (−1.21)	−0.000002 (−0.12)	−0.000001 (−0.05)
Foreign debt (percent of GDP)	−0.0007*** (−5.40)	−0.0008*** (−6.72)	−0.00086*** (−5.66)	−0.0008*** (−5.65)	−0.0006** (−2.17)	−0.0007** (−2.59)
Dummy for oil exporter	0.26* (1.82)	0.20** (2.00)	0.17 (1.22)	0.24* (1.73)	0.25 (1.17)	−0.002 (−0.02)
Corruption (ICRG)	−0.22*** (−3.73)	−0.19*** (−5.72)	−0.11** (−2.14)	−0.11** (−2.12)	−0.21* (−1.89)	−0.28*** (−6.12)
Other control variables[1]	Yes	Yes	Yes	Yes	Yes	Yes
Regional dummies	No	No	Yes	No	No	No
Country dummies	Yes	Yes	No	No	Yes	Yes
Adjusted R^2	...	...	0.37	0.31	0.88	0.97
F-statistic/Wald χ^2	3286.53	6347.99	287.42	315.26	30790.82	78554.14
P-value	0.00	0.00	0.00	0.00	0.00	0.00
Number of observations	1426	1426	1426	1426	1426	1426
Number of groups	74	74	74	74	74	74

Source: See text.
Significance at the 10, 5, and 1 percent levels is indicated by *, **, and ***, respectively.
[1] Agriculture and industry value added in percent of GDP; real per capita income; and trade (exports plus imports in percent of GDP).

assistance to developing countries. Such an initiative could have important fiscal consequences.

This chapter examined the revenue response to inflows of foreign aid in 107 countries during 1970–2000. In particular, it investigated whether the impact of aid on revenues depends on the composition of aid—that is,

Table 6. Foreign Aid and Domestic Revenue: Accounting for Serial Correlation with Sub-Sample of Corrupt Countries[1]

(t-statistics in parentheses; dependent variable is the log revenue in percent of GDP)

	FGLS (Panel-Specific AR1)		Baltagi-Wu		Panel-Corrected Standard Errors (Panel-Specific AR1)	
	Lower Half (1)	Lowest Quartile (2)	Lower Half (1)	Lowest Quartile (2)	Lower Half (3)	Lowest Quartile (4)
Loan	0.013*** (3.70)	0.009 (1.41)	0.007* (1.77)	−0.004 (−0.60)	0.011*** (2.88)	0.009 (1.38)
$(Loan)^2$	−0.0002** (−2.51)	0.0004 (1.30)	−0.0001 (−0.98)	0.001** (2.40)	−0.0002*** (2.10)	0.0004 (0.94)
Grant	−0.036*** (−6.26)	−0.083*** (−8.57)	−0.022*** (−3.02)	−0.052*** (−3.56)	−0.046*** (−4.92)	−0.084*** (−7.04)
$(Grant)^2$	0.002*** (11.44)	0.003*** (13.83)	0.001*** (4.82)	0.001*** (4.55)	0.002*** (5.64)	0.003 (10.42)
Inflation	0.00005 (0.63)	0.0004*** (4.21)	0.00006 (0.52)	0.0003* (1.82)	0.0001 (1.21)	0.0004*** (4.43)
Dummy for oil exporter	−0.029 (−0.32)	−0.12 (−0.77)	0.38* (1.72)	0.79** (2.18)	0.12 (0.63)	1.52*** (6.41)
Foreign debt (percent of GDP)	−0.001*** (−3.78)	−0.0007* (−1.65)	−0.001*** (−2.85)	−0.001** (−2.09)	−0.0006* (−1.76)	−0.00008 (−0.15)
Corruption (ICRG)	−0.47*** (−6.27)	−0.23** (−2.37)	−0.13 (−1.27)	0.14 (−0.59)	−1.06*** (−15.12)	−1.35*** (−13.96)
Other control variables[2]	Yes	Yes	Yes	Yes	Yes	Yes
Adjusted R^2	...	...	0.27	0.16	0.98	0.97
F-statistic/Wald χ^2	5832.83	63000.66	146.73	85.90	443385.80	1310000
P-value	0.00	0.00	0.00	0.00	0.00	0.00
Number of observations	657	253	657	253	657	253
Number of groups	37	18	37	18	37	18

Source: See text.

Significance at the 10, 5, and 1 percent levels is indicated by *, **, and ***, respectively.

[1] The sub-samples are based on the ICRG index of corruption, averaged over 1984–2000. The lower half and lowest quartile refer to sub-samples of relatively corrupt countries.

[2] Agriculture and industry value added in percent of GDP; real per capita income; and trade (exports plus imports in percent of GDP).

grants versus loans. The results indicate that concessional loans are generally associated with higher domestic revenue mobilization, while grants have the opposite effect. The results are robust to various specifications. The results also indicate that foreign aid is non-linearly related to domestic revenue and its impact is influenced by the level of corruption.

These results have important policy implications. The efforts to increase the provision of grants to developing countries, as well as the proposal to convert concessional loans into grants, may lower revenues. This effect varies greatly, however, depending on the level of corruption in the country. For the sample as a whole, the effect is modest; a doubling of grants from an average of about 4 percent of GDP to 8 percent of GDP could decrease revenues by just 0.4 percentage point of GDP. In countries plagued with high levels of corruption, our empirical results suggest that any increase in aid would be fully offset by reduced revenues. Thus, grants to these countries cannot be expected to increase the aggregate amount of resources available to finance government expenditure. Loans, on the other hand, do not suffer from this drawback. If higher ODA targets are achieved by increased taxation in industrial countries, falling revenue-to-GDP ratios in recipient countries would shift the burden of taxation to donor countries.

Whether the decline in domestic revenues prompted by higher aid facilitates or retards a country's development will depend on each country's circumstances. In some countries, the dampening effect of aid on revenues could be part of a strategy to return resources to the private sector to accelerate economic growth. In these cases, it would be important that the reduction in the tax burden be realized through measures that improve the efficiency of the tax system (e.g., through a reduction in tax rates), rather than reduced efforts to ensure tax compliance. In many other countries, however, additional foreign aid is needed to supplement domestic revenues and help finance well-targeted poverty-reducing outlays (e.g., in primary education and basic health) to help meet the MDGs. However, the conclusions of this paper suggest that in countries with high levels of corruption, higher aid will fail in reaching this objective, unless accompanied by offsetting measures to protect the revenues of recipient countries. It also implies that the magnitude of additional resources needed for achieving the MDGs would be larger than current estimates of $40–60 billion a year. The results of the chapter's study provide further support for the view that foreign assistance should be targeted to countries with good institutions and governance.

Traditionally, donors have imposed conditions on the expenditure side on how their resources could be utilized, without taking into account the impact of assistance on revenues. For example, debt relief under the Enhanced HIPC Initiative is meant for spending on programs that reduce poverty. A similar type of requirement could be considered for the revenue side, particularly if the share of grants in aid flows is increased. Donors could impose and then monitor certain thresholds for domestic revenues to ensure that aid-receiving countries do not scale back their efforts to generate resources for poverty reduction and to reduce aid dependence. Further research could attempt to disaggregate aid flows into monetized and nonmonetized components, with a view to ascertaining the validity and strength of the above results. Another area worth exploring is to model the dynamics of the fiscal effects of aid flows, where appropriate data are available.

Appendix

Table A1. Countries Included in the Sample

Albania	Cyprus	Lebanon	Sierra Leone
Algeria	Dominican Republic	Lesotho	Singapore
Argentina	Ecuador	Madagascar	South Africa
Azerbaijan	Egypt	Malawi	Sri Lanka
Bahrain	El Salvador	Malaysia	St. Kitts and Nevis
Bangladesh	Ethiopia	Mali	St. Lucia
Barbados	Fiji	Malta	St. Vincent and
Belize	Gabon	Mauritania	the Grenadines
Benin	Gambia, The	Mauritius	Sudan
Bhutan	Georgia	Mexico	Suriname
Bolivia	Ghana	Mongolia	Swaziland
Botswana	Grenada	Morocco	Syrian Arab Republic
Brazil	Guatemala	Namibia	Thailand
Burkina Faso	Guinea	Nepal	Togo
Burundi	Guinea-Bissau	Nicaragua	Tonga
Cameroon	Guyana	Niger	Trinidad and Tobago
Central African Republic	Honduras	Nigeria	Tunisia
Chad	India	Oman	Turkey
Chile	Indonesia	Pakistan	Uganda
China, P.R.: Mainland	Iran, I.R. of	Panama	United Arab Emirates
Colombia	Jamaica	Papua New Guinea	Uruguay
Comoros	Jordan	Paraguay	Vanuatu
Congo, Dem. Rep. of	Kazakhstan	Peru	Venezuela
Congo, Rep. of	Kenya	Philippines	Vietnam
Costa Rica	Korea	Rwanda	Yemen
Côte d'Ivoire	Kuwait	Senegal	Zambia
Croatia	Kyrgyz Republic	Seychelles	Zimbabwe

Table A2. Summary Statistics for Selected Variables, 1970–2000[1]

Variable	Mean	Standard Deviation	Minimum	Maximum
Net foreign aid (percent of GDP)	5.6	7.5	−0.5	58.7
Loans (percent of GDP)	1.5	2.6	−8.6	43.5
Grants (percent of GDP)	4.0	5.8	0.0	52.5
Domestic revenue (percent of GDP)	21.6	10.4	0.1	91.3
Real GDP per capita	2,392.1	3,671.2	84.7	37,841.2

[1]The summary statistics cover a common sample of 107 countries with 1,943 observations based on the baseline specification.

References

Alesina, Alberto, and David Dollar, 2000, "Who Gives Foreign Aid to Whom and Why?" *Journal of Economic Growth*, Vol. 5 (March), pp. 33–63.

Azam, Jean-Paul, Shantayanan Devarajan, and Stephen A. O'Connell, 1999, "Aid Dependence Reconsidered," World Bank Policy Paper No. 2144 (Washington: World Bank).

Beck, Nathaniel, and Jonathan N. Katz, 1995, "What to Do (and Not to Do) with Time-Series—Cross-Section Data," *American Political Science Review*, Vol. 89, Issue 3, pp. 634–47.

Bräutigam, Deborah, 2000, *Aid Dependence and Governance* (Stockholm: Almqvist & Wiksell).

Bulíř, Aleš, and A. Javier Hamann, 2001, "How Volatile and Unpredictable Are Aid Flows, and What Are the Policy Implications?" IMF Working Paper 01/167 (Washington: International Monetary Fund).

Bulow, Jeremy, 2002, "First World Governments and Third World Debt," *Brookings Papers on Economic Activity: 1*, pp. 229–55.

Cashel-Cordo, Peter, and Steven Craig, 1990, "The Public Sector Impact of International Resource Transfers," *Journal of Development Economics*, Vol. 32 (January), pp. 17–42.

Catterson, Julie, and Claes Lindahl, 1999, *The Sustainability Enigma: Aid Dependency and the Phasing Out of Projects: The Case of Swedish Aid to Tanzania* (Stockholm: Almqvist & Wiksell International).

Feeny, Simon, and Mark McGillivray, 2003, "Aid and Public Sector Borrowing in Developing Countries," *Journal of International Development*, Vol. 15 (November), pp. 989–98.

Franco-Rodriguez, Susana, Oliver Morrissey, and Mark McGillivray, 1998, "Aid and the Public Sector in Pakistan: Evidence with Endogenous Aid," *World Development*, Vol. 26 (July), pp. 1241–50.

Ghura, Dhaneshwar, 1998, "Tax Revenue in Sub-Saharan Africa: Effects of Economic Policies and Corruption," IMF Working Paper 98/135 (Washington: International Monetary Fund).

Heller, Peter S., 1975, "A Model of Public Fiscal Behavior in Developing Countries: Aid, Investment, and Taxation," *American Economic Review*, Vol. 65 (June), pp. 429–45.

———, and Sanjeev Gupta, 2004, Chapter 15 in *Helping Countries Develop: The Role of Fiscal Policy*, ed. by Sanjeev Gupta, Benedict Clements, and Gabriela Inchauste (Washington: International Monetary Fund).

IFIAC, 2000, "Report of the International Financial Institution Advisory Commission" (Washington: IFIAC, U.S. Congress). Available via the Internet: www.house.gov/jec/imf/meltzer.htm.

Kapur, Devesh, 2002, "Do As I Say and Not As I Do: A Critique of G-7 Proposals on Reforming the Multilateral Development Banks," United Nations

Conference on Trade and Development, G-24 Discussion Paper No. 20 (Geneva: UNCTAD).

Khan, Haider, and Eiichi Hoshino, 1992, "Impact of Foreign Aid on the Fiscal Behavior of LDC Governments," *World Development*, Vol. 20 (October), pp. 1481–88.

Knack, Stephen, 2001, "Aid Dependence and the Quality of Governance: Cross-Country Empirical Tests," *Southern Economic Journal*, Vol. 68 (October), pp. 310–29.

Leuthold, Jane H., 1991, "Tax Shares in Developing Economies: A Panel Study," *Journal of Development Economics*, Vol. 35 (January), pp. 173–85.

Lotz, Jorgen R., and Elliott R. Morss, 1967, "Measuring 'Tax Effort' in Developing Countries," *IMF Staff Papers*, Vol. 14, pp. 478–99.

———, 1970, "A Theory of Tax Level Determinants for Developing Countries," *Economic Development and Cultural Change*, Vol. 18, No. 3, pp. 328–41.

McGillivray, Mark, and Akhter Ahmed, 1999, "Aid, Adjustment and Public Sector Fiscal Behaviour in the Philippines," *Journal of the Asia-Pacific Economy*, Vol. 4, No. 2, pp. 381–91.

McGillivray, Mark, and Oliver Morrissey, 2001, "A Review of Evidence on the Fiscal Effects of Aid," CREDIT Research Paper No. 01/13 (Nottingham: Centre for Research in Economic Development and International Trade).

Odedokun, Matthew, 2003, "Economics and Politics of Official Loans versus Grants," WIDER Discussion Paper No. 2003/04 (Helsinki: United Nations University, World Institute for Development Economics Research).

Otim, Samuel, 1996, "Foreign Aid and Government Fiscal Behavior in Low-Income South Asian Countries," *Applied Economics*, Vol. 28 (August), pp. 927–33.

Pack, Howard, and Janet Pack, 1990, "Is Foreign Aid Fungible? The Case of Indonesia," *Economic Journal*, Vol. 100 (March), pp. 188–94.

Rogoff, Kenneth, 2003, "Unlocking Growth in Africa," *Finance & Development*, Vol. 40 (June), pp. 56–57.

Sanford, Jonathan E., 2002, "World Bank: IDA Loans or IDA Grants," *World Development*, Vol. 30 (May), pp. 741–62.

Schmidt, Wilson E., 1964, "The Economics of Charity: Loans versus Grants," *Journal of Political Economy*, Vol. 72 (August), pp. 387–95.

Singer, H.W., 1961, "Trends in Economic Thought or Underdevelopment," *Social Research*, Winter 1961, No. 4, 387–414.

Stotsky, Janet G., and Asegedech WoldeMariam, 1997, "Tax Effort in Sub-Saharan Africa," IMF Working Paper 97/107 (Washington: International Monetary Fund).

Svensson, Jakob, 2000, "Foreign Aid and Rent-Seeking," *Journal of International Economics*, Vol. 51 (August), pp. 437–61.

Tanzi, Vito, 1989, "The Impact of Macroeconomic Policies on the Level of Taxation and the Fiscal Balance in Developing Countries," *IMF Staff Papers*, Vol. 36 (September), pp. 633–56.

————, 1992, "Structural Factors and Tax Revenue in Developing Countries: A Decade of Evidence," in *Open Economies: Structural Adjustment & Agriculture*, ed. by Ian Goldin and L. Alan Winters (Cambridge: Cambridge University Press), pp. 267–81.

Tavares, Jose, 2003, "Does Foreign Aid Corrupt?" *Economics Letters*, Vol. 79 (April), pp. 99–106.

U.S. Department of the Treasury, 2000, "Response to the Report of the International Financial Institution Advisory Commission" (Washington: U.S. Department of the Treasury, June 8). Available via the Internet: http://www.treas.gov/press/releases/reports/response.pdf.

White, Howard, 1993, "Aid and Government: A Dynamic Model of Aid, Income, and Fiscal Behavior," *Journal of International Development*, Vol. 5 (May–June), pp. 305–12.

World Bank, 1998, *Assessing Aid: What Works, What Doesn't, and Why* (Washington: World Bank).

15

More Aid—Making It Work for the Poor

Peter S. Heller and Sanjeev Gupta

There has been a renewed call within the international community for industrial countries to meet the goal of devoting 0.7 percent of their GNP for official development assistance (ODA). Originally proposed by the Pearson Commission in 1968, only a few countries are currently meeting this target and the average ODA level is only a third of the target. Raising ODA to 0.7 percent of industrial country GNP is an important element in the strategy for reducing global poverty and meeting the Millennium Development Goals (MDGs) by 2015. It could also lead to an expanded supply of needed global public goods.

If industrial countries were to meet the ODA target, financial aid would increase to about $175 billion, slightly more than three times current levels. This could pose challenges—both macroeconomic and microeconomic—for developing countries, particularly if the funds were distributed primarily to the world's poorest countries. Transfers of extremely large amounts of money to a developing country relative to the size of its economy can be problematic. To ensure that enhanced ODA is used efficiently in the fight against global poverty, it is crucial that the international community examine closely alternative approaches to allocating the aid, both among countries and for complementary global poverty reduction programs.

Reprinted with permission from *World Economics*, Vol. 3, No. 4 (October–December), 2002. Peter S. Heller and Sanjeev Gupta are members of the Fiscal Affairs Department, International Monetary Fund. They wish to thank Eduardo Aninat, Gabriela Inchauste, Erwin Tiongson, Shamit Chakravarti, and Solita Wakefield for extensive help in preparing this paper. Michael Hadjimichael, Timothy Lane, Kevin Fletcher, and Edward Frydl also provided useful comments on an earlier draft.

Concerns and Challenges

The Scope of the Challenge

If one were to distribute the full 0.7 percent of GNP in aid only to the world's least developed countries as defined by the OECD's Development Assistance Committee (DAC) (and conditional on these countries' satisfying certain governance criteria or establishing a track record of successful policy implementation)—the scale of transfers would be massive relative to these economies' size. Moreover, applying such a distributional criterion would result in enormous differences in per capita transfers to the "absolute poor" of the world (individuals with incomes of less than $1 a day). It would mean that no transfers would go to poor people living in countries with per capita incomes above the DAC-defined threshold. Thus, some of the largest countries in the world would be excluded. The excluded countries would include those with higher annual per capita incomes, which are classified as "other low-income countries" (such as India, Nigeria, Pakistan, and Vietnam), as well as "lower-middle-income countries" (including China, Indonesia, and the Philippines). The allocation of a 0.5 percent target for ODA—equivalent to $125 billion and representing the level of increase estimated to respond to the MDGs—would yield broadly similar results.

If the increased ODA resources were distributed according to a different criterion—for example, proportional to the share of the world's absolute poor in a country—the macroeconomic issues associated with resource transfers would be significantly diminished. However, the bulk of aid would then go, not to the poorest countries in the world, but to the larger countries listed above. Different scenarios illustrate these points:[1]

Scenario 1

In this scenario, aid is assumed to go to those least developed countries (as defined by DAC) that have good economic policies (based on Collier and Dollar's (1999) criteria),[2] but with the amounts scaled up to reflect the ODA target of 0.7 percent of GNP. As shown in Figure 1, the average ratio of ODA to GDP in recipient countries would be 32 percent, almost two and a half times what it is now, and the revenues available for government programs would almost triple.

---

[1] Detailed discussions of these and other scenarios are provided in Heller and Gupta (2002).

[2] Paul Collier and David Dollar (1999) of the World Bank recently carried out an analysis of how aid might be reallocated if countries with severe poverty and good policies were targeted and if countries with civil strife or poor policies were excluded.

Figure 1. Two Scenarios
(Unweighted averages)

Scenario 1: If aid is increased to 0.7 percent of industrial country GNP but is channeled primarily to the poorest countries, the ratio of ODA to GDP would be more than double what it is today.

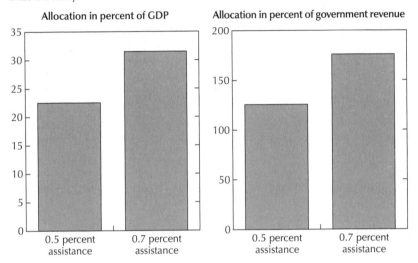

Scenario 2: Increasing the allocation to China and India would reduce problems of absorbing aid flows in the poorest countries.

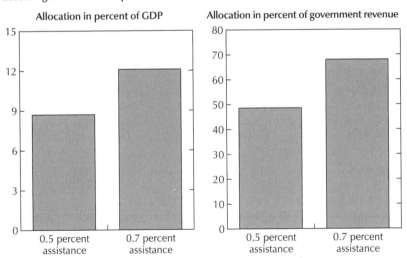

Source: Poverty-efficient aid allocation based on Collier and Dollar (1999).
Note: Scenario 1 is based on Collier and Dollar's (1999) poverty-efficient allocation of aid. The implied share of total aid for each country in the dataset was calculated, and then $175 billion and $125 billion were allocated accordingly, corresponding to 0.7 and 0.5 percent of industrial country GNP.

For many countries, however, the ratio of ODA to GDP would be much higher—90 percent in Ethiopia, 52 percent in Uganda, 60 percent in Burundi, 48 percent in Vietnam, 43 percent in Nicaragua, 57 percent in Guyana, and 74 percent in the Kyrgyz Republic. One problem with Scenario 1 is that aid to China and India—countries that have large numbers of absolute poor and that have pursued good policies—would account for no more than 11 percent of total ODA.

Scenario 2

Here, the Collier-Dollar criteria are used but with the allocation to China and India allowed to increase. ODA would then average about 12 percent of GDP, diminishing the problems related to absorption, but still with some important exceptions among the least developed countries. (For example, ODA transfers would be 33 percent of Ethiopia's GDP.) China and India together would receive about $116 billion of the projected total of $175 billion, while Nigeria, Pakistan, the Philippines, and Vietnam would receive about $25 billion. Only about $30 billion of the increased ODA would be allocated to the least developed countries and about one-third of this would go to Bangladesh. Sub-Saharan African countries would receive no more than $20 billion, with $4 billion going to Nigeria.

Absolute poverty is not limited to the poorest countries. Indeed, in Scenario 3 (not shown), if ODA were distributed to countries in relation to the proportion of population living below US$1 a day, China and India together would receive about $112 billion—almost the same total as in Scenario 2. However, India would receive more ($73 billion) than China ($39 billion) because it has a greater concentration of individuals in absolute poverty, whereas, in Scenario 2, China would receive $76 billion and India $40 billion. Similarly, using the criterion of the number of individuals living in absolute poverty, countries in sub-Saharan Africa would receive no more than $33 billion in ODA. Recipients among the least developed countries would receive ODA transfers averaging about 32 percent of GDP, compared with 8 percent for low income countries.

Macroeconomic and Microeconomic Policy Challenges

Why are large aid flows relative to the size of an economy problematic? Here we underscore some of the factors and bottlenecks that would have to be addressed if a significant expansion of ODA were to occur for many countries.

Macroeconomic Issues of Absorption

The likelihood of significant macroeconomic problems will depend both on the size of the external resource transfers relative to the scale of the recipient economy *and* the extent to which such transfers take the form of financial transfers for spending on domestic goods and services rather than imports. If ODA were spent entirely on imports, the balance of payments would be unchanged; the increase in imports would be completely financed by foreign inflows. In this case, there would be no direct impact on the money supply or aggregate demand in the domestic economy.[3] For example, a significant expansion of externally financed imports of antiretrovirals for the treatment of AIDS could be readily absorbed with only negligible macroeconomic effects.

In contrast, if a significant share of foreign inflows were to be spent on nontraded goods, the price of domestic goods and services would increase. To make local purchases, foreign exchange would need to be converted into local currency that in turn would expand the monetary base. This would fuel an increase in domestic demand, some of which would be met by expanded imports, contributing to a weakening of the trade balance. However, there would also be a significant increase in demand for nontraded goods. Because the worsening of the trade balance would be more than offset by foreign inflows, the pressure of demand for nontraded goods, coupled with supply constraints on their production, would contribute to an increase in their prices, leading to an increase in the overall domestic price level. In the case of a fixed exchange rate regime, the pressure of expanded liquidity on domestic demand and prices of nontraded goods would lead to a real exchange rate appreciation, as the domestic price level would rise while the nominal exchange rate would remain unchanged.

In the case of a flexible exchange regime, the increased supply of foreign currency, not wholly absorbed by imports of goods and services, would drive up the price of the domestic currency, in effect leading to an appreciation in the nominal exchange rate.[4] Neither situation would be conducive to growth or poverty reduction. When domestic inflation is high, the poor and middle-income groups are likely to suffer. But the poor would also suffer if the competitiveness of the goods they produce were adversely affected by an exchange rate appreciation. Likewise, a poor country's capacity to compete in world markets, and ultimately to

---

[3] If government spending substitutes for existing private consumption, private consumers may shift resources to other uses, thus possibly generating second-round effects.

[4] Hjertholm, Laursen, and White (2000) suggest that foreign aid that eases local supply bottlenecks can have a deflationary impact, which may, in turn, exceed the upward pressure on the real exchange rate resulting from significant external resource transfers.

be weaned from ODA, would suffer if the competitiveness of its export industries were to be undermined by a real exchange rate appreciation.

This phenomenon, where large inflows of foreign currency into an economy have harmful consequences, is termed the "Dutch disease" problem. It is not a new problem. The debate on the relationship between international payments and the real exchange rate (the so-called transfer problem) dates back to the 1920s when the issue of German war reparations arose. Effecting a large capital transfer requires a flow of *real* goods and services or the appreciation of real exchange rates (Mundell, 1991). The sharp increase in oil prices in the 1970s, and subsequently, the macroeconomic policy management challenges confronting some of the poorer countries that have benefited from substantial aid flows, have all led to a resurgence of interest in this topic.[5]

Resolving the macroeconomic policy challenges posed by significant external resource transfers can be difficult, given that there are limits as to how much direct commodity imports can be readily absorbed without incurring adverse domestic disincentive effects. For most poor countries, with limited infrastructure and human capital, absorptive capacity bottlenecks cannot be quickly removed.

A large inflow of donor funds may leave a country facing a trade-off between selling foreign exchange or treasury bills in order to mop up the excess liquidity generated from these inflows. Such an operation could lead to a real exchange rate appreciation and an increase in interest rates. Both outcomes would have adverse effects on growth, as the real appreciation of the exchange rate would hurt competitiveness while the selling of government securities would crowd out private sector credit. In addition, increased foreign inflows could potentially have an adverse impact on domestic revenue mobilization efforts, creating a disincentive for policy makers to incur the political cost of a strengthening in tax administration.

Another policy challenge that can arise with heavy reliance on external assistance for financing basic public services is an increase in fiscal uncertainty, making long-term planning more difficult. The disbursement of donor aid is often conditional not only on satisfactory progress in the efficient use of resources but also on other factors. These include political concerns, the various requirements of donors, and the often cumbersome procedures for disbursing aid flows. Time-series data show that donor commitments systematically exceed disbursements

---

[5]Bulíř and Lane (2002) review the theoretical and empirical literature on the Dutch disease. They find substantial evidence of aid-induced exchange rate appreciation. Evidence of Dutch disease has also been found for Burkina Faso, Côte d'Ivoire, Senegal, and Togo (Adenauer and Vagassky, 1998) as well as for Sri Lanka (White and Wignaraja, 1992).

and that aid flows cannot be predicted reliably on the basis of donor commitments alone (Bulíř and Javier Hamann, 2001).[6] Aid in such circumstances can become a source both of instability and of year-to-year fiscal volatility. Consumption volatility has significant social costs and its welfare consequences are much higher in poorer countries (Pallage and Robe, 2003). Over the longer term, the permanent increase in expenditure commitments may also have a negative impact on long-run fiscal sustainability, as countries are expected to eventually "graduate" from their dependence on aid.

Microeconomic Absorption Issues

There are a number of microeconomic challenges that would need to be addressed if external inflows were to be substantially increased, reflecting the limited domestic absorption capacity of many potential recipient countries. First, studies show that large inflows of aid can overwhelm the management capacity of governments.[7] Over the 1990s, ODA commitments of the European Union exceeded gross disbursements by more than US$1.6 billion each year, peaking at US$2.2 billion in 1994 (OECD, 1998). This has been attributed, in part, to the limited absorptive and administrative capacities of the recipient countries. It is also possible that the existing administrative infrastructure is such that recipient countries may be unable to use additional resources efficiently, thus leading to wastage and a congestion externality.

This is particularly true for countries where fiscal decentralization has gone hand in hand with donor support and where increasingly the resources are being channeled through subnational governments for strengthening local service delivery. In Uganda, for example, the large expansion of resources for education, health, and water supply has exposed administrative difficulties, such as deficiencies in payroll systems. This could reduce the productivity of increased expenditures unless these deficiencies are directly addressed.

Second, it would be critical to ensure that increased aid does not reduce the incentive of countries to adopt good policies and discourage efforts to reform inefficient institutions. This is analogous to the observed

---

[6]The cross-country evidence on the volatility of aid, however, is mixed. Collier (1999) found that aid to Africa has been both less volatile than other revenue sources and is negatively correlated with them. In contrast, recent studies by Bulíř and Javier Hamann (2001) and Pallage and Robe (2001) suggest that aid is more volatile than revenues, that the relative volatility increases with the degree of aid dependency, and that aid flows are significantly procyclical, suggesting that aid flows may not smooth out fluctuations in consumption among recipient countries.

[7]See, for example, Kanbur, Sandler, and Morrison (1999).

"welfare dependency" among poor households, where welfare payments create high implicit marginal tax rates and discourage work. For recipient countries, the implicit marginal tax rates would correspond to a situation where donors would reduce aid flows in response to rising per capita income levels. As such, aid may create perverse incentives for recipient governments, creating, in effect, a "moral hazard" problem. In addition, foreign aid may undermine progress in institutional development, such as in the recipient government's efforts to strengthen revenue collection (Azam and others, 1999).

Third, in the past, aid dependence has been said to weaken accountability and encourage rent seeking and corruption. Aid can impede the development of a healthy "civil society," with recipient governments becoming accountable to donors rather than to domestic taxpayers. Unless donors' commitment and disbursement practices change, with higher levels of external assistance, recipient governments will need to increase further the time spent fulfilling the requirements of donors.[8] In addition, because aid may be used for patronage purposes, such as the provision of subsidies to state-owned enterprises and increased public employment, it can represent a potential source of rents, thus leading to unproductive, rent-seeking activities. Using cross-country data for about 80 countries, Knack (2000) finds that indeed higher aid levels may erode the quality of governance.[9]

A Multi-Pronged Approach to Allocating an Expanded ODA Effort for Poverty Reduction

In seeking to meet the MDGs and obtain a dramatic reduction in the incidence of world poverty, the world community has set out ambitious but realistically achievable objectives. Many believe that the long-standing goal of raising ODA to 0.7 percent of industrial country GNP should be an important element of this overall strategy. There is some urgency in moving quickly to realize this target. Within 10 to 15 years,

---

[8] With increased aid, however, recipient governments also have more resources for fulfilling donor requirements.

[9] Recent reviews of the impact of aid on growth and economic development have concluded that the record of aid has, at best, been mixed. The World Bank (1998) found that foreign aid has been "highly effective, totally ineffective, and everything in between." In addition, the review suggested that aid has had a beneficial impact only in countries that have made substantial progress with reform of policies and institutions. Easterly (2001) has suggested that aid has tended to reward poor performance, going to countries with poor policies where aid is wasted, rather than countries with good policies where aid could have high payoffs.

the industrial countries of the world will begin to confront the budgetary pressures of aging populations. Industrial countries are likely to have more budgetary room in the next decade for an expanded ODA effort than they will thereafter.

We now describe a number of strategies that can be pursued to address the challenges raised above with respect to the effective allocation and utilization of expanded ODA. In essence, we believe the world community should adopt a multi-pronged strategy that has five essential elements. First, by reconsidering the criteria according to which ODA is distributed, much of ODA should be channeled to countries for which the macroeconomic absorptive challenges would not be significant, and yet where there are large parts of the population in absolute poverty. Second, policy programs must intensely focus on ways to relax the key microeconomic and institutional bottlenecks that limit a country's capacity to absorb significant external financial resources. This is critical to enable higher real resource transfers, consistent with macroeconomic stability and adequate incentives for sustainable and rapid real growth.

Third, there is considerable scope for investments in research and development (R&D) that could lead to technological innovations readily absorbable by the poorest countries in their agricultural and manufacturing sectors. By expanding the range of technologies relevant to the situation of poor countries, there is greater scope to expand production capacity and foster productivity growth. Recognizing absorptive capacity limitations in the poorer countries, such investments might need to be made in some of the more advanced developing countries in a region.

Fourth, ODA can be mobilized now, with the intention of deferring its distribution, pending a strengthening of the absorptive capacity of some of the poorer countries. The increased emphasis on the accumulation of trust funds in multilateral institutions illustrates this approach. Fifth, some resources could be channeled to finance the removal of the barriers that now prevent access, by the poorest countries, to the markets of the industrial economies.

Reconsidering the Distributional Criteria for Expanded ODA

Earlier, we underscored the need to channel some of the increased ODA funds to countries that are not normally seen as the poorest.[10] Simply to respond to the problems of absolute poverty, this would appear appropriate. But it would also be consistent with the present distribution of ODA. Donor countries have multiple objectives in the

---

[10]This appears to be implicitly recognized by both the UN and the Zedillo Commission. They advocate that between US$37.5 billion (0.15 percent of GDP) and US$50 billion (0.2 percent of GDP) should be earmarked for the least developed countries.

granting of external assistance in addition to a country's per capita income level or its incidence of poverty. Political considerations obviously enter, e.g., as relates to aid to post-conflict and transition countries, or on the basis of geopolitical considerations. An expanded ODA effort is not likely to mean a reduction of such assistance. But equally, if the objective of the expanded ODA effort is to achieve the MDGs and to reduce poverty, then additional resources should be directed to where the poor are. This would imply far greater ODA to countries in South and East Asia. But low- and middle-income countries with high concentrations of poverty must do their part as well, utilizing ODA to narrow the significant prevailing inequalities in income distribution and to address the sources of endemic poverty.

Facilitating an Expanded Direct Flow of ODA to the Poorest Countries

For the least developed countries, the scale of the resource transfer associated with the realization of the 0.7 percent target would still be large relative to the size of their domestic economies. This would be true even if much of the resources were provided in the form of imports and services. Over the short to medium term, this puts a premium on limiting the expansion of domestically produced services involving nontradable goods and services, particularly within the public administration.

Much of the ODA in the short term would thus need to be concentrated on imported goods and services. But there are many imported goods that could still make an enormous difference in addressing critical needs in many poor countries. One need only mention pharmaceutical products, including antiretrovirals (ARVs) to address the HIV/AIDS crisis. Of course, since it may take some time before overall aid flows actually attain the 0.7 percent target, a gradual enhancement in absorption capacity may occur naturally. An enhanced role of external technical assistance—the supply of skilled manpower to address initial shortages—may facilitate this process.[11]

Careful monitoring of the macroeconomic situation in the poorest countries will be critical. Some macroeconomic pressures in the form of inflation and real exchange rate depreciation are probably inevitable, but there are limits beyond which such effects will undermine the very sustainability of the desired development effort. But a testing of the limits will be necessary, and particularly with a significant risk of some

---

[11]Many would argue that the more intensive importation and delivery of ARVs to treat HIV/AIDS must be accompanied by an adequate buildup of clinical and research services to monitor treatment and prevent the possible emergence of resistant strains of the HIV virus.

inflationary pressure, social safety net schemes need to be in place in order to minimize the burden on the poorest groups within a country. Gradual augmentation of ODA levels may be needed for some countries, particularly if simply increasing the scale of imports is inappropriate for the country's development needs.

The recent emphasis on the production of poverty reduction strategy papers (PRSPs) in low-income countries remains critical. It ensures both local ownership in terms of decisions on how the enhanced resources are used and provides some check on the governance process. Efforts to strengthen public expenditure and budget management (PEM) systems will be even more important if adequate accountability is to be provided to donor nations for this enhanced aid effort. Given the scale of the expansion of the public sector that would be implied by greater ODA, resource flows must be *sustained* and *dependable*, in order to avoid disruptions in the provision of public services.

Some enhanced aid could be allocated to strengthen public institutions and improve the quality of governance (Knack, 2000). Many low-income countries have identified governance and/or institutional strengthening as critical in their poverty reduction strategies (e.g., Madagascar and Cameroon). The New Partnership for Africa's Development (NEPAD) is promoting peer reviews of economic and corporate governance practices to make recommendations on appropriate standards and codes of good practice. One could even consider targeting aid to countries that have taken steps to reduce corruption or increase accountability and transparency (Bräutigam, 2000). For countries that are undertaking reforms to strengthen their PEM systems, aid should be provided in the form of direct budgetary support. Budgetary resources are fungible. General budgetary support provides recipient governments with the greater flexibility to build administrative capacity, particularly when donors are not designing and implementing projects, or providing tied aid and technical assistance (Knack, 2000).

Finally, aid flows should not create perverse incentives for the recipients. Good performance would have to be an explicit criterion for allocating aid.

Expanding the Potential for Increased Technological Innovations Benefiting the Poorest Countries

Some expanded ODA could be directed to the production and provision of global public goods. The recent report of the WHO-sponsored Commission on Macroeconomics and Health (2001) argues for expanded outlays on a significant R&D effort directed at the principal disease problems underlying excess mortality among the poor. It also urges the provision of commercial distribution incentives for any drugs and vaccines developed under such a program.

In a similar vein, R&D on alternative technologies to replace fossil fuels will be particularly important in the coming decades to provide low-cost alternatives for developing countries seeking to substitute for inefficient and carbon-emitting energy facilities or technologies. The consequences of climate change in coming decades are likely to be the most adverse for developing countries. While much R&D effort is under way in the industrial world, it is important that affordable and efficient energy technologies relevant for developing countries are also developed and commercially brought on stream. This may require the financing of directed research that would not necessarily emerge from industrial countries.

Additional financial support will also be needed for R&D on agricultural technologies that will facilitate adaptation by tropical countries in response to climate change (Heller and Mani, 2002). Such R&D may also be critical if countries that are heavily dependent on traditional agriculture are not to suffer adverse consequences from prospective technological developments in the agricultural sector. A critical focus of efforts of major commercial investors in agricultural R&D in the industrial countries is the development of "genetic use restriction technologies" (GURTs).[12] Recent research suggests that, over time, such GURTs could inhibit significant diffusion of technological gains and weaken the prospects for agricultural productivity growth in the poorest countries most susceptible to food shortages and high population growth. To facilitate their capacity to absorb and profit from new agricultural technology developments, many developing countries will need to develop a capacity for R&D in the agricultural biotech sector (Swanson, 2002) and enhanced ODA could finance such efforts.[13]

Finally, there is a need to focus on areas of key vulnerability in the future. If the industrial countries galvanize the necessary ODA resources, it will be desirable to proactively consider investments in the developing world that would frontally address some of the most important looming potential shortages that will affect both development and global stability in coming decades. For example, pressures on available water supplies—as a consequence of population growth, economic development, and climate change—may prove a particularly dangerous source of political and economic vulnerability in coming decades. Such shortages are particularly worrisome in the Middle East and South Asia.

---

[12]These relate to plant varieties that cannot subsequently be reproduced by the purchaser in subsequent growing seasons.

[13]Only a limited number of developing countries, principally low- and low-to-middle-income countries, have such a capacity for agricultural biotech research (Swanson, 2002).

A multinational effort to consider alternative approaches to addressing potential emerging pressures can have a high payoff in terms of the problems of poverty in the future.

Trust Funds for the Accumulation of ODA Resources

Given that there may be limits on how much ODA can be sustainably transferred to some of the poorest countries, one possible option is to accumulate resources in a trust fund. Most industrial countries are likely to have more budgetary room for an expanded ODA effort now than in the future. Given current absorptive capacity constraints in many poor countries, it may be desirable to sever the temporal link between disbursement of aid and its expenditure. Some increased ODA could thus be paid into internationally controlled "trust fund" arrangements and released on a pre-determined schedule or according to observable milestones related to improvements in absorptive capacity. Such a trust fund already exists to finance debt relief initiative for highly indebted poor countries (HIPCs). The total cost of HIPC assistance— estimated at about US$33 billion in 2000—is financed by both bilateral creditors and multilateral lenders. The multilateral component of the initiative has been provided through the HIPC Trust Fund, administered by the World Bank, the total pledges for which have reached US$2.6 billion, with paid-in contributions amounting to almost US$1 billion. Should ODA increase gradually over time, the need for inter-temporal planning will be less critical.

Specialized global trust funds are also starting to emerge to finance the provision of selected global public goods. These act as endowments for future earmarked pro-poor programs, sometimes focused on specific sectors, and managed at the center, provincial, or community levels, in a developing country. For example, a global fund was recently set up to pool, manage, and allocate new resources to fight AIDS, tuberculosis, and malaria, diseases that collectively cause 25 percent of deaths worldwide. This global fund, which is supported by a small secretariat based in Geneva, already has committed US$1.6 billion to 40 programs in 31 severely affected countries.

Addressing Barriers to Industrial Country Market Access by the Poorest Countries

A strengthening of social policy instruments in industrial countries may be a necessary investment to soften some opposition to the removal of trade barriers in these countries. Most observers recognize that the opening up of industrial country markets to the products of the developing world is as essential as additional ODA for engendering self-sustaining development.

Concluding Remarks

In conclusion, any significant expansion of ODA must be accompanied by a concerted effort by all partners in the development community to anticipate the macro and microeconomic challenges associated with utilizing external resources effectively. This is an issue that extends beyond simply the multilateral and bilateral donors. It will also entail a collaborative partnership with aid recipients, external NGOs, civil society, and the private sector. The central objectives are to achieve the MDGs in the years ahead and to foster self-sustaining development by the poorest countries of the world. The potential channels and instruments through which additional ODA funds can play a productive role are many. This paper outlines only a few.

In addition to ensuring good usage of ODA resources and pursuing effective policies, the paper emphasizes the importance of targeting ODA as much on the basis of the size of a country's population in absolute poverty as on whether it is among the least developed countries. It also suggests that modalities other than direct bilateral ODA transfers may contribute to the goal of world poverty reduction.

But it will not be easy to secure consensus on both the allocation and institutional modalities for creative and effective use of these resources. At the same time, the importance of moving quickly to achieve such a consensus is great. Much goodwill would be lost if additional resources are inefficiently used or diverted from their principal objectives.

References

Adenauer, Isabell, and Laurence Vagassky, 1998, "Aid and the Real Exchange Rate: Dutch Disease Effects in African Countries," *Intereconomics: Review of International Trade and Development,* Vol. 33 (July/August), pp. 177–85.

Azam, Jean-Paul, Shantayanan Devarajan, and Stephen A. O'Connell, 1999, "Aid Dependence Reconsidered," World Bank Policy Paper No. 2144 (Washington: World Bank).

Bräutigam, Deborah, 2000, *Aid Dependence and Governance* (Stockholm: Almqvist & Wiksell International).

Bulíř, Ales, and A. Javier Hamann, 2001, "How Volatile and Predictable Are Aid Flows and What Are the Policy Implications?" IMF Working Paper 01/167 (Washington: International Monetary Fund).

Bulíř, Ales, and Timothy Lane, 2002, "Aid and Fiscal Management," IMF Working Paper 02/112 (Washington: International Monetary Fund).

Collier, Paul, 1999, "Aid Dependency: A Critique," *Journal of African Economies*, Vol. 8, No. 4, pp. 528–45.

———, and David Dollar, 1999, "Aid Allocation and Poverty Reduction," World Bank Policy Research Working Paper No. 2041 (Washington: World Bank).

Commission on Macroeconomics and Health, 2001, *Macroeconomics and Health: Investing in Health for Economic Development* (Geneva: World Health Organization).

Easterly, William, 2001, *The Elusive Quest for Growth: Economists' Adventures and Misadventures in the Tropics* (Cambridge: MIT Press).

Financing for Development, prepared by the staff of the World Bank and the IMF for the Development Committee.

Heller, Peter S., and Muthukumara Mani, 2002 "Adapting to Climate Change," *Finance & Development*, Vol. 39 (March), pp. 29–31.

Heller, Peter S., and Sanjeev Gupta, 2002, "Challenges in Expanding Development Assistance," IMF Policy Discussion Paper No. 02/5 (Washington: International Monetary Fund).

Hjertholm, Peter, Jytte Laursen, and Howard White, 2000, "Macroeconomic Issues in Foreign Aid," University of Copenhagen, Institute of Economics Discussion Paper No. 00–05.

Kanbur, S. M. Ravi, Todd Sandler, and Kevin M. Morrison, 1999, *The Future of Development Assistance: Common Pools and International Public Goods*, Policy Essay No. 25 (Washington: Overseas Development Council).

Knack, Stephen, 2000, "Aid Dependence and the Quality of Governance: A Cross-Country Empirical Analysis," World Bank Policy Paper No. 2396 (Washington: World Bank).

Mundell, Robert, 1991, "The Great Exchange Rate Controversy: Trade Balances and the International Monetary System," in C. Fred Bergsten, ed., *International Adjustment and Financing: The Lessons of 1985–1991* (Washington: Institute for International Economics).

OECD, 1998, "European Community," *Development Cooperation Review Series No. 30* (Paris: Organization for Economic Co-operation and Development).

Pallage, Stéphane and Michel Robe, 2001, "Foreign Aid and the Business Cycle," *Review of International Economics*, Vol. 9, No. 4, pp. 641–72.

Pallage, Stéphane and Michel Robe, 2003, "On the Welfare Cost of Economic Fluctuations in Developing Countries," *International Economic Review*, Vol. 44 (May), pp. 677–98.

Swanson, Timothy, ed., 2002, *Biotechnology, Agriculture and the Developing World: The Distributional Implications of Technological Change* (Cheltenham: Edward Elgar).

White, Howard and Ganeshan Wignaraja, 1992, "Exchange Rates, Trade Liberalization and Aid: The Sri Lankan Experience," *World Development*, Vol. 20 (October), pp. 1471–80.

World Bank, 1998, *Assessing Aid: What Works, What Doesn't, and Why* (Washington: Oxford University Press).

16

Aid and Fiscal Management

ALEŠ BULÍŘ AND TIMOTHY LANE

Foreign aid has dwindled in the budgets of many donor countries during the past several years, but it continues to loom very large for
many of the recipients.[1] In many developing countries, foreign aid receipts are an important source of revenue and thus a key element in fiscal policy. Where domestic resources are very limited, aid may be an
indispensable source of financing, in particular for expenditures in areas
such as health, education, and public investment that are essential to
raise the living standards of poor people in developing countries.

Given that aid is limited, it is particularly important to use it wisely.
This requires not only establishing appropriate systems to manage aid
funds with a view to avoiding corruption and mismanagement—
important though this aspect is—but also designing aggregate fiscal
policy to take proper account of the macroeconomic implications of
aid-financed spending. Both aspects are essential to maximize the

The authors thank for comments Alberto Alesina, Ernesto Hernández-Catá, and participants at the IMF conference on Macroeconomics and Poverty, held on March 14–15, 2002
and an IMF seminar. Ivetta Hakobyan and Siba Das provided expert research assistance.

[1] The first fact—that industrial countries presently devote only about 0.25 percent, significantly less than the goal of 0.7 percent, of GNP to foreign aid—has received more attention than the second fact that aid has hardly declined in importance to the countries
that continue to receive it. In recent years, donors seem to have become more selective
vis-à-vis economic policies pursued by recipient countries, and an increasing share of aid
is being distributed based on economic and social considerations (World Bank, 2002) as
opposed to geopolitical and historical considerations (Alesina and Dollar, 2000).
Easterly (2002), however, challenges the World Bank's findings and claims that until 1999
no link between economic performance and aid disbursements could be observed.

benefits for the recipients—and thereby convince donors that aid is money well spent.

This chapter focuses on the macroeconomic aspects of fiscal policy management in aid-receiving countries. The chapter first discusses the implications of aid in the economy as a whole. Second, it discusses the implications of aid for short-term fiscal policy management—in particular, how actual or anticipated changes in aid receipts should be reflected in government spending.

In discussing the fiscal implications of aid, a basic question is whether aid receipts are any different from other sources of revenue. The literature has focused on two elements. First, in the long run, aid—unlike, for instance, tax revenues—tends to taper off as the economy develops (and, in some cases, much sooner); this should be taken into consideration in determining the appropriate intertemporal fiscal policy. Second, while all revenues are subject to uncertainty, the nature of the uncertainty is different for aid than for domestic tax revenues, as the former stems from the spending processes of donor countries and the design of conditionality. Thus, an important empirical question is how the uncertainty of aid compares with that of tax revenues. To the extent that aid receipts are relatively uncertain, the issue from the donors' standpoint is how to reduce this uncertainty and, from the recipients' standpoint, how to take it into account in designing fiscal policy.[2]

Macroeconomic Implications of Aid

Aid generally expands the recipient country's opportunities by expanding consumption and investment beyond the level of domestically generated income and saving, respectively. Aid has been sizable in many countries and reasonably stable during the 1990s (Table 1). The sheer magnitude of aid in a number of countries suggests that it may

---

[2]Discussions of the role of aid in fiscal policy have, at times, been overshadowed by the question of how to measure the fiscal deficit: with or without grants? There is a strong case for using the definition that includes grants, provided that grants are measured accurately (and projected realistically), since grants by definition do not generate an obligation to repay. A second issue is whether the grant element of concessional borrowing should be included as revenues. To avoid double counting, this would need to be offset on the expenditure side by imputing the costs of servicing outstanding concessional debt at market rates. But imputing the entire net present value of interest subsidy when the loan is received while spreading the interest costs paid with the subsidy over the life of the loan would seem to reduce, rather than enhance, the clarity of the accounts. Moreover, the imputation of the implicit grant element would depend heavily on assumptions regarding future exchange rates and interest rates.

Table 1. Official Development Assistance and Foreign Direct Assistance in Selected Aid-Dependent Countries, 1989–91[1]

(Percent of gross national income, unless stated otherwise)

	1990–99 Average	1990	1999	Compared with 1989, Aid in 1999 Was:	Foreign Direct Investment (percent of GDP)	Gross Domestic Product[2]
Bhutan	22.6	17.6	16.1	Lower	0.1	656
Cape Verde	27.2	31.7	23.7	Lower	1.9	1,461
Djibouti	21.3	—	14.2	Lower	0.0	742
Guinea-Bissau	51.5	55.1	25.7	Lower	0.7	183
Kiribati	25.5	36.0	25.6	Lower	0.0	600
Malawi	26.7	28.6	25.1	Lower	1.3	156
Mauritania	23.7	22.0	23.6	Higher	0.5	483
Micronesia, Fed. States of	34.5	—	48.9	Higher	0.0	1,707
Mongolia	23.6	—	25.4	Higher	1.8	457
Mozambique	45.0	42.4	23.2	Lower	2.7	198
Nicaragua	40.7	33.6	33.0	Lower	4.4	472
Rwanda	29.8	11.3	19.2	Higher	0.2	235
Samoa	25.2	31.5	12.9	Lower	2.7	1,011
Saõ Tomé and Principe	112.7	104.2	65.1	Lower	0.0	337
Vanuatu	20.5	30.6	16.3	Lower	11.7	1,347
Zambia	26.5	16.0	20.8	Higher	3.5	389

Source: World Bank, *World Development Indicators,* and authors' calculations.
[1]Countries where the 1990–99 average ratio of aid to gross national income was higher than 0.2.
[2]In constant 1995 U.S. dollars; per capita terms.

have important macroeconomic effects.[3] These can be considered at two levels: the allocative effects on the structure of production, consumption, and relative prices; and the effects on economic growth.

Allocative Effects

Theory

The allocative effects of aid-financed spending can be illustrated first of all in a simple two-sector general equilibrium model with tradables and nontradables (Michaely, 1981). See Figure 1. The economy produces and consumes tradable and nontradable goods, constrained by the production possibility frontier PQ. The initial equilibrium relative

---

[3]Some economists have argued that aid is an inefficient instrument for spurring development in low-income countries and that it played a significantly negative role in those countries by encouraging waste and corruption (Bauer, 1979).

Figure 1. The Effect of Aid on the Relative Price of Traded and Nontraded Goods

Nontradable goods

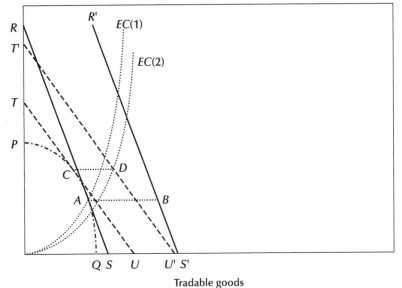

Tradable goods

price *RS*—which also gives the economy's consumption possibilities—determines the optimum at point A. We also draw an Engel curve, *EC*(1), with the income elasticity of demand for nontraded goods being greater than one, an assumption fairly common in the literature (White, 1992).[4]

In this framework, aid can be represented as transfer in the form of traded goods (AB), expanding the country's consumption possibility frontier to *R'S'*. Assuming that the aid is provided as an in-kind transfer of tradables to residents, the new consumption equilibrium at unchanged domestic relative prices would be at point B. However, this would imply excess supply of traded goods, lowering their price relative to that of nontraded goods. The equilibrium relative price would be *TU* (or *T'U'*), corresponding to the new Engel curve *EC*(2), and equilibrium consumption would be at point D. Production remains on the production possibility frontier at point C, but its composition is shifted toward nontradables, reflecting their higher relative price.

---

[4]Given that the bulk of nontradables comprises services and construction, they both can be seen as "luxuries." In any case, changing the elasticity to one or even to less than one does not affect the results substantially.

What is the overall impact? Consumers are obviously better off: they consume more of both tradable and nontradable goods, while the change in relative shares of tradable and nontradable goods depends on the elasticity assumptions. Depending on the relative price change, the structure of the economy and factor rewards change also. If labor and capital are free to move between sectors, the factor used intensively in the nontradables sector gains and the other factor loses; on the usual assumption that nontradables are more labor-intensive than tradables, economywide real wages rise and real returns to capital fall.[5] Suppliers of any factor of production that is specialized in nontradables—e.g., workers with specialized skills—tend to gain at the expense of specialized factors used in the tradables sector. Donors provide aid mostly with a view to easing the domestic saving constraint and, hence, contributing to investment. It is relatively easy to adjust the model to reflect this effect by relaxing the assumption that aid is provided as a direct consumption transfer. First, there is the possibility that donors may insist that aid is consumed as tradables, say by financing projects that use only imported materials. In such a case, the impact on the relative price and composition of traded-to-nontraded goods will depend on fungibility of aid. If aid merely frees domestic resources that would have been used to finance these projects irrespective of aid—that is, if aid is fully fungible—the effect of aid would be identical to that described above.

A second possibility is that aid is used for investment in productive capacity that would not have been implemented in the absence of aid. In this case, the production possibility frontier would shift outward, with the nature of this shift depending on whether the investment is allocated to the production of tradables or nontradables. The effect on the structure of demand also depends on the extent to which aid-financed investment involves tradable versus nontradable goods as inputs.

This model illustrates the possibility that aid-financed spending could lead to "Dutch disease"—that is, a reduction in the recipient country's production of tradable goods.[6] But in this model, there is nothing wrong with the shift in production away from tradables; it is merely an efficient adaptation of the economy to the receipt of a transfer, which is unambiguously welfare improving for the recipient country. For the effects of

---

[5]This is, of course, a result of the Stolper-Samuelson theorem: a change in relative prices benefits the factor used intensively in the industry that expands (Stolper and Samuelson, 1941).

[6]In practice, the upward pressure on the real exchange rate will be greater (1) the greater the marginal propensity to spend on nontradable goods, (2) the lower the supply responsiveness of nontradable goods, (3) the higher the demand responsiveness to price changes, and (4) the lower the policy coordination to sterilize aid inflows.

aid to be a problem, some other elements would need to be taken into consideration.[7] First, the shift away from tradables production can generate distortions, such as the possibility of a loss of positive externalities associated with "learning by doing."[8] In that case, however, the distortion ought to be tackled directly as opposed to discouraging aid inflows. Second, aid may be temporary, in which case the intertemporal use of aid is at issue: it would not be desirable for the structure of production and consumption to adapt fully to aid received this period if the aid will not continue next period. Finally, large aid inflows may lead to a relaxation of tax discipline, effectively keeping the resource constraint at the pre-aid level, but with a less sustainable fiscal position.

Empirical Evidence

The simple model just presented illustrates that aid-financed spending may increase the relative price of nontradables and reduce the production of tradables—that is, cause "Dutch disease." But it is an empirical question whether this hypothetical negative effect of aid outweighs the positive effect on productive capacity of aid-financed investment and the welfare effect of aid-financed consumption.

As a starting point, we may consider the behavior of aid flows and real exchange rates in a number of aid-receiving countries. Figure 2 shows a diverse sample of aid-receiving countries, illustrating that aid inflows and appreciation of real exchange rates have often gone hand in hand.

This impression is borne out by a substantial body of more systematic empirical evidence.[9] Traces of aid-induced real exchange rate appreciation were found by van Wijnbergen (1986) and Elbadawi (1999) in two samples of African countries, and these early results were subsequently confirmed by Younger (1992), Vos (1998), and Atingi-Ego and

---

[7]Another class of models dealing with the impact of aid looks at the political economy impact of aid flows and these models are mostly skeptical about any positive aid effects. The most prominent are (1) "the war of attrition" models (Bulow and Klemperer, 1999), whereby aid results in bad policies because individual factions in the recipient country cannot agree on how aid should be allocated and spent and (2) "the voracity effect" models (Tornell and Lane, 1999), whereby weak institutional structure combined with fractionalization of the governing elite produce wasteful spending of aid inflows. Empirical support for these models is provided by Casella and Eichengreen (1996) and Alesina and Weder (2002), respectively.

[8]This argument goes back to Romer (1986). See also Lucas (1988) and Barro and Sala-i-Martin (1995).

[9]Dutch disease models—see Edwards and van Wijnbergen (1989) for a model and White (1992) for a review—were originally formulated for countries with sudden discoveries of natural resources, but were eventually extended to the effects of aid inflows in developing countries and even foreign direct investment surges in transition and emerging economies (Frait and Komárek, 1999).

Figure 2. Real Effective Exchange Rate and Aid in Selected Countries
(1990=100 and in percent of gross national income)

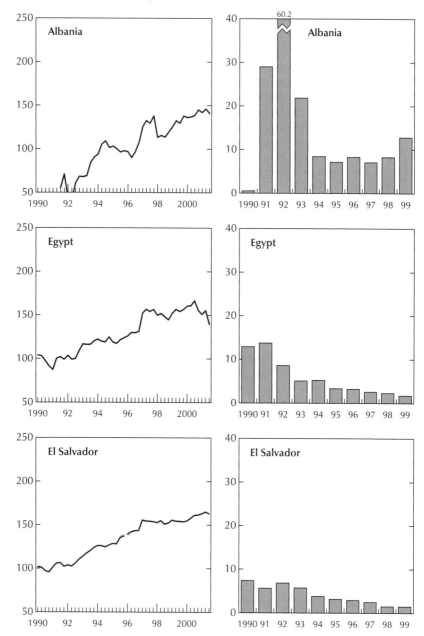

Figure 2. *(continued)*

(1990=100 and in percent of gross national income)

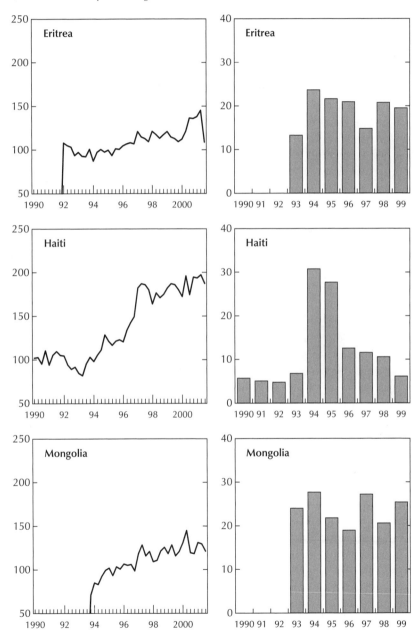

Figure 2. *(concluded)*
(1990=100 and in percent of gross national income)

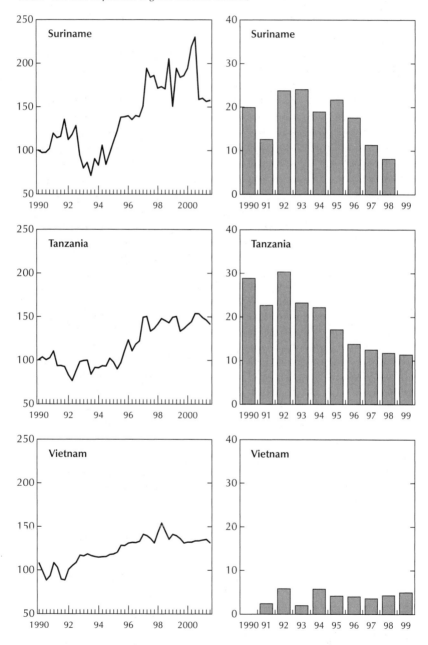

Sources: IMF, *Information Notice System,* and World Bank, *World Development Indicators.*

Sebudde (2000) for Ghana, Pakistan, and Uganda, respectively. However, Nyoni (1998) found aid inflows to depreciate the real exchange rate in Tanzania, and Dijkstra and van Donge (2001) found no impact in Uganda.[10]

Of course, real appreciation may not necessarily depress exports; moreover, other developments, such as the terms of trade, the overall fiscal balance, or country's openness, can mitigate or even offset the change in relative prices. There are several channels that can negate the impact of appreciation on exports.[11] First, the aid-induced inflow of foreign commodities may have a deflationary impact by increasing the supply of commodities or by easing supply bottlenecks in the economy; see Hjertholm, Laursen, and White (2000). Second, real appreciation can be beneficial. As long as imports are used toward "productive" investments in a broad sense, say, physical, capital, health, or education products, appreciated currency will accommodate more of those imports, ultimately contributing to future growth.[12] Third, some shift of resources out of tradable goods may be desirable, providing the increase in aid is permanent (Adam and others, 1994). Falck (2000) claims to have found evidence of the latter effect in Mozambique. Finally, aid may lower transaction costs of doing business in low-income countries (Collier, 2000). But it is unclear to what extent such effects may mitigate, or dominate, the effects of real appreciation on production of tradables.[13]

Empirical evidence on the exchange rate–exports nexus of Dutch disease has not been convincing, a result that is to be expected given the circumstances in most aid-dependent countries. Exports in countries such as Ghana, Uganda, or Tanzania were falling before the surge in aid in the 1980s and 1990s both because the official exchange rate made those exports uncompetitive and because of high transaction

---

[10]From a technical point of view, the single-country studies are vulnerable to sample changes and regime switching: most of these countries have had alternating periods of very low and very high periods of aid inflows, casting doubts on the stability of the estimated parameters. Moreover, those models invariably use short time series only.

[11]These channels also seem to imply that the traditional thinking about private investment crowding out through higher real interest rates is less relevant in developing economies.

[12]This may not be an easy assumption to make. Even in relatively well-run countries, diversion of public funds may reach staggering proportions. For example, Reinikka and Svensson (2002) report that in Uganda ". . . on average, during the period 1991–95, schools received only 13 percent of what the central government contributed to the schools' nonwage expenditures. The bulk of the allocated spending was either used by public officials for purposes unrelated to education or captured for private gain."

[13]Elbadawi (1998) estimated the relative role of endowment, transaction costs, and exchange rates for manufacturing exports in a sample of African countries. He found that high transaction costs and exchange rates misalignment explain the bulk of Africa's export underperformance vis-à-vis East Asia.

costs owing to dilapidating infrastructure, bad macroeconomic policies, and high export taxes. Consequently, many of these economies have been able to increase their overall exports at appreciated real exchange rates simply on account of policies to lower barriers to trade.

It has been argued recently that Dutch disease may affect the structure of exports rather than their overall level. In these models, aid supports employment in the low-skill nontradables sector and the correspondingly high wages then crowd out employment in the traded goods sector. There seems to be more evidence to support this hypothesis: manufactured good exports in many of the less developed countries are substantially below what is predicted on the basis of the countries' labor and capital endowments, and the rate of growth of exports is slower than predicted. These results have been documented in single-country studies for Ghana, Cameroon, and some South Pacific states by Teal (1999), Söderling (2000), and Laplagne, Treadgold, and Baldry (2001), respectively, and in a large panel-data study of African countries by Sekkat and Varoudakis (2000).

We find that the tradable sector has shrunk dramatically in most aid-dependent countries between 1985 and 1999 (Figure 3).[14] The average decline in constant prices was more than 8 percentage points of GDP, while the decline increased to more than 10 percentage points of GDP when measured in current prices. Historically, the share of nontraded goods on GDP has been growing in all countries, especially in those that reached a certain level of development. In contrast, output in per capita terms either declined or stagnated in all but three of our sample countries (Bhutan, Burkina Faso, and Uganda). In other words, these results imply an absolute decline in tradable output per capita as opposed to a relative decline in developed countries.

Aid and Growth

Conceptual Issues

There are different ways of modeling the linkage between aid and growth. From one perspective, aid fosters growth by enabling the country to finance more rapid accumulation of capital, supplementing private savings. This perspective is represented by the Harrod-Domar model, in which the effectiveness of aid in contributing to growth

---

[14]We approximate the share of traded goods by the share of agriculture (including fishing), mining, and manufacturing. We show results for those countries in Table 1 where the appropriate data were available. Our results are similar to those reported by Laplagne (1997), who reported the share of tradable goods for a sample of small South Pacific economies.

Figure 3. Developments in Traded Goods Sector in Selected Countries, 1985–99[1]
(Percent of GDP)

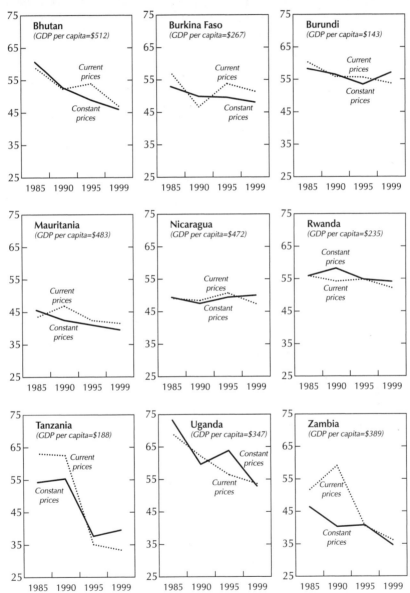

Source: IMF, Recent Economic Developments reports and Statistical Appendixes, various countries and issues.

[1]The traded goods sector is approximated by agriculture, mining, and manufacturing. Data for Uganda are for the following fiscal years: 1984/85, 1989/90, 1994/95, 1998/99; and the 1986 data are used for Mauritania and Nicaragua.

depends on the productivity of capital, as represented by the incremental capital output ratio (ICOR). This assumes that there is no scarcity of complementary factors of production such as labor. According to this model, a sustainable growth path may generate a financing gap, which can be filled through aid or other sources of financing.

The Harrod-Domar model was supplanted in the academic literature about 40 years ago by the Solow growth model, which allows for the possibility of substitution between capital and labor. It implies that the economy approaches a steady state in which the economy's savings are balanced by the need for investment to maintain a constant capital-labor ratio given labor force growth and productivity increases. In this model, the steady state growth rate is equal to the rate of population growth plus the rate of technical change. A flow of aid thus does not affect the economy's growth rate once it reaches the steady state, but it does imply that this growth rate is reached at a higher level of GDP—itself a desirable outcome—and moreover, implies a higher growth rate during the transition.

Endogenous growth models emerged during the 1980s, motivated by concerns that the Harrod-Domar and Solow models did not explain some of the key stylized facts about development in an international perspective—notably, the persistence of international differences in per capita incomes and in growth rates (Lucas, 1988). Endogenous growth models explain growth on the basis of some form of increasing returns to scale, often linked to human capital accumulation and positive externalities associated with "learning-by-doing." Because endogenous growth models leave open the possibility that the equilibrium growth rate is path-dependent (i.e., it depends on the previous history of production in the country), they open the way to empirical work on various factors that influence growth. In particular, in an endogenous growth model, aid may influence growth to the extent that it is used to add to human capital. This has focused attention in particular on the role of health and education spending in development. A related literature has focused on the role of institutions in influencing total factor productivity (Ensminger, 1997).

Empirical Evidence

The literature showed rather convincingly that aid inflows are associated with higher rates of growth (Hansen and Tarp, 2001a). It has also been shown, however, that too much aid can be detrimental to economic growth, even though the estimates are rather imprecise as to what is the exact amount of aid necessary to bring about negative returns of aid (Durbarry, Gemmell, and Greenaway, 1998; Lensink and

White, 1999; or Elbadawi, 1999). It is troubling, however, that in none of the major development success stories, such as in Taiwan Province of China, China, Botswana, Korea, or Chile, does aid seem to have played an important role. In these cases either aid was small through the whole period or the country was weaned off aid early.

The empirical literature offers little agreement on what actually explains the growth performance of less-developed countries and what has been the role of aid during the past three decades. Nevertheless, the results can be summarized relatively easily. First, most studies found that aid increases total savings, albeit by less than the amount of aid inflows. In the underlying Harrod-Domar model, aid relaxes the saving constraint on investment and, hence, should contribute positively to economic growth. Second, the results from reduced-form regressions imply that the aid-investment link is positive and that whenever aid increases saving, it also increases investment and growth. Aid does not, however, generate any multiplier effect: although the estimated coefficients are positive, they are generally smaller than one. Third, whether "good economic policies" are necessary for aid to be effective is debated. Although countries with "good policies" obviously grow faster than those with "poor policies," it is not clear that aid given to the latter countries is simply wasted or that "good-policies" countries with sufficient aid can be assured of success in their economic development.[15] Finally, there is an apparent paradox in the aid effectiveness literature: on the one hand, numerous microeconomic studies have shown that most development projects yield respectable rates of return; on the other hand, U.S. dollar per capita GDP barely moved in the poorest countries that are major aid recipients.

The empirical findings on the aid-growth nexus provide limited insights on the quality of economic growth in aid-recipient countries. One of the key results from endogenous growth models is that an economy's ability to make use of new technologies is an important determinant of its growth. In this regard, many poor, aid-dependent countries fail and the level of foreign direct investment remains well below the level necessary to achieve sustainable growth (Table 1).[16] Although many alternative explanations have been suggested to account for this failure, the

---

[15] See Hadjimichael and others (1995), Burnside and Dollar (2000), and Collier and Dehn (2001) for the good policies–aid-growth nexus and the critiques by Lensink and White (2000), Guillaumont and Chauvet (2001), Dalgaard and Hansen (2001), Hansen and Tarp (2001b), and Easterly (2002). In contrast, Easterly (2001) argues that neither good policies nor exogenous shocks can explain much of the poor growth performance in developing countries and finds a strong link to the rate of growth in OECD countries in the context of a leader-follower model.

[16] See, for example, Ajayi (2001) or Basu and Srinivasan (2002).

aid-driven expansion of the nontradable sector and a lack of support for the high-skill, traded goods sector is clearly one of them. Indeed, the causality may run in the opposite direction: foreign direct investment tends to flow into countries with vibrant tradable good sectors, which tend to deteriorate with large aid inflows (Figure 3). Effectively, aid has left nontradables-driven growth vulnerable to its fluctuations.[17]

Policy Implications

The models used to examine the impact of aid and the accompanying empirical results have implications for the appropriate time profile of aid. The Harrod-Domar and Solow models both imply that the bulk of aid should be provided when the country is poorest, as this is when additional capital financed through aid will be most productive. Consequently, that analysis suggests that aid should taper out as the economy develops. Endogenous growth models, on the other hand, suggest that the productivity of capital may instead increase as the economy develops, suggesting that aid may do more good at a later stage. Empirical studies suggesting that aid is more effective in promoting growth in good policy environments also indicate that aid should "taper in" rather than "taper out" (Gunning, 2000). This path also implies that, during the early years of development, the aid ought to be used to support a higher level of government spending and/or to lower the burden of distortionary taxes on the country.

As a general principle, the argument for aid that "tapers in" seems rather compelling: it would provide support for infrastructure and human capital development while enabling the country to maintain a minimum level of consumption, especially for the poor. But applying this approach poses a number of challenges (Lancaster, 1999). First, one would need to project an appropriate path for development and financing, to identify the points at which aid should be increased, and at which it should taper out. For example, the recipient country authorities and donors could specify a comprehensive, long-term development plan with clear progress toward the goal of a sustainable path.[18] Second, donors would need to commit themselves to financing such a path, giving substance to the promise to deliver more aid—in a predictable manner—sometime in the future. The latter aspect is particularly

---

[17]See Guillaumont and Chauvet (2001) for a similar argument in the context of the Dollar-Burnside regression: once "structural vulnerability" is taken into account, the aid-policy interactive term becomes insignificant.

[18]Past attempts at formulating such long-term paths, such as the 25-year, UNDP-funded Vision 2020, that were formulated for a number of developing countries in the mid-1990s, failed to garner support from both the authorities and key donors.

important in view of the poor track record of aid commitments in predicting actual disbursements (see the concluding section below).

The view that the contribution of aid to growth depends very much on the policies in place focuses greater attention on the policy conditionality associated with aid. It can be used to justify a significant level of conditionality regarding economic governance, particularly on the management of budgetary resources. In other words, conditionality would be attached to measures to build better institutions. At the same time, the argument that aid should be back-loaded (i.e., "tapering in") goes hand in hand with a shift toward outcomes-based conditionality— in contrast to traditional conditionality based on policy actions taken by the authorities. Outcomes-based conditionality is intended to ensure that aid is disbursed in the most productive environment while also giving recipient countries more freedom in selecting their policies. Its drawback from the standpoint of the recipient country is that it exposes the country to greater uncertainty regarding future disbursements, as aid would continue to flow only if outcomes meet donor expectations (International Monetary Fund, 2002).[19]

Regardless of the form of conditionality, the issue remains whether the conditions attached to aid can in fact ensure that it is disbursed in a supportive policy environment. On the one hand, the evidence suggests that the number of conditions typically attached to aid has increased but, on the other hand, countries with higher ratios of aid to gross national income have tended to meet fewer of those conditions (Figure 4, upper panel).[20] More generally, it is increasingly believed that economic reforms are likely to be implemented only to the extent that they are strongly supported within the country itself (Svensson, 2000; Khan and Sharma, 2001).

Aid and Short-Term Fiscal Management

Large aid inflows, sustained or temporary, have a powerful impact on the short-term conduct of fiscal and monetary policies. If aid is volatile, then some of the potential positive effects of aid may not materialize: volatility is welfare reducing and more so in developing countries that

---

[19] It is not difficult to imagine a situation in which the domestic authorities would bargain with the donor agencies about interpretation of outcomes in the same way they presently bargain about the thrust of future policies.

[20] For example, IMF-supported programs during 1993–96 contained somewhat more structural measures in aid-dependent countries than in those where the role of aid has been negligible. The estimated parameter in regression of the number of structural conditions on aid in percent of GDP is statistically significant at the 90 percent level.

Figure 4. Aid Dependency and Program Ownership in Selected Countries
(Sample of 33 countries with IMF-supported programs during the 1990s)

Number of structural conditions

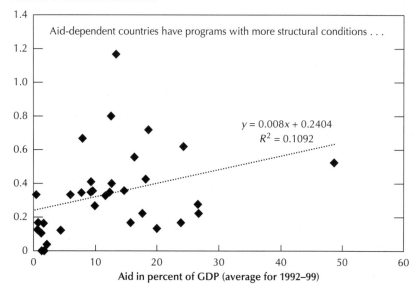

Percentage of structural conditions implemented

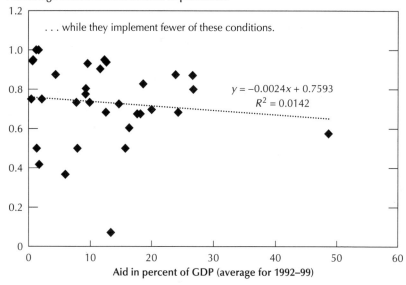

Source: Data are from Bulíř and Moon (2003).
Note: The number of structural conditions is normalized by the length of the program.

have limited domestic financial instruments to offset external shocks. Aid-heavy budgets may take the overall fiscal stance outside the control of the recipient country, owing to limited predictability of aid disbursements. Also, to the extent that donors place conditions on spending, such budgets may lack flexibility on the expenditure side.

Volatility of Aid

Most empirical studies that have examined the volatility of aid have found aid to be significantly more volatile than domestic fiscal revenue (Gemmell and McGillivray, 1998; Pallage and Robe, 2001; and Bulíř and Hamann, 2003).[21] Of course, some volatility of aid is to be expected and may indeed have a stabilizing impact: certain forms of aid, such as food aid or balance of payment support, are disbursed only if the country is hit with an exogenous shock (say, a drought or a sudden drop in terms of trade). To confirm this hypothesis, one would require aid disbursements to be negatively correlated with those shocks. In fact, however, most researchers have reported that aid is positively correlated with economic activity—that is, aid is weakly procyclical (Gemmell and McGillivray, 1998; Barrett, 2001; and Bulíř and Hamann, 2003).[22] Highly volatile and procyclical aid is obviously less beneficial to recipient countries than a similar mean level of aid delivered in a less volatile form (Pallage and Robe, 2003); aid volatility is also likely to substantially attenuate the growth effects of aid (Lensink and Morrissey, 2000).

The results presented below, drawn from Bulíř and Hamann (2003), show that aid—measured by the OECD as the total development assistance—has been much more volatile than domestic fiscal revenue, up to seven times more volatile in the case of heavily aid-dependent countries (Table 2). The volatility of aid increases with the aid dependency: when the sample is narrowed down to countries with an aid-to-revenue ratio of 50 percent or more, the relative volatility increases by an additional 50–75 percent as compared with sample countries with aid-to-revenue ratio of 10 percent or more. The volatility of aid depends on whether aid is measured in U.S. dollar terms or in percent of

---

[21]One widely cited and influential paper reports the opposite result (Collier, 1999), but this is mainly a reflection of some particular features of the empirical methodology used, including the failure to de-trend the data and the exclusive focus on U.S. dollar measures of aid and tax revenues (discussed below). For a discussion of empirical issues in estimating the volatility of aid, see Bulíř and Hamann (2003).

[22]Collier (1999) reported that aid was negatively correlated with revenue in a sample of African countries; however, his estimated covariance term incorporates the same empirical features as mentioned in the previous footnote, and moreover it is not significantly different from zero.

Table 2. Which Is More Volatile: Aid or Revenue?[1]

(Ratio of variances of aid and revenue)

	Countries with an Aid-to-Revenue Ratio of 10 Percent or More	Countries with an Aid-to-Revenue Ratio of 50 Percent or More
Aid and revenue in percent of GDP		
Average	4.96**	7.42**
Median	2.19**	4.91**
Correlation coefficient (average)	0.08	0.05
Number of countries	57	33
Aid and revenue in U.S. dollars per capita		
Average	1.73**	3.00**
Median	0.80	2.25
Correlation coefficient (average)	0.09*	0.11
Number of countries	55	29

Source: Data from Bulíř and Hamann (2003). The data set covers the period from 1975 to 1997 and excludes countries with end-period population of less than 400,000.
[1] The statistical significance of the average and median estimates is measured by the *F*-test and "runs test," respectively. Significance at the 95 percent and 99 percent levels is indicated by one and two asterisks, respectively.

domestic GDP, each measure having some limitations. The former metric would be relevant if aid and tax revenues were spent entirely on tradables with prices fixed in U.S. dollars; the latter would be relevant if the government wanted to use aid and tax revenues to finance spending equivalent to a given slice of GDP. In addition, there is not much evidence of a countercyclical character of aid. While in a few countries the correlation coefficient between aid and revenue was negative, on average aid appears to be modestly procyclical, although this result is not statistically significant in most samples.[23]

These results suggest that aid is quite volatile in relation to other sources of revenues, and this may pose challenges for short-term fiscal management.[24] Of course, there is little reason to assume that aid volatility and procyclicality must be taken as given. Indeed, there is significant room for both aid recipients and donors to improve the pattern of aid disbursements.

---

[23] Aid was found to be countercyclical mostly in countries with large, short-lived shocks and in post-conflict countries. From the donor perspective, French-speaking countries were more likely to receive aid in a countercyclical pattern but, as before, the results do not seem to be robust.

[24] These results do not mean that aid-financed budgets are necessarily more variable than budgets financed by the same level of tax revenues: the variance of total revenues equals the sum of the variances of aid and non-aid revenues plus their covariance—an effect analogous to portfolio diversification. But it will be true in most cases, given that aid is several times as volatile as tax revenues and the covariance term is either zero or positive in most countries.

One major source of aid variability is conditionality—not only the conditions attached by bilateral donors, but also frequently the requirement by donors that aid recipients have the seal of approval of an ontrack, IMF-supported program. There are two sides to this issue. From the country's point of view, it means that complying with conditionality is important not only because of the merits of the policies to which conditions are attached but also because it reduces volatility in aid inflows. But from the perspective of the donors and the international financial institutions, there is an obvious tension between the need to ensure that "good policies" are being implemented versus the negative impact of disruptions in aid disbursements. This gives a particular point to recent efforts to ensure that conditionality is appropriately focused on those elements that are genuinely needed—a key element in the IMF's recent review of conditionality (IMF, 2001a, 2001b).

However, there are also factors that lead to disruptions in aid disbursements over which the recipient country has less control: the tendency for aid commitments to be scaled down through the domestic budget-making processes in the donor countries. This will be discussed in the next subsection.

Predictability of Aid

There has long been a perception that aid commitments err on the optimistic side of what is likely to be deliverable, even when the country's economic policy program remains on track. To the extent that this occurs, it implies that such commitments are a weak basis on which to base spending plans, particularly when aid is a large component of the budget. In turn, projected fiscal deficits including committed aid will tend to overstate the strength of the fiscal position.

Bulíř and Hamann (2003) examine aid commitments as a predictor of disbursements and find that aid commitments explain only a negligible part of the actual disbursement in a simple time-series model and that short-term predictions—even those unrelated to commitments— have been excessively optimistic. These findings are robust to the type of aid: project aid versus program aid or loans versus grants.[25] Moreover, conditionality does not seem to be a factor here: the poor record of predicting aid has been found also for countries with on-track programs.

---

[25] Project ("tied") aid constitutes payments for investment projects agreed between the donor and recipient and its fungibility depends on whether the authorities intended to finance these projects themselves prior to the aid commitment (White, 1992). In contrast, program aid (also called balance of payments support or "untied" aid) generally comes in a "cash" form and is perfectly fungible—the authorities have complete control over the use of these resources.

Table 3. How Good Are Short-Term Predictions of Aid?

(Percent of GDP; sample averages)

	Aid Projections		Aid Disbursements	
	Average	Median	Average	Median
Total aid				
All countries	9.2	7.6	7.4	5.9
Of which:				
No program interruption	9.3	7.4	7.7	5.8
Program interruption	8.5	7.8	5.8	7.5
Project aid				
All countries	5.2	5.1	4.8	4.1
Of which:				
No program interruption	5.3	4.8	4.7	3.9
Program interruption	4.6	5.8	5.2	7.5
Program aid				
All countries	4.7	3.6	3.2	1.9
Of which:				
No program interruption	5.0	3.6	3.7	2.2
Program interruption	3.4	3.6	0.6	0.7

Source: Data from Bulíř and Hamann (2003), a survey based on responses from IMF desk economists for 37 countries. The period covered is 1998 for most countries. Aid projections correspond to projections in IMF-supported programs.

Total aid disbursements in countries with IMF-supported programs were on average some 20 percent less than what was projected at the beginning of the period (Table 3).[26] Contrary to intuition, these results change only little when the sample is divided into countries with and without interruptions in their programs.[27] We find, however, that the prediction error differs markedly for project and program aid. Average project aid disbursements were about 10 percent below predictions, although the median estimate was again about 20 percent. We also find that project aid disbursements are independent of the status of their IMF-supported programs: countries with program interruptions received on average more project aid than was predicted, while countries with program interruptions received some 10 percent less. In contrast, average program aid disbursements were some 32 percent and 25 percent smaller than commitments in all countries and in countries without program interruptions, respectively. The penalty for program interruption was sizable: aid in those countries fell by more than 80 percent below the committed level.

---

[26] See Table 4 for the list of countries.

[27] Program interruption occurs if either (1) the last scheduled program review was not completed or (2) all scheduled reviews were completed but the subsequent annual arrangement was not approved in Enhanced Structural Adjustment Facility/Poverty Reduction and Growth Facility arrangements.

Table 4. List of Countries Used in the Survey[1]

Country	Period	Type of IMF Arrangement[2]
Albania	January 1998–December 1998	ESAF
Algeria	July 1998–June 1999	EFF
Azerbaijan	January 1998–December 1998	ESAF
Bolivia	January 1998–December 1998	ESAF
Burkina Faso	January 1998–December 1998	ESAF
Cambodia	January 1998–December 1998	ESAF
Cameroon	July 1998–June 1999	ESAF
Cape Verde	January 1998–December 1998	Stand-By
Central African Republic*	January 1998–December 1998	ESAF
Côte d'Ivoire	January 1998–December 1998	ESAF
Djibouti	January 1998–December 1998	ESAF
Dominican Republic	January 1998–December 1998	None
Ecuador	January 1998–December 1998	None
Egypt	June 1998–June 1999	Stand-By
El Salvador	December 1997–December 1998	Stand-By
Macedonia, FYR	January 1998–December 1998	ESAF
Gabon	January 1998–December 1998	EFF
Ghana	January 1998–December 1998	ESAF
Guyana	January 1998–December 1998	ESAF
Indonesia	April 1998–March 1999	Stand-By/EFF
Jordan	January 1998–December 1998	EFF
Kyrgyz Republic	January 1998–December 1998	ESAF
Lao P.D.R.	October 1997–September 1998	None
Madagascar	January 1998–December 1998	ESAF
Mauritania	January 1998–December 1998	ESAF
Mongolia	January 1998–December 1999	ESAF
Mozambique	December 1997–December 1998	ESAF
Nepal	July 16, 1998–July 15, 1999	None
Nigeria	January 1998–December 1998	None
Panama	January 1998–December 1998	EFF
Papua New Guinea*	January 1998–December 1998	None
Republic of Congo*	December 1997–December 1998	ESAF
Sierra Leone	January 1998–December 1998	ESAF
Tajikistan	July 1998–June 1999	ESAF
Yemen	January 1998–December 1998	ESAF
Zambia*	January 1998–December 1998	ESAF
Zimbabwe*	January 1998–December 1998	Stand-By

[1]Countries denoted with an asterisk had an interruption in the IMF-supported program.
[2]Enhanced Structural Adjustment Facility, Extended Fund Facility, and Stand-By Arrangement.

Aid cannot be predicted reliably on the basis of donors' commitments, as there seems to be a tendency for all parties involved (donors, the local authorities, and the IMF itself) to systematically overestimate aid disbursements.[28] The prediction errors are not symmetric—more countries experience unexpected shortfalls in aid than unexpected increases in aid.

---

[28]To some extent, this may reflect the strategic behavior by the IMF, given its role in giving a "seal of approval" as the basis for other external assistance.

What Are the Policy Alternatives for Aid Recipients?

If aid is volatile or unpredictable, or both, the recipient countries have two basic options: they could devise a flexible fiscal framework in which tax and spending plans can be adjusted in response to aid receipts, or they could try to smooth out fluctuations in aid disbursements by running down international reserves. A third option is to rely on domestic nonmonetary financing to handle variations in aid. Each of these options will be discussed in turn.

From a fiscal perspective, aid can be used to increase expenditure, lower taxes, reduce debt, or a combination of all three. The actual composition should reflect expectations of the nature of aid: for example, temporary aid increases should not be used for permanent tax reductions or for an increase in mandatory expenditures (entitlements), but should mainly be saved. In contrast, expected "permanent" increases could be channeled into higher spending or lower taxes with little consequences for fiscal stability.

The empirical evidence suggests that countries tend to treat all aid inflows as permanent in the long run, but as a financing item in the short run (see Heller, 1975, and White, 1992). First, the available studies noted that past temporary increases were mostly consumed, leading to a permanently higher level of expenditure—a ratchet effect of aid-induced expenditure (McGillivray and Morrissey, 2001a). Second, the strongest short-term interactions were found between aid and government borrowing, implying that aid windfalls or shortfalls tend to be mirrored in adjustments in deficits (see Gemmell and McGillivray, 1998). McGillivray and Morrissey (2001b) report similar findings from a sample of fiscal response studies. In other words, there is little evidence that aid recipients try to make the distinction between permanent and temporary aid flows.

Budgets can be designed to accommodate aid disbursements in excess of the conservative fiscal baseline, providing that established budgetary procedures are made more flexible. For example, domestic-currency funds could be released to the line ministries only after the equivalent foreign currency–denominated aid has been deposited at the central bank. But the flexibility of fiscal frameworks to make up for variations in aid receipts is limited. Fiscal flexibility is an idea that harks back to the heyday of Keynesian fiscal activism, when it was thought that taxes and spending plans could be shut on and off in response to new information on macroeconomic conditions.

In industrial countries, enthusiasm for the concept of fiscal flexibility was dampened by further analysis and experience. On the revenue side, variations in tax rates to compensate for temporary fiscal shortfalls shifts uncertainty onto the taxpayers and, through their effects on expectations, may result in changes in behavior that vitiate these intended effects (time inconsistency problem). On the expenditure side, it is generally disruptive to turn expenditures on and off at short notice unless these expenditures are not serving an important purpose in the first place. Moreover, expenditures that are turned off for short-term reasons are often difficult to turn on again. For this reason, industrial countries have relied increasingly on "built-in fiscal flexibility" stemming from the income sensitivity of tax and spending items, rather than hoping to fine-tune activist policies. It is hard to believe that low-income countries can succeed where industrial countries failed.

The second option, allowing foreign exchange reserves to ride out fluctuations in aid receipts, poses different but equally daunting problems. It implies that if aid falls short of projected levels, reserves are allowed to decline below the levels envisaged and domestic credit expands to finance a larger-than-projected fiscal deficit. This approach requires that the country plan to follow conservative fiscal and monetary policies in order to build a cushion of reserves that can be drawn down to cover aid shortfalls;[29] this cushion represents resources that could be put to better use in the country if aid were delivered more reliably. Moreover, to the extent that aid shortfalls are chronic, as discussed in the previous subsection, this approach introduces an element of artificiality into fiscal plans, making fiscal targets look more conservative than probable outturns.

The third option mentioned, using domestic bond financing to maintain spending plans in the face of aid shortfalls, can be also be used, subject to quantitative limitations. A necessary condition for this approach is to have functioning domestic financial markets. But even if those markets exist, there is a limit to the amount the government can finance domestically: for example, the evidence suggests that most sub-Saharan African countries cannot issue more domestic debt than equivalent to 15 percent of GDP without recourse to printing money. Moreover, given the shallowness of domestic financial markets in most aid-dependent countries, heavy use of these markets by the government may significantly crowd out private borrowing. Finally, the cost of domestic financing is generally higher than that of concessional external financing, even when the impact of devaluation is taken into account (Beaugrand, Loco, and Mlachila, 2002).

Thus, any of these ways of adapting to short-term variations in aid—fiscal flexibility, using a cushion of reserves, or domestic borrowing—

---

[29]Most IMF-supported programs include adjusters to ensure that quarterly spending plans can continue even if aid falls short of projected levels. See IMF (2002), Annex I, for a discussion.

has limitations.[30] As long as uncertainties on aid receipts remain substantial, it is likely that some combination of the three will need to be used, depending on the extent to which variations in aid are expected to be permanent or transitory. But these considerations also point to the need for aid recipients to formulate their fiscal plans on the basis of more realistic projections of the aid that is likely to materialize, and for donors to make stronger efforts to keep their promises.

Conclusions

Despite the declining share of aid in budgets of donor countries, aid continues to play an important role in many developing countries. While the impact of aid is typically divided between supplementing domestic saving and contributing to consumption, there is less agreement on the potential effects of aid on growth. The impact of large aid inflows on the relative price of traded and nontraded goods is well known, and several recent papers confirmed the importance of real exchange rate appreciation for the decline of the traded goods sector in developing countries. But in a dynamic context, the effects of aid depend on how aid-financed spending affects the productive capacity of the economy. While several empirical studies suggest that aid tends to enhance growth, they also suggest that the linkage is neither direct nor automatic, but depends very much on the environment that influences the use of aid.

The positive impact of aid has been undermined in some cases by the volatility and unpredictability of aid. Aid is significantly more volatile than domestic fiscal revenue, and its volatility increases with a country's aid dependency. In addition, aid is procyclical vis-à-vis domestic fiscal revenue: rather than smoothing out cyclical shocks, it tends to exacerbate them. Moreover, aid is not well predicted even in countries with "on-track" programs and the prediction error is asymmetric: aid commitments are more likely to overestimate disbursements than vice versa.

This chapter has highlighted a number of issues that aid poses for fiscal management. None of these findings alters the view that donors should be more generous with aid. However, it is important to take these issues into account to ensure that aid has its intended effect of boosting growth and alleviating poverty.

---

[30] As a related issue, empirical evidence on a direct impact of aid in the monetary area is rather scanty and outdated (see White, 1992, for a review). Recently, Fanizza (2001) illustrated, in the case of Malawi, inflationary pressures resulting from the government's inability to sell sufficient amount of foreign exchange, owing to the country's small and isolated foreign exchange market.

References

Adam, Chris, and others, 1994, *Evaluation of Swedish Development Co-Operation with Tanzania: A Report for the Secretariat for Analysis of Swedish Development Assistance* (Stockholm: Secretariat for Analysis of Swedish Development Assistance, Ministry for Foreign Affairs).

Ajayi, S. Ibi, 2001, "What Africa Needs to Do to Benefit from Globalization," *Finance & Development*, Vol. 38 (December), pp. 6–8.

Alesina, Alberto, and David Dollar, 2000, "Who Gives Foreign Aid to Whom and Why?" *Journal of Economic Growth*, Vol. 5 (March), pp. 33–63.

Alesina, Alberto, and Beatrice Weder, 2002, "Do Corrupt Governments Receive Less Foreign Aid?" *American Economic Review*, Vol. 92 (September), pp. 1126–37.

Atingi-Ego, Michael, and Rachel Kaggwa Sebudde, 2000, "Uganda's Equilibrium Real Exchange Rate and Its Implications for Non-Traditional Export Performance," *Bank of Uganda Staff Papers*, Vol. 2, No. 1, pp. 1–43.

Barrett, Christopher B., 2001, "Does Food Aid Stabilize Food Stability?" *Economic Development and Cultural Change*, Vol. 49 (January), pp. 335–49.

Barro, Robert J., and Xavier Sala-i-Martin, 1995, *Economic Growth* (Cambridge, Massachusetts: MIT Press).

Basu, Anupam, and Krishna Srinivasan, 2002, "Foreign Direct Investment in Africa—Some Case Studies," IMF Working Paper 02/61 (Washington: International Monetary Fund).

Bauer, Peter T., 1979, "Foreign Aid Viewed Differently," *Aussenwirtschaft*, Vol. 34 (September), pp. 225–39.

Beaugrand, Philippe, Boileau Loko, and Montfort Mlachila, 2002, "The Choice Between External and Domestic Debt in Financing Budget Deficits: The Case of Central and West African Countries," IMF Working Paper 02/79 (Washington: International Monetary Fund).

Bulíř, Aleš, and A. Javier Hamann, 2003, "Aid Volatility: An Empirical Assessment," *IMF Staff Papers*, Vol. 50, No. 1, pp. 64–89.

Bulíř, Aleš, and Soojin Moon, 2003, "Do IMF-Supported Programs Help Make Fiscal Adjustment More Durable?" IMF Working Paper 03/38 (Washington: International Monetary Fund).

Bulow, Jeremy, and Paul Klemperer, 1999, "The Generalized War of Attrition," *American Economic Review*, Vol. 89 (March), pp. 175–89.

Burnside, Craig, and David Dollar, 2000, "Aid, Policies, and Growth," *American Economic Review*, Vol. 90 (September), pp. 847–68.

Casella, Alessandra, and Barry Eichengreen, 1996, "Can Foreign Aid Accelerate Stabilisation?" *Economic Journal*, Vol. 106 (May), pp. 605–19.

Collier, Paul, 1999, "Aid 'Dependency': A Critique," *Journal of African Economies*, Vol. 8 (December), pp. 528–45.

————, 2000, "Africa's Comparative Advantage," in *Industrial Development and Policy in Africa: Issues of De-Industrialization and Development Strategy*, ed. by Hossein Jalilian, Michael Tribe, and John Weiss (Cheltenham, United Kingdom: Edward Elgar), pp. 11–21.

————, and Jan Dehn, 2001, "Aid, Shocks, and Growth," World Bank Policy Research Working Paper No. 2688 (Washington: World Bank).

Dalgaard, Carl-Johan, and Hendrik Hansen, 2001, "On Aid, Growth, and Good Policies," *Journal of Development Studies*, Vol. 37 (August), pp. 17–41.

Dijkstra, A. Geske, and Jan Kees van Donge, 2001, "What Does the 'Show Case' Show? Evidence of and Lessons from Adjustment in Uganda," *World Development*, Vol. 29 (May), pp. 841–63.

Durbarry, Ramesh, Norman Gemmell, and David Greenaway, 1998, "New Evidence on the Impact of Foreign Aid on Economic Growth," CREDIT Research Paper, No. 98/8 (University of Nottingham: Centre for Research in Economic Development and International Trade).

Easterly, William, 2001, "The Lost Decades: Developing Countries' Stagnation in Spite of Policy Reform 1980–1998," *Journal of Economic Growth*, Vol. 6 (June), pp. 135–57.

————, 2002, "The Cartel of Good Intentions: The Problem of Bureaucracy in Foreign Aid," *Journal of Policy Reform*, Vol. 5 (December), pp. 223–50.

Edwards, Sebastian, and Sweder van Wijnbergen, 1989, "Disequilibrium and Structural Adjustment," Chapter 28 in *Handbook of Development Economics*, Vol. II, ed. by H. Chenery and T.N. Srinivasan (New York: North-Holland).

Elbadawi, Ibrahim A., 1998, "Can Africa Export Manufactures? The Role of Endowment, Exchange Rates, and Transaction Costs," World Bank Policy Research Working Paper No. 2120 (Washington: World Bank).

————, 1999, "External Aid: Help or Hindrance to Export Orientation in Africa?" *Journal of African Economies*, Vol. 8 (December), pp. 578–616.

Ensminger, Jean, 1997, "Changing Property Rights: Reconciling Formal and Informal Rights to Land in Africa," in *The Frontiers of the New Institutional Economics*, ed. by John N. Droback and John V.C. Nye (San Diego, California: Academic Press), pp. 165–96.

Falck, Hans, 2000, "Mozambique: Dutch Disease in Mozambique?" SIDA Country Economic Report 2000:1 (Stockholm, Sweden: Swedish International Development Cooperation Agency).

Fanizza, Domenico, 2001, "Foreign Aid, Macroeconomic Stabilization, and Growth in Malawi," in *Malawi—Selected Issues and Statistical Appendix*, IMF Country Report No. 01/32 (Washington: International Monetary Fund), pp. 11–30.

Frait, Jan, and Luboš Komárek, 1999, "Dlouhodobý rovnovážný reálný měnový kurz koruny a jeho determinanty" (Long-Term Equilibrium Real Exchange Rate of the Koruna and Its Determinants), Working Paper No. 9–99 (Prague: Czech National Bank). Available via the Internet: http://www.cnb.cz/pdf/c-vp9-99.pdf.

Gemmell, Norman, and Mark McGillivray, 1998, "Aid and Tax Instability and the Government Budget Constraint in Developing Countries," CREDIT Research Paper No. 98/1 (University of Nottingham: Centre for Research in Economic Development and International Trade).

Guillaumont, Patrick, and Lisa Chauvet, 2001, "Aid and Performance: A Reassessment," *Journal of Development Studies*, Vol. 37 (August), pp. 66–92.

Gunning, Jan W., 2000, "Rethinking Aid," paper presented at the 12th Annual Bank Conference on Development Economics (Washington: World Bank). Available via the Internet: http://www.worldbank.org/research/abcde/washington_12/pdf_files/gunning.pdf.

Hadjimichael, Michael T., and others, 1995, *Sub-Saharan Africa: Growth, Savings, and Investment, 1986–93*, IMF Occasional Paper No. 118 (Washington: International Monetary Fund).

Hansen, Henrik, and Finn Tarp, 2001a, "Aid and Growth Regressions," *Journal of Development Economics*, Vol. 64 (April), pp. 547–70.

———, 2001b, "Aid Effectiveness Disputed," *Journal of International Development*, Vol. 12, pp. 375–98.

Heller, Peter S., 1975, "A Model of Public Fiscal Behavior in Developing Countries: Aid, Investment, and Taxation," *American Economic Review*, Vol. 65 (June), pp. 429–45.

Hjertholm, Peter, Jytte Laursen, and Howard White, 2000, "Macroeconomic Issues in Foreign Aid," University of Copenhagen, Institute of Economics Discussion Paper No. 00/05 (Copenhagen: University of Copenhagen).

International Monetary Fund, 2001a, "Conditionality in IMF-Supported Program—Policy Issues" (Washington: International Monetary Fund). Available via the Internet: http://www.imf.org/external/np/pdr/cond/2001/eng/policy/021601.pdf.

———, 2001b, "Streamlining Structural Conditionality: Review of Initial Experience" (Washington: International Monetary Fund). Available via the Internet: http://www.imf.org/external/np/pdr/cond/2001/eng/collab/review.htm.

———, 2002, "The Modalities of Conditionality—Further Considerations" (Washington: International Monetary Fund). Available via the Internet: http://www.imf.org/external/np/pdr/cond/2002/eng/modal/010802.htm.

Khan, Mohsin S., and Sunil Sharma, 2001, "IMF Conditionality and Country Ownership of Programs," IMF Working Paper 01/142 (Washington: International Monetary Fund).

Lancaster, Carol, 1999, "Aid Effectiveness in Africa: The Unfinished Agenda," *Journal of African Economies*, Vol. 8, pp. 487–503.

Laplagne, Patrick, 1997, "Dutch Disease in the South Pacific: Evidence from the 1980s and Beyond," *Pacific Economic Bulletin*, Vol. 12 (June), pp. 84–96.

———, Malcolm Treadgold, and Jonathan Baldry, 2001, "A Model of Aid Impact in Some South Pacific Microstates," *World Development*, Vol. 29 (February), pp. 365–83.

Lensink, Robert, and Oliver Morrissey, 2000, "Aid Instability as a Measure of Uncertainty and the Positive Impact of Aid on Growth," *Journal of Development Studies*, Vol. 36 (February), pp. 31–49.

Lensink, Robert, and Howard White, 1999, "Is There an Aid Laffer Curve?" CREDIT Research Paper No. 99/6 (University of Nottingham: Centre for Research in Economic Development and International Trade).

———, 2000, "Assessing Aid: A Manifesto for Aid in the 21st Century?" *Oxford Development Studies*, Vol. 28 (February), pp. 6–17.

Lucas, Robert, 1988, "On the Mechanics of Economic Development," *Journal of Monetary Economics*, Vol. 22 (July), pp. 3–42.

McGillivray, Mark, and Oliver Morrissey, 2001a, "Aid Illusion and Public Sector Fiscal Behaviour," *Journal of Development Studies*, Vol. 37 (August), pp. 118–36.

———, 2001b, "A Review of Evidence on the Fiscal Effects of Aid," CREDIT Research Paper No. 01/13 (University of Nottingham: Centre for Research in Economic Development and International Trade).

Michaely, Michael, 1981, "Foreign Aid, Economic Structure, and Dependence," *Journal of Development Economics*, Vol. 9 (December), pp. 313–30.

Nyoni, Timothy S., 1998, "Foreign Aid and Economic Performance in Tanzania," *World Development*, Vol. 26 (July), pp. 1235–40.

Pallage, Stéphane, and Michel A. Robe, 2001, "Foreign Aid and the Business Cycle," *Review of International Economics*, Vol. 9 (November), pp. 636–67.

———, 2003, "On the Welfare Cost of Economic Fluctuations in Developing Countries," *International Economic Review*, Vol. 44 (May), pp. 677–98.

Reinikka, Ritva, and Jakob Svensson, 2002, "Explaining Leakage of Public Funds," CEPR Discussion Paper Series No. 3227 (London: Centre for Economic Policy Research).

Romer, Paul M., 1986, "Increasing Returns and Long-Run Growth," *Journal of Political Economy*, Vol. 94 (October), pp. 1002–37.

Sekkat, Khalid, and Aristomene Varoudakis, 2000, "Exchange Rate Management and Manufactured Exports in Sub-Saharan Africa," *Journal of Development Economics*, Vol. 61 (February), pp. 237–53.

Söderling, Ludvig, 2000, "Dynamics of Export Performance, Productivity and Real Effective Exchange Rate in Manufacturing: The Case of Cameroon," *Journal of African Economies*, Vol. 9 (December), pp. 411–29.

Stolper, Wolfgang F., and Paul A. Samuelson, 1941, "Protection and Real Wages," *Review of Economic Studies*, Vol. 9 (November), pp. 58–73. Reprinted in *Comparative Politics and the International Political Economy*, Vol. 1 (Aldershot, United Kingdom: Elgar, 1995), pp. 255–70.

Svensson, Jakob, 2000, "When Is Foreign Aid Policy Credible: Aid Dependence and Conditionality," *Journal of Development Economics*, Vol. 61 (February), pp. 61–84.

Teal, Francis, 1999, "Why Can Mauritius Export Manufactures and Ghana Not?" *World Economy*, Vol. 7 (September), pp. 981–93.

Tornell, Aaron, and Philip R. Lane, 1999, "The Voracity Effect," *American Economic Review*, Vol. 89 (March), pp. 22–46.

van Wijnbergen, Sweder, 1986, "Macroeconomic Aspects of the Effectiveness of Foreign Aid: On the Two-Gap Model, Home Goods Disequilibrium and Real Exchange Rate Misalignment," *Journal of International Economics*, Vol. 21 (August), pp. 123–36.

Vos, Rob, 1998, "Aid Flows and 'Dutch Disease' in a General Equilibrium Framework for Pakistan," *Journal of Policy Modeling*, Vol. 20 (February), pp. 77–109.

White, Howard, 1992, "The Macroeconomic Impact of Development Aid: A Critical Survey," *Journal of Development Studies*, Vol. 28 (January), pp. 163–240.

World Bank, 2002, *Global Development Finance* (Washington: World Bank).

Younger, Stephen D., 1992, "Aid and the Dutch Disease: Macroeconomic Management When Everybody Loves You," *World Development*, Vol. 20 (November), pp. 1587–97.

17

Foreign Aid and Consumption Smoothing: Evidence from Global Food Aid

SANJEEV GUPTA, BENEDICT CLEMENTS, AND ERWIN R. TIONGSON

1. Introduction

The debate on aid effectiveness has largely focused on the impact of aggregate "development assistance" on economic growth or economic development more broadly (Easterly, 2001; World Bank, 1998). As a result, relatively little attention has been paid to how well certain components of foreign aid achieve their stated objectives, such as disaster relief, humanitarian assistance, and food aid. In this paper, we focus on one particularly important component of foreign aid—food aid—and evaluate whether it helps stabilize consumption in recipient countries, and whether it has been targeted to those countries most in need.

Aid inflows (including food aid) impact government revenues and economic activity. This is the case when aid flows through the budget and if part or all of the commodity aid is sold in local markets. Wide variations in the receipt of commodity aid can thus lead to volatility in both government revenues and economic activity and make fiscal

Reprinted from the *Review of Development Economics*, Vol. 8, Sanjeev Gupta, Benedict Clements, and Erwin R. Tiongson, "Foreign Aid and Consumption Smoothing: Evidence from Global Food Aid," © 2004, with permission from Blackwell.

The authors wish to thank Abbassian Abdolreza, Rina Bhattacharya, Aleš Bulíř, Chris Barrett, Paul Cashin, Bikas Joshi, Menachem Katz, Noureddine Krichene, Wojciech Maliszewski, Srobona Mitra, Paulo Neuhaus, Stéphane Pallage, Michel A. Robe, Tobias Roy, Ratna Sahay, George Simon, Shahla Shapouri, Thierry Tressel, Luis Valdivieso, Mario Zejan, and an anonymous referee for helpful comments on an earlier draft. George Simon and Giampiero Lucarini (WFP) generously provided data on food aid.

management more problematic. This paper also seeks to shed light on this issue by empirically assessing whether the timing of food aid has contributed to the volatility of government revenues and economic activity in recipient countries.

The rest of this paper is structured as follows: Section 2 reviews the relevant literature. Section 3 presents the empirical framework and the data sources. Section 4 reports the empirical results and Section 5 concludes.

2. Literature Review

A number of recent papers have also documented a pattern of aid volatility and aid procyclicality with respect to output and fiscal revenues (Gemmell and McGillivray, 1998; and Pallage and Robe, 2001). The procyclicality of aid implies that aid flows cannot stabilize fluctuations in consumption; direct (humanitarian) intervention does not take place when it is needed most. Food aid is usually made available free or on highly concessional terms. Counterpart funds generated by commodity aid including food aid provide critical budget support.

The size of counterpart funds is substantial in many recipient countries (Colding and Pinstrup-Andersen, 2000). Counterpart funds (from food aid, commodity aid, and project aid) accounted for about 30% of government revenue in Mozambique in the early 1990s (Riley, 1992). In Albania, counterpart funds from food aid sales amounted to 5% of government expenditure and 3% of GDP during the same period. In Georgia, revenues from food aid sales accounted for about 15% of total expenditures in the mid-1990s (UNDP, 1996).

Fluctuations in food aid can have important macroeconomic consequences. In particular, the timing of food aid and its sale could be viewed as an "automatic stabilizer" for the economy; when food output in a country falls, government revenues decline and spending increases. Monetization of food aid flows in these circumstances stabilizes flows to the budget in addition to shielding food consumption levels in the country. Furthermore, food aid (including commodities distributed directly to households) is critical for alleviating spending pressures on the budget to offset the adverse consequences of food shortages.

A handful of case studies of individual food aid programs and time series studies of global food aid and world commodity prices suggest that food aid is *not* effective in addressing transitory food insecurity (Clay et al., 1996), and that food aid and world prices move inversely (Benson, 2000). Therefore, food aid fails to mitigate transitory food insecurity. However, these studies do not provide information on the relationship between food aid and cyclical fluctuations in aggregate domestic food availability by country. With respect to cross-country econometric studies, the literature has examined the cyclicality of either individual food aid programs alone or multilateral food aid programs for small samples of countries. The empirical findings are mixed (Barrett, 2001; Mellor and Pandya-Lorch, 1992; and Trueblood et al., 2001). Evidence on how well food aid is targeted to countries with the greatest need is also mixed (Shapouri and Missiaen, 1990; Diven, 2001; and Barrett, 2001).

A number of important issues remain unresolved in the empirical literature on food aid. First, because food aid is typically provided by a number of donors, evaluating the performance of individual programs in responding to food shortages can be misleading. An evaluation of the performance of global food aid would be more appropriate. Second, the cyclical properties of food aid with respect to revenues and overall deficit have not been examined. Because food aid can provide additional revenue and because food shortages can be symptoms of a more fundamental economic downturn, the magnitude and direction of co-movements between food aid and measures of economic activity provide useful information. Third, recent research has found that the results of business cycle studies are sensitive to the choice of filter (Canova, 1999). This implies that the robustness of results from empirical studies of food aid should be tested against various filtering techniques and model specifications. Fourth, the literature on food aid has noted a change in the composition of food aid toward emergency aid, raising the question of whether its cyclical properties have also changed. Finally, while the literature has noted that foreign aid is not necessarily progressive, the issue of whether this also applies to global food aid per se has yet to be settled.

3. Methodology and Data

Methodology

This paper employs two strategies for assessing the cyclical properties of foreign aid with respect to domestic food availability in recipient countries: (1) the calculation of correlation coefficients between food aid and domestic food availability detrended by the Hodrick-Prescott filter; and (2) a two-step Tobit regression of food aid on a measure of relative shortfalls in consumption and a measure of absolute shortfalls in consumption. As explained below, the second strategy also provides a test for the progressivity of food aid distribution.

Hodrick-Prescott Filter

First, following the literature, we measure business cycles as deviations from trend. We detrend nonconcessional food availability using the Hodrick and Prescott (1997) filter, which for a series x extracts the

growth component x^g and the cyclical component $x^c = x - x^g$ by minimizing the following loss function:

$$\sum_t x^{c2} + \lambda \sum_t \left(\left(x^g_{t+1} - x^g_t \right) - \left(x^g_t - x^g_{t-1} \right) \right)^2, \tag{1}$$

where λ is a weight that reflects the relative variance of growth and cyclical components. For annual data, $\lambda = 100$ by convention.[1] The logarithm
of x is used to calculate percentage deviations from trend. The correlations between global food aid and the cyclical component of domestic
food availability are calculated contemporaneously, and with leads and
lags up to two years. For comparison, we also calculate the correlations
between food aid and the cyclical components of log per capita income
as a measure of economic activity and a proxy for consumption shortfalls.

Two-Step Estimation

The empirical literature on food aid and consumption smoothing has
examined how food aid flows respond to shortfalls in food availability
by first measuring food availability in terms of deviations from a trend
(Mellor and Pandya-Lorch, 1992; Shapouri and Rosen, 2001), and then
examining the statistical relationship between food aid and such deviations. We use the same two-step estimation procedure, but adopt the
specification in Barrett (2001); and Barrett and Heisey (2002). Their
method has the added feature of providing a measure of progressivity
(that is, whether food aid flows are, on average, targeted toward countries with greater absolute shortfalls in food availability).

The first step requires estimating the growth rate in nonconcessional
food availability (NA) using a logarithmic trend regression for each
country in the sample:

$$\ln\left(NA_t \right) = \alpha_{0N} + \alpha_{1N} Year + \varepsilon_{nt}, \tag{2}$$

where ε_{nt} captures the deviations around the trend nonconcessional
NA. NA is measured using the FAO data as the sum of domestic food
production (PROD) plus total food imports (IM).

The second step involves the regression of food aid per capita (FA)
on ε_{nt} and the level of NA. Because FA is a nonnegative variable often

---

[1] Given the uncertainty about the nature of business cycles in developing countries,
we recognize that there could be a case for using different values of λ to assess the robustness of the results. Instead, we opt to use alternative detrending techniques (as described below) as a robustness test. In addition, recent research indicates that traditional
values for λ are appropriate for most countries (Marcet and Ravn, 2001).

taking zero value, the relationship is estimated using a panel data Tobit specification:

$$\tilde{FA}_{it} = \beta_0 + \beta_1 \varepsilon_{nit} + \beta_2 NA_{it} + \sum_r \lambda_r D_{ir} + \sum_t \theta_t Y_{it} + \omega_{it} \quad \text{if } FA_{it} > 0 \quad (3a)$$

$$\tilde{FA}_{it} = 0 \quad \text{if } FA_{it} = 0, \quad (3b)$$

where i is the index of the recipient country, t is the year, and r is region.[2] In Eq. (3a), β_1 is a measure of the stabilization effect of food aid and β_2 is the measure of progressivity, controlling for fixed effects of regions and years (as captured by the dummy variables D and Y for regions and years, respectively). The method thus distinguishes relative shortfalls (ε_{nt}) from absolute shortfalls (NA) in food availability. In particular, $\beta_1 < 0$ indicates that global food aid is countercyclical, $\beta_1 > 0$ indicates that it is procyclical, and $\beta_1 = 0$ indicates that it is acyclical. The sign of β_2, on the other hand, indicates whether food aid is progressive. $\beta_2 > 0$ would indicate the progressivity of global food aid.

Barrett and Heisey (2002) note two possible sources of bias in the estimation of Eqs. (3a) and (3b): (1) omitted variables bias, and (2) endogeneity bias due to reverse causality between food aid (FA) and food availability (NA), through commercial imports (IM = NA – PROD).

First, control for lagged food aid may be required because a number of studies note that food aid flows are persistent. In particular, Diven (2001) finds a strong incremental trend in food aid "programming," where policymakers appear to use shipments from the previous year as a starting point for marginal adjustments. Evidence from micro data confirms some spatial inertia in food aid allocations as well, which means that food aid allocation to certain regions persist (Clay et al., 1996; and Jayne et al., 2002), for various reasons including significant fixed costs in food aid operations.

Second, food aid flows may have an effect, both lagged and contemporaneous, on commercial food imports by the recipient, as some imports are displaced by food aid. There is thus some reverse causality between food aid and food availability, via food imports. Though an argument could be made that food aid flows may also depress production, there is no evidence that food aid (FA_{it}) has any contemporaneous effect on domestic food production ($PROD_{it}$) (Barrett, 2002).

To correct for these biases, Barrett and Heisey (2002) suggest reestimating Eqs. (3a) and (3b) as follows:

---

[2]Given our interest in assessing whether food aid responds to food needs across (as well as within) countries, country fixed effects are not included.

$$\tilde{F}A_{it} = \varphi_0 + \varphi_1\varepsilon_{pit} + \varphi_2 PROD_{it} + \varphi_3 FA_{it-1} + \sum_r \sigma_r D_{ir} \tag{4a}$$
$$+ \sum_t \omega_t Y_{it} + \omega_{it} \quad \text{if} \ \ FA_{it} > 0$$

$$\tilde{F}A_{it} = 0 \quad \text{if} \ \ FA_{it} = 0, \tag{4b}$$

where ε_{pit} is a measure of fluctuations in domestic food production as in Eq. (2), FA_{it-1} is lagged food aid, and $PROD_{it}$ is a measure of domestic food production per capita. $PROD_{it}$ may be treated as exogenous. The sign of φ_1 indicates the cyclical properties of global food aid.

Modifications

To test the robustness of the results to the choice of filters, we employ other filtering or detrending techniques in both procedures. In addition to the Hodrick-Prescott filter, we employ linear and quadratic detrending. In particular, we decompose a data series into a cyclical component and a linear function of time:

$$x_t = \alpha + \beta * t + c_t. \tag{5}$$

This is similar to Eq. (2), where an OLS regression yields residuals (ε_t) that are the cyclical component of the series (c_t). The quadratic trend adds a second term to equation (5):

$$x_t = \alpha + \beta * t + \gamma * t^2 + c_t. \tag{6}$$

We also use an approximation of the band-pass filter developed by Christiano and Fitzgerald (1999). This filters both high frequency "noise" and low frequency "trends," thus leaving fluctuations within a specified band at typical business cycle frequencies (1.5 to 8 years). Using the new filtering procedures, one possible modification to the two-step method would be to estimate ε_{nt} as deviations from a nonlinear trend (ε_{nt}^N) rather than from a linear time trend implied by equation (2). Eq. (3a), for example, is then estimated as

$$\tilde{F}A_t = \beta_0 + \beta_1\varepsilon_{nit}^N + \beta_2 NA_t + \sum_r \lambda_r D_{ir} + \sum_t \theta_t Y_{it} + \omega_{it} \quad \text{if} \ FA_{it} > 0 \tag{3a'}$$

$$\tilde{F}A_t = 0 \qquad\qquad\qquad\qquad\qquad\qquad \text{if} \ FA_{it} = 0. \tag{3b'}$$

A test of the null hypothesis $\beta_1 = 0$ versus the alternate hypothesis $\beta_1 < 0$ is again a direct test of the procyclicality of global food aid. A similar procedure may be applied to Eqs. (4a) and (4b).

Data

This paper uses comprehensive data on global food aid flows over 30 years, 1970–2000, covering some 150 recipient countries. Global food aid data are drawn from the WFP's *Food Aid Flows* (various issues) and the Food and Agriculture Organization's (FAO) FAOSTAT database. Data on population, domestic food production, and total food imports are from the FAOSTAT database. All food data are measured in volumes (metric tons). We proxy total food production, food imports, and global food aid using cereal volumes. All series are measured in per capita terms.

Data for GDP per capita, total government revenue (in percent of GDP), and overall deficit (in percent of GDP) are from the World Economic Outlook (WEO) database. The data generally cover the 1970–2000 period, though the period may vary across countries.

4. Results

Correlations

Table 1 provides the summary information on the correlations between global food aid and cyclical fluctuations in nonconcessional food availability, by region.[3] The estimates are based on food availability up to two periods in leads and lags, using linear and quadratic detrending as well as the band-pass and Hodrick-Prescott filters (not reported). The results indicate that food aid is overwhelmingly acyclical across all regions. Some 100 out of the 150 countries in the sample have correlation coefficients less than zero. However, these are mostly within the intervals judged not significantly different from zero. At the most, only in 28 countries is food aid significantly countercyclical. The results are invariant to the choice of filter.

Tobit Regressions

Baseline Regressions

Table 2 presents the results of the Tobit regression of Eqs. (3a) and (3b). For the sample as a whole, the results indicate that global food aid follows a significantly progressive distribution. This means that food aid has been responsive to absolute shortfalls in nonconcessional food availability across countries.

---

[3]Country-level results (not reported) are available on request from the authors. The correlations between food aid and the cyclical components of log per capita income—a proxy for consumption shortfalls—show similar patterns (not reported).

Table 1. Cyclical Properties of Food Aid

(Unweighted averages; comovement with domestic nonconcessional food availability)

	Sample Size	Linear Detrending					Quadratic Detrending				
		Two-period lag	One-period lag	Zero lag	One-period lead	Two-period lead	Two-period lag	One-period lag	Zero lag	One-period lead	Two-period lead
Asia	27.0	-0.03	-0.03	-0.06	0.00	-0.10	0.00	-0.08	-0.03	0.01	-0.06
Middle East and North Africa	16.0	0.06	-0.04	-0.04	0.10	0.10	-0.05	-0.05	0.00	0.08	0.02
Sub-Saharan Africa	48.0	0.03	0.01	-0.02	0.01	-0.06	-0.03	0.00	0.01	0.04	0.02
Transition	24.0	-0.08	-0.06	0.00	0.07	-0.06	0.03	0.20	0.10	-0.21	-0.26
Western Hemisphere	33.0	0.06	-0.06	-0.11	-0.03	0.01	0.03	0.01	0.08	-0.06	-0.06
Others	5.0	-0.09	-0.13	-0.09	-0.07	-0.12	-0.04	-0.01	-0.01	0.05	0.00

Sources: FAO database; WFP database; and authors' calculations.

Table 2. Baseline Tobit Regression Results for All Countries: Linear Detrending[1]

	(1)	(2)	(3)	(4)
β_1 (cyclicality)	0.0136***	0.0096**	0.0118**	0.0079*
	(2.92)	(2.03)	(2.52)	(1.66)
β_2 (progressivity)	−0.0422***	−0.0241***	−0.0425***	−0.0246***
	(−8.53)	(−3.69)	(−8.61)	(−3.78)
Regional dummies	No	Yes	No	Yes
Year dummies	No	No	Yes	Yes
LR statistic	79.05	171.36	120.44	213.41
P-value	0.00	0.00	0.00	0.00
Number of observations	3,720	3,720	3,720	3,720

Source: See text.

(***), (**), and (*) denote significance at the 1, 5, and 10 percent level, respectively.

[1]Specification varies from one column to the next, depending on the inclusion or exclusion of regional or year dummies.

An equally interesting result is the progressivity of food aid flows among low-income countries (not reported). In fact, the relationship between per capita income and food aid is negative and significant, but the coefficient size is small (−0.03). Food aid to these low-income countries appears to have been triggered by absolute shortfalls in consumption.

However, the preliminary results from Tobit regressions further confirm that, on average, food aid flows have not generally been responsive to fluctuations in food availability. In fact, there is evidence that food aid disbursements have been procyclical rather than countercyclical.

Accounting for bias arising from the absence of lagged food aid and the endogeneity of commercial food imports, as noted above, lagged food aid and domestic production (PROD)—to proxy nonconcessional food availability (NA)—are added to the baseline regressions, following Eqs. (4a) and (4b). The regression results in Table 3 confirm that for the sample as a whole, global food aid is generally progressive and responds to absolute gaps across countries.

Furthermore, the sign of φ_1 suggests that food aid is countercyclical for the sample as a whole but insignificant. We run the modified Tobit regressions for selected subsamples: the food-insecure (defined as the bottom quartile of countries ranked by nonconcessional food availability) and low-income countries (defined as the bottom quartile of countries ranked by per capita income). The results suggest that for the most food-insecure and low-income countries, food aid has been disbursed countercyclically. We further test whether this holds for sub-Saharan Africa given the absence of correlation between business cycles in donor countries and in sub-Saharan Africa. The results indicate that food aid is significantly progressive and countercyclical in Africa.

Table 3. Modified Tobit Regression Results: Linear Detrending

	All Countries	All Countries	All Countries	Most Food-Insecure[1]	Low-Income[2]	Sub-Saharan Africa
φ_1 (cyclicality)	-0.0012 (-0.49)	-0.0029 (-1.17)	-0.0033 (-1.28)	-0.007** (-2.21)	-0.0107*** (-7.16)	-0.004*** (3.10)
φ_2 (progressivity)	-0.0392*** (-8.05)	-0.0192*** (-3.22)	-0.0195*** (-3.28)	0.017 (1.04)	-0.0084** (-2.01)	-0.021*** (-4.05)
Food aid ($t-1$)	0.3705*** (69.02)	0.3779*** (55.62)	0.3765*** (53.07)	0.66*** (20.88)	0.6684*** (25.26)	0.89*** (65.47)
Regional dummies	No	Yes	Yes	Yes	Yes	No
Year dummies	No	No	Yes	Yes	Yes	Yes
LR statistic	460.24	527.95	568.42	471.45	659.78	1980.25
P-value	0.00	0.00	0.00	0.00	0.00	0.00
Number of observations	3,558	3,558	3,558	900	810	1,310

Source: See text.

(***), (**), and (*) denote significance at the 1, 5, and 10 percent level, respectively.

[1] Bottom quartile of countries ranked by average nonconcessional food availability during 1970–2000.

[2] Bottom quartile of countries ranked by average per capita income during 1970–2000.

The results in Table 3 imply that food aid covers a minuscule amount of food needs. In particular, food aid covers only about 7 kilograms out of every contemporaneous metric ton shortfall in food-insecure countries. This confirms previous findings in the literature that food aid mitigates consumption shortfall in some countries, but is far from sufficient to cover the entire consumption shortfall (Barrett and Heisey, 2002, and Lavy, 1992).

Finally, the coefficient on lagged food aid (φ_3) is relatively large across specifications and significant, confirming previous findings that there is a persistence or inertia in food aid distributions.

Other Filters

The regression results reported in Tables 2 and 3 are based on the linear detrending technique. We reestimate Eqs. (4a) and (4b) and substitute measures of transitory shortfalls in food availability using the quadratric trend, band pass filter, and the Hodrick-Prescott filter for the sample as a whole. The results are generally invariant to the choice of filter.[4]

Food Aid in the 1990s

Have food aid flows become more countercyclical over time? To test changes over time, we divide the sample into 10-year periods. As indicated in Table 4, food aid is consistently progressive; if anything, there is some evidence that it has become more progressive over time. In contrast, the responsiveness of food aid flows to transitory shortfalls in consumption has varied over time. In terms of decades, it was significantly countercyclical over the 1980s. Contrary to expectations, food aid has not become countercyclical in recent years. Dividing the sample into 15-year periods and 20-year periods reinforces these findings. The results hold for a linearly detrended measure of food availability and are robust to other measures of cyclical fluctuations. An expansion of the regression equation to include dummy variables for the 1980s and the 1990s and their interaction with other independent variables also indicates that food aid is consistently progressive but has not become more countercyclical over time.[5] There is some evidence that the incremental trend in food aid has become weaker over time, as the coefficient estimates for lagged food aid suggest.

---

[4]The results are available from the authors upon request.

[5]Results are available from the authors upon request. The 1970s act as the base period in this analysis. Using dummy variables for the 1980s and 1970s, with the 1990s as the base period, yields qualitatively similar results.

Table 4. Modified Tobit Regression Results: Food Aid Flows Over Time
(Linear detrending)

	10-Year Periods			15-Year Periods		20-Year Periods	
	1971–80	1981–90	1991–2000	1971–85	1986–2000	1971–90	1981–2000
φ_1 (cyclicality)	-0.0002 (-0.15)	-0.0048*** (-2.67)	0.0027 (0.38)	-0.0030*** (-3.24)	0.0036 (0.76)	-0.0030*** (-2.66)	-0.0027 (-0.74)
φ_2 (progressivity)	-0.0144*** (-5.06)	-0.0154*** (-4.18)	-0.0369*** (-2.98)	-0.0162*** (-6.15)	-0.0393*** (-4.56)	-0.0157*** (-6.51)	-0.0433*** (-6.31)
Food aid (t–1)	0.8176*** (43.61)	0.9104*** (45.93)	0.1436*** (4.08)	0.88*** (55.36)	0.3158*** (11.32)	0.8818*** (63.65)	0.3155*** (53.45)
Regional dummies	No	No	No	No	No	No	No
Year dummies	No	No	No	No	No	No	No
LR statistic	1118.66	1222.36	26.56	1780.00	95.59	2309.19	229.59
P-value	0.00	0.00	0.00	0.00	0.00	0.00	0.00
Number of observations	1,189	1,186	1,183	1,784	1,774	2,257	2,369

Source: See text.
(***), (**), and (*) denote significance at the 1, 5, and 10 percent level, respectively.

Food Aid and Fiscal Variables

Previous studies suggest that counterpart funds generated by monetized food aid account for a significant share of the government budget in some countries. Using the same econometric framework as in Eqs. (3) and (4), we now examine how food aid moves with relative and absolute revenue shortfalls. We use the Hodrick-Prescott filter to detrend the revenue series and estimate relative revenue shortfalls.

The results are provided in Table 5. The columns marked "Balance" and "Revenue" indicate coefficient estimates from a regression of food aid on (absolute and relative) shortfalls in general government fiscal balances and general government revenues, respectively. The results suggest that countries that have the largest revenue shortfall or largest overall fiscal deficit receive proportionately more aid. Food aid thus responds to absolute shortfalls in domestic resources and may provide critical budget support, to the extent that monetized food aid generates counterpart funds and non-monetized food aid alleviates spending pressures. However, food aid is not statistically associated with relative shortfalls in government revenue or the government fiscal balance. This reinforces the findings from previous sections: food aid responds to measures of absolute, but not relative, need.

The results in Table 5 are based on aggregate food aid. Because counterpart funds are generated from the sale of commodities provided through aid, a more accurate measure would be an analysis of the component that is sold in local markets.[6] Data on the volume of food aid sold, by country, are available from WFP for 1988 onward. They indicate that, on average, the share of sold food in aggregate food aid has fallen from about 45% to 30%.

Using these data and employing the same econometric framework utilized above, we examine the impact of food aid volume sold in local markets on relative and absolute revenue shortfalls and the overall budget deficit. The results are reported in Table 6. They suggest that food aid has benefited countries with large overall deficits.[7] The magnitude is much larger than reported in Table 5 using aggregate food aid. However, there is no measurable association between food aid sold on local markets and revenue shortfall, whether in absolute or relative terms.

---

[6]However, non-monetized food aid is also critical for alleviating spending pressures on the budget. In this respect, aggregate food aid (rather than just the volume of food sold in local markets) may be a more accurate measure.

[7]It can be argued that fiscal balances are *jointly* determined with food aid flows, as recipient governments incur new expenses associated with food aid agreements. However, given the very small share of food needs covered by contemporaneous food aid, this is not likely to have an impact on the empirical results.

Table 5. Tobit Regression Results: Fiscal Variables
(Hodrick-Prescott filter)

	All Countries		Aid-Dependent Countries[1]		Low-Income Countries[2]	
	Balance	Revenue	Balance	Revenue	Balance	Revenue
φ_1 (cyclicality)	0.0002*	0.0001	0.0002	0.0001	0.0001	0.00003
	(1.78)	(1.30)	(1.47)	(1.24)	(0.83)	(0.92)
φ_2 (progressivity)	-0.0002**	-0.00012**	-0.0003**	-0.0001**	-0.0002**	0.0001
	(-5.13)	(-3.20)	(-3.88)	(-2.41)	(-2.03)	(1.24)
Food aid (t−1)	0.83**	0.85**	0.82**	0.84**	0.67**	0.67**
	(59.30)	(60.84)	(44.10)	(45.20)	(19.93)	(19.67)
Regional dummies	Yes	Yes	Yes	Yes	Yes	Yes
Year dummies	Yes	Yes	Yes	Yes	Yes	Yes
LR statistic	2378.71	2366.29	1349.58	1340.44	427.99	426.45
P-value	0.00	0.00	0.00	0.00	0.00	0.00
Number of observations	2,414	2,414	1,382	1,382	500	500

Source: See text.
(**), (*), and (*) denote significance at the 1, 5, and 10 percent level, respectively.
[1] Bottom quartile of countries ranked by average aid per capita during 1970–2000.
[2] Bottom quartile of countries ranked by average per capita income during 1970–2000.

Table 6. Tobit Regression Results: Food Aid Sales and Fiscal Variables, 1989–2000
(Hodrick-Prescott filter)

	All Countries		Most Food-Insecure[1]		Aid-Dependent Countries[2]	
	Balance	Revenue	Balance	Revenue	Balance	Revenue
φ_1 (cyclicality)	−0.044 (−0.27)	−0.166 (−1.09)	−0.07 (−0.39)	0.05 (0.29)	−0.26 (−0.67)	−0.48 (−1.14)
φ_2 (progressivity)	−0.18** (2.28)	0.05 (0.97)	−0.24*** (−3.55)	−0.02 (−0.49)	−0.30* (−1.87)	0.24 (1.55)
Food aid (t−1)	0.83*** (31.20)	0.83*** (30.71)	0.68*** (11.18)	0.84*** (15.72)	0.76*** (13.54)	0.76*** (13.51)
Regional dummies	Yes	Yes	Yes	Yes	Yes	Yes
Year dummies	Yes	Yes	Yes	Yes	Yes	Yes
LR statistic	721.23	715.62	194.60	180.35	212.31	209.24
P-value	0.00	0.00	0.00	0.00	0.00	0.00
Number of observations	940	940	231	231	265	265

Source: See text.
(***), (**), and (*) denote significance at the 1, 5, and 10 percent level, respectively.
[1] Bottom quartile of countries ranked by average nonconcessional food availability during 1970–2000.
[2] Bottom quartile of countries ranked by average aid per capita during 1970–2000.

5. Discussion and Policy Implications

The empirical evidence examined in this paper suggests that global food aid has been allocated to where it is most needed. Based on data covering a large sample of recipient countries during 1970–1999, the evidence suggests that countries with larger absolute shortfalls in food availability have received more aid. Food aid has also been counter-cyclical within countries with the greatest need. The results are robust to various specifications and filtering techniques.

Food aid has nonetheless fallen short of its objectives. For the sample of food-insecure countries for which food aid has been counter-cyclical, quantities have not been enough to stabilize consumption. For other recipient countries, food aid has not been significantly counter-cyclical. Thus, in these countries, food aid does not function as a social safety net. In addition, the responsiveness of food aid flows to transitory shortfalls in consumption has varied over time. In terms of decades, it was significantly countercyclical over the 1980s, but not significantly countercyclical over the 1990s. With respect to fiscal variables, food aid has benefited countries with large overall fiscal deficits. However, there is no measurable association between food aid sold on local markets and revenue shortfall, whether in absolute or relative terms.

The acyclicality of food aid has two implications for macroeconomic and fiscal management. First, to the extent that recipient governments rely on counterpart funds as a revenue source and food aid is not disbursed in a countercyclical manner, the instability of budgetary revenues is not alleviated. Second, shortfalls in food supply increase demands on the government budget for programs to shield the consumption of the population. In the absence of counterpart funds from food aid, the government will have to rely on domestic resources to fund such programs. Falling revenues and rising demand for budgetary programs are likely to complicate macroeconomic management for the food aid–receiving countries. In the circumstances, the "automatic stabilizer" benefits of countercyclical food are largely not met.

References

Barrett, C.B., 2001. Does food aid stabilize food availability? Economic Development and Cultural Change 49, 335–349.

Barrett, C.B., 2002. Food security and food assistance programs. In: Gardner, B.L., Rausser, G.C. (Eds.), Handbook of Agricultural Economics. Elsevier Science, Amsterdam.

Barrett, C.B., Heisey, K.C., 2002. How effectively does multilateral food aid respond to fluctuating needs? Food Policy 27, 477–491.

Benson, C., 2000. The food aid convention: an effective safety net? In Clay, E., Stokke, O. (Eds.), Food Aid and Human Security. Frank Cass, London, 102–119.

Canova, F., 1999. Does detrending matter for the determination of the reference cycle and the selection of turning points? Economic Journal 109, 126–150.

Christiano, L., Fitzgerald, T.J., 1999. The band pass filter, NBER Working Paper No. 7257.

Clay, E., Dhiri, S., Benson, C., 1996. Joint Evaluation of European Union Programme Food Aid. Overseas Development Institute, London.

Colding, B., Pinstrup-Andersen, P., 2000. Foreign aid as an aid instrument: past, present and future. In: Tarp, F., Hjertholm, P. (Eds.), Foreign Aid and Development. Routledge, London.

Diven, P. J., 2001. The domestic determinants of US food aid policy. Food Policy 26, 455–474.

Easterly, W., 2001. The elusive quest for growth: economists' adventures and misadventures in the tropics. MIT Press, Cambridge, MA.

Gemell, N., McGillivray, M., 1998. Aid and tax instability and the government budget constraint in developing countries. CREDIT Research Paper No. 98/1, University of Nottingham.

Hodrick, R., Prescott, E., 1997. Postwar U.S. business cycles: an empirical investigation. Journal of Money, Credit and Banking 29, 1–16.

Jayne, T. S., Strauss, J., Yamano, T., Molla, D., 2002. Targeting of food aid in rural Ethiopia: chronic need or inertia? Journal of Development Economics 68, 247–288.

Lavy, V., 1992. Alleviating transitory food crises in sub-Saharan Africa: international altruism and trade. World Bank Economic Review 6, 125–138.

Marcet, A., Ravn, M.O., 2001. The HP-filter in cross-country comparisons. Universitat Pompeu Fabra and London Business School Economics Working Paper No. 588.

Mellor, J., Pandya-Lorch, R., 1992. Food aid and development in the MADIA countries. In: Lele, U., (Ed.), Aid to African Agriculture: Lessons from Two Decades of Donors' Experience. Johns Hopkins University Press, Baltimore.

Pallage, S., Robe, M.A., 2001. Foreign aid and the business cycle. Review of International Economics 9, 641–672.

Riley, B., 1992. An analysis of the use of counterpart funds in Mozambique. IDS Bulletin 23, 41–45.

Shapouri, S., Missiaen, M., 1990. Food aid: motivation and allocation criteria. U.S. Department of Agriculture, Economic Research Service Foreign Agricultural Economic Report No. 240.

Shapouri, S., Rosen, S., 2001. Food security and food aid distribution, Issues in Food Security. U.S. Department of Agriculture Information Bulletin No. 765.

Trueblood, M.A., Shapouri, S., Henneberry, S., 2001. Policy options to stabilize food supplies: a case study of southern Africa. U.S. Department of Agriculture Information Bulletin No. 764.

UNDP, 1996. Human Development Report: Georgia. United Nations Development Programme, New York.

World Bank, 1998. Assessing Aid: What Works, What Doesn't, and Why. Oxford University Press, New York.

World Food Programme, 2002. 2001 Food Aid Flows. World Food Programme, Rome.

18

Fiscal Consequences of Armed Conflict and Terrorism in Low- and Middle-Income Countries

SANJEEV GUPTA, BENEDICT CLEMENTS, RINA BHATTACHARYA, AND SHAMIT CHAKRAVARTI

1. Introduction

Contrary to expectations, the end of the Cold War has not been a harbinger of peace. There has been a proliferation of armed conflicts around the world over the past dozen years. In particular, terrorist groups have become increasingly sophisticated, daring, and destructive. More than 4 million people are estimated to have perished in violent conflicts between 1989 and 2000, and 37 million people have been displaced as refugees, either inside or outside their countries (World Bank, 2000). In 2000, there were 25 major armed conflicts around the world, of which 23 were intrastate conflicts (*SIPRI Yearbook 2001*).[1] International terrorist

Reprinted from the *European Journal of Political Economy*, Vol. 20, Sanjeev Gupta, Benedict Clements, Rina Bhattacharya, and Shamit Chakravarti, "Fiscal Consequences of Armed Conflict and Terrorism in Low- and Middle-Income Countries," © 2004, with permission from Elsevier.

The authors would like to thank Emanuele Baldacci, Hamid Davoodi, Stefano Fassina, Hong-Sang Jung, Mansoob Murshed, Erwin Tiongson, an anonymous referee, and participants of the DIW workshop for useful comments and suggestions.

[1] The Stockholm International Peace Research Institute (SIPRI) publishes a yearly review of armaments, disarmament, and international security. A major armed conflict is defined in the *SIPRI Yearbook 2000* as "a contested incompatibility that concerns government and/or territory over which the use of armed force between the military forces of two parties, of which at least one is the government of a state, has resulted in *at least 1000 battle-related deaths* over the duration of the conflict."

attacks increased from an average of about 342 a year between 1995 and 1999 to 387 a year between 2000 and 2001.[2] Most of the armed conflicts and terrorist activities have taken place in low- and middle-income countries. Between 1996 and 2000, almost 70% of the major armed conflicts, more than 20% of all international terrorist attacks, and over 70% of all casualties due to such attacks took place in Asia and Africa.

While the literature has documented the economic costs of armed conflict and terrorism, a cross-country examination of their fiscal consequences is yet to be undertaken. Armed conflict and prolonged terrorist activities can strongly influence the revenues and expenditures of countries, and in turn affect their economic growth. Although armed conflict and terrorism are often treated as distinct phenomena, experience from different parts of the world shows that there is a close link between the two. This paper analyzes the effects of armed conflict and terrorism on fiscal balances and economic growth in low- and middle-income countries.

The remainder of this paper is structured as follows. Section 2 provides a brief overview of the literature, followed in Section 3 by a description of the channels through which armed conflict and terrorism can affect the fiscal accounts and economic growth. Section 4 sets out the methodology for the empirical analyses presented in the paper. Section 5 compares the evolution of various macroeconomic variables and socioeconomic indicators before, during, and after 22 episodes of armed conflict in a number of low- and middle-income countries. Section 6 estimates an integrated system of equations for real per capita income growth, government revenue, and government spending, to highlight the main channels through which armed conflict and terrorism affect the fiscal accounts. Section 7 concludes.

---

[2] Data on terrorist activities and casualties are drawn from a report prepared by the U.S. Department of State (2002). There is no consensus regarding how terrorism should be defined. Title 22 of the United States Code, Section 2656f(d) defines terrorism as "premeditated, politically motivated violence perpetrated against noncombatant targets by sub-national groups or clandestine agents, usually intended to influence an audience." The Columbia Encyclopedia, 6th Edition, 2001, defines terrorism as "the threat or use of violence, often against the civilian population to achieve political ends. Terrorism involves activities such as assassinations, bombings, random killings, hijackings, and skyjackings. It is used for political, not military purposes, and by groups too weak to mount open assaults."

2. Review of the Literature

Several studies have assessed the economic costs of armed conflicts.[3] Richardson and Samarasinghe (1991) estimate that the total accumulated economic cost of the armed conflict in Sri Lanka in the five years between 1983 and 1988 was about U.S.$4.2 billion, or 68% of Sri Lanka's GDP in 1988. Arunatilake et al. (2001) perform a similar exercise for a longer period and estimate that the conflict between 1983 and 1996 cost Sri Lanka about twice the country's 1996 GDP. In a similar vein, several empirical studies, based on different techniques, approaches, and data, have found an inverse relationship between different measures of political instability and violence on the one hand, and growth or investment on the other (Veneiris and Gupta, 1986; Barro, 1991; Alesina and Perotti, 1993 and 1996; Alesina et al., 1996; and Rodrik, 1999).

Armed conflict impacts on a country's financial development. Addison et al. (2002) conclude that conflict can (1) adversely affect the process of financial deepening by undermining confidence in the domestic currency due to fear of inflation and depreciation; (2) encourage the movement of funds away from productive assets (bank deposits, capital) to nonproductive assets (gold); and (3) affect the regulation and supervision of the financial system. Their model, applied to 79 countries, shows that conflict significantly reduces financial development, and that the negative effect increases as conflict intensifies.

Prolonged terrorist activities, like armed conflict, also lower growth, both directly and indirectly. Abadie and Gardeazabal (2003) find that after the outbreak of terrorism in the 1970s, per capita GDP in the Basque region of Spain declined by about 10% relative to a "synthetic" control region, and that this gap widened in response to spikes in terrorist activity. Some studies have empirically assessed the impact of terrorism on tourism, both domestic and regional, and have found the expected negative effect (Drakos and Kutan, 2001; Enders and Sandler, 1991; and Enders, Sandler, and Parise, 1992). For example, in a study covering Greece, Israel, and Turkey, and using Italy as a "control variable," Drakos and Kutan (2001) found that the intensity (measured by number of casualties) of terrorist incidents has significant domestic and cross-country effects on the market shares of the affected

---

[3]Over and above the economic costs, prolonged armed conflicts can impose significant social and political costs that are difficult to estimate. For example, it is not possible to quantify the intangible costs of violence and insecurity, the human suffering and trauma, the breakdown in law and order, the animosity and mistrust that are created among warring parties, and the adverse effects of the reduced stock of health and education endowments on the long-run growth prospects of a country.

countries, and that there are significant contagion effects from terrorism within the region.

Terrorist threats raise the transaction costs of doing business and trade. Nitsch and Schumacher (2002) show that terrorist acts and large-scale violence adversely affected bilateral trade flows for more than 200 countries for the period 1960–93. A doubling of the number of terrorist incidents is associated with a decrease in bilateral trade by about 6%. Moreover, additional security measures put in place to deter terrorist attacks can impede the flow of goods and services. Walkenhorst and Dihel (2002) estimate the global welfare losses due to tighter security precautions that have been put in place following the attacks of September 11, 2001 at about US$75 billion.

As noted earlier, a cross-country examination of the fiscal consequences of armed conflicts is yet to be undertaken. However, recent case studies and related empirical studies of military spending and growth suggest channels through which armed conflict and terrorism can have an effect on fiscal accounts and economic growth.

3. Fiscal Effects of Armed Conflict and Terrorism: Potential Channels

Armed conflict and terrorism can affect the fiscal accounts by disrupting economic activities, eroding the tax base, lowering the efficiency of tax administration, and distorting the composition of public spending. Tax receipts, for example, vary with the health of the economy. Economic downturns due to insecurity and violence can lead to a decline in tax revenues. Beyond their effects on real activity, armed conflict and terrorism (especially if prolonged) can destroy part of the tax base (e.g., through the destruction of business firms,) and weaken the efficiency of tax administration. For example, Ndikumana (2001) notes that, following the outbreak of armed conflict in two countries in Africa, not only did the tax base collapse, but tax administration was also hampered. With the return of peace and the resumption of normal production in one of the two countries, tax revenues recovered progressively, and by 1998 exceeded the preconflict level.

Military expenditures typically increase in response to conflict and terrorism, and tend to remain high even after cessation of violence.[4] Higher spending for security can also affect the composition of public

---

[4]In Sri Lanka, for example, between 1983 and 1996, defense spending increased from 1.4% to 6% as a share of GDP, and from 4.4% to 21.6% as a share of total government spending (Arunatilake et al., 2001).

spending by decreasing outlays for education, health, and other productive items. Moreover, the destruction of physical infrastructure and human capital due to violence, and the indirect effects on trade, tourism, and business confidence, all weaken the fiscal position and adversely affect economic growth, as noted earlier.

Defense spending can affect the long-run sustainable growth rate both negatively and positively (Shieh et al., 2002). First, there is a "crowding out effect," whereby an increase in defense expenditures by the government reduces the resources available to the economy for private investment and for public spending on sectors that have a strong and positive impact on growth. Second, there is a "spin-off" effect from the positive supply-side spillover effects of defense expenditure on the nondefense sectors of the economy. This effect is likely to be small in low- and middle-income conflict-affected countries, since the majority of defense spending tends to be on imported armaments. Third, there is a "resource mobilization" effect on savings and investment: defense spending provides both internal and external security, and hence, boosts private savings and investment and attracts foreign investment. This has a positive effect on growth.[5]

Earlier studies have suggested that defense spending has a positive effect on economic growth in less-developed countries (Benoit, 1978). However, more recent empirical research shows that cutting military spending fosters economic growth (Arora and Bayoumi, 1993; Bayoumi et al., 1993; Knight et al., 1996). These papers argue that lower military spending can encourage growth by increasing capital formation and improving the efficiency with which resources are utilized in the economy. Cessation of conflict and terrorism can result in a "peace dividend," releasing fiscal resources to be used for deficit reduction, lowering taxes, or raising the allocation for spending in social sectors.[6]

4. Empirical Methodology

The empirical analysis in this paper is based on two approaches. The first approach assesses the impact of armed conflict *within* conflict-affected countries, by examining the evolution of macrofiscal and socioeconomic variables before, during, and after 22 episodes of

---

[5]This effect is likely to be highly nonlinear: up to a certain basic level of spending on defense, there is a positive impact on savings and investment, but after this threshold is passed, higher government spending on defense is unlikely to promote further private sector savings and investment.

[6]Conflict and violence can itself be affected by the perceived inequities in the distribution of the tax burden and in the pattern of public spending (Addison and Murshed, 2001).

conflict in 20 low- and middle-income countries.[7] The sample includes those episodes of armed conflict that either began or were ongoing in 1985 or later, and which ended by 1999, based on SIPRI's definition of major armed conflicts.[8]

SIPRI draws data on armed conflicts from the Uppsala Conflict Data Project of the Department of Peace and Conflict Research, Uppsala University, Sweden. The Uppsala Conflict Data Project divides armed conflicts into the following three categories based on the level of casualties:

- Minor armed conflict: At least 25 battle-related deaths a year and fewer than 1,000 battle-related deaths during the course of the conflict.

- Intermediate armed conflict: At least 25 battle-related deaths a year and an accumulated total of at least 1,000 deaths but fewer than 1,000 in any given year.

- War: At least 1,000 battle-related deaths a year.

SIPRI's characterization of a major armed conflict covers the two most severe levels of conflict, i.e., "intermediate" armed conflict and war (Gleditsch et al., 2001). This paper does not include "minor" armed conflicts, since these are unlikely to have *measurable* effects on the fiscal accounts and the economic growth of the affected countries.

One shortcoming of the SIPRI index is that it applies an absolute criterion for the number of battle-related deaths. Thus, a country with a large population will be classified as being in conflict even though the number of deaths may be small relative to its population. Moreover, the number of battle-related deaths may not adequately capture the economic impact of armed conflict; it is possible that a number of sporadic, low-intensity incidents affecting mainly the local population will have a different impact on business and consumer confidence and international perception of risk in the country concerned than a single dramatic event affecting mainly the tourist sector or key sectors linked to foreign trade. Despite these drawbacks, the

---

[7]Because of the problems of defining terrorism and of the sensitivity involved in classifying countries as victims or as perpetrators of terrorism, the preconflict, conflict and postconflict analysis is restricted only to countries that have experienced armed conflicts as defined by SIPRI. See Appendix A.

[8]See footnote 1 for the definition of armed conflict used in this paper. Appendix A lists the sample countries for this as well as for the subsequent econometric analysis.

SIPRI index is broadly consistent with the conflict index produced by the Heidelberg Institute for International Conflict Research (HIIK).[9]

The second approach followed compares the economic consequences of armed conflict and terrorism *across* countries by estimating an integrated system of equations for real per capita income growth, government revenue, and government spending. The International Country Risk Guide (ICRG) ratings on internal conflict are used as a proxy for the *combined risk from terrorism and conflict.*[10] The ICRG ratings provide an overall assessment of violence in a country due to civil war, terrorism, and civil disorder, and the actual or potential impact on governance. The highest rating is given to those countries ". . . where there is no armed opposition to the government and the government does not indulge in arbitrary violence, direct or indirect, against its own people." The lowest rating is given to a country embroiled in an ongoing civil war and/or facing terrorist attacks. Given the difficulty of reaching a consensus on a universally acceptable definition of terrorism as well as of measuring terrorist activities, separate risk ratings for terrorism are not available. One advantage of the ICRG ratings is that they provide ratings of risk due to internal conflict and terrorism for a wide range of countries, and not just for those that have had major armed conflicts as defined by SIPRI.[11] The SIPRI index of armed conflicts (proportion of each 5-year period during which there were armed conflicts) is used to check the robustness of the results. The SIPRI index has been used in other empirical studies, such as Davoodi et al. (2001).

---

[9]Unlike SIPRI, the Heidelberg Institute does not consider a cutoff level of 1,000 conflict-related deaths to classify a country as being affected by conflict. It defines conflict broadly as "the clashing of interests (positional differences) on national values and issues (territory, independence, self-determination, autonomy, ideology, power, resources) of some duration and magnitude between at least two parties (states, groups of states, organizations, or organized groups) that are determined to pursue their interests and win their case."

[10]Because more than 90% of all major armed conflicts since 1990 have been internal (SIPRI Annual Yearbooks), only the ICRG internal conflict rating is used in the econometric estimation. The ICRG ratings are compiled by a U.S.-based consultancy service, the Political Risk Services Group. Details are available via the Internet: http://www.prsgroup.com/index.html.

[11]Where ICRG internal conflict ratings are available for the corresponding episodes of the conflict, preconflict, and postconflict analysis (for 14 of the 20 countries), there is a broad match between low ICRG ratings (of about 8 or less) and countries that have been classified as conflict-affected by SIPRI and HIIK. The average ICRG internal conflict score for these 14 countries is 3.7 between 1984 and 1989, 6.4 between 1990 and 1994, and 8.2 between 1995 and 1999.

5. Macroeconomic and Fiscal Variables and Socioeconomic Indicators: Preconflict, Conflict, and Postconflict Periods

The results from comparing the conflict, preconflict, and postconflict phases of 22 episodes of armed conflicts in lower- and middle-income countries are presented in Figures 1–5 and Table 1. The data on real GDP are consistent with the hypothesis of a significant pickup in growth in the immediate postconflict years. There is a dramatic pickup in inflation during the conflict period, followed by a significant decline in the immediate postconflict period (see Figures 1 and 2). The data show a notable increase in the share of gross fixed-capital formation to GDP in the immediate postconflict years, particularly in the private sector (see Figure 3).

Figures 4–5 show the evolution of fiscal variables over the preconflict, conflict, and postconflict periods. Due to data constraints, government revenue and foreign grants are used as a proxy for government revenue.[12] The available data for the sample of countries show that the share of government revenue in GDP tends to fall during the conflict period, and to pick up somewhat in the immediate postconflict period. On the expenditure side, there appears to be a significant increase in government expenditure and net lending as a percent of GDP during the conflict period compared with the preconflict period, followed by a notable decline in the immediate postconflict period. In particular, the available data suggest high government spending on defense during the conflict period and in the period immediately preceding it, followed by a significant fall in the immediate postconflict period. However, high defense spending during the conflict period and in the years immediately preceding it tends to be at the expense of macroeconomic stability (as reflected for example in higher budget deficits and a pickup in inflation) rather than at the cost of lower spending on education and health as a share of GDP. Nevertheless, since conflict is associated with lower real GDP growth, the implication is lower growth in real per capita government spending on education and health during conflict periods.

Turning now to the socioeconomic indicators, Table 1 shows a significant decline in the rate of improvement of life expectancy at birth during the conflict period, but the trend for improvement in life expectancy picks up again in the immediate postconflict period. There is also a significant deterioration in the rate of improvement of infant mortality during conflict years, but the deterioration continues into the

---

[12]Grants, on average, are much lower than revenue. For example, for a sample of 31 low-income countries with programs supported by the IMF since 1999, grants were only 3.5% of GDP, compared with revenue of about 18% of GDP (Gupta et al., 2002).

Figure 1. Real GDP Growth in Conflict Countries[1]
(Average annual percentage change)

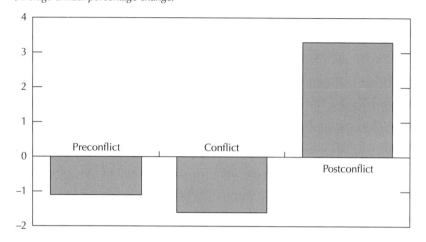

Sources: IMF, *World Economic Outlook*; World Bank, *World Development Indicators 2001*; and IMF staff calculations.

[1]Based on a sample of 12 countries. The real GDP per capita growth corresponding to the preconflict, conflict, and postconflict periods are –1.1, –1.6, and 3.3 percent a year, respectively.

Figure 2. Consumer Price Inflation in Conflict Countries[1]
(Average annual percentage change)

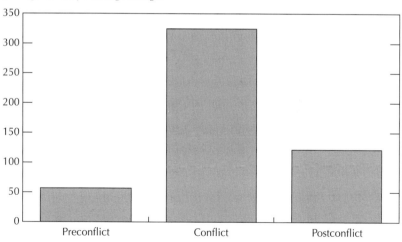

Sources: IMF, *World Economic Outlook*; World Bank, *World Development Indicators 2001*; and IMF staff calculations.

[1]Based on a sample of 9 countries.

Figure 3. Capital Formation in Conflict Countries[1]
(Percent of GDP)

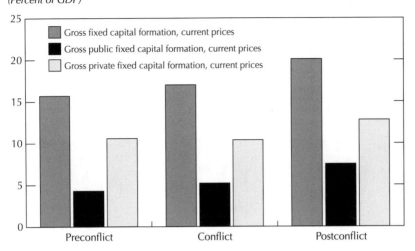

Sources: IMF, *World Economic Outlook*; World Bank, *World Development Indicators 2001*; and IMF staff calculations.

[1]Based on a sample of 17 countries for gross fixed capital formation, and on 11 countries each for gross public and private capital formation.

Figure 4. Fiscal Aggregates in Conflict Countries[1]
(Percent of GDP)

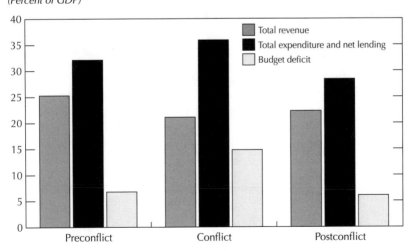

Sources: IMF, *World Economic Outlook*; World Bank, *World Development Indicators 2001*; and IMF staff calculations.

[1]Based on a sample of 14 countries.

Figure 5. Composition of Government Spending in Conflict Countries[1]
(Percent of GDP)

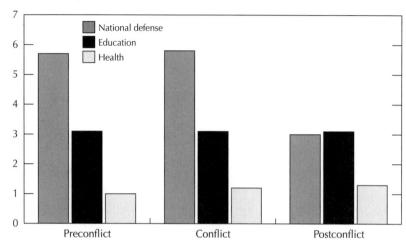

Sources: IMF, *World Economic Outlook*; World Bank, *World Development Indicators 2001*; and IMF staff calculations.

[1]Based on a sample of 12 countries for defense expenditure and on 6 countries each for education and health spending.

immediate postconflict period. The available data also show a marked improvement in gross enrollment rates (at all three levels—primary, secondary, and tertiary) following the end of armed conflict.

While a useful exercise, the conclusions drawn from the before-during-after analysis should be interpreted with caution. This analysis does not control for other factors that affect macroeconomic and fiscal outcomes, independent of armed conflict and terrorism, which may have also changed over the periods of violence. To isolate more rigorously the effects of conflict and terrorism, the following section presents the econometric estimation of a system of interlinked equations covering a wider range of countries, including those not affected by conflict and terrorism.

6. Econometric Estimates

As mentioned earlier, there are three main ways in which armed conflict and terrorism can affect the fiscal accounts: by influencing real economic activity (GDP) and therefore, government revenues; by adversely affecting both the tax base and the efficiency of the tax administration; and by changing the composition of government spending. These fiscal

Table 1. Selected Social Indicators in Countries Experiencing Armed Conflicts[a]

(Average annual rates of change, percent)

	Preconflict[b]	Conflict[b]	Postconflict[b]	Number of Countries for Which Data Are Available
Life expectancy at birth, total (years)	0.4	−0.5	0.4	5
Mortality rate, infant (per 1,000 live births)[c]	3.8	0.6	0.0	7
Gross primary enrollment rate	...	2.6	3.2	9
Gross secondary enrollment rate	...	1.1	2.1	9
Gross tertiary enrollment rate	...	−1.5	2.1	9

Sources: IMF, *World Economic Outlook;* World Bank, *World Development Indicators 2001;* and authors' calculations.

[a] Combines all the low-income, lower-middle-income, and upper-middle-income countries affected by armed conflict as discussed in the paper. Countries are classified into income categories based on the World Bank's criteria in terms of level of 1998 GNP per capita—low-income, US$760 or less; lower-middle-income, US$761 to US$3,030; and upper-middle-income, US$3,031 to US$9,360.

[b] Conflict period refers to the period over which a country experienced armed conflict (as defined by SIPRI); preconflict refers to the average of three years preceding the conflict, and postconflict refers to the average of three years following the conflict (depending upon availability of data).

[c] Positive rates of growth signify an improvement in the variable.

consequences can have repercussions on economic growth, which would further affect the public finances. To capture all these effects, a structural model with three equations is specified: the first for economic growth, the second for the ratio of government revenue to GDP, and the third for the composition of government spending measured by the share of defense spending in total government expenditure.

In the structural model, the equations for per capita income growth (equation (1)), government revenue to GDP (equation (2)), and defense expenditure as a share of total government spending (equation (3)) are specified as follows:

$$GRPCY_{i,t} = \alpha_r + \alpha_1 PCYINI_{i,t} + \alpha_2 GSECINI_{i,t} + \alpha_3 DEFEXPD_{i,t} + \quad (1)$$
$$\alpha_4 AGEDEP_{i,t} + \alpha_5 CONF_{i,t} + \alpha_6 INVGDP_{i,t} + \mu_{1i,t}$$

$$GREVGDP_{i,t} = \beta_r + \beta_1 PCY_{i,t} + \beta_2 NONAGRX_{i,t} + \beta_3 CONF_{i,t} + \quad (2)$$
$$\beta_4 AGRVA_{i,t} + \beta_5 URBPOP_{i,t} + \mu_{2i,t}$$

$$DEFEXPD_{i,t} = \lambda_r + \lambda_1 DEFGDPN_{i,t} + \lambda_2 CONF_{i,t} + \mu_{3i,t}, \quad (3)$$

where

$GRPCY$ = growth of real per capita income (GDP).

$PCYINI$ = real per capita income (GDP, in US\$) in the initial year of the sample period.

$GSECINI$ = gross secondary school enrollment rate in the initial year of the sample period.

$DEFEXPD$ = share of defense expenditure in total government spending.

$AGEDEP$ = age-dependency ratio.

$CONF$ = a conflict variable (discussed below).

$INVGDP$ = total investment in percent of GDP.

$GREVGDP$ = government revenue as a ratio of GDP.

PCY = real per capita income (in US\$).

$NONAGRX$ = share of nonagricultural exports in GDP.

$AGRVA$ = agriculture value added in percent of GDP.

$URBPOP$ = urban population as a share of total population.

$DEFGDPN$ = (unweighted) average of neighboring countries' ratio of defense spending to GDP.

α_r, β_r, and λ_r are region-specific factors, and $\mu_{1i,t}$, $\mu_{2i,t}$ and $\mu_{3i,t}$ are the usual error terms. The subscript (i,t) for the main explanatory variables refers to country and time period, respectively. The endogenous variables in the system are the three dependent variables and the investment ratio. The model is estimated using 5-year averages of annual data for each country over four time periods: 1980–84, 1985–89, 1990–94, and 1995–99. Region and time dummies were included in the estimated equations.

Some authors have argued that conflict and terrorism are, in a sense, endogenous due to the possibility of reverse causation, i.e., that prolonged poor growth performance may help engender conflict. Violence and unrest may not only be a cause but may also arise from fluctuations in economic variables. Indeed, instrumental variable techniques have been used in some of the studies to correct for reverse causation, but the validity of instruments in cross-country regressions has been questioned by some authors (Abadie and Gardeazabal, 2003). However, given the difficulty of empirically modeling conflict and terrorism, and in finding suitable instruments, they are taken to be exogenous in line with a number of other studies (e.g., Davoodi et al., 2001; Gupta et al., 2001; Hess, 2003).

The above structural model was estimated using the Generalized Method of Moments (GMM) estimation technique so as to address the underlying problems of autocorrelation and heteroscedasticity that typically arise in estimating a structural panel model with endogenous variables. Following the standard approach, the instruments used in the estimation were all the exogenous variables of the structural model—i.e., all the variables in the system except for the three dependent variables and the investment ratio—plus an ICRG corruption index and inflation volatility. The latter two are used as proxies for the investment climate to instrument for the investment ratio.[13] All of the results presented below pass the Sargan test for validity of the instrument set.

The data used in estimation of the structural model were taken from the IMF's *World Economic Outlook*, the World Bank's *World Development Indicators 2001*, Yearbooks of the Stockholm International Peace Research Institute, and the *International Country Risk Guide*. Due to the limited availability of time series data on tax revenues, data on revenues and foreign grants are used as a proxy for domestic government revenues.

Baseline Regressions

Model 1a (Table 2) uses the ICRG measure of internal conflict and terrorism. Note that a *higher* value of the ICRG conflict rating implies a

---

[13] See, for example, Brunetti and Weder (1998), who find that economic volatility and corruption are detrimental to investment.

lower risk of internal conflict and terrorism.[14] As in the standard Barro growth equations (Barro, 1991), the coefficient on the initial level of per capita income is negative and statistically significant at the 5% level. However, the coefficient on the initial stock of human capital (proxied by the gross secondary school enrollment rate) is not statistically significant. The implication is that, at least for the sample of countries included in this study, convergence toward a common level of real per capita income is not dependent on the initial stock of human capital. The age dependency ratio is also not statistically significant, and neither is the ICRG rating for internal conflict and terrorism. Consistent with our hypothesis, the ratio of defense spending in total government expenditure has a negative and statistically significant effect on growth.

The structural equation for the government revenue-to-GDP ratio is based on studies such as Bahl (1971), Tanzi (1992), and Ebrill et al. (2001). The estimates are consistent with their findings that the share of government revenue in GDP in developing countries is a function of the level of development (proxied by real per capita income) and of the openness of the economy (proxied by the ratio of nonagricultural exports to GDP). However, the internal conflict and terrorism variable does not have any significant effect on the government revenue-to-GDP ratio, and neither does the structure of the economy (proxied by the ratio of value added in agriculture to GDP). One reason why stronger results are not obtained for this equation could be the inclusion of foreign grants in the measure of revenues; some of the structural variables explaining government tax revenues, for example, may not have an impact on grants in the same way.

The third equation for the share of defense in government expenditure is consistent with the finding in Davoodi et al. (2001) that higher spending on defense by neighboring countries—which could be interpreted as a measure of regional tensions—is associated with a significantly higher share of defense in total government spending. Moreover, the coefficient for internal conflict and terrorism is positive and statistically significant at the 1% level.[15]

---

[14]For the sake of brevity, the estimates of the time dummy and regional dummy coefficients are not presented in Table 2.

[15]Collier and Hoeffler (2002b) find, based on data for the period 1960–1999, that military expenditure by a country is strongly influenced by the level of military expenditure of its neighbors. They estimate that an initial exogenous increase in military expenditure by one country is more than doubled in both the originating country and its neighbors. Potentially, there is an offsetting public good effect if rebellions are deterred by military expenditure. However, instrumenting for military expenditure, Collier and Hoeffler find no deterrence effect of military spending on the risk of internal conflict. Hence, there appears to be no regional public good effect offsetting the public bad arising from a neighborhood arms race.

Table 2. Regression Results

	Growth of Real Per Capita Income	
Dependent Variable	Model 1a	Model 1b
Per capita income, initial	−0.0004 (−2.33)**	−0.0005 (−3.20)***
Gross secondary enrollment, initial	−0.017 (−1.22)	−0.02 (−1.40)
Ratio of defense spending to government expenditure	−0.37 (−7.01)***	−0.28 (−5.65)***
SIPRI rating for major armed conflicts		−1.72 (−1.90)
ICRG internal conflict rating (civil wars and terrorism)	−0.15 (−0.91)	
Age dependency ratio	−4.04 (−1.30)	−6.84 (−2.22)**
Total investment	0.17 (1.10)	−0.01 (−0.05)
R-squared	0.18	0.24

	Revenue (in percent of GDP)	
Dependent Variable	Model 1a	Model 1b
Real per capita income	0.001 (2.76)***	0.001 (2.70)***
Ratio of nonagricultural exports to GDP	0.23 (4.85)***	0.22 (4.75)***
SIPRI rating for major armed conflicts		−0.34 (−0.30)
ICRG internal conflict rating (civil wars and terrorism)	0.06 (0.30)	
Agriculture value added	−0.07 (−1.09)	−0.09 (−1.38)
Urbanization	0.02 (0.41)	0.02 (0.42)
R-squared	0.58	0.58

	Defense Spending (in percent of government spending)	
Dependent Variable	Model 1a	Model 1b
Average defense spending of neighbors (in percent of GDP)	0.97 (2.61)***	1.26 (3.38)***
SIPRI rating for major armed conflicts		2.68 (1.31)
ICRG internal conflict rating (civil wars and terrorism)	−0.80 (−3.87)***	
R-squared	0.46	0.43
Number of observations	137	127
p-values[a]	0.70	0.78

White's heteroscedastic consistent t-statistics are in parentheses; (***), (**), and (*) denote significance at the 1%, 5%, and 10% levels, respectively.

[a]The p-values refer to the test of overidentifying restrictions implied by the exogeneity of instruments. The instruments used are: corruption, inflation volatility, and all the exogenous variables in the system (i.e., all variables except for the three dependent variables and the ratio of total investment to GDP).

In summary, the empirical results using the ICRG rating for internal conflict and terrorism suggest that violence and insecurity raise the share of defense spending in total government expenditure, which in turn has a negative effect on growth by diverting resources away from spending on sectors (education, health, infrastructure) that promote economic growth over the long term. The risk from conflict and terrorism does not seem to have any additional negative impact on growth, over and above its impact on the composition of government spending. Moreover, conflict and terrorism do not seem to have any impact on government revenue.

Robustness Tests

To assess the robustness of the results, the above model is reestimated using a different measure of conflict: the proportion of years during each 5-year period when the country was in conflict according to the SIPRI index. The results (Model 1b) tell a somewhat different story from the Model 1a estimates; the ratio of defense spending to government expenditure still has a statistically significant and negative effect on growth, but (unlike in Model 1a) the SIPRI-based conflict variable does not have a statistically significant impact on the composition of government spending. However, the SIPRI-based measure of armed conflict has a *direct* negative effect on growth which is statistically significant at the 10% level. In addition, the age dependency ratio now becomes statistically significant as well. In short, the results using the SIPRI-based conflict variable suggest that conflict has a *direct* negative impact on growth, rather than an *indirect* effect through the composition of government spending.

The results using the SIPRI-based conflict index may differ from those using the ICRG rating for internal conflict and terrorism because the former is discrete for any given year (either 0 or 1). By contrast the ICRG rating for internal conflict and terrorism is a more continuous variable, and varies from 0 to 12 with changes in the perceived risk from violence and insecurity.

Some authors have argued that ethnic fractionalization also has an impact on growth (e.g., Easterly and Levine, 1997). A variable measuring fragmentation, however, is not found to have a statistically significant effect (Table 3). Furthermore, the SIPRI-based measure of armed conflict remains a statistically significant determinant of growth, while the results using the ICRG measure of internal conflict and terrorism are broadly unchanged.

7. Conclusions

The empirical literature on economic costs of armed conflicts and terrorism has yet to provide a comprehensive, cross-country examination of their fiscal consequences. This study provides a cross-country examination using two approaches. First, the evolution of various

Table 3. Regression Results: Robustness Test

	Growth of Real Per Capita Income	
Dependent Variable	Model 1a	Model 1b
Per capita income, initial	−0.0004 (−3.52)***	−0.0006 (−4.76)***
Gross secondary enrollment, initial	−0.001 (−0.07)	−0.008 (−0.51)
Ratio of defense spending to government expenditure	−0.36 (−8.74)***	−0.27 (−5.73)***
SIPRI rating for major armed conflicts		−2.17 (−2.16)**
ICRG internal conflict rating (civil wars and terrorism)	−0.13 (−0.86)	
Age dependency ratio	−3.58 (−0.92)	−6.79 (−1.80)*
Total investment	−0.005 (−0.042)	−0.08 (−0.51)
Ethnic fragmentation	0.01 −0.99	0.01 −1.10
R-squared	0.19	0.24

	Revenue (in percent of GDP)	
Dependent Variable	Model 1a	Model 1b
Real per capita income	0.0008 (1.81)*	0.0008 (1.91)*
Ratio of nonagricultural exports to GDP	0.18 (4.74)***	0.18 (4.48)***
SIPRI rating for major armed conflicts		0.60 (0.60)
ICRG internal conflict rating (civil wars and terrorism)	−0.29 (−1.75)*	
Agriculture value added	−0.08 (−1.33)	−0.09 (−1.49)
Urbanization	0.08 (1.70)*	0.05 (1.24)
R-squared	0.51	0.49

	Defense Spending (in percent of government spending)	
Dependent Variable	Model 1a	Model 1b
Average defense spending of neighbors (in percent of GDP)	0.79 (2.30)**	1.12 (2.79)***
SIPRI rating for major armed conflicts		1.56 (0.57)
ICRG internal conflict rating (civil wars and terrorism)	−0.67 (−2.58)**	
R-squared	0.44	0.34
Number of observations	126	127
p-values[a]	0.74	0.96

White's heteroscedastic consistent *t*-statistics are in parentheses; (***), (**), and (*) denote significance at the 1%, 5%, and 10% levels, respectively.

[a]The *p*-values refer to the test of overidentifying restrictions implied by the exogeneity of instruments. The instruments used are: corruption, inflation volatility, and all the exogenous variables in the system (i.e., all variables except for the three dependent variables and the ratio of total investment to GDP).

macroeconomic and fiscal variables and socioeconomic indicators during 22 episodes of conflict, and in the years immediately preceding and following the conflicts, was analyzed. Second, an integrated system of equations for real per capita income growth, government revenue, and government spending was estimated to examine the main channels through which armed conflict and terrorism affect the fiscal accounts.

The empirical results using the ICRG measure for internal conflict and terrorism are consistent with the hypothesis that armed conflict and terrorism lead to a higher share of defense spending in total government expenditure, which has a negative effect on growth by diverting resources away from spending on socially and economically productive sectors that promote economic growth. The results using the SIPRI-based conflict measure, however, suggest that conflict has a *direct* and significant negative impact on growth, rather than an *indirect* effect through its impact on the composition of government spending. The results using the SIPRI-based conflict index may differ from those using the ICRG rating for internal conflict and terrorism because the former is discrete for any given year (either 0 or 1). By contrast, the ICRG rating for internal conflict and terrorism is a more continuous variable, and varies from 0 to 12 with changes in the perceived risk from violence and insecurity.

The findings from the econometric estimation are generally consistent with the conclusions of the before-during-after conflict analysis. The share of government revenue in percent of GDP tends to fall during the conflict period, and to pick up somewhat in the immediate post-conflict period. This analysis also suggests that armed conflict leads to higher government spending on defense, but this tends to be at the expense of macroeconomic stability (reflected, for example, in significantly higher budget deficits and a pickup in inflation) rather than at the cost of lower spending on education and health—at least when measured as a percent of GDP. However, since conflict is associated with lower real GDP growth, the result is lower growth in real per capita government spending on education and health during conflict periods. Not surprisingly, the data are consistent with an increase in the share of investment in GDP in the immediate postconflict period, and in the share of private sector investment. The available data also show a dramatic pickup in inflation during the conflict period, followed by a significant decline in the immediate postconflict period.

The results suggest sizable economic gains in terms of economic growth, macroeconomic stability, and the generation of tax revenues to support poverty-reducing spending, for countries that end conflicts and tackle terrorism. Ending violence and restoring security can be expected to lower the share of the budget allocated to military spending. These results confirm those of earlier studies, underscoring the potential for the "peace dividend" to contribute to economic development. For example, a recent study by Hess (2003) finds that the pure economic welfare losses from conflict are quite large. The authors estimate that these losses are typically four times larger than the welfare costs of business cycles as calculated by Lucas (1987), and that, on average, individuals would give up over 6% of their current annual level of consumption as a one-time payment in order to live in a world of perpetual peace.

Successful reconstruction after conflict involves rebuilding damaged institutions and infrastructure, renewing the social contract, generating a sense of trust among the warring parties, and ensuring that grievances due to economic disparities or perceived biases in fiscal policies are addressed. All this takes time. The continued involvement (and not just one-shot assistance) of the donors and the international community is therefore critical, especially in countries that have experienced prolonged conflicts.[16]

International institutions (such as the IMF) have been involved in lending for reconstruction to postconflict countries. As part of its emergency assistance facility to help members emerging from conflicts rebuild capacity and recover economic stability, the IMF, for example, has provided US$300 million over the period 1995–2000 to seven postconflict countries. The findings of this paper have implications for the design of macroeconomic and fiscal policies for countries emerging from conflicts. In particular, the results suggest that conflict- and terrorism-affected countries are likely to experience a pickup in government tax revenues and a reduction in military spending (albeit with a lag) following the cessation of violence, and this would help in restoring macroeconomic stability.

Appendix A. Sample Countries

For the preconflict, conflict, and postconflict analysis, a sample of 20 countries (22 episodes of major armed conflicts based on SIPRI data) where conflict began or was ongoing after 1985, but ended by 1999, is used. The sample includes 15 low-income countries (Armenia,

---

[16]This is emphasized by Collier and Hoeffler (2002a), who find that during the first three postconflict years, absorptive capacity on average is no greater than normal, but that in the rest of the first postconflict decade, it is approximately double its normal level. Thus, ideally, aid and donor involvement should be phased over several years following the end of the conflict. Collier and Hoeffler find that historically, aid has not been higher on average in postconflict societies, and indeed it has tended to taper off over the course of the decade following the cessation of conflict.

Azerbaijan, Bangladesh, Cambodia, Chad, the Republic of Congo, Georgia, Guinea-Bissau, the Lao People's Democratic Republic, Mozambique, Nicaragua, Senegal, Tajikistan, Uganda, and the Republic of Yemen), 3 lower-middle-income countries (Albania, El Salvador, and Guatemala) and 2 upper-middle-income countries (Croatia and Lebanon).

Where ICRG country ratings on internal conflict are also available for the corresponding episodes (for 14 of the 20 countries), there is a broad match between low ICRG ratings of 8 or less (the lower the ICRG rating, the higher the risk of internal conflict) and countries that have been classified as conflict-affected by SIPRI.[17] The average ICRG internal conflict score (where available) for these 20 countries is 3.7 between 1984 and 1989, 6.4 between 1990 and 1994, and 8.2 between 1995 and 1999. This is a reflection of the fact that in most of these 20 countries, the conflicts took place mainly during the 1980s (or before) and during the first half of the 1990s.

For the econometric analysis, a larger set of 66 countries including conflict and nonconflict, low- and middle-income countries is used (see list below). Of these 66, the following countries—Armenia, Azerbaijan, Croatia, El Salvador, Guatemala, Mozambique, Nicaragua, Senegal, and Uganda—were classified by SIPRI as countries experiencing major armed conflicts. Problems of data availability, which are particularly severe for countries affected by armed conflict, constrained the sample considerably.

Countries Used in the Econometric Analysis

Albania, Angola, Argentina, Armenia, Azerbaijan, Belarus, Bolivia, Brazil, Bulgaria, Cameroon, Chile, Colombia, Côte d'Ivoire, Croatia, Czech Republic, Ecuador, Egypt, El Salvador, Estonia, Ethiopia, Gabon, The Gambia, Guatemala, Honduras, Hungary, India, Indonesia, Iran, Jamaica, Jordan, Kazakhstan, Kenya, Latvia, Lithuania, Madagascar, Malawi, Malaysia, Mali, Mexico, Moldova, Morocco, Mozambique, Nicaragua, Niger, Nigeria, Oman, Pakistan, Paraguay, Philippines, Poland, Romania, Saudi Arabia, Senegal, Slovak Republic, South Africa, Sri Lanka, Syrian Arab Republic, Tanzania, Thailand, Tunisia, Turkey, Uganda, Uruguay, Venezuela, Zambia, and Zimbabwe.

---

[17]On the 0–12 ICRG scale, 0 denotes Very High Risk of Conflict and 12 denotes Very Low Risk. For example, Liberia had an average ICRG (internal conflict) rating of 2.1 between 1990 and 1994.

References

Abadie, A., Gardeazabal, J., 2003. The economic costs of conflict: a case study of the Basque country. American Economic Review 93, 113–132.

Addison, T., Murshed, S.M., 2001. The fiscal dimensions of conflict and reconstruction. WIDER Discussion Paper No. 2001/49. World Institute for Development Economics Research, United Nations University, Helsinki.

Addison, T., Chowdhury, A.R., Murshed, S.M., 2002. By how much does conflict reduce financial development? WIDER Discussion Paper No. 2002/48. World Institute for Development Economic Research, United Nations University, Helsinki.

Alesina, A., Perotti, R., 1993. Income distribution, political instability, and investment. NBER Working Paper No. 4486. National Bureau of Economic Research, Cambridge, MA.

Alesina, A., Perotti, R., 1996. Income distribution, political instability, and investment. European Economic Review 40, 1203–1228.

Alesina, A., Ozler, S., Roubini, N., Swagel, P., 1996. Political instability and economic growth. Journal of Economic Growth 1, 189–212.

Arora, V., Bayoumi, T., 1993. Economic benefits of reducing military expenditure, Annex II in World Economic Outlook. International Monetary Fund, Washington, DC.

Arunatilake, N., Jayasuriya, S., Kelegama, S., 2001. The economic cost of the war in Sri Lanka. Research Studies: Macroeconomic Policy and Planning Series No. 13. Institute of Policy Studies of Sri Lanka, Colombo.

Bahl, R.W., 1971. A regression approach to tax effort and tax ratio analysis. IMF Staff Papers 18, 570–612.

Barro, R.J., 1991. Economic growth in a cross section of countries. Quarterly Journal of Economics 106, 407–443.

Bayoumi, T., Hewitt, D., Schiff, J., 1993. Economic consequences of lower military spending: some simulation results. IMF Working Paper No. 93/17. International Monetary Fund, Washington, DC.

Benoit, E., 1978. Growth and defense in developing countries. Economic Development and Cultural Change 26, 271–280.

Brunetti, A., Weder, B., 1998. Investment and institutional uncertainty: a comparative study of different uncertainty measures. Weltwirtschaftliches Archiv/Review of World Economics 134, 513–533.

Collier, P., Hoeffler, A., 2002a. Aid, policy and growth in post-conflict economies. Paper presented at a Joint World Bank-IMF Seminar, Washington, DC.

Collier, P., Hoeffler, A., 2002b. Military expenditures: threats, aid, and arms races. Paper presented at a Joint World Bank-IMF Seminar, Washington, DC.

Davoodi, H., Clements, B., Debaere, P., Schiff, J., 2001. Military spending, the peace dividend, and fiscal adjustment. IMF Staff Papers 48 (2), 290–316.

Drakos, K., Kutan, A.M., 2001. Regional effects of terrorism on tourism: Evidence from three Mediterranean countries. Center for European Integration Studies (ZEI), Working Paper No. 26. Rheinische Friedrich-Wilhelms-Universität, Bonn.

Easterly, W., Levine, R., 1997. Africa's growth tragedy: policies and ethnic divisions. Quarterly Journal of Economics 112, 1203–1250.

Ebrill, L., Keen, M., Bodin, J.P., Summers, V., 2001. The Modern VAT. International Monetary Fund, Washington, DC.

Enders, W., Sandler, T., 1991. Causality between transnational terrorism and tourism: the case of Spain. Terrorism 14, 49–58.

Enders, W., Sandler, T., Parise, G.F., 1992. An econometric analysis of the impact of terrorism on tourism. Kyklos 45, 531–554.

Gleditsch, N.P., Strand, H., Eriksson, M., Sollenberg, M., Wallensteen, P., 2001. Armed conflict 1946–1999: a new dataset. Paper presented at the Euroconference on: Identifying Wars: Systematic Conflict Research and Its Utility in Conflict Resolution and Prevention. Uppsala University, Uppsala, Sweden.

Gupta, S., de Mello, L., Sharan, R., 2001. Corruption and military spending. European Journal of Political Economy 17, 748–777.

Gupta, S., Plant, M., Dorsey, T., Clements, B., 2002. Is the PRGF living up to expectations? Finance and Development 39, 17–20.

Hess, G.D., 2003. The economic welfare cost of conflict: an empirical assessment. Working Paper, Department of Economics, Claremont McKenna College, CA.

Knight, M., Loayza, N., Villanueva, D., 1996. The peace dividend: military spending cuts and economic growth. IMF Staff Papers 43, 1–37.

Lucas Jr., R.E., 1987. Models of Business Cycles. Blackwell, Oxford.

Ndikumana, L., 2001. Fiscal policy, conflict, and reconstruction in Burundi and Rwanda. WIDER Discussion Paper No. 2001/62. World Institute for Development Economics Research. United Nations University, Helsinki.

Nitsch, V., Schumacher, D., 2002. Terrorism and trade. Paper presented at the German Institute for Economic Research (DIW) workshop, The Economic Consequences of Global Terrorism. Available via the Internet: http://www.diw.de/deutsch/service/veranstaltungen/ws_consequences.

Richardson Jr., J.M., Samarasinghe, de A.S.W.R., 1991. Measuring the economic dimensions of Sri Lanka's ethnic conflict. In: Samarasinghe, de A., Coughlan, R. (Eds.), Economic Dimensions of Ethnic Conflict. St. Martin's Press, New York.

Rodrik, D., 1999. Where did all the growth go? external shocks, social conflict, and growth collapses. Journal of Economic Growth 4, 385–412.

Shieh, J.-Y., Ching-Chong, L., Wen-Ya, C., 2002. Endogenous growth and defense expenditures: a new explanation of the Benoit hypothesis. Defense and Peace Economics 13, 179–186.

Stockholm International Peace Research Institute, SIPRI Yearbook, 2001. Armaments, Disarmament and International Security. Oxford University Press, Oxford.

Tanzi, V., 1992. Structural factors and tax revenue in developing countries: a decade of evidence. In: Goldin, I., Winters, L.A. (Eds.), Open Economies: Structural Adjustment and Agriculture. Cambridge University Press, Cambridge, UK.

U.S. Department of State, 2002. Patterns of global terrorism—2001 (Washington). Available via the Internet: http://www.state.gov/s/ct/rls/pgtrpt/2001/html.

Venieris, Y.P., Gupta, D.K., 1986. Income distribution and sociopolitical instability as determinants of savings: a cross-sectional model. Journal of Political Economy 94, 873–883.

Walkenhorst, P., Dihel, N., 2002. Trade impacts of the terrorist attacks of September 11, 2001: a quantitative assessment. Paper presented at the German Institute for Economic Research (DIW) workshop, The Economic Consequences of Global Terrorism. Available via the Internet: http://www.diw.de/deutsch/service/veranstaltungen/ws_consequences.

World Bank, 2000. Economic causes of civil conflict and their implications for policy. Press Briefing, June 15, Washington, DC. Available via the Internet: http://www.worldbank.org/html/extdr/extme/pr061500.htm.

19

A Comparison Between Two Public Expenditure Management Systems in Africa

IAN LIENERT

One important objective of the enhanced HIPC (Heavily Indebted Poor Country) debt reduction initiative is to redirect the budgetary resources released from servicing external debt toward poverty-reducing expenditures. Several questions arise in this context. First, are African countries' public expenditure management systems robust enough to allow specific poverty-reducing expenditures to be identified in annual budgets and tracked in countries' accounting systems? Second, does the expenditure control system allow poverty-reducing expenditures to be protected from cuts should there be unforeseen shortfalls in revenues? Third, are internal and external audit mechanisms effective, so as to ensure the integrity of expenditure reports, both in-year and annually? To answer these, and other questions, an assessment of the entire public expenditure management system is required in each country.

Such a study was published in 2002.[1] The public expenditure management systems of 24 low-income countries were assessed on the basis of a common set of 15 questions in the three areas of budget preparation, budget execution, and fiscal reporting. Figure 1 shows the overall results—both regions attained only about 35 percent of the required

The author wishes to thank colleagues of the IMF's Fiscal Affairs Department, particularly Dominique Bouley, Jack Diamond, Pokar Khemani, Annalisa Fedelino, and Davina Jacobs, as well as Mike Stevens of the World Bank for helpful comments.

[1] See IMF and World Bank (2002).

Figure 1. Relative Performance of Public Expenditure Management Systems in Africa

Percentage of countries meeting benchmarks

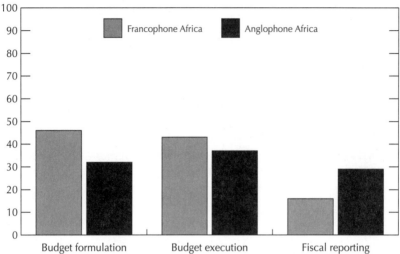

Source: IMF and World Bank (2002).
Note: 15 benchmarks were established: 7 for budget formulation and 4 each for budget execution and fiscal reporting. The francophone countries in the sample are Benin, Burkina Faso, Cameroon, Chad, Guinea, Madagascar, Mali, Mauritania, Niger, and Senegal. The anglophone countries in the sample are The Gambia, Ghana, Malawi, Tanzania, Uganda, and Zambia.

benchmarks—well below that required to meet the objectives of effective public expenditure management systems (see the subsection on potential strengths of the individual public expenditure management systems for details). Information on the progress in implementing action plans built on the initial assessment has also been published.[2]

This chapter focuses on one question: "Is there a specific public expenditure management system in Africa that consistently performs better than other systems?" Since most countries in Africa have inherited either a French-based or a British-based management system, the comparison is limited to these two systems.[3] Other studies have documented the common weaknesses of the anglophone and francophone systems, respectively.[4] This chapter complements this research by conducting a comparative analysis.

---

[2]See IMF (2003).

[3]Lusophone countries inherited a Portuguese-based system and the Democratic Republic of the Congo, Rwanda, and Burundi inherited a Belgian system, which differs somewhat from the French-based system.

[4]For example, see Lienert and Sarraf (2001) for weaknesses in anglophone African countries, and Bouley, Fournel, and Leruth (2002) and Moussa (2004) for weaknesses in francophone African countries.

A study of this nature necessarily includes generalizations: countries in the two areas have experienced different developments of their public expenditure management systems since independence. The study focuses on the countries that have benefited from IMF technical assistance over the past decade.[5] The emphasis is therefore on describing or evaluating how public expenditure management systems actually operate, rather than how they ought to operate on the basis of each system's regulatory framework.

Budget Preparation

This section first examines the legislative framework for budget making, as it provides the foundation of the budget preparation system. It then reviews common features of budget preparation in the two regions.

Legislative Basis for Budget Preparation

Constitutions in francophone countries typically include a statement that the annual budget law (*loi de finances*) determines the resources and expenses of the state. They also include provisions on the timing of the presentation of the law to parliament (often in October for a budget year that begins on January 1) and permissable actions by the executive branch when the annual budget is not adopted on time by parliament. Typically, governments begin executing the new budget on the basis of monthly authorizations equal to 1/12th of the previous year's budget.

Constitutions of anglophone countries vary considerably in their provisions for the budget process. Some countries have very few, if any, articles on budgeting in their constitutions (e.g., Uganda). Others have considerably more detail than francophone countries (e.g., Nigeria). A typical constitutional requirement is that money may not be withdrawn from the consolidated fund unless provided for by another law.

In the French-based system, organic budget laws spell out five well-known principles for budget preparation: annual basis, unity, universality, specificity, and equilibrium (balance).[6] In francophone Africa, organic budget laws are based largely on that adopted in France

---

[5] These are the 15 countries listed in Figure 1, plus Côte d'Ivoire, Djibouti, Kenya, Lesotho, Nigeria, Togo, and Zimbabwe. South Africa is excluded since it is more advanced in budget management than a typical African country.

[6] Attiogbe (1999) recalls these principles for the case of Togo. These principles were developed during the 3rd and 4th French Republics, 1871–1958; see Chapter 1 of Lord (1973).

in 1959.[7] They typically define or specify (1) current and capital expenditures, and loans/advances; (2) the broad categories of the economic classification of expenditures;[8] (3) the nature of documents to be submitted to parliament; and (4) procedures for preparing and adopting the annual budget law.

Budget laws in anglophone countries differ from those of the francophone countries. The closest equivalent to an "organic budget law" in anglophone countries are "finance and audit acts." Although these may include a chapter on budget preparation, there is strong emphasis on budget execution and ex post audit. In both regions, ministries of finance provide guidance to budget preparation, through budget circulars or other administrative notices.

Common Features of Budget Preparation in the Two Regions

The processes involved in budget preparation are similar in the two regions (see Box 1).

Since the abandonment of national planning,[9] budgets have traditionally only been annual, at least for current expenditures. In recent years, initiatives have been made to develop medium-term budget frameworks, especially in the anglophone countries (e.g., Ghana, Tanzania, and Uganda). In the case of Uganda, a Budget Act was adopted in 2000, which, among other things, provides legal underpinning for medium-term budget frameworks.

In francophone countries, multiyear budget provisioning for capital expenditures is provided for in organic budget laws. Multiyear budget appropriations (*autorisations de programme*) allow ministries to commit expenditures for capital projects for periods exceeding one year. Accompanying these appropriations are limits on annual payments (*crédits de paiements*), which are included in the annual budget law. At year-end, any unspent payments within the annual limit can be carried over to the new fiscal year. In contrast, in anglophone countries, unspent appropriations are generally cancelled at year-end and reappropriated in the following year's budget.

Donors dominate the financing of public investment programs.[10] In both sets of countries, donors finance most investment budget spending.

---

[7] See *Ordonnance du 2 janvier, 1959 portant Loi Organique relative aux Lois de finances.*

[8] See, for example, Directive No. 05/97/CM/WAEMU concerning budget laws. Available via the Internet: www.uemoa.int.

[9] In the initial years after independence, many countries prepared national development plans. However, these were poorly linked with annual budgets and policy debates.

[10] Central government investment budgets are usually a subset of public investment programs, as the latter cover all public investment projects, including those executed by local governments and public enterprises.

> **Box 1. Common Features of Budget Preparation Systems in Francophone and Anglophone Africa**
>
> - Annual basis for the budget, but no medium-term expenditure framework.
> - One budget for current expenditures and another budget for investments.
> - Detailed line-item budgeting.
> - Budget generally limited to central government, plus a few autonomous funds. Local governments and extrabudgetary funds are excluded.
> - Decentralization of budgeting to lower levels of government is under way.
> - Unrealistic costings of expenditures; some line items are underprovisioned.
> - Timing—budget preparation allows little time for parliamentary discussion.
> - Absence of focus on results or effectiveness of government programs.

Although projects in the public investment programs should be prioritized according to objective criteria, in practice, donor preferences have heavily influenced the composition of projects included in public investment programs. However, there is an increasing tendency for some donors to provide nontargeted budgetary assistance.

Dual budgeting has been widespread. Separate budgets are often prepared for current expenditures and "investment" expenditures. The latter—sometimes called "development budgets"—often contain considerable recurrent expenditures. The absence of medium-term budget frameworks and the existence of nonintegrated budgets also result in the failure to appreciate the recurrent expenditure implications of investment projects. It is now recognized that, in both sets of countries, "dual budgeting may well be the most important culprit in the failure to link planning, policy, and budgeting" (see Box 3.11 of World Bank, 1998).

The budget has traditionally been prepared mainly on a detailed line-item basis. In both regions, the main budget document may run into hundreds of pages. Such detail complicates budgetary management. Budget classification is generally similar: the budget is adopted by organizational classification (e.g., ministry, administrative unit, and province) and by economic classification (e.g., salaries, current goods and services, transfers, and capital spending). It is rare in both regions to classify expenditures by program or by function. In both regions the rules for reallocation between budget lines are well defined, although in practice, they are not always respected.

In both sets of countries, the budget adopted is generally limited to central government. In the annual budget, parliament approves central government transfers to lower levels of government. Estimates of the revenues of subnational governments are usually not provided as background information. Revenues collected and retained by autonomous agencies (e.g., hospitals) dependent upon budget transfers for their main source of income are often not shown in the budget.

In both regions, semiautonomous budgets, extrabudgetary funds, and off-budget activities are important. In the francophone countries, although organic budget laws refer to the principle of *unity* of spending from one common fund and *universality* (all spending should be in the budget), in practice there are several exceptions. In particular, there are budget annexes and special treasury accounts of various types.[11] Although these are presented to parliament for adoption and subject to public accounting rules, in practice accounting records are poorly maintained. In anglophone countries, extrabudgetary activity appears to be a more important problem than in francophone countries:[12] off-budget "below-the-line" funds have caused problems in budget execution in several countries (e.g., The Gambia and Zimbabwe). Road funds are usually integrated with the budget preparation process, but they are managed autonomously. Social security or pension funds are generally outside the budget preparation process in both regions.[13]

Revenue projections have often been unrealistic. In both regions, there has been a tendency for revenues to fall short of projections (e.g., the impact of the reduction in external tariffs in WAEMU countries has been underestimated). However, in some countries, there has been improvement in recent years, especially for tax revenue projections, which are generally projected more conservatively (e.g., in Tanzania). However, there is a persistent problem of shortfalls in revenues (relative to projections) for donors' grants, resulting in an underexecution of the development budget.

Some specific current expenditures are underestimated in the budget, particularly those on electricity, telephone, water, and other expenditures whose commitment cannot be postponed (e.g., food for the army and for prisoners). This is partly because budget departments of ministries of finance lack qualified staff who can critically examine the expenditure estimates on the basis of well-maintained databases of ministry-specific unit costs and consumption volumes of these items. Also, there is often a very tight timetable for bilateral budget discussions at the technical level.

---

[11] In most francophone countries, the revenues and expenditures of the Post and Telecommunications Offices are presented as a budget annex to the annual budget law. The budgets for the national pension funds, the debt management agency, and the social security office are not systematically included in the budget.

[12] Of the 10 francophone countries listed in Figure 1, 90 percent reported that "government activities are not funded through extrabudgetary resources to a significant degree" whereas in the 6 anglophone countries only one-third met this benchmark—see IMF and World Bank (2002).

[13] One exception is the pension funds for retired civil servants and military.

Following agreement of the budget at the technical level, important political decisions affecting spending are sometimes made late in the budget cycle. Also, after the budget is adopted by parliament, political authorities—not necessarily the minister of finance—may make decisions that weaken the capacity of the ministry of finance to finance all budgeted expenditures.

One specific feature of francophone countries is the distinction between existing and new policies. As early as the 1960s, the annual budgets of several francophone countries showed, for each line item, a split between policies already in place (*services votés*) and new measures (*mesures nouvelles*). However, the quality of the estimates for the new measures was often not high, as these were largely based on extrapolations of previous-year budget projections. Nonetheless, a formal distinction between existing and new policies was not part of the system adopted in anglophone Africa.

Budgets are often adopted late in both groups of countries. Although in francophone countries constitutions and/or organic budget laws lay out the key dates for budget presentation and adoption by parliament, these are not always respected. For example, in Côte d'Ivoire, the budget for 2001, covering January–December, was adopted in July 2001. Similarly, in anglophone countries, where budget preparation calendars are also clearly spelled out, the budget may be presented to parliament just before the beginning of a new fiscal year (e.g., Kenya, Tanzania, and Uganda), and not adopted until the second or third month of the new fiscal year (see Fölscher, 2002, for a five-country survey).

The budget is usually not discussed extensively by parliament. In the United Kingdom and France, parliamentary budget commissions have traditionally played an active role in examining the budget prior to its formal adoption by parliament. This has not been the case in Africa, reflecting lack of capacity and inadequate attention to the role of parliament in the budget process. However, parliamentary budget subcommittees are becoming active in a few francophone countries and several anglophone countries (e.g., Mali, Tanzania, and Uganda), in line with greater democratization.

Performance-oriented budgeting is beginning in both regions (e.g., Mali and Uganda). This is necessitated by the challenge of implementing country-owned poverty-reduction strategies that link specific objectives—especially in education and health—with budgeted expenditures needed to achieve the desired changes. However, the capacity to administer the additional data and analytical requirements of output/outcome budgeting is often lacking. Moreover, where they exist, "programs" are not well conceived; they are often simply a provisioning of present organizational structures within ministries.

Budget Execution

In contrast to the considerable similarities of the two public expenditure management systems for budget preparation, when it comes to budget execution there are some important differences. The key contrasts between the two systems revolve around the degree of (de)centralization of responsibility for budget management to spending ministries. These differences are elaborated below and in successive subsections.

Key Actors in the Expenditure Process and Their Respective Roles

The British approach can be characterized as one of decentralized management—spending ministries are mainly responsible for budget execution. In contrast, the French-based system is one in which the central ministry of finance plays an important role at each step of the spending process. The balance of powers and key players are illustrated in Figure 2.

In anglophone countries, officials in spending ministries are charged with initiating and authorizing expenditures at each stage, from commitment to payment. Following adoption of the budget, the minister of finance[14] issues quarterly or annual warrants to "accounting officers," who are generally the heads ("permanent secretaries") of spending ministries and have extensive responsibilities (Box 2). The warrants convey the legal authority to vote holders to authorize expenditure from public funds. Accounting officers, in turn, may delegate disbursement authority to officers in their ministry.

In the francophone system, such wide-ranging responsibilities are not provided to spending ministries. On the contrary, the closest equivalent to accounting officers (*gestionnaires de crédit*) have a rather limited role—mainly that of initiating expenditures at the commitment stage, within the budget provision. They do not have authority to issue payment orders (*ordonnancement*); this is the role of the payment authorizing officer (*ordonnateur*). However, in most African francophone countries, the minister of finance is the sole authorizing officer (*ordonnateur unique*).[15]

---

[14]Traditionally, this was done via the "paymaster-general," a high-ranking official of the ministry of finance appointed by the minister for controlling the issue of public moneys to accounting officers.

[15]The directives by the West African Economic and Monetary Union (WAEMU) to the eight West African francophone countries contain such a provision. This system dates from the time from when there was a single governor of France in the colony. Upon independence, the governors' powers were transferred to the ministers of finance. Similarly, in Mauritania, with the exception of the minister of defense, the minister of finance is the sole authorizing officer; in practice, this function is delegated to the budget director.

Figure 2. Relative Influence of Ministry of Finance and Spending Ministries in Budget Execution

Ministry of Finance

**Sector Ministries'
Spending Agencies**

Anglophone African Countries

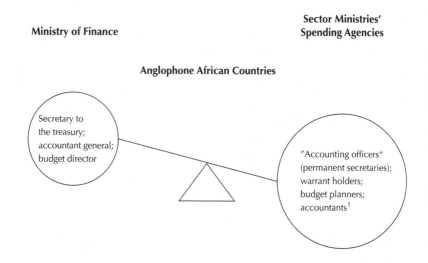

Secretary to the treasury; accountant general; budget director

"Accounting officers" (permanent secretaries); warrant holders; budget planners; accountants[1]

Francophone African Countries

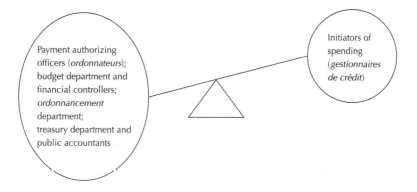

Payment authorizing officers (*ordonnateurs*); budget department and financial controllers; *ordonnancement* department; treasury department and public accountants

Initiators of spending (*gestionnaires de crédit*)

[1]Accountants report to the accounting officer of the ministry or agency, but are usually posted to the unit by the accountant general of the ministry of finance, who sets professional standards.

Box 2. Responsibilities of Accounting Officers in Spending Ministries of Anglophone Countries

- Preparing budget projections for their ministry.

- Ensuring that no head of expenditure is exceeded and that no subhead or item is exceeded without proper authority.[1]

- Delegating authority to spend to authorized officers in his/her ministry— subwarrant holders—and ensuring that delegated officers do not overspend.

- Endorsing the Annual Accounts of the ministry and defending the ministry's budget outcome before the Public Accounts Committee of parliament.

---

[1] Accounting officers can generally reallocate funds from one subhead to another within current budgets (but not capital budgets). However, they are not authorized to transfer budget allocations for salaries to nonsalary current expenditures or vice versa.

Various departments of the ministry of finance of francophone countries play all the important roles in budget execution. The key players are financial controllers (*contrôleurs financiers*), who are generally under the budget department of the ministry of finance, and approve expenditure commitments on advance basis and, often, the issuance of payment orders to the treasury;[16] and public accountants (*comptables publics*) in the treasury.

A key principle of the francophone public expenditure management system is the separation of the payment authorizing officer and the treasury officer responsible for payment. Since both of these functions are centralized in the ministry of finance, financial management in spending ministries is diluted: the minister of finance is both the sole authorizing officer and the overseer of the functioning of the treasury and the countrywide body of public accountants. Thus, despite the principle of the separation of the payment authorizing officer and the public accountant, the minister of finance performs both roles.

As a consequence, the minister of finance has unique powers in expenditure management, without parallel in the anglophone system. The system in Africa is even more centralized than in France, where both cabinet ministers and central government representatives at the local level (*préfets*) are payment authorizing officers. The system in francophone Africa therefore confers virtually no responsibility for effective financial management on government ministers or the heads of spending ministries.

---

[16] In some countries *sous-ordonnateurs* exist for authorizing payment orders at the regional level (e.g., Madagascar) or in specific ministries (e.g.. Ministry of Defense, Mauritania). However, such delegated officers are still under the authority of the *ordonnateur principal*, usually the minister of finance.

Expenditure Control

In the anglophone system, expenditure control is largely exercised by the warrant system. In principle, the ministry of finance can control the issuance of warrants for nonstatutory expenditures.[17] Annual warrants are usually provided for salaries, and quarterly or monthly warrants for other current expenditures. Warrant control is a major instrument of expenditure control in some countries (e.g., Kenya and Lesotho). In principle, accounting officers record expenditure commitments in their "vote books" and should report these to the ministry of finance. However, in several countries (e.g., Malawi and Zambia), ministries' reports on commitments are incomplete and received late by the ministry of finance; as a consequence, the ministry of finance has been unable to exercise control over expenditure commitments.

"Cash budgeting" arrangements were introduced in a number of anglophone countries, especially during the 1990s (e.g., Kenya, Tanzania, and Zambia), mainly because expenditure control was not being exercised.[18] Under this system, cash allocations to ministries are limited to that dictated by cash availability—that is, the amount that ministries are authorized to spend is subject to cash limits. Since cash limits were often below the warrant limits—and the latter are consistent with the annual budget appropriations—accounting officers often did not ensure that expenditure commitments were contained within the cash limits. As a result, expenditure arrears—overdue unpaid invoices—became a pervasive problems in many anglophone African countries.

The expenditure control system in francophone countries is quite different, with formal controls at the commitment, payment order issuance, and payment stages of expenditure approval (see Figure 3). However, the formal duties exercised by the ministry of finance are limited largely to compliance with budget appropriations.

In the francophone countries, controls overlap, and at no stage in the expenditure process is it questioned whether or not the expenditure should take place. The treasury's "control" of expenditures is limited to checks of the conformity of expenditure payment requests with existing financial regulations. Such checks have already been done twice by the financial controller. Also, they seldom take into consideration the amount of cash available for expenditure. Thus, although the treasury

---

[17] Statutory expenditures are those that must be paid irrespective of budget projections, because another law requires it. Included are debt servicing, salaries of certain high officials (e.g., auditor general), etc. A similar category of budget appropriations (*crédits évaluatifs*) exists in francophone countries.

[18] There were both revenue shortfalls and expenditure overruns. To deal with the former, warrant authority can be withdrawn under the British system. However, in Africa, warrant withdrawal was extremely rare.

Figure 3. Key Differences in Budget Execution and Expenditure Control

Anglophone Africa		Stage of Spending Process	Francophone Africa		
Spending ministry	Ministry of finance		Ministry of finance		Spending ministry
		↓	Budget department and/or financial controller	Treasury	
	Warrants issued by ministry of finance to spending ministries	**Allocation of annual appro- priations**	Allocates *crdits ouverts*		
Orders placed by minsitries		**Commitment (government liable for future payment)** ↓	A priori commitment control: first visa:		Initiates spending
Orders placed					Orders placed
Goods and services received		**Accrual (goods/ services received and debt incurred)** ↓	Invoices received from spending ministries		Attests goods received
Prepares payment voucher		**Payment order issuance** ↓	Prepares payment voucher *(ordonnance- ment)* second visa control		
			[separation of *ordonnateur* and *comptable*]		
Pays invoice (when decentralized)	Pays invoice (when centralized payment)	**Payment**	Payment order received, checked, and invoice paid		

may provide a visa "good for payment" on payment vouchers, the treasury's coffers may be empty and payment arrears arise. This is largely because, in most francophone countries, monthly cash management systems, if developed, are poorly integrated with treasury procedures.

Some expenditures in francophone countries do not require formal controls at every stage. Payments for salaries and debt servicing are examples. For such payments, there are special expenditure control arrangements, usually executed by special centralized agencies. For example, control over salary payments is conferred mainly to a special division of the ministry of finance, which, in collaboration with the civil service ministry and the treasury, should make salary payments only to civil servants whose existence is verified. In practice, owing mainly to the lack of integration with personnel records, salary control is often weak. As a result, salaries have been paid to nonexistent or "ghost" workers. A similar problem has arisen in anglophone African countries (Lienert and Modi, 1997).

Special debt agencies, responsible for orderly debt payments, have been established in some francophone countries.[19] These agencies— *caisses autonomes d'amortissement*—were set up (and later abandoned in some countries), largely to ensure that external debt was serviced, as the treasury was not always able to perform this function effectively. Despite the establishment of these debt agencies, payment arrears on debt, especially external, occurred in several francophone countries—a reflection of poor internal control and management, and/or lack of coordination within the ministry of finance (notably with the treasury).

Payment

In anglophone countries, payment is either centralized or decentralized. The basic model at independence was a centralized payment system, with subtreasuries for regional payments. However, in some countries, both payment authorization and actual payment was devolved to spending ministries. Such is the case in Malawi and Zambia. In others, payment remains centralized (e.g., The Gambia, Lesotho, and Tanzania). In the case of Tanzania, the re-centralization of the payment function in 1996 facilitated the installation of an integrated computerized accounting and payment system.

In francophone countries, it would be inconceivable for payment to be made outside the treasury. Consistent with its inheritance of the strong centralized role played by the treasury in France, all payments are effected by the treasury.

---

[19] See Box 5 of Bouley, Fournel, and Leruth (2002).

Internal Control and Internal Audit [20]

In anglophone countries, internal control is semi-decentralized. In several countries, the officers who perform the internal control function in spending ministries are employees of the internal audit department of the ministry of finance (e.g., in The Gambia, Kenya, Uganda, and Malawi). These officers are outposted to spending ministries to ensure compliance with financial regulations issued by the ministry of finance and are viewed by accounting officers as agents of the ministry of finance, as they report principally to the ministry of finance, with copies of reports addressed to the accounting officers. In a few countries (e.g., Ghana until recently), spending ministries recruit and manage their own internal auditors to assist the accounting officer in financial management. In such countries, internal auditors' reports are prepared principally for the accounting officers, with copies for the internal audit department of the ministry of finance.

Francophone countries' ministries of finance have a strong system of centralized internal control. At the expenditure commitment stage, the financial controller, who may be outposted to the spending ministry, checks the regularity and conformity of the commitment against budget appropriations. The payment authorizing officer issues a payment order to the treasury, for which a second visa (approval) is required from the financial controller. A third control is made by the treasury accountant, who makes the payment. Internal control is therefore highly centralized, as all of the above are ministry of finance staff.

In addition to an elaborate system of internal control, most francophone countries have established an internal audit unit (*l'inspection des finances*). These units are also located in the ministry of finance: generally they are attached to the minister of finance's office. The inspectorates have broad responsibilities for internal audit, as opposed to the internal control activities of financial controllers, who perform routine checking. The inspectorates audit not only the financial management units located in the ministry of finance (tax/customs administrations, budget department, treasury), but any public sector entity. These inspectorates generally report directly to the minister of finance. Some anglophone countries (e.g., Uganda) also have an inspectorate division in the ministry of finance, with functions similar to those of these inspectorates.

In some francophone countries, an even higher-level agency (*contrôle générale d'état*), with investigative powers and responsibilities broader

---

[20]For fuller details on the operation of internal control and audit in Africa, see Diamond (2002). For a distinction between internal control and internal audit, see Chapter 10 of OECD (2001).

than the high-level inspectorate, has been established. These high-level units, under the presidency, perform audits internal to the executive branch. The closest equivalent agencies in anglophone countries are the anti-corruption offices/commissions that have been established in several countries (e.g., Nigeria, Uganda: see http://www.unodc.org/unodc/en/corruption_projects.html).

Government Accounting, Fiscal Reporting, and Banking Arrangements

This section examines the similarities and differences in the accounting systems, as summarized in Box 3. It then discusses the common problem of not producing timely accounts in both regions. Banking arrangements are also reviewed.

Accounting Framework

The francophone countries' accounting system is typically specified formally by decree, or even law.[21] These decrees/laws are modeled largely on the Public Accounting Decree adopted in France in 1962 (which is under revision given the intention of France to move to accrual accounting). Accounting regulations in anglophone countries are prepared by the ministry of finance and hence can be modified easily.

The French-based accounting system is more complete, incorporating some accrual information. Although the accounts are cash based in both public expenditure management systems, in the anglophone countries, the accounting system is single-entry and does not require regular reporting of financial assets and liabilities *within the year* (although external and domestic debt is usually recorded, with varying degrees of quality). In francophone countries, from the payment order stage for expenditures, the accounting system becomes a double-entry one. Both revenues and expenditures, as well as financial assets and liabilities, are recorded according to a well-specified chart of accounts.[22] This allows identification of bills that have been sent to the treasury for payment but have not been paid. Such information is not obtainable from the accounting system of the anglophone countries, although special recording arrangements have been put in place (e.g., in Malawi, Uganda, and Zambia) to capture this missing information.

---

[21] In Mali, in addition to a decree, an Accounting Law has been adopted.

[22] There are usually nine standard "classes" of accounts, based on the system used in France.

**Box 3. Similarities and Differences in Accounting
and Banking Arrangements**

Similarities:
- cash basis for accounting;
- poorly maintained accounting records that often lack reconciliation with bank records; and
- annual accounts not available within statutory deadlines.

Differences francophone countries have:
- a more formal and complex accounting framework;
  treasury balances are an integral part of the system;
- accounting centralized in the ministry of finance;
- a complementary accounting period for accounts closure; and
- a single treasury account (with some exceptions).

Differences anglophone countries have:
- spending ministries responsible for preparing annual accounts and providing in-year accounting reports to the ministry of finance; and
- a multiplicity of government bank accounts (particularly in countries where payment is decentralized to spending ministries).

Spending ministries in francophone countries are not responsible for preparing accounts, which are centralized in the ministry of finance. Nonetheless, line ministries should maintain accounting records of expenditures at the commitment and verification stages; their records for commitments should be cross-checked with the "master" records held in the ministry of finance, usually the budget department. In practice, the quality of accounting information at the prepayment stage is variable in francophone African countries, although it is often better than treasury information.

Annual Accounts

In the anglophone countries, accounting officers prepare and submit annual accounts to the accountant general. The main account is the "appropriation account," which shows actual expenditures against expenditures appropriated by parliament. The accounting officers also have to prepare statements on (1) the annual revenues collected by his/her ministry; (2) the amounts outstanding for loans for which the accounting officer is responsible; and (3) other statements, as specified by the accountant general. The accountant general consolidates all departmental accounts into the annual accounts of government. These are forwarded to the auditor general for external audit (see the next section). The ministry of finance's financial regulations contain the deadlines for submission by the accountant general of the annual accounts to the auditor general. Although the prescribed period for completing the accounts is usually six months,[23] in practice, long delays are experienced in some countries.

Spending ministries in francophone countries are absolved of the responsibility of preparing annual accounts. The preparation of annual accounts by the ministry of finance is a more complex process: a double set of accounts is prepared. First, the administrative accounts (*comptes administratifs*), providing details of revenues and expenditures up until, and including, the issuance of payment orders is prepared. This task is generally performed by the budget department. Second, the treasury accounts (*comptes de gestion*) show the account balances and transactions at the encashment stage for revenues and at the cash payment stage for expenditures. In the treasury accounts, there should be a reconciliation of stocks and flows: opening treasury balances for a new fiscal year should equal the opening treasury balances of the previous fiscal year plus all flows during the previous fiscal year. Any discrepancies between closing balances from one year and opening balances of the new year should be fully explained. However, such reconciliations are seldom performed, as the administrative capacity and/or willingness to operate the accounting system is often lacking.

There are important differences concerning the delays for the closing of annual accounts. In the anglophone countries, accounts are generally closed on the final day of the fiscal year; in practice, a few days may be allowed for processing transactions that have occurred at the end of the year. In contrast, for the francophone countries, there is a relatively long complementary period for closing the accounts. Payment orders may be issued up until the final day of the fiscal year.[24] To allow payment to be made after the end of the fiscal year, a complementary period of two to three months is authorized (payments for the preceding year can be made after December 31 but recorded as if they had taken place before January 1 of the new year). Long complementary periods have the inconvenience of keeping two books of accounts open for the early months of a new fiscal year. In some countries (e.g., Togo), extensions to the mandated complementary period are made. As

---

[23] A further three months is generally prescribed for their auditing.

[24] In some cases, issuance of payment order may be closed earlier, e.g., December 15, rather than December 31.

a result, the processing of transactions relating to the previous fiscal year continue for several months after the end of the fiscal year.

Both regions have suffered from a common problem of nonavailability of annual accounts. The IMF's Code of Good Practices in Fiscal Transparency prescribes that final accounts should be presented to parliament within 12 months of the end of the fiscal year. This implies that accounts must be presented to the external audit agency 6–9 months after the end of a fiscal year. There are very few African countries that meet this deadline: in a sample of 17 francophone and anglophone countries, only two countries (Chad and Uganda) presented their annual accounts to parliament within this deadline.[25] In some anglophone countries (e.g., The Gambia and Lesotho) the delay has been 5–10 years, whereas some francophone countries have not produced a coherent set of annual accounts for many years, if at all (e.g., Madagascar and Mauritania). However, since the late 1990s, a number of francophone countries have begun to prepare annual accounts (e.g., Benin, Burkina Faso, Côte d'Ivoire, Cameroon, Guinea, Niger, and Senegal), after years of neglect in some cases.

In-Year Reporting

In anglophone Africa, regular reporting by the spending ministries to the ministry of finance is critical for preparing in-year fiscal reports. The managers of spending agencies are required to ensure that vote books are kept up-to-date and sent regularly to the accountant general's office for recording in the government general ledger. Spending ministries' vote books should be reconciled with the data maintained in the accountant general's office. In countries with manual recording systems, expenditure commitments are often poorly recorded and monthly expenditure reports are either not received in a timely fashion or are of poor quality. Only in a few countries have recording systems been computerized; these provide online data simultaneously in spending ministries and the ministry of finance (e.g., Tanzania).

In francophone countries, in-year reporting is centralized in the ministry of finance. Accounting for expenditure commitments and payment order issuance is the responsibility of the budget department.[26]

---

[25] See IMF and World Bank (2002).

[26] Practices vary in the countries where the financial control function is not under the ministry of finance. For example, in Madagascar, the most reliable source of information on commitments is the financial control unit under the presidency, although the data are not fully reconciled with the records of the budget ministry (there is also a ministry of finance in Madagascar). In contrast, in Mauritania, the financial control entity, under the presidency, relies on the computerized records of the budget department of the ministry of finance.

Full accounting records for revenues received and expenditure payments are maintained by the treasury. However, for payments, transactions are not necessarily posted to final accounts with the same nomenclature as the budget—the treasury's accounting nomenclature is not necessarily identical to the budgetary nomenclature of the budget department. As a result, it is often difficult to track payments of specific budgetary expenditures.

Comprehensive reconciliation of accounting ledger data with bank account records is not always undertaken systematically in either region, thereby undermining the reliability of monthly fiscal reports. Nonreconciliation of data appears to be more acute in anglophone countries, especially those with a multiplicity of bank accounts (see the subsection below). This is despite the provisions of financial regulations, which lay down the need for regular reconciliation.

Government Banking Arrangements

In principle, a treasury single account, held at the central bank, is an integral component of both systems. In practice, there are a number of "special" accounts outside the treasury single account. In both regions, donors—who finance much of the capital expenditure—typically require that a separate bank account be opened, usually in a commercial bank, as they are distrustful of payments being effected by local treasuries.

In the anglophone countries that have decentralized the payment function, the number of government bank accounts may exceed 1,000 (e.g., Zambia). In such countries, each ministry has a separate account for each type of spending. Accounts have been opened in a multiple number of commercial banks, in addition to those opened at the central bank. Commercial banks are not used this way in francophone countries. The treasuries of francophone countries ensure that funds are pooled—not only those of central government, but also those of local governments, semi-autonomous public agencies, and public enterprises. In principle, this helps to manage cash balances more effectively

Dedicated funds, each with a separate bank account, are commonplace in both regions. Autonomous agencies, set up by specific laws, receive earmarked government revenues for dedicated spending. For example, road funds managed by boards independent of the ministry of finance have been set up (Potter, 1997). Off-budget funds for receiving oil revenues were, in the past, a source of nontransparency in oil-producing countries in both regions, notably in Cameroon and Nigeria. In francophone countries (e.g., Senegal), the existence of many special accounts whose balances are not pooled results in ineffective cash management: unremunerated deposit balances build up and at the same time the government borrows domestically at high interest rates. This is especially the case in anglophone countries, where treasury bill markets are relatively well developed.

External Audit and Parliamentary Control

The external audit agencies reflect the historical inheritance from the corresponding institutions in the United Kingdom and France. In the anglophone African countries, offices of the auditor general have been set up. A major task of the auditor general is to prepare an annual report on the government's accounts, for review by the public accounts committee (*commission des finances*) of parliament. The auditor general is usually appointed by the country's president, conjointly with parliament. In most francophone countries, chambers of accounts (*chambres des comptes*) have been set up (e.g., in Benin, Chad, Guinea, Madagascar, and Mali); in a few countries there is no external audit agency.[27] The external audit institution in francophone countries is seen as part of a triple set of controls: administrative, jurisdictional, and parliamentary.

Unlike the British-based system, the francophone countries' chambers of accounts are legally independent of both the executive and the legislative. They are under the judiciary branch of government, being presided over by a magistrate. As in France, the president of the chamber of accounts is appointed solely by the executive branch. If available, the chamber of accounts' annual report is normally transmitted to parliament, as well as to the president of the country. In some countries, parliament does not receive the entire external audit report.[28]

Auditors general have financial independence, whereas chambers of accounts are dependent on the supreme court for their annual budgets. In anglophone countries, the auditor general's salary is a statutory expenditure. As the accounting officer for his or her office, the auditor general oversees the preparation of the annual budget for his or her office and submits it to the ministry of finance (which may cut it). After end-year, the auditor general defends his/her budget outcome in parliament. A different situation prevails in most francophone countries: since the chamber of accounts is only one of several chambers of the supreme court, its annual budget is not determined exclusively by its president. For this reason, some countries (e.g., Burkina Faso and Senegal) have set up financially independent courts of accounts and

---

[27]For example, Cameroon, although an external audit agency is now envisaged.

[28]For example, in Mauritania, only parts of the annual report are required to be sent to parliament.

the WAEMU Commission is encouraging the other six member countries to transform chambers of accounts into independent courts of accounts. However, the case of Burkina Faso illustrates that this is not an easy process: the constitution needed to be changed in 2001 to establish an independent court. Mali, for instance, decided in 2001 to postpone the required constitutional change needed to transform its audit department (*section des comptes*) (of the Supreme Court) into an independent court of accounts.

In the francophone system, the chamber of accounts is required to issue a certificate of conformity that indicates that the annual accounts are internally consistent. The usefulness of this requirement is questionable, since each transaction of the two sets of accounts (the treasury's accounts and the administrative accounts) should already have been checked by the treasury for consistency.

In francophone countries, parliaments verify—or should verify—the annual accounts by a formal law. The budget execution law (*loi de règlement*) records the outturns for revenues and expenditures, and compares these with the budget estimates, inclusive of any modifications to the original budget—either via reallocation between budget lines or by supplementary estimates. In principle, the budget execution law can only be presented to parliament once the chamber of accounts has certified that the treasury's accounts and administrative accounts are fully compatible. In several countries, budget execution laws have either not been adopted at all (because annual accounts are unavailable), or have been adopted without verification by the chamber of accounts (because it has inadequate capacity).

In both regions, the follow-up mechanisms for implementing the recommendations of annual reports of the external audit agencies are inadequate. This is not a result of system design, but rather due to the lack of material and human resources devoted to the external audit function. In anglophone countries, when (if) the auditor general's report is presented to the legislative branch, it may be reported in the media, but then quickly forgotten. Although accounting officers are required to follow up on the recommendations of the auditor general, by presenting written reports to the public accounts committee of parliament on the actions taken to address concerns raised, enforcement of such provisions is weak. The ministry of finance is also supposed to report action taken to implement the auditor general's recommendations, but this is seldom done.

In francophone countries, the focus is on the accuracy of the accounts and approval by parliament of any difference between the original budget and the actual outturn. Although the chamber of accounts has authority to hold public accountants personally responsible for any misreporting, there is seldom any prosecution. If misdemeanors are made by payment authorizing officers—those who commit government to pay—the chamber of accounts has no authority to initiate actions against them. In France, there is a second body, a court of budget and financial discipline, to deal with non-treasury officials who inappropriately manipulate funds. In Africa, such courts have not been set up.[29]

Is One Public Expenditure Management System Superior?

The previous sections have shown that the main differences between the two public expenditure management systems are in budget execution, fiscal reporting, and audit. For budget preparation, similarities dominate, although it could be argued that, with respect to investment spending, the francophone system has a favorable feature—it allows carryovers of unspent commitments, thereby facilitating better forward planning of investment expenditures.

This section examines more closely the distinctive features of the "British-" and "French-based" public expenditure management systems, and discusses whether they contribute to better financial management. It then compares the common weaknesses of the two public expenditure management systems and suggests that there are additional factors causing the mediocre performance of public expenditure management systems in both regions.

Potential Strengths of the Individual Public Expenditure Management Systems

The key distinctive features of the two systems are summarized in Table 1. In the discussion below, it is argued that the French-based public expenditure management system should, in principle, give better results for achieving macroeconomic stability, an important objective for any public expenditure management system. Neither management system is geared toward obtaining efficiency objectives. Discussion of results-oriented budgeting is beyond the scope of this paper, as performance-oriented budgeting is yet to be introduced in most African countries.

Expenditure Control and Payment Arrears

It could be argued that the centralized French-based system, with controls by the ministry of finance at each stage of the expenditure

---

[29]Senegal is an exception—such a court has been established under the independent court of accounts.

Table 1. Potential Relative Strengths of Public Expenditure Management Systems

Area of Public Expenditure Management	Anglophone Countries	Francophone Countries
Expenditure control	Spending ministries are primarily responsible for expenditure control.	Ministry of finance exercises expenditure control prior to payment.
Internal audit	Internal audit partly decentralized to spending ministries.	Centralized internal control and internal audit.
Accounting system and fiscal reporting	Simpler accounting; no split between responsibilities of the payment authorizing officer and the accountant (*ordonnateur* and *comptable*); spending ministries are responsible for preparing the primary records of expenditure commitments and payments.	Accounting framework is logical: changes in treasury balances should equal flows of transactions. Expenditure is recorded and reported at each stage; accounts payable can be identified. Centralized accounting should facilitate accurate fiscal reporting.
Banking arrangements		Greater centralization of bank accounts in central bank (no payment by spending ministries).
Fiscal rules		To support the fixed exchange rate regime of the CFA franc, borrowing from the central bank has always been limited (it is now proscribed).
External audit and parliamentary control	Heads of spending agencies and/or ministers must defend budget outcomes in parliament.	External audit agency is independent of both the executive and legislative branches.

process, results in better expenditure control. In the French-based system, the ministry of finance takes a lead role in controlling expenditures at the prepayment stage, and in theory, it is able to integrate information on expenditure commitments into the cash planning process. Such strong central surveillance could be considered necessary to counteract weak administrative capacity and limited accountability of line ministries' budget managers.

In view of this, expenditure commitment control systems are being put in place in various anglophone African countries (e.g., Malawi, Tanzania,[30] Uganda, and Zambia). However, there has been mixed success in controlling expenditure commitments and, especially, in preventing expenditure payment arrears, which is a pervasive problem in several anglophone countries. This reflects the generalized lack of financial discipline. Although expenditures could in principle be controlled by warrant withdrawal, in practice, this instrument is not used sufficiently.[31]

In some francophone countries, when revenues fall short of projections, expenditure commitments can be closed earlier than usual. Should it become transparent during the year that there is insufficient cash for meeting all payments, the budget department of the ministry of finance can instruct ministries to no longer commit expenditures after a certain date (e.g., mid-November instead of end-November). Similarly, the ministry of finance can stop payment order issuance before the close of the fiscal year (e.g., mid-December). Although these tools have been used in several francophone countries, their effectiveness has been limited, because only a small proportion of discretionary expenditures is postponable, important exceptions are accorded, and the instructions are not always fully enforced. Worse, in several countries, there is not an awareness of the need to freeze commitments, owing to defective cash management procedures, poor accounting information, or a lack of willingness to control expenditures.

The problem of expenditure payment arrears is also pervasive in several francophone countries. Whereas in a few countries nearly all government invoices are paid on time (e.g., Benin, Mali, and Mauritania), in other countries, the size of expenditure arrears has surpassed the worst-case anglophone countries, even exceeding 10 percent of GDP in Djibouti and Togo. This suggests that there are other important factors

---

[30] In Tanzania, expenditure commitment control is computerized. In the other three countries, manual systems have been, or are being, put in place to control expenditure commitments.

[31] Financial regulations of anglophone countries usually provide that the unspent balance of any warrant may, at any time, be withdrawn by the minister of finance. Once a withdrawal warrant has been issued, the accounting officer may not permit expenditure to exceed the remaining balance.

> ## Box 4. Exceptional Expenditure Procedures in Francophone Countries
>
> Francophone countries adhere to the following exceptional expenditure procedures.
>
> - Direct payment by the treasury (*ordres de paiement*), under which the treasury is directed to make payment without the usual a priori controls on commitments and payment order issuance.
>
> - Imprest accounts (*caisse d'avances*), which are usually reserved for small or specific expenditures, under tightly defined rules. In some countries, ministries use this procedure for many expenditures of a particular type (e.g., all defense expenditures in Madagascar).
>
> - Special accounts/funds, used for payments that do not require prior approval at the payment order stage.
>
> The main objective of these procedures is to accelerate payment. For transactions conducted by these "exceptional" procedures, regularization of accounting is supposed to be rapid. In practice, such expenditures may never be recorded with clarity. In some countries, the "exceptional" procedures have become the standard way of executing nonsalary expenditure. Moreover, when arrears arise, the treasury director has discretion as to which bills should be paid first, which is an open door to corruption in the payment process.

at play in francophone countries that are preventing effective control of expenditure commitments.

In several francophone countries, expenditure arrears are partly caused by the bypassing of the normal expenditure control procedures. Because the system of a priori expenditure control by the ministry of finance at both the commitment and payment order stages is complex, contains redundancies, and is slow to permit payment for goods or services, francophone countries have introduced, or overexploited, "simplified" expenditure procedures that bypass the central controls (Box 4).

The lack of feedback from the treasury to the budget department and spending ministries is a particularly acute problem in francophone countries. The split between the payment authorizing officer and the accountant has an unfortunate consequence. The budget department considers that its work is complete when it sends documents to the treasury for payment. The "lack of resources" problem is perceived by the budget department to be the treasury's problem alone. There is no feedback from the treasury to the budget department. When there are shortfalls in cash revenues, instead of examining ways in which the rate of approval of expenditures at the commitment stage could be slowed, the budget department disavows responsibility for unpaid bills. In these circumstances, unpaid suppliers approach the treasury directly to hasten payment, perhaps with some added incentives to ensure prompt transfer of funds. The lack of feedback between the accountant general's department and budget department is also a problem in anglophone countries. In both regions, budget departments fail to provide good guidance to the treasury concerning payments that are in the pipeline.

Ineffective cash management also contributes to the arrears problem. Even in the relatively well-managed francophone countries, expenditure commitment "control" is simply a check against budget appropriations. With the possible exception of closing commitments earlier than usual at end-year, budgeted expenditure commitments are not adjusted downward during the year should cash not be available. This is partly due to inadequate coordination between the budget department and the treasury.

Internal Audit

It could be argued that the centralized internal control and audit systems of the francophone countries result in better financial management than the decentralized systems in anglophone countries. First, the internal control mechanisms associated with expenditure control are well established in the francophone countries: a body of financial controllers, under the budget department of the ministry of finance, is an essential part of the expenditure control system in all countries. In contrast, internal audit divisions of ministries of finance of anglophone countries—which provide internal auditors to spending ministries—are usually a less prominent part of the public expenditure management system. Second, in the francophone countries that have established inspectorate units, there is potential for investigating and reporting on malpractices in the public expenditure management system as a whole. Few anglophone countries have such inspectorates. Third, when human capacity is weak in spending ministries, and the rule of law/regulations is not respected, strong central control is needed—decentralization of the internal audit function requires well-trained teams of auditors, with effective oversight from the management of spending ministries. This is usually lacking in anglophone countries.

However, there is little evidence to suggest that francophone countries have more effective internal audits. According to surveys conducted in 10 francophone countries, only one was deemed to have effective internal audits.[32] This finding for francophone countries is

---

[32] In the same survey, only one out of six anglophone countries had effective internal audit. Internal audit was found to be one of the areas of the public expenditure management system of HIPC countries that needed the most upgrading. See item 9 of Figure 2 in IMF and World Bank (2002).

partly because financial controllers lack the necessary independence and/or willingness to enforce financial regulations. For example, it is well known that not all goods or services are delivered according to contractual conditions, suggesting that financial controllers may collude with accounting officers, suppliers, and/or receiving officers (*comptables matières*) who certify that goods or services have been delivered when in fact full delivery has not taken place. There may also be little effective control over overinvoicing. Concerning the internal audit unit, these bodies may not have been provided with sufficient financial, material, or human resources, or may often lack the necessary dynamism, to carry out their functions fully.

Accounting System and Fiscal Reporting

It could be argued that the francophone countries' accounting system contributes to better financial management. In principle, the French-based accounting system is capable of providing budget managers with richer and more consistent information for financial management. First, the accounting framework is laid out comprehensively in accounting regulations and a formal chart of accounts (very similar to that used in France). The accounting system includes some accruals-basis information, with financial assets and liabilities identified in accounts. Cash flow statements are, in principle, reconciled with treasury balances. In turn, treasury accounts and bank records of revenues and expenditures are reconciled.[33] In anglophone countries, accounting instructions and charts of accounts also exist, but the partial accrual information is missing. Second, in the francophone system, expenditure is recorded and reported in at least three stages: commitment, issuance of payment orders, and payment. In addition, spending ministries hold records at the accrual (*liquidation*) stage—when economic transfer takes place. In the anglophone countries, at best, commitments and payments are recorded. Third, the francophone accounting system is double-entry for treasury transactions, enabling accounts payable at the treasury to be identified. It is impossible to obtain data on expenditure arrears from traditional anglophone accounting systems. Fourth, since accounting is centralized, timely fiscal reporting should be easier.

The potential advantages of the francophone countries' accounting systems are not exploited, mainly because it has proven difficult to operate and maintain solid accounts. The complexity of the accounting system, operated in most countries on a manual basis (until recently),

---

[33] Seventy percent of the francophone countries assessed in 2002 (see IMF and World Bank, 2002) reported that "fiscal and banking data reconciliation is undertaken regularly." This is considerably higher than the 33 percent of anglophone countries.

has resulted in very poor accounting records being kept in most francophone countries. A particular problem is the artificial split between the payment authorizing officer and the accountant, which has resulted in fragmentation, and even inconsistencies, in accounting information. In most countries, budget departments maintain the expenditure records for commitments and issuance of payment orders, although some countries have institutional fragmentation even at this level.[34] While treasuries maintain—or should maintain the "downstream" accounting records, including the general ledger from which fiscal reports should be generated—in many countries, timely and consistent treasury balance information is unavailable. Additionally, because several francophone countries have maintained different classification systems for the "upstream" and "downstream" expenditure records,[35] it is extremely difficult to track expenditure at each stage. It is mainly for these reasons that, in the survey of francophone and anglophone countries' accounting systems conducted in 2002, the anglophone countries performed relatively better, although the performance of these countries was also completely unsatisfactory.[36]

Besides the fragmentation of responsibilities *within* the ministry of finance, the noninvolvement of spending ministries in maintaining the primary records deprives the ministry of finance of maintaining expenditure records at the crucial accrual (*liquidation*) stage. If francophone countries begin to move toward implementing full accrual accounting, it will be a challenge to change institutional arrangements so that accounting is devolved to spending ministries, as is presently the case in anglophone countries.

The francophone sanction system has a flaw. More importantly, sanctions are rarely applied in both regions. In the francophone countries, the entire responsibility for preventing abuse in financial management rests on the shoulders of the public accountants, whose accounts are judged by an independent agency—the chamber (court)

---

[34] In some countries (e.g., Togo), an *ordonnancement* (or "finance") department has been established, separate from the budget department. Also, financial controllers in some countries are outside the ministry of finance (e.g., under the presidency), and may keep independent accounting records.

[35] The lack of consistency between the budget and the accounting nomenclatures can be traced to the system used in France until recently.

[36] No francophone country closed accounts within two months of the fiscal year, whereas one-third of anglophone countries do so. No francophone country was capable of producing final accounts on a functional classification basis, whereas one-third of anglophone countries were doing so in 2001. In contrast, the francophone countries performed relatively better in terms of *presenting* the budget on a functional classification basis. This apparent paradox reflects the fact that the francophone countries' budgeted expenditures cannot necessarily be traced through to final accounts.

of accounts—to detect any malpractice. Since public accountants are responsible for checking the validity of prepayment documents received in the treasury, they alone bear "pecuniary and personal responsibility." In contrast, the regulations usually impose no sanctions on the upstream players—especially the payment authorizing officers of the ministry of finance's budget department or of spending ministries (in the few cases where issuance of payment orders has been decentralized). In contrast, the accounting officers in anglophone countries are, in principle, responsible for preventing overspending (see Box 2). Although there may be some sanctions in financial regulations, such as the preparation of a written report to the minister of finance when overspending occurs, such provisions are often not enforced. In many anglophone countries, the president of the country appoints the accounting officers and, should abuses occur, accounting officers are understandably reluctant to report.

Banking Arrangements

The centralization of all bank accounts at the central bank, with no payments being made directly by spending ministries, appears to be another potential advantage of the public expenditure management system in francophone countries. Some anglophone countries, too, have reinstituted a central payment system from a treasury single account, as this contributes to more effective cash management and reduces the scope for maintaining unutilized balances in multiple bank accounts. Despite this advantage, both anglophone and francophone countries abandon this principle for donor-financed expenditures, for which commercial bank accounts controlled by donors, not treasuries, are used. Also, in francophone countries, public enterprises are often obliged to deposit any surplus funds at the treasury; to the extent that the treasury allows enterprise deposit accounts to go into overdraft, the government is lending to these enterprises in a nontransparent manner.[37]

Fiscal Rules

A unique feature of the francophone countries is the very strict limit on government borrowing from the central bank. Such a limit aims at supporting the fixed exchange rate vis-à-vis the euro. Until 2000, the total government borrowing limit from the two regional central banks of the CFA franc zone was fixed at 20 percent of tax revenues; since then, government borrowing from the central banks has been prohibited. In fact, WAEMU countries are now obliged to repay outstanding

---

[37] See Bouley, Fournel, and Leruth (2002) for a fuller discussion of the treasury circuit.

government credits. Whereas this fiscal rule has kept inflation rates low in francophone countries, it has also resulted in cash shortages and banking crises, as formal rules were bypassed in an indirect way.[38] In contrast, some anglophone countries experienced bouts of high inflation in the early 1990s, owing to central bank financing of unplanned fiscal deficits; at that time, it was relatively easy to exceed any limits on "ways and means" advances from central banks.

External Audit and Parliamentary Control

It could be argued that the system of external audit and parliamentary control in anglophone countries results in more effective public expenditure management. First, the auditor general's offices have had a long tradition of preparing annual reports. In contrast, the chambers of accounts in francophone countries are more recent creations. Second, the chambers of accounts concentrate very heavily on the legality of expenditures and compliance with financial rules, and review of the draft budget execution law, whereas anglophone countries have a wider mandate and are moving toward efficiency and effectiveness audits. Third, parliamentary public accounts committees—which are essential for the follow-up of external auditors' recommendations—have been more active in the democratic anglophone countries than have their counterparts in francophone countries.

In practice, in both regions, the external audit function has not been accorded the priority it deserves. In both regions, external audit offices are often deprived of the necessary financial, human, and material resources for carrying out their mandates. Very few African countries are able to present audited annual accounts to parliament within 12 months (see IMF and World Bank, 2002). Finally, when reports become available, they are not acted upon with the seriousness they deserve.

Common Weaknesses of Public Expenditure Management Under Both Systems

The francophone countries' public expenditure management systems appear to have performed slightly better than those in anglophone countries in attaining benchmarks for budget preparation, about the same for budget execution, and considerably worse for fiscal reporting.

---

[38]Masson and Pattillo (2002) describe the indirect deficit financing in CFA franc zone countries: "Much activity was initially kept off the fiscal accounts, as governments pushed state-owned banks to make loans to public enterprises." These banks were able to obtain refinancing from the BCEAO at concessional rates.

However, the differences are not significant: statistical tests indicate that one cannot confirm (at standard confidence levels) the hypothesis that the francophone and anglophone countries' averages shown in each panel of Figure 1 are dissimilar.

Thus, any unique and favorable features of the francophone countries' public expenditure management system have not necessarily contributed to a consistently better performance. The main area in which the francophone countries were slightly better than anglophone countries was budget preparation. There are potentially two areas where the francophone countries' public expenditure management systems are effectively advantageous. First, there is a distinction between existing and new policies, and second, there is a requirement for medium-term investment projections. However, the "better" results for budget preparation shown in Figure 1 are largely due to the francophone countries having relatively lesser recourse to extrabudgetary funds, fuller integration of donor-financed expenditures into the budget, and more complete budget (but not accounting) classification systems (see the various footnotes above). These differences, however, pale compared with the generalized weaknesses of budget preparation: both regions share the common problems of budgets not being comprehensive; inadequate classification systems; poor costing of specific expenditures; and an absence of medium-term budget frameworks (until very recently).

For budget execution, the two regions have broadly similar weaknesses, which are widespread. The francophone countries show more regular reconciliation of accounting and banking information. Both regions share common problems of poor expenditure control (with considerable variation in each region), weak internal auditing systems, and incomplete reconciliation of accounting and banking data.

At first sight, it appears paradoxical that the francophone countries perform worse for fiscal reporting than do the anglophone countries. It is argued above that, in principle, the French-based accounting and reporting system has several advantages over the British-based one. However, there appears to be a large gap between theory and practice. The poor overall performance of the francophone countries suggests that the accounting system is either too complex and archaic to operate and/or the rules are flouted. Francophone countries have had a particularly severe problem producing comprehensive and timely monthly and annual accounts. As a consequence, external audit institutions are unable to perform financial audits of annual accounts, let alone implement more modern techniques, such as value-for-money audits.

Conclusions

This study analyzes the differences between the public expenditure management systems of anglophone and francophone Africa. Concerning the budget process, the following conclusions can be drawn.

- Budget preparation in the two regions is broadly similar, although the francophone countries' system has two features that arguably are advantageous relative to that of the anglophone countries.

- There are significant differences in budget execution procedures between the two systems, centering particularly around the role and powers of the ministry of finance and the degree of delegation of financial management to spending agencies.

- The francophone countries have the advantage of possessing a formal system of recording and controlling expenditures at the prepayment stages.

- Greater centralization of fiscal management in francophone countries should, in principle, produce better results for macroeconomic control since, throughout Africa, institutional capacity for operating budget execution and accounting arrangements in spending ministries is even more limited than at the central (ministry of finance) level. On the other hand, for efficiency in budget management—resource allocation and obtaining results from budgetary programs—it could be argued that the anglophone countries' decentralized systems are conducive to better performance.

- The accounting system in the francophone countries also has some potential advantages, as it should produce more comprehensive information for fiscal management.

- The anglophone countries have inherited external audit arrangements that play a relatively more important role in the budget process than they do in francophone countries. In principle, supreme audit agencies in anglophone countries provide parliament and the public with timely information on budget execution and the integrity of annual accounts.

Although the francophone countries' budget execution and government accounting systems have a number of potential advantages, these have not produced better results. On the contrary, the desirable distinctive features of the francophone public expenditure management system are not accompanied by better aggregate expenditure control, as expenditure arrears in some francophone countries are higher than in worst-case anglophone countries. Nor have the desirable features of the francophone accounting system—its greater centralization in the ministry of finance and production of partial accrual accounting information (treasury balances)—resulted in better fiscal reporting. Concerning the production of quality and timely in-year fiscal reports and annual accounts, the francophone African countries have had particularly severe problems.

Thus, any distinctive strengths of the individual public expenditure management systems do not appear to have influenced the performance of the system as a whole. In both regions, common weaknesses dominate—these being widespread at every phase of the budget cycle. At the preparation stage, budgets need to be made more comprehensive, by incorporating all foreign-financed projects and extrabudgetary activities into an integrated national budget that has been formulated with firm expenditure ceilings derived from a medium-term budget framework. Expenditure control needs improving in nearly all countries, to prevent arrears.

Improvement in data quality is a top priority. Full reconciliation of accounting and banking data, and more effective internal audit arrangements, are crucial. In both regions, the production of in-year fiscal reports and annual accounts is particularly weak. Although external audit bodies exist in nearly all countries, they have had a limited impact on improving public expenditure management systems.

To counter the various weaknesses of their public expenditure management systems, in 2002, the country authorities of all countries benefiting from the HIPC debt relief initiative identified specific short- and medium-term measures to implement. These action plans were drawn up in collaboration with the Bretton Woods institutions. By 2003, progress was being made in implementing these plans, with action initiated for over 80 percent of the identified measures. However, for short-term actions—those that should have been completed within 12 months—only 35 percent of identified measures had been completed in francophone countries, and 26 percent, in anglophone countries. So, one should not overestimate the speed at which desirable reforms can be implemented, especially given the generalized weak institutional capacity to introduce and sustain far-reaching changes in public financial management. Also, there is a need to impose budget discipline at each stage of the budget process; otherwise, expenditure overruns, the nonproduction of timely and comprehensive accounts, and ineffective internal and external audit activities will continue.

Since there are big variations *within* the francophone or anglophone groupings, it can be concluded that the disappointing features observed are due not to the public expenditure management systems themselves, but in the way they operate. Thus, even if budget legislation and implementation instructions are clarified, in the absence of changes in the attitudes of all players in the budget process—in the executive, legislative, and judicial branches of government—it is unlikely that significant improvements will occur. Critical actions will be those directed toward enhancing budget discipline and improving the accountability of all those responsible for budget preparation, execution, reporting, and evaluation.

Strong political willingness to ensure that the existing rules are enforced with rigor and that sanctions are applied where necessary will be required to bring about lasting improvements in the public expenditure management systems in both anglophone and francophone Africa. Although this is largely a domestic issue, the international community can contribute to durable solutions by not only more fully understanding the actual operation of public expenditure management systems, but also withholding assistance to those countries that persistently fail to provide their taxpayers with adequate accountability mechanisms.

References

Attiogbe, Kinvi, 1999, *Le Processus Budgétaire au Togo* (Lomé, Togo: Ministère des Finances et des Privatisations, Direction du Budget).

Bouley, Dominique, J. Fournel, and L. Leruth, 2002, "How Do Treasury Systems Operate in Sub-Saharan Africa?" IMF Working Paper 02/58 (Washington: International Monetary Fund).

Diamond, Jack, 2002, "The Role of Internal Audit in Government Financial Management: An International Perspective," IMF Working Paper 02/94 (Washington: International Monetary Fund).

Fölscher, Alta, ed., 2002, *Budget Transparency and Participation: Five African Case Studies* (Cape Town, South Africa: IDASA).

International Monetary Fund, 2003, "Update on Implementation of Action Plans to Strengthen Capacity of HIPCs to Track Poverty-Reducing Public Spending" (Washington, March 11). Available via the Internet: http://www.imf.org/external/np/hipc/ 2003/track/030703.pdf.

———, and World Bank, 2002, "Actions to Strengthen the Tracking of Poverty-Reducing Public Spending in HIPCs" (Washington, March 24). Available via the Internet: http://www.imf.org/external/np/hipc/2002/track/032202.pdf.

Lienert, Ian, and Jitendra Modi, 1997, "A Decade of Civil Service Reform in Sub-Saharan Africa," IMF Working Paper 97/179 (Washington: International Monetary Fund).

Lienert, Ian, and Feridoun Sarraf, 2001, "Systemic Weaknesses of Budget Management in Anglophone Africa," IMF Working Paper 01/211 (Washington: International Monetary Fund).

Lord, Guy, 1973, *The French Budgetary Process* (Berkeley, California: University of California Press).

Masson, Paul, and Catherine Pattillo, 2002, "Monetary Union in West Africa: An Agency of Restraint for Fiscal Policies?" *Journal of African Economics*, Vol. 11 (September), pp. 387–412.

Moussa, Yaya, 2004, "A Cross-Country Analysis of Public Expenditure Management Systems in Francophone Africa," IMF Working Paper 04/42 (Washington: International Monetary Fund).

OECD, 2001, *Managing Public Expenditure: A Reference Book for Transition Economies* (Paris: OECD).

Potter, Barry, 1997, "Dedicated Road Funds: A Preliminary View on a World Bank Initiative," IMF Paper on Policy Analysis and Assessment No. 97/7 (Washington: International Monetary Fund).

World Bank, 1998, *Public Expenditure Management Handbook* (Washington: World Bank).